Shin hanga

Shin hanga

The New Prints of Japan 1900–1960

Chris Uhlenbeck | Jim Dwinger | Philo Ouweleen

LUDION

Preface

From the late 19th century onwards, Japanese prints were appreciated and collected throughout the world. In Europe and the United States, Japanese printmaking had a profound influence on artists and the general public. In particular, the work of 18th- and 19th-century masters such as Utamaro, Sharaku, Toyokuni, Hokusai and Hiroshige caught the attention of the Western public, with literally hundreds of exhibitions being staged. Very slowly, interest shifted to more modern Japanese printmaking. While initially the focus was on the work of printmakers from the second half of the 19th century – figures such as Kuniyoshi, Kunisada and Yoshitoshi – in the 1990s attention was finally paid to 20th-century printmakers.

One can speak of an exciting period of initiation that resulted in large-scale collecting activities by museums and private individuals. Publications appeared, websites and databases were created, and the technical knowledge surrounding these modern prints increased rapidly. The 20th-century prints turned out to be extremely attractive to collectors, especially due to their technical perfection. Furthermore, because of their relatively recent creation, it was, at least initially, easy to find prints in perfect, unblemished condition. As a result, especially in the United States but also in Europe, collections of this genre really took off.

This book was initially published as a catalogue for the eponymous exhibition at the Museum für Ostasiatische Kunst in Cologne, Germany (2022), that traveled the same year to the Japan Museum SieboldHuis in Leiden, Netherlands, and the Royal Museums of Art and History in Brussels. The publication brings together the work of two Dutch collectors who have been captivated by the 'New Prints' of Japan – Tobias Lintvelt and René Scholten – both of whom have collected with a keen, critical eye for quality and condition. I would like to thank them for making their excellent collections available. The selection of prints included here is made even more striking as it is supplemented with various works from the collection of the most important Japanese publisher of prints in the 20th century, Watanabe Shōzaburō. His grandson Watanabe Shōichirō provided crucial works that filled the gaps in this overview and I greatly appreciate his support, both in terms of loans and knowledge. I would also like to thank Darrel Karl and Hein Vijverberg for allowing us to include additional prints from their collections.

This project has asked a great deal of my team – Jim Dwinger, Philo Ouweleen and Leon Oninckx. I consider myself lucky to have such colleagues: without them, the project would have stalled amid good intentions. In addition, my thanks go to the editors, Nausikaä de Blaauw, Robert Anderson and Sara Harrison. Gratitude is also due to the publisher, Ludion, which had the vision to plunge into this Japanese adventure.

Chris Uhlenbeck

Introduction

Who doesn't recognize them: *The Great Wave off the Coast of Kanagawa* (1832) (Fig. 1) by Katsushika Hokusai (1760–1849), Utagawa Hiroshige's *Sudden Shower over the Great Bridge at Atake* (1857) (Fig. 2), the countless beautiful women prints by Kitagawa Utamaro (1753–1806) and the actor heads of Tōshūsai Sharaku (active 1794–95)?

All of these prints are part of an illustrious group of universal iconic images that are in the same league as Leonardo's *Mona Lisa*, Munch's *The Scream*, Van Gogh's *The Starry Night* and Picasso's *Guernica*, to name but a few.

The aforementioned 18th- and 19th-century Japanese artists were highly appreciated. They were the heroes of Japonists in Europe and the United States during the last decades of the 19th century. Early Western collectors initially had an eye only for these big names. Everything that happened after 1860 in the field of ukiyo-e (images of the floating world) printmaking was overlooked. Tsukioka Yoshitoshi (1839–92), Kawanabe Kyōsai

(1831–89), Toyohara Kunichika (1835–1900) and Kobayashi Kiyochika (1847–1915), for example, were ignored until well after the Second World War. The changed use of colour, with brighter pigments and visible Western influences, was not appreciated, regarded as an affront to the original Japanese aesthetic. Appreciation for these artists would come only much later. What is remarkable, however, is that in Japan, in the first half of the 20th century, the work of the artists presented in this catalogue in particular was as highly appreciated as that of the great names of more than a hundred years earlier.

A changing Japan

In the early 17th century, Japan closed itself off from the outside world. This situation would change only in 1853, under threat of American military force. In 1858 negotiations eventually resulted in a trade agreement with the United States and, shortly after, with various European powers. This was an extremely complex period. In Japan, the search was

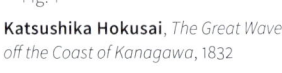

Fig. 1
Katsushika Hokusai, *The Great Wave off the Coast of Kanagawa*, 1832

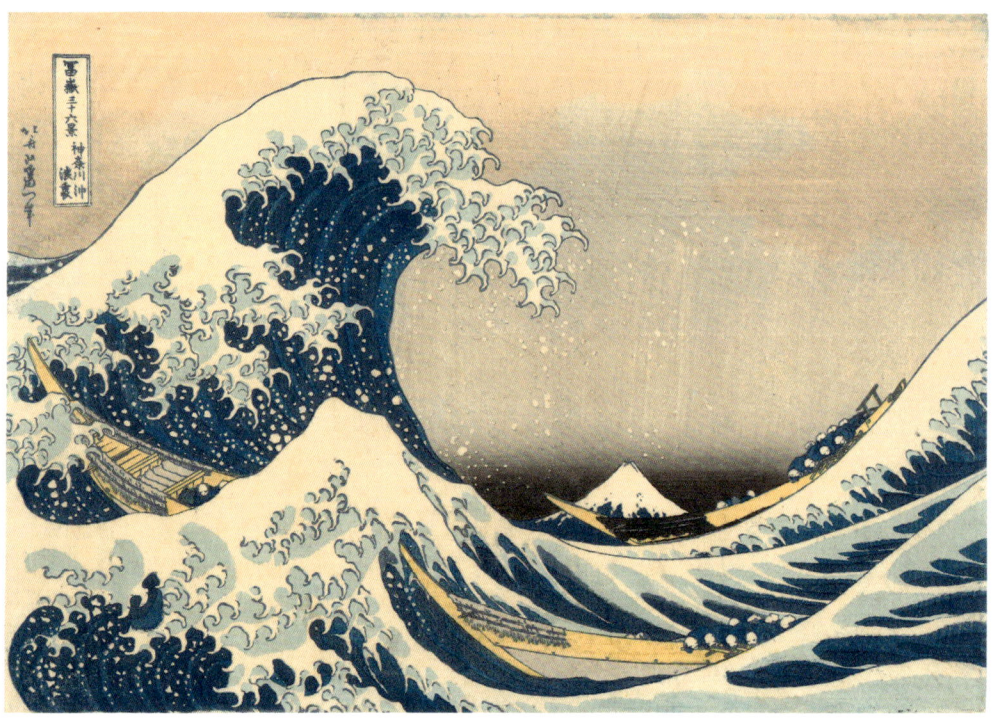

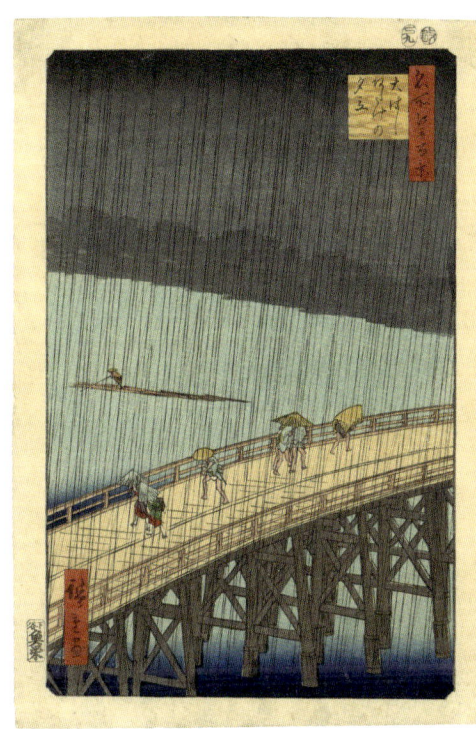

relative political stability. Education was well organized, and the literacy rate was very high.

The Japanese government realized that economic development was not the only way of achieving the status of a modern nation. It decided to hire foreign specialists (*o-yatoi*) in a multitude of domains, including the cultural field. And so, in 1876, the Italian painter Antonio Fontanesi (1818–82) arrived at the Technical Art Academy (*Kōbu Bijutsu Gakkō*) in Tokyo to set up an art department based on the Western model. It created an opportunity for students to receive training in the arts in a way other than through the traditional master–apprentice system that had prevailed in Japan for centuries. The introduction of Western ideas was not limited to art education: the influx of illustrated newspapers, magazines and books from Europe increased steadily, creating a direct and fruitful visual confrontation between Japanese and European methods of representation. In addition, alternative technologies of reproduction made their appearance and proved extremely fruitful for the development of Japanese printmaking. Photography had already gained a foothold by the 1860s, and the introduction of chromolithography via the Italian specialist Edoardo Chiossone (1833–98), coupled with steam-driven printing presses, enabled the mechanical production of magazines, newspapers and books. It was precisely this development of alternative media that threatened the existing technology for reproducing images – woodblock printing. For three centuries this technology had been extremely successful in Japan and led to an immense output of illustrated and non-illustrated books, pamphlets, calendars, packaging materials, games, invitations, announcements and, of course, the famous prints.

Photography and (chromo-)lithography initially seemed to pose a threat to this traditional industry, but it quickly transpired that artists could just as well provide illustrations for the new media. In addition to providing prints and paintings, typical Meiji

on for a balanced relationship with the outside world, based on an extremely weak military position and a system divided between shogunal and imperial factions. All of this caused enormous unrest, but gradually the power of the shogunate diminished in favour of the emperor.

Emperor Meiji (1852–1912) assumed the position of supreme ruler in 1868. He was one of the greatest advocates of the modernization of Japan. The country acquired fresh ideas and knowledge from Europe and the United States at breakneck speed, emerging as a superpower that could rival the world's greatest countries, culminating initially in the victory over China in the First Sino-Japanese War of 1894–95. Economic development was so successful because the preconditions for rapid growth had already been created in Japan's pre-industrial society. There was a developed infrastructure, a high degree of specialization and a long period of artists such as Ogata Gekkō (1859–1920) also contributed illustrations to newspapers and magazines that were produced by means of modern presses.

Towards the end of the 19th century, traditional printmaking gradually lost its share of the visual representation market. Several important artists were still at work, such as Tsukioka Yoshitoshi, Toyohara Kunichika, Kobayashi Kiyochika and the aforementioned artist Ogata Gekkō, but their numbers were dwindling, as was the number of traditional publishers. The last major boom in print production took place in the years 1904–5, during the Russo-Japanese War. Numerous artists created triptychs to document the conflict, as they had during the Sino-Japanese War of 1894–5.

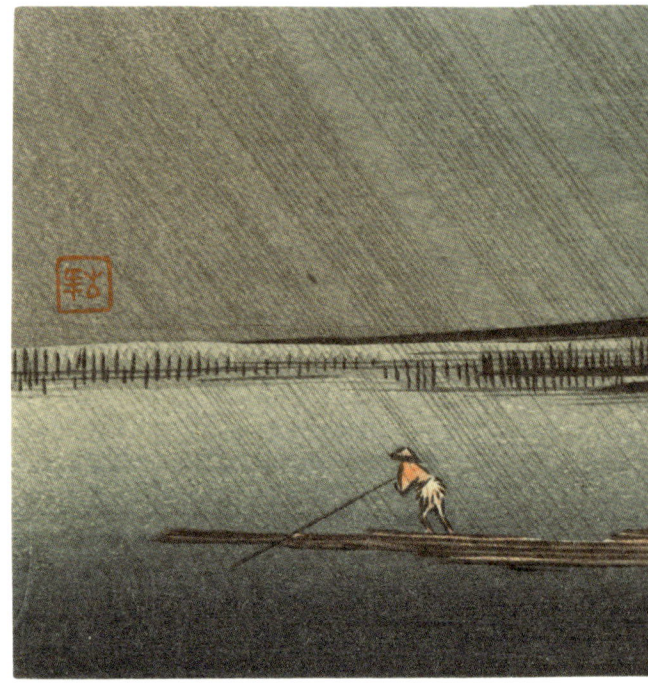

Rescuing printmaking

Just after the turn of the 20th century, the 17-year-old Watanabe Shōzaburō (1885–1962) was apprenticed to the dealer, publisher and collector Kobayashi Bunshichi (1864–1923), whose firm focused on the sale of 18th- and 19th-century original ukiyo-e as well as issuing high-quality reproductions and publishing new work.

In doing so, Bunshichi satisfied the demand among foreigners and tourists for prints that confirmed the traditional image of Japan – as a land of temples, red bridges, bamboo forests and rainswept landscapes (see Fig. 3). After a four-year apprenticeship, however, the young Watanabe felt strong enough to start his own business, and in 1906 he established himself as an independent publisher in Hama-chō, Tokyo. In 1909 he moved to the Kyōbashi district located between the upscale Ginza and Nihonbashi, the traditional heart of downtown Tokyo. From 1907 onwards he supplied prints by Takahashi Hiroaki (Shōtei, 1871–1945) and Itō Sōzan (1884–?) to an antique shop in the mountain tourist resort of Karuizawa, to which many foreigners travelled to avoid the capital's summer heat and to enjoy skiing in winter. Both artists designed prints

in the *tanzaku* format (c. 36 × 16 cm); Sōzan dealt largely with prints of flowers and birds. From 1907 until the earthquake of 1 September 1923, Hiroaki created at least 200 landscape compositions for Watanabe. Watanabe classified these first attempts as *shinsaku hanga* (newly made prints). However, the style of these now rare landscapes was not what Watanabe had in mind; they were too much like an updated version of Hiroshige's work. In the majority of these designs, Watanabe did not include his publisher's mark, possibly an indication that he was not completely satisfied. It is unclear how extensive this trade was: early prints of Hiroaki are extremely rare and are seldom found in museum collections, either in Japan or in the West. This may be evidence of short runs or of a low 'survival rate' – in the latter case because they were generally cheap and not lavishly executed and therefore neither cherished nor preserved.

Even so, these prints were readily bought by foreigners in Japan. Watanabe understood the potential of the foreign market, within Japan and abroad, and for this reason entered into relationships with, among others, the large art dealer Yamanaka and Co., which had had offices in New York, Boston and London since the end of the 19th century.

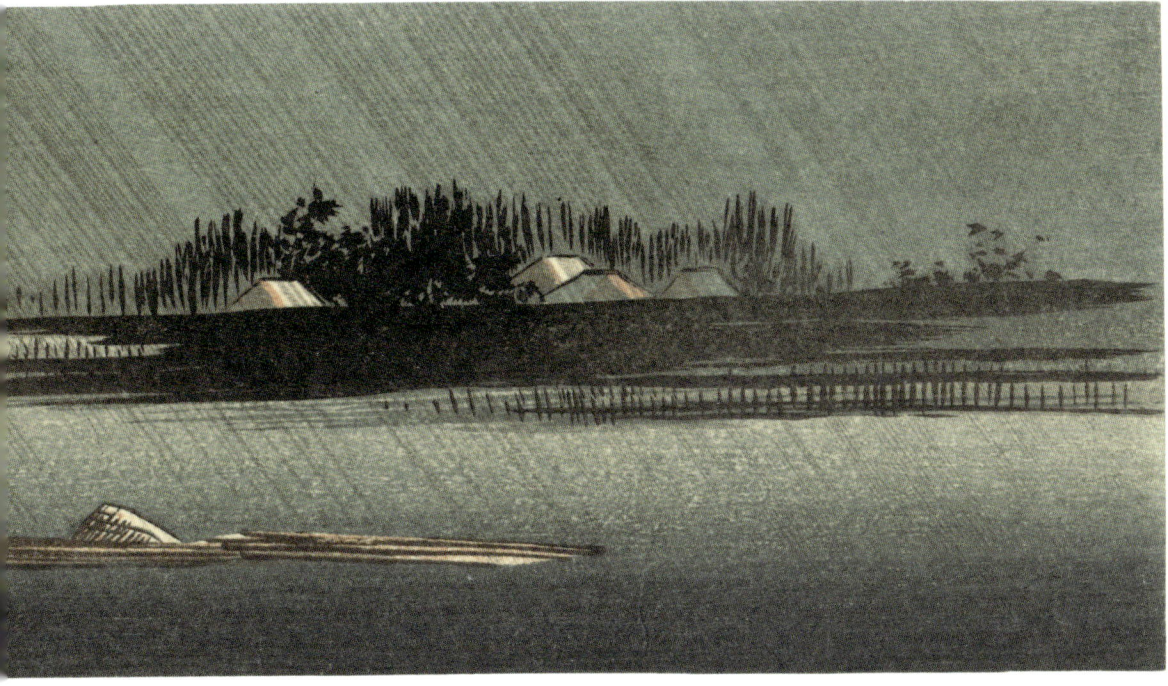

Fig. 3

Uehara Konen, *River in the Rain*, published by Kobayashi Bunshichi, c. 1910

Watanabe Shōzaburō was initially driven by three considerations. First, he had observed the massive export of Japanese prints to the United States and Europe during the last two decades of the 19th century. Japanese traders such as Hayashi Tadamasa (1853–1906) were responsible for the export of an immense number of Japanese prints to Paris. Hayashi alone is believed to have sold more than 160,000 prints in Paris over a ten-year period.[1] In addition, prominent collectors on the east coast of the United States purchased the prints extensively, thus laying the foundation for the largest museum collections of Japanese prints in the world (for example, the Museum of Fine Arts in Boston). This concerned Watanabe, through it did not stop him from becoming involved in the trade himself. He also tried to stimulate interest in traditional ukiyo-e in Japan, possibly in order to prevent the finest specimens from moving abroad. He attempted to achieve this by organizing a memorial exhibition of Hiroshige's work in 1917.[2]

Second, Watanabe was aware that the emergence of rival printing techniques eroded the traditional skills required for making the blocks and prints. He feared the disappearance of this technical knowledge and skill. In 1916 he therefore published a series of extremely luxurious reproductions of prints by the great masters from the 18th and 19th centuries. The series known as *Ukiyo-e hanga kessakushū* (Collection of Ukiyo-e Masterpieces) consisted of six portfolios of the most beautiful reproductions and showcased the incredible craftsmanship of woodblock cutters and printers.

Third, Watanabe also knew that printmaking could recover only if a new language of style and form was developed, without compromising the high technical standards. He seemed to realize that the printmaking that typified the Meiji Period could never appeal to the Western public in the same way the masterpieces of 18th- and 19th-century masters did.

Towards a new style

It was not easy for Watanabe to come up with a new style. He searched for new ideas and found them, in 1915, at an exhibition in Tokyo of the work of the Austrian artist Fritz Capelari (1884–1950) (Cat. 9). After seeing his paintings and watercolours, Watanabe invited Capelari to submit designs to be made into prints. That same year he published 12 prints by Capelari and thereby made clear the new path he wished to take. From 1915 onwards

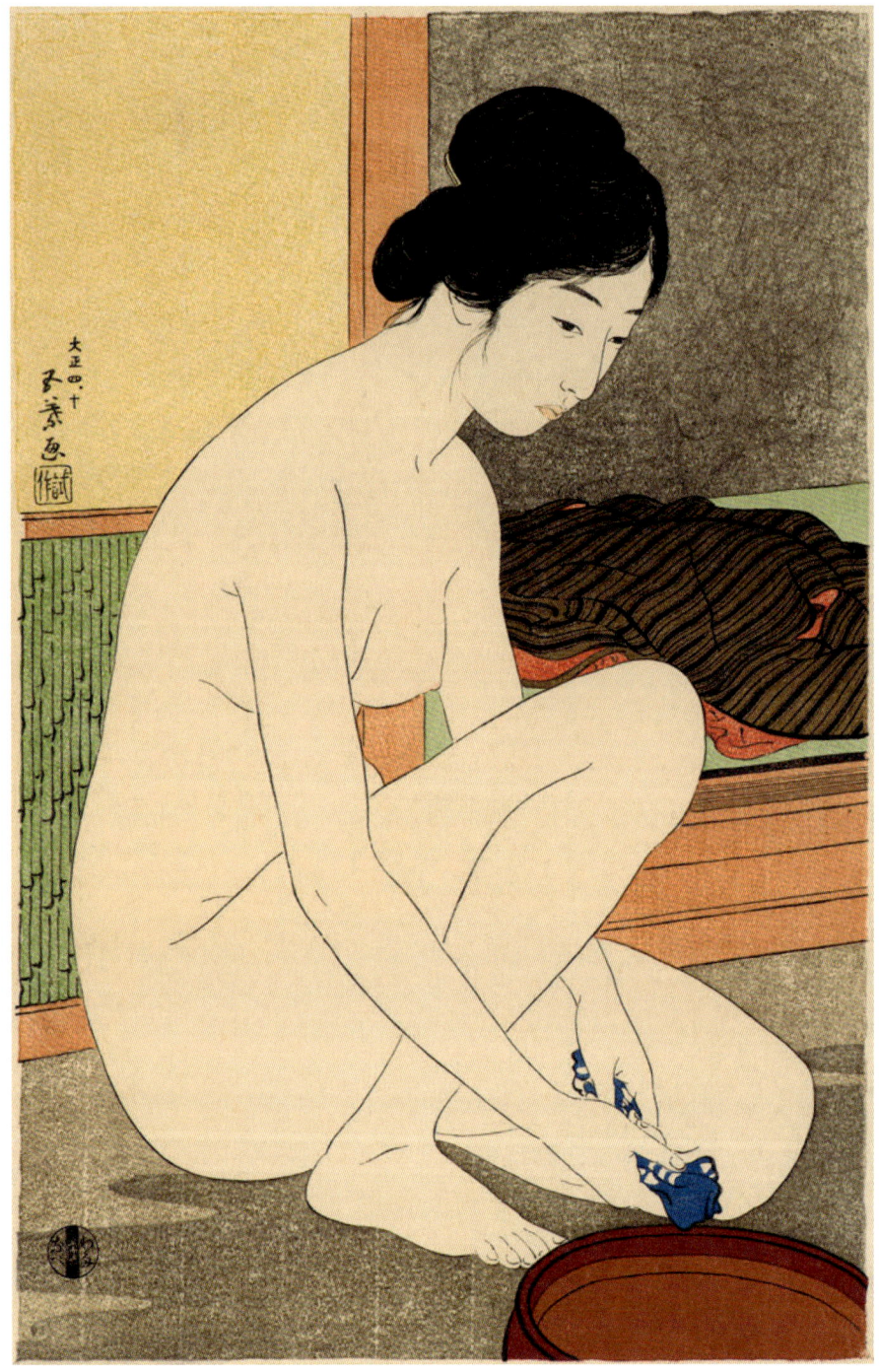

developments accelerated. It was in this year the first print by Hashiguchi Goyō (1881–1921) was published (see Fig. 4), and Watanabe teamed up with the artist Itō Shinsui and, soon after, with Kawase Hasui. This collaboration with Shinsuii resulted in a series of impressive landscape designs in the small *chūban* format (19 × 25.5 cm) that would inspire Hasui. He then made a number of extraordinary *bijin-ga* (beautiful women) prints, taking his cue from Capelari's early examples.

After his first print, Goyō decided to move forward without Watanabe's guiding hand. He chose to self-publish his prints, possibly as a result of a disagreement with Watanabe about the printing techniques used by his printers. This is a clear indication that Watanabe had strong opinions and granted his artists only relative freedom. In this respect, Watanabe was a classic, charismatic and dominant publisher working in the old tradition. However, there is no doubt that the works Watanabe published from 1915 onwards completely broke with what had been produced in traditional printmaking up to that point. In the new *bijin-ga* prints the women show emotion, while the landscapes are more impressionistic and less conventional than those made by Hiroaki for Watanabe until then.

Traditional Japanese print production

Printmaking as it developed from the end of the 17th century was an extremely commercial art form: the aim was to sell as many copies of a design as possible. As such, the art form was not 'free', in the sense that it was not the artist himself who decided what to produce. It was commission-driven art, with the publisher (*hanmoto*) giving the assignment in 90 per cent of cases. He knew the market and asked artists to create designs that he anticipated would sell in numerous impressions. During the heyday of printmaking – the late 18th and first half of the 19th century – it was the publisher who asked an artist to design, for example, a temple in the snow or an actor in a specific role in which he was scheduled to appear on stage. The artist presented his proposal in the form of a sketch to the publisher, who then added any remarks or suggested changes. After processing the comments, the artist came up with the final sketch that the publisher then scheduled for production. A block cutter then cut the blocks, and a printer carried out the final printing. The publisher was responsible for marketing and selling the prints. In essence, Watanabe and his 20th-century colleagues followed this time-honoured process. Having the highest-quality artisans in-house was paramount to the success of a publisher. Watanabe Shōzaburō's grandson Shōichirō, who followed in his grandfather's footsteps, would later complain in an interview that it had become increasingly difficult for him to find talented young printers.[3]

The partnership between publisher, artist, block cutter and printer is often referred as the 'ukiyo-e quartet'. In the 20th century, while people no longer spoke of ukiyo-e – because printmaking was no longer dominated by the imagery of the transient lifestyle of 18th- and 19th-century Edo – Watanabe's production system remained basically the same.

The first signs of change

For the first time in history, however, this production system was under pressure: from the last decades of the 19th century onwards, artists started to look abroad and discovered different ideas about art and artistic freedom. At the beginning of the 20th century, this led to the emergence of a rival printmaking movement under the name *sōsaku hanga* (creative prints).

The artists who belonged to this movement wanted to retain control over the entire process, from design to final product. Personal expression was paramount. In theory, they did not want to use publishers, although this was at times unavoidable in view of their marketing needs. Greater control over the entire process and the removal of the block cutter and printer as 'filters' between their original design and the end product brought them closer to Western ideas about originality. Subsequently, they started to embrace the un-Japanese custom of publishing prints in small, numbered editions. They also chose different subject matter and, in their social behaviour, too, imitated the numerous artistic coteries that characterized, for example, the Paris art scene around the turn of the century. They founded magazines, organized exhibitions, and

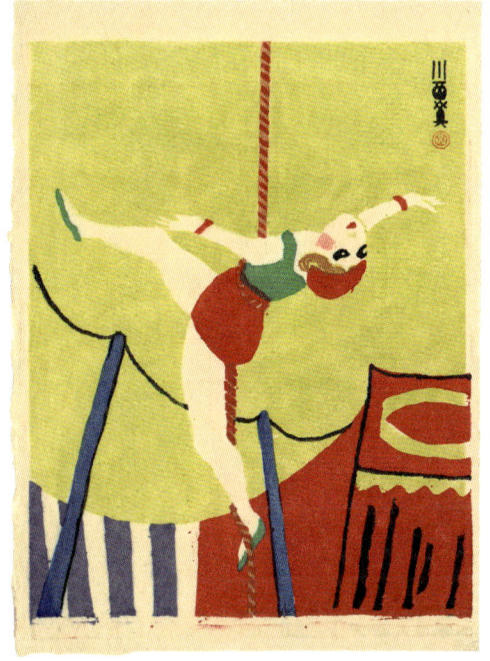

were politically and socially engaged. This societal involvement was almost totally absent among the *shin hanga* artists. The contrast between these two movements sometimes led to harsh words being exchanged: *sōsaku hanga* artists accused their *shin hanga* colleagues of being subordinate to the commercial wishes of the publishers, while, conversely, the *shin hanga* practitioners regarded their opponents as 'amateurs', upbraiding them for their lack of technical skills. But, in reality, the differences between the two movements were not that extreme. Some *sōsaku hanga* artists worked with publishers or with *hanpukai* (distribution clubs).[4] Even the most important *sōsaku hanga* artist, Onchi Kōshirō (1890–1955), often had his blocks printed by an apprentice. Conversely, some *shin hanga* artists resisted the control of publishers. Yoshida Hiroshi (1876–1950), for example, decided, after a short collaboration with Watanabe, to supervise the production process himself and added the two characters meaning *jizuri* (self-printed) to the margin. Nonetheless, the permanent presence

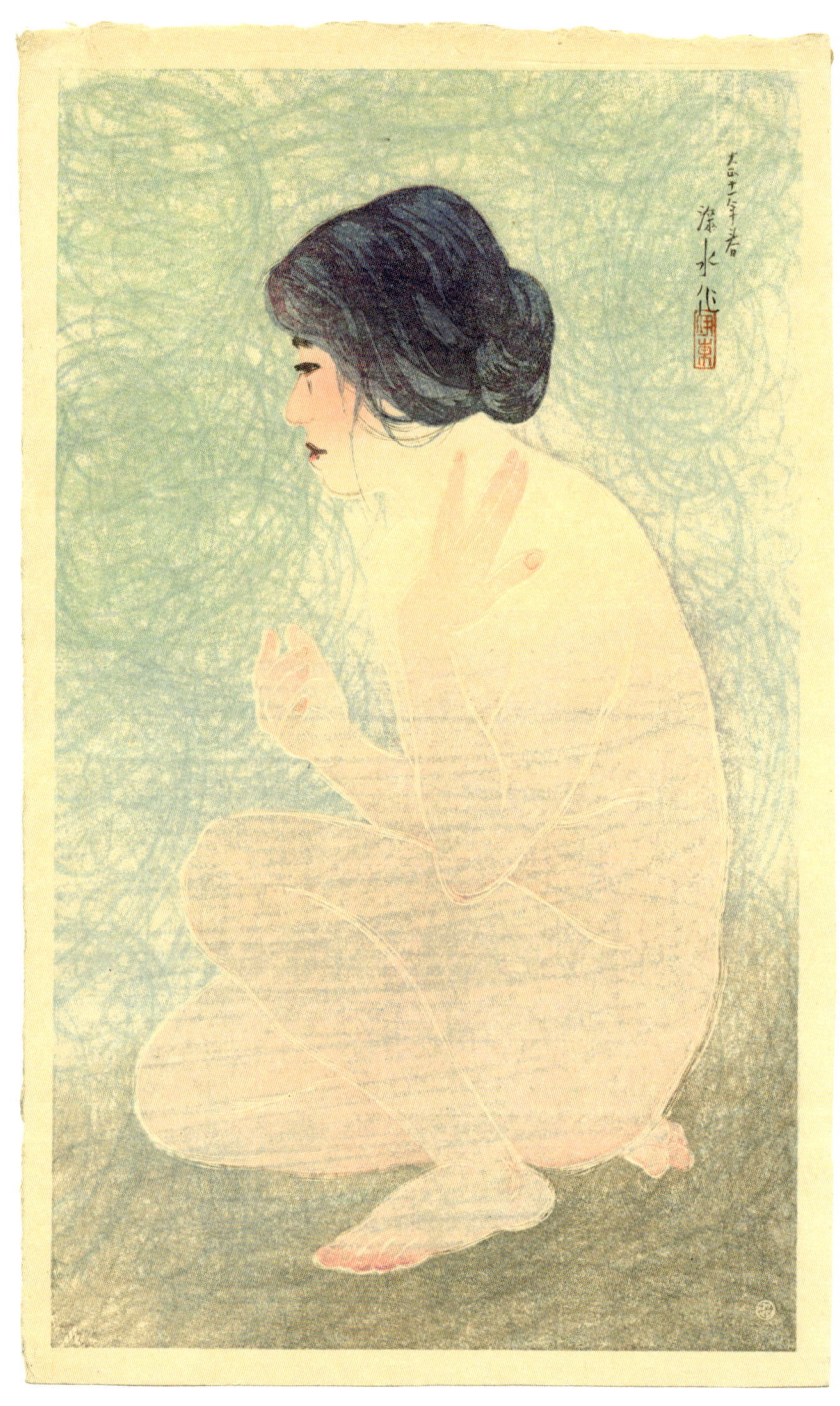

Fig. 6

Itō Shinsui, *Bathing in Early Summer*, 1922. The rough contour lines are accentuated by the use of blind printing.

of the *sōsaku hanga* movement certainly influenced the development of *shin hanga* printmaking. Watanabe was well aware of the criticism aimed at his production and introduced a number of innovations to the printing style of the work of the artists in his stable. The intentionally coarser contours of the prints of naked women (see, for example, Itō Shinsui's *Bathing in Early Summer* [Fig. 6]) was one such stylistic adaptation.

Ideologically, there was also the contrast between the emphasis on Japanese identity and the acceptance of a more Western approach to art. The exhibitions created by the *sōsaku hanga* coteries regularly featured prints and even reproductions by Western artists, thereby indicating how much they were part of an international movement. Watanabe was not interested in this: he wanted to produce innovative traditional Japanese art. Nevertheless, he realized the importance of the Western market and understood that it was still mainly oriented towards traditional designs and not looking for the style expressed by the *sōsaku hanga* movement. To help counter this, from early on he published English-language sales catalogues. One issue he struggled with was that of the size of the print run. Foreign customers were somewhat suspicious if a print was not numbered and from an unlimited edition. In response, he initially numbered some of his series by Itō Shinsui and Kawase Hasui.

These prints were sold through a system of subscription. Later, in 1930 and 1936, when he organized sales exhibitions in Toledo, Ohio, the catalogue entries suggested that the print run was limited to 100, 250 or 300 pieces. This was clearly a marketing ploy that did not quite match reality.

After 1923 Watanabe gradually abandoned numbering, basically following the practice of generations of publishers before him – reproducing a print for as long as it sold. Today, in 2022, the Watanabe firm is still printing from original blocks made between fifty and almost a hundred years ago.

Shin hanga reaches full maturity

Watanabe's experiments with Takahashi Hiroaki in the landscape genre and his attempts, in collaboration with the Austrian Fritz Capelari, to come up with a new style of printmaking resulted in a considerable output from 1916 onwards. *Shin hanga* had truly been born.

It was Itō Shinsui, however, who brought about real innovation in the design of landscape prints,

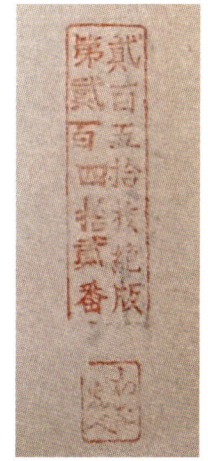 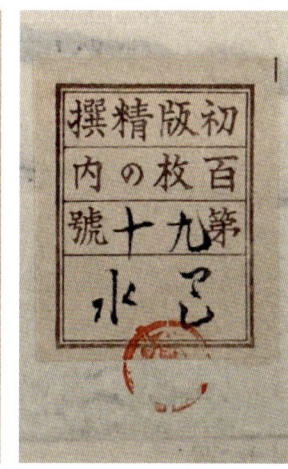

particularly in the early years. His earliest landscapes in the *chūban* format were extremely atmospheric and characterized by exquisite colour transitions. The landscapes were empty, devoid of people. Typical is the presence of a white border round the composition. The margins are much wider than in the early landscapes of Hiroaki, and compositions that bleed off the page, as in the works by Konen (Fig. 3 and Cat. 1), have now become a thing of the past. Shinsui also nods to Hiroshige, his predecessor from the 19th century, by giving his first landscape series (1917) the classic and often used title *Ōmi hakkei* (Eight Views of Ōmi).

The title is analogous to the series titles used by the great masters, such as *Fuji sanjūrokkei* (Thirty-Six Views of Mount Fuji) or *Mutamagawa* (Six Jewel Rivers), some of the most common series titles in traditional Japanese printmaking. But this link with

Fig. 7a–b
Two examples of numbering. *Left*: a stamp on the reverse of a print by Shinsui, issued by Watanabe, stating it to be no. 104 from an edition of 500. *Right*: a label, on the reverse of a Hasui print issued by Sakai-Kawaguchi, stating it to be no. 90 of an edition of 100 impressions, sealed with Hasui's distinctive red round seal.

Fig. 8
Kawase Hasui, *Snow at Dawn (Ogi Port, Sado)*, 1921, with the description from the 1930 Toledo catalogue, no. 66

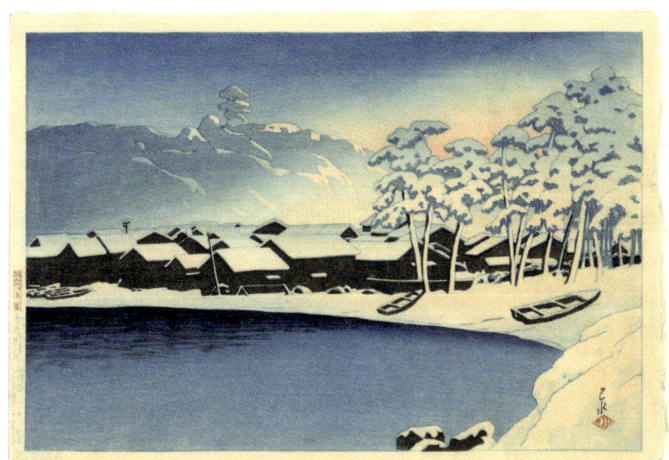

66   SNOW DAWN AT OGI PORT, SADO (Yuki no Akebono Sado Ogi Minato)

Snow-enveloped landscape; blue-green ice-covered water reflecting the sky; grey-black houses with light tints of morning above the blue-white trees and no the grey-blue snowy mountain.

Signed, "Hasui"; also his seal. Imprint of publisher, Watanabe. Margin: "Tabi Miyage, Dai Ni Shu" (Souvenirs of Travels, Second Series). "Yuki no Akebono, Sado Ōgi Minato" (Snow Dawn, Ogi Port, Sado). Dated, "Taisho Ju Nen Ju-ni Gatsu". Edition, 100 impressions.   9⁹⁄₁₆'' x 14³⁄₈''

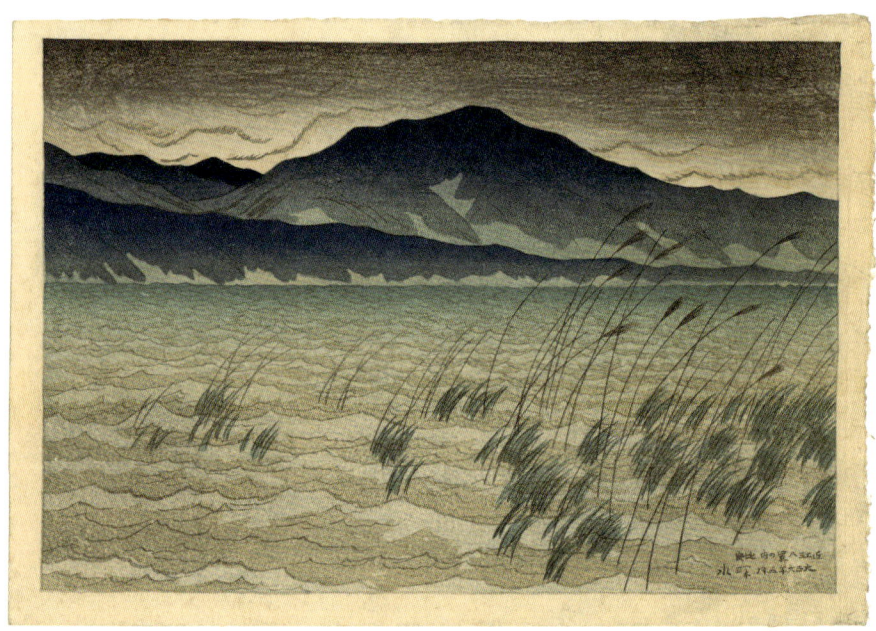

Fig. 9
Itō Shinsui, *Mount Hira*, from the series *Eight Views of Ōmi*, 1917

the past is an exception. Shinsui, and later Hasui in particular, did not depict Japan's 'famous places' (*meisho*) as Hiroshige had. The emphasis was on the typical characteristics of the Japanese landscape, untouched by modernization. This nostalgic attitude was reflected in printmaking as well as in the novels and poetry of the period.

Hasui indicated that it was Shinsui's work that had inspired him to devote himself fully to landscapes. He saw Shinsui's *Ōmi hakkei* at an exhibition in 1918 and decided to follow suit. It is remarkable that subsequently, within the group of artists considered to be from Watanabe's stable, Shinsui developed into the designer par excellence of prints of beautiful women while Hasui limited himself entirely to landscapes.

A major disaster

On 1 September 1923, at lunchtime, Tokyo was struck by a massive earthquake, which was followed by extensive fires. Much of the city lay in ruins, and more than 100,000 people died. Watanabe's workshops were razed to the ground, and the woodblock sets as well as stocks of prints already produced were lost. This terrible event led to a caesura in the classification of 20th-century Japanese prints: in almost

all cases, the term 'Pre-earthquake' in a description means that the print is a great rarity because so many of the existing stock (and copies already sold) were lost. The destruction of the woodblocks made printing of additional copies impossible. Even so, Watanabe resumed production fairly quickly after the earthquake. He moved to the location in Ginza, where his grandson still runs the business today.

At around this time other publishers appeared on the scene. From 1925 Yoshida Hiroshi began publishing his own prints. The Takamizawa Mokuhansha company had been operating since 1911, selling excellent reproductions, but now it shifted its focus to new designs (Fig. 10).

From 1929 the Sakai-Kawaguchi firm gained some market share. Sakai Shōkichi and Kawaguchi Jirō were responsible for a number of beautiful Hasui prints with extra-wide borders, which were also numbered (see Fig. 7b), as well as a series of beautiful women prints by Torii Kotondo. The latter artist later switched to the Ikeda publishers, also new to the scene. These firms were all located in Tokyo. Outside of Tokyo there was only one major publisher, based in Kyoto: Satō Shōtarō. Like Watanabe, Satō sold traditional prints, issued reproductions and released original designs. Satō also participated in the major Toledo exhibitions of 1930 and 1936, where he showed work by his two main artists, Yoshikawa Kanpō (1894–1979) (Fig. 14 and Cats. 123–25) and Miki Suizan (1887–1957).

Still, no one could match Watanabe's output. His firm was responsible for approximately 1,000 *shin hanga* designs, roughly one-third of an estimated total of 3,000 pieces that can be classified as belonging to the *shin hanga* genre. Compared to their 19th-century colleagues, individual artists had very small oeuvres. The most prolific, Kawase Hasui, created no more than a tenth of Hiroshige's estimated number, 700 versus 7,000. An important figure in the *shin hanga* movement, Itō Shinsui, made 'only' 146 prints in total, although it should be

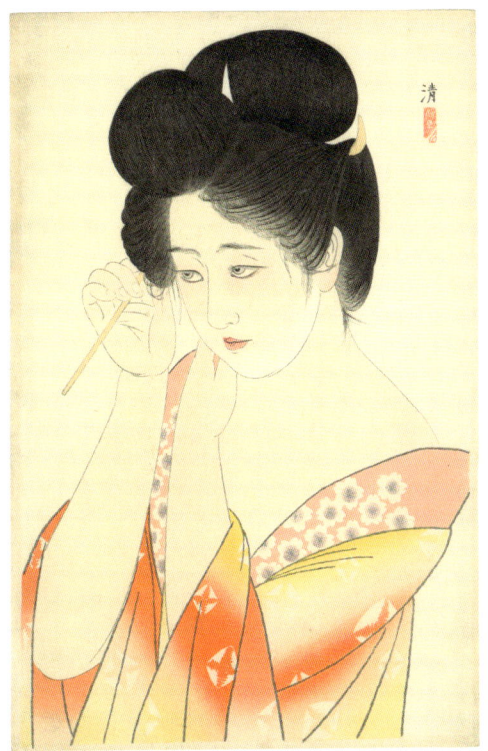

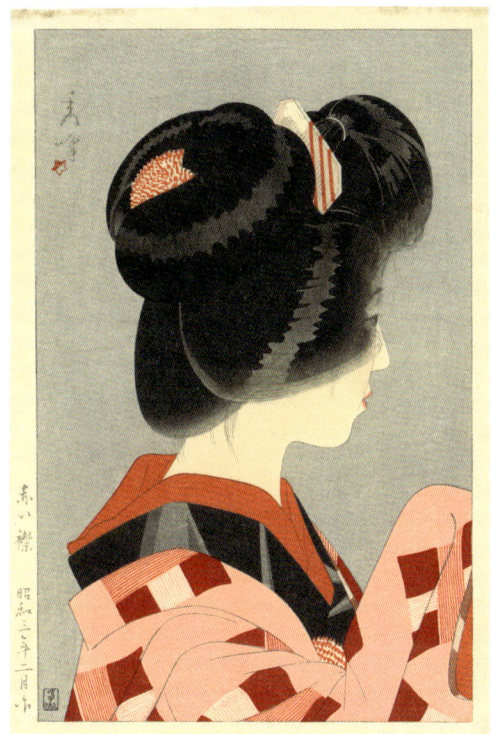

remembered that Shinsui was first and foremost a painter, receiving many commissions from wealthy clients for expensive paintings on silk.

The artists

Just as Watanabe Shōzaburō was fundamental to the commercial development of *shin hanga*, the artistic aspect of the movement was also heavily determined by the ideas and influence of a single man: Kaburaki Kiyokata (1878–1972). Kiyokata was the son of an important pioneer in the development of the modern newspaper in Japan. His father was the founder of the newspapers *Nichi-nichi shimbun* and *Yamato shimbun*. When he was 13 years old, his father sent him to the studio of the ukiyo-e artist Tsukioka Yoshitoshi and later to that of Mizuno Toshikata (1866–1908). His father wanted him to become a professional illustrator so he could later join him at his own newspapers.

Kiyokata was an esteemed designer of so-called *kuchi-e*, woodblock prints that illustrated machine-printed novels and magazines. These prints, whose purpose was to capture the essence of the story, were folded in three and loosely bound into the novels. The print was a bonus and considered a collector's item. However, Kiyokata's great ambition was to become a painter, especially of the female subjects.

In 1901 he founded a group, the Ugokai, aimed at reinvigorating the *bijin-ga* genre. Later he established Kinreisha, the academy for *nihonga*, or Japanese-style painting. Watanabe recruited four artists who attended this academy: the aforementioned Kawase Hasui and Itō Shinsui, together with Yamakawa Shūhō (1898–1944) (Fig. 11) and Kasamatsu Shirō (1898–1991).

Kiyokata was also the teacher of Kobayakawa Kiyoshi (1899?–1948) and Torii Kotondo (1900–76). With the exception of Hasui and Shirō, all of these artists, whose work has become known to a wider audience outside Japan, created more paintings than prints. In 1915 Kiyokata's students united in a group called the Kyōdokai, which regularly organized exhibitions. It was at one of those exhibitions that Watanabe saw a painting by Shinsui. After Kiyokata's intervention, Watanabe persuaded Shinsui to have one of his designs made into a print. This design was *Before the Mirror* (Cat. 25).

The subjects

Woodblocks were traditionally used for printing cards, books, stationery, amulets, games, models,

Fig. 10
Kobayakawa Kiyoshi, *Doing her Hair*, published by Takamizawa Mokuhansha, 1931

Fig. 11
Yamakawa Shūhō, *Red Collar*, published by Bijutsu-sha, 1928

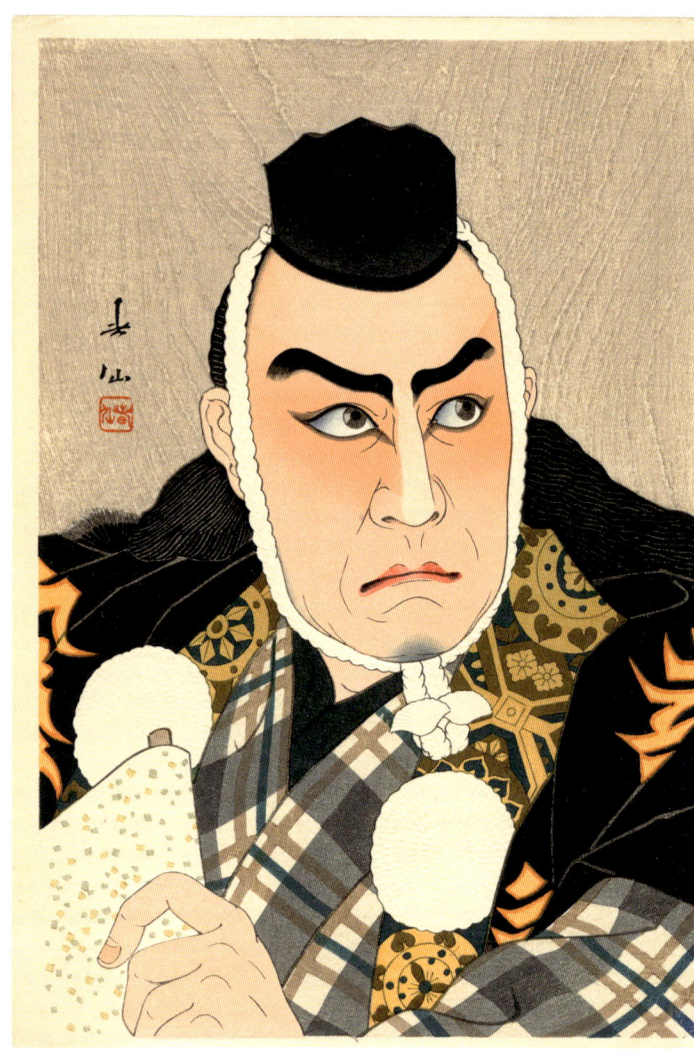
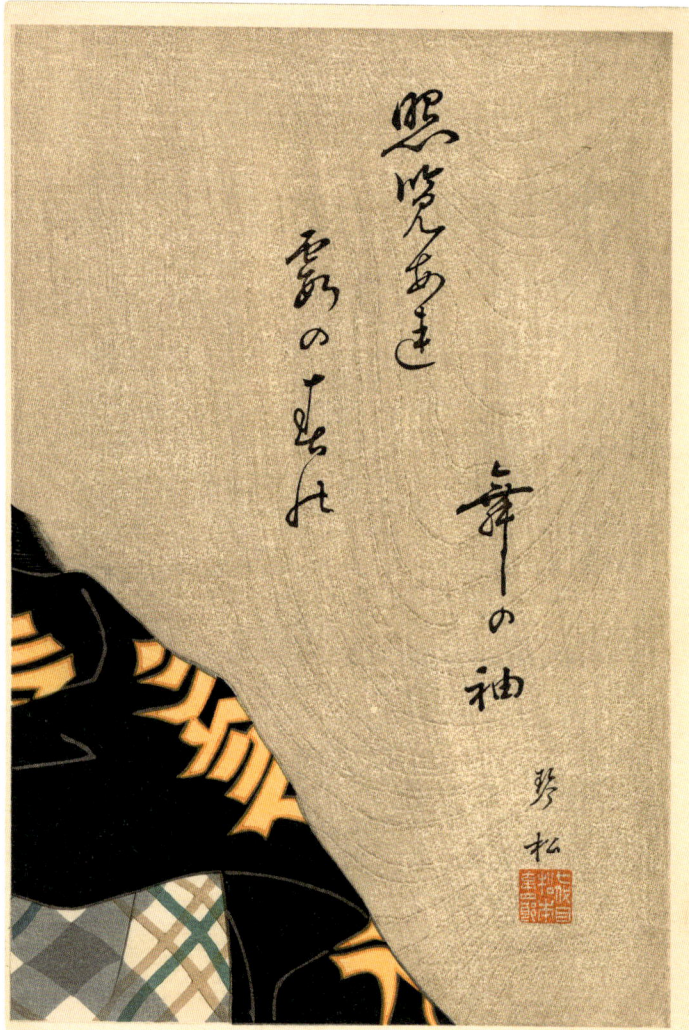

Fig. 12

Natori Shunsen, *The Actor Matsumoto Kōshirō VII as Benkei*, *ōban* diptych, published in 1935. This is the only *shin hanga* diptych within the *shin hanga* tradition. Courtesy Nihon no hanga, Amsterdam.

invitations and so on. This changed at the beginning of the 20th century. Traditional publishers, including Watanabe, still produced postcards and calendars, but modern machine printing techniques such as chromolithography were used for all other purposes. Certain prominent genres disappeared, such as the historical and heroic prints in the style of Kuniyoshi and Yoshitoshi. It seems that publishers were concerned about their reputation for 'modernity'. They felt that referring to a samurai past with an emphasis on swords, violence and rolling heads did not fit the modern image Japan now wanted to convey. The same applied to the erotic images known as *shunga* (literally 'spring images'), which almost completely disappeared as a genre. Of course, *shunga* continued to exist in all kinds of underground publications, in photography and also in painting, but no longer in the form of prints, which had still been widely produced in the late 19th century. An important reason for the dis-

appearance of *shunga* was the strict enforcement of the censorship laws instituted during the Meiji Period.

Multi-sheet compositions disappeared as well. As late as 1904–5, hundreds of triptychs depicting the Russo-Japanese War were made, but within the *shin hanga* movement only one such diptych was published, by Natori Shunsen (1886–1960) (Fig. 12).

The average print size increased slightly. The common *ōban* format (c. 38 × 26 cm), for example, was often enlarged by several centimetres for use within the beautiful women genre of prints. Landscapes were sometimes printed in extremely large formats as well (Cat. 44).

The quality of the paper used by the artists improved significantly. Twentieth-century paper was much heavier (and more expensive) than paper from the 18th and 19th centuries. This improvement gave printers even more options for printing colour over colour, without the risk of paper breaking due

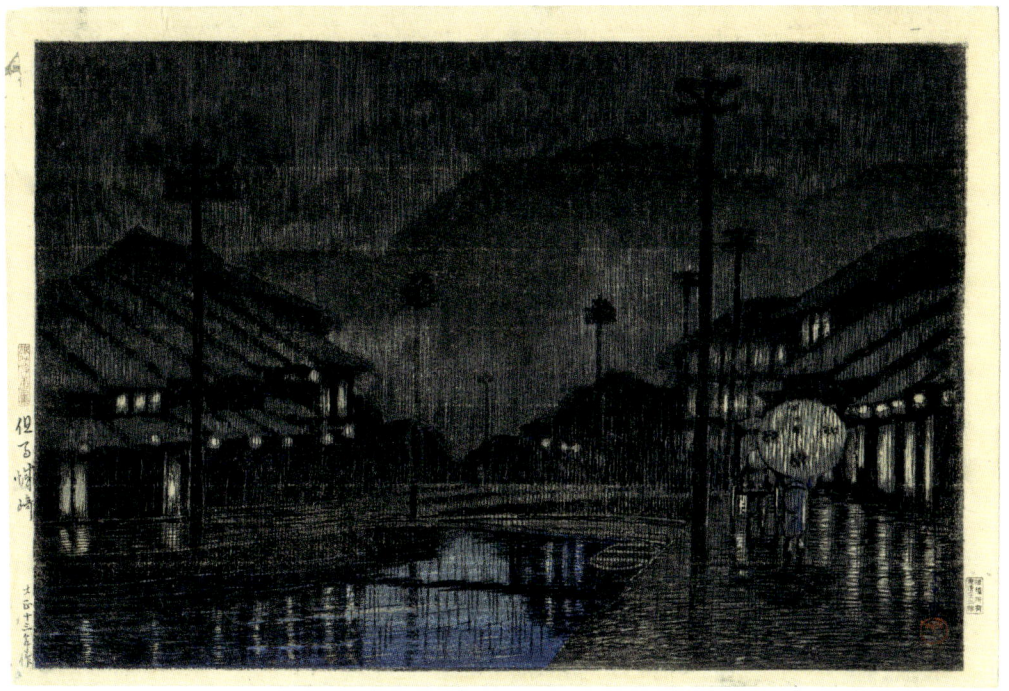

Fig. 13

Kawase Hasui, *Kinosaki, Tajima*, published by Watanabe Shōzaburō, 1924. Featuring heavy rain and lamp reflections, this is a typical example of a print by Hasui. In the left margin is the print title and the date, in the right margin the publisher's mark, and in the right corner, on the image itself, Hasui's unobtrusive signature and his red artist's seal.

to oversaturation by the ink. All this illustrates that, in the first half of the 20th century, the emphasis had shifted from a mass product to a more exclusive form of expression. To illustrate: Utagawa Hiroshige gave his name to approximately 7,000 prints over a period of 40 years between 1818 and 1858. Each of these prints – and this is a conservative estimation – had an average print run of around 3,000 pieces. This means that, within a period of 40 years, approximately 21 million prints carrying the name Hiroshige saw the light. If we compare the total production, between 1900 and 1960, of all *shin hanga* artists combined, we arrive at approximately 3,000 designs with an average circulation per copy of 1,000 pieces, amounting to a total output of 3 million pieces. Both are estimates but nonetheless give a good picture of the enormous difference in the scale of production.

Fūkei ga: landscape prints

Of Kiyokata's students, first Shinsui and then Hasui and Shirō became the main exponents of the landscape genre. The market for landscapes was fed by the enduring image of the countryside as a symbol of the social order and community that were gradually disappearing in the face of rapid urbanization. The survival of this 'agrarian myth' coincided with the need felt by some bureaucrats to support ag-

ricultural production and innovation as a counterweight to the unremitting urban sprawl. 'Agriculture as the foundation of the nation' was a popular slogan in 20th-century Japan.[5] All of this created a market for landscape artists, especially from the *shin hanga* movement. This constituted a problem for Kasamatsu Shirō, who, unlike Hasui, was reluctant to venture out into the countryside. He preferred to stay in Tokyo and thus created mainly urban scenes.[6] The contrast between town and country, resulting from the strong division between modern and traditional Japan, thus also expressed itself within the *shin hanga* movement.

In the numerous landscapes illustrated in this publication, the interaction between location and weather conditions is striking. Rain and snow dominate, symbolizing humanity's struggle with the elements (Cats. 67, 69). Additionally, the work of Hasui, in particular, brings to the fore the subtle play of light on water: the moon shining through the clouds and leaving a long glittering path across the sea (Cat. 51), or lamplight from a farmhouse that illuminates a canal, thereby emphasizing the atmosphere of loneliness and emptiness (Cat. 52). Furthermore, the compositions are not cluttered by cartouches for the signature or title, as was customary during the 19th century, especially in the landscapes of Hiroshige and his students. Print titles were positioned in the margins of the landscapes, as were, in most cases, the publisher's seals and dates.

Whereas Hasui, Shirō and Hiroaki found their subjects within Japan, Yoshida Hiroshi ventured abroad. He travelled to the United States and, upon his return to Japan, converted his sketches of the Niagara Falls, the Grand Canyon and Yosemite into prints. He also visited Switzerland, India, China and Egypt. Half of his total production of approximately 200 prints have non-Japanese subjects.

Bijin-ga: prints of beautiful women

During the 18th and 19th centuries, the *bijin-ga* genre was defined by its relationship to the Yoshiwara, Edo's brothel district. The prints depicted the most beautiful and famous geisha and courtesans. They were pin-ups or fashion pictures or disguised advertisements for teahouses, restaurants and textile merchants. By the end of the 19th century, the relationship between prints of beautiful women and night-time entertainment had started to fade. At the beginning of the 20th century, models were used for the first time, and the women portrayed gradually became recognizable as individuals. Hashiguchi Goyō (1880–1921) left dozens of drawings of his favourite model (Cats. 18, 19, 21). The focus is on the woman's pose as she combs her hair, applies make-up in front of the mirror, or engages in her bathing ritual. Her expression is often pensive, somewhat melancholic and introverted.

Within this genre, Itō Shinsui comes first in terms of numbers and importance. He produced 77 prints of women, 65 of which were published by Watanabe. Not all are masterpieces, perhaps because Watanabe and Shinsui regularly disagreed about the intention of the design and the printed end result. In some cases these quarrels led to serious production delays. Shinsui was constantly striving to achieve through printmaking that which was not possible in painting. For him it was all about texture, expressiveness and transparency.[7] Torii Kotondo was an artist from the Kiyokata school who, for reasons unknown, never associated himself with Watanabe. He comes from a long line of printmakers; he originally belonged to the renowned Torii lineage that has its origins in the 17th century and is active to this day; Kotondo's father was the seventh-generation head of the Torii school. The school specialized in prints of actors as well as theatre programmes (*banzuke*) and wooden theatre billboards (*kanban*).

After initially occupying himself with the world of the theatre – also during his period with Kiyokata – Kotondo became interested in female portraits. And although he made only 23 such prints, some of them represent the absolute pinnacle of the *shin hanga* movement, both in terms of atmosphere and technical perfection.

The *shin hanga* prints of beautiful women were highly appreciated abroad, even in the early 1920s. New York auctions sold prints by Goyō and Shinsui at premium prices. At a 1921 auction where Hokusai's *The Great Wave off the Coast of Kanagawa* went for US$ 280 (today it holds the all-time world auction record for a Japanese print, US$ 1.6 million), Shinsui's *Bathing in Early Summer* (Fig. 6) went for US$ 100, while in Japan these prints had originally cost between 3 and 15 yen from the publisher (at the time, a yen was worth about 50 cents).

Kabuki actors

In the 18th and 19th centuries, the genre of actor prints was one of the pillars of Japanese printmaking. During the first half of the 19th century in particular, tens of thousands of actor print designs were created by members of the Utagawa school. The majority of kabuki prints were released in direct relation to kabuki theatre: artists depicted actors in a specific role in a specific play on a specific day. This close relationship between performance and print completely disappeared in the 20th century; the prints now became individual portraits of actors in their best-known roles, and were not directly linked to performances in the kabuki theatres.

For publishers who wanted to revive the publishing business in the 20th century, the genre of the kabuki print was not the most obvious choice. After all, such prints could be sold only to a domestic clientele familiar with the names and roles of the famous actors of the time. Watanabe tried it anyway and was successful. First he worked with Natori Shunsen, and then with Yamamura Kōka (1885–1942). Both were excellent artists with a passion for their subject. Shunsen, in particular, set himself up as a vocal expert in the genre. Comparisons were drawn with early greats such as Tōshūsai Sharaku (active 1794–95), Utagawa Toyokuni (1769–1825) and Utagawa Kunichika (1835–1900), the last kabuki specialist of the Utagawa lineage. Contemporary critics were full of praise: as with Sharaku, the actors' heads were dramatically set against a plain background, sometimes printed with glittering mica. This was also the case with the prints by a third artist from Kyoto, Yoshikawa Kanpō (1894–1979) (Fig. 14).

Shunsen's and Kōka's prints were sold through a subscription system tied to distribution clubs. Watanabe was the producer. The name of the distribution organization was directly linked to the artist. Shunsen and Watanabe published two series, the most famous of which (from 1925) consisted of 36 designs, with a supplement of 15 pieces. Nevertheless, the kabuki genre was, and remained, a relatively small affair, with barely more than 100 *ōban* prints in very limited editions.

Kachō-ga: flowers and birds

The genre of flowers and birds has always been popular among foreigners visiting Japan, making it all the more surprising that publishers did not really pursue this avenue.

Prints of flowers and birds virtually ceased to exist after the death of Hiroshige in 1858, and the subject matter of birds and flowers became the

domain of painters. From 1880 onwards a large number of woodblock-printed books with flowers and birds appeared on the market, especially by painters such as Kono Bairei (1844–95), Shiokawa Bunrin (1808–77) and Watanabe Seitei (1851–1918). Individual prints of flowers and birds were rare. At the very end of the 19th century, however, this suddenly changed when the publisher Daikokuya issued large numbers of square prints (*shikishiban*, literally: 'square paper format', c. 23 × 21 cm) onto the market. Some of these prints were by artists who

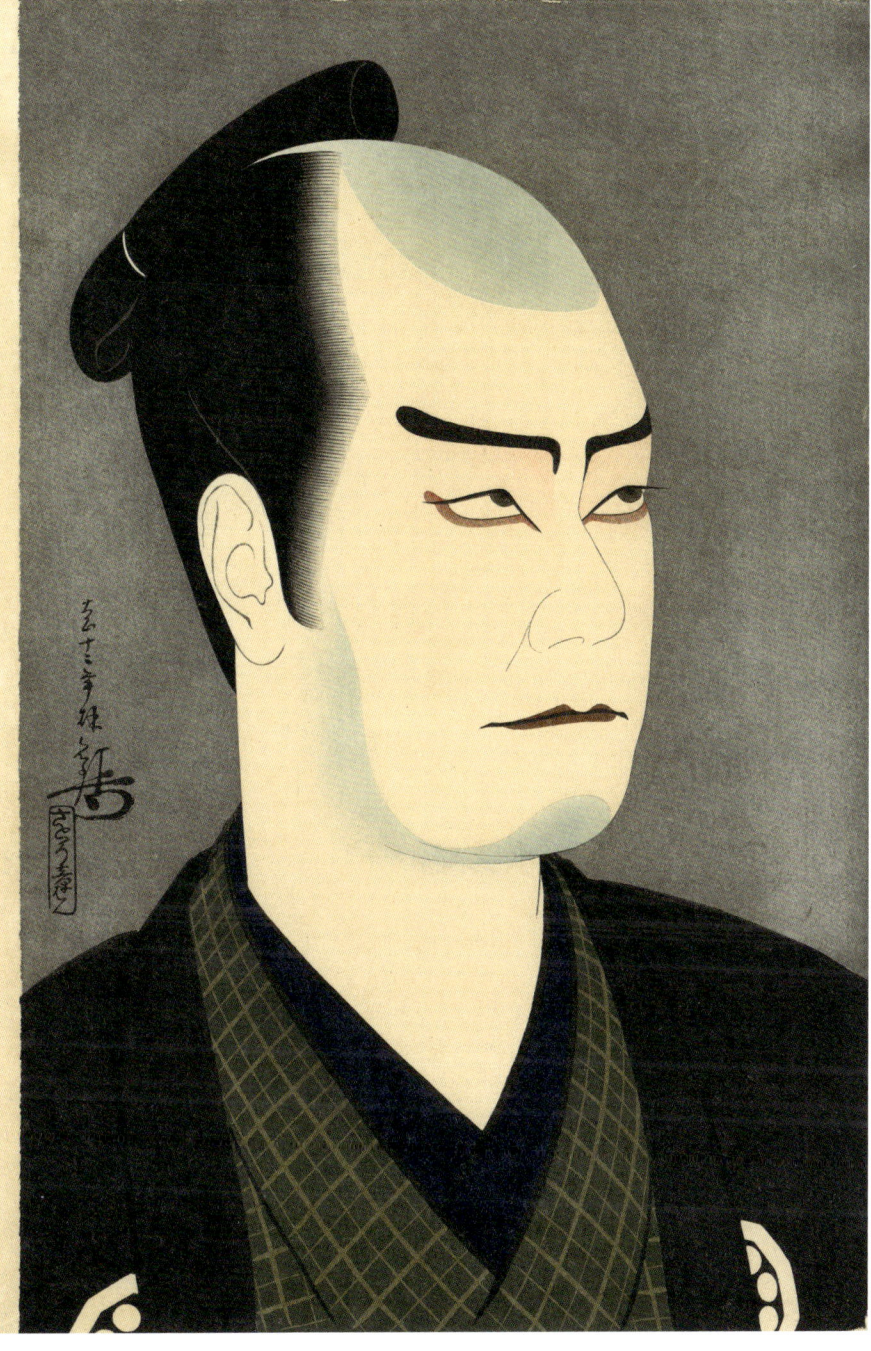

Fig. 14
Yoshikawa Kanpō, *[Ichikawa Sadanji II in the play Imayō Satsuma uta as] Gengobei of the Takashimaya Guild*, 1923

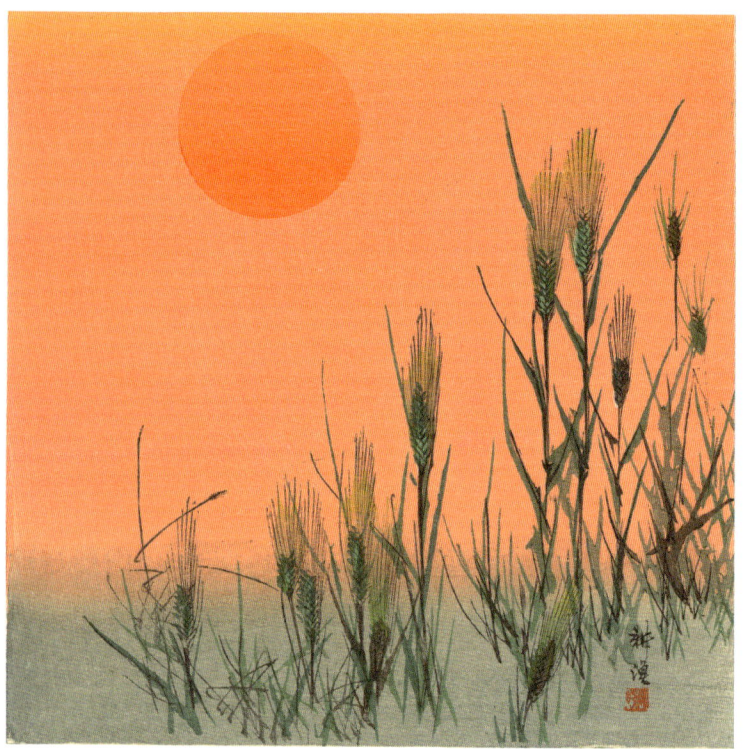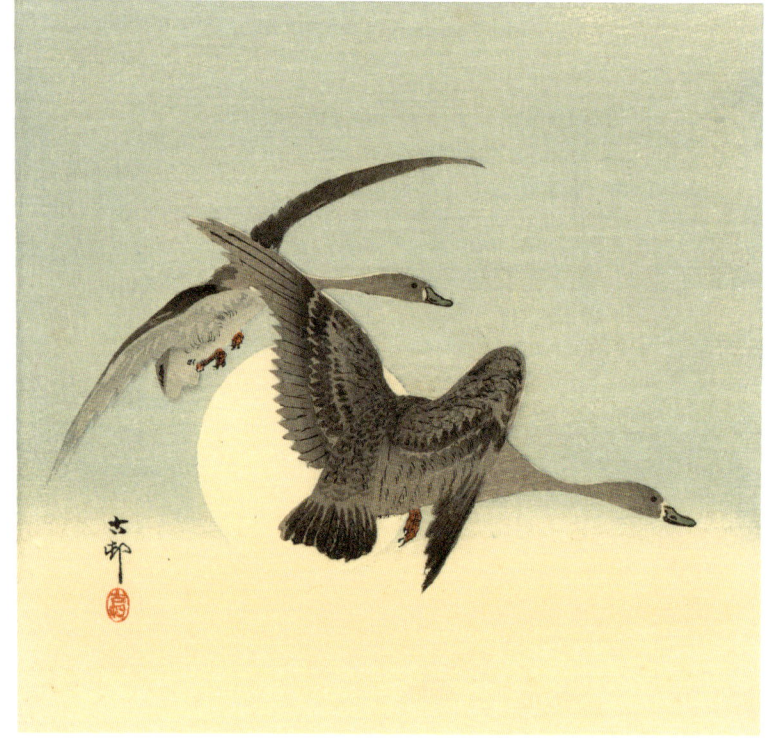

Figs. 15 and 16

Two examples of a *shikishiban* print
published by Daikokuya, c. 1908–10.
Left: **Tsukioka Kōgyo**, *Setting Sun*
Right: **Ohara Koson**, *Geese in Flight*

had passed away, such as Shibata Zeshin (1807–91).
The most important artists in this genre, who were
still alive at the time, were Ogata Gekkō, Tsukioka
Kōgyo (1869–1927) and Ohara Koson (1877–1945).

The *kachō-ga* genre was closely associated with
painting. The *shikishiban* size was derived from the
shikishi paintings, made on paper or silk glued to
cardboard. They were shown in *shikishigake*, scrolls
that enabled the display of *shikishi*. Daikokuya produced hundreds of prints in this format, over a
period of at least 25 years. This included the earliest
work of Ohara Koson. Koson was the 20th-century
flower-and-bird artist par excellence, although he
did not truly become part of the *shin hanga* tradition until 1926, when he joined the Watanabe stable. Everything in his early print work is aimed at
imitating the art of painting, even the proportions
of the format. His prints, moreover, 'bleed', that is,

they do not have the wide margin characteristic of
almost all *shin hanga* prints. Under Watanabe, his
work became more graphic. It was printed with a
lighter colour palette and was framed by margins,
like other *shin hanga* prints. It is interesting to note
that Koson did not receive recognition in Japan
until recently (2015). Since then, however, several
major retrospective exhibitions have been devoted
to him.

Modernity

While the members of the *shin hanga* movement
can be considered a conservative group of artists and publishers seeking to revive and renew
an older art form – a group that was criticized by
the more modern and cosmopolitan *sōsaku hanga*
artists – Watanabe and his colleagues did, in fact,
pay attention to the more ostentatious aspects of

modernizing Japan. This is evident in their designs of urban landscapes in which the modern city life of the 1930s was a central theme (Fig. 17).

They also chose the nude as a subject, an extremely controversial theme that Watanabe was not afraid to explore (see Fig. 4, 6). Other publishers also ventured into this genre, which, outside of illegal erotica, was new in Japanese art. This may indicate that people were aware of the role of the nude in Western painting and, by including it in their visual expressions, demonstrated how greatly they valued modernity and cosmopolitanism. Additionally, images appeared of the 'Modern Girl', *modan gāru* in Japanese (abbreviated to *moga*). The concept of the *moga* emerged around 1924. It describes the free, (financially) independent woman who makes her own choices and enjoys modern Western life. She shops in the department stores of the Ginza district and can be recognized by her cropped hair. The ultimate example of a *moga* print is Kobayakawa Kiyoshi's *Tipsy (no. 1)* (Cat. 144). Kiyoshi is the foremost designer of prints in this genre.

It is important to realize that the government looked upon this sociological phenomenon of the *moga* with great suspicion: the Tokubetsu Kōtō Keisatsu (Special Higher Police), nicknamed the 'Thought Police', had been active since the 1920s, and expressions of excessive sensuality were prosecuted.[8] The relatively small number of *moga* prints published within the *shin hanga* tradition during a time that is described as the *ero jidai* (era of eroticism) shows in part the movement's general conservatism, but possibly also indicates the successful repression of representations that were considered too licentious.

Shin hanga in decline

As the Second World War escalated and expanded from December 1941 onwards, print production in Japan came almost to a halt. Watanabe still published prints on a modest scale, but his foreign

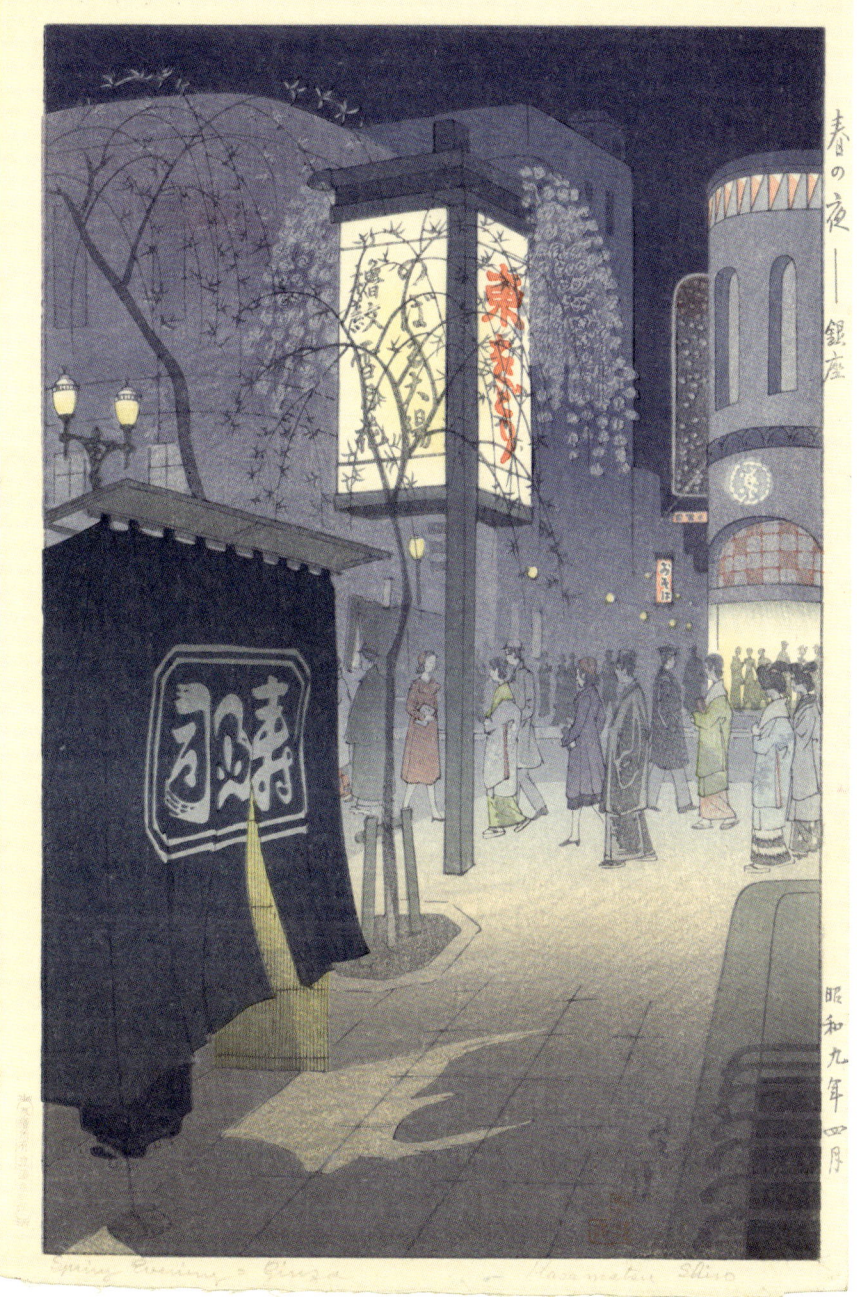

clientele was gone. Materials such as wood and paper became extremely scarce, and late in the war systematic firebombing by the Americans destroyed Tokyo, together with Watanabe's shop. In 1946, however, Watanabe quickly returned to market. The American occupying army paradoxically offered enormous sales opportunities, as many soldiers purchased prints to take back home as souvenirs. Nevertheless, one gets the impression that the landscape compositions by Hasui and the beautiful women prints of Shinsui lost some of their artistic quality after the war. The landscapes increasingly

Fig. 17

Kasamatsu Shirō, *Spring Night, Ginza*, published by Watanabe, 1934 turned into enlarged postcards, with often harshly accentuated contours. The beautiful women prints lack spirit and are rather staid. While they often seem to be trying to evoke the traditional Japanese image of women, they suffer from a certain stiffness and inexpressiveness. That is why only a limited number of post-war prints have been included in this selection. The 'New' in 'New Printmaking' was becoming somewhat stale, and the movement was unable to reinvent itself.

Epilogue

Although *shin hanga* artists and their publishers were naturally aware of the rich heritage of Japanese printmaking, it is remarkable how different the prints of *shin hanga* artists are from those of their famed 18th- and 19th-century predecessors.

The beautiful women prints of Shinsui only remotely resemble those of Utamaro, just as the landscapes of Hasui differ enormously from those of Hokusai or Hiroshige. The reason for this difference is that, essentially, 18th- and 19th-century artists were primarily genuine graphic artists, artists who were particularly aware of the power of the black line. Twentieth-century *shin hanga* artists, on the other hand, focused on texture and colour nuance; imitating painting and achieving painted effects was central to their goals. This makes sense because, with a few exceptions, almost all *shin hanga* artists were also painters and painting often accounted for a much larger part of their oeuvre. The technology and production systems may have hardly changed over the centuries, but the end results varied greatly.

Moreover, the large print runs that characterized the print industry of the late 18th and much of the 19th century became a thing of the past in the first half of the 20th. In fact, it can be concluded that the print changed from being a simple consumer product to a luxury item produced by highly competent and meticulous craftsmen. It is evident to today's collectors of *shin hanga* that these prints were the fruits of the extreme dedication of artists as they sought to transform their artistic intentions into beautiful products. And that is why the owners of the prints in this publication put their heart and soul into collecting *shin hanga*.

Chris Uhlenbeck

1   See Chris Uhlenbeck, 'The Japanese prints of Vincent van Gogh', in Chris Uhlenbeck et al., *Japanese Prints: The Collection of Vincent van Gogh* (Amsterdam: Van Gogh Museum, 2018), p. 48.

2   The exhibition was held in November–December 1917, accompanied by a beautiful catalogue written by Watanabe, with a woodblock-printed copy of Kunisada's memorial portrait of Hiroshige. In 1918 a limited-edition English translation was published.

3   See Watanabe Shōichirō and Chris Uhlenbeck, 'The *Shin Hanga* publisher Watanabe Shōzaburō : an interview with Setsuko Abe and Junko Nishiyama', in C. Uhlenbeck et al., *Waves of Renewal: Modern Japanese Prints, 1900–1960* (Leiden: Hotei Publishing, 2016), pp. 33–40.

4   See Setsuko Abe and Junko Nishiyama, 'Modes of dissemination, *hanpukai* distribution clubs', in Uhlenbeck et al., *Waves of Renewal*, pp. 62–4.

5   For an excellent discussion of the development of the ideology of the agrarian myth, see Carol Gluck, *Japan's Modern Myths: Ideology in the Late Meiji Period* (Princeton: Princeton University Press, 1985), pp. 178–204.

6   See Uhlenbeck et al., *Waves of Renewal*, p. 36.

7   See Setsuko Abe, 'A question of beauty: Itō Shinsui and Watanabe Shōzaburō's vision of *shin hanga*', in Uhlenbeck et al., *Waves of Renewal*, p. 44.

8   'Individualism, materialism and feminism were regarded as threats to the Japanese nation […]. References to "purity", and prevention of "decadence" and degeneration indicate the need felt by authorities for a moral cleansing of the nation'. See Elise K. Tipton, 'Cleansing the nation: urban entertainments and moral reform in interwar Japan', *Modern Asian Studies*, vol. 42, no. 4 (July 2008), p. 707.

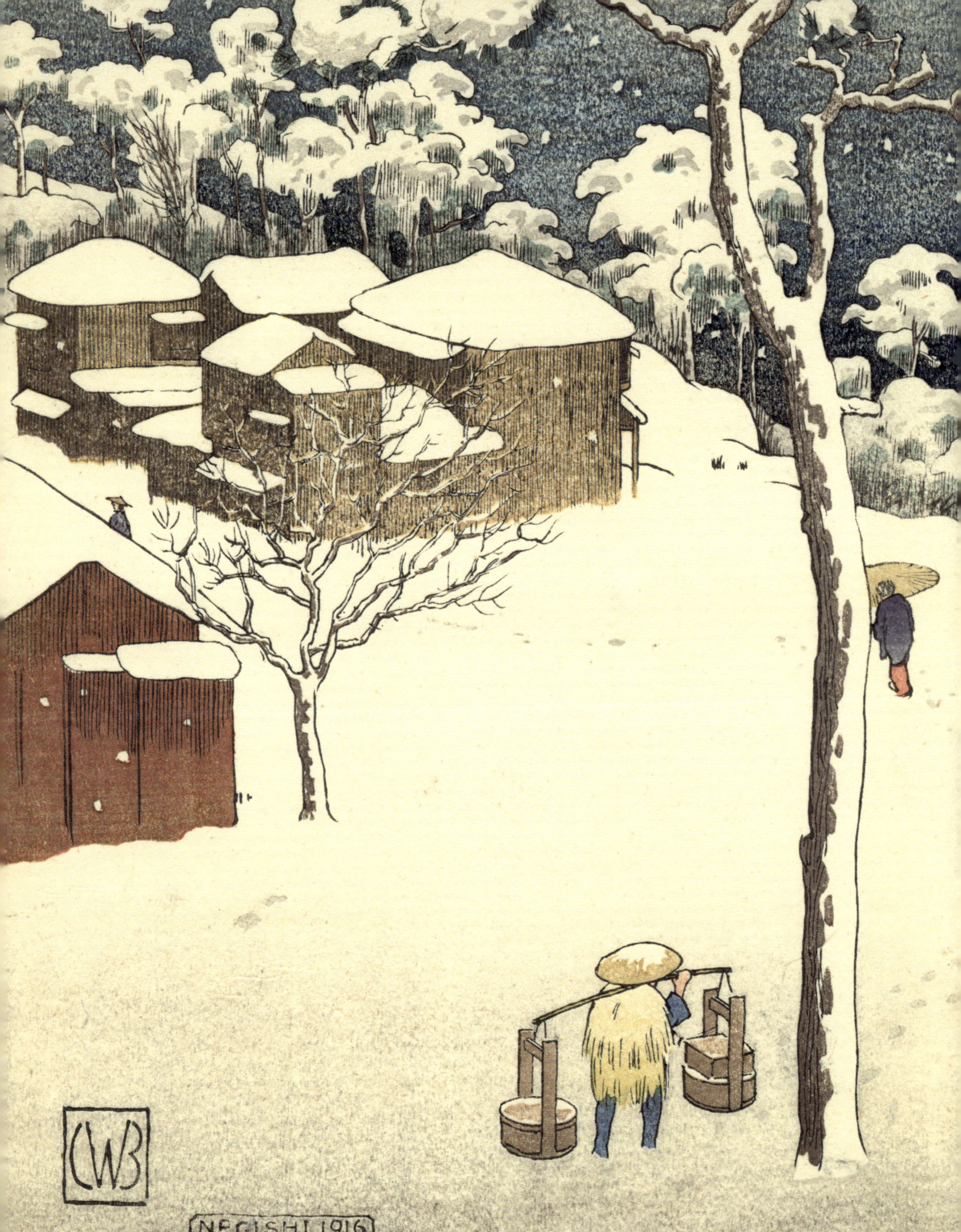

NEGISHI. 1916.

The Formative Years

Around 1906 the publisher Watanabe Shōzaburō began his search for a new style that would revitalize the traditions of Japanese printmaking for posterity. Starting off close to home, he eventually found inspiration in the works of foreign artists who came to Japan.

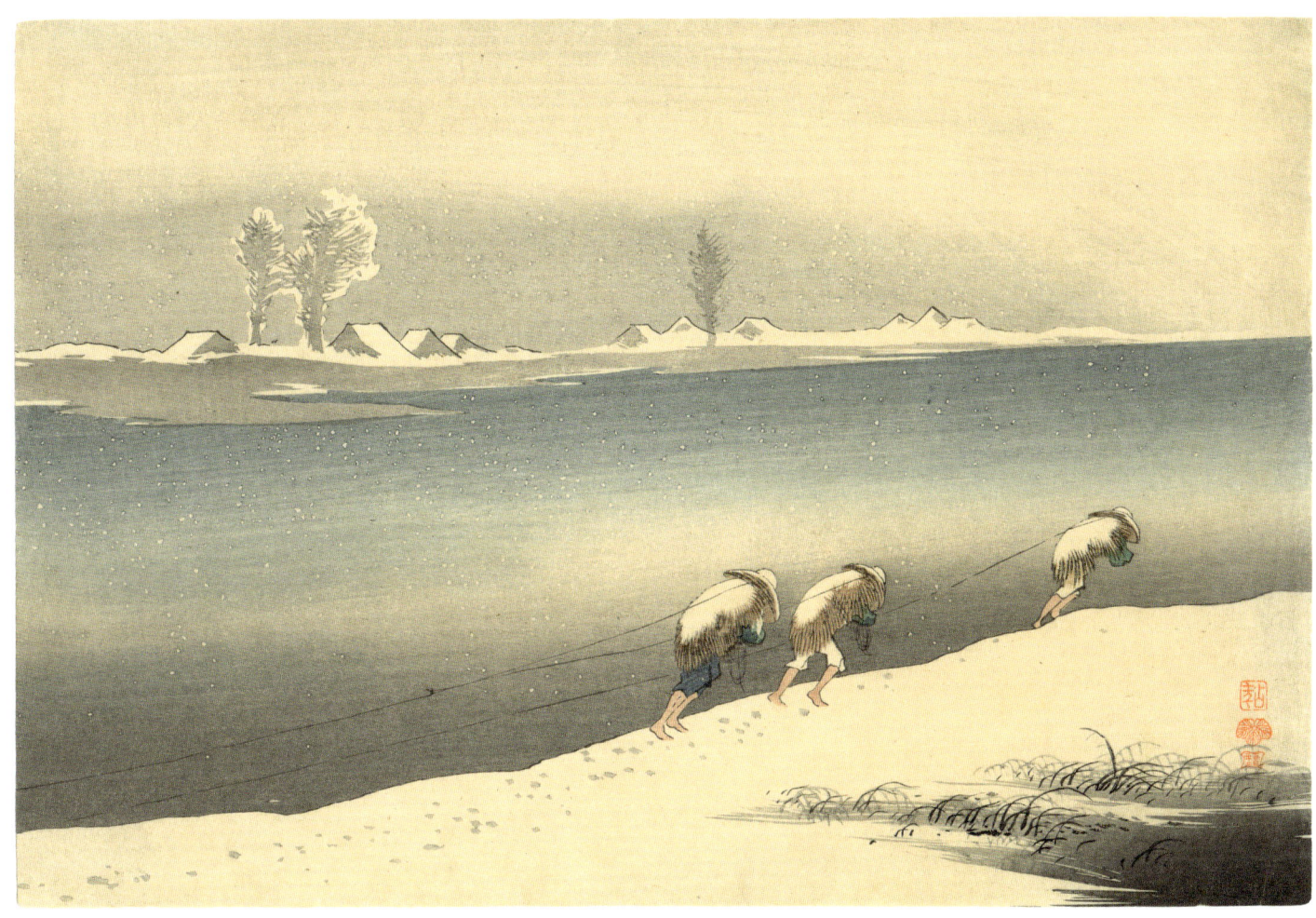

The first seven prints in this catalogue by the artists Uehara Konen and Takahashi Hiroaki are examples of the first ventures by the publishers Bunshichi and Watanabe in their search for a new style. The designs differ rather radically from what was produced in the way of landscape design by the late Meiji ukiyo-e artists. The prints are 'bleeding', meaning that they are covering the entire sheet without symmetric framing by white margins. The print quality is very good, but they were not published as luxurious productions. These were mostly sold through souvenir shops around Japan, and targeted a foreign clientele.
(PO)

Cat. 1

Uehara Konen 上原古年
(1878–1940)

Winter Landscape

Date: c. 1910
Artist's seal: *Konen*
Stock number: 322
Publisher: Kobayashi Bunshichi
Size: 23.7 × 35.5 cm
Collection Scholten

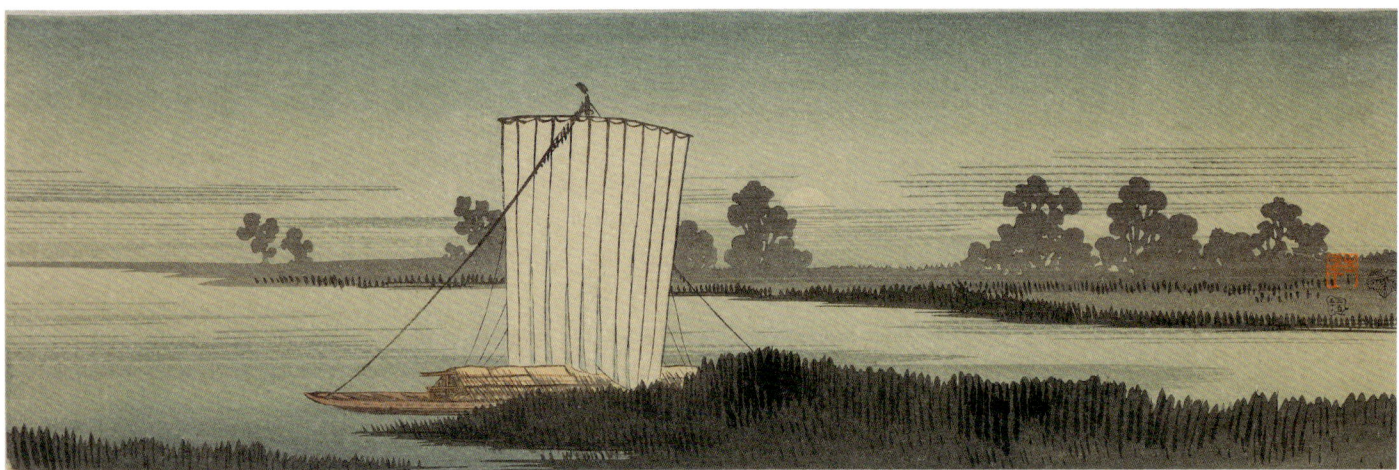

Cat. 2

Uehara Konen 上原古年
(1878–1940)

**Boat on the River towards
Evening**

Date: before 1910
Artist's seal: *Konen*
Stock number: 259
Publisher: Kobayashi Bunshichi
Size: 12 × 37 cm
Collection RMAH – JP.05896

This format was called *mitsugiriban*, meaning that three designs were printed on one block. After printing, the sheet was cut up into three individual prints. This practice posed a restriction on colour use: all designs needed to be printed in a more or less similar palette.
(PO)

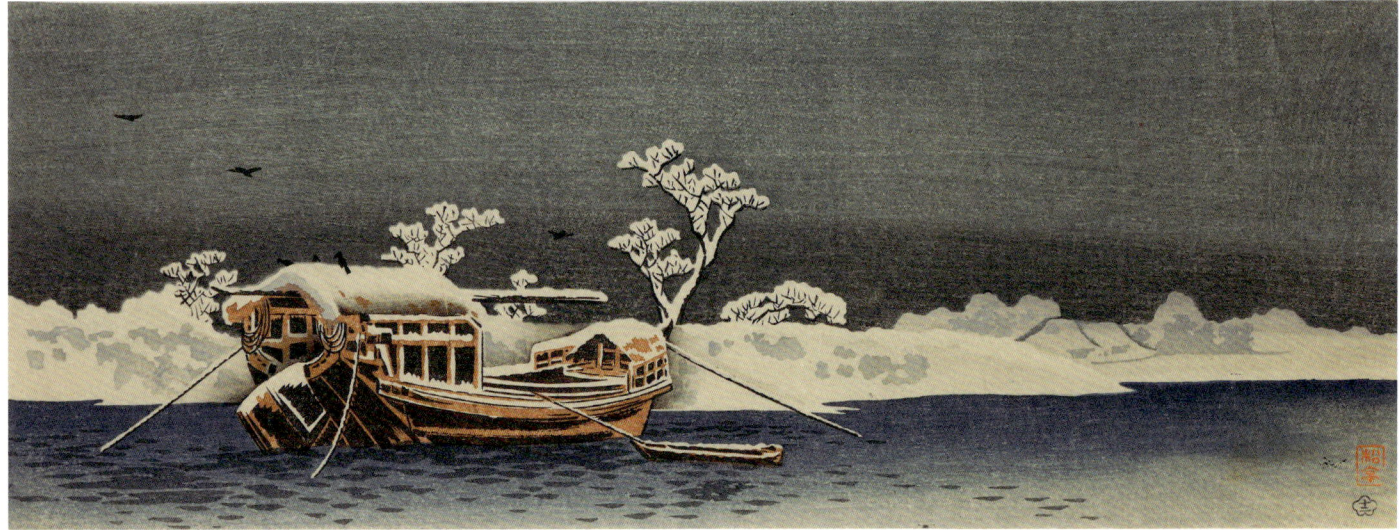

Cat. 3

Takahashi Hiroaki (Shōtei)
高橋弘明 (松亭) (1871–1945)

Boat on River in Snow

Date: before 1910
Artist's seal: *Shōtei*
Stock number: 12
Publisher: Watanabe Shōzaburō
Size: 13.4 × 36.5 cm
Collection RMAH – JP.06147

This was one of the first *shinsaku hanga* (newly made prints) by Hiroaki made in collaboration with Watanabe. Depicted is an anonymous location, with a striking contrast between the dark sky, the snowy landscape and the cold-looking water. Like the previous works, this print was numbered, but it is not certain what these numbers refer to.
(PO)

Cat. 4

Takahashi Hiroaki (Shōtei)
高橋弘明 (松亭) (1871–1945)

**Littleneck Clams Fishing Boat
at Kawasaki**

(*Kawasaki asarifune*
河さきあさ利船)

Date: before 1916
Artist's seal: *Shōtei*
Publisher: Watanabe Shōzaburō
Size: 17 × 38 cm
Collection Scholten

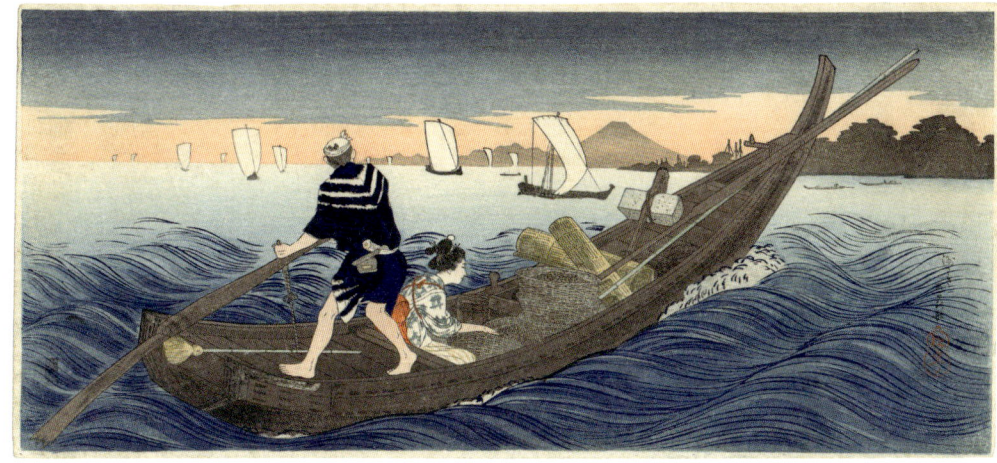

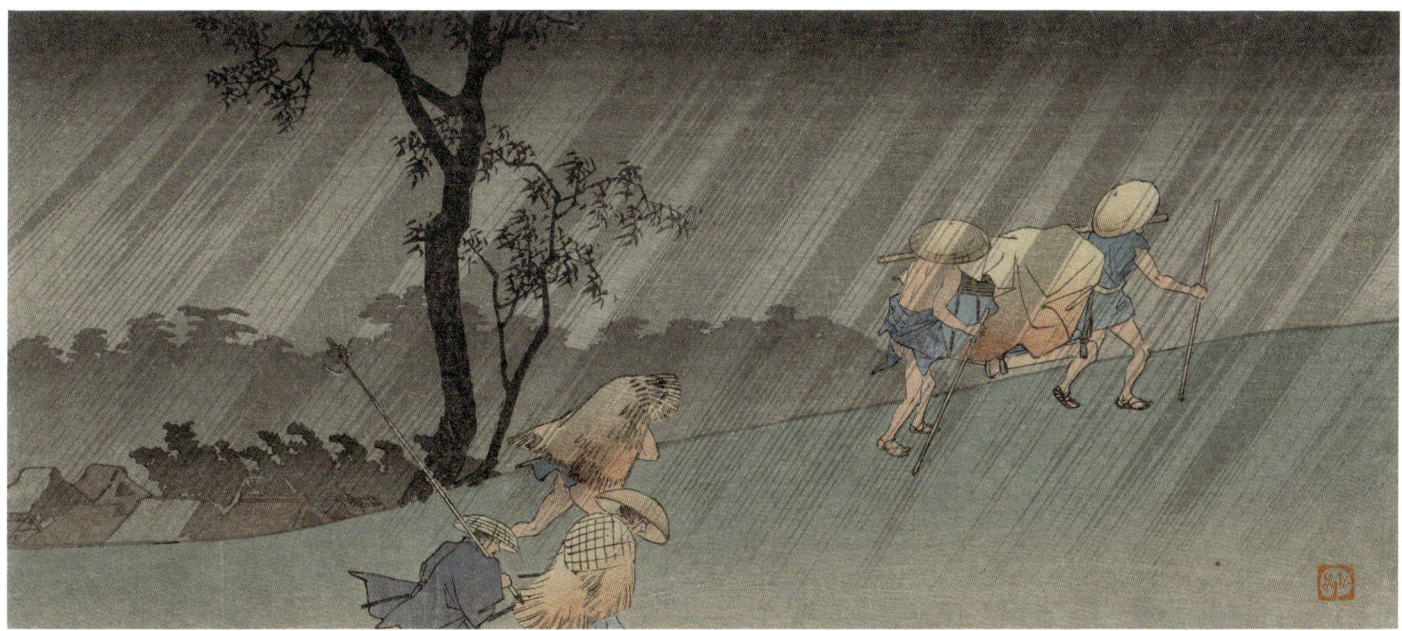

Similarly to the other Hiroaki prints in this format, the print is untitled. The composition, however, would quickly be picked up by ukiyo-e enthusiasts as a reference to Utagawa Hiroshige's iconic *White Rain at Shōno*, from his most famous series *The Fifty-three Stations of the Tōkaidō* published by Hoeidō from c. 1830. The figures hurriedly make their way upwards through the streaking rain.
(PO)

Cat. 5

Takahashi Hiroaki (Shōtei)
高橋弘明 (松亭) (1871–1945)

Shōno in Rain

(*Shōno no ame* 庄野の雨)

Date: c. 1909–23
Artist's seal: *Shōtei*
Publisher: Watanabe Shōzaburō
Size: 16 × 37 cm
Collection Scholten

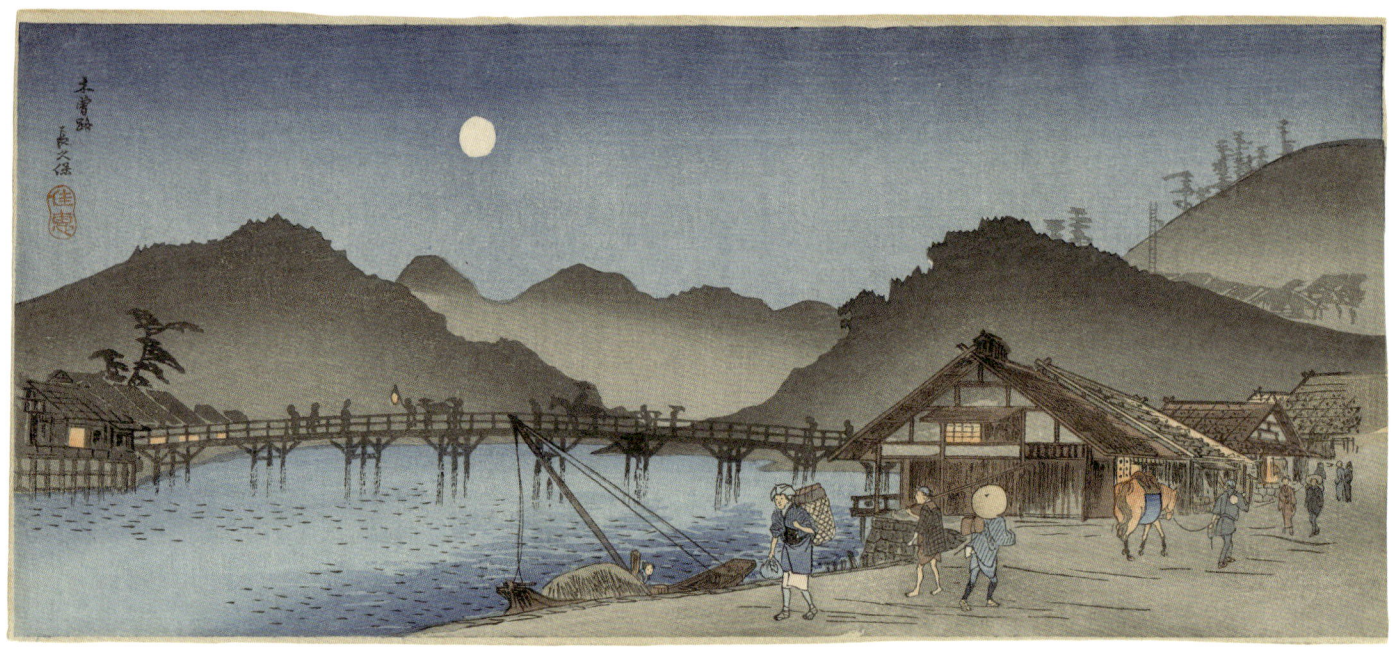

Cat. 6

Takahashi Hiroaki (Shōtei)
高橋弘明 (松亭) (1871–1945)

Bridge and Village in the Evening

Date: before 1923
Artist's seal: *Kakei*
Publisher: Watanabe Shōzaburō
Size: 17 × 38 cm
Collection Scholten

This print is rare, as the woodblock was destroyed in the Great Kantō Earthquake of 1923. The *Kakei* signature signals that this print is from the early phase of collaboration between Watanabe Shōzaburō and Hiroaki.

(PO)

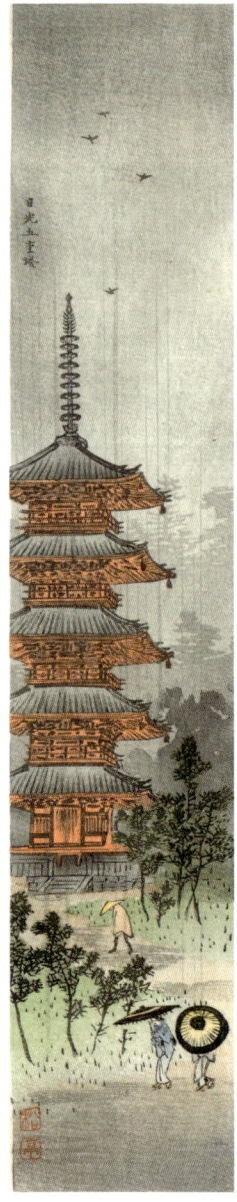

Cat. 7

Takahashi Hiroaki (Shōtei)
高橋弘明 (松亭) (1871–1945)

Nikkō – The Five-Storey Pagoda

(*Nikkō gojūnotō* 日光五重塔)

Date: before 1923
Artist's seal: *Shōtei* (two seals, *Shō* and *Tei*)
Publisher: Watanabe Shōzaburō
Size: 37.7 × 7.8 cm
Collection Scholten

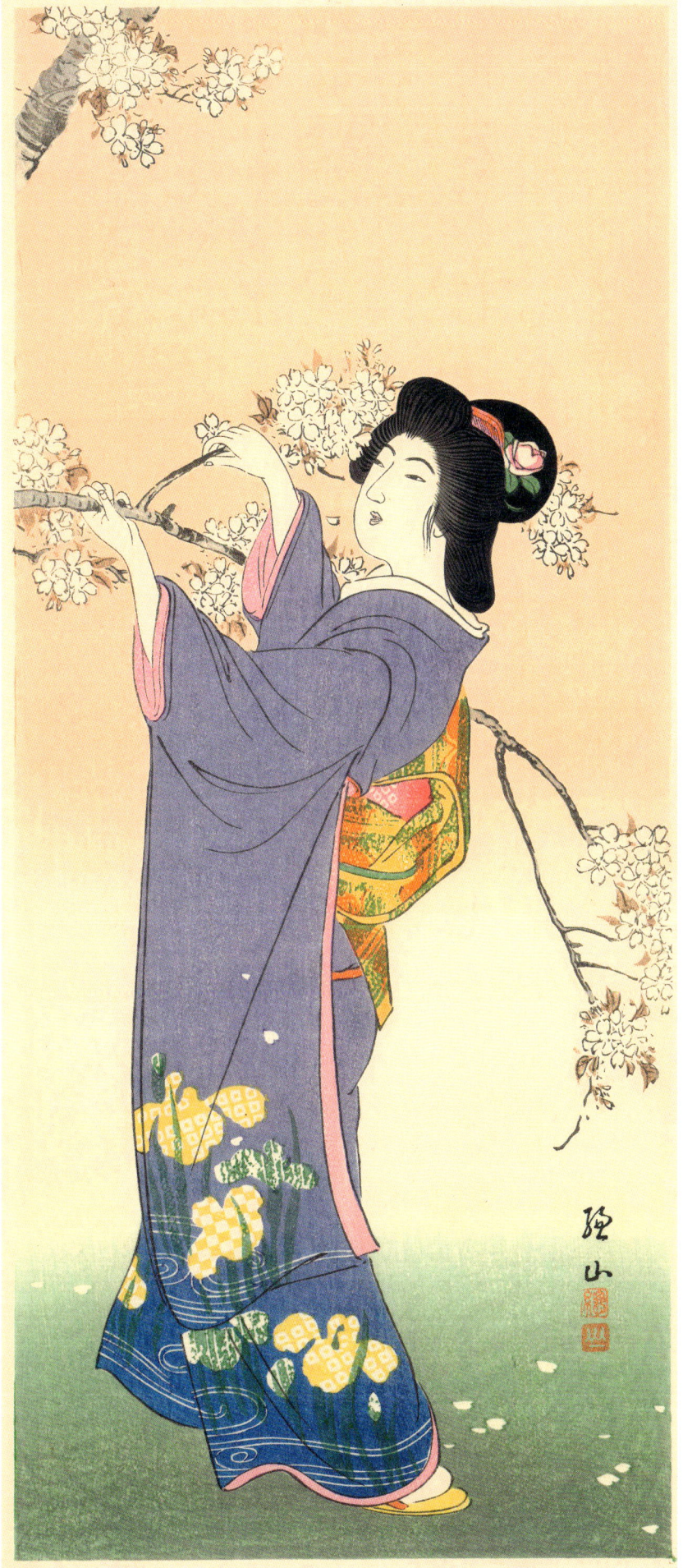

Itō Sōzan was the third artist who was making *shinsaku hanga* (newly made prints) commissioned by Watanabe Shōzaburō at this time. Together with two other prints in the same format, this design is a rare example of a *bijin* in an oeuvre that is formed mostly of *kachō-ga* (pictures of birds and flowers). *Setsugekka* (snow, moon and flowers) is a theme that often appears in Japanese visual culture and it has its origins in China. It derives from a poem by the famous Tang Dynasty poet Bo Juyi (772–846):

Lute, poetry, wine – my friends
all have deserted me;
snow, moon, flowers – these seasons,
I most often think of you.

(PO)

Cat. 8
Itō Sōzan 伊藤総山
(1884–?)
Flowers
(*Hana* 花)

Series: *Snow, Moon and Flowers*
(*Setsugekka no uchi* 雪月花のうち)
Date: designed in the Taishō Period,
re-carved and reissued after 1923.
Signature: *Sōzan*
Artist's seal: *Sōzan*
Publisher: Watanabe Shōzaburō
Size: 38 × 17 cm
S. Watanabe Color Print Co.

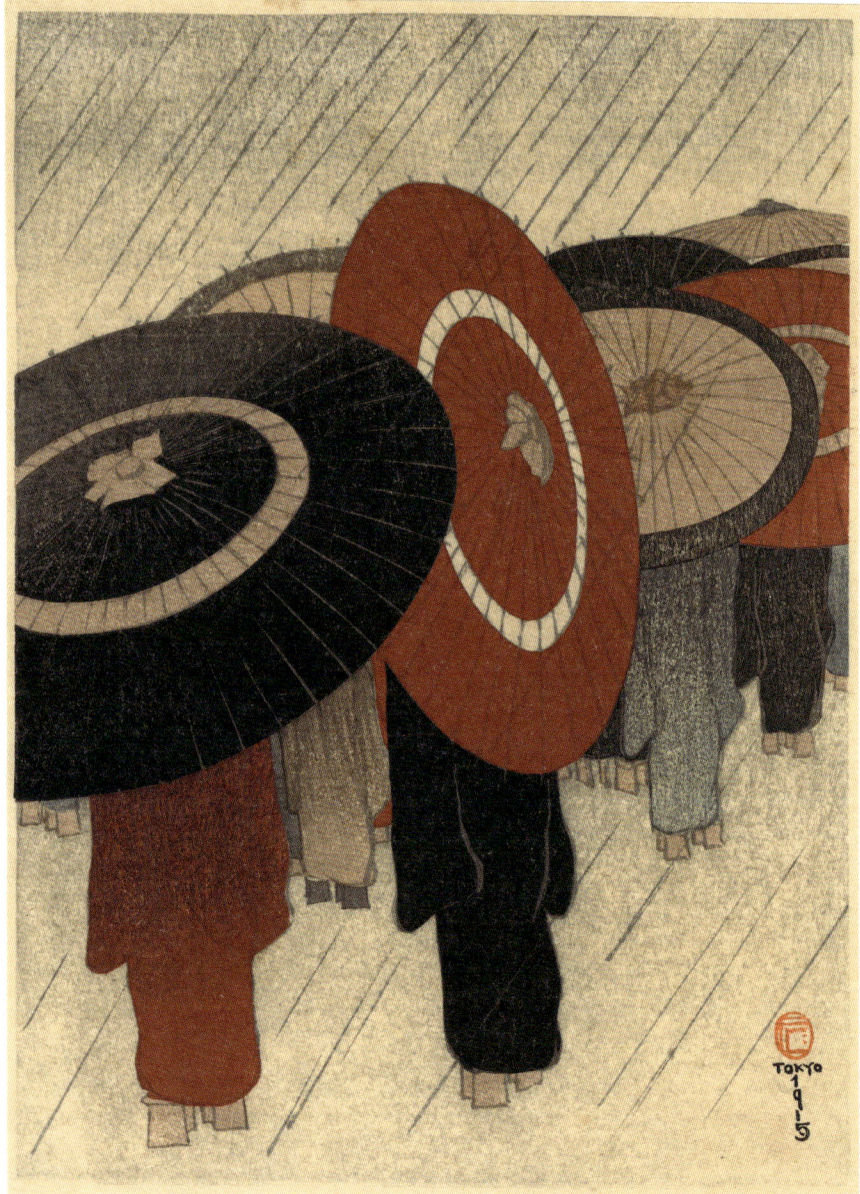

Fritz Capelari – the Austrian artist Watanabe turned to in order to find a new direction for his Japanese prints (see Introduction, pp. 11–12) – based this print on a design by Katsushika Hokusai (1760–1849), *Figures in Snow and Rain*, from the first volume of his popular *Hokusai manga*. Both compositions feature an anonymous group of people seen from a high vantage point, with their umbrellas taking up the main part of the image. Another similarity is the clear visibility of the traditional sandal-like footwear known as geta (see Fig. 1).

(PO)

Fig. 1

From: *Hokusai manga* (Sketches by Hokusai), vol. 1, 1814

Cat. 9

Friedrich (Fritz) Capelari
(1884–1950)

Returning Home in the Rain

Date: 1915
Artist's seal: *FC*
Publisher: Watanabe Shōzaburō
Size: 27.4 × 20.3 cm
Collection Scholten

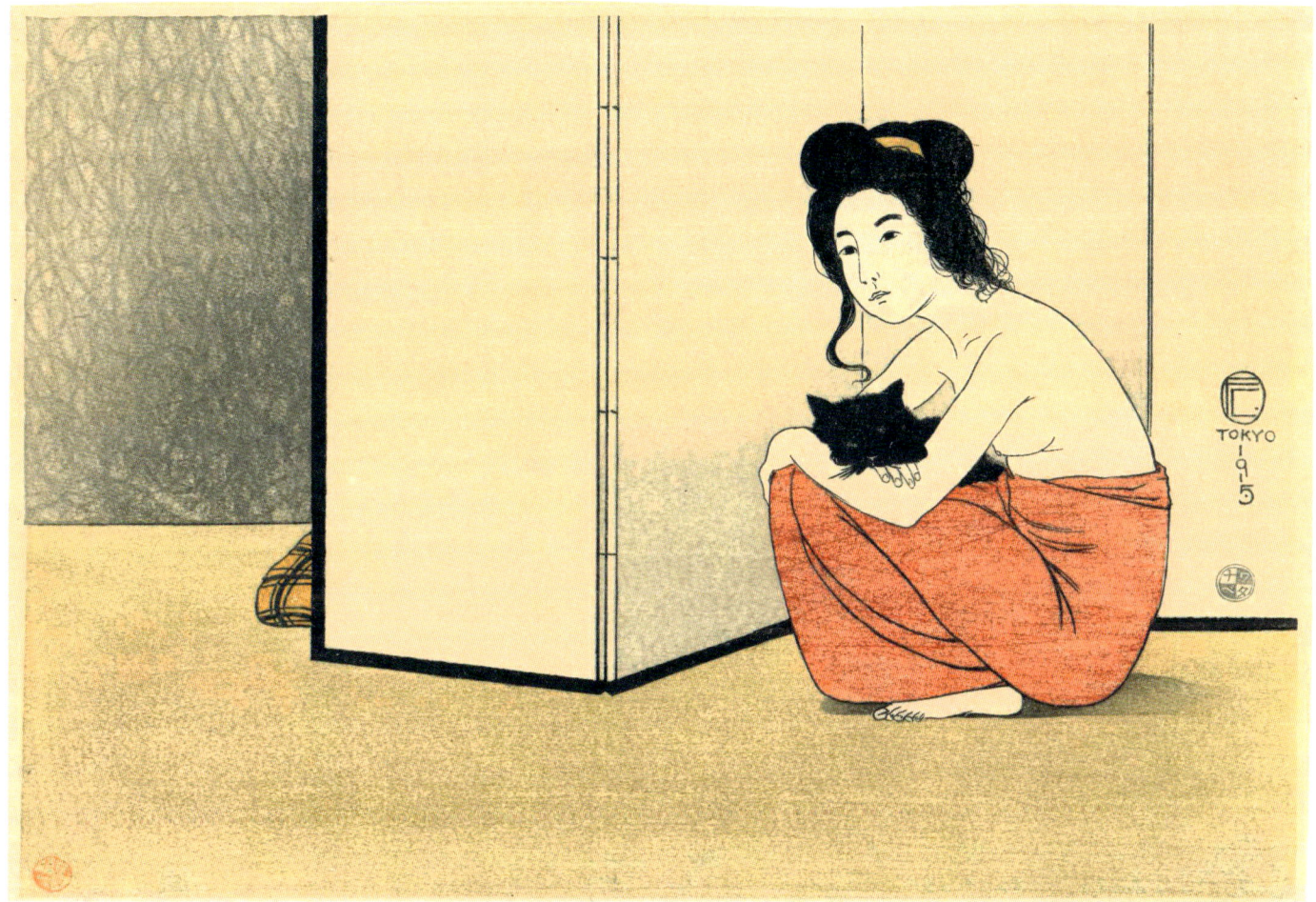

This design perhaps provides the strongest link between the example set by Capelari and subsequent *shin hanga* beautiful women by Itō Shinsui. The similarity between this design, despite the horizontal format, and Shinsui's *After a Bath* (1917, see Cat. 26) has often been noted.
(PO)

Cat. 10

Friedrich (Fritz) Capelari
(1884–1950)

Woman Holding a Black Cat

Date: 1915
Artist's seal: *FC*
Publisher: Watanabe Shōzaburō
Size: 21 × 31.5 cm
S. Watanabe Color Print Co.

Cat. 11

Friedrich (Fritz) Capelari
(1884–1950)

Woman with a Pekinese

Date: 1915
Artist's seal: *FC*
Publisher: Watanabe Shōzaburō
Size: 39 × 17.5 cm
S. Watanabe Color Print Co.

Cat. 12

Friedrich (Fritz) Capelari
(1884–1950)

Woman before a Mirror

Date: 1915
Signed: *Kaperari* (in *katakana* on
the fan in the foreground)
Artist's seal: *FC*
Publisher: Watanabe Shōzaburō
Size: 41 × 18 cm
S. Watanabe Color Print Co.

Two designs from 1915 featured a standing woman in a horizontal composition. The setting of a figure against a plain background is reminiscent of the classical prints of beautiful women by Suzuki Harunobu (1724?–70).

(PO)

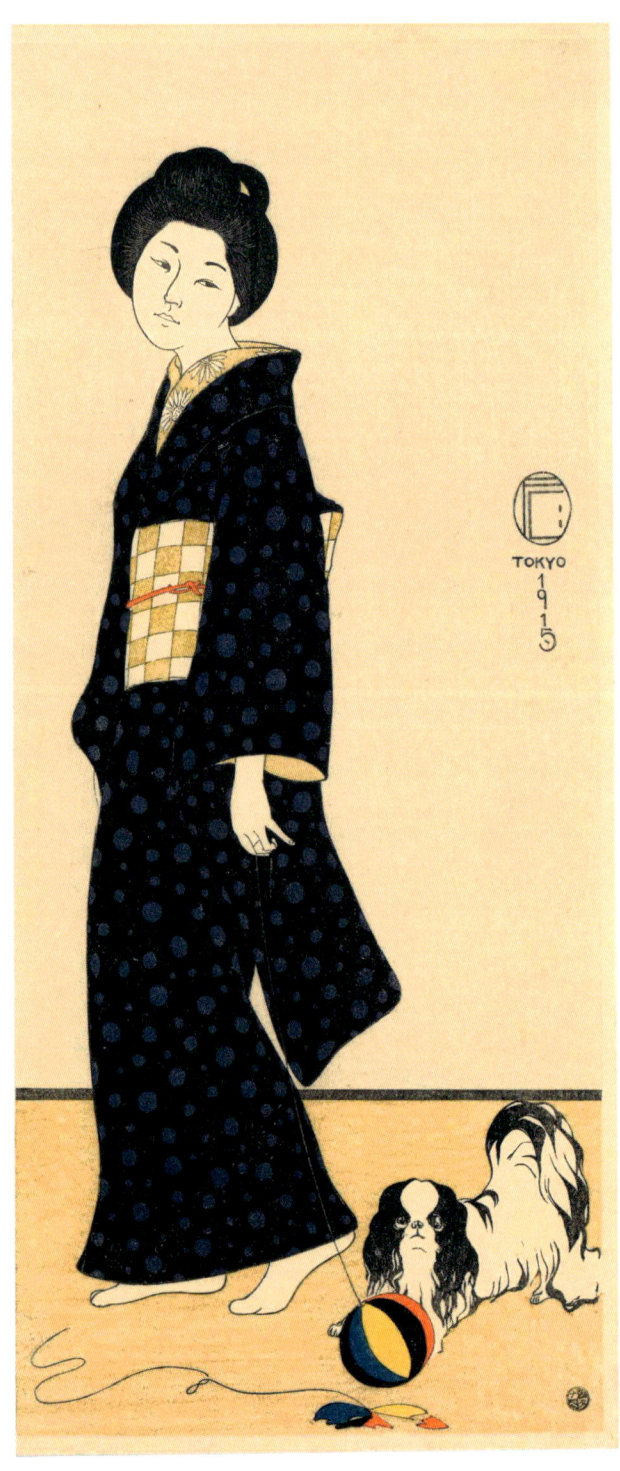

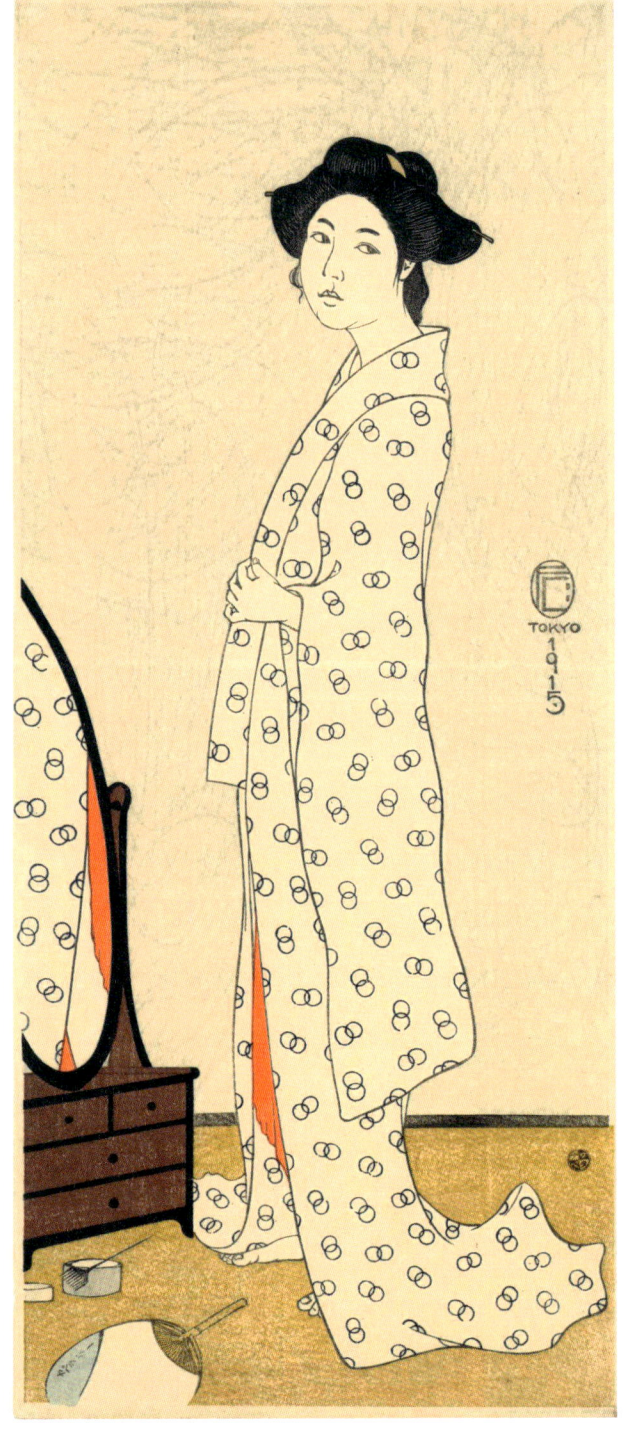

Cat. 13

Charles William Bartlett
(1860–1940)
Negishi

Date: 1916
Artist's seal: *CWB*
Publisher: Watanabe Shōzaburō
Size: 38.7 × 25.7 cm
Collection Scholten

This rare print was one of the 38 woodblock designs that Bartlett made in 1916. Watanabe Shōzaburō published most of these prints between 1916 and 1919, and a few more in later years. Bartlett's set was featured in various exhibitions in both Japan and overseas, for example in New York City. A reviewer praised Bartlett's compositions after an exhibition held at the Shirokiya department store in 1921 and said that *Negishi* was among the finest of his displayed works. The composition is a clear nod to the vertical *ōban* landscape style that Utagawa Hiroshige (1797–1858) developed in his final years. (JD)

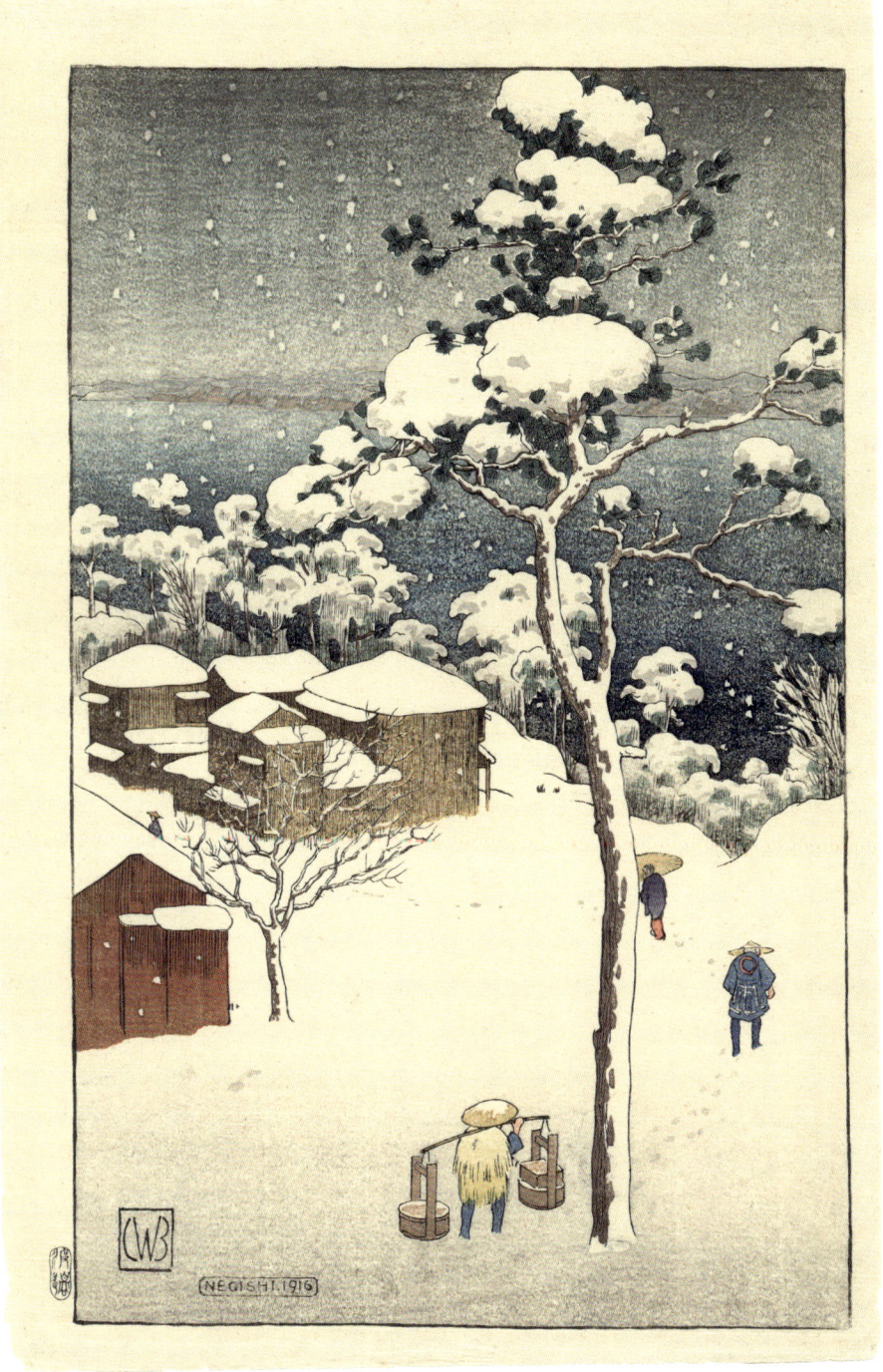

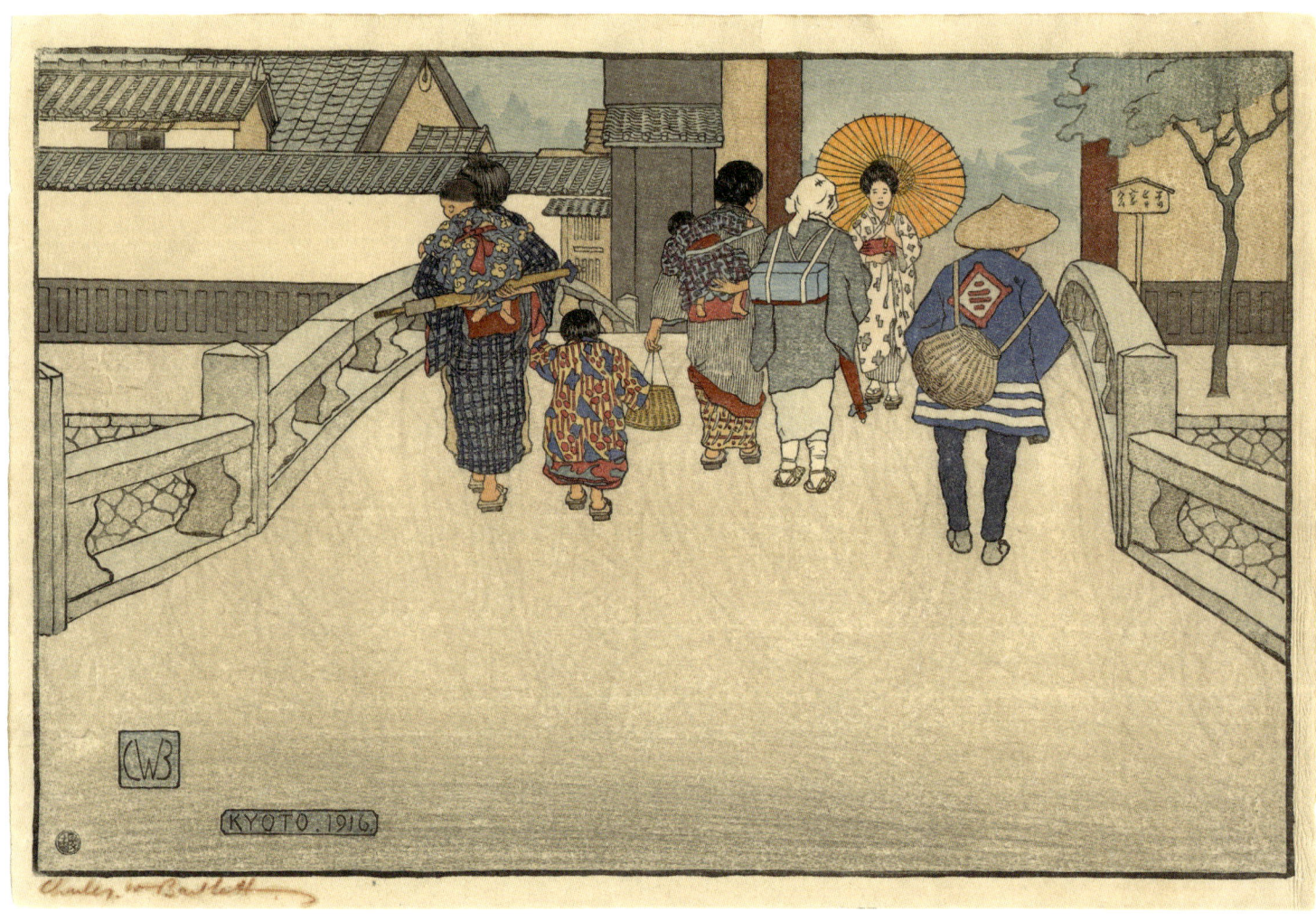

Cat. 14

Charles William Bartlett
(1860–1940)

Kyoto

Date: 1916
Signature: *Charles W. Barlett*
(left bottom corner)
Artist's seal: *CWB*
Publisher: Watanabe Shōzaburō
Size: 24.8 × 37.3 cm
Collection Scholten

As with the previous design, this print may have borrowed from compositions by Utagawa Hiroshige, particularly his famous depiction of a procession crossing the bridge at Nihonbashi. The figures in the print, however, take on a more Western style and may remind one of the designs of Prague-born artist Emil Orlík (1870–1932), who also worked in Japan and created his own woodblock prints.

(JD)

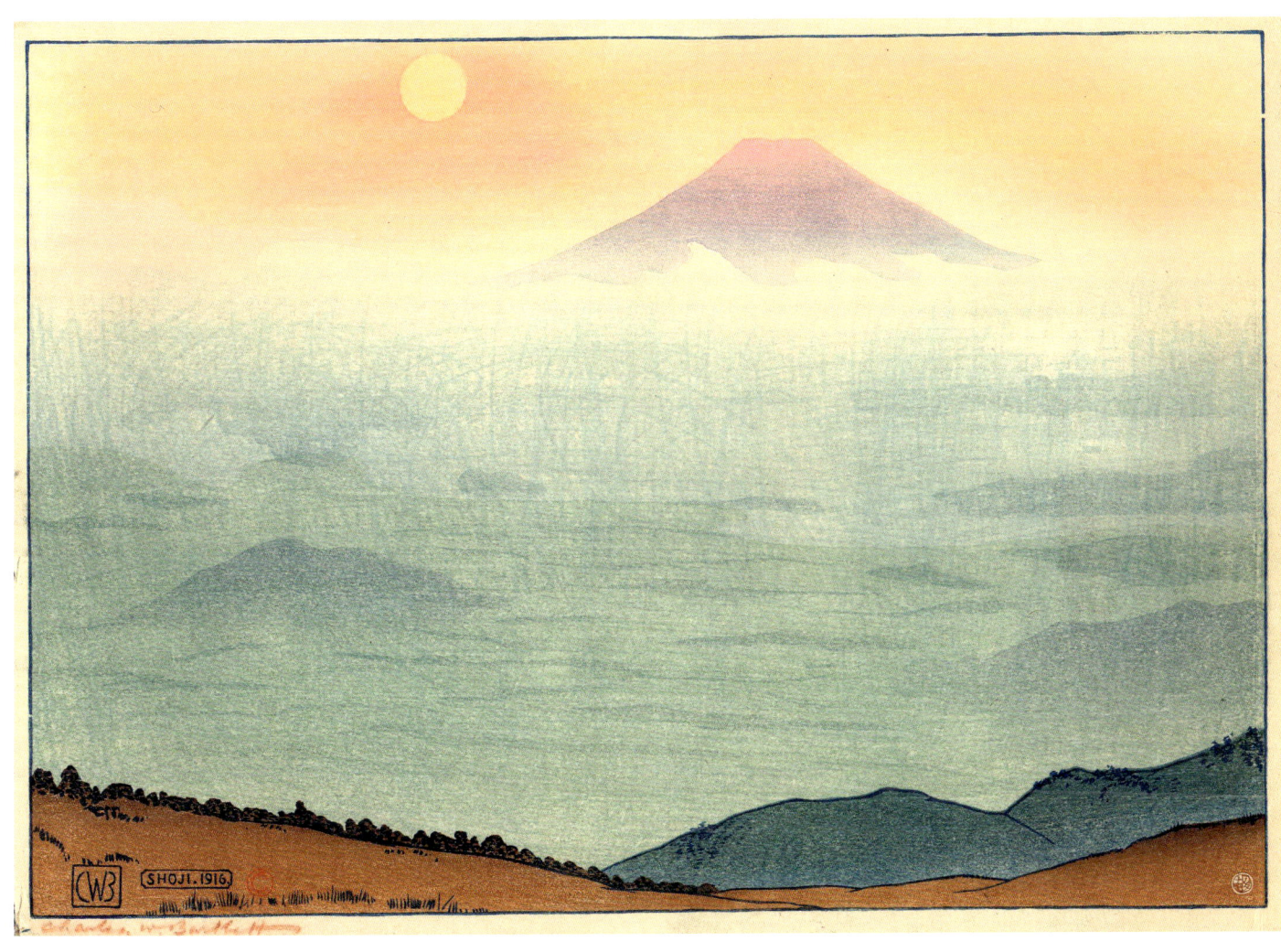

Cat. 15

Charles William Bartlett
(1860–1940)

Mount Fuji Seen from Lake Shōji

Date: 1916
Signature: *Charles W. Bartlett*
(left bottom corner)
Artist's seal: *CWB*
Publisher: Watanabe Shōzaburō
Size: 28 × 39 cm
S. Watanabe Color Print Co.

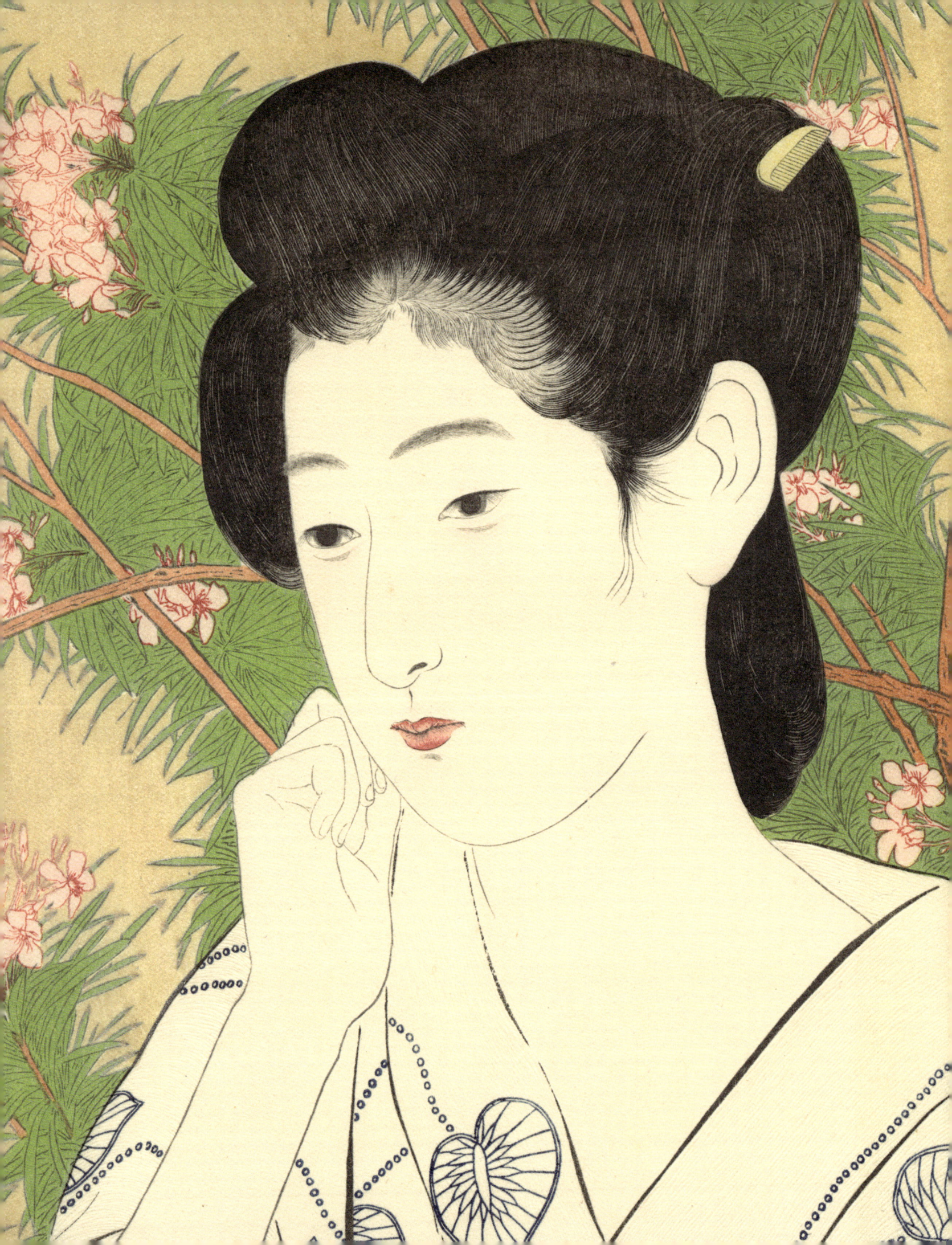

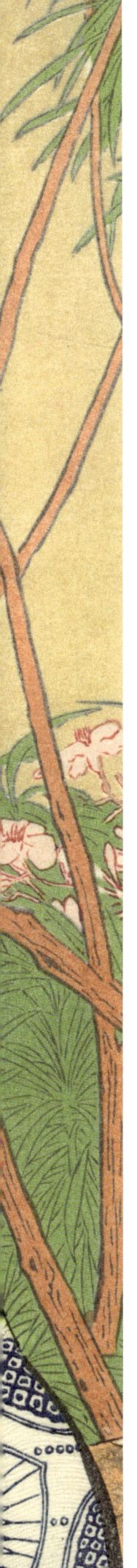

Pre-Earthquake
Beautiful Women

From 1915 the *shin hanga* movement enjoyed its first flowering, but its development was disrupted by the disastrous Great Kantō Earthquake of 1 September 1923. During those first eight years, however, iconic images of beautiful women by Hashiguchi Goyō and Itō Shinsui set the standard for years to come.

Cat. 16

Hashiguchi Goyō 橋口五葉
(1881–1921)

Woman Applying Make-up

(*Keshō no onna* 化粧の女)

Date: 1918
Signature: *Goyō ga*
Artist's seal: *Goyō*
Publisher: self-published
Block cutter: *Takano Shichinosuke*
Printer: *Somekawa Kanzō*
Size: 55.3 × 39.3 cm
Collection Scholten

This is one of the first prints that Goyō published himself. Three years previously Goyō briefly worked together with the publisher Watanabe Shōzaburō. This led to his first woodblock print, *Woman at her Bath* (*Yuami no onna*, 1915, printed 1916; see Fig. 4, p. 12 in the Introduction).

Unhappy with the outcome, Goyō decided that in future he would self-publish his work, resulting in luxury prints of an extremely high quality. He supervised every step of the process and worked together with some of the finest block cutters and printers of the day. Goyō also carefully selected premium materials to create his prints, using the highest-quality pigments and paper as well as wood for the blocks.

Woman Applying Make-up is a good example of his work: skilfully printed on thick paper, with the shimmering mica pigment lavishly applied onto a plain background. Goyō repeats this kind of composition in *Woman after a Bath* (Cat. 21) and *Woman Combing her Hair* (Cat. 18).

(PO)

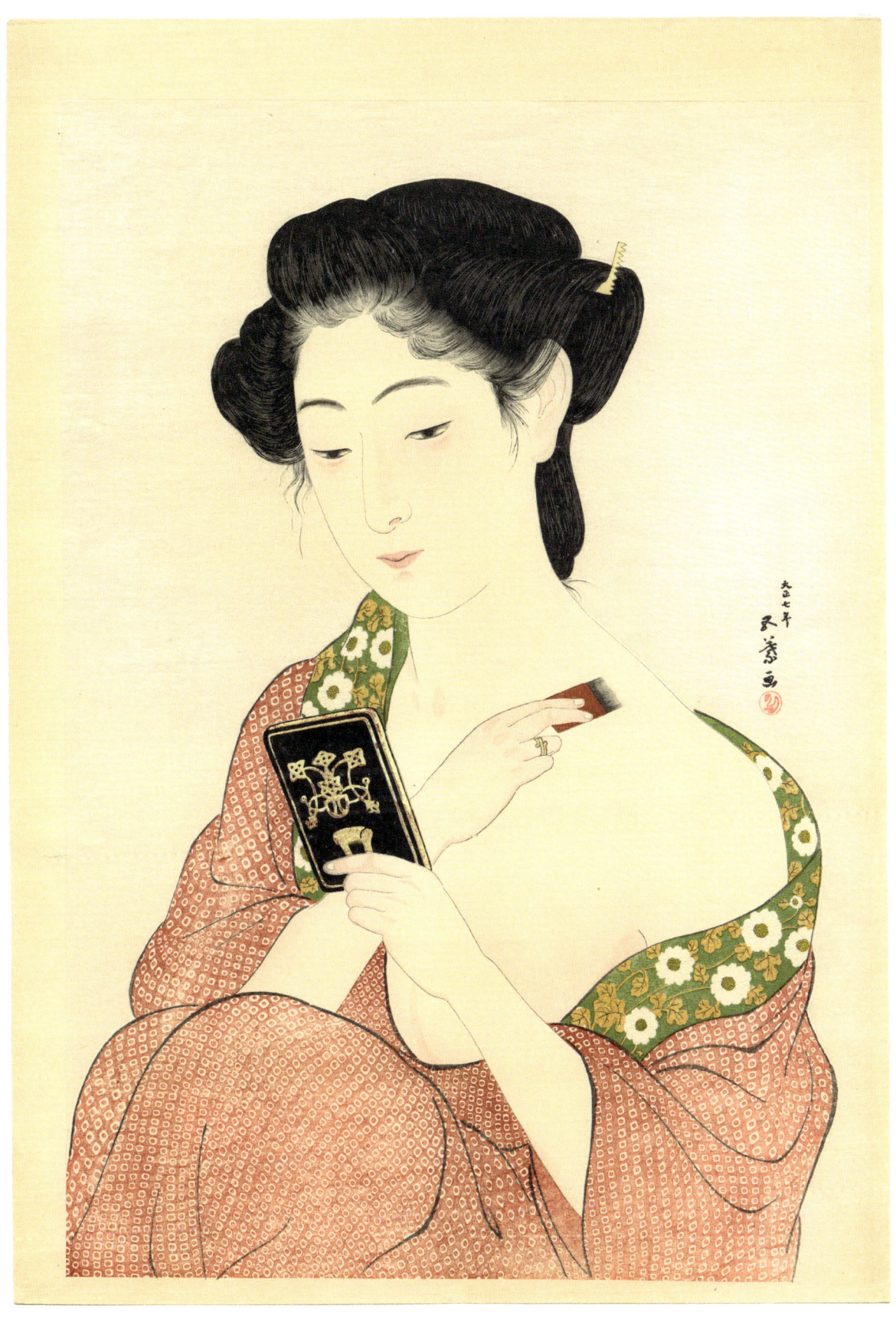

Cat. 17

Hashiguchi Goyō 橋口五葉
(1881–1921)

Woman with a Tray

(*Bon moteru onna* 盆持てる女)

Date: January 1920
Signature: *Goyō ga*
Publisher: self-published
Block cutter: *Takano Shichinosuke*
Printer: *Somekawa Kanzō*
Size: 40 × 27 cm
Private collection, the Netherlands

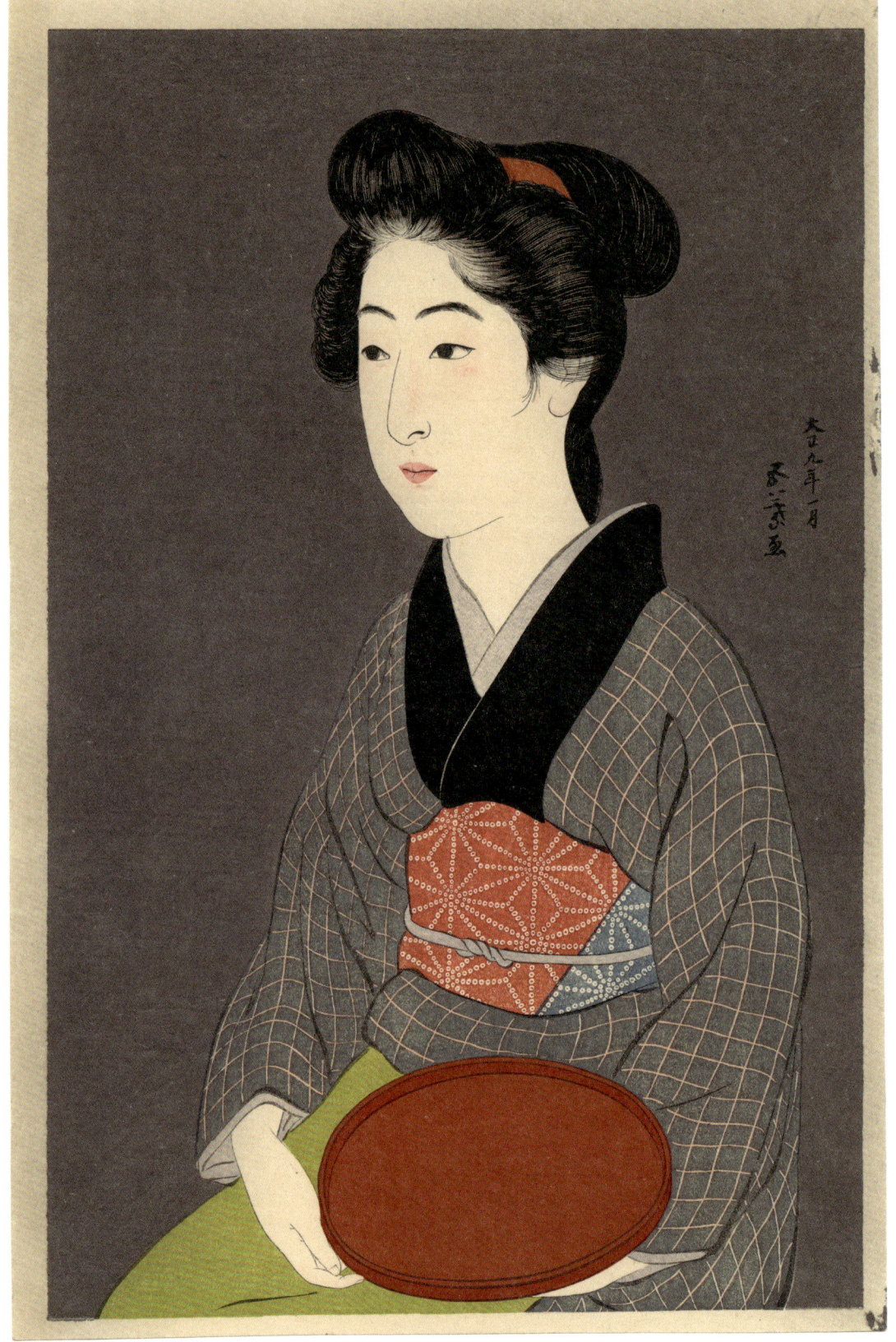

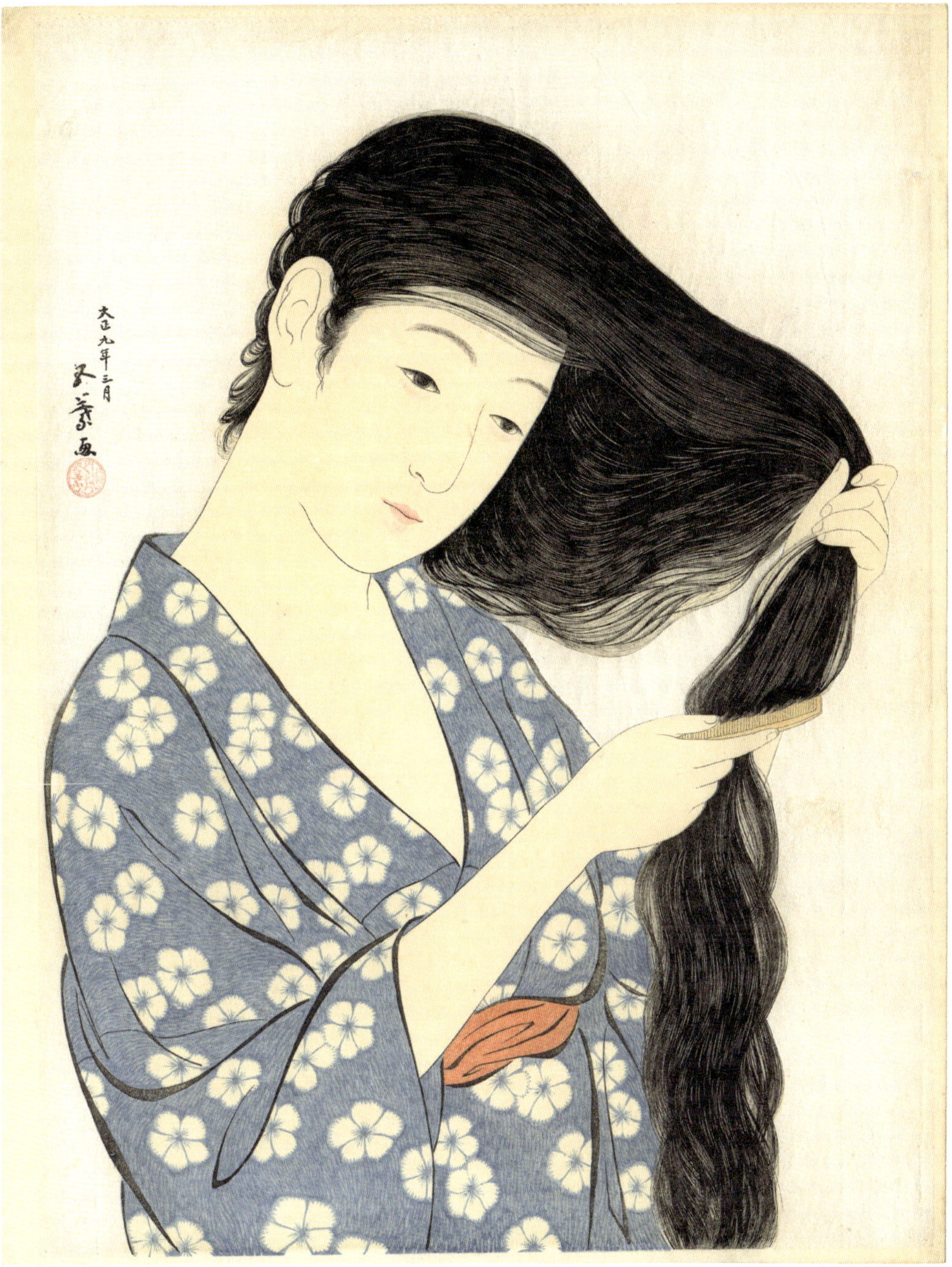

Cat. 18
Hashiguchi Goyō 橋口五葉
(1881–1921)

Woman Combing her Hair

(*Kami sukeru onna* 髪梳ける女)

Date: March 1920
Signature: *Goyō ga*
Artist's seal: *Hashiguchi Goyō*
Publisher: self-published
Block cutter: *Koike Masazō*
Printer: *Somekawa Kanzō*
Size: 44.6 × 34.5 cm
Private collection, the Netherlands

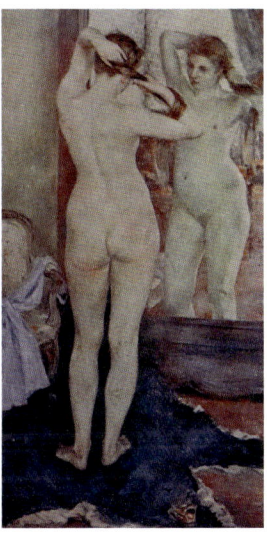

Fig. 2
Kuroda Seiki, *Morning Toilette*, 1893;
destroyed in the Second World War

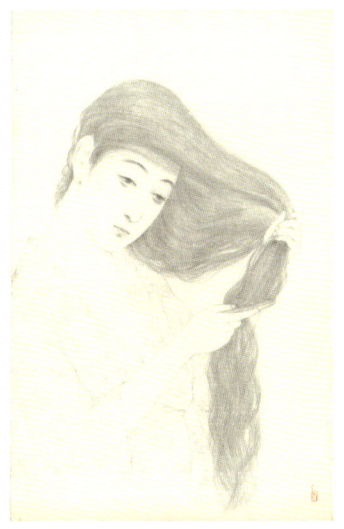

Fig. 3
Pencil study for *Woman Combing her Hair*
Artist's seal: *Goyō*
Size: 49.4 × 32.3 cm
Private collection, the Netherlands

Goyō was a prolific sketcher. He frequently worked together with models, a practice that undoubtedly added to the quality of his now iconic *bijin* prints. Kodaira Tomi modelled for this design and frequently posed for the artist. *Woman in Long Undergarments* (Cat. 19) and *Woman after a Bath* (Cat. 21) are also based on a number of drawings of this model.

His pencil studies are well preserved, and Goyō's erotic sketches in particular show the influence of his study of the *yōga* tradition (Western-style painting) and of the works of his distant relative Kuroda Seiki (1866–1924). Seiki was an influential painter in the *yōga* tradition, whose *Morning Toilette* (1893) (Fig. 2) caused great controversy when it became, in 1895, the first nude painting to be publicly exhibited in Japan.

Building upon the centuries-long tradition of *bijin-ga*, Goyō infused his beauties with lifelike qualities and a profound understanding of anatomy. With *Woman Combing her Hair*, Goyō created one of the most important works of the modern Japanese print movement.
(PO)

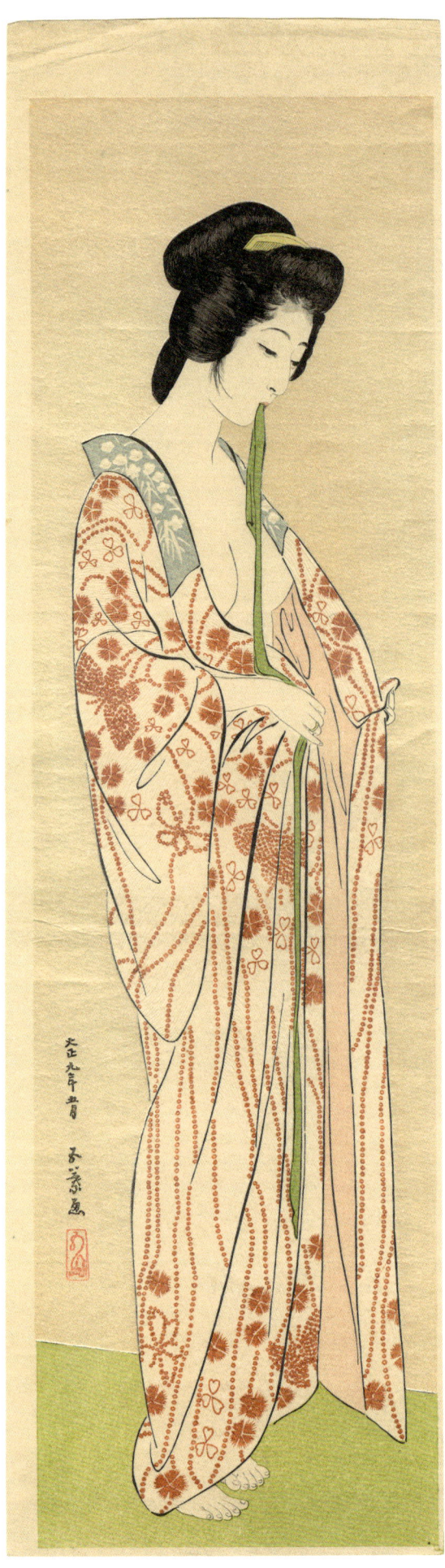

Cat. 19

Hashiguchi Goyō 橋口五葉
(1881–1921)

Woman in Long Undergarments

(*Nagajuban no onna* 長襦袢の女)

Date: May 1920
Signature: *Goyō ga*
Artist's seal: *Goyō*
Edition: 13/70
Publisher: self-published
Block cutter: *Koike Masazō*
Printer: *Akimoto Shōzaburō*
Size: 49.5 × 14.8 cm
Collection Scholten

A woman is pictured getting dressed: she holds the sash in her mouth while fixing her garment, her breasts partly exposed. Goyō based this design on sketches of the model Kodaira Tomi (see also *Woman after a Bath* [Cat. 21] and *Woman Combing her Hair* [Cat. 18]).

The unusual long and narrow format of this print directs the focus of this design on the undergarment – beautifully highlighted with detailed *karazuri* (blind-printing) – and the model's slender figure. This intimate moment is rendered in a subtle colour palette.

The result is an elegant and captivating image, and the print quickly became extremely popular and was reissued multiple times. At least three versions are known, each having a different background colour. In an interview from 1969, Watanabe Tadasu – the son of the publisher Watanabe Shōzaburō – mentions that the price for this print far exceeded that of, for example, the landscape prints by Kawase Hasui. These sold for roughly 2–3 yen per sheet, while Goyō's design went for as much as 15–35 yen. (PO)

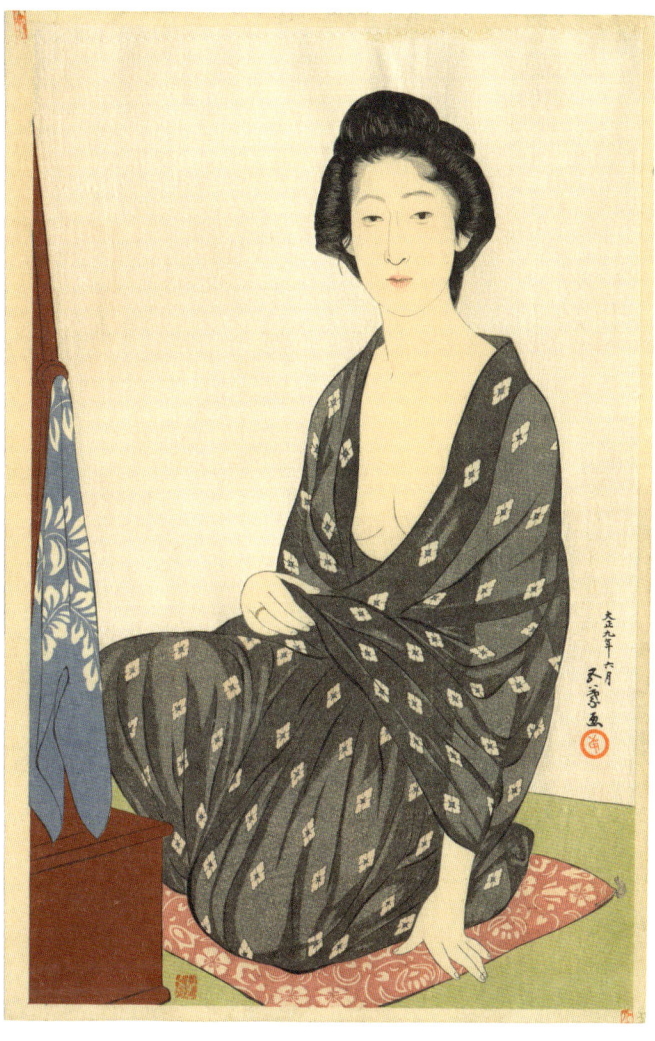

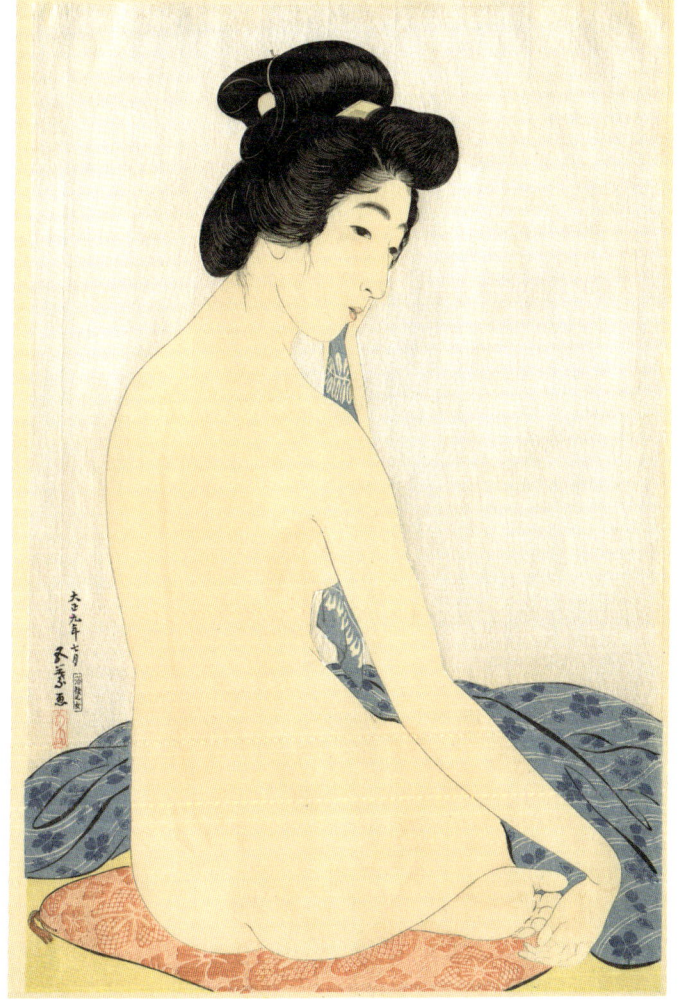

Cat. 21

Hashiguchi Goyō 橋口五葉
(1881–1921)

Woman after a Bath

(*Yokugo no onna* 浴後之女)

Date: July 1920
Signature: *Goyō ga*
Artist's seal: *Goyō*
Publisher: self-published
Block cutter: *Takano Shichinosuke*
Printer: *Somekawa Kanzō*
Size: 44.5 × 30 cm
Collection Scholten

Cat. 20

Hashiguchi Goyō 橋口五葉
(1881–1921)

Woman in a Summer Kimono

(*Natsugoromo no onna* 夏衣の女)

Date: June 1920
Signature: *Goyō ga*
Artist's seal: *GY* (round seal),
Hashiguchi (square seal), 'deer' seal
(top left margin, partly obscured)
Publisher: self-published
Block cutter: *Koike Masazō*
Printer: *Akimoto Shōzaburō*
Size: 45 × 29.5 cm
Collection Scholten

Cat. 22

Hashiguchi Goyō 橋口五葉
(1881–1921)

Hot-Spring Inn

(*Onsen yado* 温泉宿)

Date: July 1920, printed 1952
Signature: *Goyō ga*
Artist's seal: *Goyō* (left of signature),
Hashiguchi (bottom left margin)
Publisher: Goyō hanga kenkyūjo
(Goyō Print Institute)
Block cutter: *Koike Masazō* (key
block cutter)/*Maeda Kentarō*
(colour block cutter)
Printer: *Hirai Kōichi*
Size: 44.5 × 26.6 cm
Collection Scholten

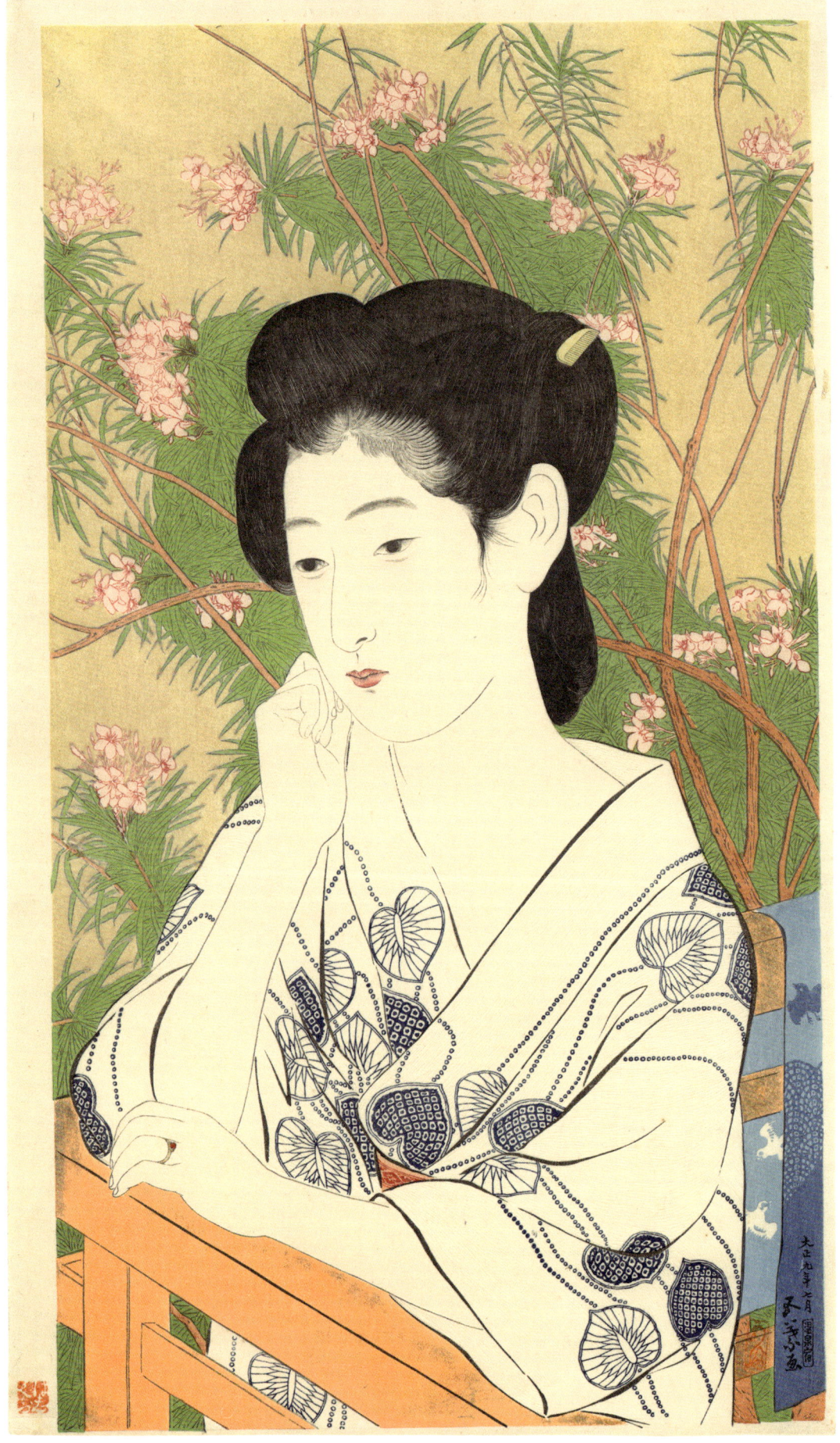

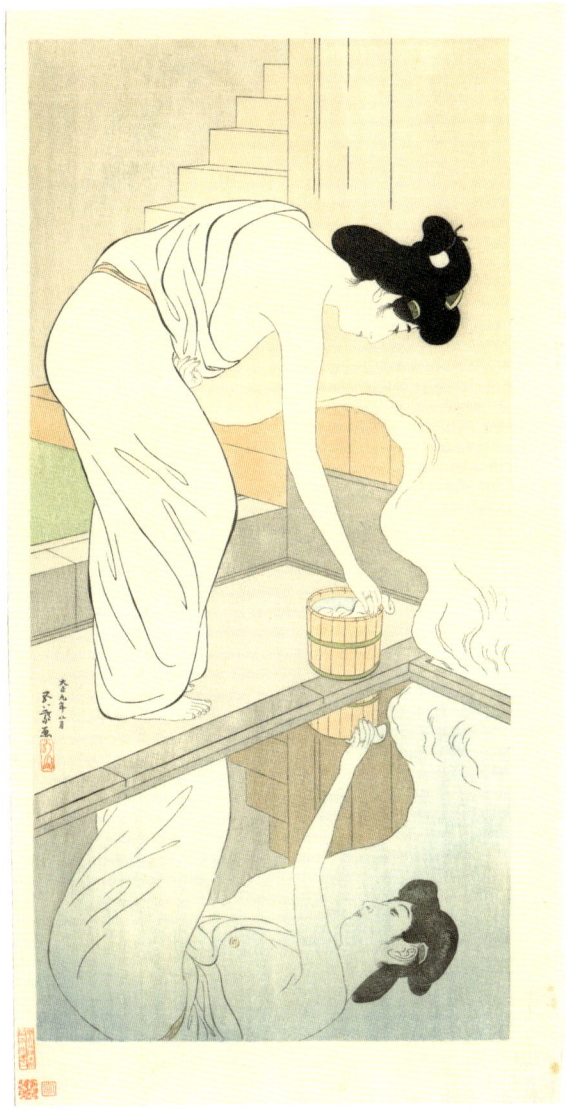

At the time of his death, 18 of Goyō's print designs remained unfinished. Goyō's nephew Hashiguchi Yasuo continued his legacy, issuing prints based on old sketches and trial prints. To do so he established the Goyō Print Institute (*Goyō hanga kenkyūjo*). *Woman at a Hot-Spring Inn* is based on a trial sheet made in 1920 and was printed posthumously in 1950–52.

(PO)

Cat. 23

Hashiguchi Goyō 橋口五葉
(1881–1921)

Woman at a Hot-Spring Inn

(*Onsen yado no onna* 温泉宿の女)

Date: August 1920, printed 1950–52
Signature: *Goyō ga*
Artist's seal: *Goyō* (below signature),
Hashiguchi (bottom left margin)
Edition: -/150 (edition number left blank)
Publisher: Goyō hanga kenkyūjo
(Goyō Print Institute)
Block cutter: *Maeda Kentarō*
Printer: *Hirai Kōichi*
Size: 56 × 28.9 cm
Private collection, the Netherlands

Cat. 24

Hashiguchi Goyō 橋口五葉
(1881–1921)

Young Woman in Summer Kimono

(*Natsu yosōi no musume* 夏装之娘)

Date: 1920, posthumously printed in 1952
Signature: *Goyō ga*
Artist's seal: *Goyō*
Publisher: self-published
Size: 52.9 × 30.3 cm
Private collection, the Netherlands

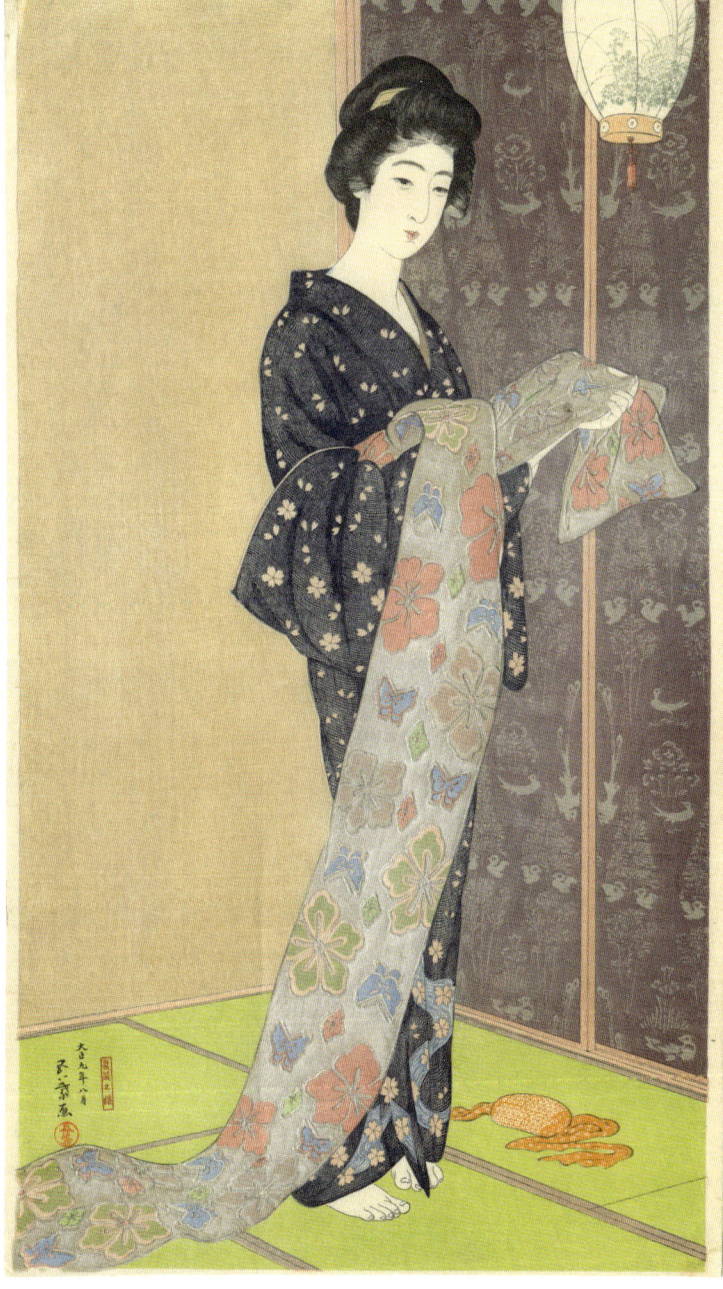

Cat. 25

Itō Shinsui 伊東深水 (1898–1972)

Before the Mirror

(*Taikyō* 対鏡)

Date: July 1916, *shihitsu* (trial work)
Signature: *Shinsui*
Artist's seal: *Tatsumi*
Edition: 74/100
Publisher: Watanabe Shōzaburō
Size: 44 × 29 cm
Private collection, the Netherlands

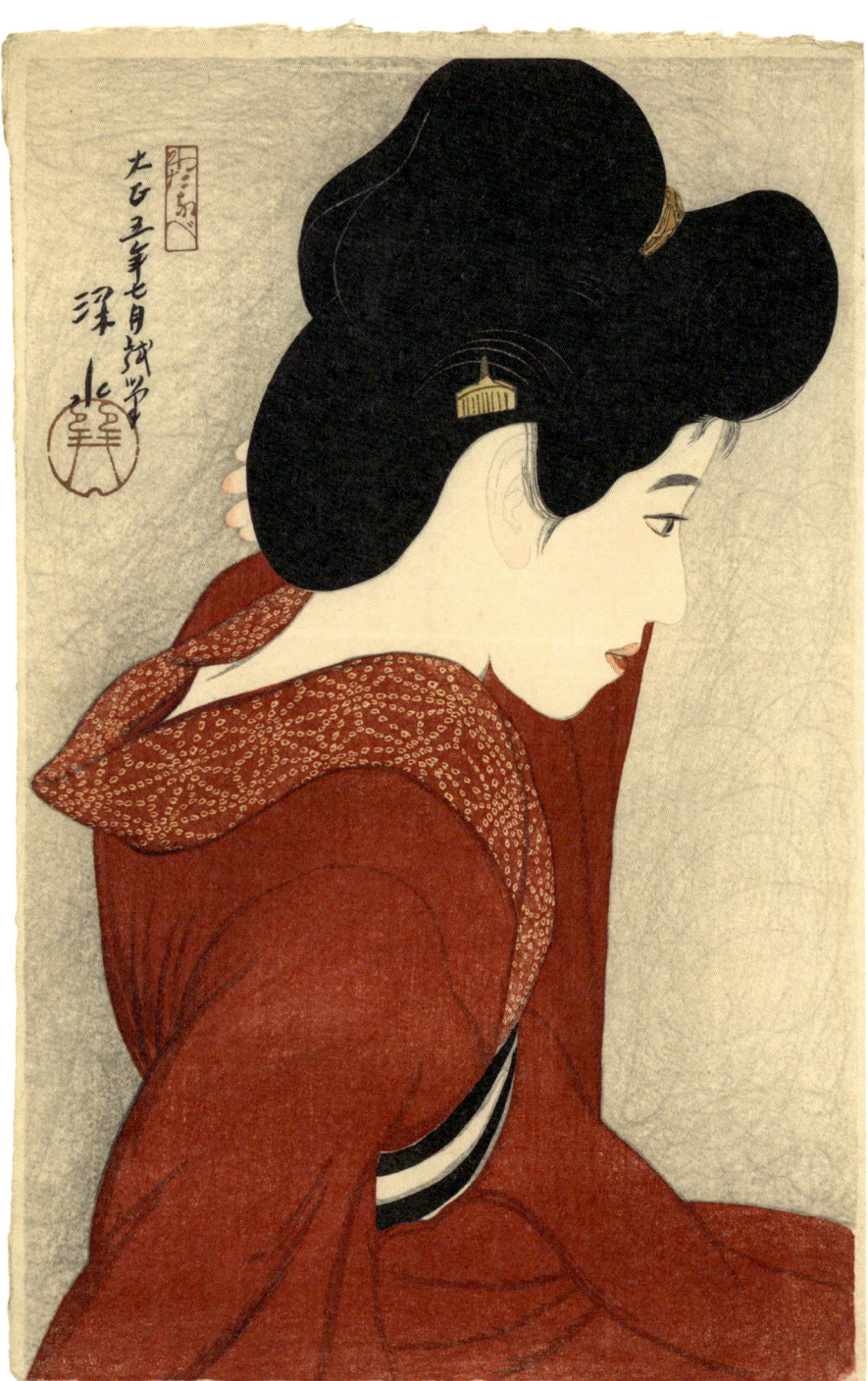

Before entering the world of *shin hanga*, Shinsui was, like many of his colleagues, a *nihonga* painter. *Before the Mirror* marks the first *shin hanga* work by Shinsui as well as his first collaboration with Watanabe Shōzaburō. Watanabe discovered his work at one of the Kyōdokai exhibitions organized by Shinsui's teacher, Kaburaki Kiyokata. He was charmed by one painting in particular: a composition of a woman glancing to the side, with its minimalistic colour palette of black, red and white. Watanabe expressed the desire to recreate the work as a print and pursuaded Kiyokata to put him in contact with Shinsui. Their collaboration proved to be fruitful: in the period between their first print and the 1923 earthquake alone they published 41 designs.

However, the two men did not always agree. Watanabe had initially suggested that the print be titled 'The Scarlet Lady', due to the bright red of the kimono and with a foreign clientele in mind. This title shifts the focus away from the clever composition, in which the mirror is putatively positioned outside the frame and the woman's downcast gaze suggests her being deep in thought.

Another quality of the print is the tension between the flat red and black surfaces and the textured background. The rubbing lines were created by applying pressure with the edge of the *baren* (printing tool).

(PO)

In this print a woman is pictured from behind, wringing out a small towel. It has been often noted that this print owes an artistic debt to Fritz Capelari's design *Woman Holding a Black Cat* (Cat. 10). It can be considered one of the most iconic images in the *shin hanga* tradition. It is also of the utmost rarity, published in an issue of no more than fifty impressions.

Shinsui himself did not care much for the design, stating: 'This picture was made at the request of Mr Watanabe. Personally I have no interest in it, but can say it has some value as showing my effort to express the quality of the face-powder around the neck without the use of colour, simply using the original paper colour.'
(PO)

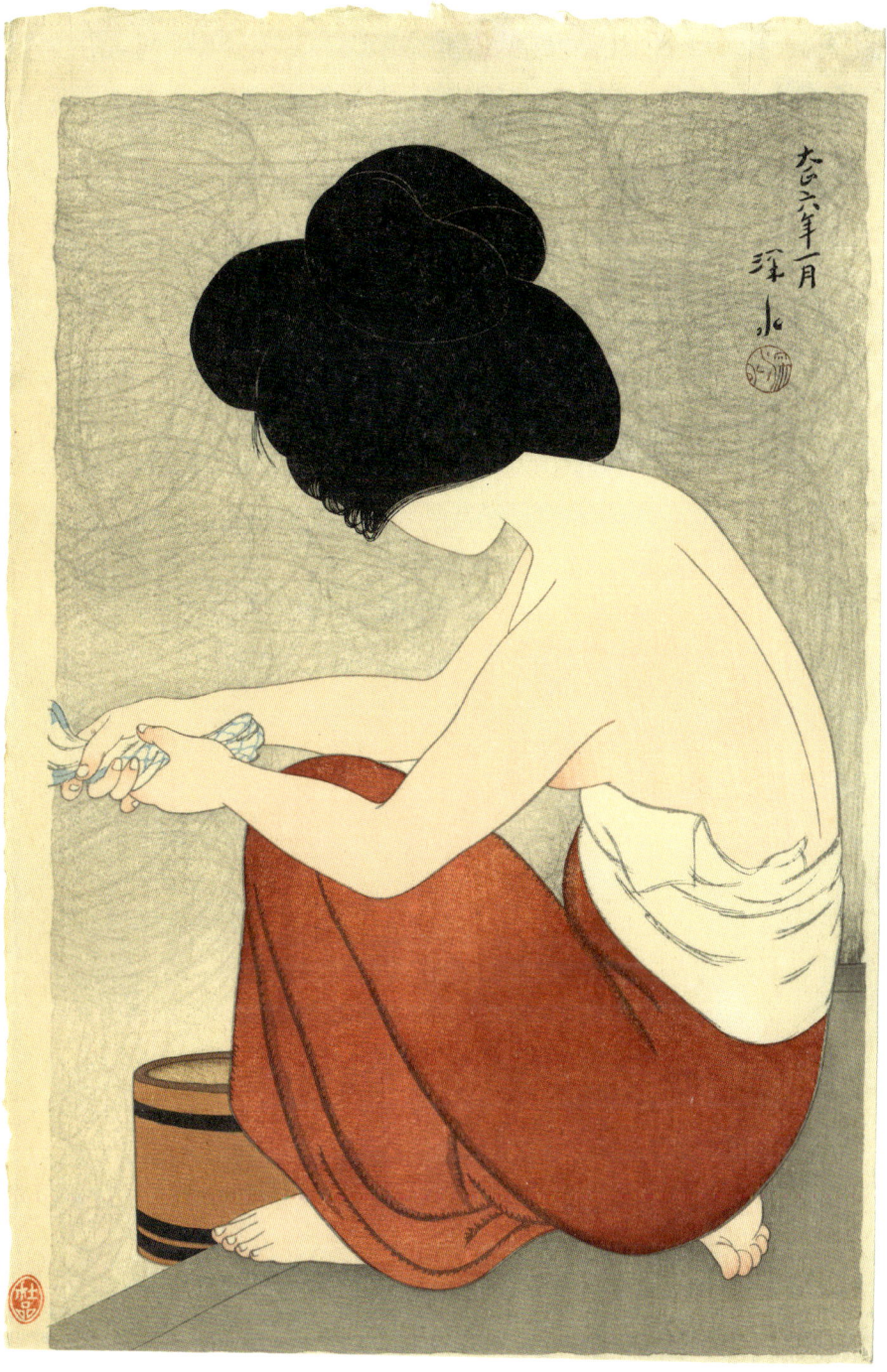

Cat. 26

Itō Shinsui 伊東深水 (1898–1972)

After a Bath

(*Yokugo* 浴後)

Date: January 1917
Signature: *Shinsui*
Artist's seal: *Shinsui*
Edition: 20/50
Publisher: Watanabe Shōzaburō
Size: 45 × 30.5 cm
Private collection, the Netherlands

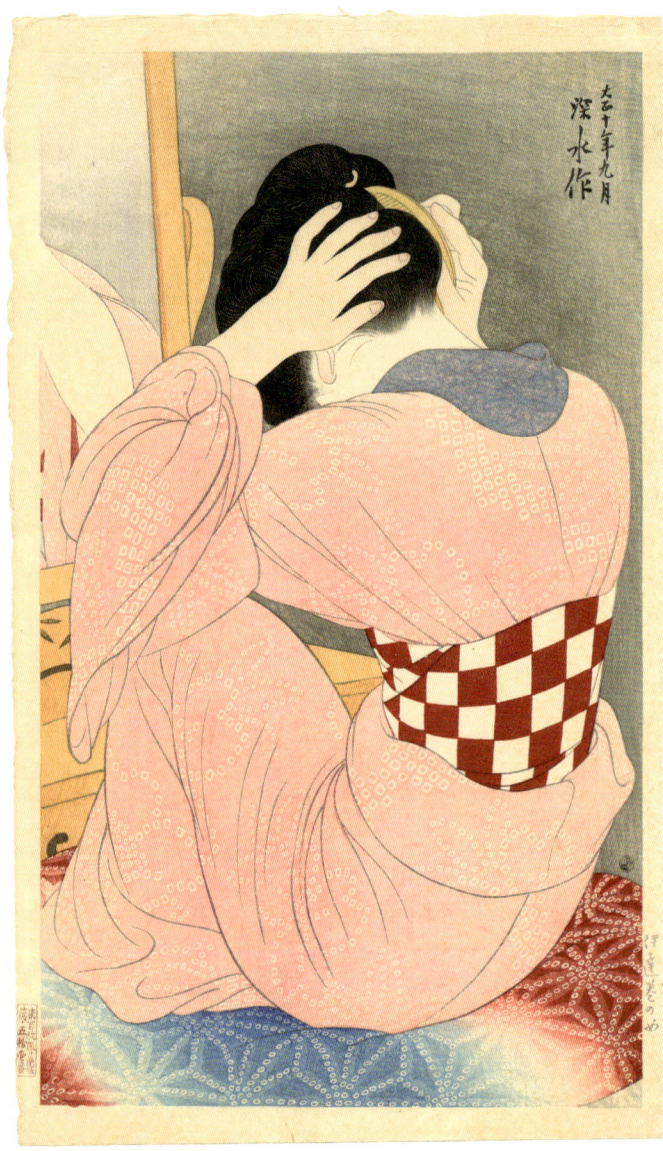

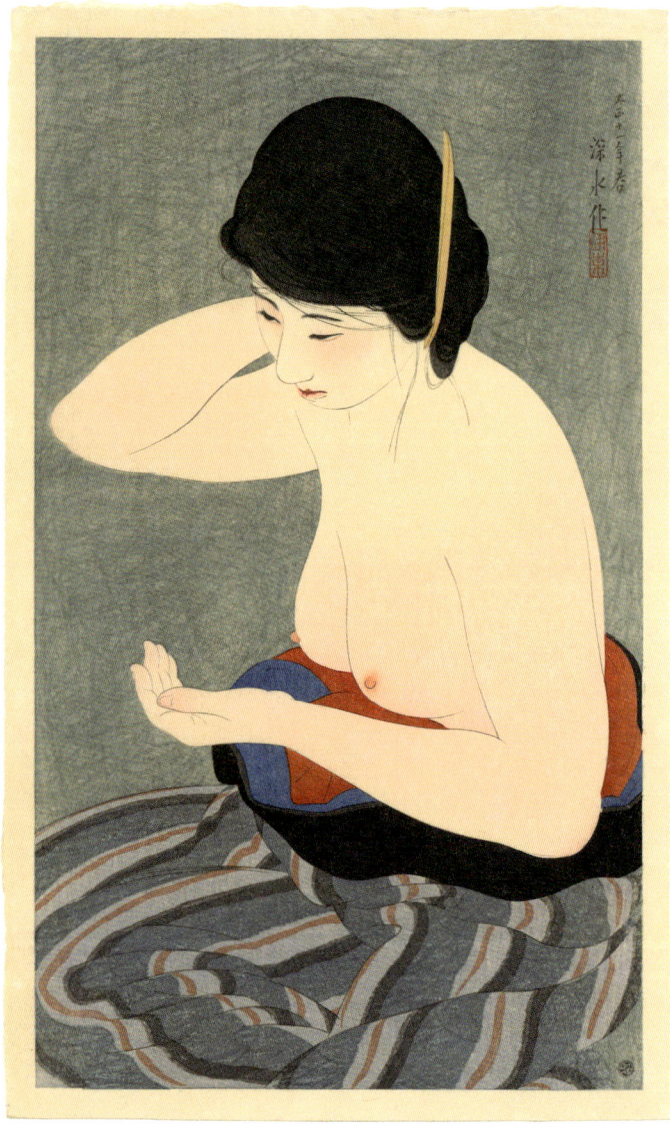

Cat. 27

Itō Shinsui 伊東深水 (1898–1972)

Woman Wearing an Under-Sash

(*Datemaki no onna* 伊達巻の女)

Date: September 1921
Signature: *Shinsui saku*
Edition: 51/200
Publisher: Watanabe Shōzaburō
Size: 43.3 × 26 cm
Collection Scholten

Cat. 28

Itō Shinsui 伊東深水 (1898–1972)

Make-up

(*Keshō* 化粧)

Series: *Twelve Forms of New Beauties*
(*Shin bijin jūnishi* 新美人十二姿)
Date: Spring 1922
Signature: *Shinsui saku*
Artist's seal: *Itō*
Edition: 29/200
Publisher: Watanabe Shōzaburō
Size: 43 × 26.8 cm
Collection Scholten

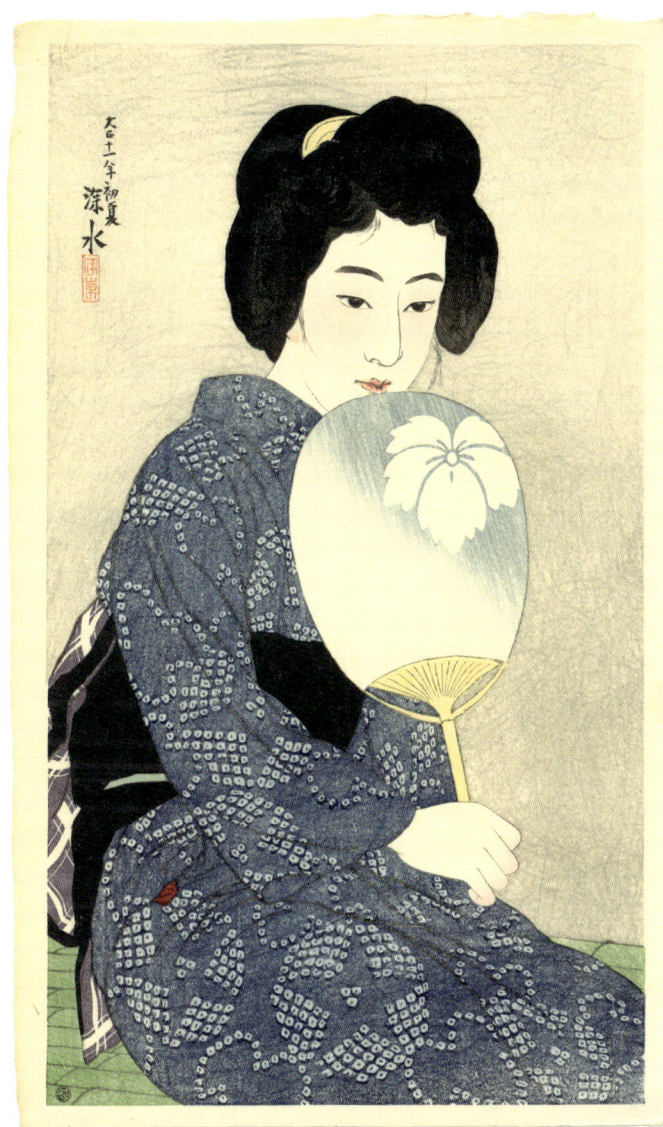

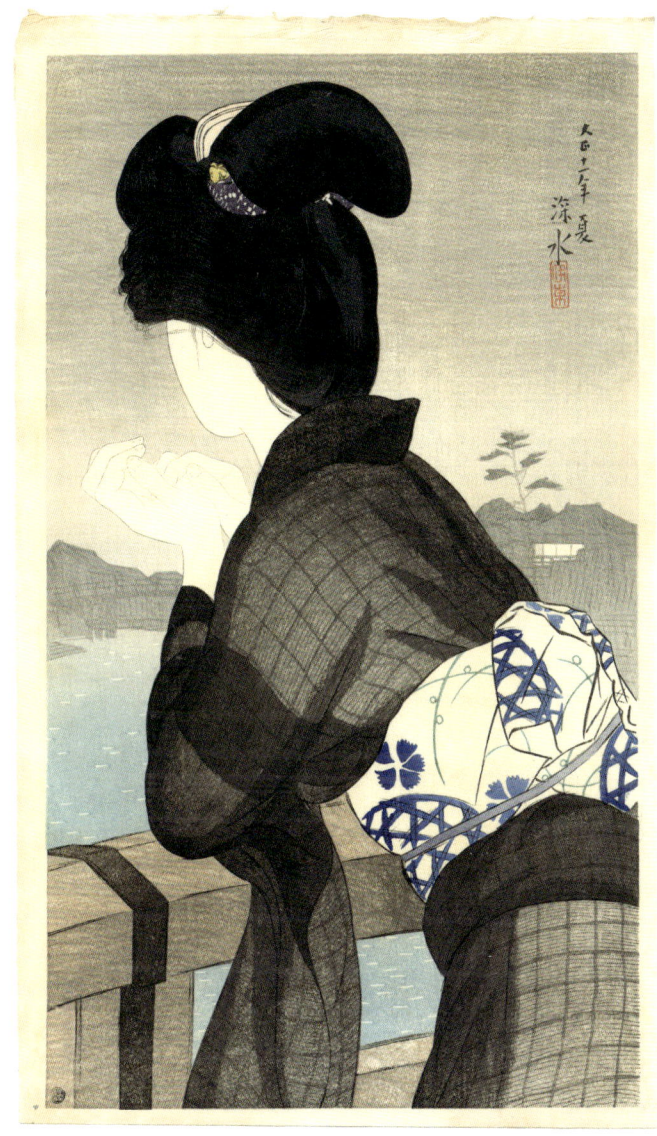

Cat. 29

Itō Shinsui 伊東深水 (1898–1972)

Cotton Kimono

(*Yukata* 浴衣)

Series: *Twelve Forms of New Beauties*
(*Shin bijin jūnishi* 新美人十二姿)
Date: Early summer 1922
Signature: *Shinsui*
Artist's seal: *Itō*
Edition: 83/200
Publisher: Watanabe Shōzaburō
Size: 43.2 × 26.3 cm
Collection Scholten

Cat. 30

Itō Shinsui 伊東深水 (1898–1972)

Evening Cool

(*Suzumi* 涼み)

Series: *Twelve Forms of New Beauties*
(*Shin bijin jūnishi* 新美人十二姿)
Date: Summer 1922
Signature: *Shinsui*
Artist's seal: *Itō*
Edition: 25/200
Publisher: Watanabe Shōzaburō
Size: 43.5 × 26.3 cm
Collection Scholten

The series *Twelve Forms of New Beauties* was commissioned by the Ukiyo-e Research Society (*Ukiyo-e kenkyūkai*) and was sold in an edition of 200 prints per design. Eleven prints were published in 1922–23, with the last design, *Contemplating the Coming of Spring*, postponed until 1924 because of the Great Kantō Earthquake.

(JD)

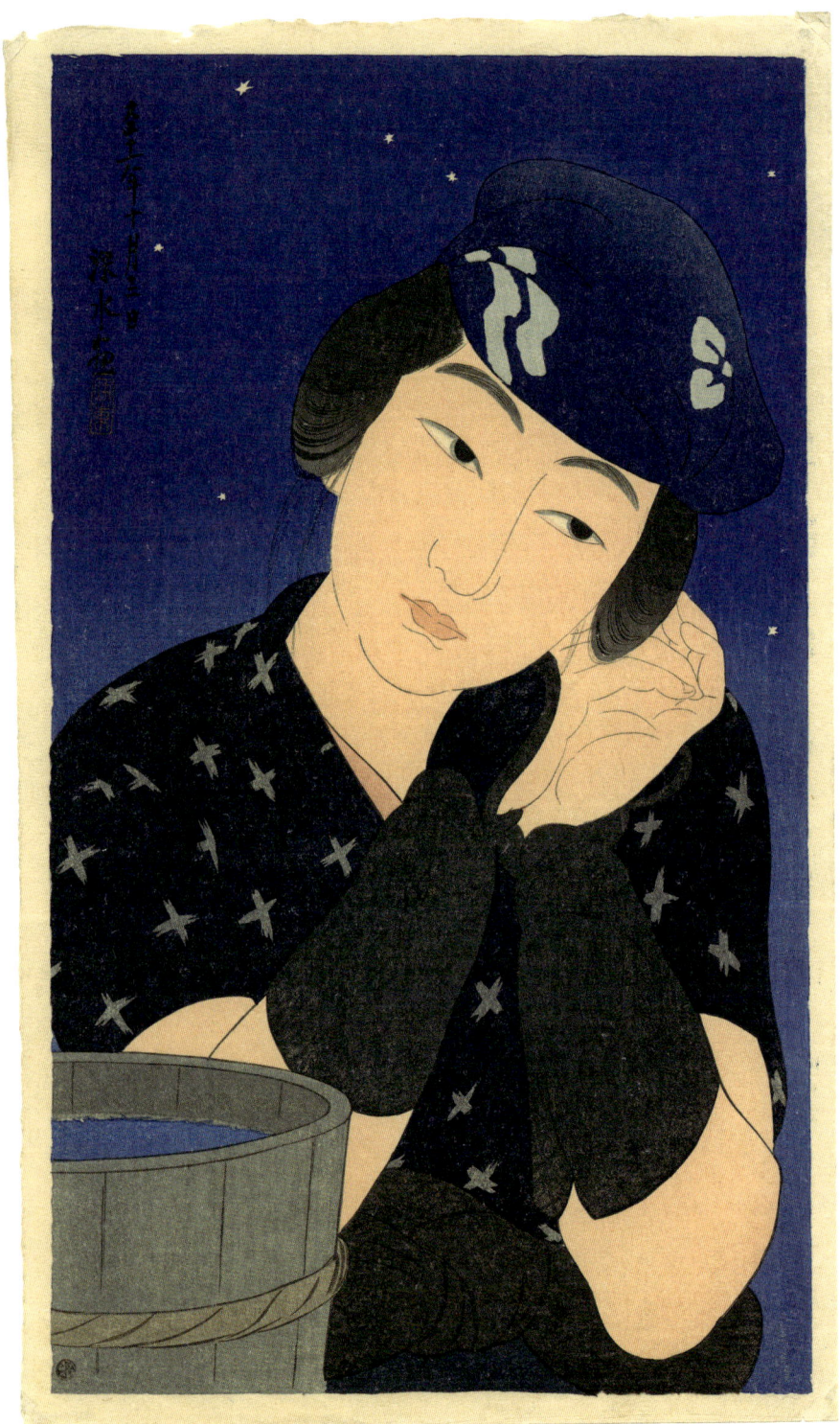

Cat. 31

Itō Shinsui 伊東深水 (1898–1972)

[Ōshima] Island Woman

(*Shima no onna* 島の女)

Series: *Twelve Forms of New Beauties*
(*Shin bijin jūnishi* 新美人十二姿)
Date: October 1922
Signature: *Shinsui ga*
Artist's seal: *Itō*
Edition: 192/200
Publisher: Watanabe Shōzaburō
Size: 42.9 × 25.9 cm
Collection Scholten

In *Shima no onna* (literally: 'woman from an island'), Shinsui deviates from his usual city-dwelling geisha and depicts Ōshima's so-called *anko-san* (Ōshima dialect for 'big sis'). *Anko-san* are typically young unmarried Ōshima women who are recognizable by their traditional indigo-coloured clothing and the water buckets or heaps of firewood that they carry on their heads. Of the many volcanic islands south of the coast between Izu Peninsula and the Bay of Tokyo, Ōshima is the largest and closest to the mainland. On the woman's head rests a small cotton hand towel (*tenugui*) to ease the weight of the water. She is set against a clear, starry night sky, far away from the light pollution of modernized downtown Tokyo.

(JD)

54

Prints from the series *Twelve Forms of New Beauties* were issued monthly to 200 subscribers. This was an attempt by Watanabe to appeal to foreign customers and promote a sense of exclusiveness and luxury. However, the numbered editions were often followed by unnumbered ones. Moreover, with the exception of Shinsui's beautiful women prints, Watanabe would later return to the practice of all ukiyo-e publishers before him: casting numbering aside and continuing to print until the market was saturated.

(PO)

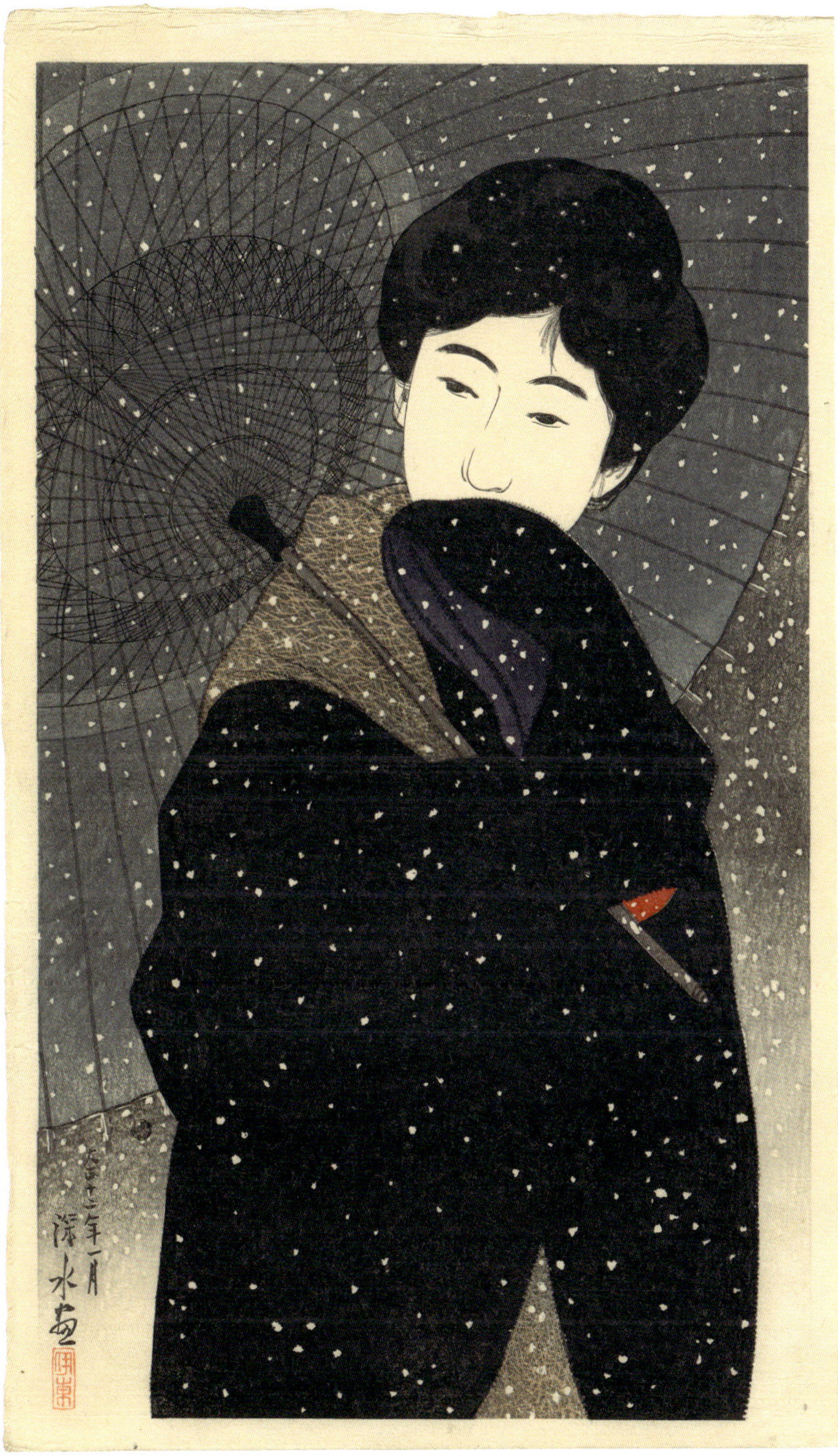

Cat. 32

Itō Shinsui 伊東深水 (1898–1972)

Snowy Night

(*Yuki no yo* 雪の夜)

Series: *Twelve Forms of New Beauties*
(*Shin bijin jūnishi* 新美人十二姿)
Date: January 1923
Signature: *Shinsui ga*
Artist's seal: *Itō*
Edition: 30/200
Publisher: Watanabe Shōzaburō
Size: 43 × 26 cm
Collection Scholten

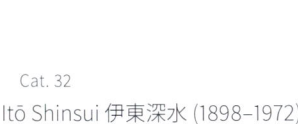

Kitano Tsunetomi 北野恒富
(1880–1947)

**Winter (Shinchi): Before
the Mirror**

(*Fuyu [Shinchi] kagami no mae*
冬 [新地] 鏡の前)

Series: *Four Seasons of the
Pleasure Quarters*
(*Kuruwa no shunjū* 廓の春秋)
Date: 1918
Signature: *Tsunetomi hitsu*
Publisher: Nakajima Seikadō
(Nakajima Jūtarō)
Printer: *Tadokoro Rikimatsu*
Size: 39.4 × 26 cm
Collection Scholten

This print portrays a woman from the northern Shinchi district of Osaka, still today an area known for its prostitution. It is part of a set of four prints, released in a limited edition of 500, of which this is the final design.

The series was announced in the prominent newspaper *Tōkyō asahi shinbun* and advertised as 'reflecting the manners and customs of contemporary pleasure quarters'.

With softly printed grey contour lines, large flat blocks of colour and a limited colour palette, this design radiates a tranquil atmosphere. No wonder, perhaps, that the *Tōkyō asahi shinbun* of 1914 lists a price of 25 sen (for the first image from the series), and four years later the same newspaper mentions a sharp increase to 1 yen 50 sen.

(PO)

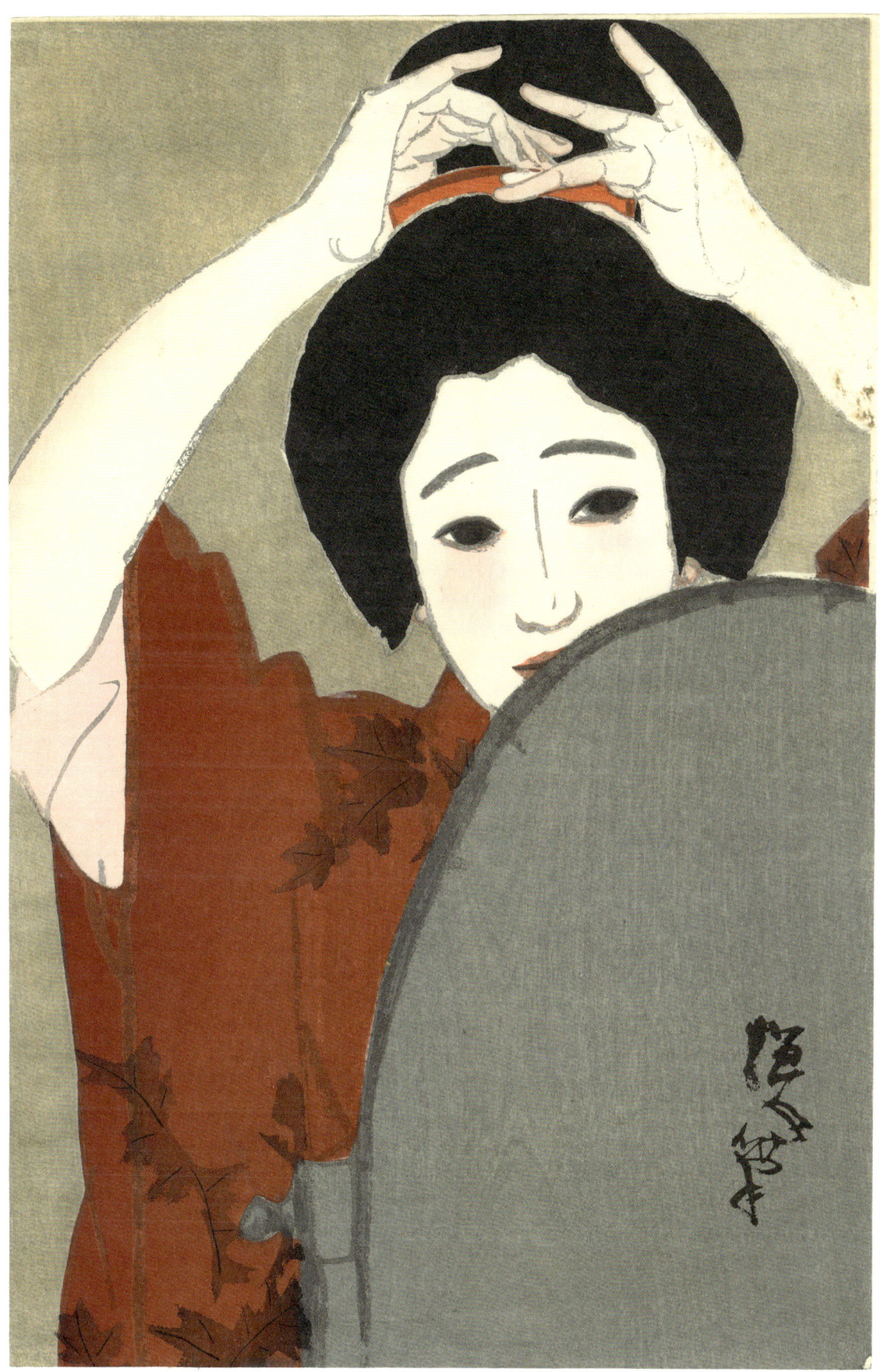

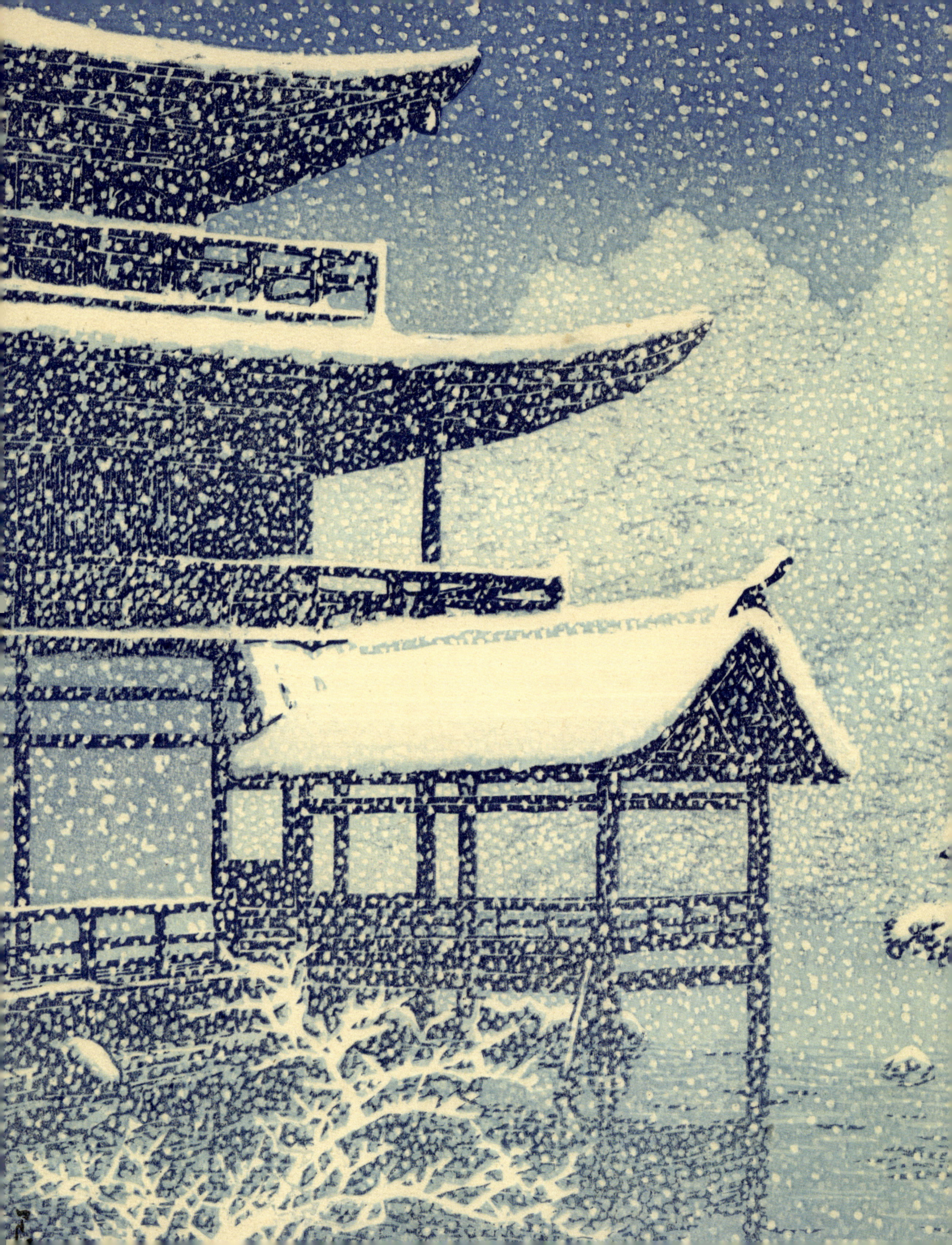

Pre-Earthquake Landscapes

It was not only in the beautiful women genre that *shin hanga* revolution-
ized Japanese printmaking, but also in the landscape genre. Shinsui, followed by Kawase Hasui soon after, portrayed quintessential Japanese
landscapes but without recourse to its famous beauty spots ... until,
that is, the Great Kantō Earthquake destroyed their prints, blocks
and sketches.

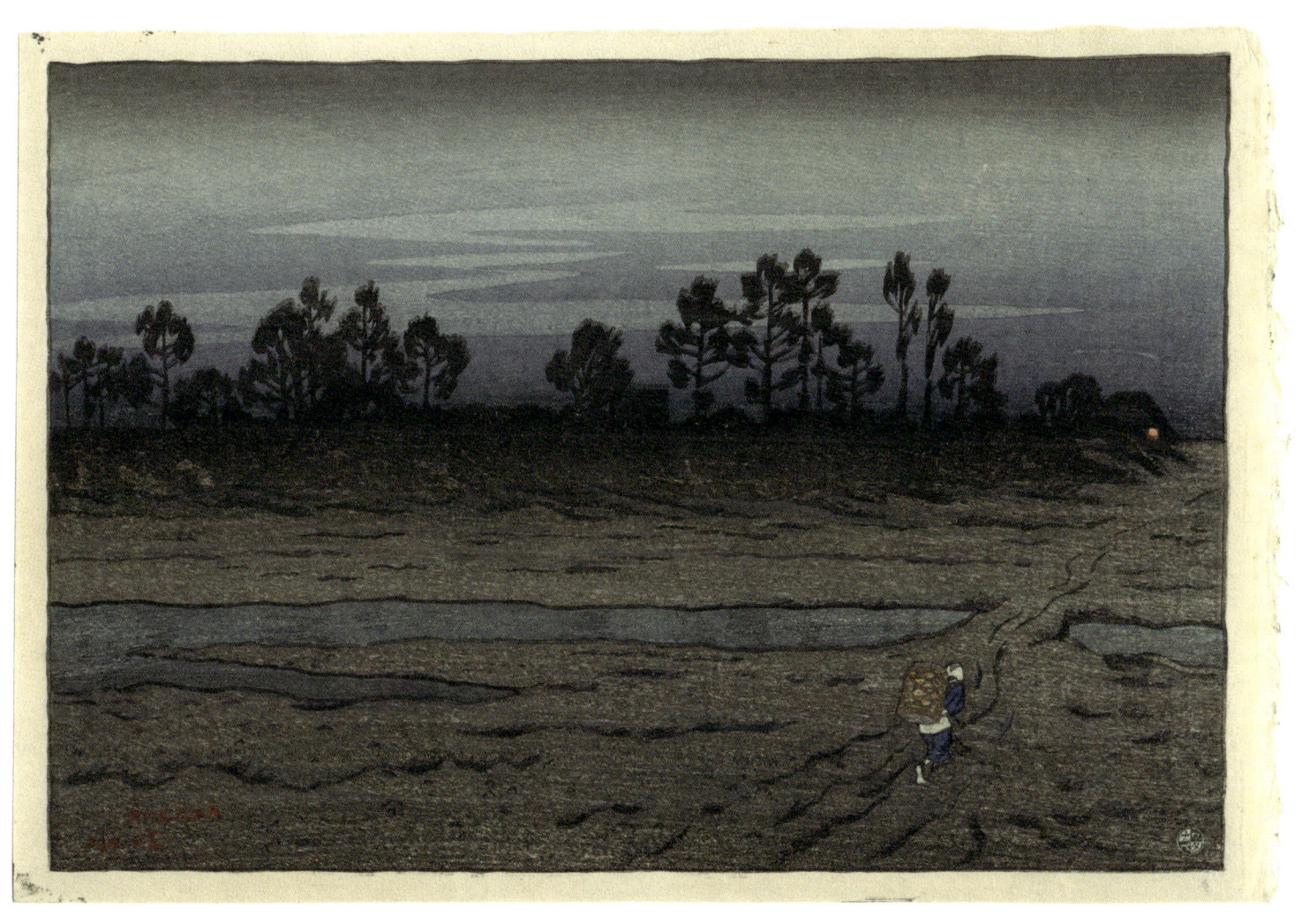

Cat. 34
Itō Shinsui 伊東深水 (1898–1972)
Evening at the Tama Riverbed
(*Tamagahara no yū* 多摩川原の夕)

Date: February 1917
Signature: *Shinsui*
Publisher: Watanabe Shōzaburō
Size: 22 × 32.4 cm
Collection Scholten

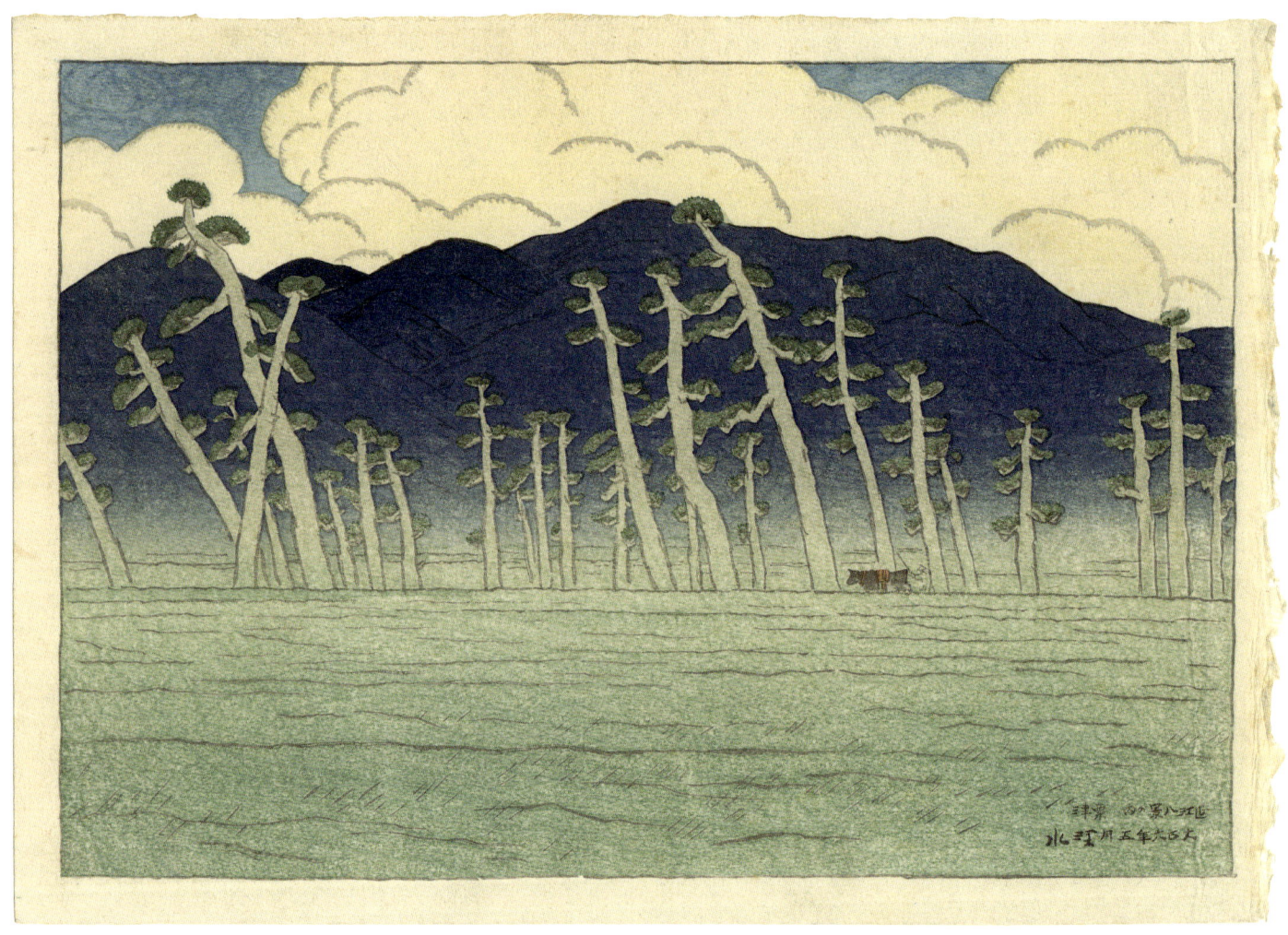

Cat. 35a

Awazu

(*Awazu* 粟津)

Cats. 35a–h

Itō Shinsui 伊東深水 (1898–1972)

Series: *Eight Views of Ōmi*
(*Ōmi hakkei no uchi* 近江八景の内)
Date: May 1917
Signature: *Shinsui*
Edition: 13/200 (a-g), 49/200 (h)
Publisher: Watanabe Shōzaburō
Size: 22 × 32 cm
Private collection, the Netherlands

About a year after designing his first prints for Watanabe, Shinsui made *Eight Views of Ōmi*, the works that inspired his friend and colleague Kawase Hasui to join the *shin hanga* scene. The 'eight views' theme comes from Chinese traditions in poetry and painting which, since its introduction in Japan in the Muromachi Period, had centred on various locations around Lake Biwa, in Ōmi Province, near Kyoto. However, departing from tradition, Shinsui omitted various poetic elements such as the flock of geese that is usually associated with Katada (Cat. 35h), the snow that is supposed to decorate the peaks of Mount Hira (Cat. 35b), and the rain in the midst of night at the great pine tree of Karasaki (Cat. 35g). Instead, rather than designing his prints using the canonical imagery, Shinsui visited the actual locations and sketched what he saw. He then worked closely with the craftsmen of Watanabe's studio to translate his sketches into the expressive painterly style that is representative of his early landscapes.

(JD)

Mount Hira
(*Hira* 比良)

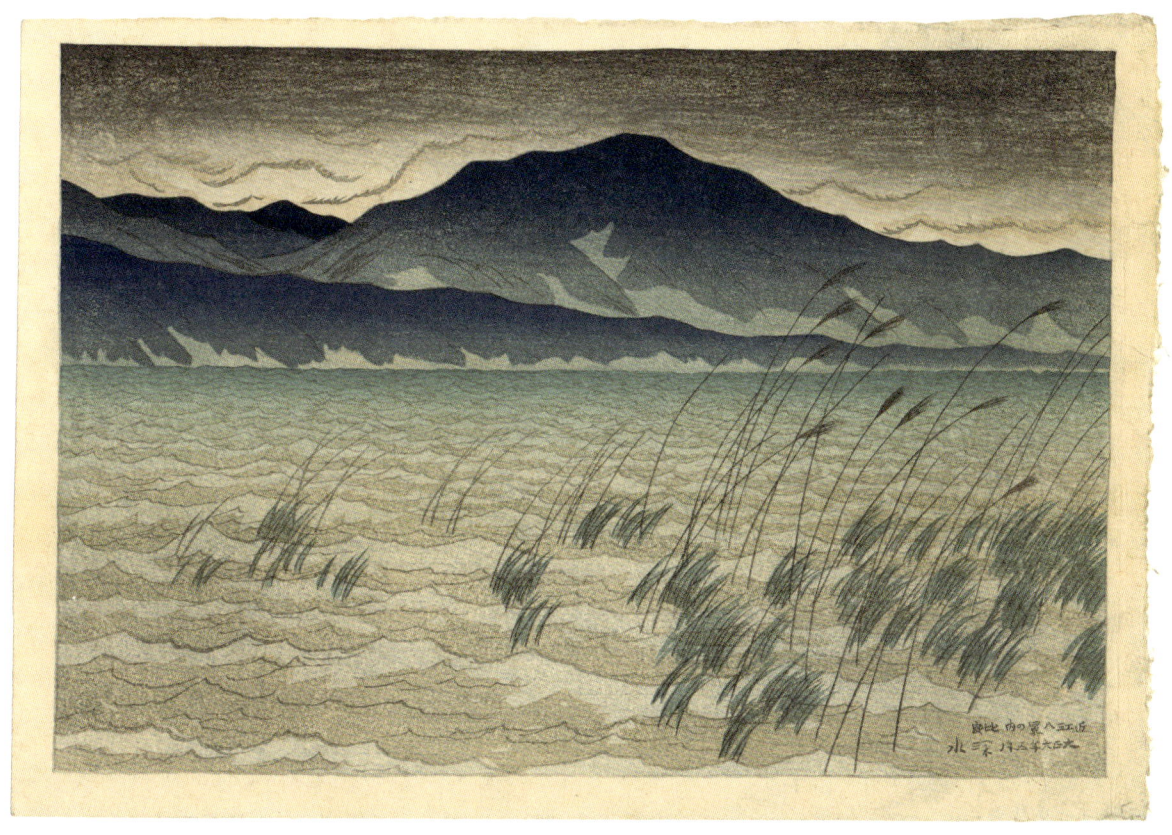

Cat. 35c
Yabase
(*Yabase* 矢橋)

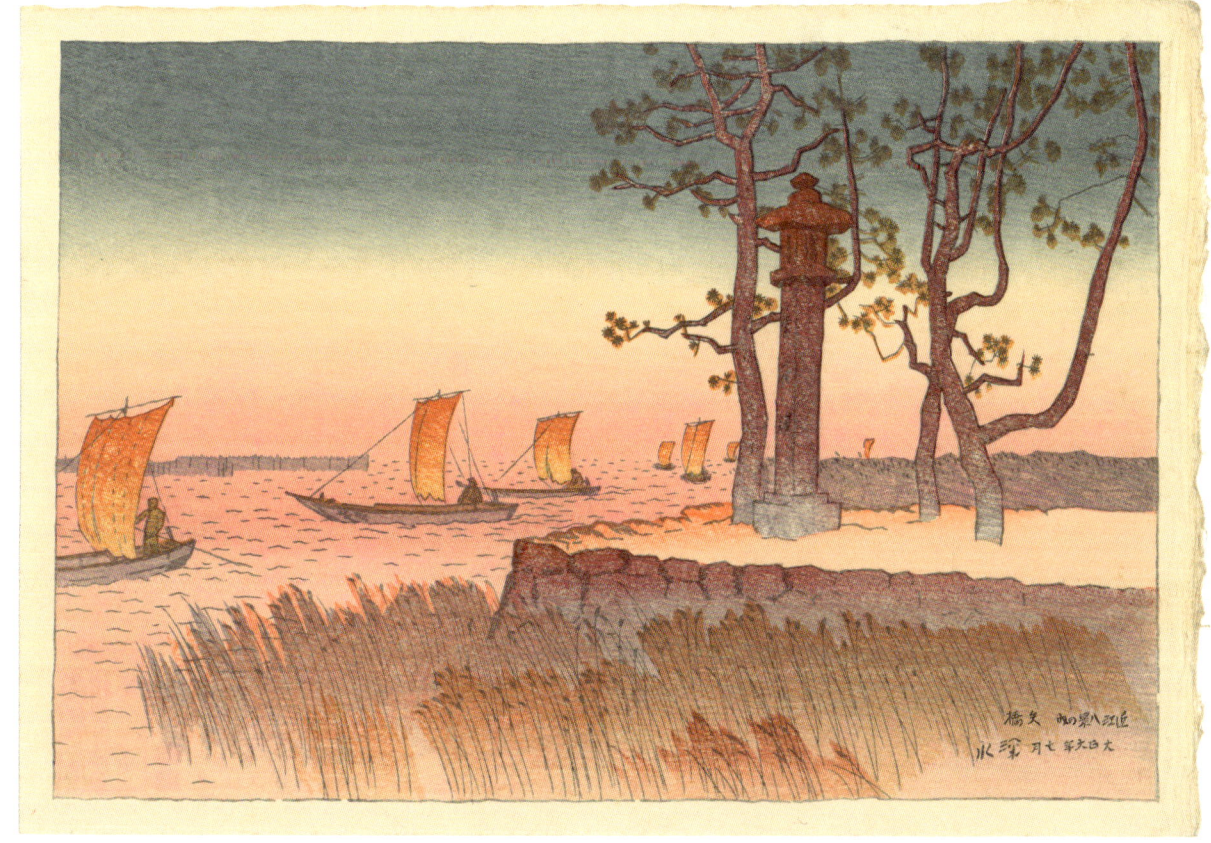

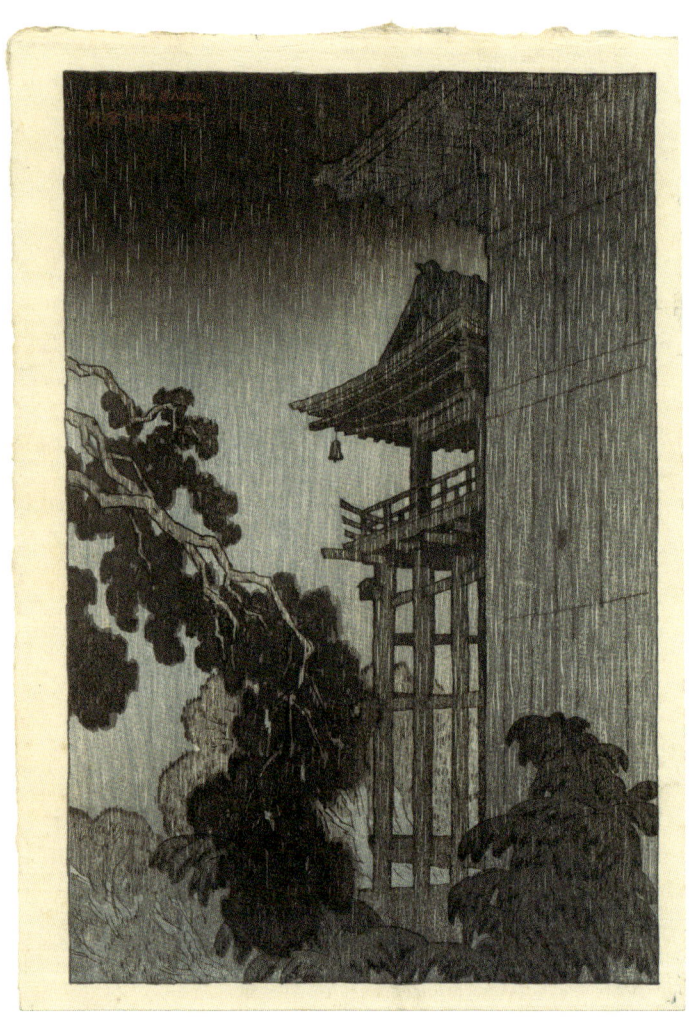

Cat. 35d

Miidera

(*Miidera* 三井寺)

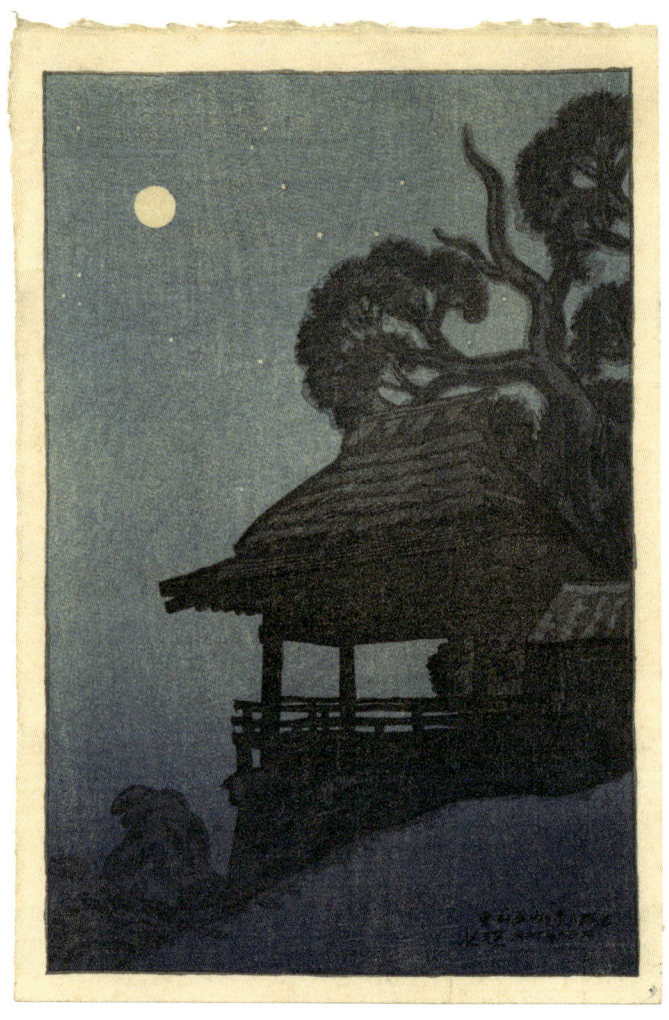

Cat. 35e

Ishiyamadera

(*Ishiyamadera* 石山寺)

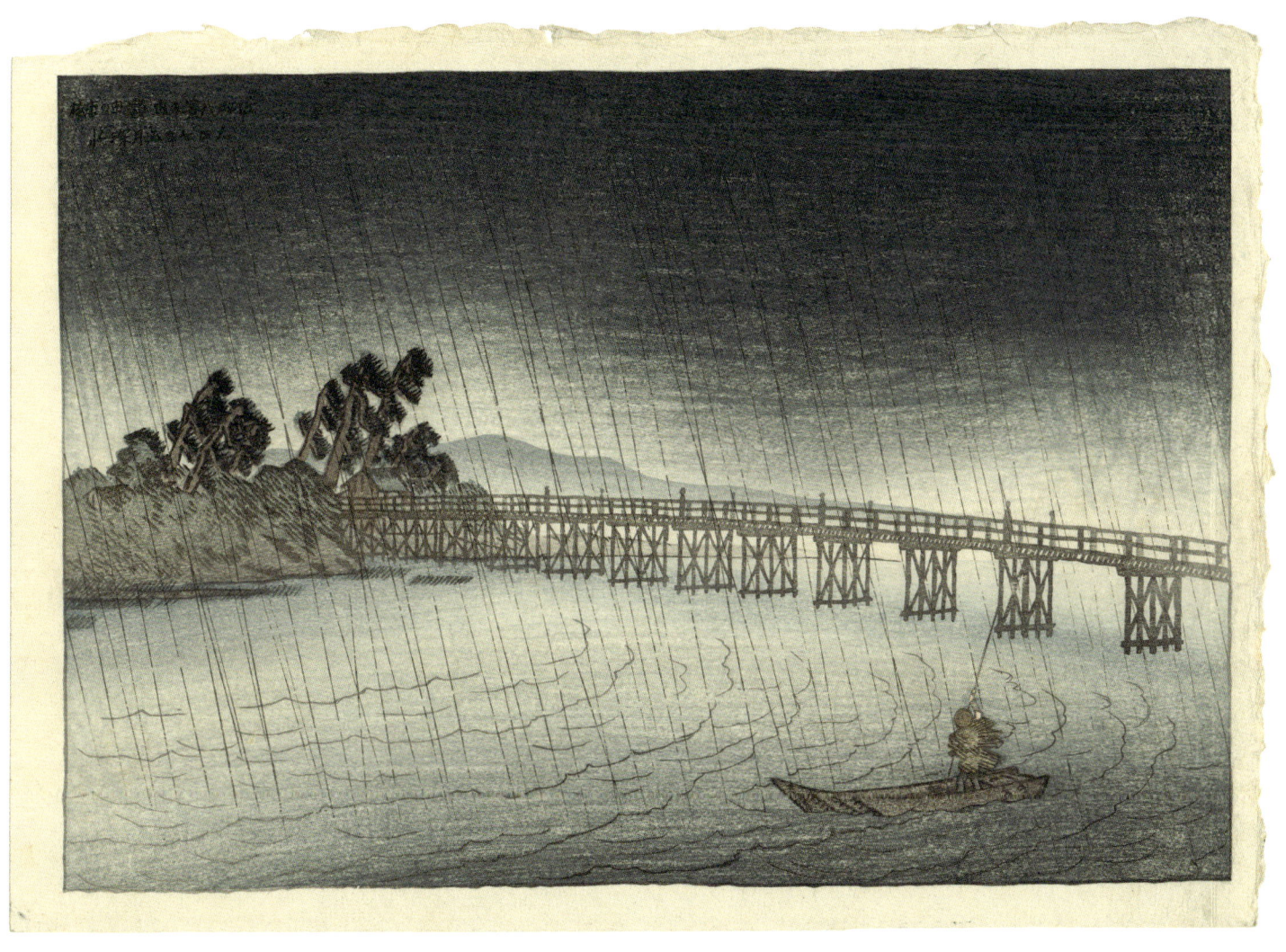

Cat. 35f

Karahashi, Seta

(*Seta no Karahashi* 瀬田の唐橋)

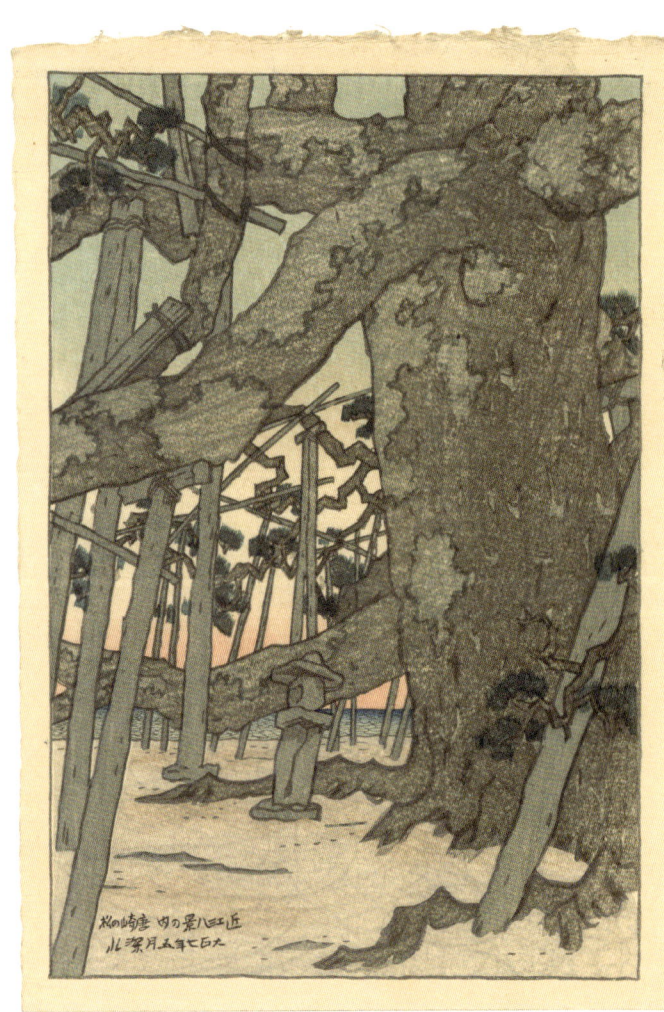

The Pine Tree at Karasaki

(*Karasaki no matsu* 唐崎の松)

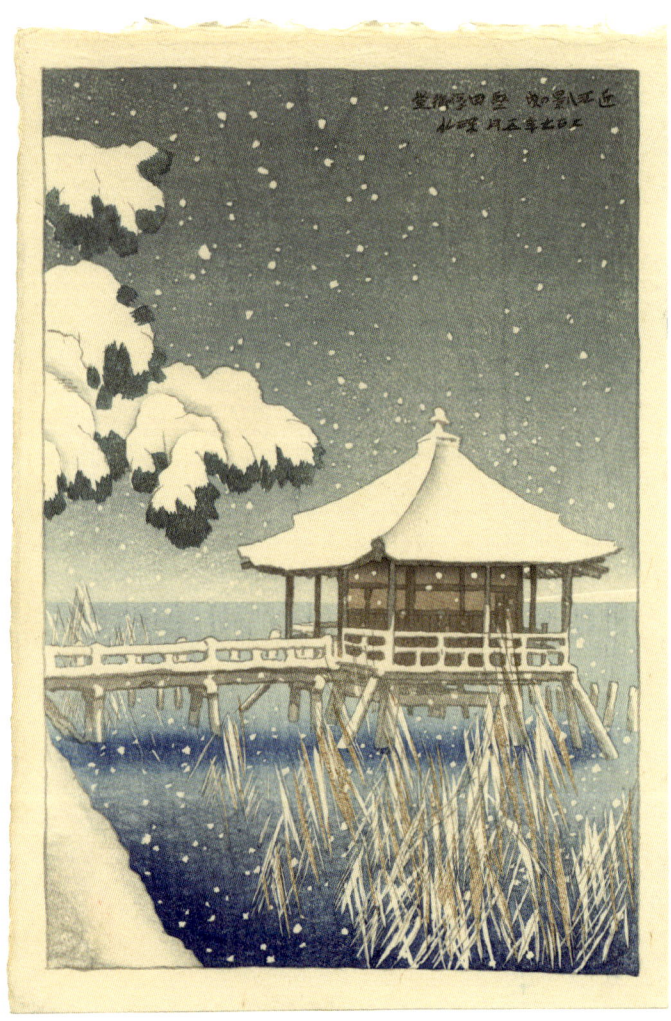

**The Floating Pavilion
[Ukimidō], Katada**

(*Katada Ukimidō* 堅田浮御堂)

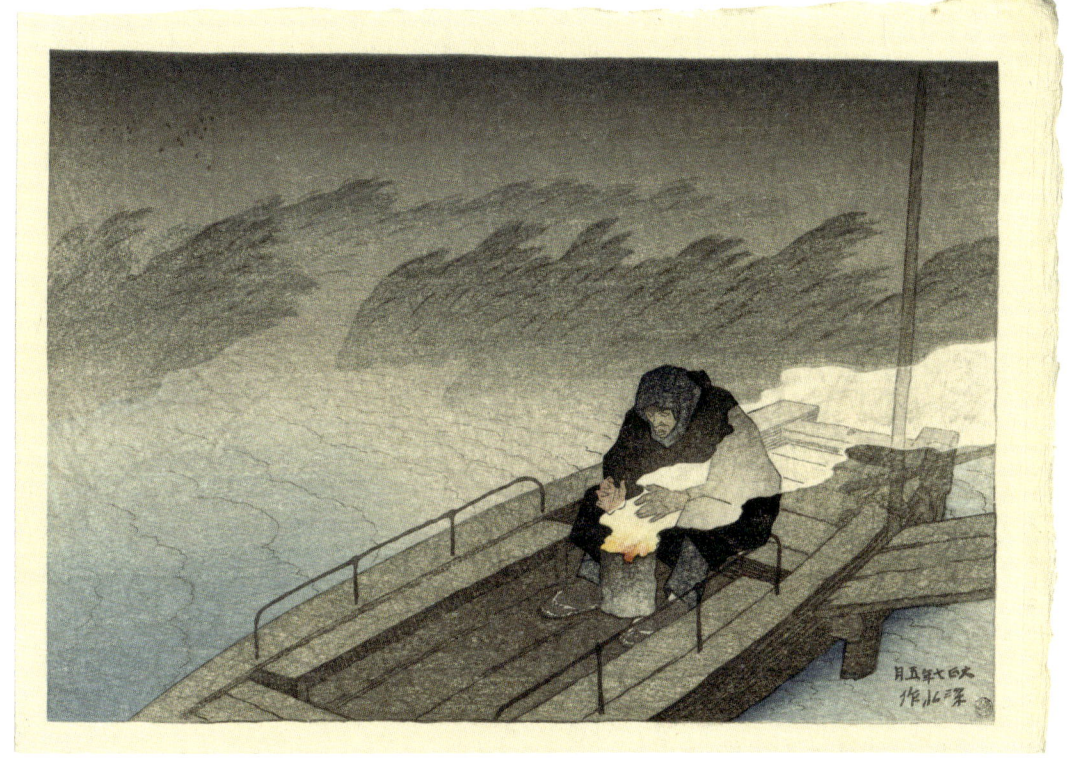

Cat. 36

Itō Shinsui 伊東深水 (1898–1972)

Ferryman

(*Watashimori* 渡し守)

Date: May 1918
Signature: *Shinsui saku*
Edition: 17/200
Publisher: Watanabe Shōzaburō
Size: 22.5 × 32.5 cm
Private collection, the Netherlands

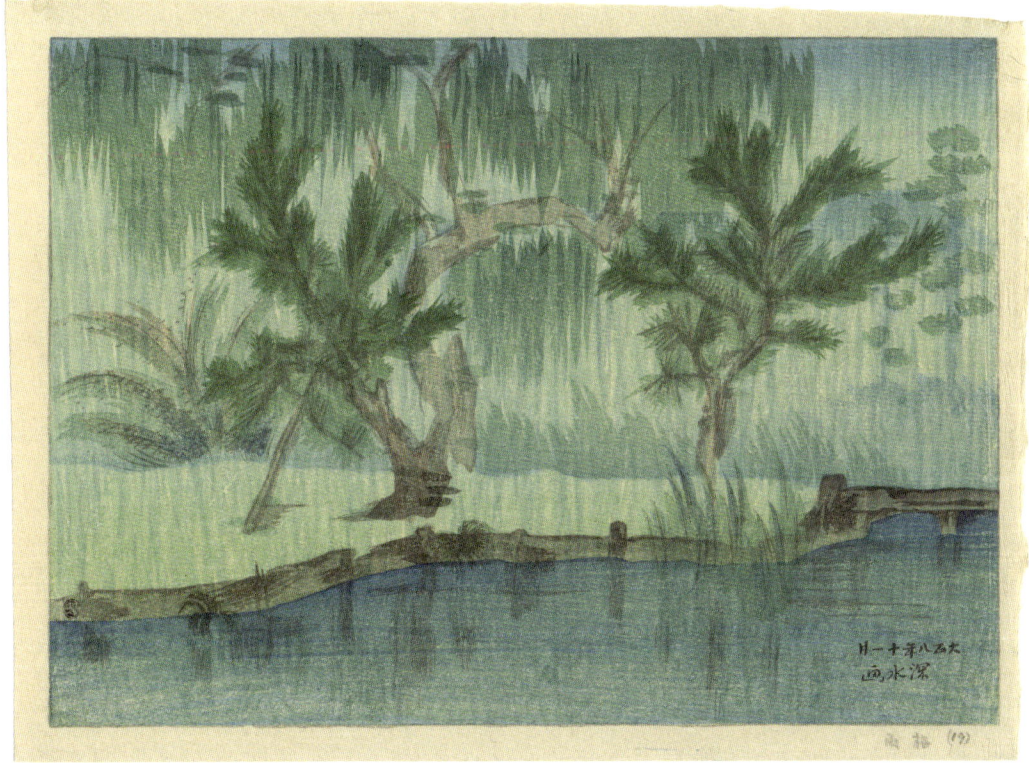

Cat. 37

Itō Shinsui 伊東深水 (1898–1972)

Rainy Season

(*Tsuyu* 梅雨)

Date: November 1919
Signature: *Shinsui ga*
Publisher: Watanabe Shōzaburō
Size: 25.2 × 35 cm
Collection Scholten

Itō Shinsui 伊東深水 (1898–1972)

Dawn [at the Tachiai River]

(*Reimei* 黎明)

Date: November 1919
Signature: *Shinsui ga*
Publisher: Watanabe Shōzaburō
Size: 26 × 35.9 cm
Collection Scholten

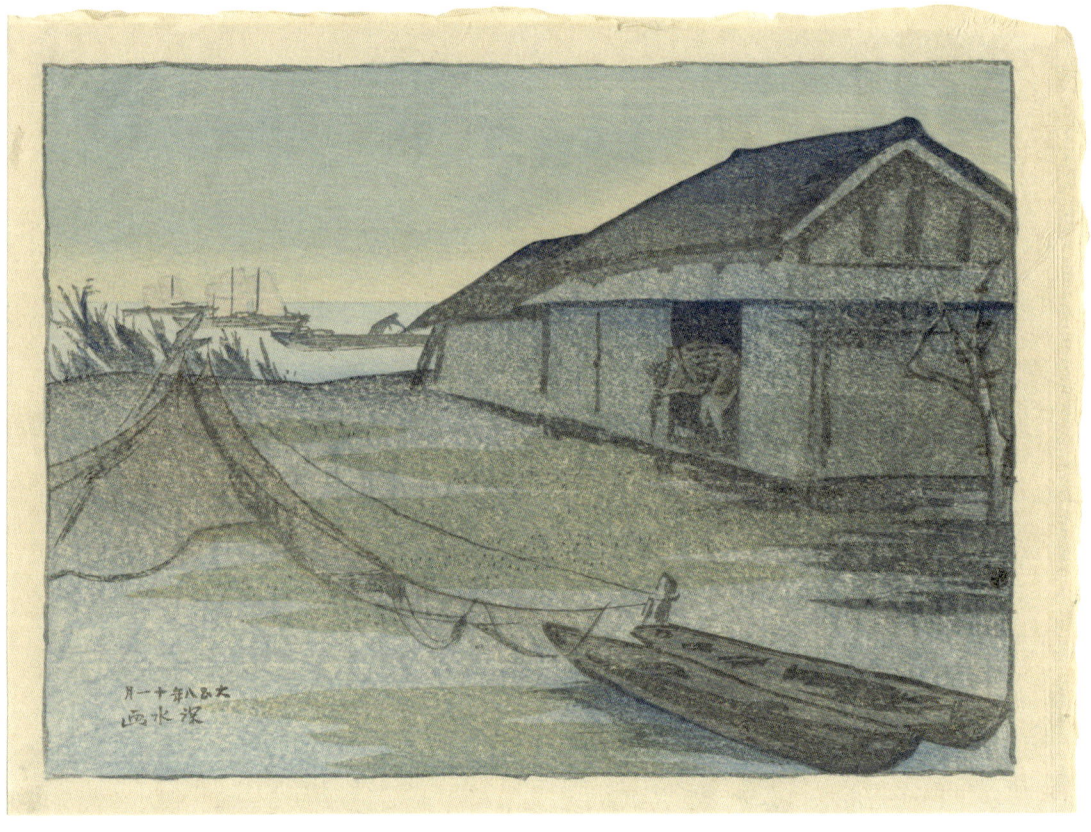

Cat. 39

Itō Shinsui 伊東深水 (1898–1972)

Before a Thunderstorm

(*Kandachimae* 神立前)

Date: March 1920
Signature: *Shinsui ga*
Publisher: Watanabe Shōzaburō
Size: 33.2 × 23.3 cm
Private collection, the Netherlands

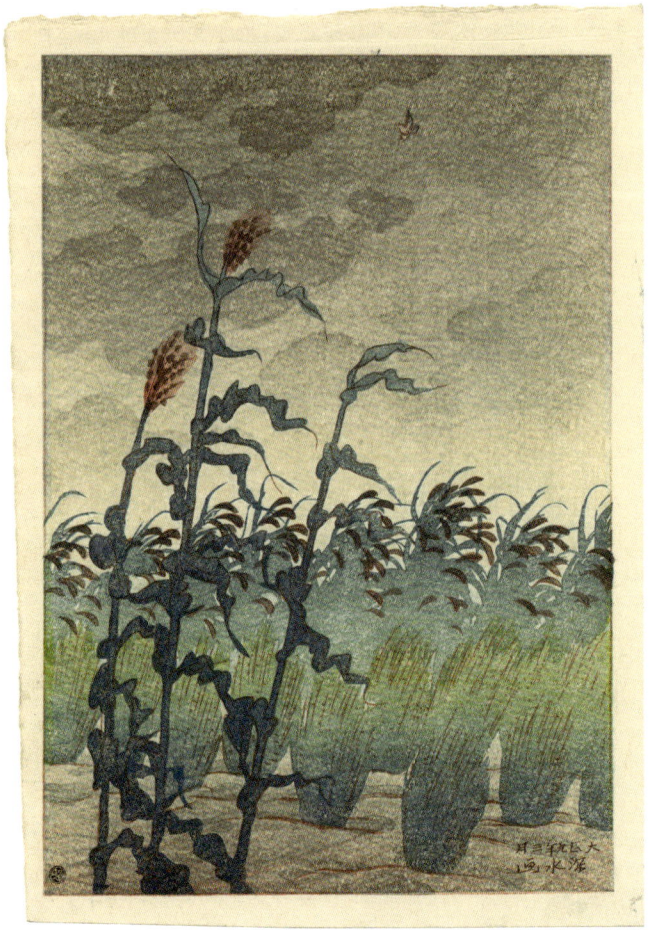

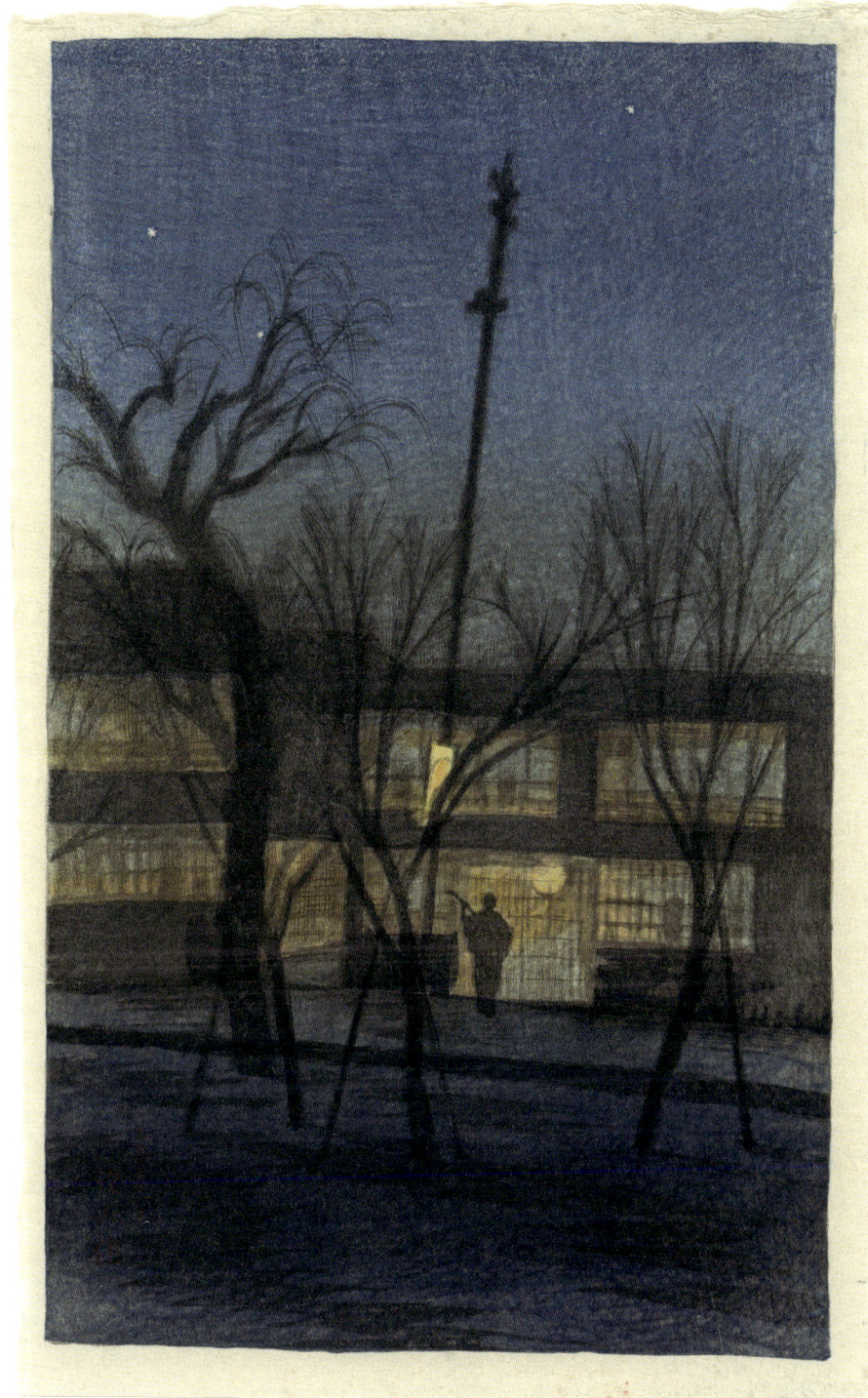

Cat. 40

Itō Shinsui 伊東深水 (1898–1972)

Ikenohata at Night

(*Yoru no Ikenohata* 夜の池之端)

Date: January 1921
Signature: *Shinsui saku*
Edition: 71/100
Publisher: Watanabe Shōzaburō
Size: 41.3 × 26.3 cm
Private collection, the Netherlands

The reverse of this print carries a note written by Watanabe in which he mentions that the *Edo-e kanshōkai* (Society for the Appreciation of Edo Pictures) would commission a print whenever they had a yearly surplus. The previous year they had commissioned *Mount Ibuki in Snow* by Hashiguchi Goyō (Cat. 45), and this year they celebrated by publishing Shinsui's nightscape. Ikenohata is a neighbourhood in Ueno, Tokyo, right next to the Shinobazu Pond. According to Watanabe's note, Shinsui was impressed by the sight he witnessed from the pond's edge, the lights from inside the houses contrasting with the dark silhouettes of the night. Watanabe asked Shinsui to freely supervise the carvers and printers, which resulted in this atmospheric evening scene.
(JD)

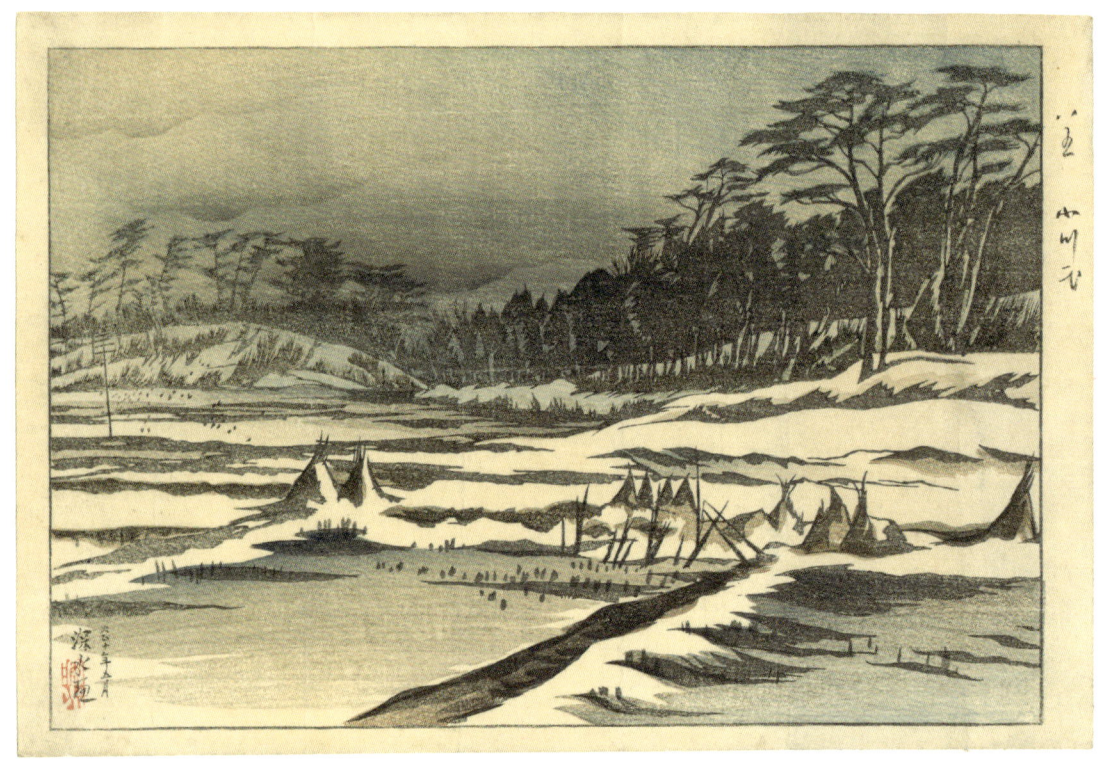

Cat. 41

Itō Shinsui 伊東深水 (1898–1972)

After the Snow

(*Yuki no ato* 雪の後)

Date: May 1921
Signature: *Shinsui ga*
Artist's seal: *Shinsui*
Publisher: Watanabe Shōzaburō
Size: 25.9 × 39 cm
Collection Scholten

Cat. 42

Itō Shinsui 伊東深水 (1898–1972)

Setting Sun in Autumn

(*Aki no rakujitsu* 秋の落日)

Date: May 1921
Artist's seal: *Shinsui*
Publisher: Watanabe Shōzaburō
Size: 26.3 × 37.7 cm
Collection Scholten

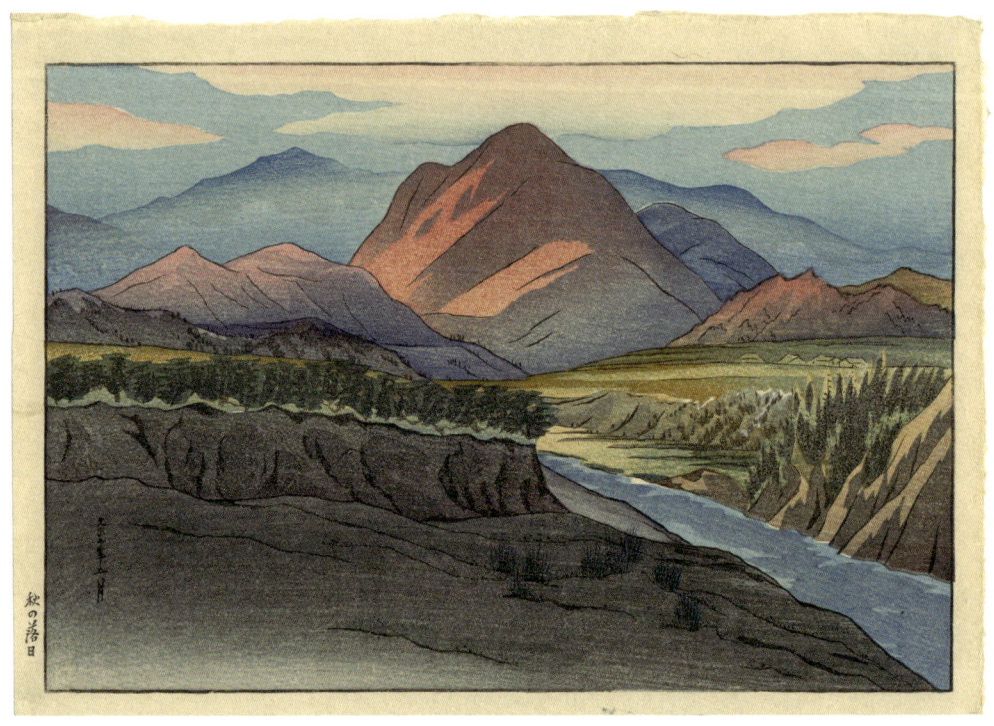

Itō Shinsui 伊東深水 (1898–1972)

Rainbow

(*Niji* 虹)

Date: September 1921
Signature: *Shinsui saku*
Publisher: Watanabe Shōzaburō
Size: 43.5 × 25.8 cm
Collection Scholten

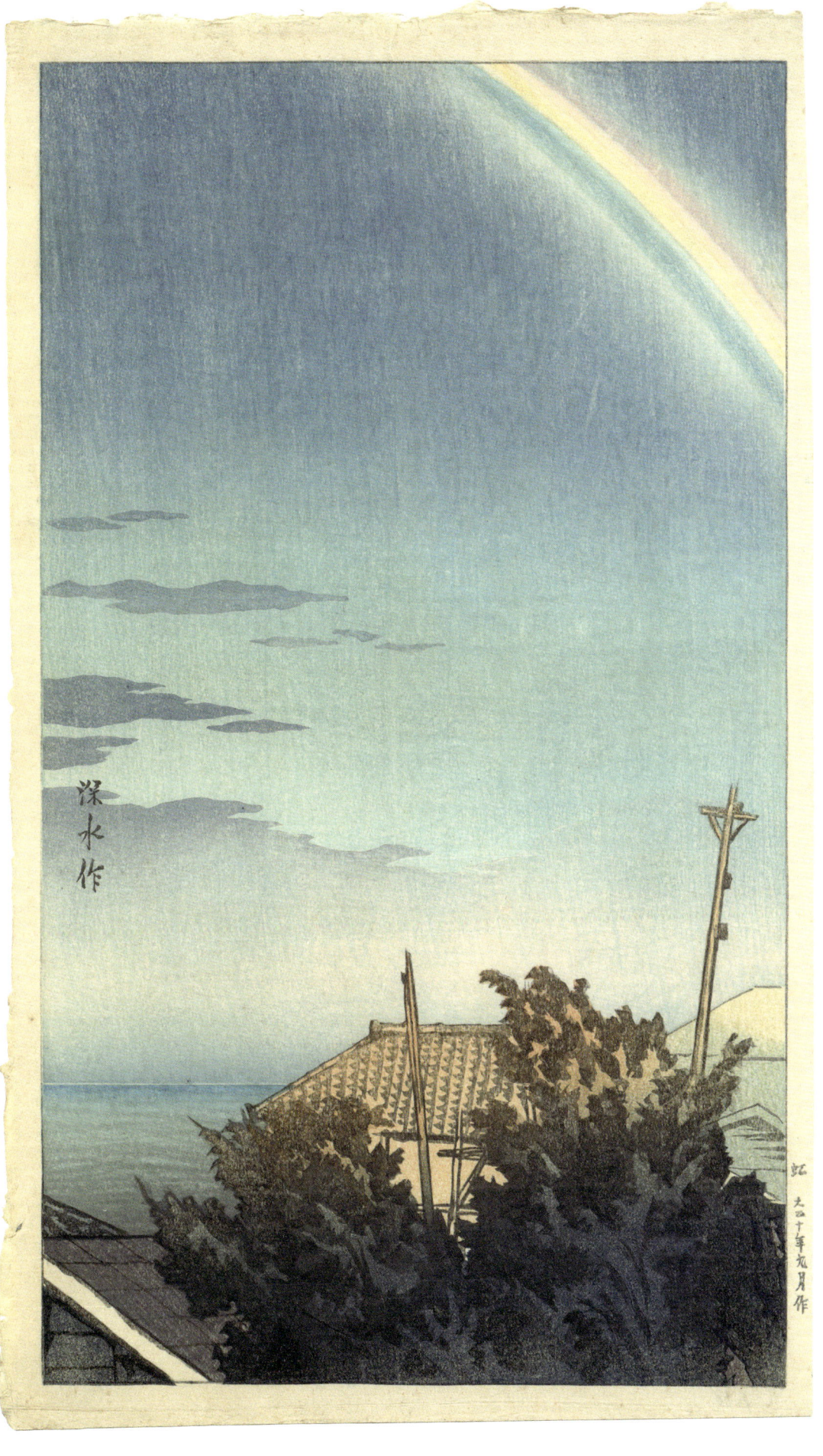

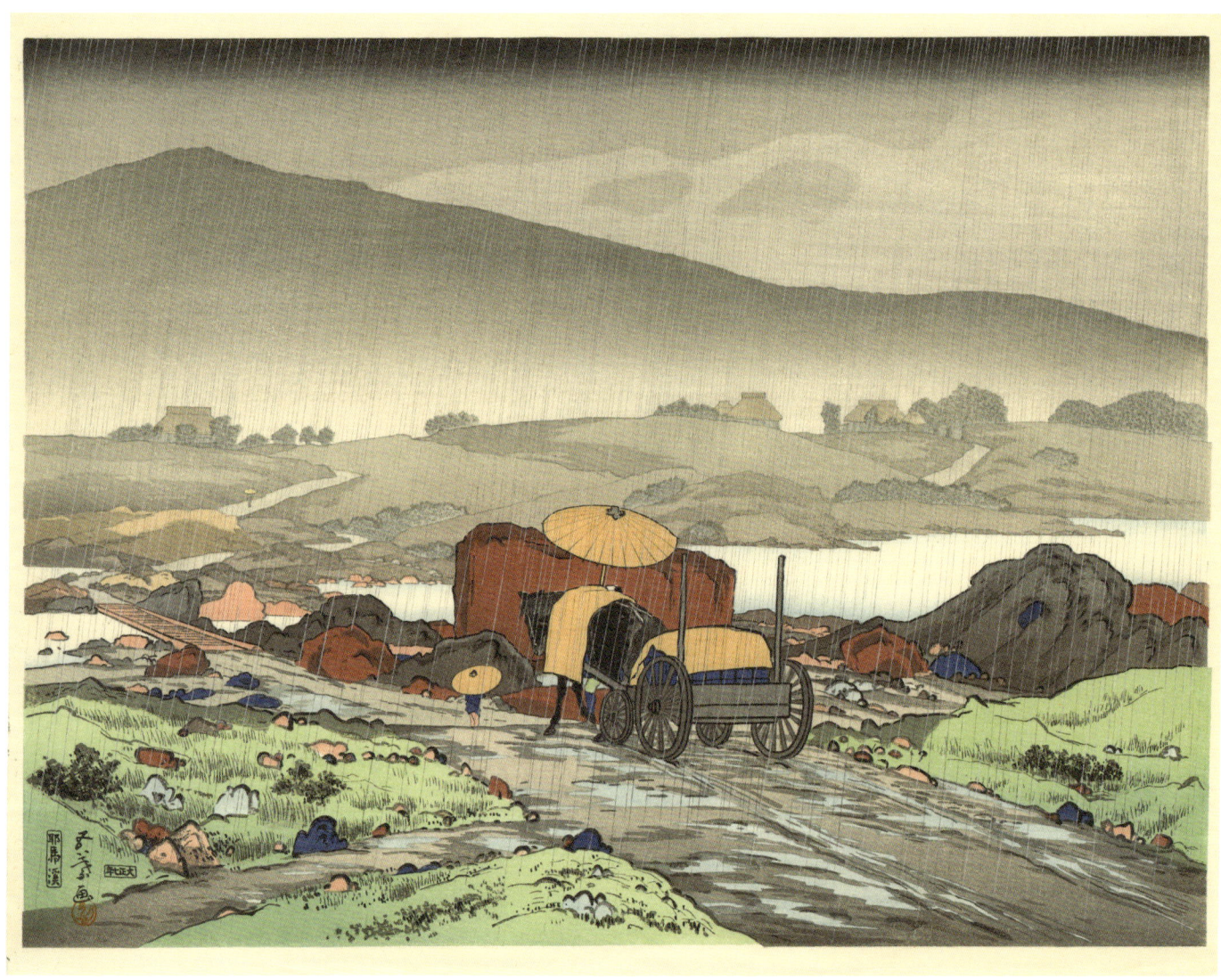

Cat. 44

Hashiguchi Goyō 橋口五葉
(1881–1921)

[The Valley of] Yabakei

(*Yabakei* 耶馬渓)

Date: 1918
Signature: *Goyō ga*
Artist's seal: *Goyō*
Publisher: self-published
Block cutter: *Takano Shichinosuke*
Printer: *Somekawa Kanzō*
Size: 40.5 × 51.1 cm
Private collection, the Netherlands

Along with *Woman Applying Make-up* (Cat. 16), this rendition of the valley of Yabakei in an unusually large format was among Goyō's first self-published prints. In the summer of 1911, Goyō had visited the north-eastern part of Kyūshū, and he became particularly fond of the valley, of which he made various sketches and paintings during and after his travels. It was a fitting topic for one of the first designs produced by his own studio. His knowledge of traditional 19th-century landscape prints is evident in the foreground, with its vivid contrasting colours and the rocks depicted with clearly defined, brush-like contours. The background, however, with its subtle tints of grey, is much more in line with what would become characteristic of the *shin hanga* tradition, with gradual colour transitions and painterly effects. The glimmering mica applied to the lines of rain attests to the quality of craftmanship involved in the production of this print.
(JD)

Cat. 45

Hashiguchi Goyō 橋口五葉
(1881–1921)

Mount Ibuki in Snow

(*Yuki no Ibukiyama* 雪の伊吹山)

Date: January 1920 ('year of the
Metal Monkey' in lower left seal)
Signature: *Goyō ga*
Edition: 71/100
Publisher: Watanabe Shōzaburō,
for the *Edo-e kanshōkai* (Society for
the Appreciation of Edo Pictures)
Size: 25.6 × 40 cm
Private collection, the Netherlands

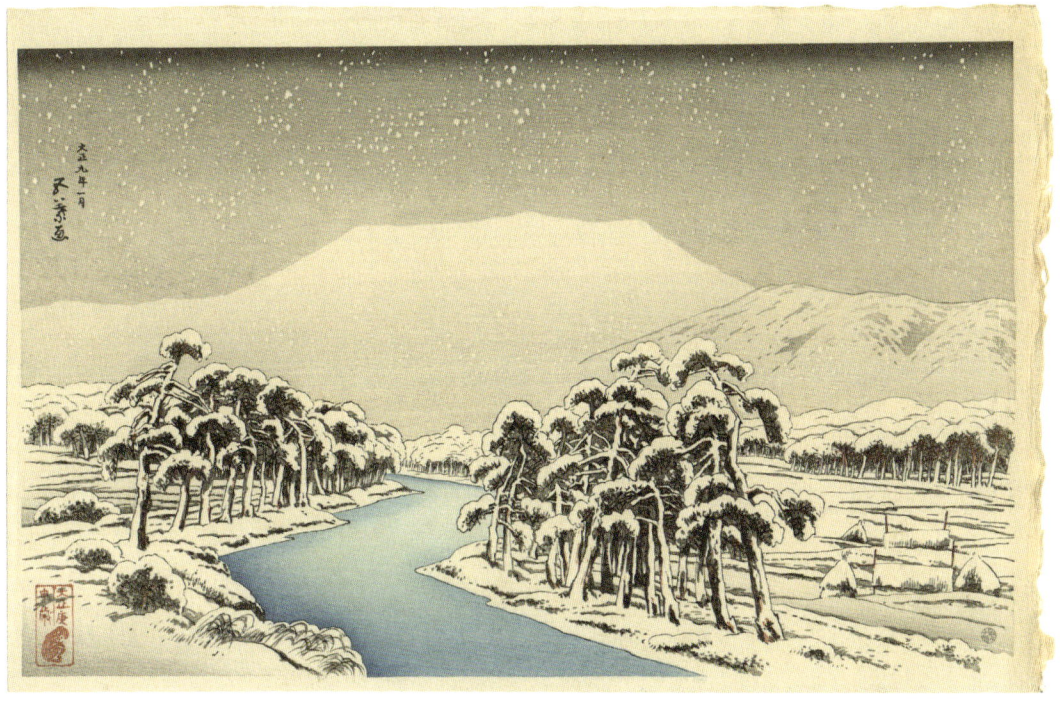

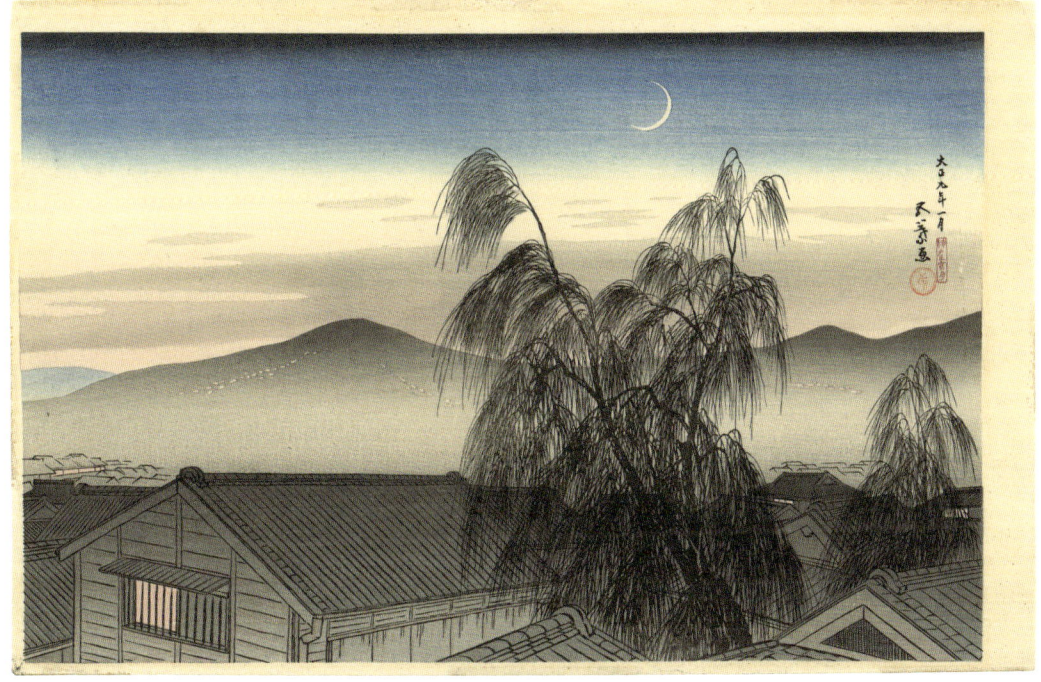

Cat. 46

Hashiguchi Goyō 橋口五葉
(1881–1921)

Evening Moon at Kobe

(*Kobe no yoizuki* 神戸之宵月)

Date: January 1920
Signature: *Goyō ga*
Artist's seal: *GY*
Publisher: self-published
Block cutter: *Takano Shichinosuke*
Printer: *Somekawa Kanzō*
Size: 30.2 × 47.5 cm
Private collection, the Netherlands

Cat. 47

Kawase Hasui 川瀬巴水 (1883–1957)

Shiogama, Shiobara

(*Shiobara Shiogama* 塩原塩釜)

Date: Autumn 1918
Signature: *Hasui*
Artist's seal: *Hasui*
Edition: 41/350
Publisher: Watanabe Shōzaburō
Size: 47.5 × 17.9 cm
Private collection, the Netherlands

Cat. 48

Kawase Hasui 川瀬巴水 (1883–1957)

An Overcast Day in Yaguchi

(*Kumoribi no Yaguchi* 雲り日の矢口)

Date: Early summer 1919
Signature: *Hasui*
Artist's seal: *Hasui*
Publisher: Watanabe Shōzaburō
Size: 47 × 18 cm
Collection Scholten

After seeing Itō Shinsui's 1917 series of *Ōmi hakkei*, Hasui was encouraged to partake in the *shin hanga* movement and showed some of his sketches to Watanabe Shōzaburō. These were made in 1909 during one of his many visits to Shiobara in Tochigi Prefecture, where his aunt Kakimoto Natsu lived with her husband and ran a souvenir shop until her death in 1920. Hasui spent a large part of his childhood in Shiobara, and the area was therefore particularly important to him, a fitting choice for his very first prints. In 1918 he and Watanabe proceeded to publish three of his designs in *nagaban* format, *Shiogama, Shiobara* being one of them. In this print the artist wanted to emphasize the contrast between the dark wooden buildings, the surrounding trees and the pale-yellow hue of the mountains in the background. The region was home to various hot springs, and in the lower left corner, just to the left of the woman washing clothes, a man is relaxing in one of the *onsen* baths.
(JD)

After creating his first three prints, Hasui continued to work with Watanabe and produced six more prints, one in *aiban* format (Cat. 51) and five in the *nagaban* format (three are featured in this catalogue, Cats. 48–50), based on sketches he made in various places in northern Japan during one of his annual tours. This scene shows the Tama River in south-western Tokyo rather than the northern destinations of Hasui's trips. Three figures are handling a *jarifune*, a boat for hauling gravel, which was a typical sight for this area according to the artist.
(JD)

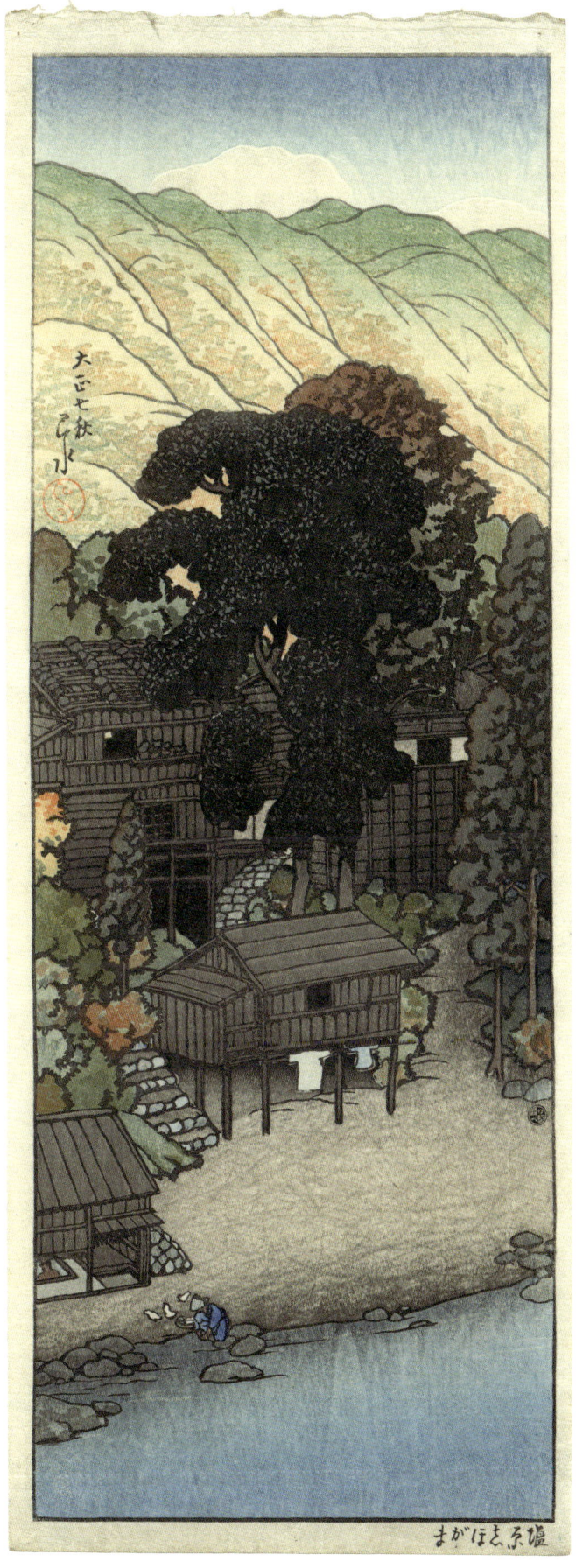

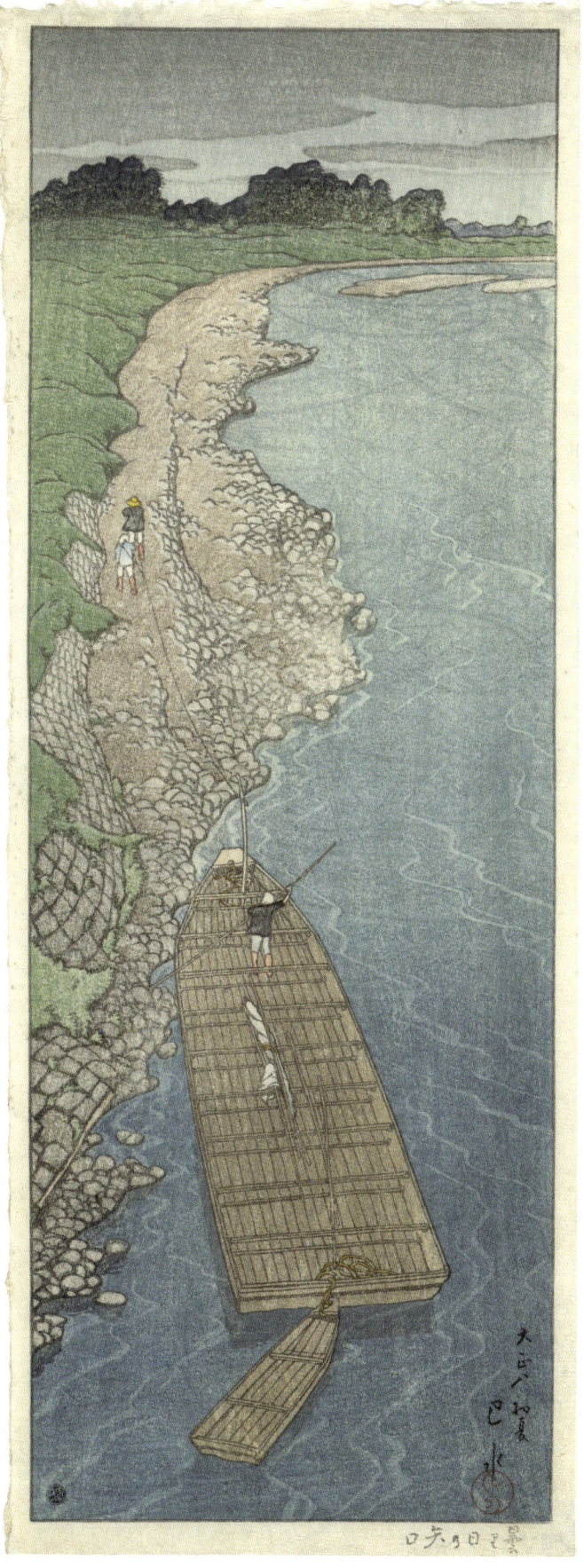

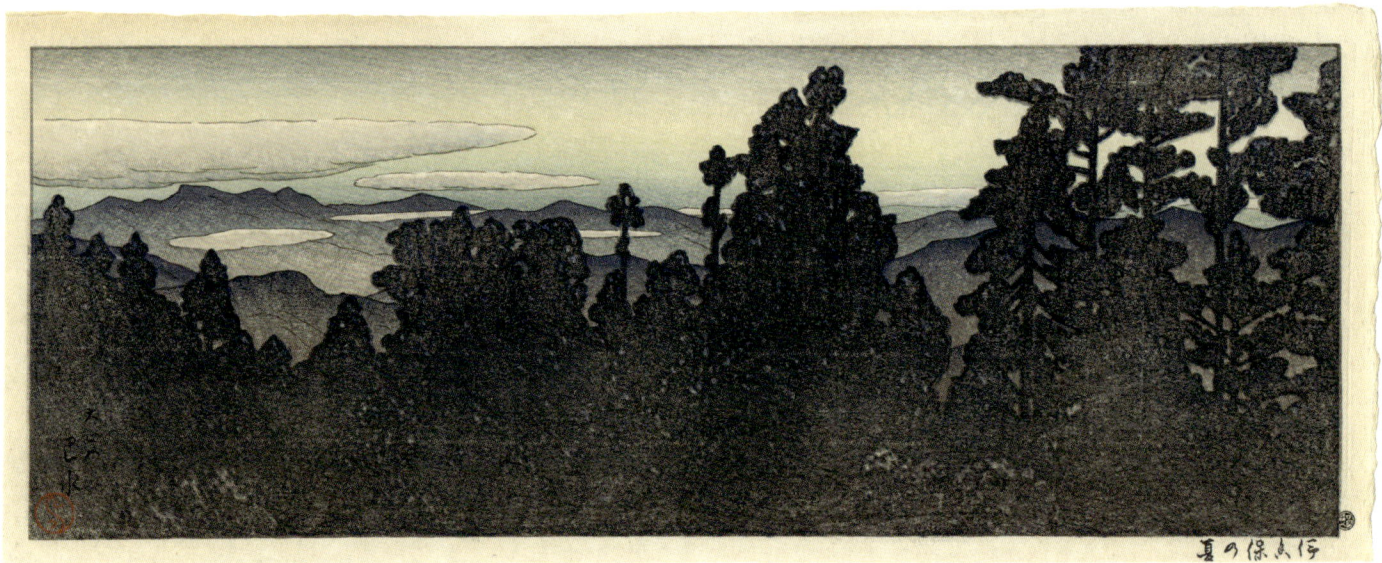

Cat. 49

Kawase Hasui 川瀬巴水 (1883–1957)

Summer in Ikaho

(*Ikaho no natsu* 伊香保の夏)

Date: Summer 1919
Signature: *Hasui*
Artist's seal: *Hasui*
Publisher: Watanabe Shōzaburō
Size: 18.4 × 47.3 cm
Collection Scholten

When Hasui visited Ikaho in Gunma Prefecture, the sight of the misty mountains visible through the shadowy thicket left a strong impression on him, and this composition was based on the memories of his stay there.
(JD)

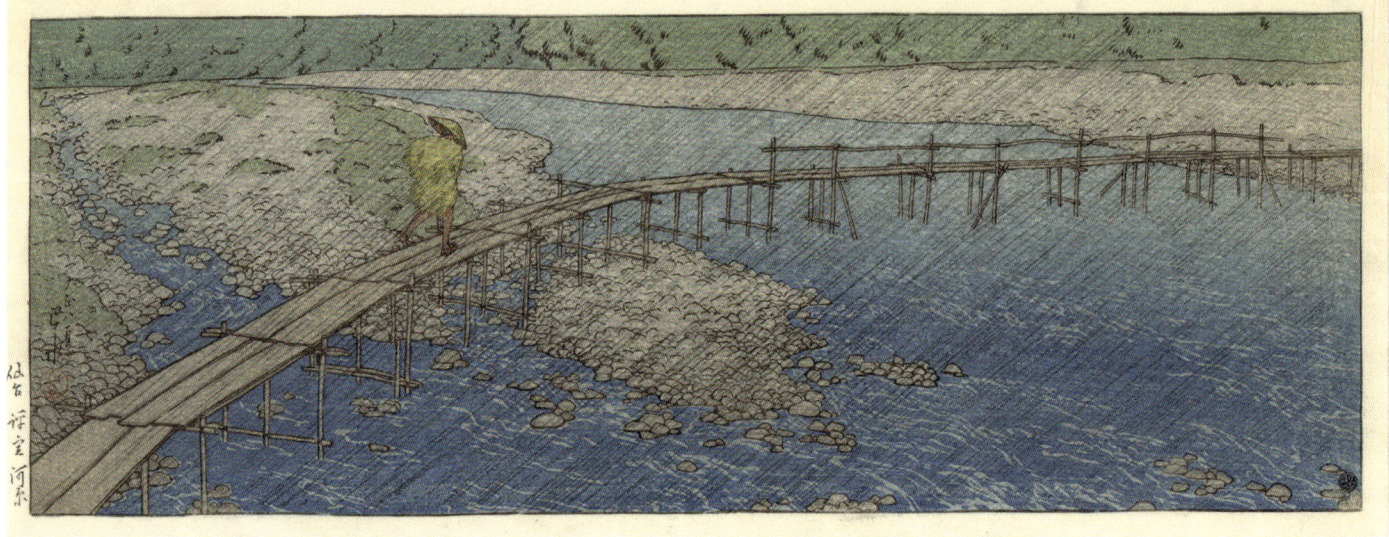

Cat. 50

Kawase Hasui 川瀬巴水 (1883–1957)

The Hyōjōgawara Riverbed in Sendai

(*Sendai Hyōjōgawara* 仙台評定河原)

Date: Summer 1919
Signature: *Hasui*
Artist's seal: *Hasui*
Publisher: Watanabe Shōzaburō
Size: 18.2 × 47.2 cm
Collection Scholten

Dressed in traditional rainwear, the man confronting stormy weather in Sendai might as well have been an Edo Period traveller, and this composition is a typical example of the romantic views of the countryside held by Hasui and other artists of his time. The gritty texture in the shade of grey in the riverbanks gives variation to the rocks and pebbles along the shoreline, while the different shades of blue in the water intensify our sense of the river's rain-fuelled current. A variant of this print exists, with different figures and without the streaking rain.

(JD)

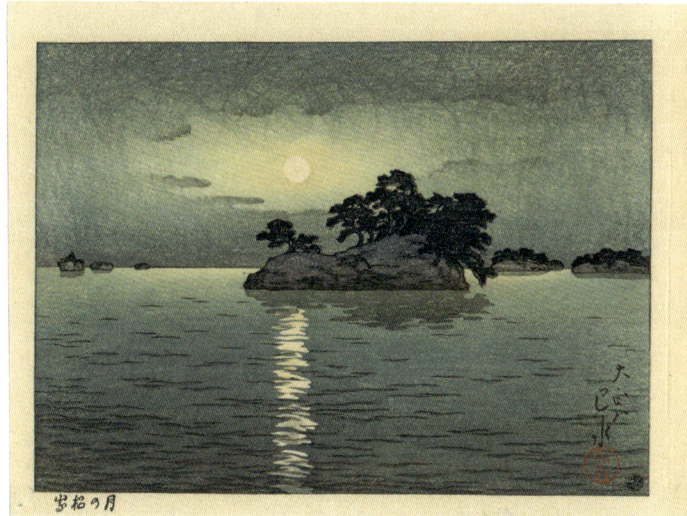

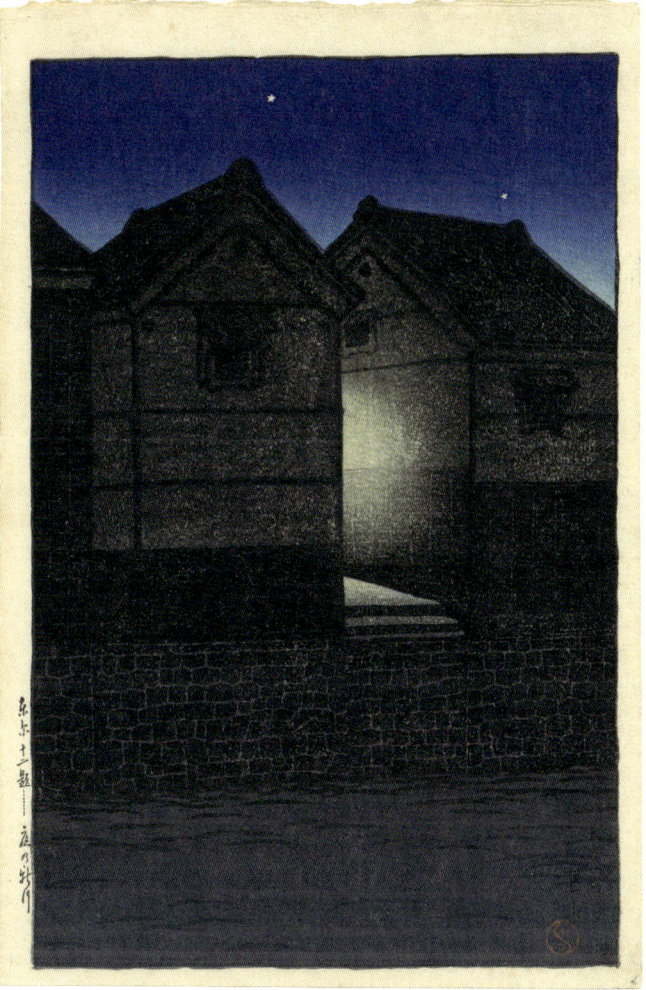

Cat. 51

Kawase Hasui 川瀬巴水 (1883–1957)

Matsushima in Moonlight

(*Tsuki no Matsushima* 月の松島)

Date: 1919
Signature: *Hasui*
Artist's seal: *Hasui*
Publisher: Watanabe Shōzaburō
Size: 19.1 × 25.8 cm
Collection Scholten

Cat. 52

Kawase Hasui 川瀬巴水 (1883–1957)

Shinkawa at Night

(*Yoru no Shinkawa* 夜の新川)

Series: *Twelve Scenes of Tokyo*
(*Tōkyō jūnidai* 東京十二題)
Date: July 1919
Signature: *Hasui*
Artist's seal: *Hasui*
Publisher: Watanabe Shōzaburō
Size: 39.3 × 26.5 cm
Private collection, the Netherlands

Cat. 53

Kawase Hasui 川瀬巴水 (1883–1957)

Komagata Embankment

(*Komagatagashi* 駒形河岸)

Series: *Twelve Scenes of Tokyo*
(*Tōkyō jūnidai* 東京十二題)
Date: Early summer 1919
Signature: *Hasui*
Artist's seal: *Kawase*
Publisher: Watanabe Shōzaburō
Size: 26 × 39 cm
Private collection, the Netherlands

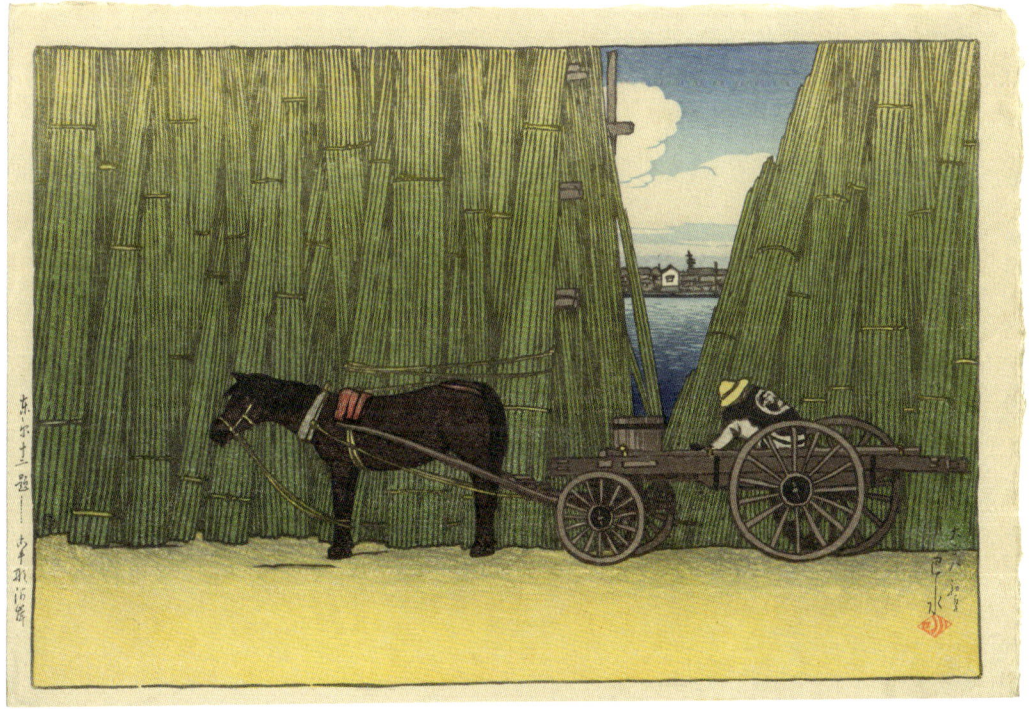

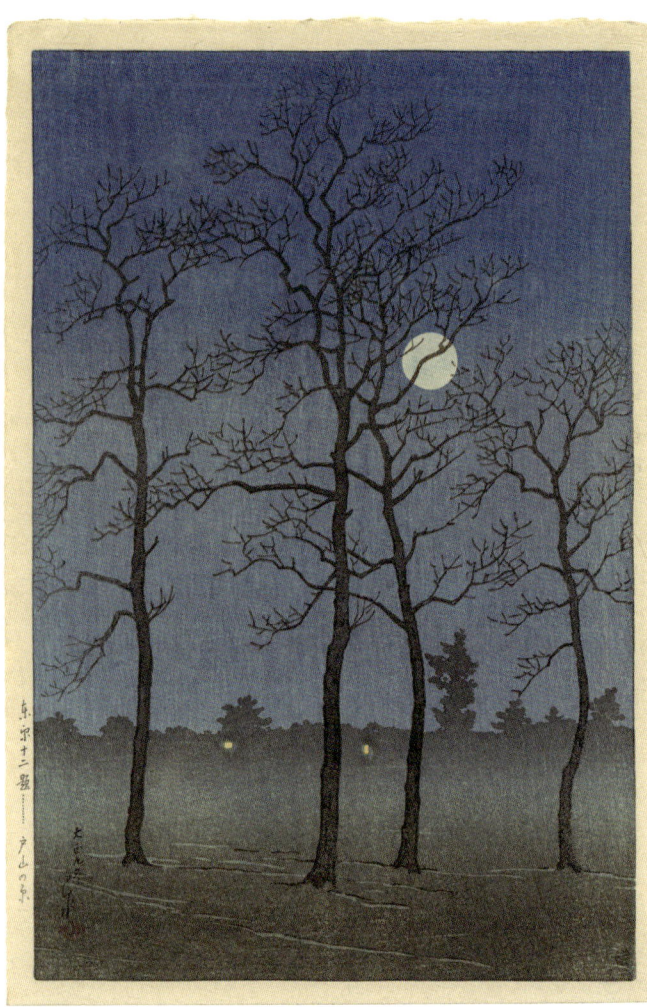

Cat. 54

Kawase Hasui 川瀬巴水 (1883–1957)

Toyama Plain

(*Toyama-no-hara* 戸山の原)

Series: *Twelve Scenes of Tokyo*
(*Tōkyō jūnidai* 東京十二題)
Date: Winter 1920
Signature: *Hasui*
Artist's seal: *Kawase*
Publisher: Watanabe Shōzaburō
Size: 38.7 × 26.5 cm
Collection Scholten

Cat. 55

Kawase Hasui 川瀬巴水 (1883–1957)

Snow at Shirahige

(*Yuki no Shirahige* 雪の白ひげ)

Series: *Twelve Scenes of Tokyo*
(*Tōkyō jūnidai* 東京十二題)
Date: Winter 1920
Signature: *Hasui*
Artist's seal: *Hasui*
Publisher: Watanabe Shōzaburō
Size: 26.2 × 39 cm
Private collection, the Netherlands

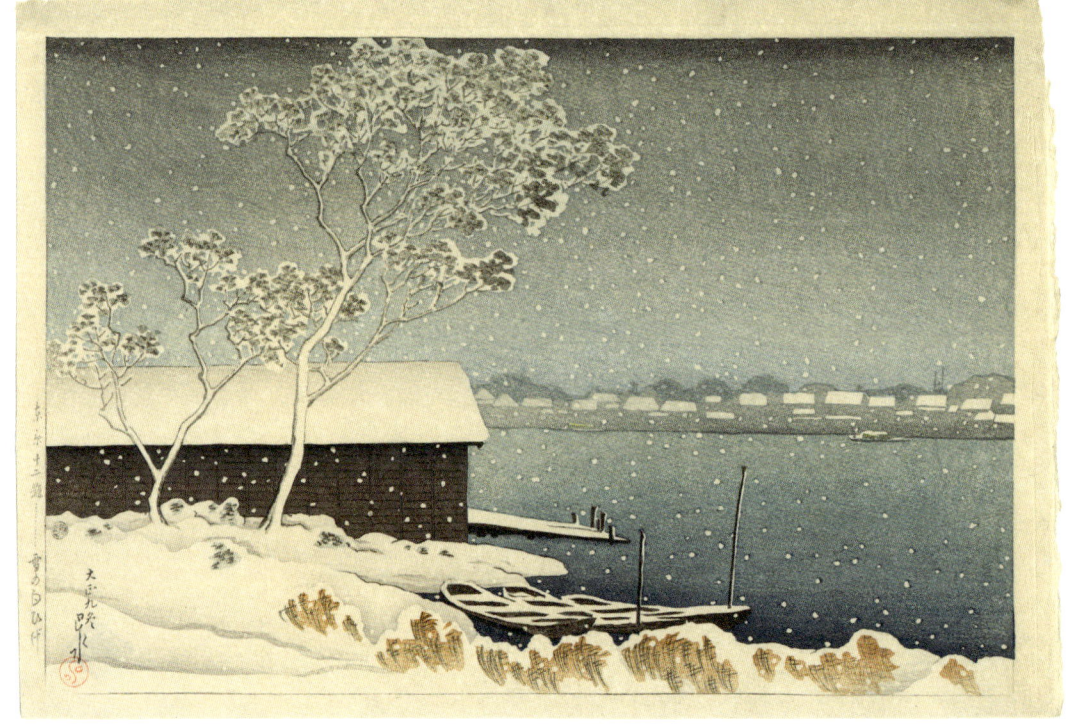

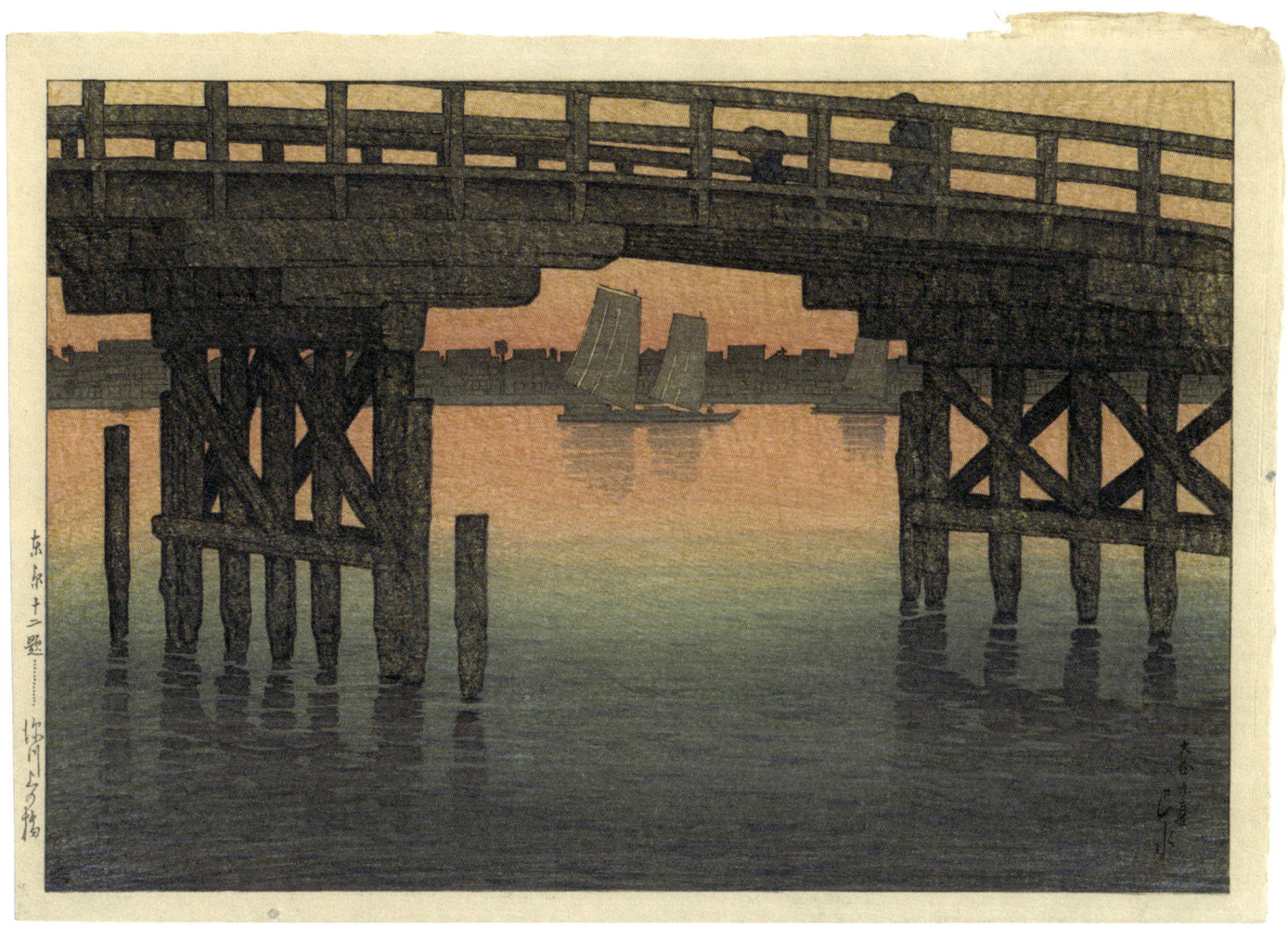

Twelve Scenes of Tokyo was published between 1919 and 1921, based on sketches Hasui made around the city. Hasui framed Tokyo with a nostalgic vision that sought to present the rapidly growing city as the quintessential Japanese village rather than the modern metropolis that it was becoming. The artist noted that, in the area near this particular bridge, 'incongruous Western-style buildings' were absent, and that it reminded him of the ukiyo-e landscapes of the early 19th century, an indication of his romantic vision of the past. Various states of this print have appeared, with different colour gradations in the sky, ranging from a very light yellow to deep orange.

(JD)

Cat. 56

Kawase Hasui 川瀬巴水 (1883–1957)
Kami(no) Bridge, Fukugawa

(*Fukugawa, Kaminohashi*
福川上の橋)

Series: *Twelve Scenes of Tokyo*
(*Tokyo junidai* 東京十二題)
Date: Summer 1920
Signature: *Hasui*
Artist's seal: *Hasui*
Publisher: Watanabe Shôzaburô
Size: 26.5 × 38.8 cm
Private collection, the Netherlands

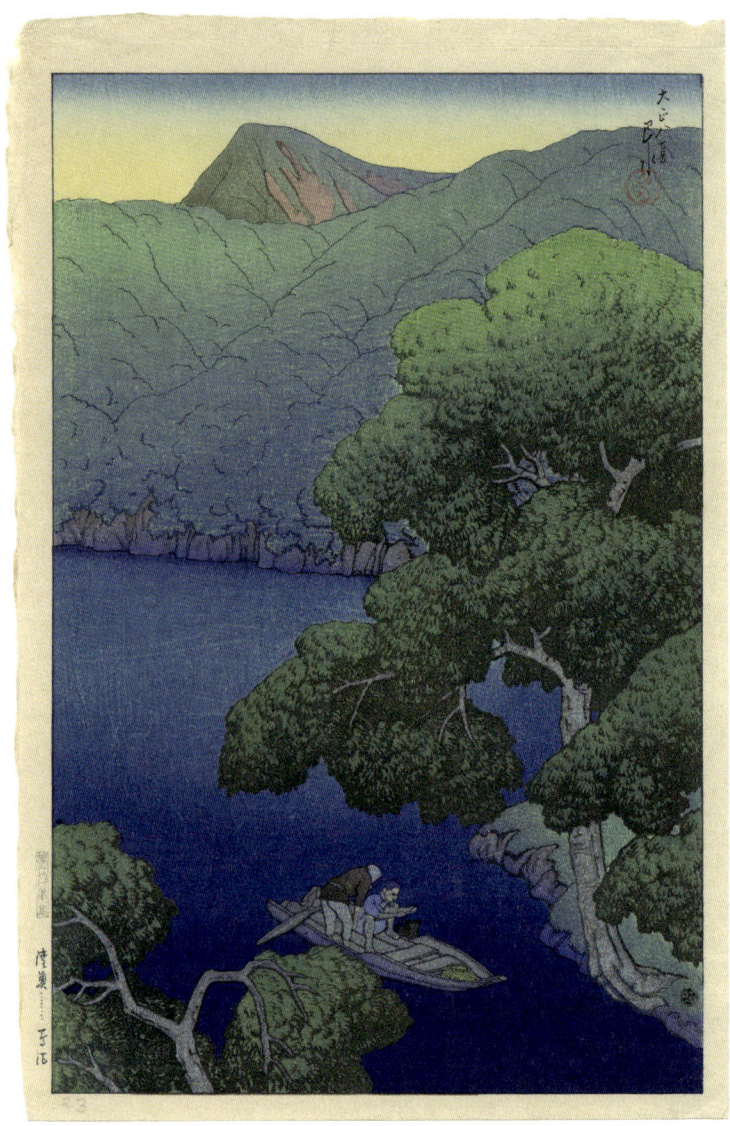

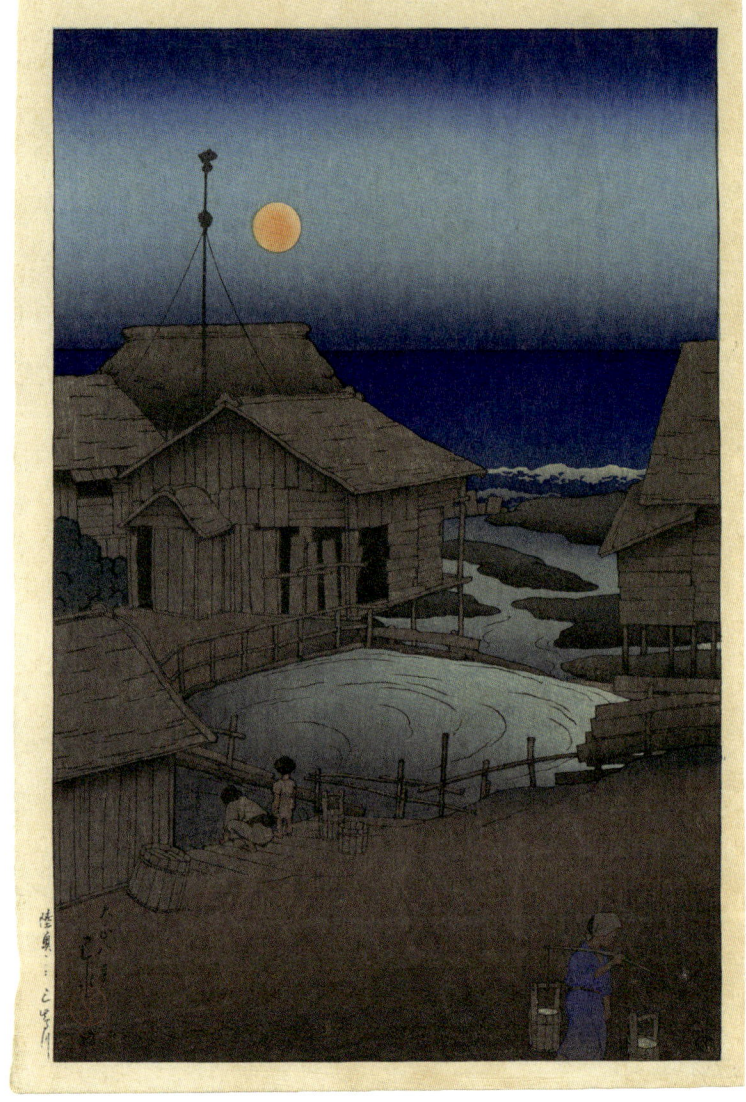

Cat. 57

Kawase Hasui 川瀬巴水 (1883–1957)

Tsuta Marsh, Mutsu

(*Mutsu Tsutanuma* 陸奥蔦沼)

Series: *Souvenirs of Travel, first series*
(*Tabi miyage dai isshū* 旅みやげ第一集)
Date: Summer 1919
Signature: *Hasui*
Artist's seal: *Hasui*
Publisher: Watanabe Shōzaburō
Size: 39.2 × 26.3 cm
Collection Scholten

Cat. 58

Kawase Hasui 川瀬巴水 (1883–1957)

Mishima River, Mutsu

(*Mutsu Mishimagawa* 陸奥三島川)

Series: *Souvenirs of Travel, first series*
(*Tabi miyage dai isshū* 旅みやげ第一集)
Date: Summer 1919
Signature: *Hasui*
Artist's seal: *Hasui*
Publisher: Watanabe Shōzaburō
Size: 38.6 × 26.5 cm
Collection Scholten

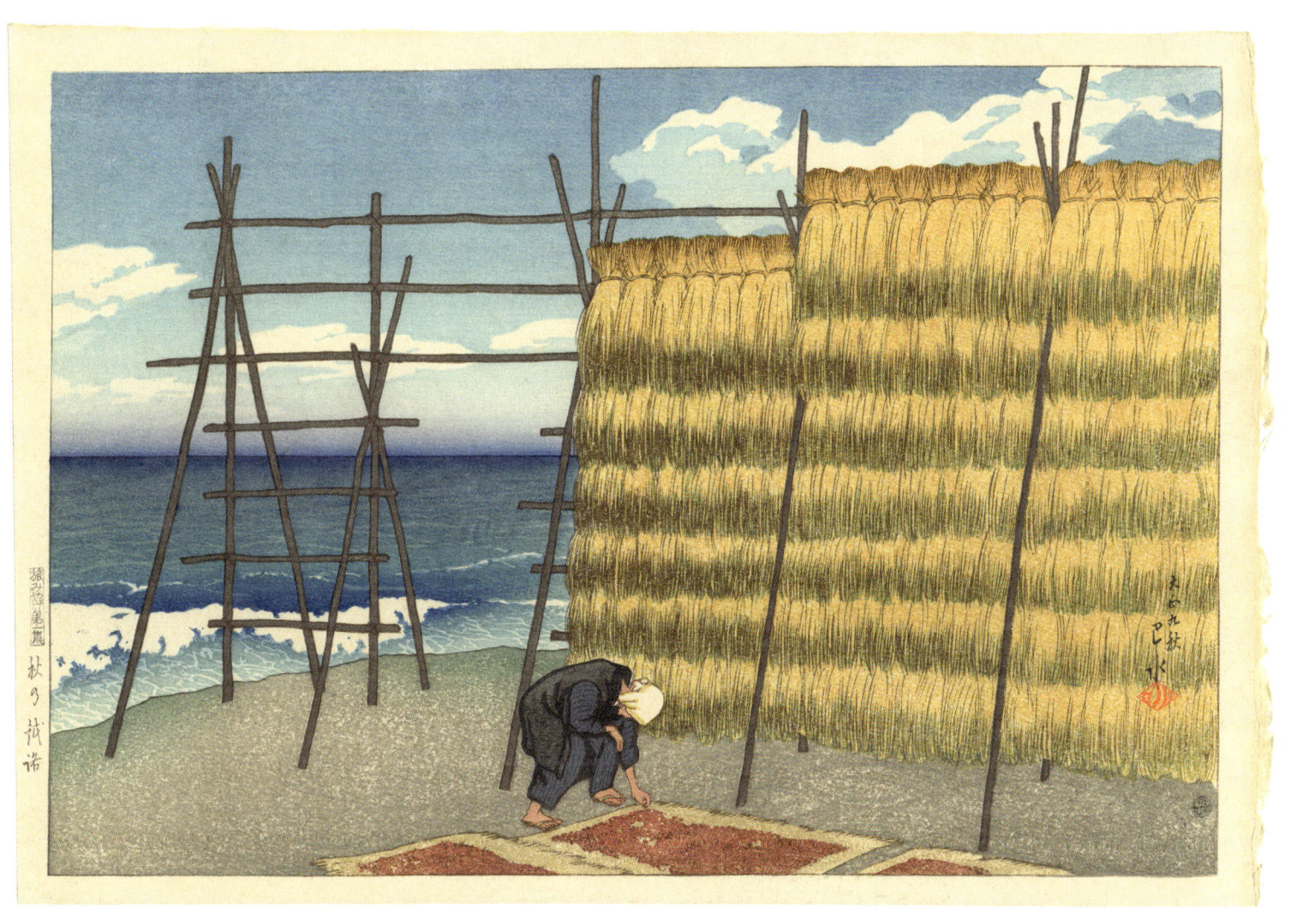

Cat. 59

Kawase Hasui 川瀬巴水 (1883–1957)

Autumn in Koshiji

(*Aki no Koshiji* 秋の越路)

Series: *Souvenirs of Travel, first series*
(*Tabi miyage dai isshū* 旅みやげ第一集)
Date: Autumn 1920
Signature: *Hasui*
Artist's seal: *Kawase*
Publisher: Watanabe Shōzaburō
Size: 26.3 × 38.5 cm
Private collection, the Netherlands

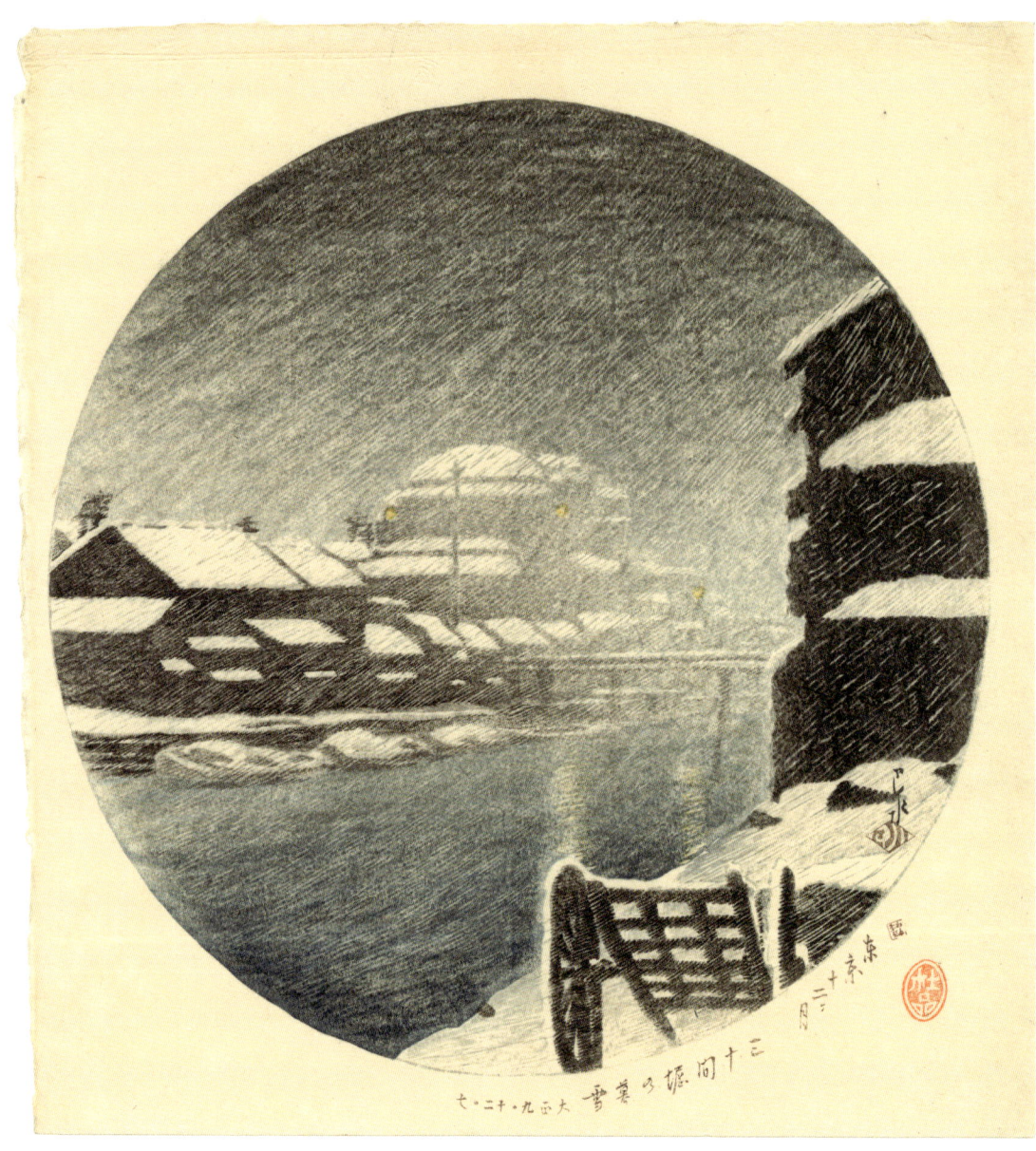

Cat. 60

Kawase Hasui 川瀬巴水 (1883–1957)
Evening Snow at Sanjūgen Canal

(*Sanjūgenbori no bosetsu*
三十間掘の募雪)

Series: *Twelve Months of Tokyo*
(*Tōkyō jūnikagetsu* 東京十二ヶ月)
Date: 7 December 1920
Signature: *Hasui*
Artist's seal: *Kawase*
Publisher: Watanabe Shōzaburō
Size: 29.7 × 27.8 cm
Collection Scholten

This is one of five prints from an unfinished series in an unusual square format with round decorative frames covering seasonal themes. Hasui mentioned in his diaries that he was not satisfied with the traditional way of depicting snowfall in woodblock prints using white dots. In an experimental attempt to convey the true intensity of a blizzard, he covered this scene of the Sanjūgen Canal in Tokyo's Chūō Ward with a dense layer of short thin lines. Hasui notes that the design was partly successful, but he felt that the technique needed further improvement. Although he often returned to the more traditional patterns of white dots, he continued to search for new ways to express heavy snowfall in later works such as *A Fine Winter's Sky, Miyajima* (Cat. 65), *Ochanomizu* (Cat. 180) and *Hataori, Shiobara* (Cat. 196).

(JD)

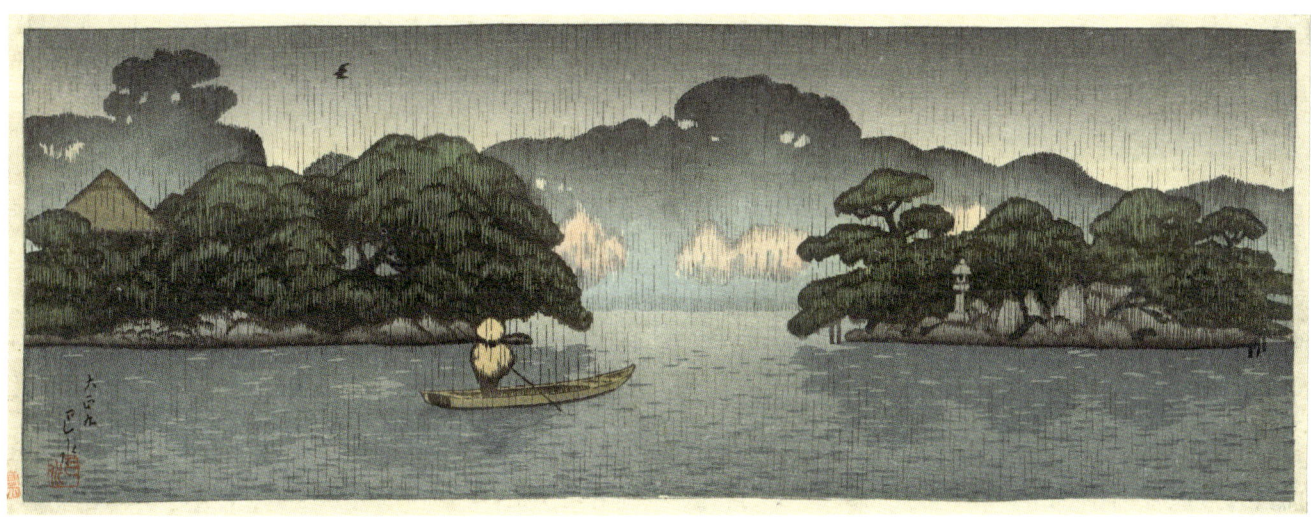

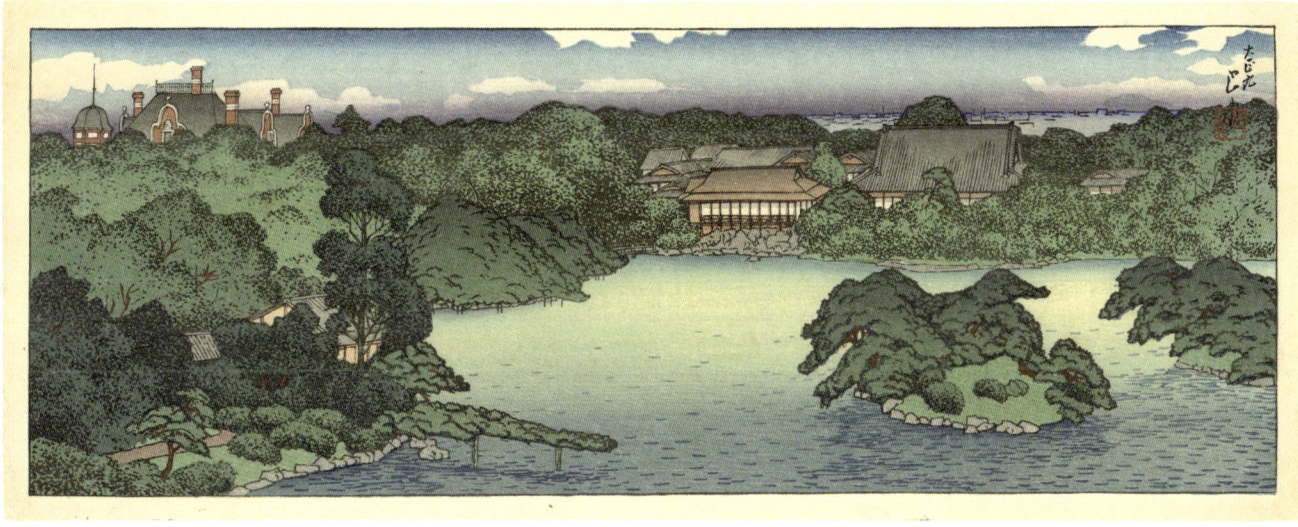

Cat. 61

Kawase Hasui 川瀬巴水 (1883–1957)

Small Boat in a Spring Shower

(*Harusame no kobune* 春雨の小舟)

Date: 1920
Signature: *Hasui*
Artist's seal: *Hasui*
Publisher: Watanabe Shōzaburō
Size: 17.5 × 46.3 cm
Collection Scholten

Cat. 62

Kawase Hasui 川瀬巴水 (1883–1957)

**Panoramic View of
the Daisensui Pond**

(*Daisensui no zenkei* 大線水の全景)

Date: 1920
Signature: *Hasui*
Artist's seal: *Hasui*
Publisher: Watanabe Shōzaburō
Size: 18.4 × 47.2 cm
Collection Scholten

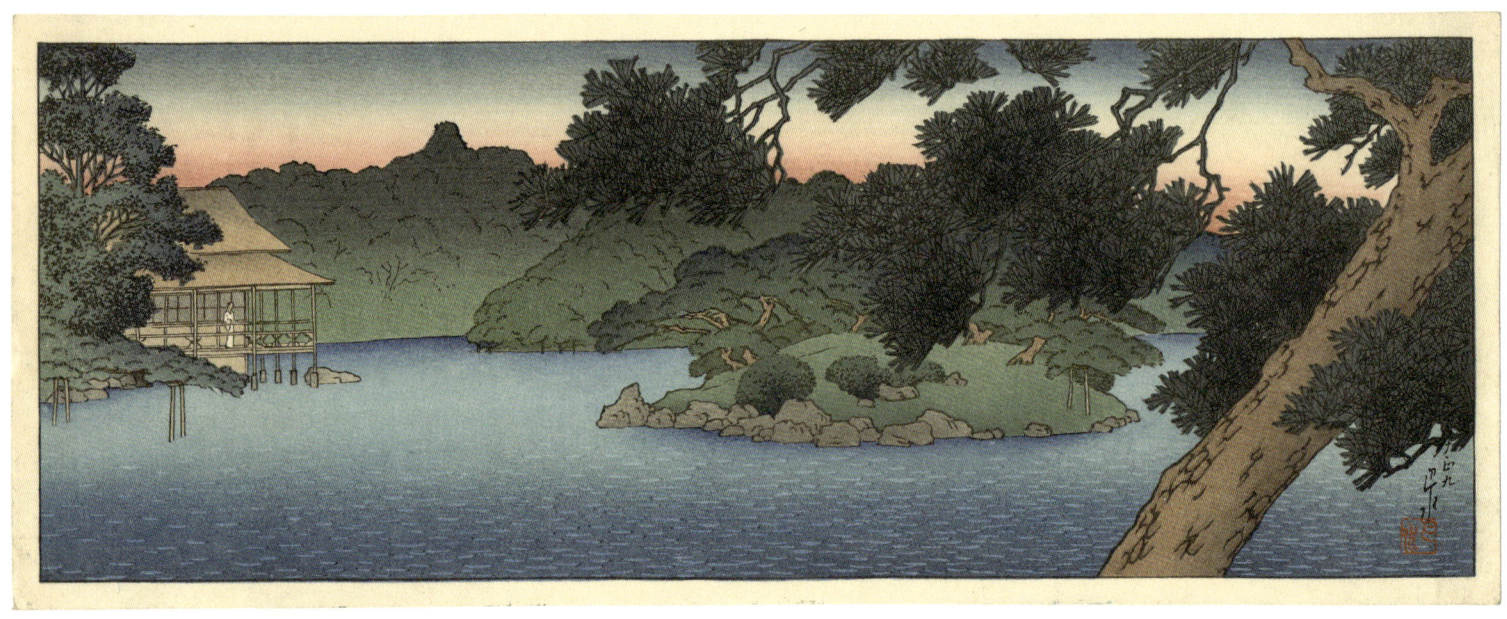

Cat. 63

Kawase Hasui 川瀬巴水 (1883–1957)

Guest House in the Pines on the Pond's Edge

(*Matsu no chihan no ryōtei* 松の池畔の涼亭)

Date: 1920
Signature: *Hasui*
Artist's seal: *Hasui*
Publisher: Watanabe Shōzaburō
Size: 18.3 × 47 cm
Collection Scholten

In 1920 Hasui was commissioned by the Iwasaki family, the owners of Mitsubishi, to create eight landscape prints of their Kiyosumi estate in eastern Tokyo. Along with five *ōban* landscapes, Hasui designed these three scenes in the long and narrow *nagaban* format. The villa and garden were founded in the Edo Period and acquired by Iwasaki Yatarō, the founder of Mitsubishi, in 1878. Following the disastrous earthquake of 1923, it served as a shelter for refugees. It has been open to the public since 1932, and its scenery can still be enjoyed today.

(JD)

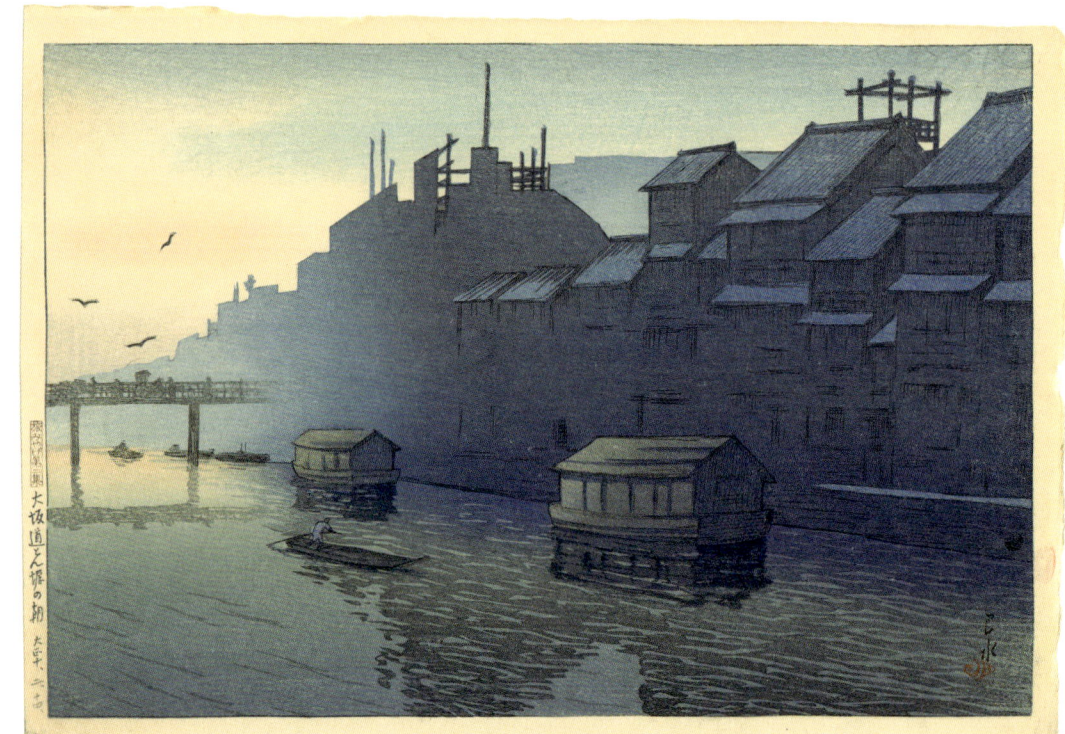

Cat. 64

Kawase Hasui 川瀬巴水 (1883–1957)

Morning in Dōtonbori, Osaka

(*Ōsaka Dōtonbori no asa* 大阪道とん堀の朝)

Series: *Souvenirs of Travel, second series*
(*Tabi miyage dai nishū* 旅みやげ第二集)
Date: 14 February 1921
Signature: *Hasui*
Artist's seal: *Kawase*
Publisher: Watanabe Shōzaburō
Size: 26 × 38.5 cm
Private collection, the Netherlands

Kawase Hasui 川瀬巴水 (1883–1957)

A Fine Winter's Sky (Miyajima)

(*Seiten no yuki [Miyajima]*,
晴天の雪 [宮島])

Series: *Souvenirs of Travel, second series*
(*Tabi miyage dai nishū* 旅みやげ第二集)
Date: 17 February 1921
Signature: *Hasui*
Artist's seal: *Kawase*
Publisher: Watanabe Shōzaburō
Size: 39.1 × 26.3 cm
Collection Scholten

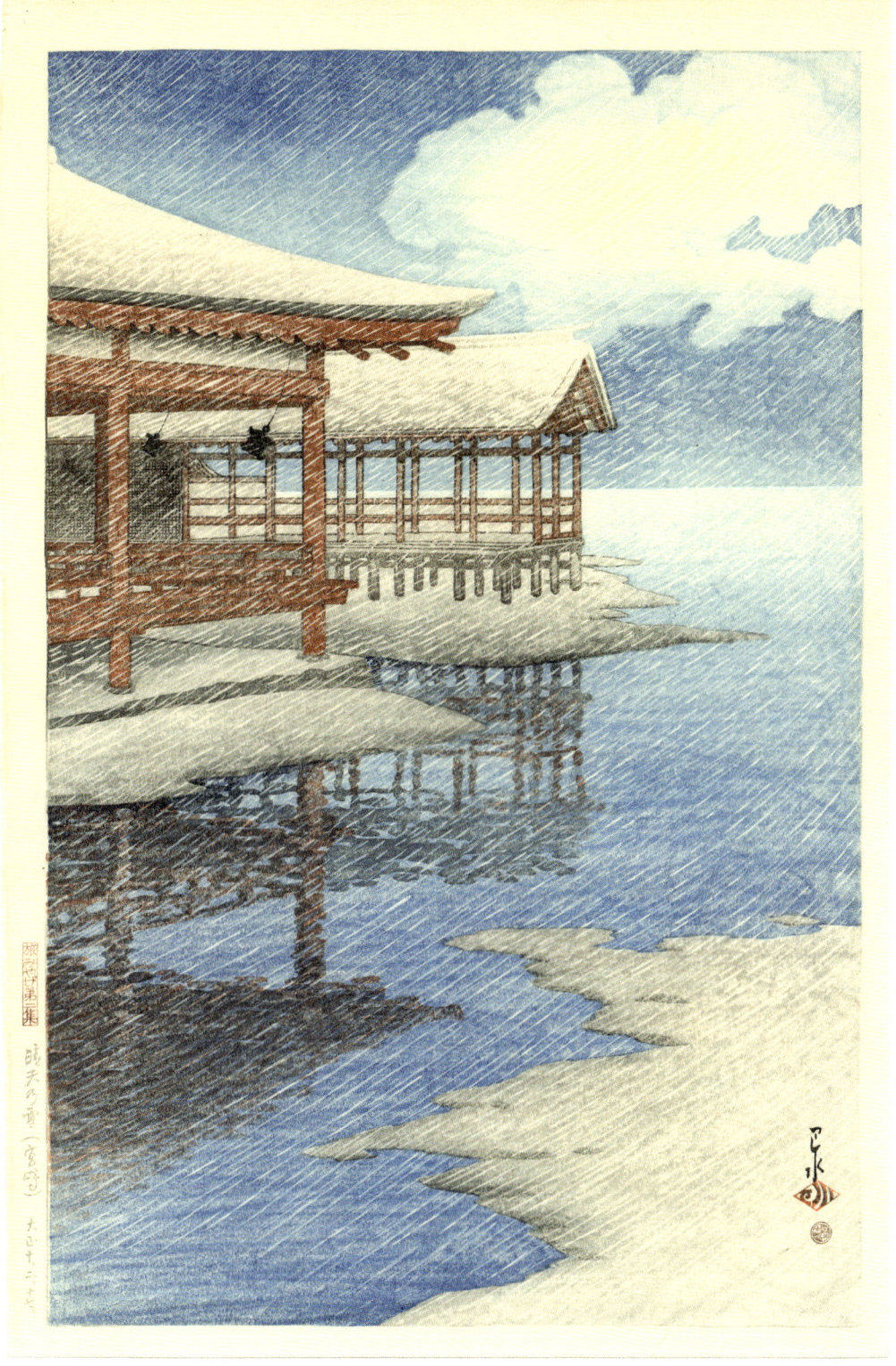

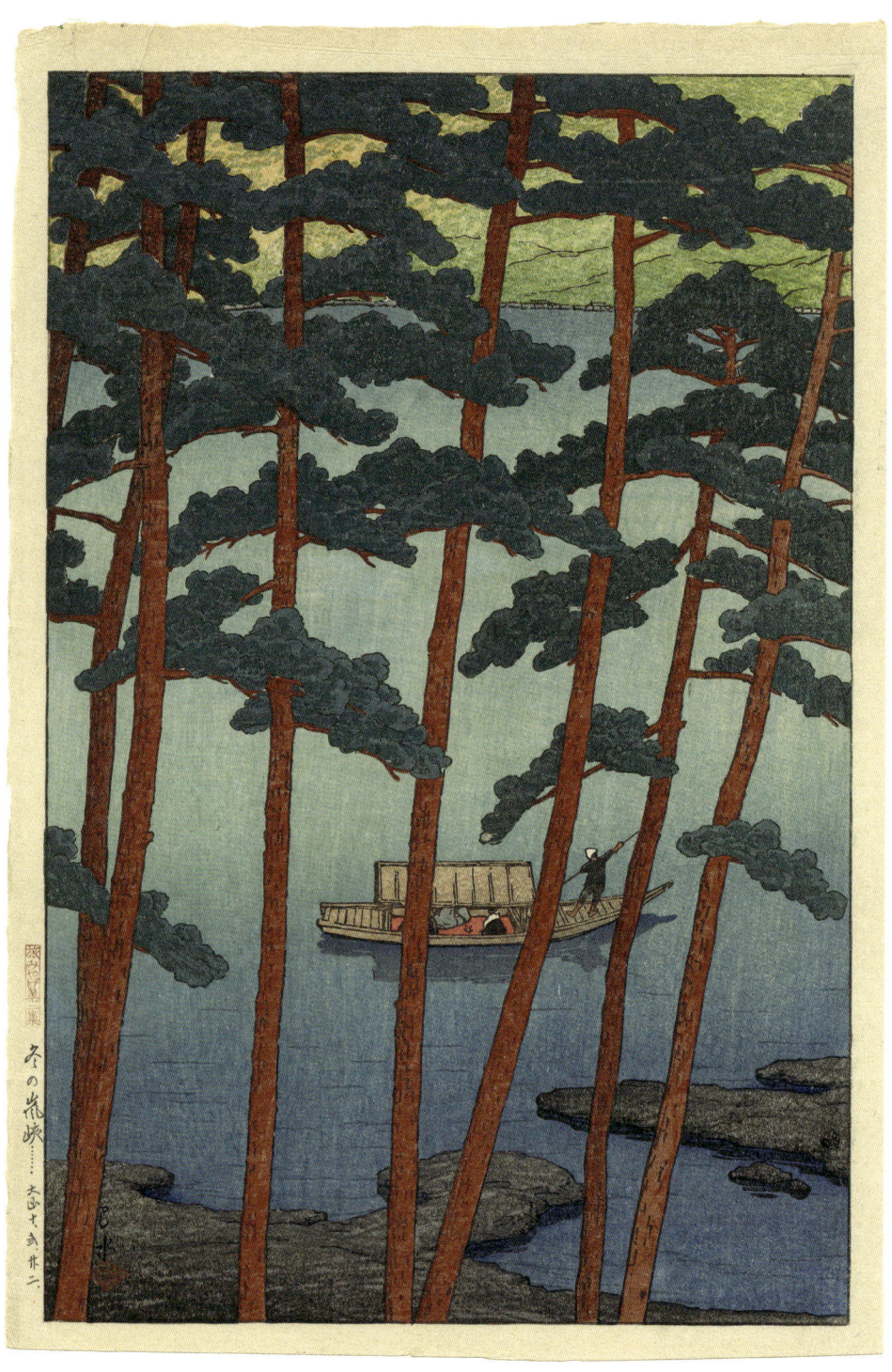

Cat. 66

Kawase Hasui 川瀬巴水 (1883–1957)

Winter at Arashiyama Gorge

(*Fuyu no Rankyō* 冬の嵐峡)

Series: *Souvenirs of Travel, second series*
(*Tabi miyage dai nishū* 旅みやげ第二集)
Date: 22 February 1921
Signature: *Hasui*
Artist's seal: *Kawase*
Publisher: Watanabe Shōzaburō
Size: 39 × 26.5 cm
Private collection, the Netherlands

In 1921 Hasui made two more trips: during the winter through western Honshū and a summer journey to the north. These two trips inspired his *Souvenirs of Travel, second series*, which consists of 28 prints. Depicted here is the Katsura River running through the gorge in Arashiyama in Kyoto, which is famed for its beauty. Through the striking red pines we can see one of the pleasure boats typical of the area. This composition reminds us of the vertical landscape prints from the series *One Hundred Famous Views of Edo* by Utagawa Hiroshige, in which the background is often partly obscured by dramatic close-ups of objects in the foreground. The scenes depicted in *Souvenirs of Travel, second series*, even of famous places such as Arashiyama, are characterized by a kind of quiet anonymity and modesty.

(JD)

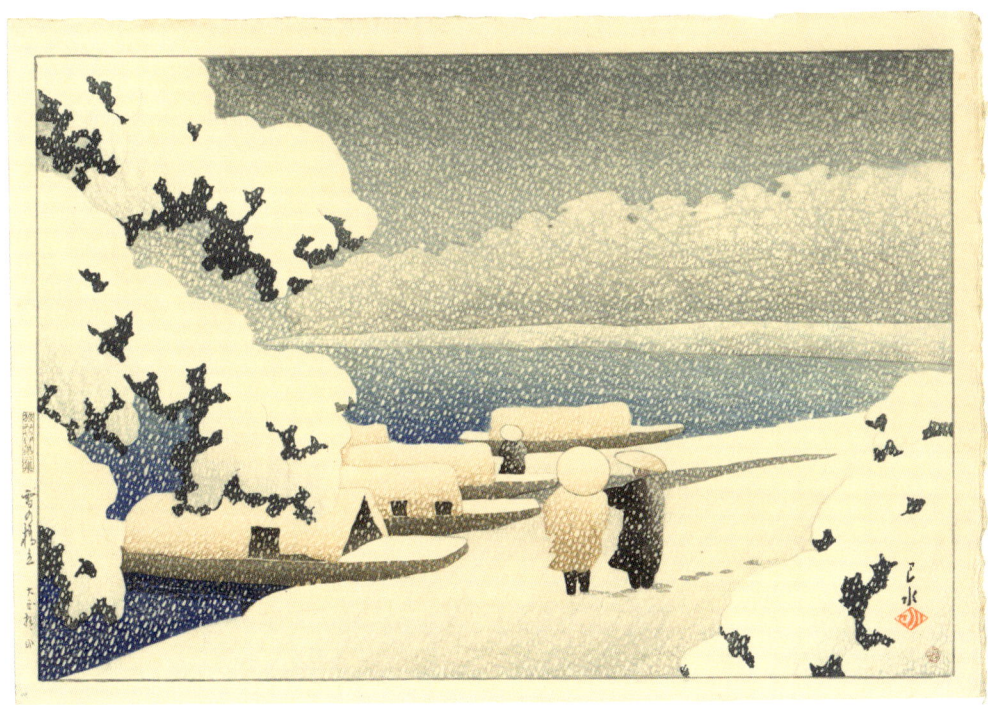

Cat. 67

Kawase Hasui 川瀬巴水 (1883–1957)

Snow at Hashidate

(*Yuki no Hashidate* 雪の橋立)

Series: *Souvenirs of Travel, second series*
(*Tabi miyage dai nishū* 旅みやげ第二集)
Date: February 1921
Signature: *Hasui*
Artist's seal: *Kawase*
Publisher: Watanabe Shōzaburō
Size: 26.2 × 39 cm
Private collection, the Netherlands

Cat. 68

Kawase Hasui 川瀬巴水 (1883–1957)

Urahama, Echigo

(*Echigo no Urahama* 越後のうら浜)

Series: *Souvenirs of Travel, second series*
(*Tabi miyage dai nishū* 旅みやげ第二集)
Date: 27 August 1921
Signature: *Hasui*
Artist's seal: *Kawase*
Publisher: Watanabe Shōzaburō
Size: 26.2 × 39 cm
Private collection, the Netherlands

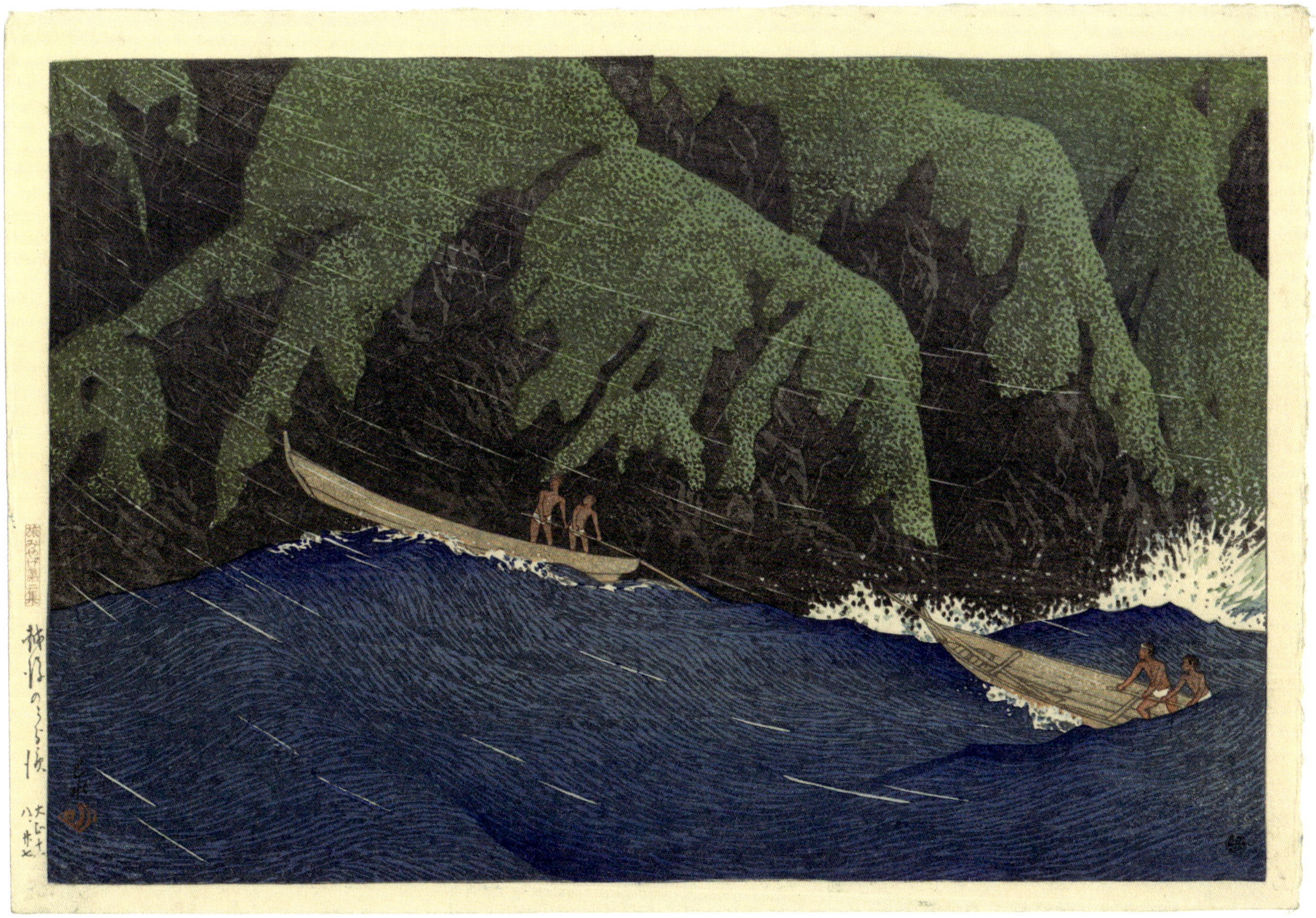

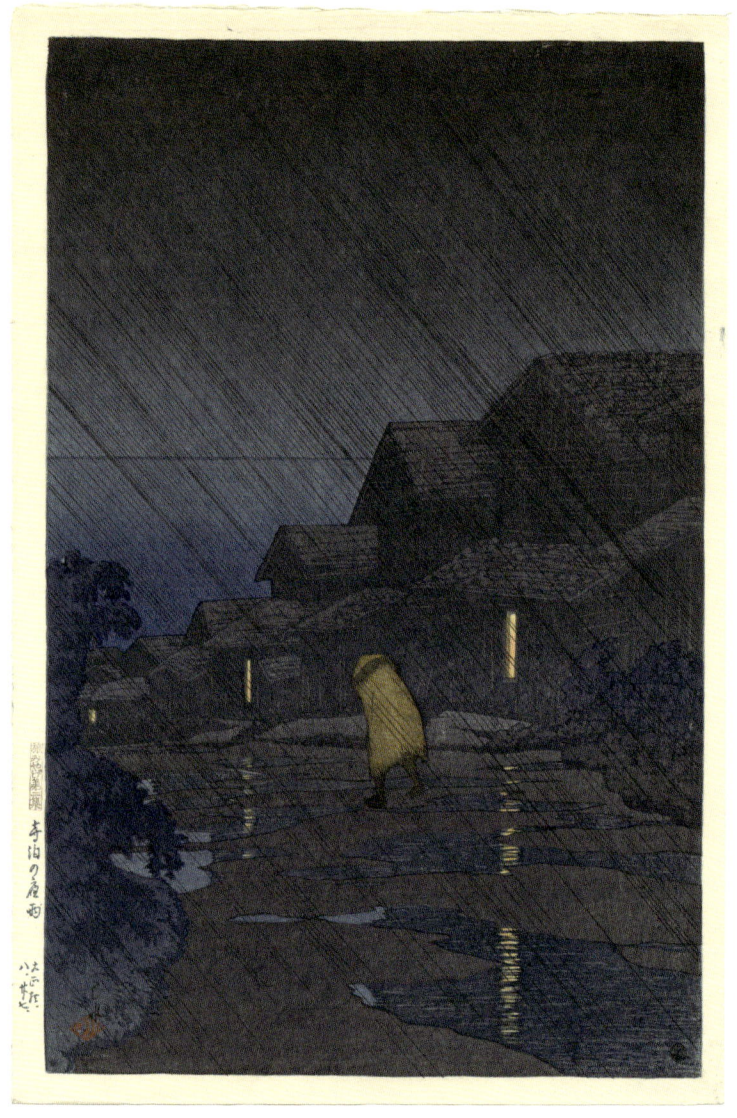

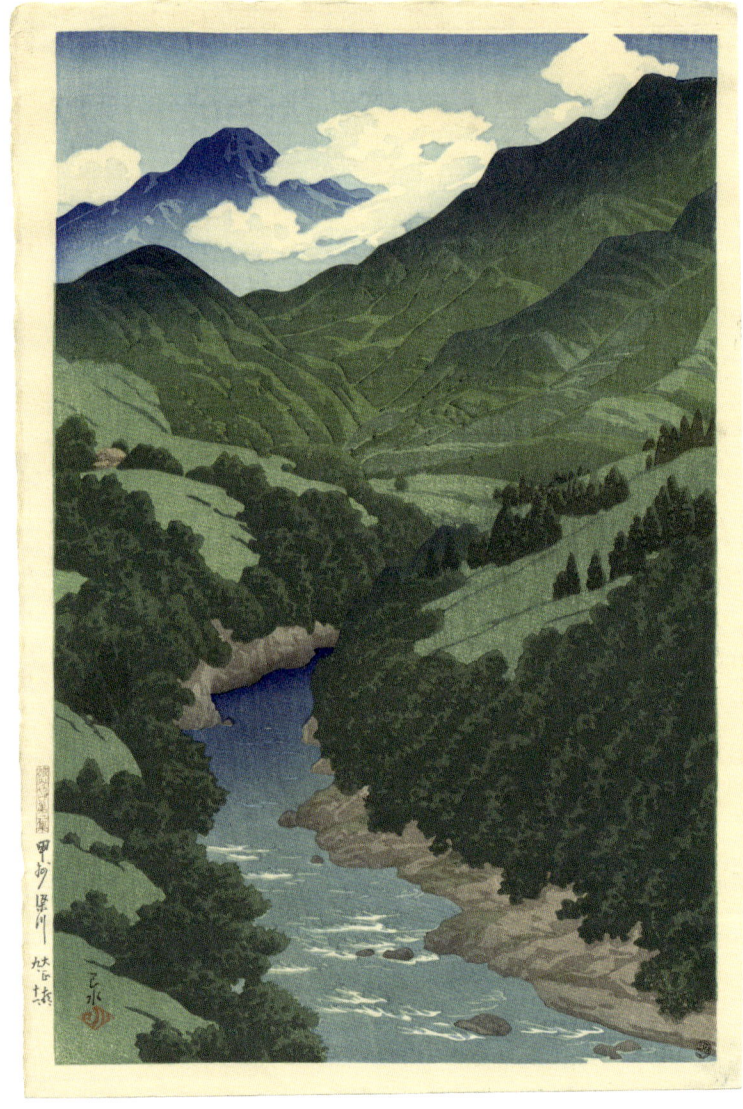

Cat. 69

Kawase Hasui 川瀬巴水 (1883–1957)

Evening Shower, Teradomari

(*Teradomari no yau* 寺泊の夜雨)

Series: *Souvenirs of Travel, second series*
(*Tabi miyage dai nishū* 旅みやげ第二集)
Date: 27 August 1921
Signature: *Hasui*
Artist's seal: *Kawase*
Publisher: Watanabe Shōzaburō
Size: 38.5 × 26.2 cm
Collection Scholten

Cat. 70

Kawase Hasui 川瀬巴水 (1883–1957)

Yana River, Kōshū

(*Kōshū Yanagawa* 甲州梁川)

Series: *Souvenirs of Travel, second series*
(*Tabi miyage dai nishū* 旅みやげ第二集)
Date: 11 September 1921
Signature: *Hasui*
Artist's seal: *Kawase*
Publisher: Watanabe Shōzaburō
Size: 38.5 × 26.6 cm
Collection Scholten

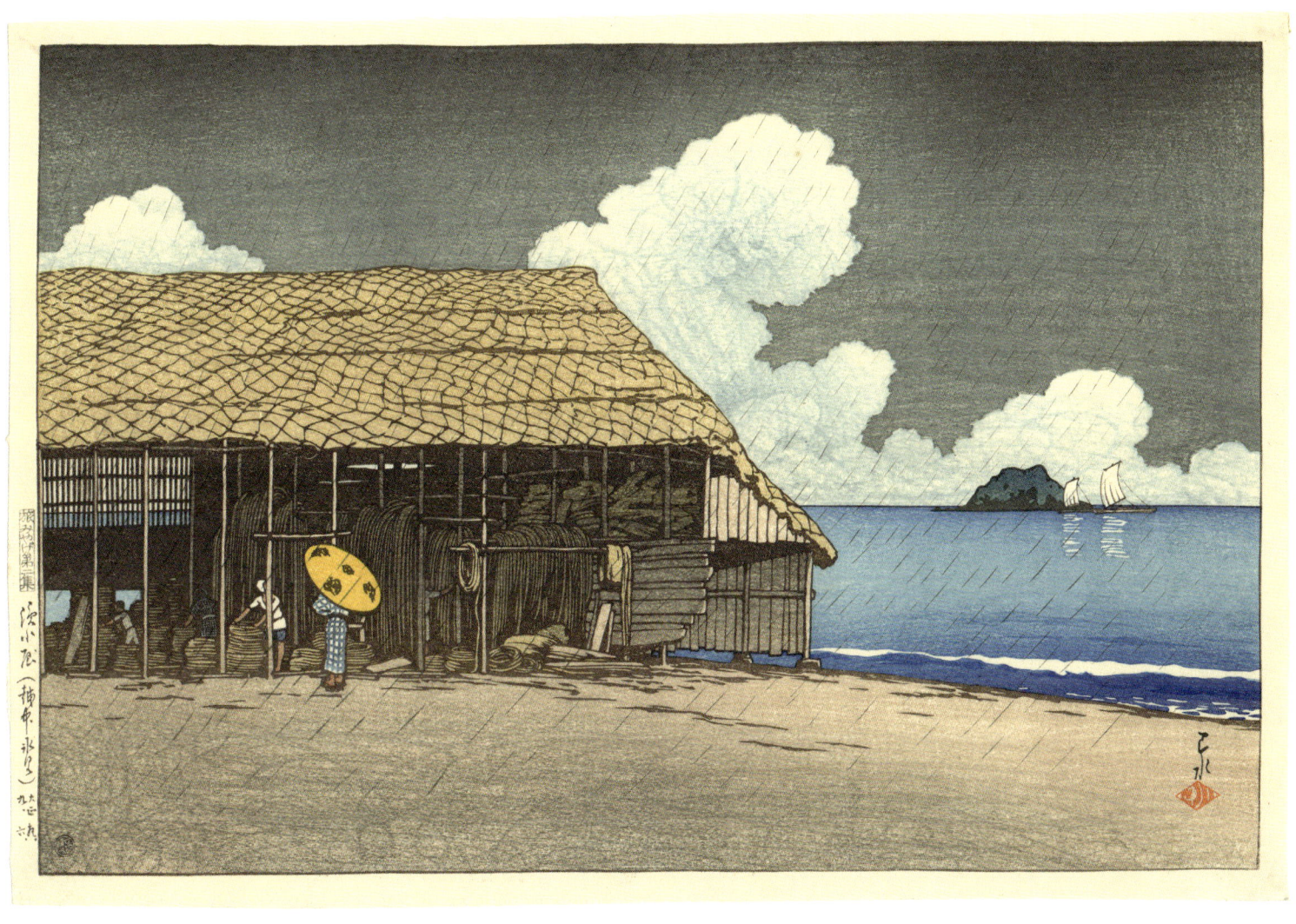

Cat. 71

Kawase Hasui 川瀬巴水 (1883–1957)

Seaside Cottage (Himi, Etchū)

(*Hama shōoku [Etchū Himi]* 浜小屋 [越中氷見])

Series: *Souvenirs of Travel, second series*
(*Tabi miyage dai nishū* 旅みやげ第二集)
Date: 6 September 1921
Signature: *Hasui*
Artist's seal: *Kawase*
Publisher: Watanabe Shōzaburō
Size: 25.7 × 38.3 cm
Private collection, the Netherlands

Cat. 72

Kawase Hasui 川瀬巴水 (1883–1957)

Nishimikawazaka, Sado

(*Sado Nishimikawazaka*
佐渡西三川坂)

Series: *Souvenirs of Travel, second series*
(*Tabi miyage dai nishū*
旅みやげ第二集)
Date: December 1921
Signature: *Hasui*
Artist's seal: *Kawase*
Publisher: Watanabe Shōzaburō
Size: 26.3 × 39.1 cm
Collection Scholten

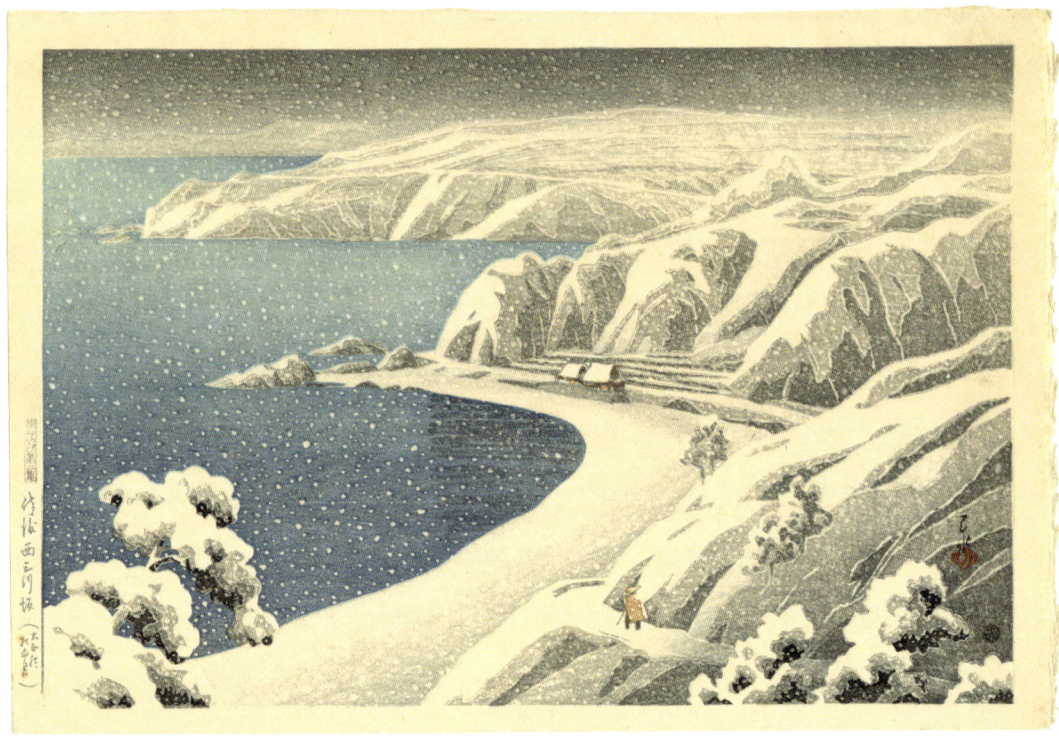

Cat. 73

Kawase Hasui 川瀬巴水 (1883–1957)

Snow at Dawn (Ogi Port, Sado)

(*Yuki no akebono [Sado Ogikō]*
雪の明ぼの [佐渡小木港])

Series: *Souvenirs of Travel, second series*
(*Tabi miyage dai nishū* 旅みやげ第二集)
Date: December 1921
Signature: *Hasui*
Artist's seal: *Kawase*
Publisher: Watanabe Shōzaburō
Size: 26.3 × 38.5 cm
Private collection, the Netherlands

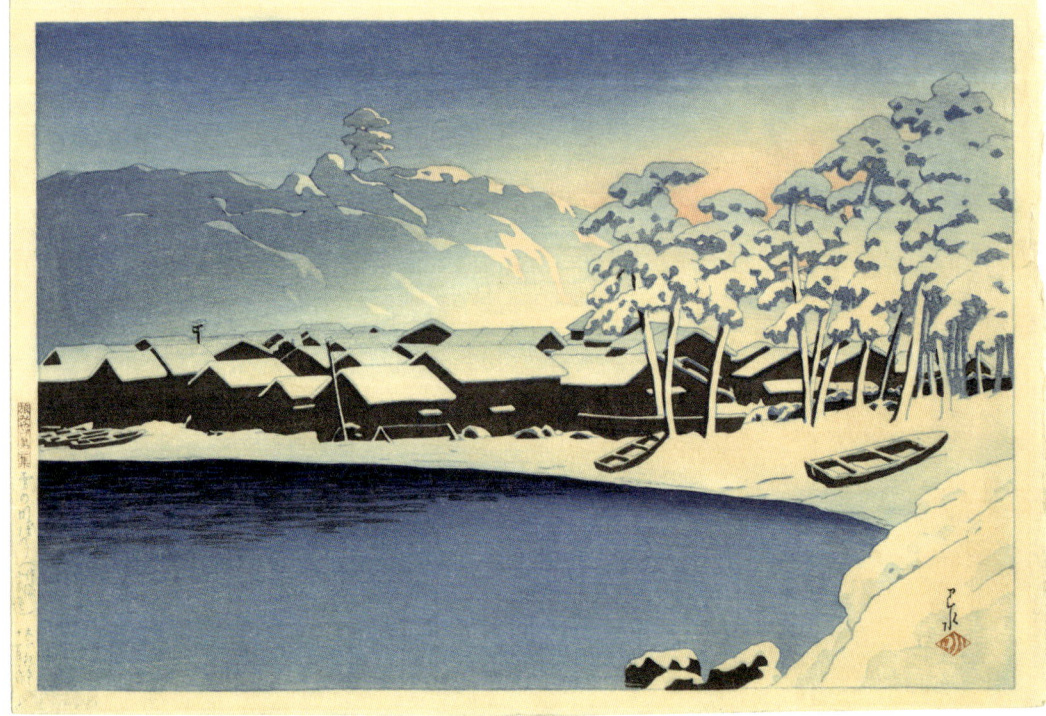

Cat. 74

Kawase Hasui 川瀬巴水 (1883–1957)

Slope at Senkō Temple, Onomichi

(*Onomichi Senkōji no saka* 尾之道千光寺の坂)

Series: *Selection of Scenes of Japan* (*Nihon fūkei senshū* 日本風景選集)
Date: 1922
Signature: *Hasui*
Artist's seal: *Kawase*
Edition: 11/300
Publisher: Watanabe Shōzaburō
Size: 30.5 × 22.8 cm
Collection Scholten

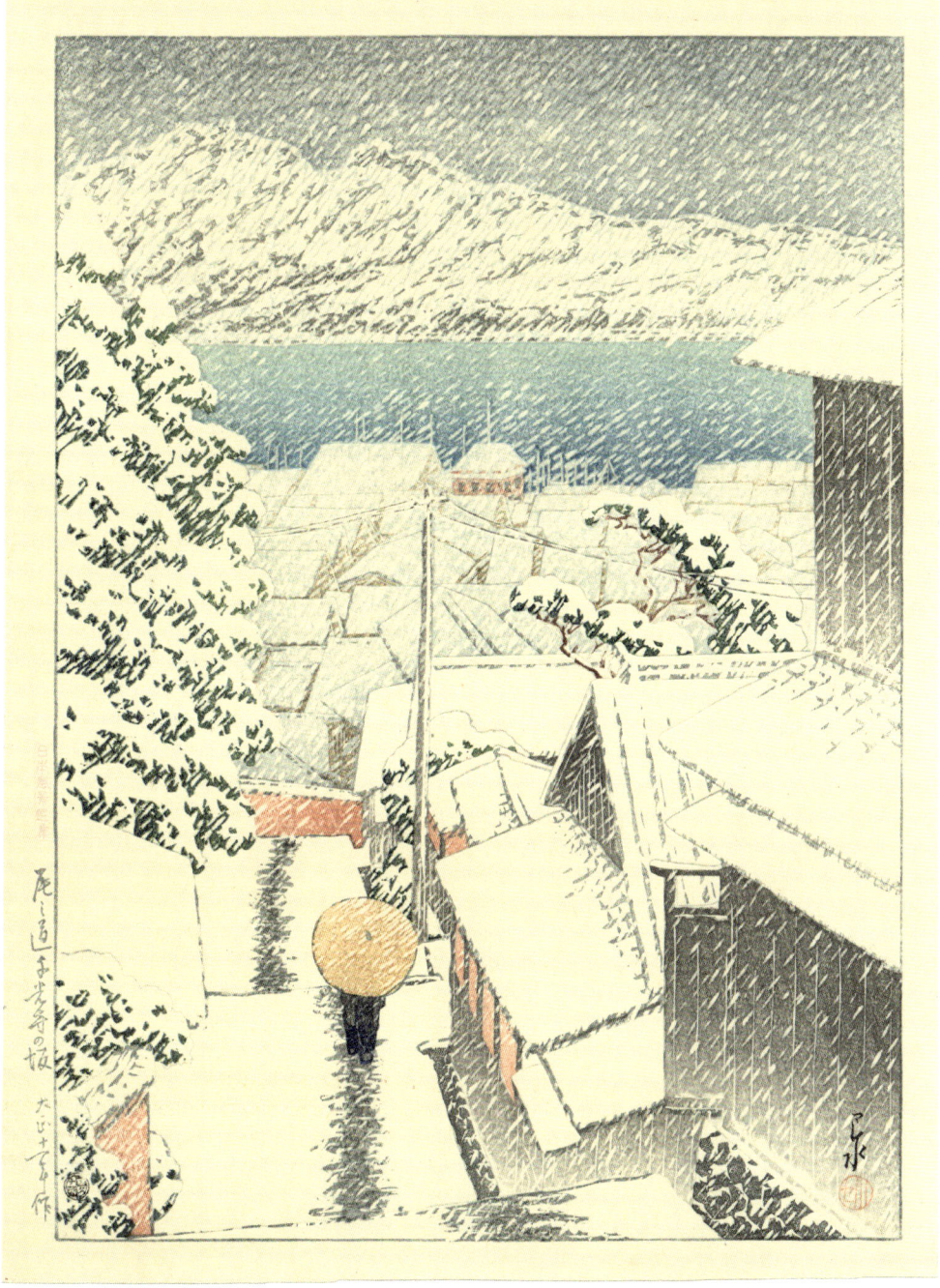

In 1922 Hasui went on one of his longest journeys, visiting various places in western Honshū and travelling round Kyūshū. Thirty-six prints in the *aiban* format were issued from the sketches he made along the road. They were sold by subscription through the Ukiyo-e Research Association (*Ukiyo-e kenkyūkai*) in 12 sets of 3, each in a titled folder. Thirty of the prints were made in 1922 and 1923 up until the Great Earthquake in September, which destroyed all of Hasui's 188 sketchbooks and most of his blocks and prints. One keyblock of an Okayama scene survived, however, and the design was printed shortly after the earthquake. The last five prints, of which *Suhara, Kiso* is included in section 8 (Cat. 174), were published from 1924 until 1926. As in his earlier works, the prints convey a sense of a timeless, 'pure' Japan. However, sometimes the scenes do feature hints of modernity such as the power lines in *Slope at Senkō Temple, Onomichi* and *Kōtsuki River, Kagoshima* (Cat. 75).

(JD)

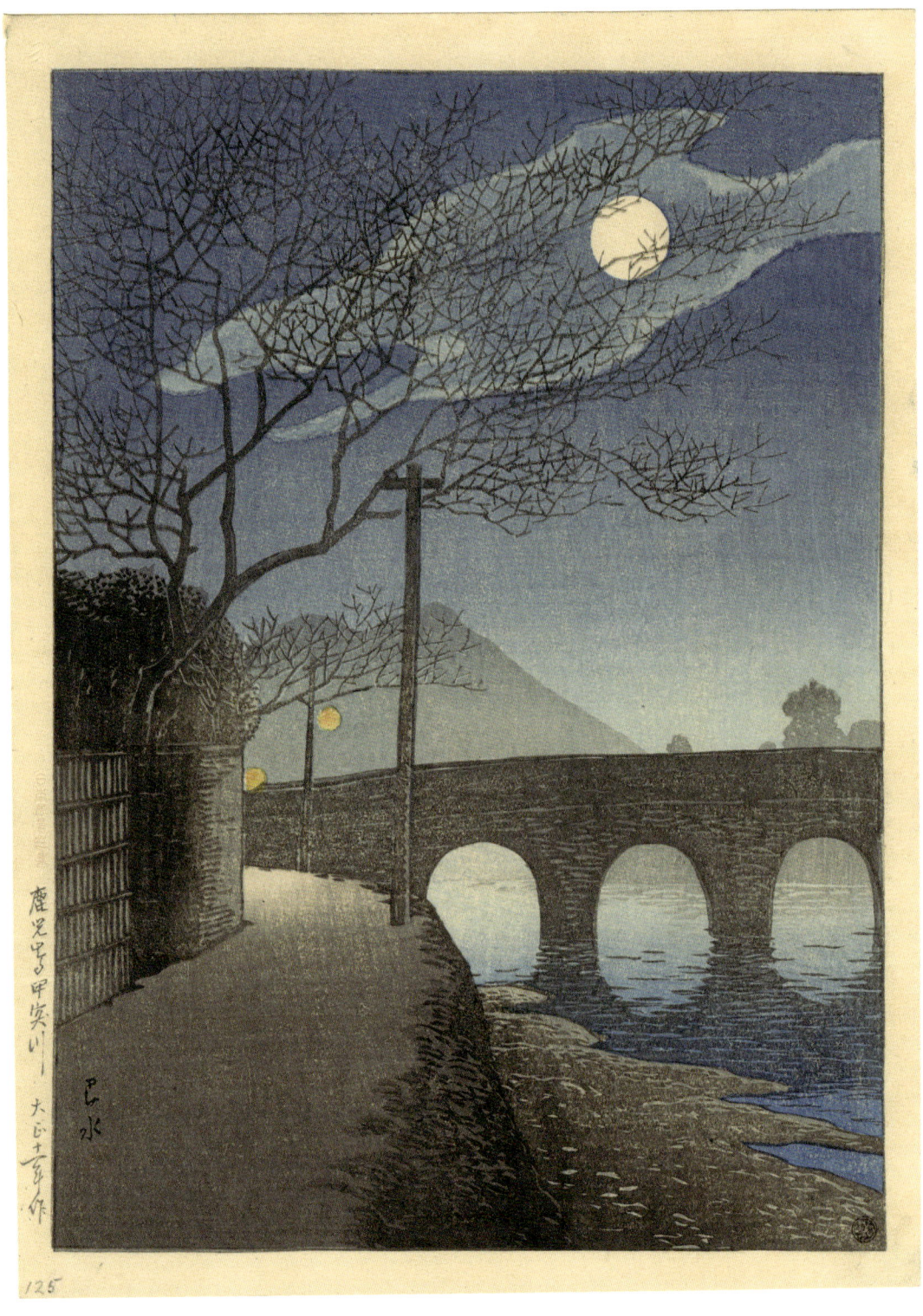

Cat. 75

Kawase Hasui 川瀬巴水 (1883–1957)

Kōtsuki River, Kagoshima

(*Kagoshima Kōtsukigawa* 鹿児島
甲突川)

Series: *Selection of Scenes of Japan*
(*Nihon fūkei senshū* 日本風景選集)
Date: 1922
Signature: *Hasui*
Artist's seal: *Kawase*
Edition: 16/300
Publisher: Watanabe Shōzaburō
Size: 30.6 × 22.5 cm
Collection Scholten

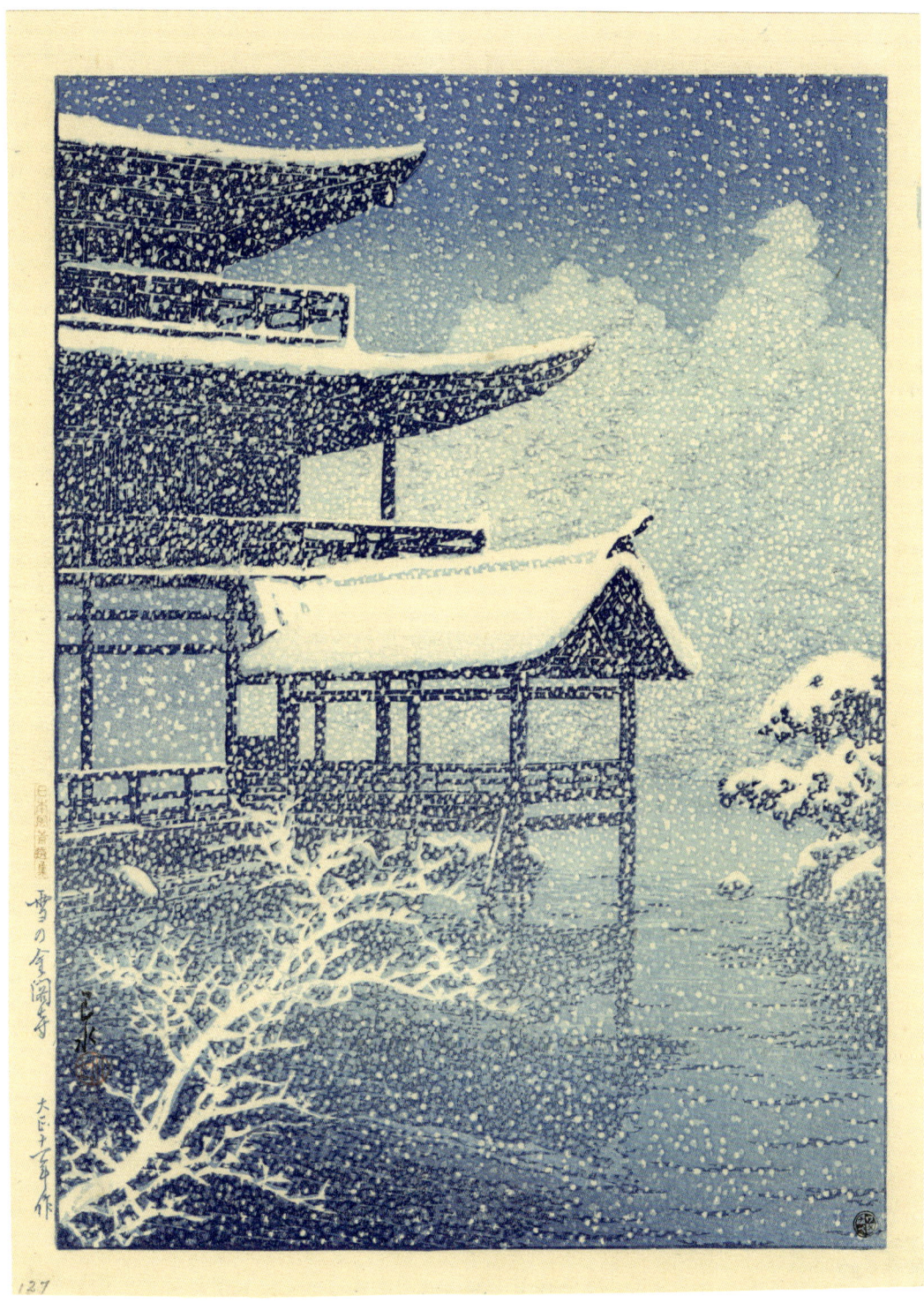

In Hasui's typical modest fashion, even famous places he depicts in his prints are shrouded in anonymity. In this view of Kyoto's Golden Pavilion, its gilt exterior – from which it takes its name – is obscured by heavy snowfall. It should be kept in mind, however, that during Hasui's time the pavilion was not as shiny as it is today: in 1950 it was torched by a fanatic and has since been reconstructed with additional decorative golden layers.
(JD)

Cat. 76

Kawase Hasui 川瀬巴水 (1883–1957)
Snow at Golden Pavilion
(*Yuki no Kinkakuji* 雪の金閣寺)

Series: *Selection of Scenes of Japan*
(*Nihon fūkei senshū* 日本風景選集)
Date: 1922
Signature: *Hasui*
Artist's seal: *Kawase*
Edition: 16/300
Publisher: Watanabe Shōzaburō
Size: 30.6 × 22.7 cm
Collection Scholten

Cat. 77

Kawase Hasui 川瀬巴水 (1883–1957)

Morning at Beppu

(*Beppu no asa* 別府の朝)

Series: *Selection of Scenes of Japan*
(*Nihon fūkei senshū* 日本風景選集)
Date: 1922
Signature: *Hasui*
Artist's seal: *Kawase*
Publisher: Watanabe Shōzaburō
Size: 30.9 × 22.7 cm
Collection Scholten

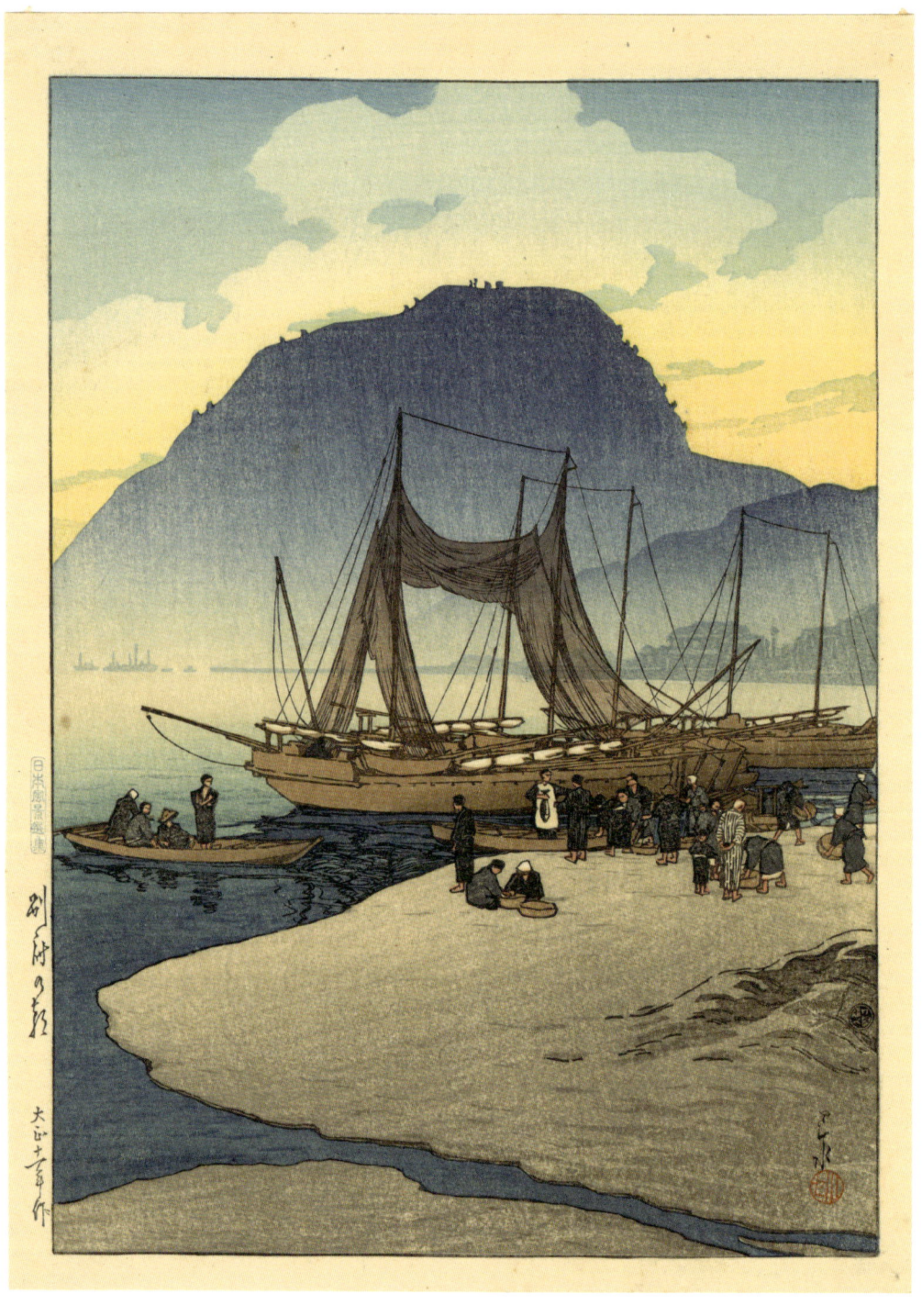

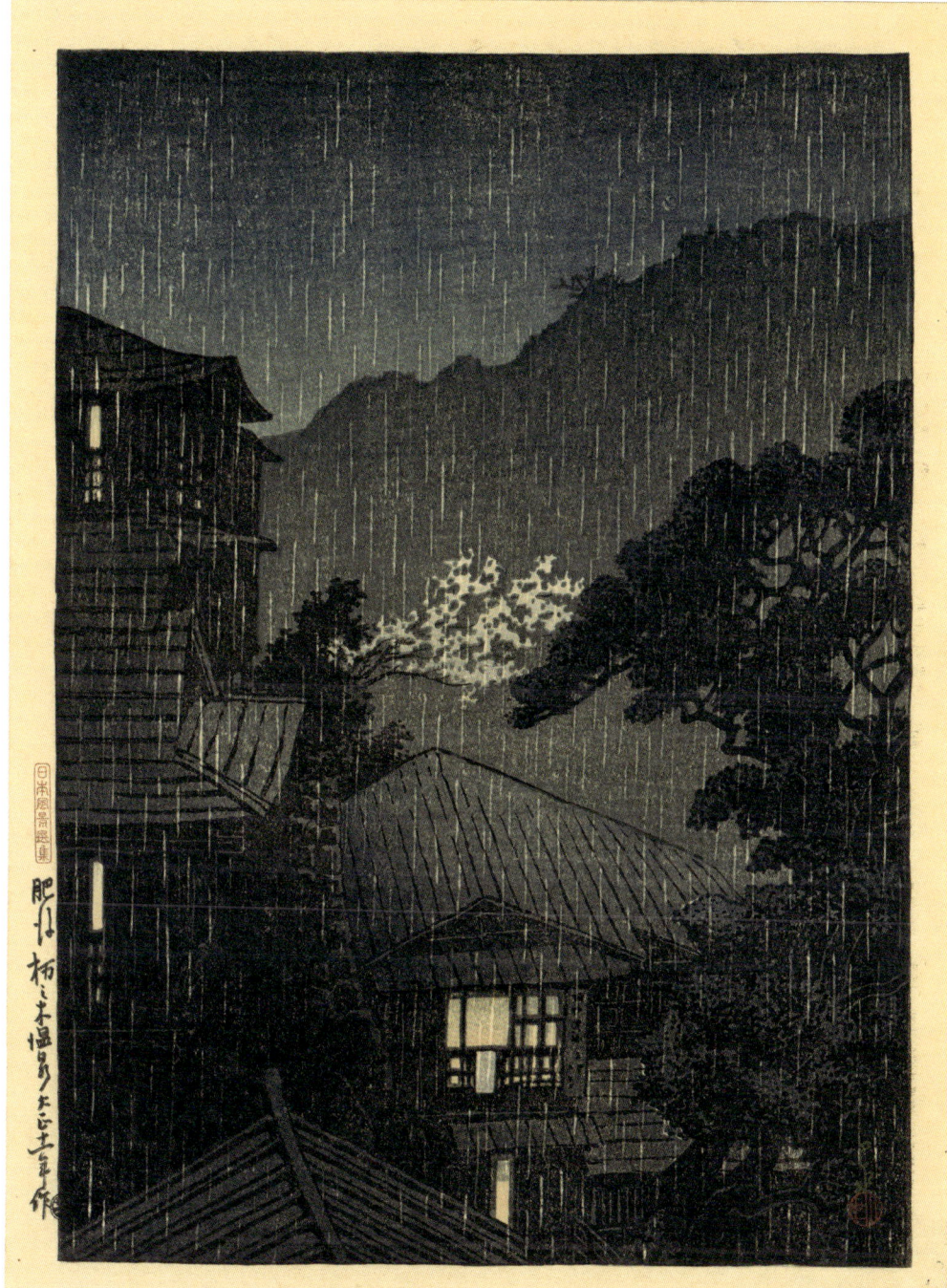

Cat. 78

Kawase Hasui 川瀬巴水 (1883–1957)

**Tochinoki Hot Springs
in Higo Province**

(*Higo Tochinoki onsen*
肥後栃の木温泉)

Series: *Selection of Scenes of Japan*
(*Nihon fūkei senshū* 日本風景選集)
Date: 1922
Signature: *Hasui*
Artist's seal: *Kawase*
Edition: 33/300
Publisher: Watanabe Shōzaburō
Size: 30.5 × 22.9 cm
Collection Scholten

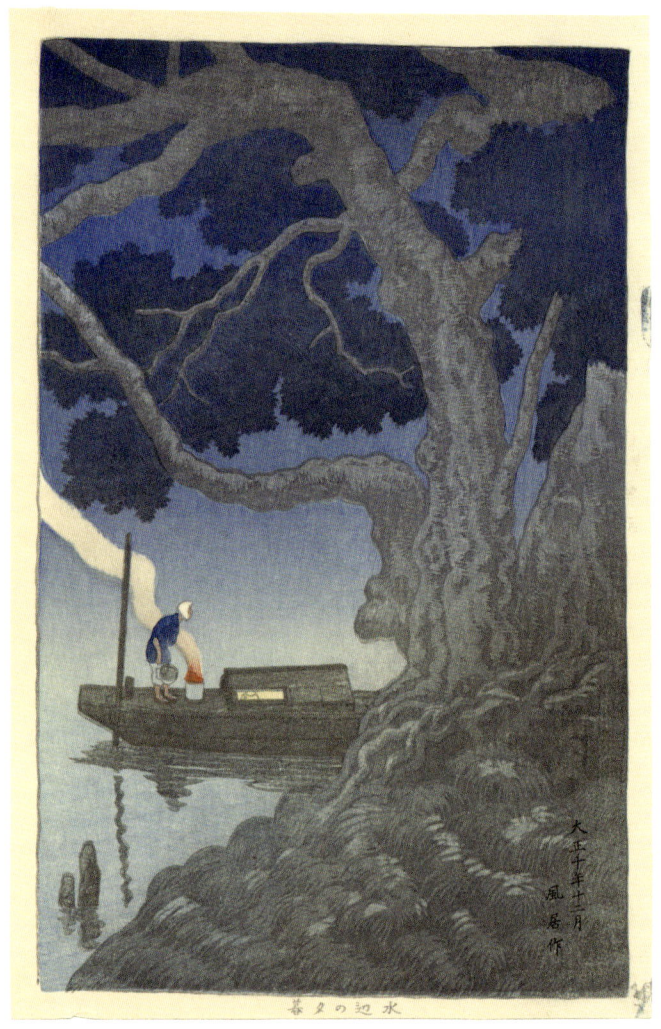

Yanagihara Fūkyo 柳原風居 (dates unknown)

Dusk at the Water's Edge

(*Mizube no yūgure* 水辺の夕暮)

Date: December 1921
Signature: *Fūkyo saku*
Publisher: Watanabe Shōzaburō
Size: 38.5 × 25.5 cm
Collection Scholten

Cat. 80

Furuya Taiken 古屋台軒 (1897–1941)

Itinerant Musicians

(*Tabi geinin* 旅藝人)

Date: December 1921
Signature: *Taiken*
Publisher: Watanabe Shōzaburō
Size: 26.1 × 36.8 cm
Collection Scholten

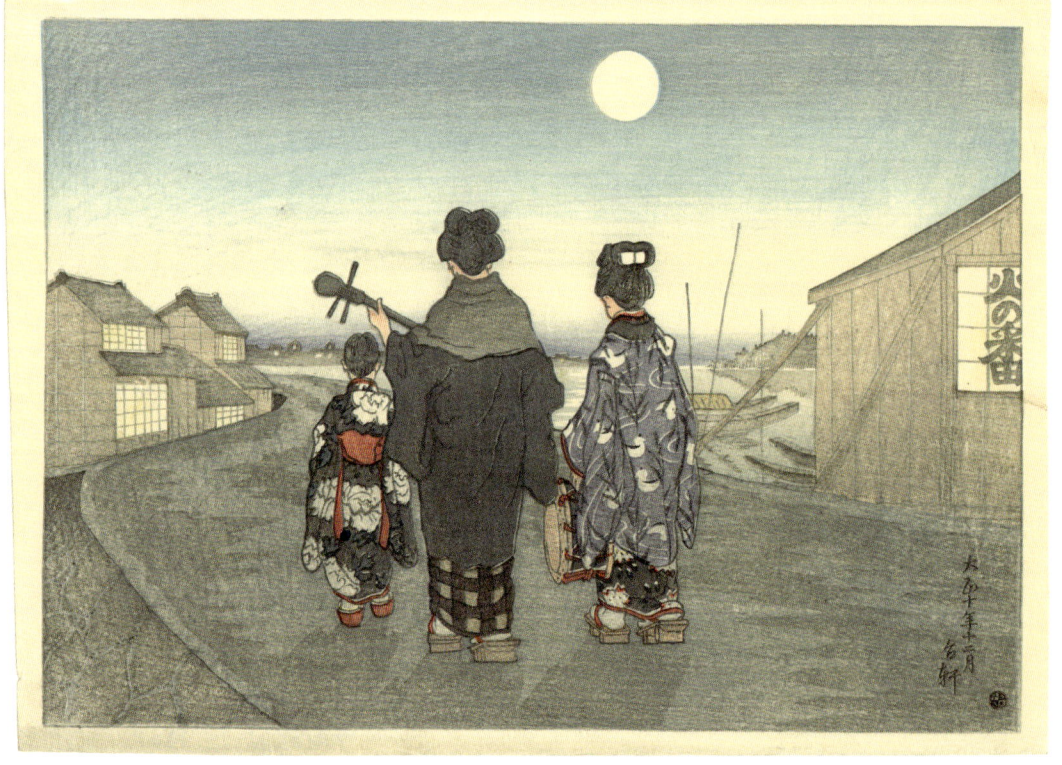

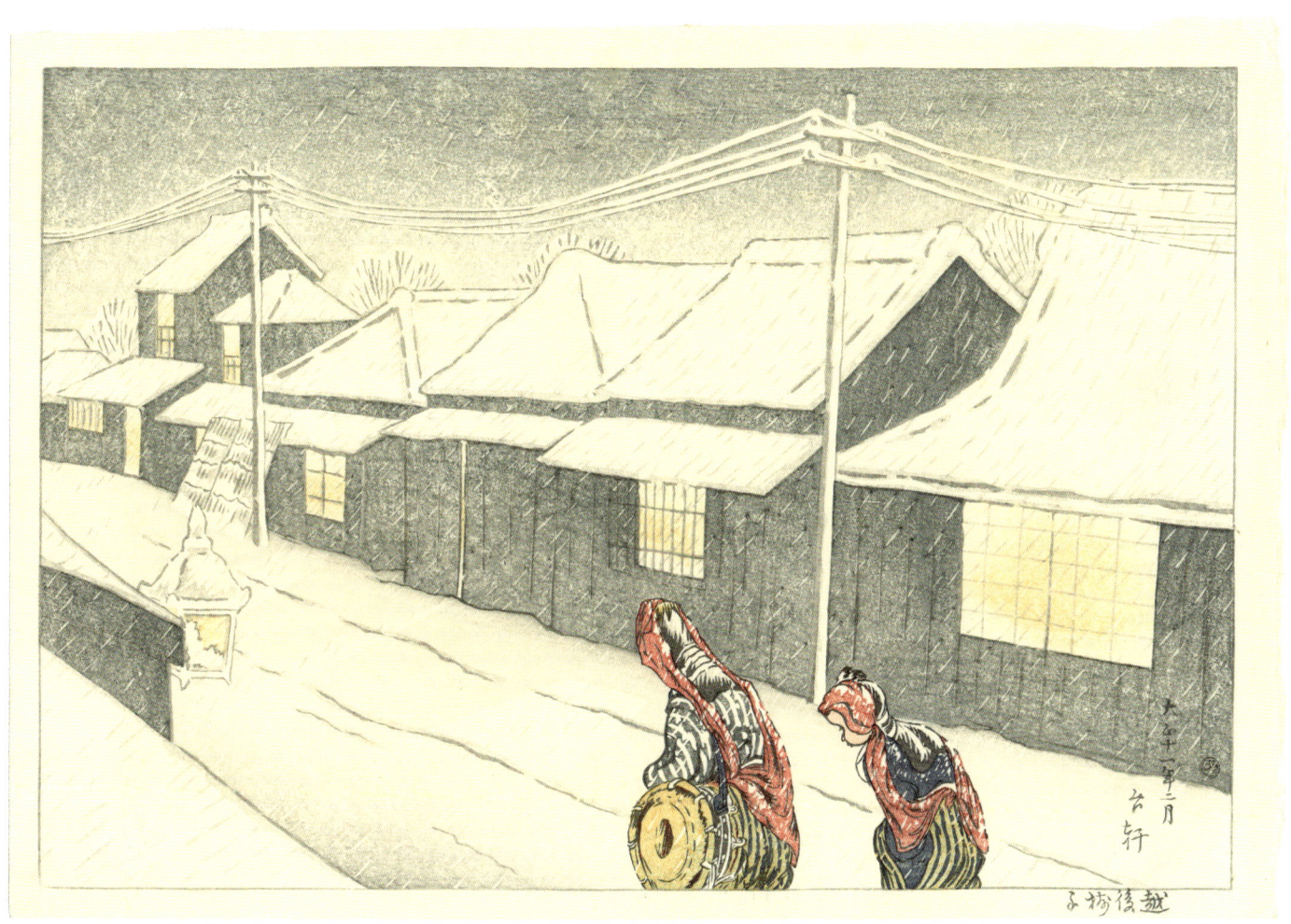

The four prints that Taiken made with Watanabe can be seen as a series, as they all fit one theme: that of *minzoku geinō* (folk music and dance). This print shows a tradition that at the time of its publication was already considered a rare sight. Two *Echigo-jishi* performers ('Chinese lions of Echigo', in present-day Nagano Prefecture) make their way through a snowy residential street at night, lights glowing from behind the windows. Their costumes featuring black-and-red headdresses are typical for this kind of street performer.

Such wandering groups were a popular form of folk entertainment. The child acrobats would wear miniature versions of *shishira* (Chinese lion-head masks) and perform gymnastics to the rhythm of the drums, played by an adult. They presented themselves from door to door and in public areas such as temples or busy streets, and would receive money or rice for their acts. The tradition lost its popularity in the Meiji Period, especially with the strict enforcement of child labour laws.
(PO)

Cat. 81

Furuya Taiken 古屋台軒 (1897–1941)
Echigo-jishi Performers
(*Echigo-jishi* 越後獅子)

Date: February 1922
Signature: *Taiken*
Publisher: Watanabe Shōzaburō
Size: 26.4 × 38.6 cm
Collection Scholten

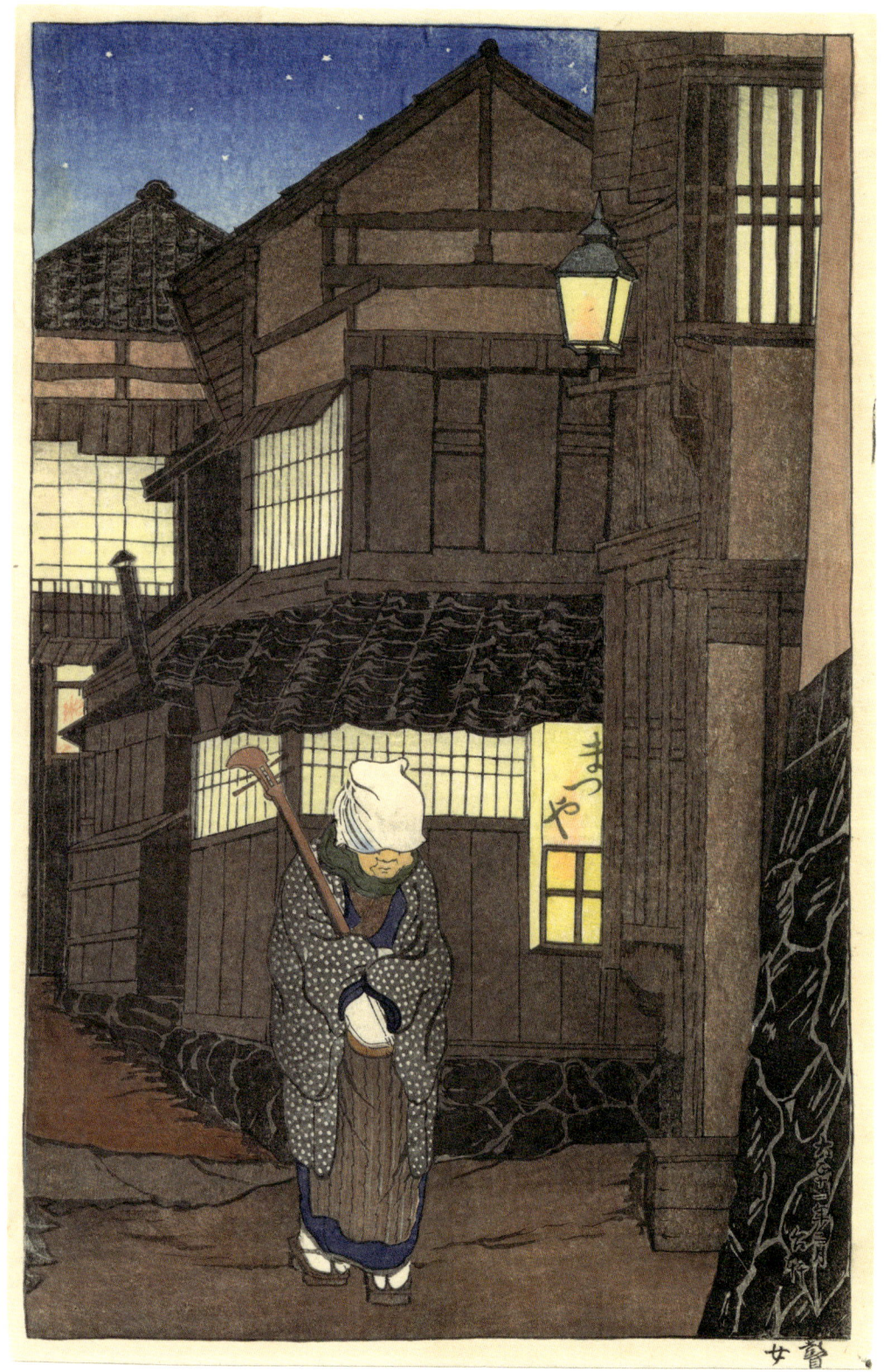

Cat. 82

Furuya Taiken 古屋台軒 (1897–1941)

Blind Shamisen Player

(*Goze* 瞽女)

Date: February 1922
Signature: *Taiken*
Publisher: Watanabe Shōzaburō
Size: 37.7 × 25 cm
Private collection, the Netherlands

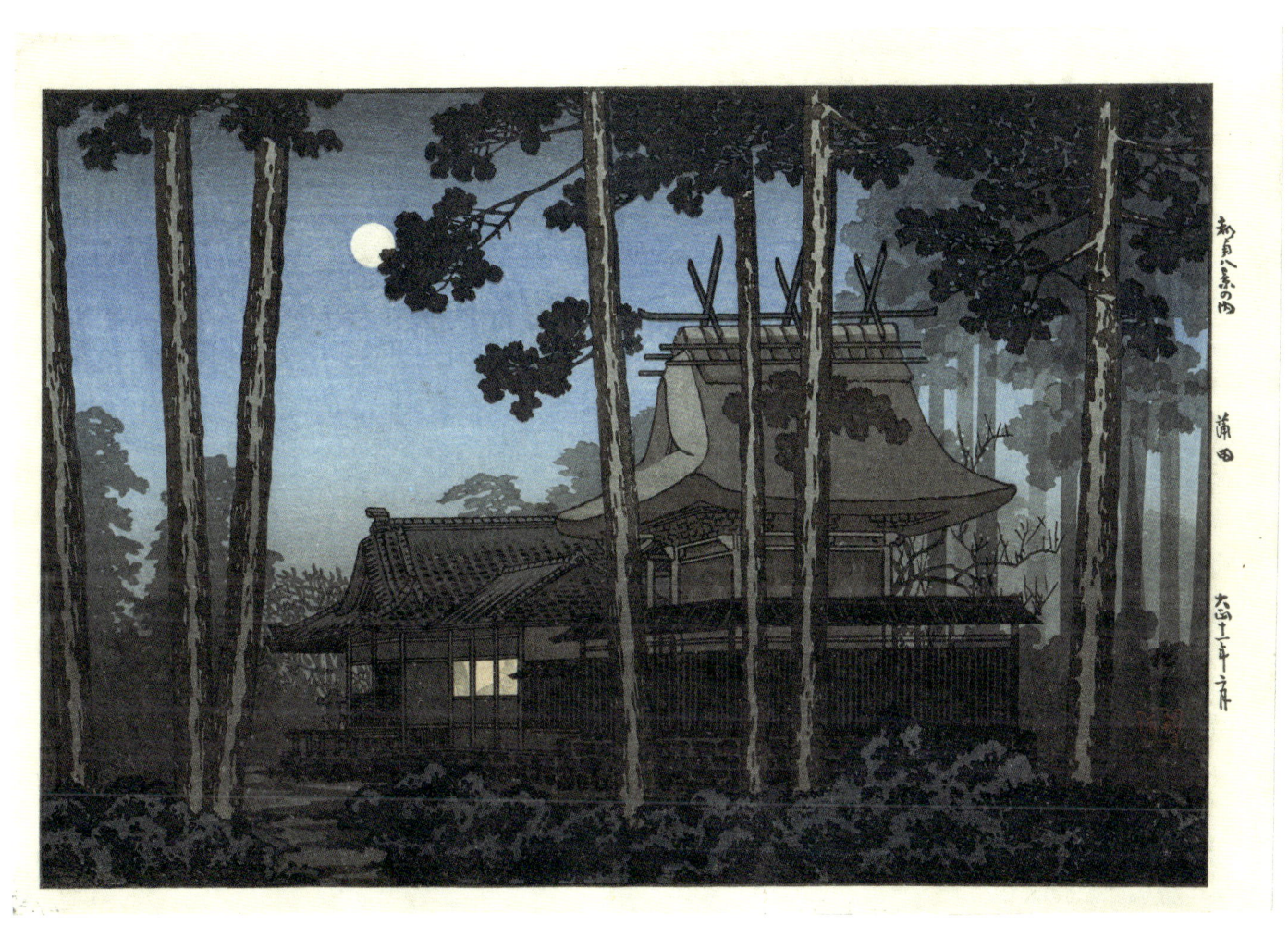

Cat. 83

Takahashi Hiroaki (Shōtei)
高橋弘明 (松亭) (1871–1945)

Kamata

(*Kamata* 蒲田)

Series: *Eight Views South of the Capital*
(*Tonan hakkei no uchi* 都南八景之内)
Date: February 1922
Signature: *Shōtei*
Artist's seal: *Shōtei*
Publisher: Watanabe Shōzaburō
Size: 26.5 × 39 cm
Collection Scholten

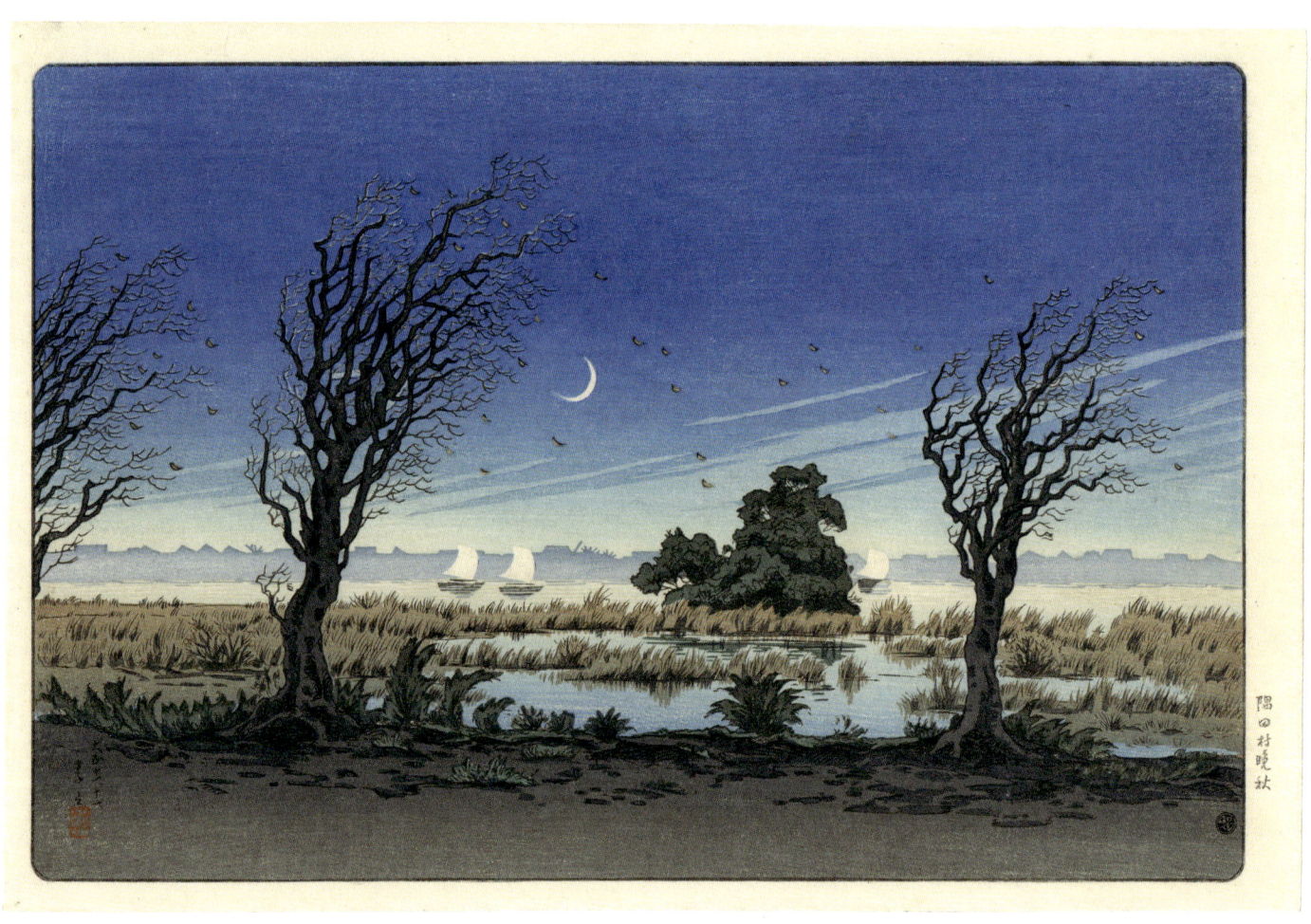

Cat. 84

Itō Takashi 伊藤孝之 (1894–1982)

Late Autumn in Sumida Village

(*Sumidamura banshū* 隅田村晚秋)

Date: December 1922
Signature: *Takashi*
Artist's seal: *Itō*
Publisher: Watanabe Shōzaburō
Size: 25.6 × 38.9 cm
Collection Scholten

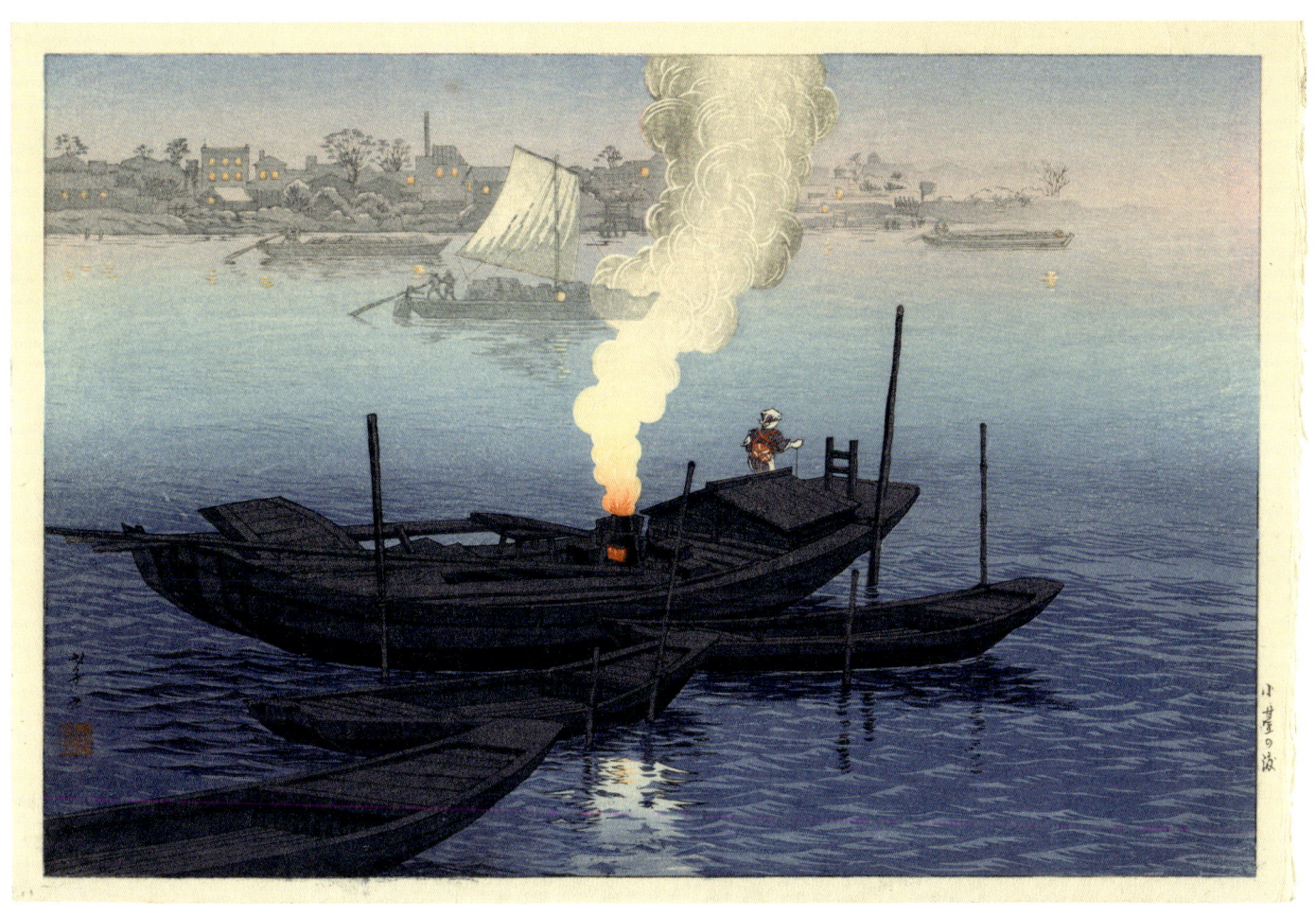

Although the original design of this print was made in 1922, the blocks were lost in the earthquake of 1923, and this edition was printed from newly carved blocks, resulting in various differences in the details. Odai is an area on the northern outskirts of Tokyo where the Sumida River and Ara River converge. The only way to cross the rivers was by ferry, until a bridge was built in 1933.
(JD)

Cat. 85

Itō Takashi 伊藤孝之 (1894–1982)
Odai Ferry
(*Odai no watashi* 小台の渡し)

Date: after 1923
Signature: *Takashi*
Artist's seal: *Itō Takashi*
Publisher: Watanabe Shōzaburō
Size: 27 × 38.6 cm
Private collection, the Netherlands

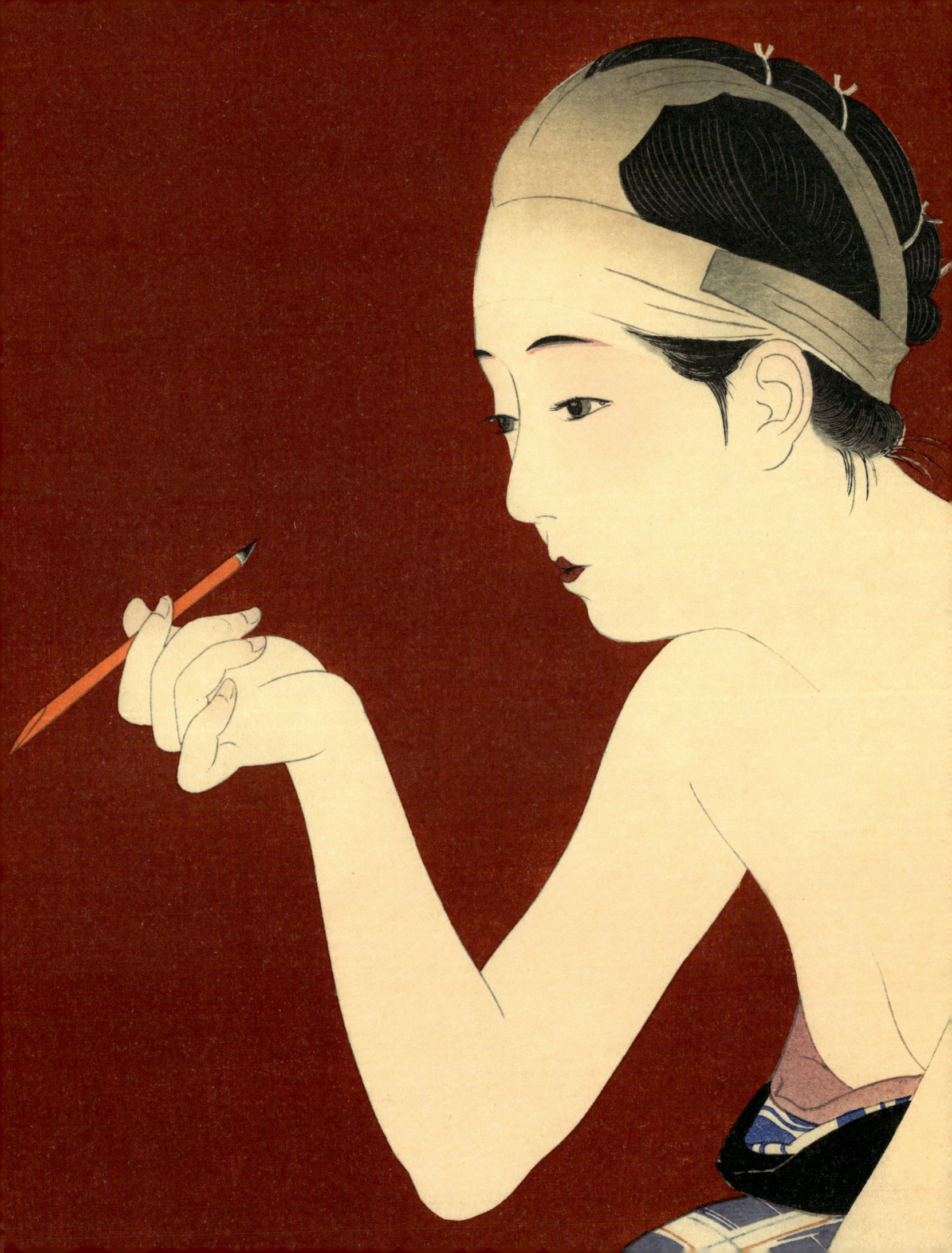

Post-Earthquake Beautiful Women

After the 1923 earthquake, the printmaking industry quickly recovered, and the students of the influential painter Kaburaki Kiyokata were invited by Watanabe Shōzaburō and other publishers to transform their paintings into print designs. The block carvers and printers showed their incredible technical abilities and created some of the most luxurious prints ever made.

Cat. 86

Kitano Tsunetomi 北野恒富
(1880–1947)

The Heron Maiden

(*Sagi musume* 鷺娘)

Date: c. 1925
Signature: *Tsunetomi hitsu*
Publisher: *Nezu Seitarō*
Block cutter: *Yamana Yoshiteru*
Printer: *Matsuno Kassui*
Size: 54.2 × 36.4 cm
Collection Scholten

One of Tsunetomi's most famous designs, this print depicts a beautiful woman who could transform into a white heron. Her origins lie in a folktale about a woodcutter who rescues a wounded heron. She later appears to him in her human form, and they get married. In their home she weaves the finest garments on condition that the woodcutter must not watch her while she works. However, he is unable to resist the temptation, and when he enters her room he finds her weaving clothes in her heron form. The white heron flies away, never to be seen again. When a standalone dance act was created for her character in the Meiji Period, the theme attracted renewed interest. The tale of the heron maiden saw another surge in popularity around 1920, when she appeared in several prints and paintings by *nihonga* and print artists such as Kaburaki Kiyokata. Among the most successful was Tsunetomi's rendition, which he originally made as a hanging scroll painting. Notable here is the exquisite use of *gofun* for the snowflakes and of mica in the background. A folder for this print has been discovered with the title *Winter* and the series title *Beauties in the Four Seasons*, which suggests that it was part of a set of four, one for each season. Only one other design that is thought to be part of this series – titled *Maiko*, shown below (Cat. 87) – is known, however.
(JD)

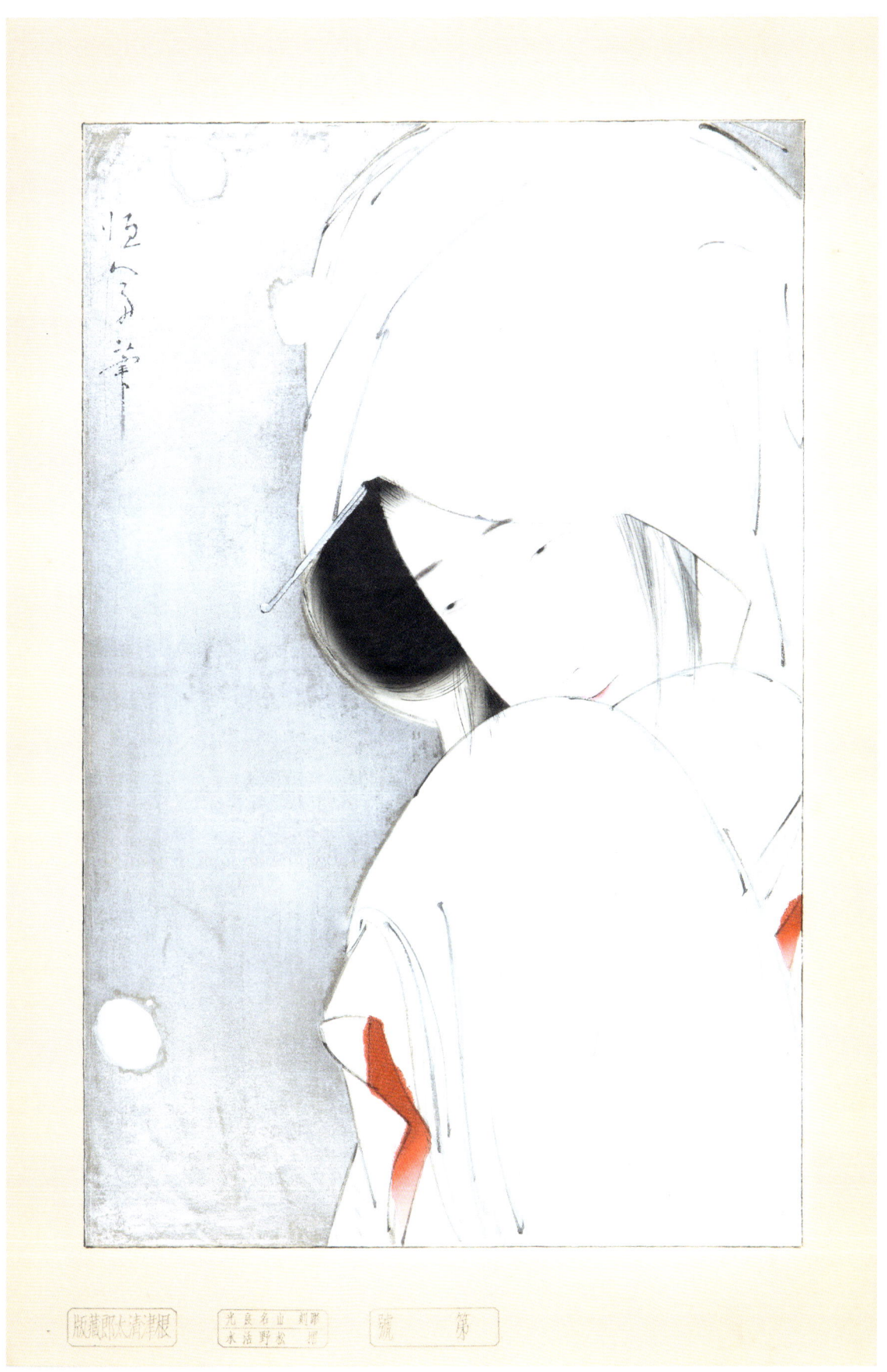

Kitano Tsunetomi 北野恒富
(1880–1947)

Maiko

(*Maiko* 舞妓)

Date: 1925
Signature: *Tsunetomi hitsu*
Artist's seal: *Tsunetomi*
Edition: Numbered 12
Publisher: Nezu Seitarō
Block cutter: *Yamana Yoshiteru*
Printer: *Matsuno Kassui*
Size: 53.5 × 36.3 cm
Collection Scholten

Itō Shinsui 伊東深水 (1898–1972)

Long Undergarment

(*Nagajuban* 長襦袢)

Date: 1927
Signature: *Shinsui ga*
Artist's seal: *Itō*
Edition: 10/200
Publisher: Watanabe Shōzaburō
Size: 43 × 27 cm
Collection RMAH – JP.06151

This print depicts a woman in a long undergarment combing her hair. It was a common trope for Shinsui to depict his *bijin* working on their appearance, such as applying make-up or doing their hair like the woman in this print. It is interesting to note that the woman in Hirano Hakuhō's *Before the Mirror* (Cat. 107) wears almost exactly the same type of undergarment as depicted here, possibly as a nod to Shinsui. This print with its mica background is in excellent condition, and the usually vulnerable red and orange colours have remained unfaded.
(JD)

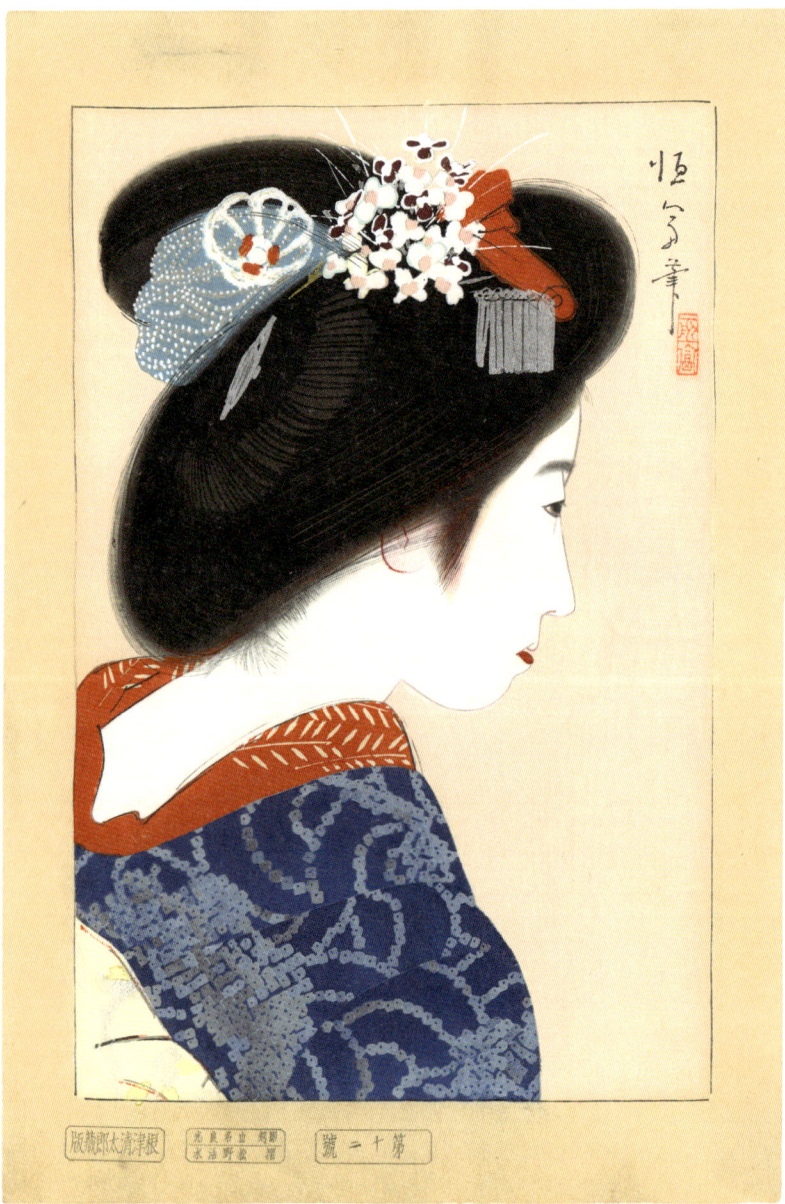

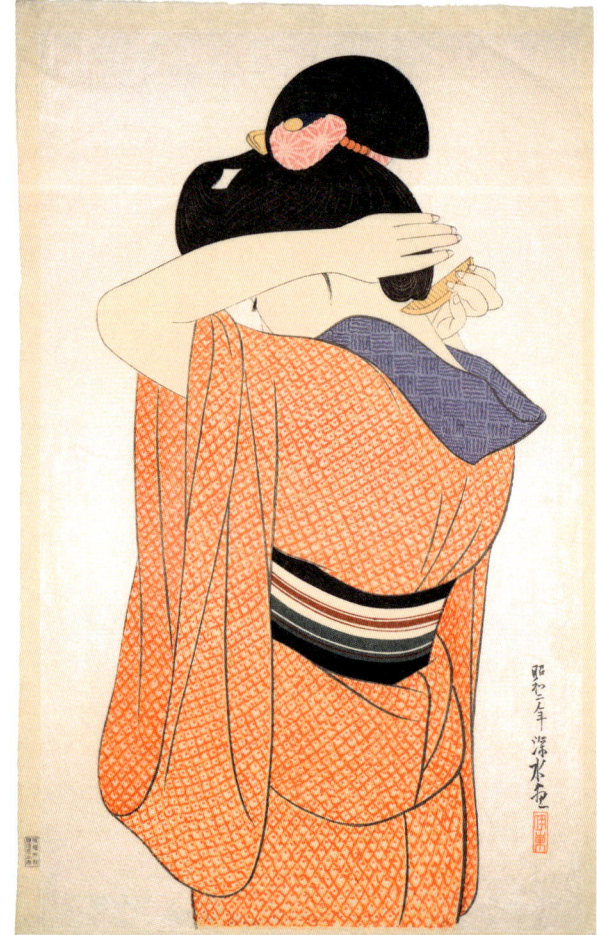

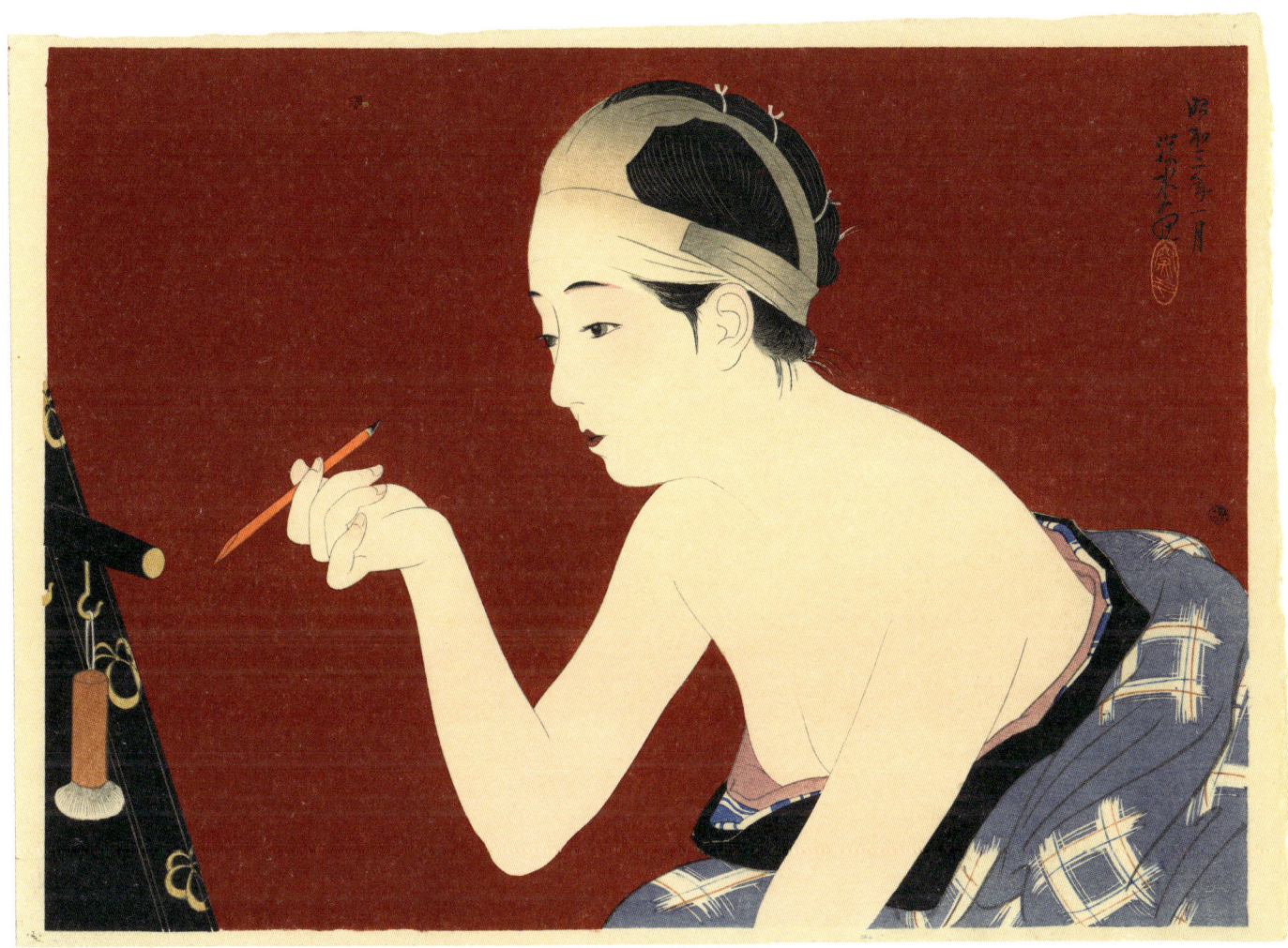

Printed in an unusual horizontal format, this design depicting an actress applying make-up sold out quickly. The model is said to be the movie and theatre star Mizutani Yaeko (1905–79). It is thought that Shinsui partly based the composition of this print on his 1924 painting *Oshiroi* (*Face Powder*). The deep-red colour in the background is the result of reprinting the same colour block multiple times, thereby creating a stark contrast with the woman's pale skin. Trial prints have been discovered with not only slightly different colour schemes but also much lighter backgrounds, from a mild pink to a colour almost similar to the figure's pale skin. These trials were quite common, and they illustrate the experimentation involved in the printing process before the final publication.

(JD)

Cat. 89

Itō Shinsui 伊東深水 (1898–1972)

Blackening the Eyebrows

(*Mayuzumi* 眉墨)

Date: January 1928
Signature: *Shinsui ga*
Artist's seal: *Shinsui*
Edition: 27/200
Publisher: Watanabe Shōzaburō
Size: 28 × 40 cm
Collection Scholten

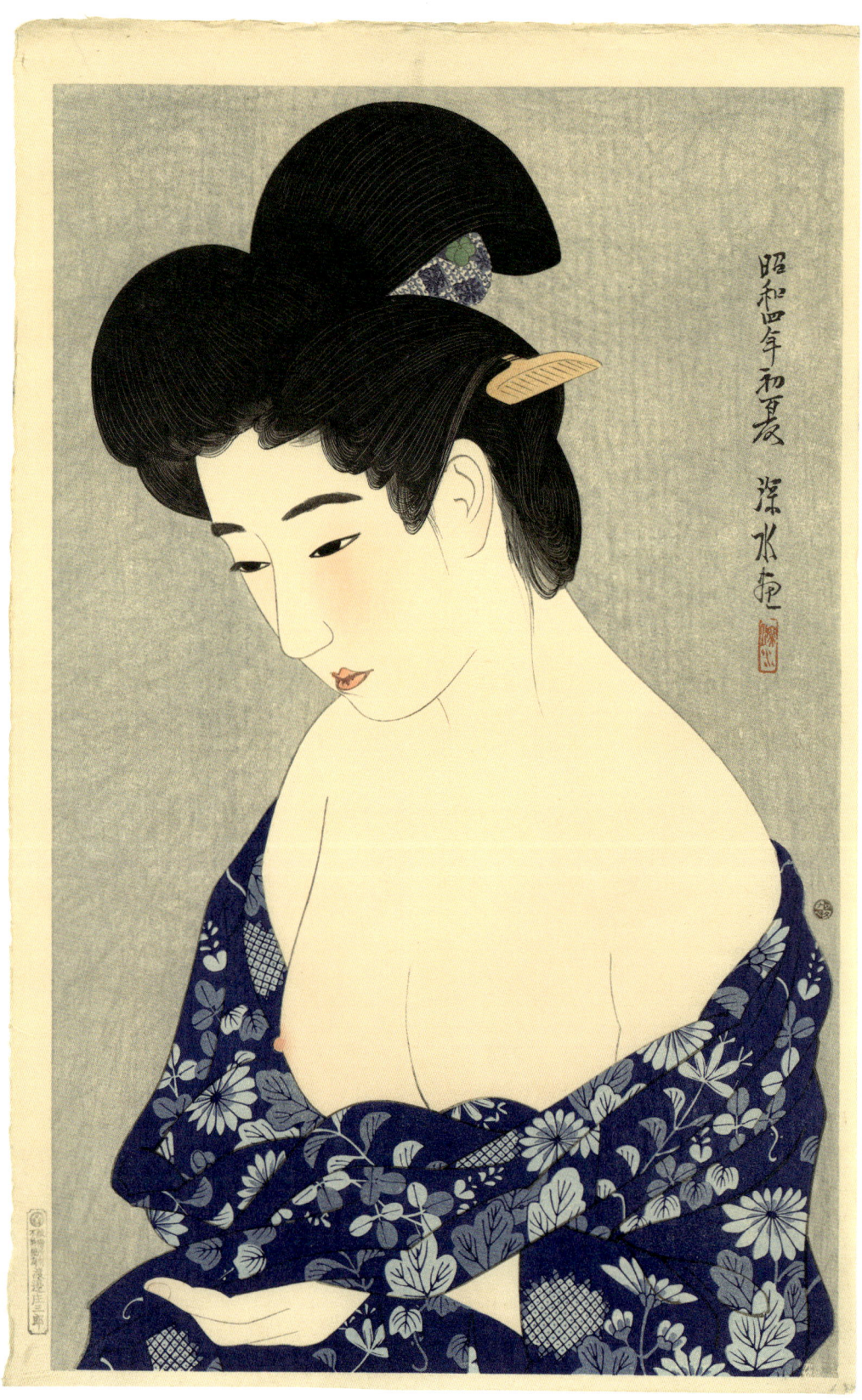

Cat. 90

Itō Shinsui 伊東深水 (1898–1972)

New Cotton Kimono

(*Hatsu yukata* 初浴衣)

Series: *The First Collection
of Modern Beauties*
(*Gendai bijinshū dai-isshū*
現代美人集第一輯)
Date: Early summer 1929
Signature: *Shinsui ga*
Artist's seal: *Shinsui*
Edition: 189/250
Publisher: Watanabe Shōzaburō
Size: 43.5 × 28 cm
Collection Scholten

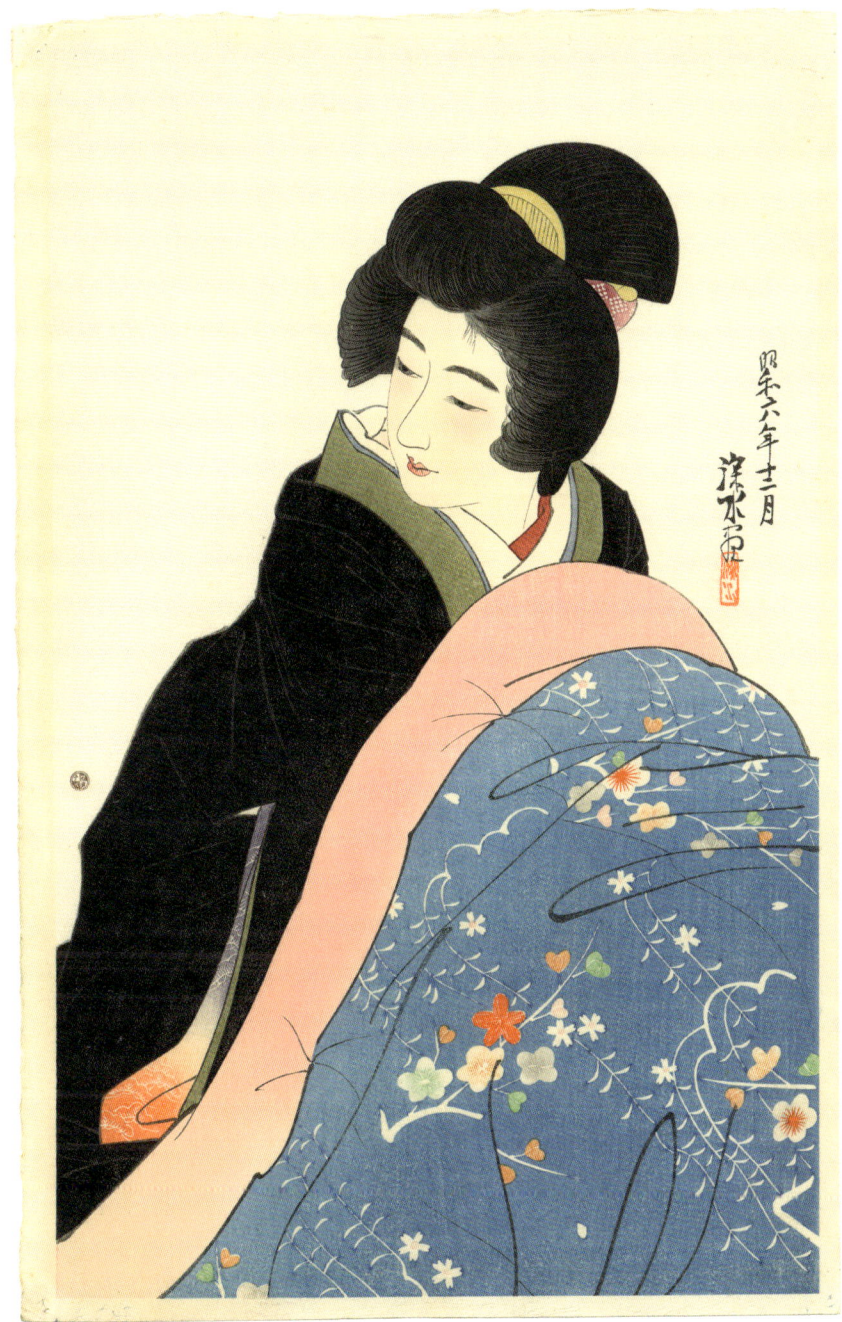

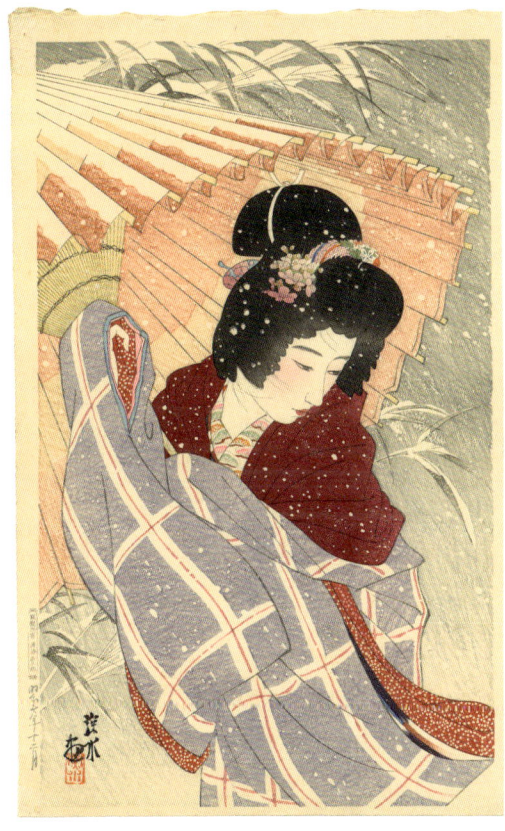

Cat. 91

Itō Shinsui 伊東深水 (1898–1972)

Footwarmer

(*Kotatsu* こたつ)

Series: *The Second Collection
of Modern Beauties
(Gendai bijinshū dai-nishū*
現代美人集第二輯)
Date: December 1931
Signature: *Shinsui ga*
Artist's seal: *Shinsui*
Edition: 196/250
Publisher: Watanabe Shōzaburō
Size: 42.9 × 27.8 cm
Collection Scholten

Still found in many Japanese households, a *kotatsu*
is a low table placed over a heat source and covered
by a thick quilt. While nowadays *kotatsu* generally
come with electric heating and can be placed any-
where in the house, in the past people would warm
their feet round the *irori*, a traditional sunken hearth
usually located in the middle of a *tatami* floor. The
kotatsu provides an inexpensive and cosy way to
stay warm in the midst of winter, especially in traditional homes with poor insulation.

(JD)

Cat. 92

Itō Shinsui 伊東深水 (1898–1972)

Snowstorm

(*Fubuki* 吹雪)

Series: *The Second Collection
of Modern Beauties
(Gendai bijinshū dai-nishū*
現代美人集第二輯)
Date: December 1932
Signature: *Shinsui ga*
Artist's seal: *Shinsui*
Edition: 240/250
Publisher: Watanabe Shōzaburō
Size: 44.2 × 27.4 cm
Collection Scholten

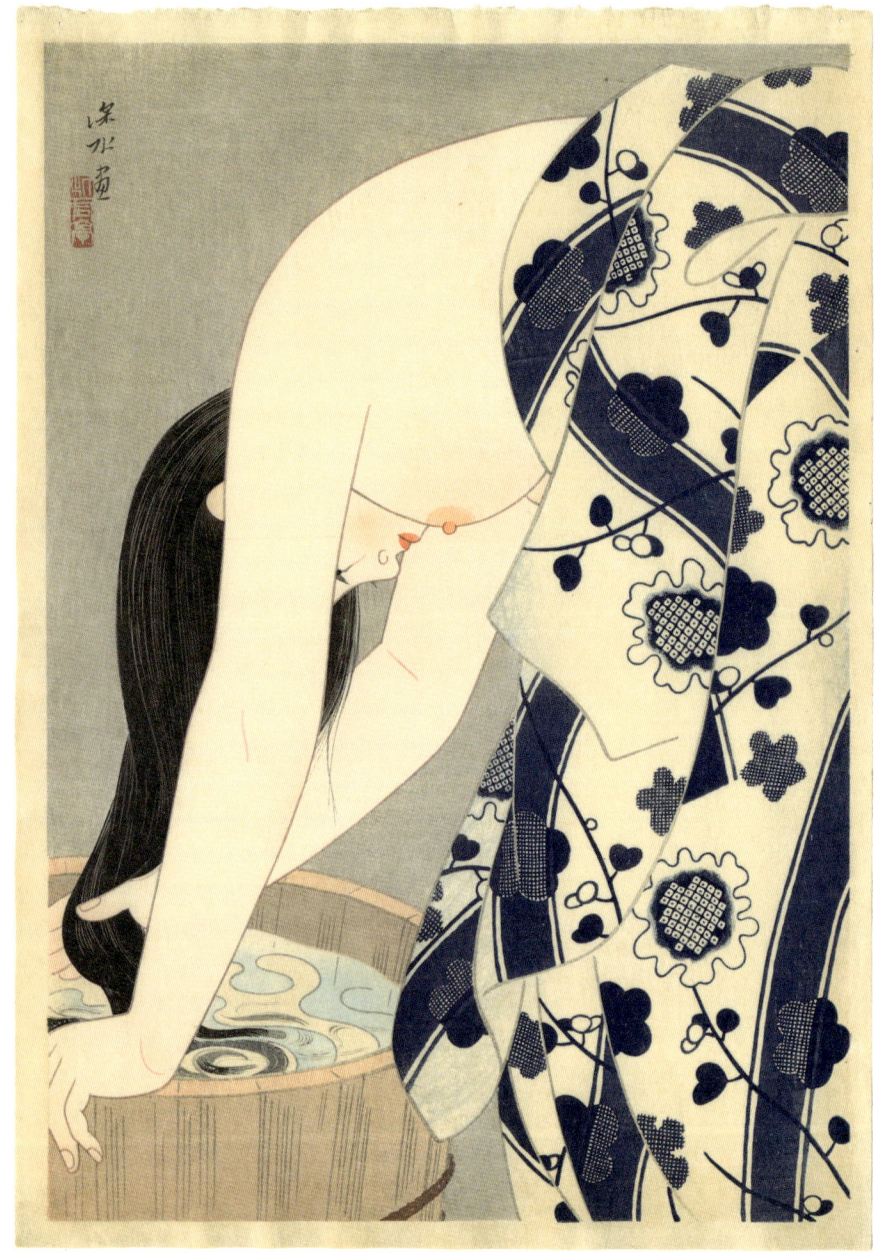

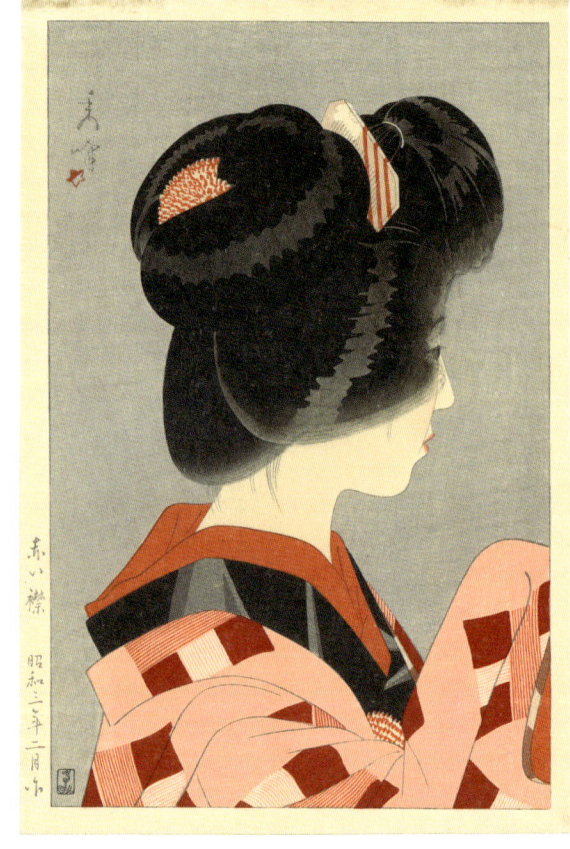

Cat. 93

Itō Shinsui 伊東深水 (1898–1972)

Washing the Hair

(*Kami* 髪)

Date: September 1952
Signature: *Shinsui ga*
Artist's seal: *Shikuntei*
Publisher: Bunkazai Hogo Iinkai
(Committee for the Protection
of Cultural Assets of Japan)
Block cutter: *Maeda Kentarō*
Printer: *Ono Gintarō*
Size: 51.9 × 37 cm
Collection Scholten

Shinsui based this design on a two-panel screen painted four years earlier. This exquisite print, made using 39 superimposed printings, is enlivened by a mica background. It was commissioned on the occasion of the designation of the traditional craft of woodblock printing as an Intangible Cultural Property (*Mukei Bunkazai Gijiutsu Hozon*). It was published by the Committee for the Protection of Cultural Assets of Japan (*Bunkazai Hogo Iinkai*). With this in mind, the print came with a label on the reverse with information in Japanese and English. (PO)

Cat. 94

Yamakawa Shūhō 山川秀峰
(1898–1944)

Red Collar

(*Akai eri* 赤い襟)

Series: *Four Images of Women*
(*Fujo yondai* 婦女四題)
Date: February 1928
Signature: *Shūhō*
Artist's seal: maple-leaf-shaped seal
Publisher: Bijutsu-sha
Size: 38.9 × 26.8 cm
Private collection, the Netherlands

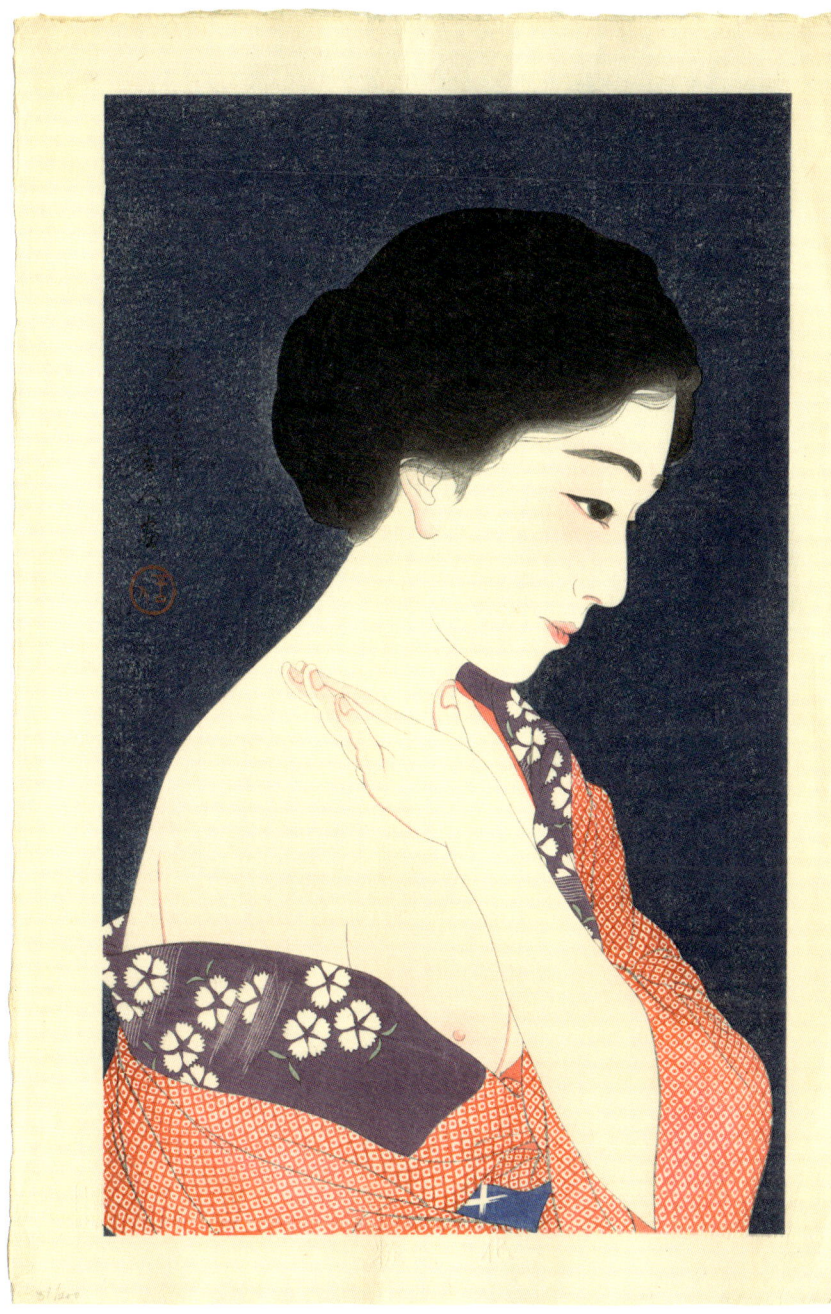

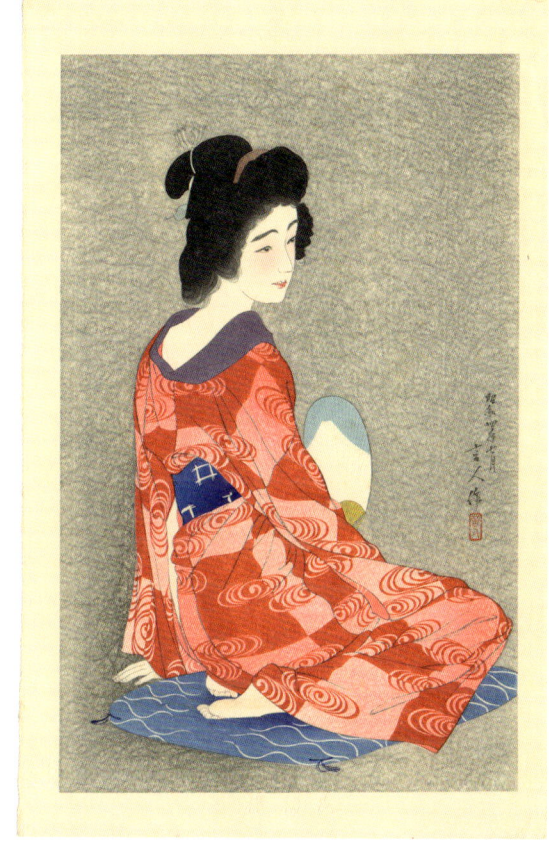

Cat. 95

Torii Kotondo 鳥居言人 (1900–76)

Make-up

(*Keshō* 化粧)

Date: June 1929
Signature: *Kotondo ga*
Artist's seal: *Kotondo*
Edition: 81/200 (labelled 'export edition')
Publisher: Sakai-Kawaguchi
Block cutter: *Itō* (full name unknown)
Printer: *Komatsu Wasakichi*
Size: 46 × 30 cm
Collection Scholten

This is a striking design of a woman elegantly raising her little finger as she powders her neck and shoulder. The gritty texture of the background is created when the printer presses his *baren* against the paper in such a way that its pressure marks become visible. In the lower left corner, in blind-printing we find the names of the joint publishing team of Sakai Shōkichi and Kawaguchi Jirō. Two hundred copies were printed of the first edition. Kawaguchi released a second edition of 300 as well as unnumbered prints.

(PO)

Cat. 96

Torii Kotondo 鳥居言人 (1900–76)

Long Undergarment

(*Nagajuban* 長襦袢)

Date: July 1929
Signature: *Kotondo saku*
Artist's seal: *Kotondo*
Edition: 63/200 (labelled 'export edition')
Publisher: Sakai-Kawaguchi
Size: 46 × 30 cm
Collection Scholten

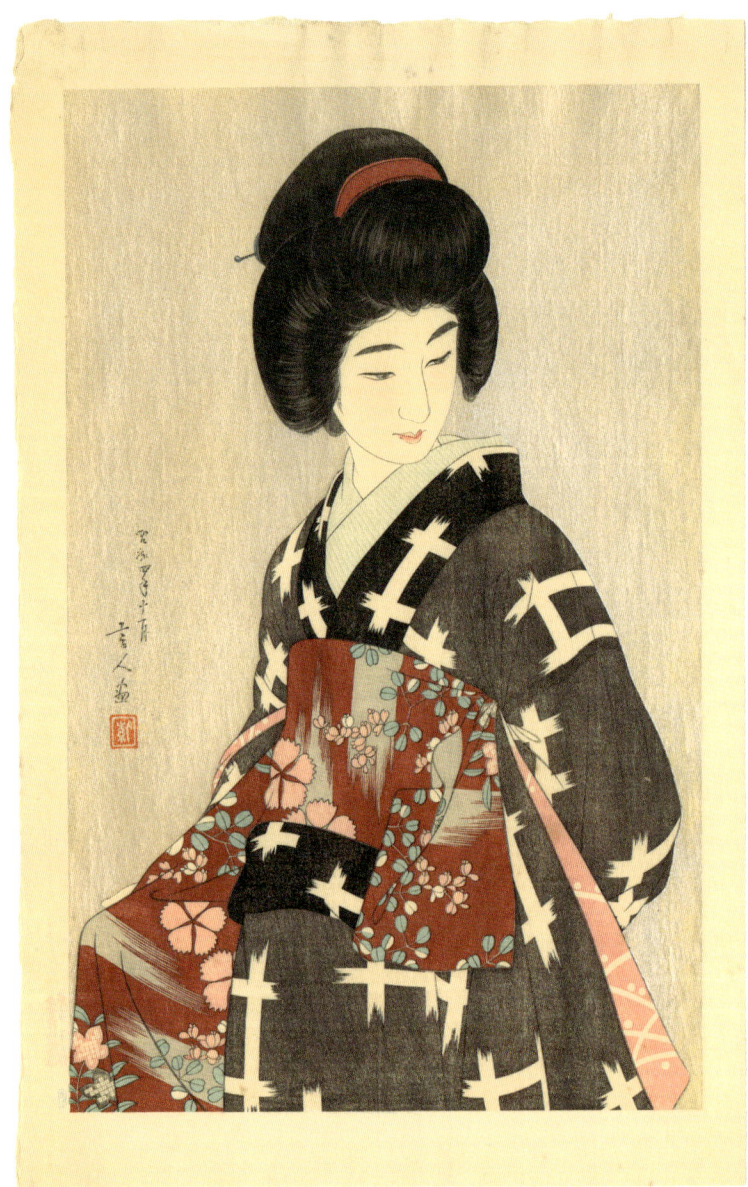 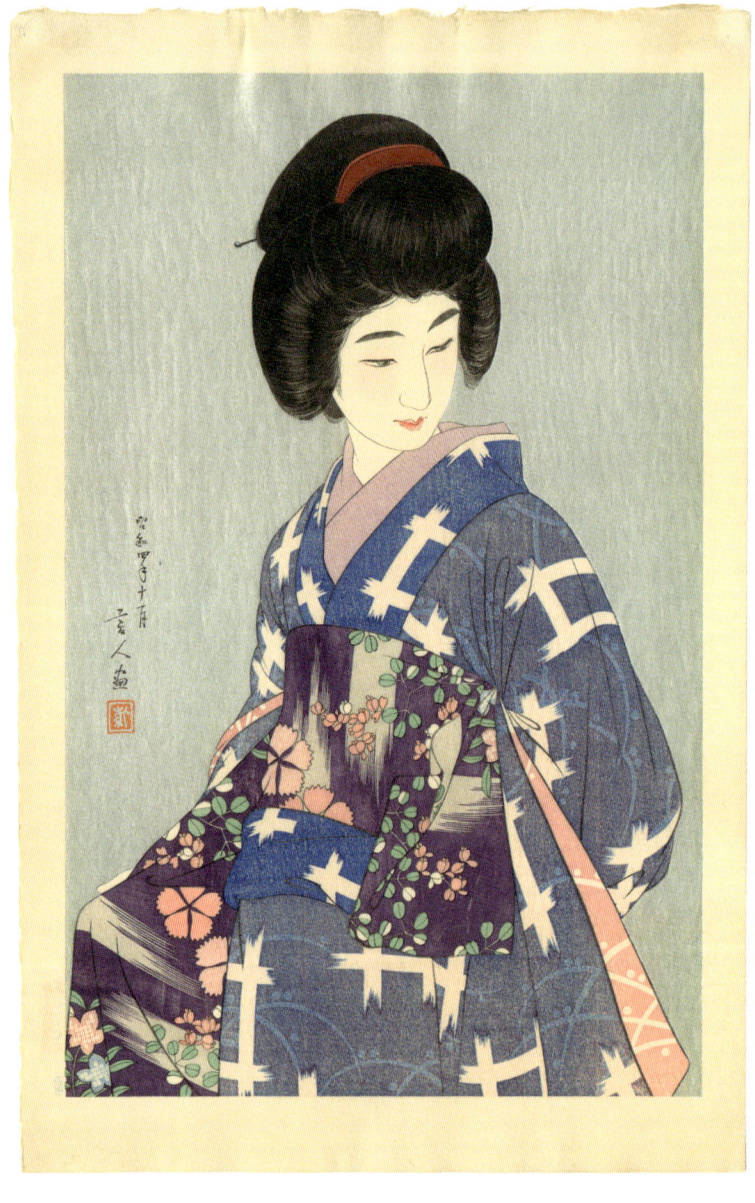

Cat. 97a (black kimono) & 97b (blue kimono)

Torii Kotondo 鳥居言人 (1900–76)

Sash

(*Obi* 帯)

Date: November 1929
Signature: *Kotondo ga*
Artist's seal: *Shi*
Edition: 139/350 (a), 125/350 (b)
Publisher: Kawaguchi
Size: 46.5 × 30 cm
Private collection, the Netherlands

This print is a fine example of how far woodblock printing technology had come under the *shin hanga* movement. The glittering layer of mica in the background was printed over a layer of ink. As the edition was printed in multiple colour combinations this resulted in dazzling scenes in various shades. Besides the two examples here, a third state that bears no publisher's information is known, possibly a trial print, in which both dress and sash are red.

(JD)

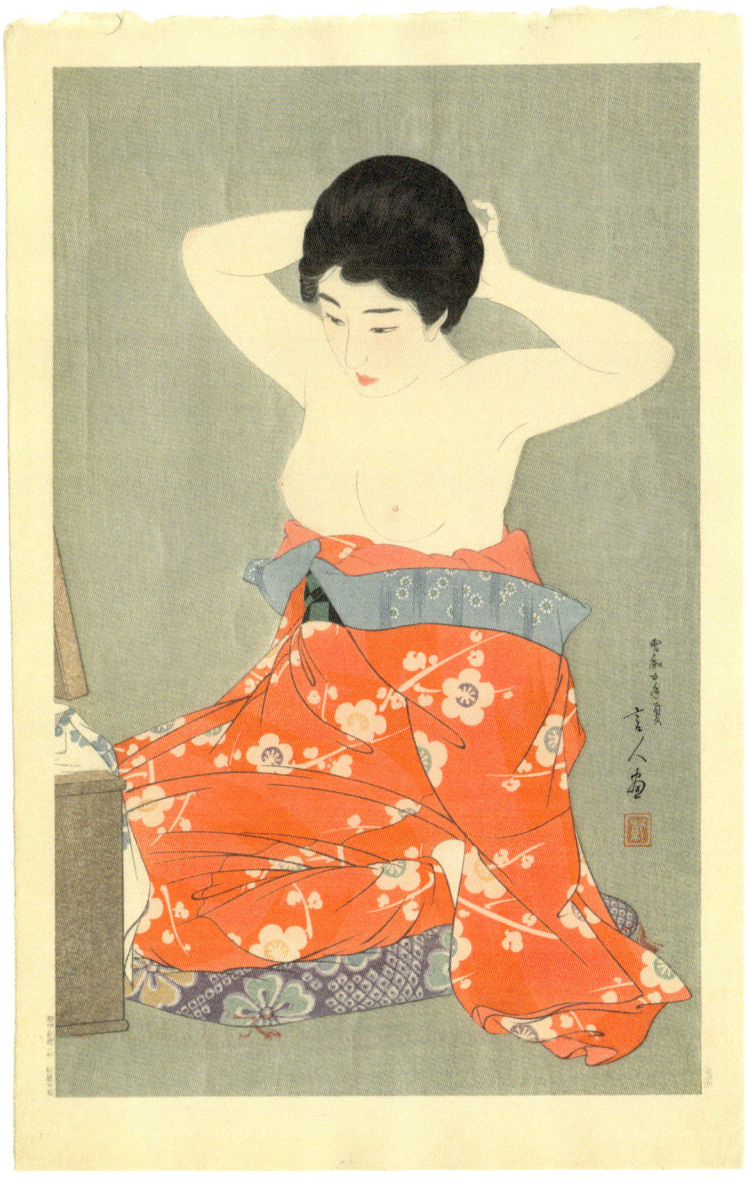

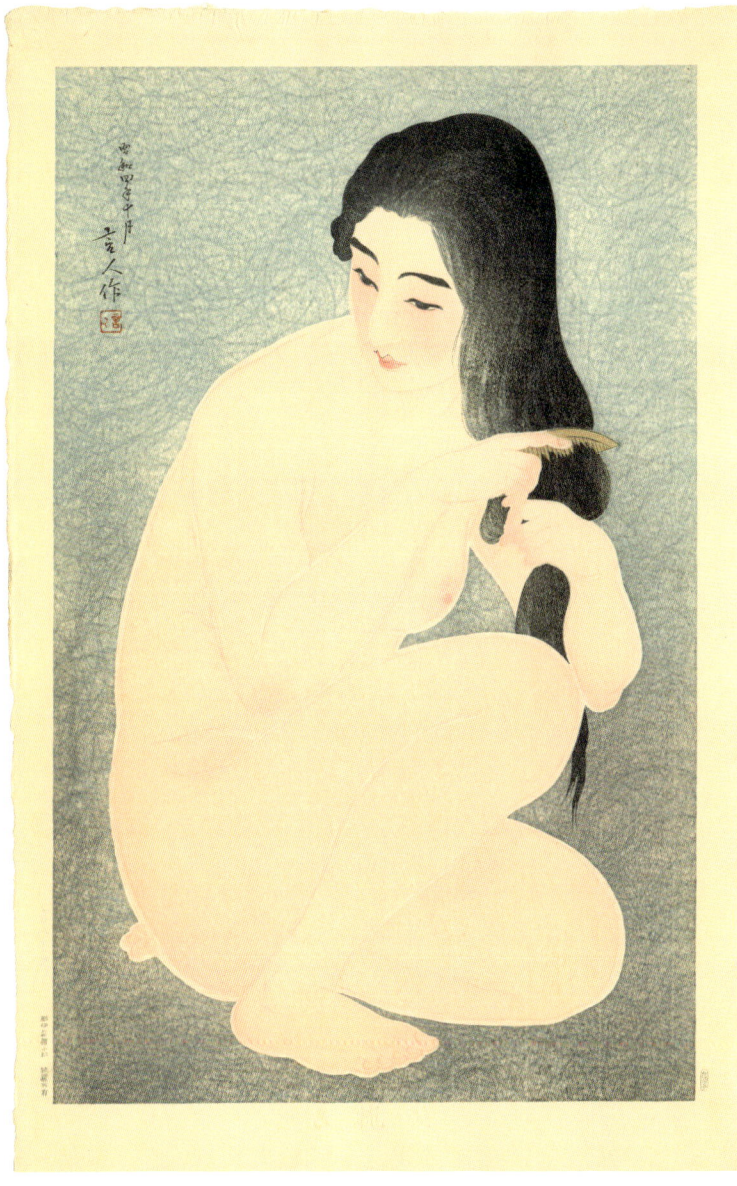

Cat. 98

Torii Kotondo 鳥居言人 (1900–76)

Make-up

(*Keshō* 化粧)

Date: Summer 1930
Signature: *Kotondo ga*
Artist's seal: *Shi*
Edition: 201/350
Publisher: Kawaguchi
Block cutter: *Itō* (full name unknown)
Printer: *Komatsu* (Komatsu Wasakichi)
Size: 46 × 29.5 cm
Collection Scholten

Cat. 99

Torii Kotondo 鳥居言人 (1900–76)

Combing her Hair

(*Kamisuki* 髪梳き)

Date: October 1930
Signature: *Kotondo saku*
Artist's seal: *Kotondo*
Edition: 187/300
Publisher: Kawaguchi
Block cutter: *Itō* (full name unknown)
Printer: *Komatsu* (Komatsu Wasakichi)
Size: 46 × 29.5 cm
Collection Scholten

The mosquito net in the background tells us that the woman is still waking up after a hot summer's night. *Asanegami*, or 'morning hair', is a poetic word used in tales and verses since at least the 8th century. It evokes the image of a woman lying in her bed and thinking of her lover. The prints published by Ikeda were of the highest quality. To guarantee his customers that his prints were truly from a limited edition, Ikeda ordered his carvers to damage the key block after the hundredth impression. His clientele would receive a monochrome print of the gouged block as proof (see Fig. 4). It is said that the authorities deemed the theme of this design too salacious, and Ikeda was forced to halt the printing after 70 impressions. Unsold prints were confiscated, making this design one of the rarest *shin hanga* prints. Both the colour print and the monochrome key block bear the red collector's seal of Mr Shimoyama, a regular patron of Kotondo. (JD)

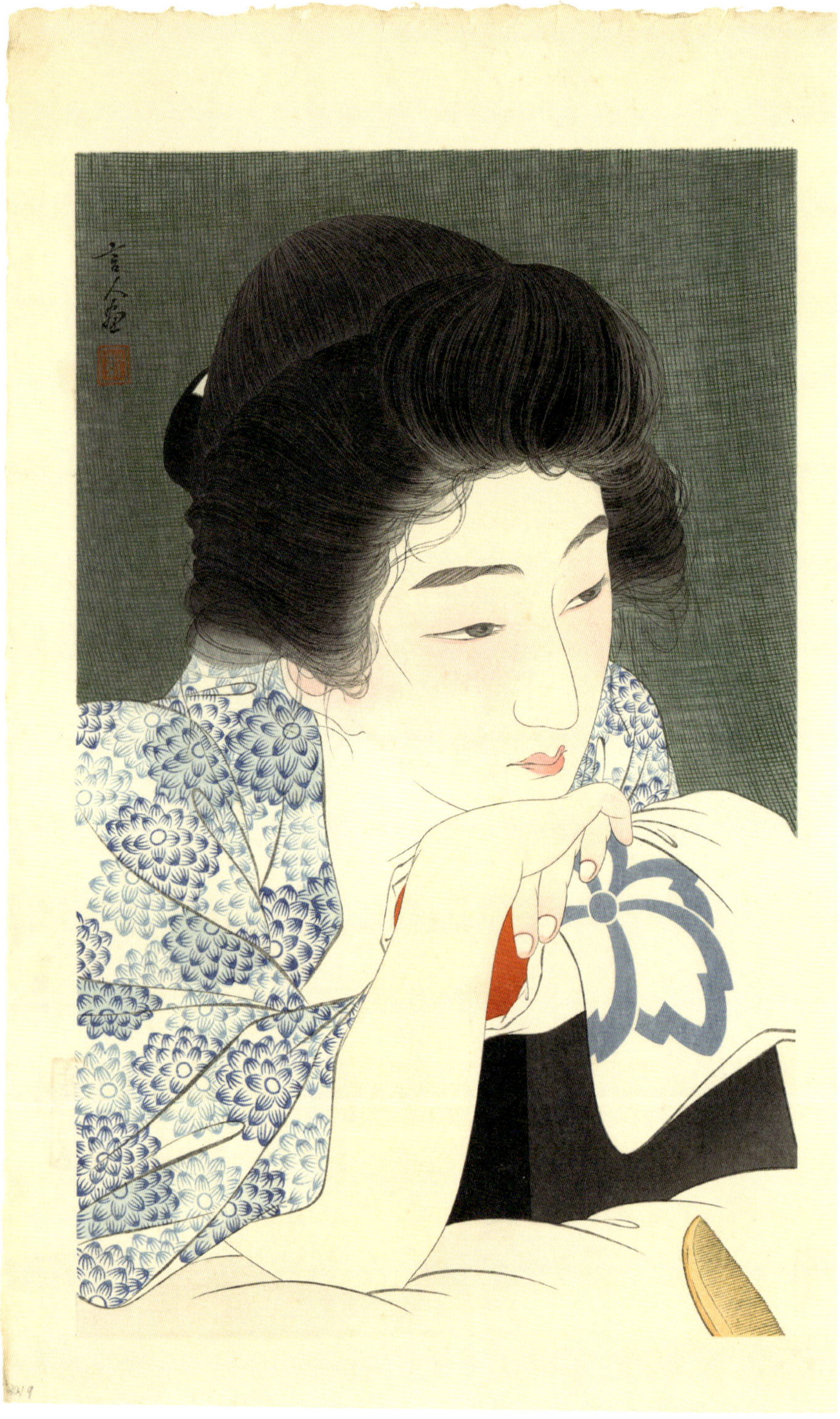

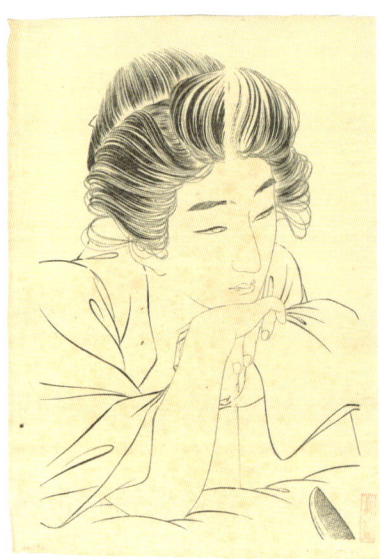

Fig. 4
Print of the destroyed key block for *Morning Hair*
Size: 42 × 29.5 cm

Cat. 100

Torii Kotondo 鳥居言人 (1900–76)

Morning Hair

(*Asanegami* 朝寝髪)

Date: November 1931
Signature: *Kotondo ga*
Artist's seal: *Kotondo*
Edition: 25/100
Publisher: Ikeda shoten (Ikeda publishing company)
Block cutter: *Maeda Kentarō*
Printer: *Maejima* (full name unknown)
Size: 48 × 29.5 cm
Private collection, the Netherlands

Torii Kotondo 鳥居言人 (1900–76)
Combing her Hair
(*Kamisuki* 紙梳き)

Date: 1933
Signature: *Kotondo ga*
Artist's seal: *Torii*
Edition: 83/100
Publisher: Ikeda shoten
(Ikeda publishing company)
Size: 47 × 29.8 cm
Private collection, the Netherlands

Unlike many other students of Kaburaki Kiyokata, Kotondo did not collaborate with Watanabe Shōzaburō but chose to work with the joint publishers' team of Sakai Shōkichi and Kawaguchi Jirō and, later in his career, with Ikeda shoten, as is the case with this print. Kotondo's beauties typically all wear traditional Japanese clothing at a time when Western fashion was becoming increasingly popular. Kotondo's beauties aim to embody the more traditional image of Japanese women, which appealed to both Japanese and Western collectors. They call to mind the aesthetic of *iki*: a refined, subdued sense of style and elegance.

(PO)

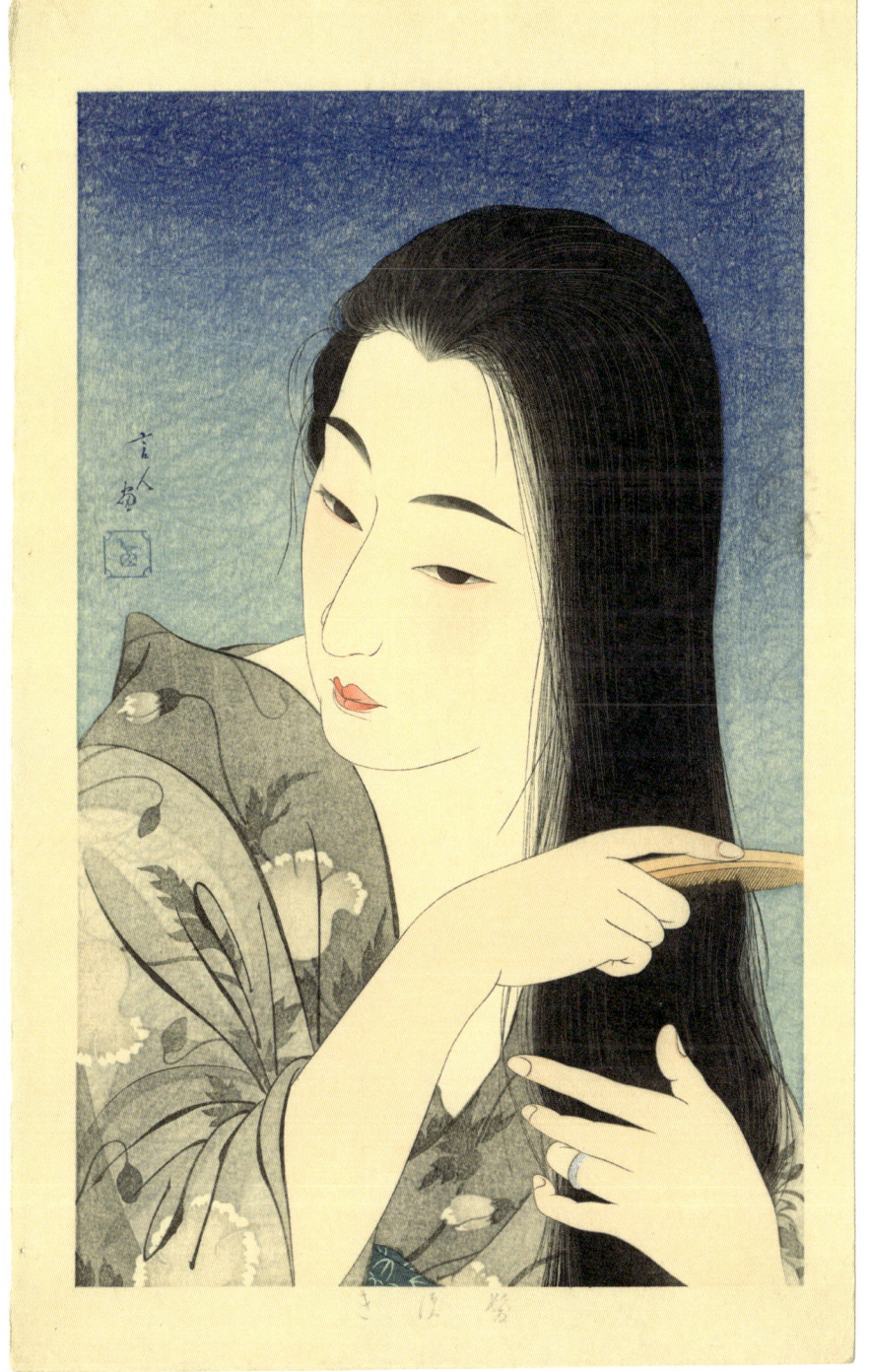

Cat. 102

Torii Kotondo 鳥居言人 (1900–76)
Coming out of the Bathhouse
(*Yugaeri* 湯がえ里)

Date: 1933
Signature: *Kotondo ga*
Artist's seal: *Kotondo*
Edition: 60/100
Publisher: Ikeda shoten
(Ikeda publishing company)
Size: 47.5 × 29.5 cm
Collection Scholten

A young woman, modelled after Kotondo's wife, is seen exiting a bathhouse, walking through the *noren* curtain hanging over its entrance. On her arm she carries a small basket, towel on top. Her face is still flushed from the hot water of the bath.
(PO)

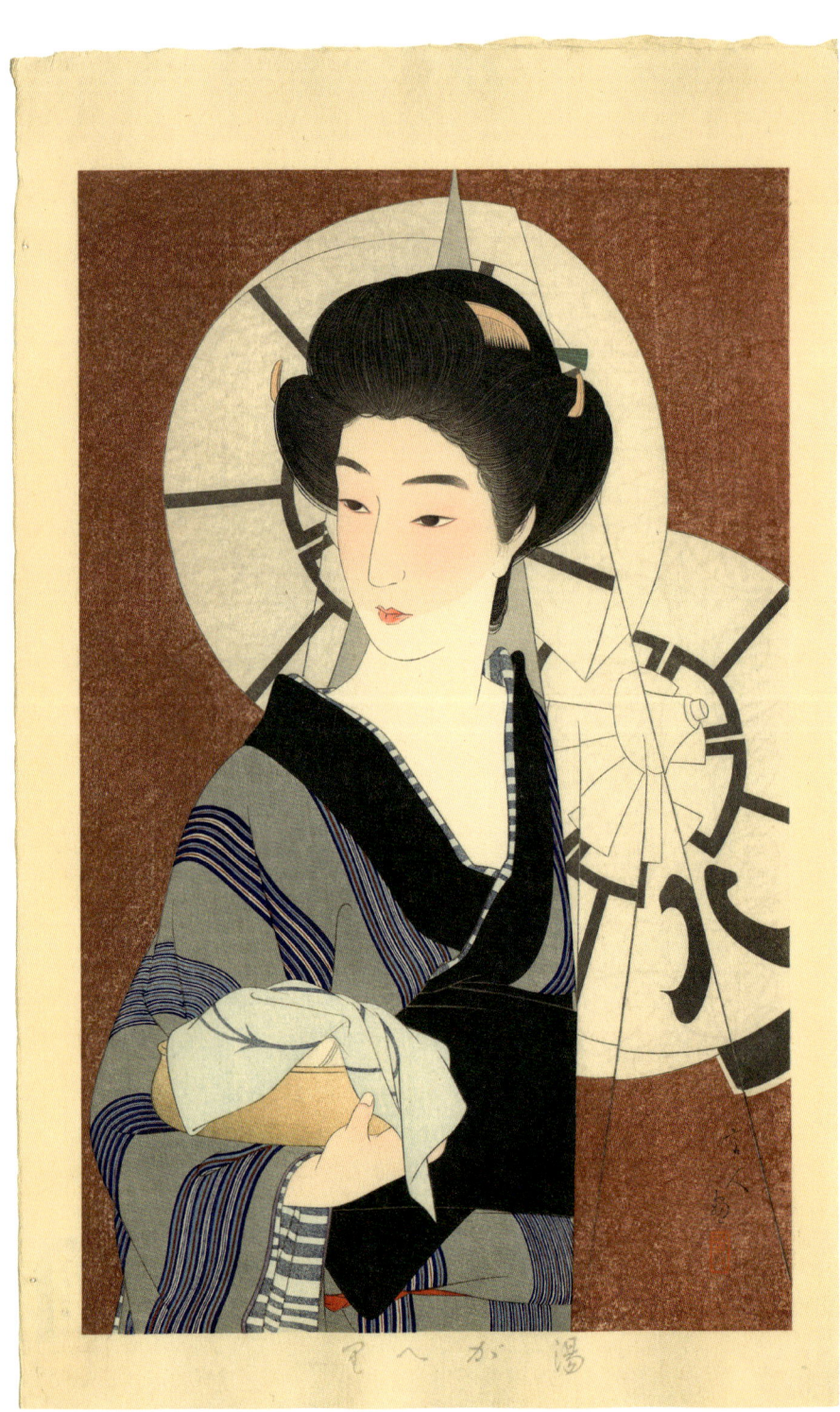

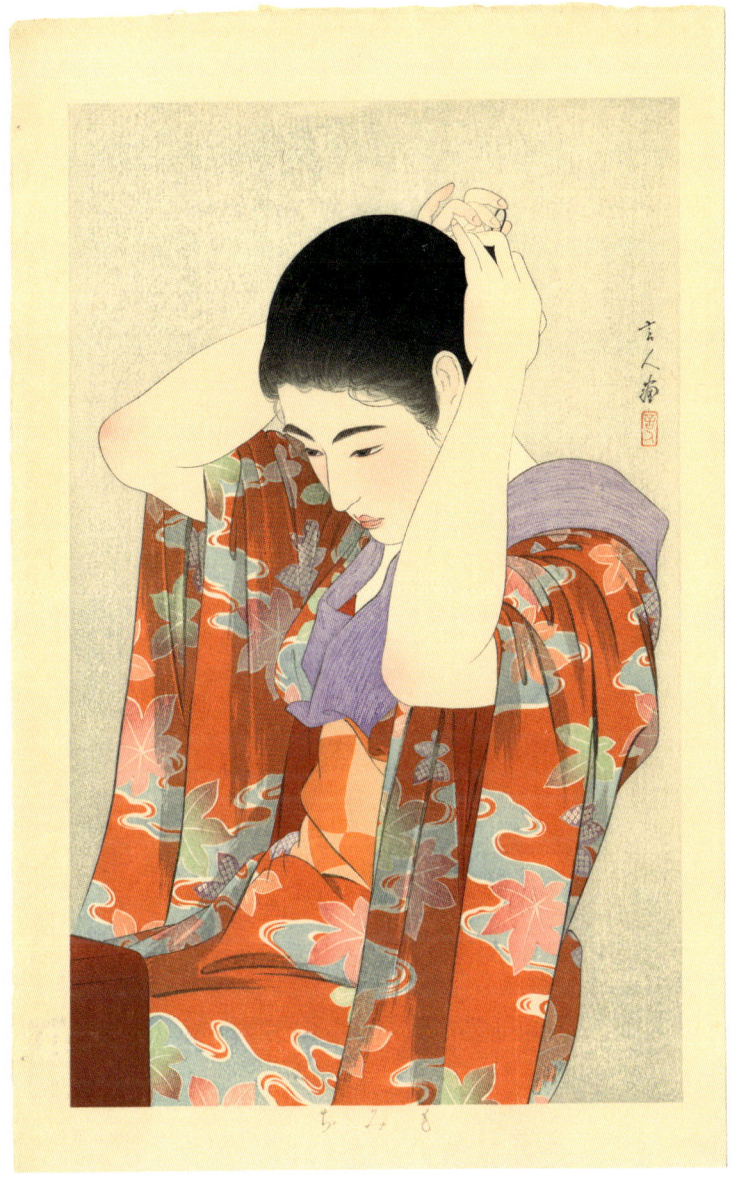

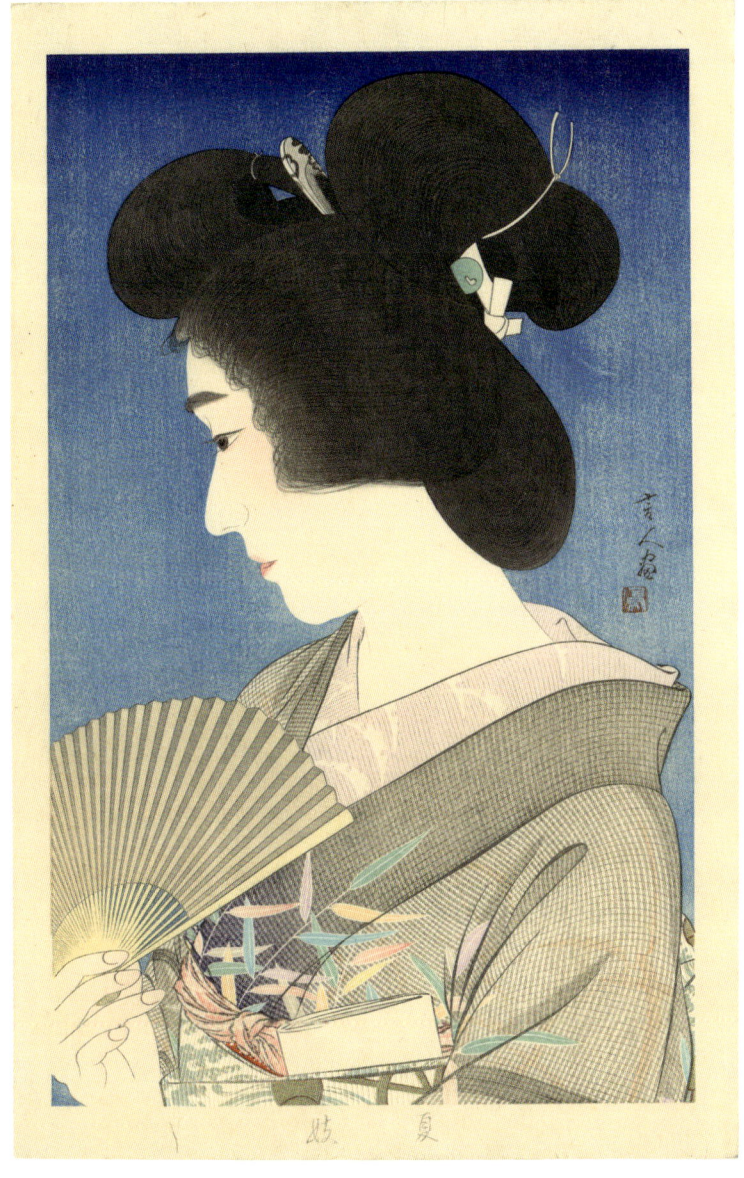

Cat. 103

Torii Kotondo 鳥居言人 (1900–76)

Autumn Leaves

(*Momiji* もみじ)

Date: 1933
Signature: *Kotondo ga*
Artist's seal: *Kotondo*
Edition: 20/100
Publisher: Ikeda shoten
(Ikeda publishing company)
Size: 47 × 29.7 cm
Private collection, the Netherlands

Cat. 104

Torii Kotondo 鳥居言人 (1900–76)

Geisha in Summer Style

(*Natsuko* 夏妓)

Date: 1934
Signature: *Kotondo ga*
Artist's seal: *Kotondo*
Edition: -/100 (blank)
Publisher: Ikeda shoten
(Ikeda publishing company)
Size: 45 × 29 cm
Private collection, the Netherlands

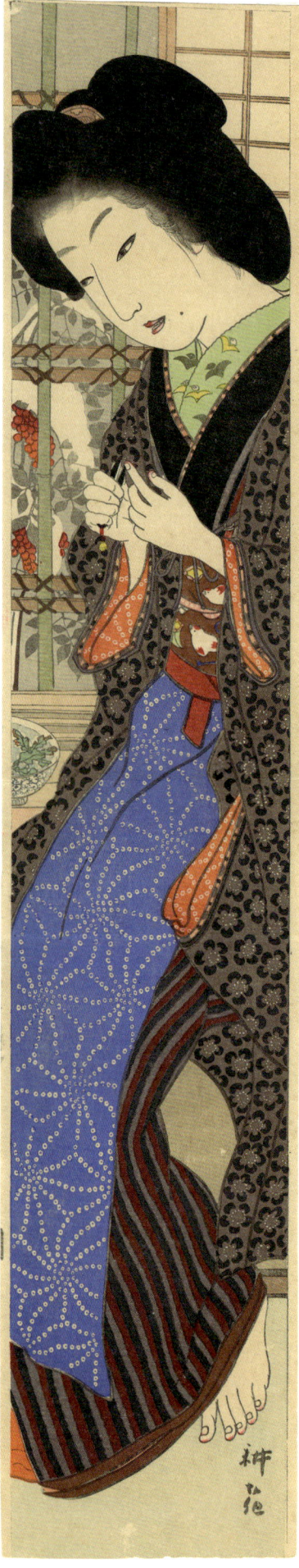

Cat. 105

Yamamura Kōka (Toyonari)
山村耕花 (豊成) (1885–1942)

**A Typical Daughter
of Downtown Edo**

(*Shitamachi no musume* 下町の娘)

Date: before 1935
Signature: *Kōka*
Publisher: unknown
Size: 74.2 × 14.7 cm
Collection Scholten

The pillar print (*hashira-e*) was an extremely popular type of print in the 18th and early 19th century, but in the 20th century only one design is known to exist in this format.
(CU)

Cat. 106

Hirano Hakuhō 平野白峰
(1879–1957)

Summer Kimono (Beppu)

(*Natsu sugata [Beppu]* 夏姿 [別府])

Date: Summer 1936
Signature: *Hakuhō*
Artist's seal: *Hakuhō*
Publisher: Watanabe Shōzaburō
Size: 50.3 × 25 cm
Collection Scholten

Hakuhō was a self-taught *nihonga* painter, who produced only six *bijin* prints in collaboration with Watanabe Shōzaburō between 1932 and 1936. In four of his six known prints, the woman's face is obscured from view, its features left to the viewer's imagination.
(PO)

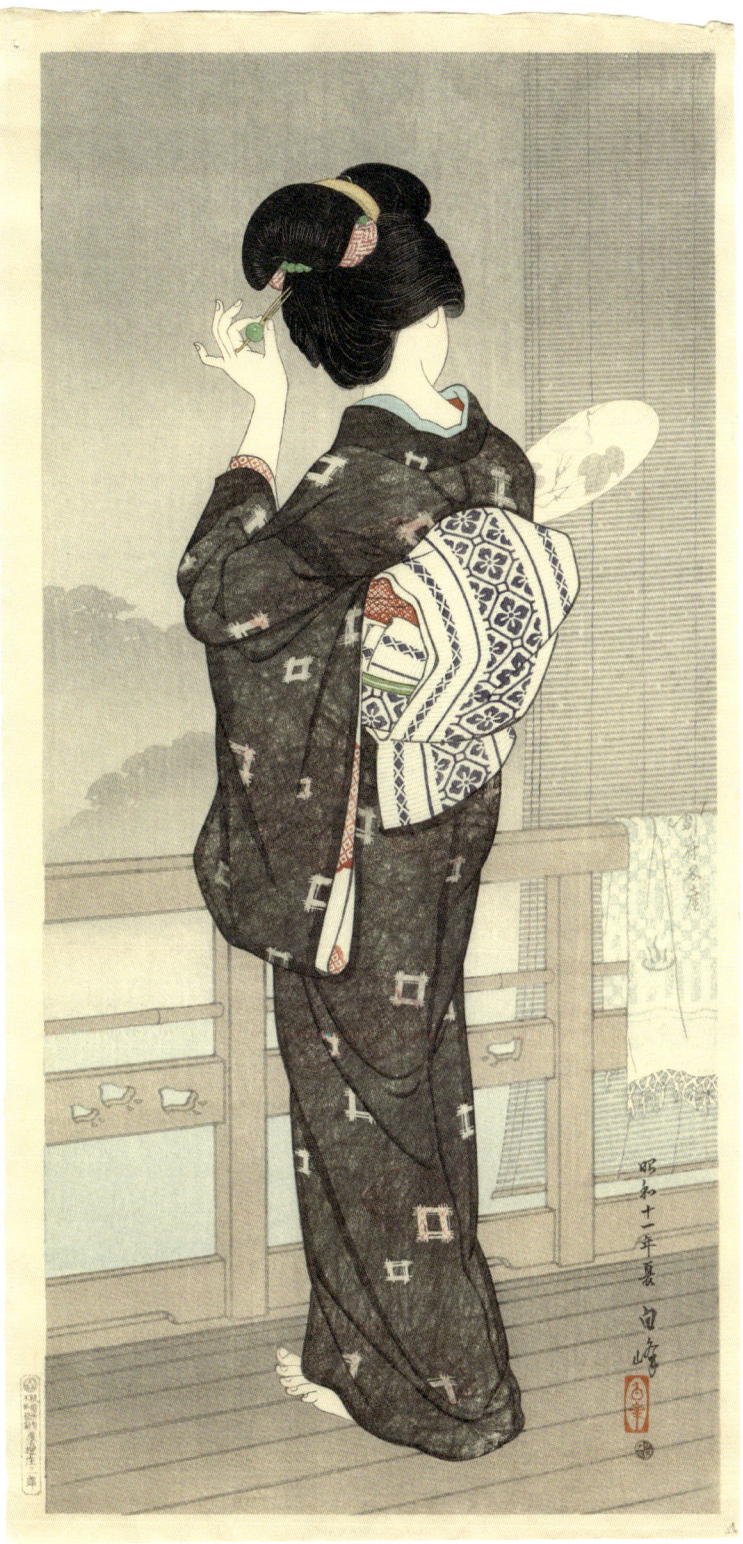

Cat. 107

Hirano Hakuhō 平野白峰
(1879–1957)

Before the Mirror

(*Kagami no mae* 鏡の前)

Date: January 1932
Signature: *Hakuhō ga*
Artist's seal: *Hakuhō*
Edition: 83/90
Publisher: Watanabe Shōzaburō
Size: 48 × 28.2 cm
Private collection, the Netherlands

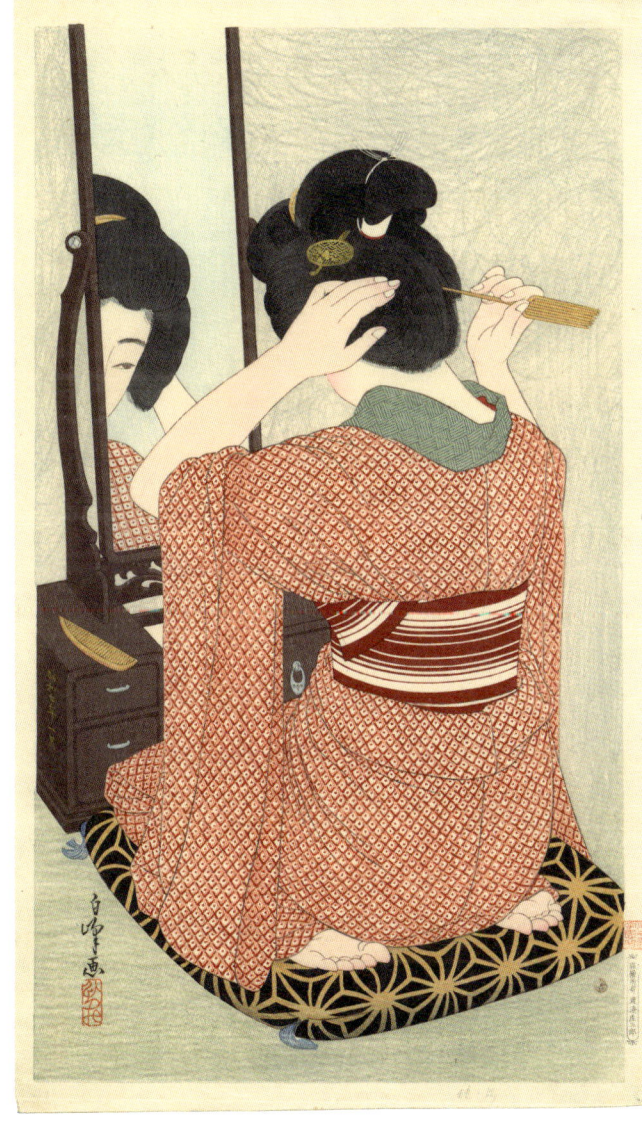

Cat. 108

Hirano Hakuhō 平野白峰
(1879–1957)

After a Bath

(*Yuagari* 湯上り)

Date: January 1932
Signature: *Hakuhō ga*
Artist's seal: *Hirano*
Edition: 18/100
Publisher: Watanabe Shōzaburō
Size: 43.6 × 27.9 cm
Collection Scholten

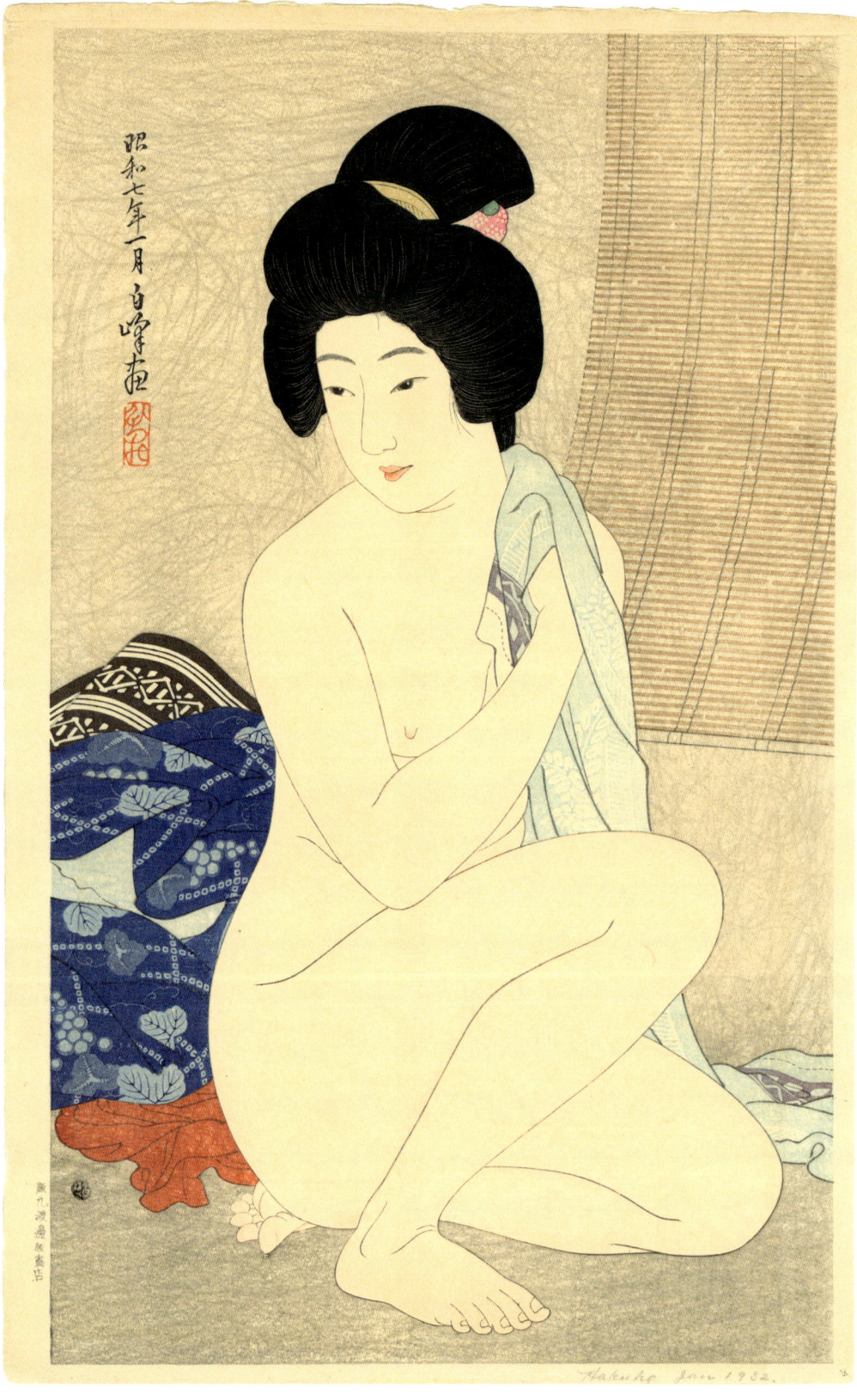

In this design the printer used the edge of the baren (the disk-shaped printing instrument) to create swirls in the background. This method was often used to add texture and more specifically, to suggest steam rising from the bath (see also Fig. 6, p. 14). Possibly Hakuhō was inspired by the (now extremely rare) and revolutionary print by Hashiguchi Goyō of a nude woman wringing out a towel. Both images feature a similar pose, with part of the chest exposed, but other private parts hidden from sight by a clever positioning of the figure's limbs (see Fig. 4, p. 12).

(CU)

This rear-view portrait of a woman before a mirror, turned slightly to her left, bears no publisher's marks but is recorded in the sales catalogue of the Watanabe Publishing company. Note the delicate pink shading on her fingers and cheek. Later impressions often lack this delicate colour (see also Cat. 99, p. 113 for a design by Kotondo with similar pinks).

(CU)

Cat. 109

Hirano Hakuhō 平野白峰
(1879–1957)
Woman before a Mirror
(*Kagami no mae no shōjo*
鏡の前少女)

Date: April 1932
Signature: *Hakuhō ga*
Artist's seal: *Haku*
Publisher: Watanabe Shōzaburō
Size: 39 × 27.9 cm
Collection Scholten

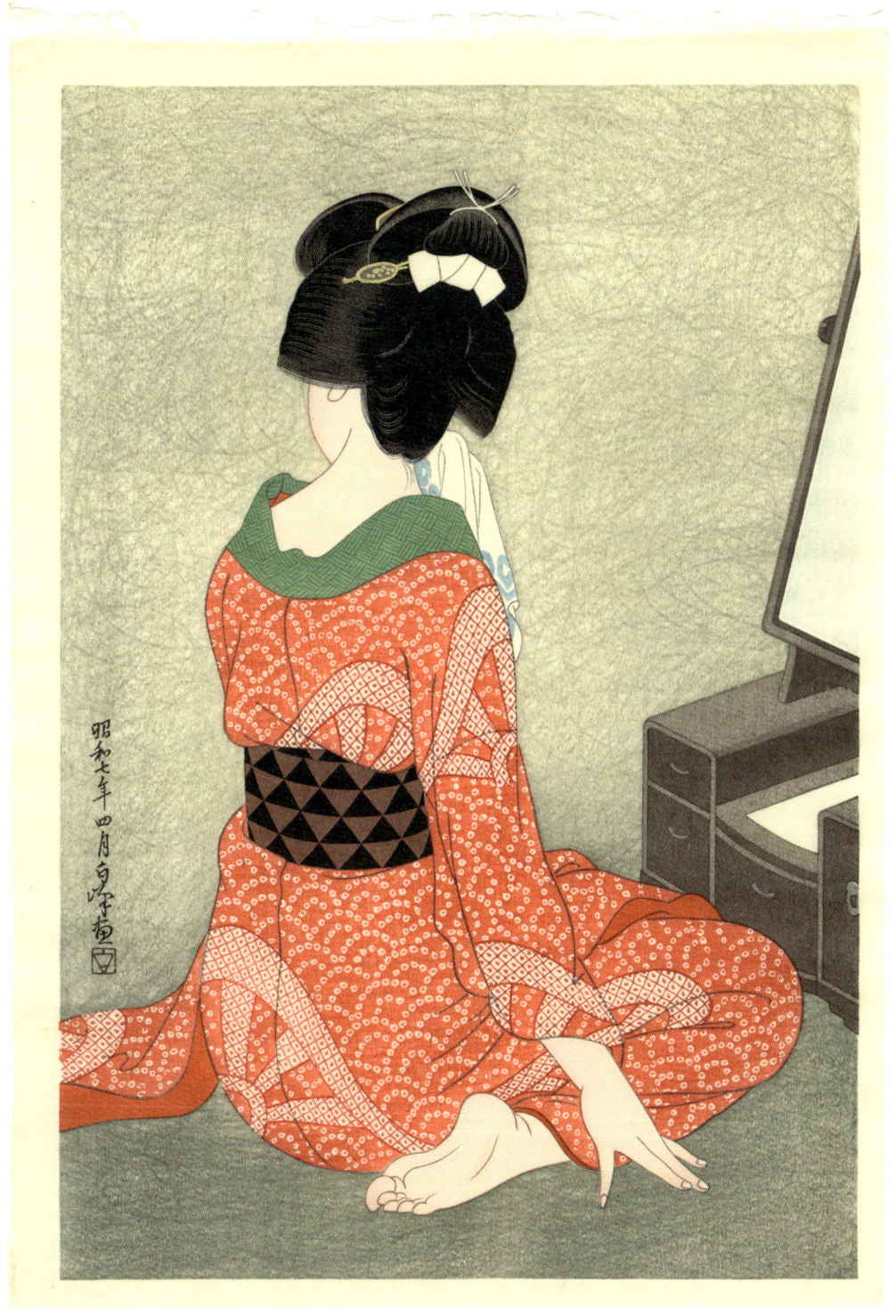

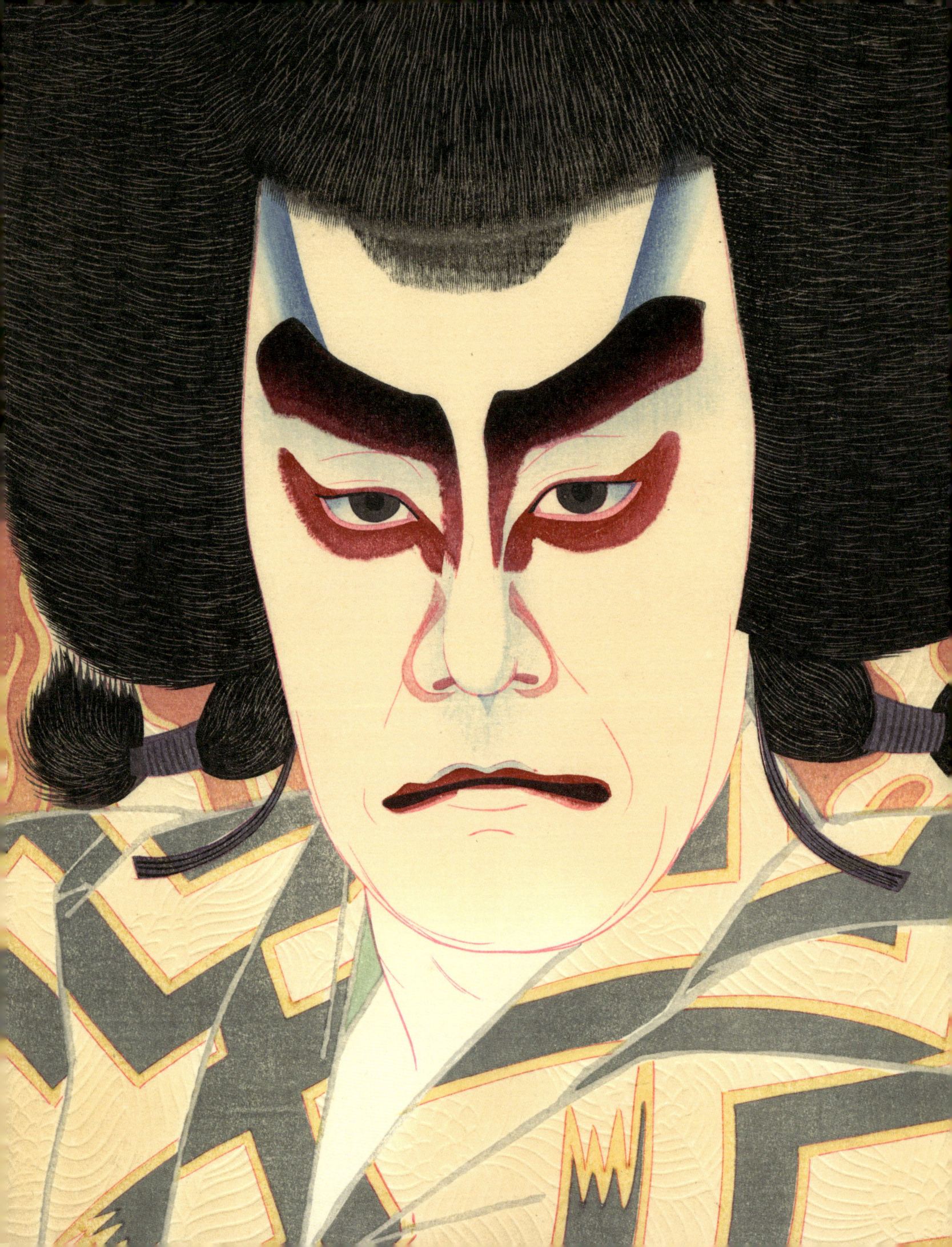

The Great Stars of the Kabuki Stage

The *shin hanga* movement could not ignore the kabuki theatre. Here the artists found inspiration in the portraits of the great 18th-century enigma Toshūsai Sharaku, reinventing his large head portraits (*ōkubi-e*) and setting them against glimmering mica backgrounds.

Cat. 110

Yamamura Kōka (Toyonari)
山村耕花 (豊成) (1885–1942)

**Kataoka Nizaemon XI as
Ōboshi Yuranosuke [in the play
Kanadehon Chūshingura]**

(*Jūissei Kataoka Nizaemon no
Ōboshi Yuranosuke* 十一世片岡仁左
衛門の大星由良之助)

Date: 1916
Signature: *Kōka ga*
Artist's seal: unread seal
Publisher: Watanabe Shōzaburō
Size: 35.5 × 24.5 cm
Private collection, the Netherlands

This print was Kōka's first *shin hanga* work, which he based on the *buromaido* (bromide) photographs of the actors. *Buromaido* was a category of commercial photographic portraits of celebrities printed on bromide paper. These were sold at performances in the kabuki theatres. He continued to model all his subsequent actor prints on such pictures. This design depicts the extremely popular Kataoka Nizaemon XI (1857–1934). Here he is shown in the role of Ōboshi Yuranosuke in the play *Kanadehon Chūshingura*, the famous story of the 47 *rōnin*, or masterless samurai, who had sworn to avenge their lord. It is thought that this print shows Yuranosuke leading the *rōnin* in a raid on the mansion of their antagonist, Moronō. The actor in this portrait has often been mistaken for the equally popular Nakamura Ganjirō I, as both actors had portrayed Yuranosuke not long before this print was made. However, this is undoubtedly Nizaemon XI, judging by the large hooked nose which characterizes his profile in other works as well (Cats. 115 and 119), as opposed to Ganjirō I's more balanced facial features (Cats. 114 and 117). Ironically, at the time this print was published there was an ongoing feud between the two performers, and they did not share a stage until they were reconciled after the earthquake of 1923.

(JD)

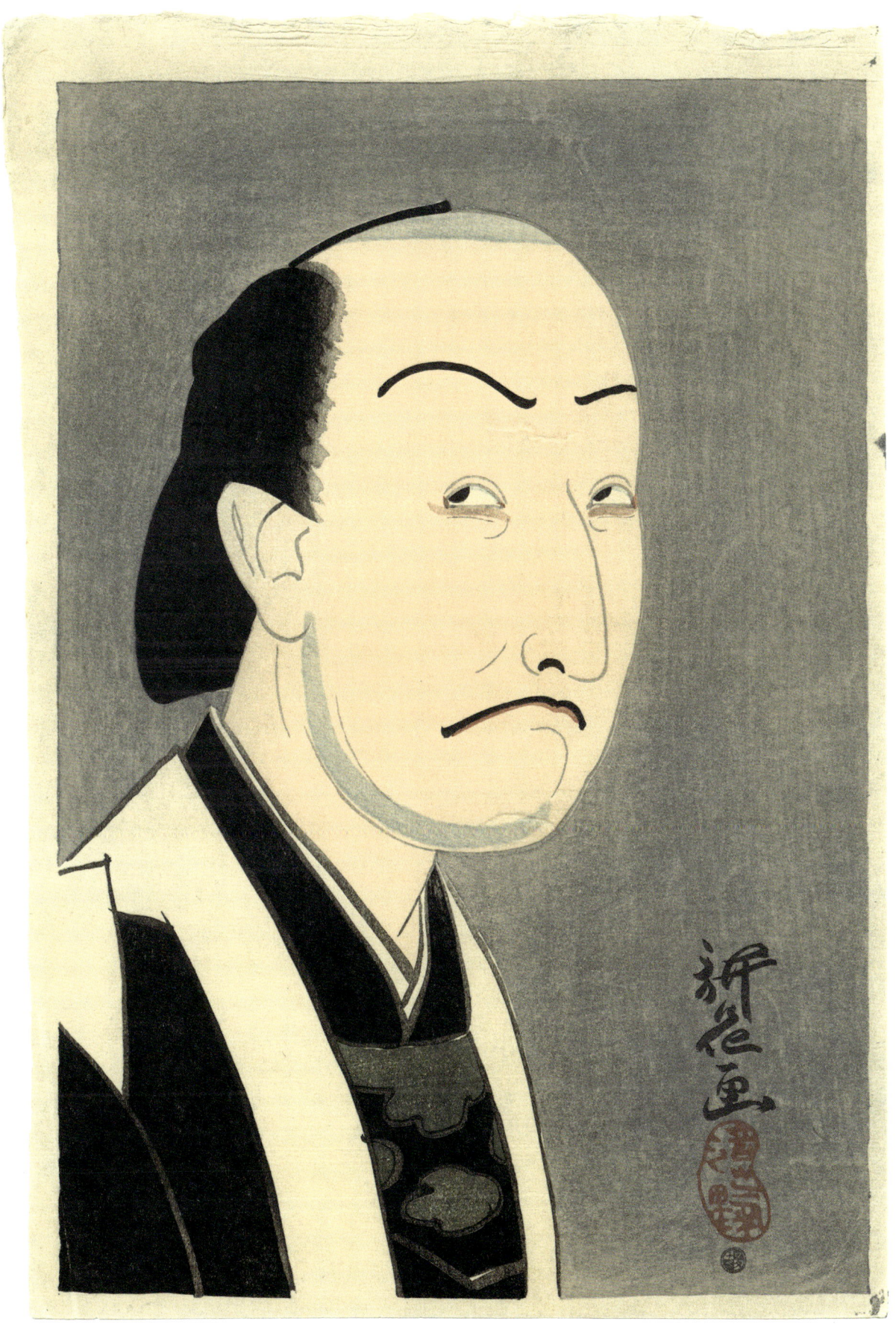

Cat. 111

Yamamura Kōka (Toyonari) 山村耕
花 (豊成) (1885–1942)

**Onoe Matsusuke IV as Kōmori
Yasu [in the play *Kirare Yosa*]**

(*Yonsei Onoe Matsusuke no Kōmori
Yasu* 四世尾上松助の蝙蝠安)

Date: 1917
Signature: *Kōka ga*
Artist's seal: *Ka*
Publisher: Watanabe Shōzaburō
Size: 41 × 29.2 cm
Collection Scholten

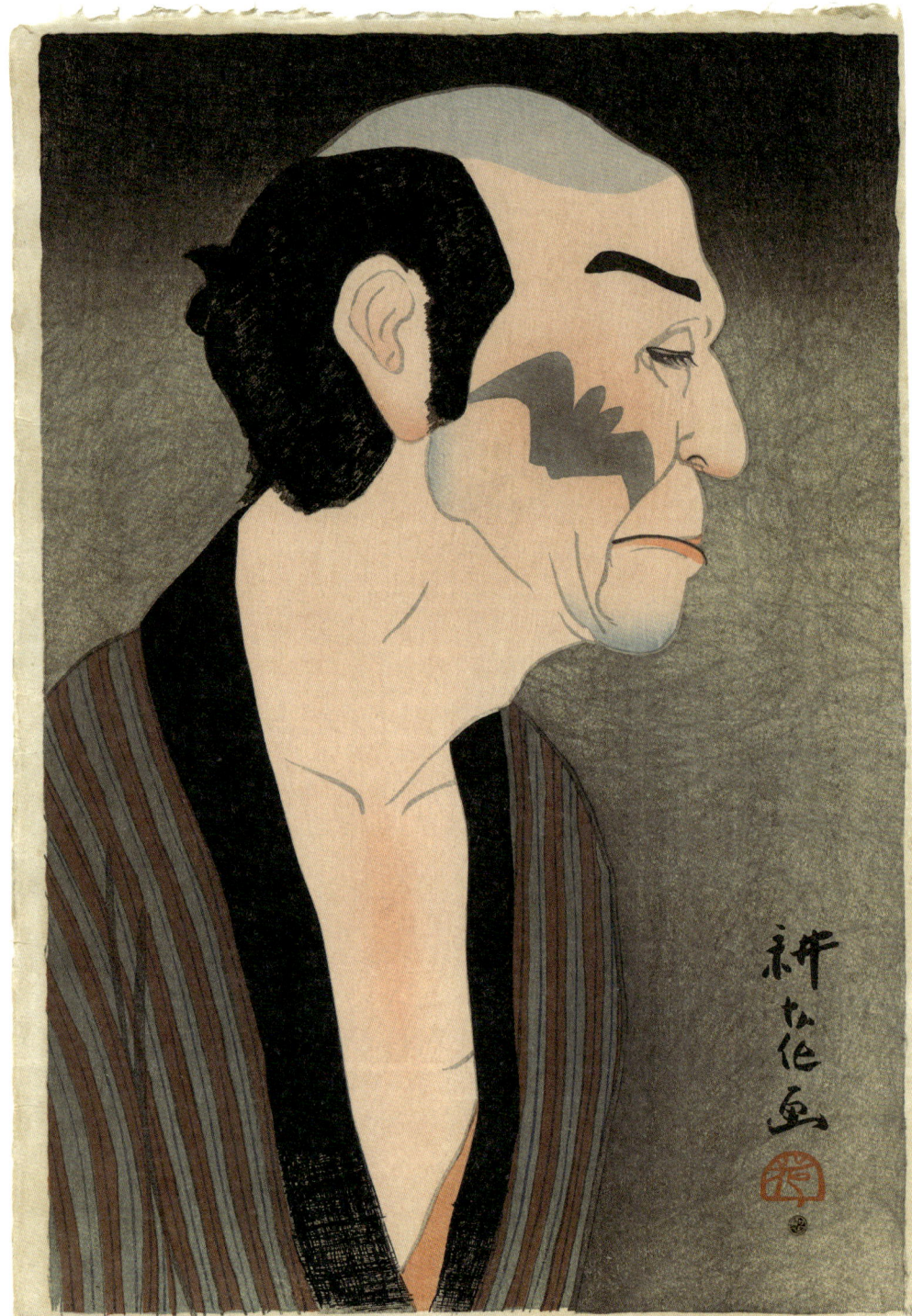

Kōka's second print, also published by Watanabe, depicts Onoe Matsusuke IV (1843–1928) in the play commonly known as *Kirare Yosa* (Carved-up Yosa). Here he is shown as Kōmori Yasu (Yasu 'the Bat'), a blackmailer who took his nickname from the bat tattoo on his face. The play centres round Yosaburō, also known as *Kirare* (Carved-up), a musician who had been mutilated with slashes because of his affair with a gang leader's mistress, Otomi. Years after the incident, he and Otomi meet again and discover that their love for each other has not faded. Kōka had depicted Matsusuke in the role of Yasu in similar fashion previously in one of his contributions to the 1915 kabuki project in issue 1 of *Shin nigao-e* (New Actor Portraits).
(JD)

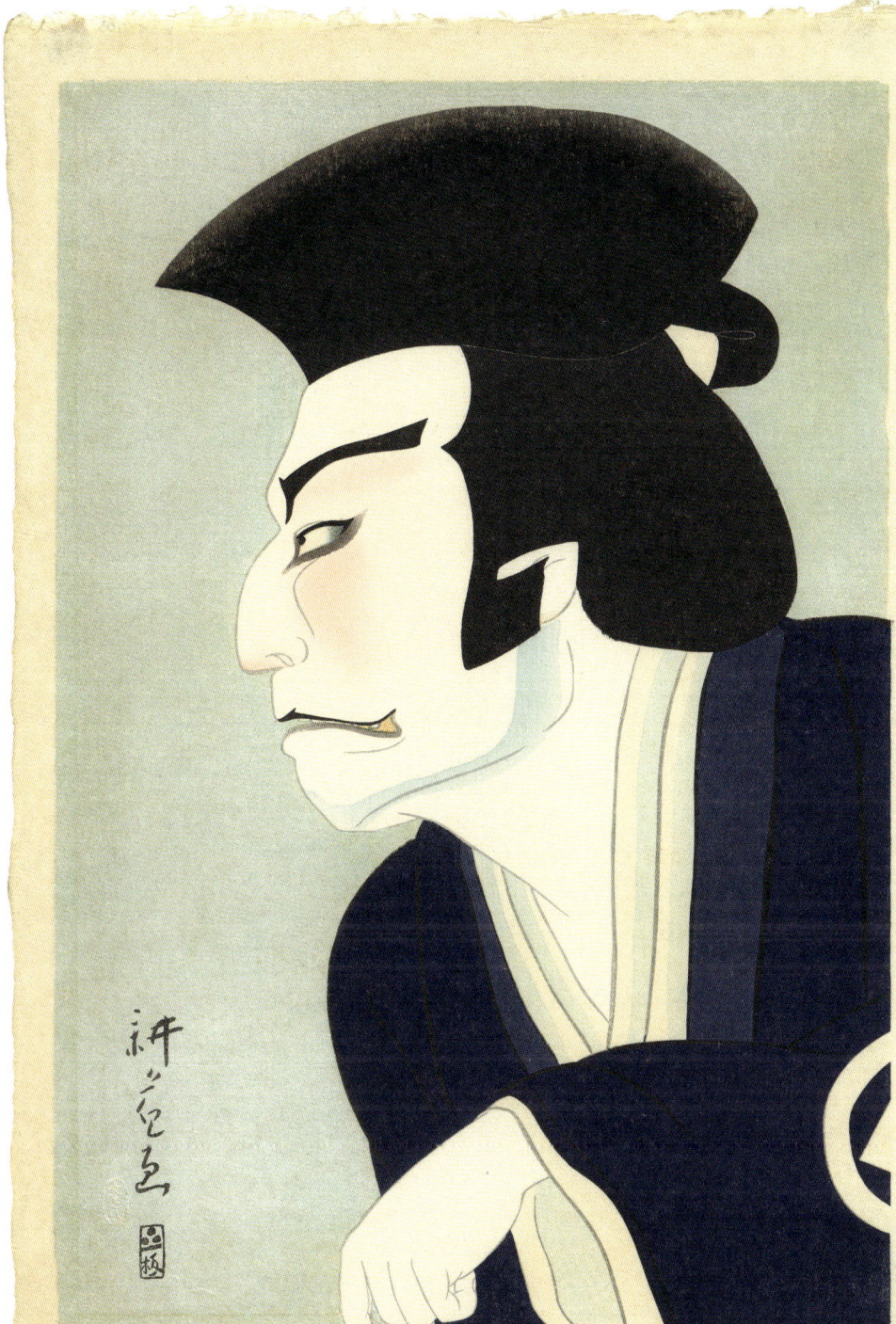

Cat. 112

Yamamura Kōka (Toyonari) 山村耕花 (豊成) (1885–1942)

Ichikawa Danshirō II as Henmi Tesshinsai [in the play *Kyōkaku harusame gasa*]

(*Nisei Ichikawa Danshirō no Henmi Tesshinsai* 二世市川段四郎の逸見鉄心斎)

Date: 1919
Signature: *Kōka ga*
Publisher: Watanabe Shōzaburō
Size: 40 × 27.6 cm
Private collection, the Netherlands

Kyōkaku harusame gasa (A Chivalrous Commoner, A Spring Rain Umbrella) was a *shin kabuki*, or new kabuki, play (see also Cat. 124) written by the noted journalist and critic Fukuchi Gen'ichirō (1841–1906), who in the late Meiji Period was active in the revitalization and reformation movements of kabuki. In January 1917 Ichikawa Danshirō II (1855–1922) performed the role of Henmi Tesshinsai, a notorious *rōnin* who exploits his samurai class privileges to terrorize the streets of Edo. His opponent, Ōguchiya Gyō'u, a *kyōkaku* – a chivalrous but rough street ruffian, also known as *otokodate* – who eventually defeats Tesshinsai and his gang, was played by Ichimura Uzaemon XV (depicted as Naozamurai in Cat. 118).
(JD)

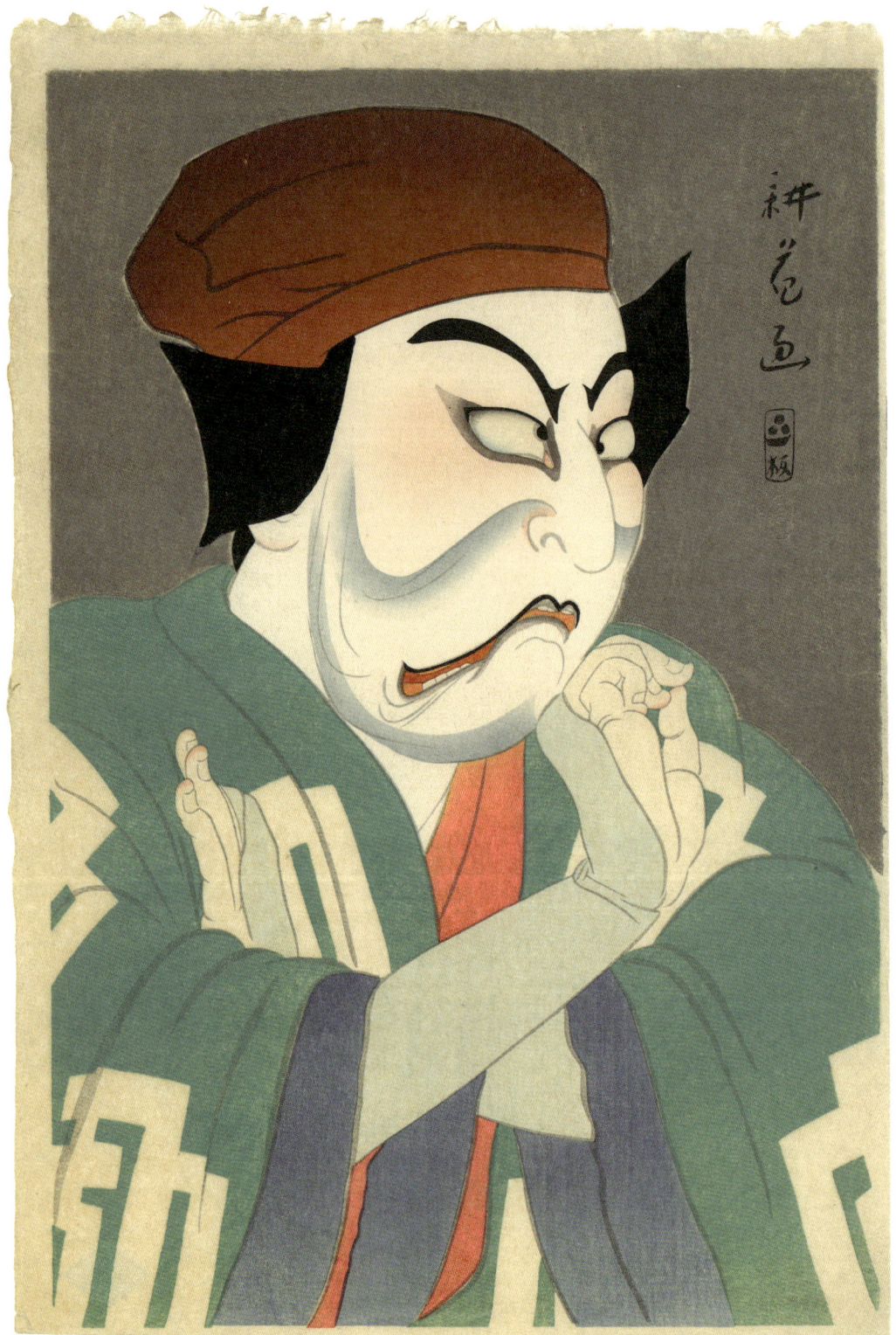

Cat. 113

Yamamura Kōka (Toyonari)
山村耕花 (豊成) (1885–1942)

Matsumoto Kōshirō VII as the Gatekeeper Sekibei [in the play *Tsumoru koi yuki seki no to*]

(Nanasei Matsumoto Kōshirō sekimori Sekibei 七世松本 幸四郎の 関守関兵衛)

Date: 1919
Signature: *Kōka ga*
Publisher: Watanabe Shōzaburō
Size: 39.9 × 27.2 cm
Private collection, the Netherlands

128

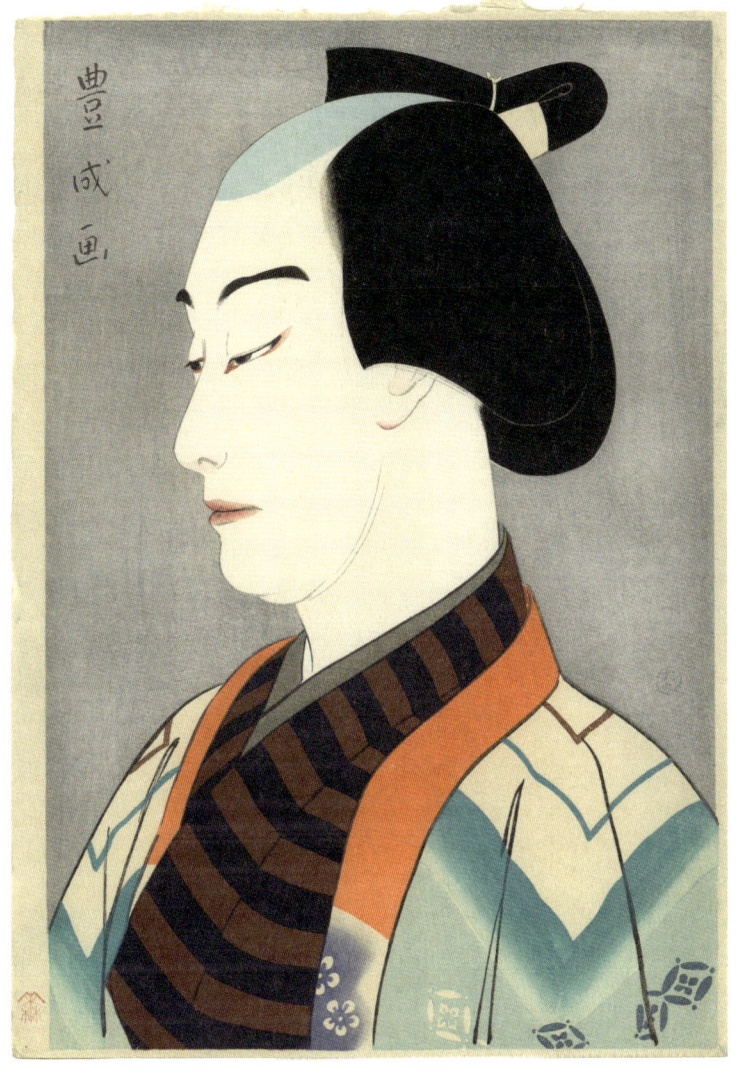

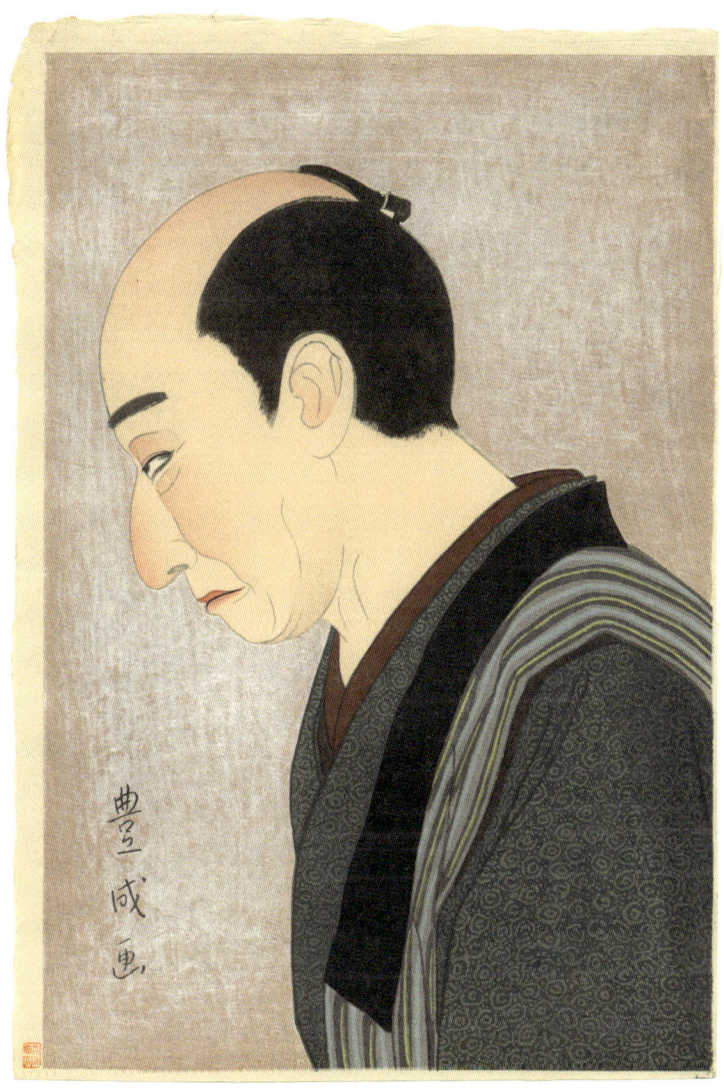

Cat. 114

Yamamura Kōka (Toyonari)
山村耕花 (豊成) (1885–1942)

**Nakamura Ganjirō I as Akaneya
Hanshichi [in the play *Sakaya*]**

(*Shosei Nakamura Ganjirō no
Akaneya Hanshichi* 初世中村鴈治郎
の茜屋半七)

Series: (Untitled series known as)
Flowers of the Theatrical World
(*Rien no hana* 梨園の華)
Date: 1920
Signature: *Toyonari ga*
Artist's seal: *Yamamori*
Publisher: Watanabe Shōzaburō,
distributed through Yamamura
Kōka Hanga Kankōkai
Size: 40.5 × 29 cm
Private collection, the Netherlands

Cat. 115

Yamamura Kōka (Toyonari)
山村耕花 (豊成) (1885–1942)

**Kataoka Nizaemon XI as
Kakiemon [in the play *Meikō
Kakiemon*]**

(*Jūissei Kataoka Nizaemon no
Kakiemon* 十一世 片岡仁左衛門の
柿右衛門)

Series: (Untitled series known as)
Flowers of the Theatrical World
(*Rien no hana* 梨園の華)
Date: 1921
Signature: *Toyonari ga*
Artist's seal: *Kōka*
Publisher: Watanabe Shōzaburō,
distributed through Yamamura
Kōka Hanga Kankōkai
Size: 41 × 28.7 cm
Collection Scholten

Cat. 116

Yamamura Kōka (Toyonari)
山村耕花 (豊成) (1885–1942)
**Morita Kan'ya XIII as Jean
Valjean [in the play _Les
Misérables_]**
(_Jūsansei Morita Kan'ya no Jan
Barujan_ 十三世守田勘弥のジャン・
バルジャン)

Series: (Untitled series known as)
Flowers of the Theatrical World
(_Rien no hana_ 梨園の華)
Date: 1921
Signature: _Toyonari ga_
Artist's seal: _Toyonari_
Publisher: Watanabe Shōzaburō,
distributed through Yamamura
Kōka Hanga Kankōkai
Size: 41 × 29 cm
Private collection, the Netherlands

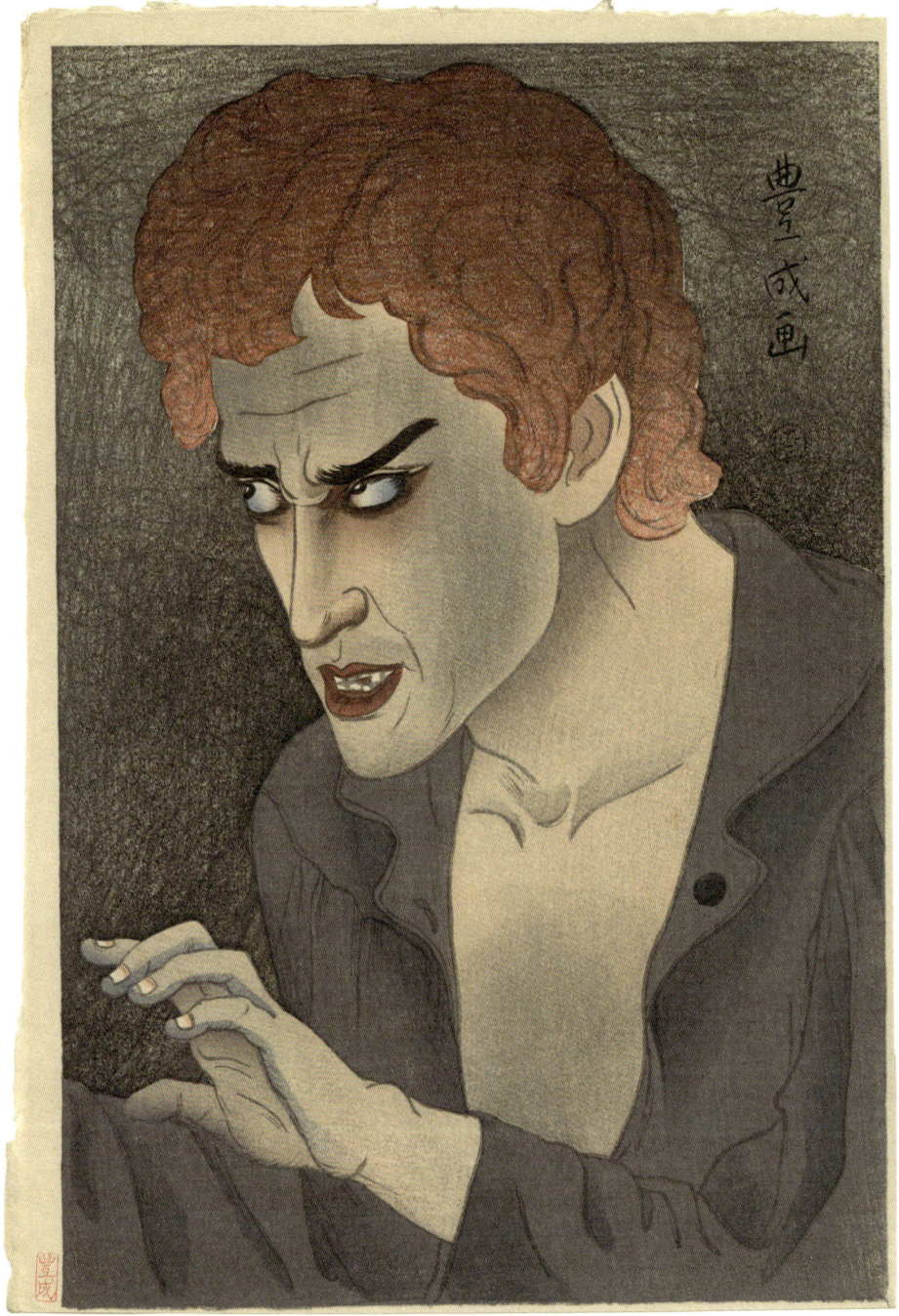

This is one of Kōka's most striking designs and distinguishes itself from the other actor portraits by its unusual subject matter. From the mid-1910s Morita Kan'ya XIII (1885–1932) had been one of the leading figures in bringing modern kabuki and Western plays onto the Japanese stage. In 1920 he performed in the Yūraku theatre in Tokyo as Jean Valjean, the lead role in _Les Misérables_, a play after Victor Hugo's novel about the many social issues of 19th-century urban France. Not only in theme but also in compositional style the print stands out from the others: Kōka aimed to evoke a more Western style with the strong swirls of the _baren_ in the background and the heavy use of shadow and fine lines in Valjean's face and hands. The untitled set of 12 prints, commonly known as _Rien no hana_ (Flowers of the Theatrical World), was published by the Watanabe company. The series was actually the first commission given to Watanabe by the Publication Society of Yamamura Kōka's Prints (_Yamamura Kōka Hanga Kankōkai_), a collective of Kōka's patrons who acted as distributors.

(JD)

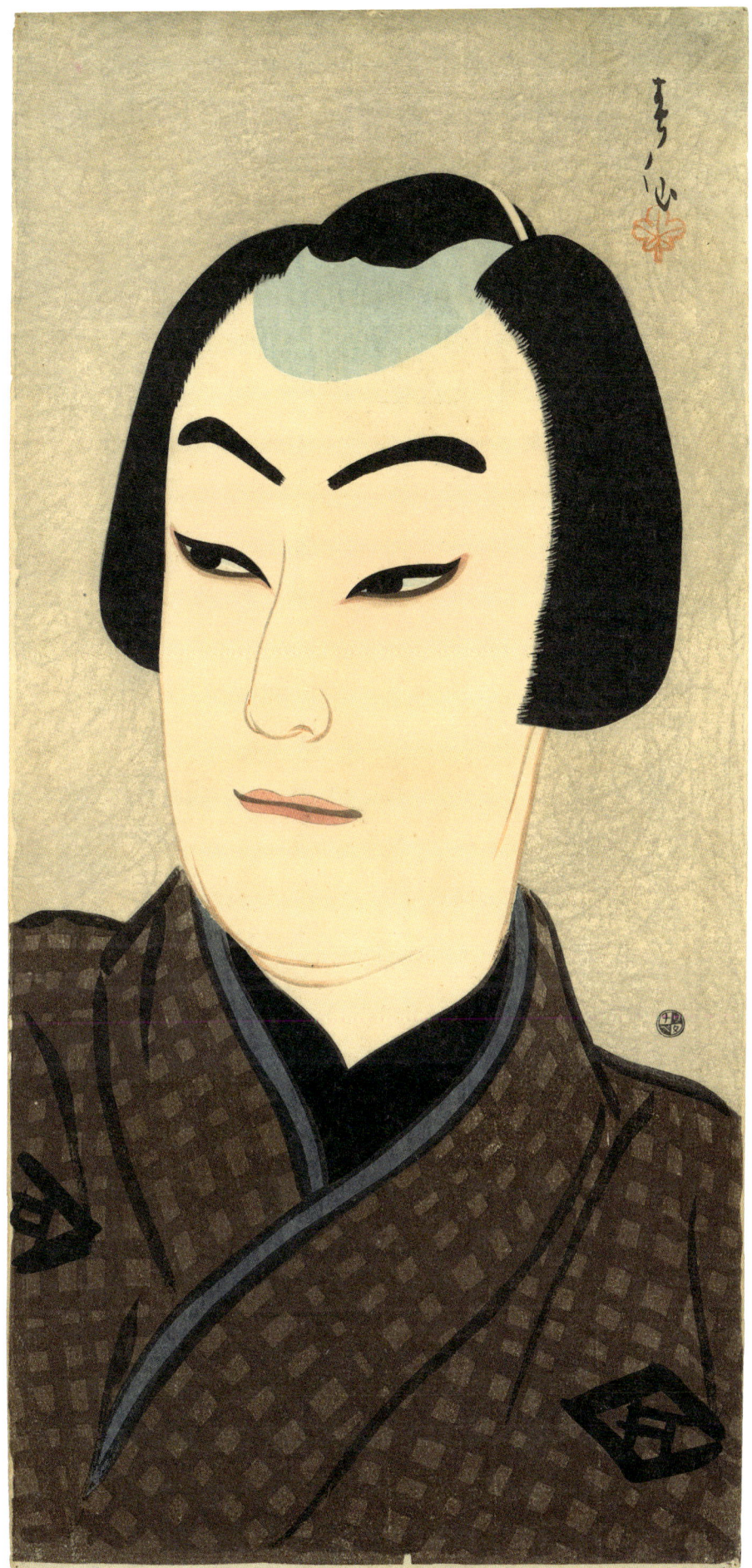

The production of this print in 1916 marked the beginning of the long and enduring collaboration between Shunsen and Watanabe. After Watanabe saw Shunsen's painting of the same subject in the second *Gekiga tenrankai* (Exhibition of Theatre-Themed Pictures), he asked the artist to reproduce the design in woodblock format. In an unusual elongated format, the kabuki star Nakamura Ganjirō I (1860–1935) is depicted as Kamiya Jihei, one of his most memorable roles. In *Shinjū ten no Amijima* (The Love Suicides at Amijima), the highly popular piece written by the Edo Period playwright Chikamatsu Monzaemon (1653–1725), Jihei is caught in a love triangle, torn between his sense of duty towards his family and his love for his mistress, Koharu. As the title suggests, he and his lover ultimately seek a way out by committing suicide together.

(JD)

Cat. 117

Natori Shunsen 名取春仙
(1886–1960)

Nakamura Ganjirō I as Kamiya Jihei [in the play *Shinjū ten no Amijima*]

(*Shodai Nakamura Ganjirō no Kamiya Jihei* 初代中村鴈治郎の紙屋治兵衛)

Date: 1916
Signature: *Shunsen*
Artist's seal: leaf-shaped seal
Publisher: Watanabe Shōzaburō
Size: 51.5 × 25 cm
Collection Scholten

Natori Shunsen 名取春仙
(1886–1960)

**Ichimura Uzaemon XV as
Naozamurai in *Iriya***

(*Jūgosei Ichimura Uzaemon Iriya no
Naozamurai* 十五世市村羽左衛門 入
谷の直侍)

Series: *A Collection of Shunsen's
Creative Print Likeness Portraits*
(*Sōsaku hanga Shunsen nigao-e
shū* 創作版画春仙似顔絵集)
Date: 1925
Signature: *Shunsen hitsu*
Artist's seal: *Shunsen* (square seal
below signature), *Natori* (oval approval
seal in lower right margin)
Publisher: Watanabe Shōzaburō,
distributed through Shunsen
Hanga Kankōkai
Size: 39.5 × 27 cm
Collection Scholten

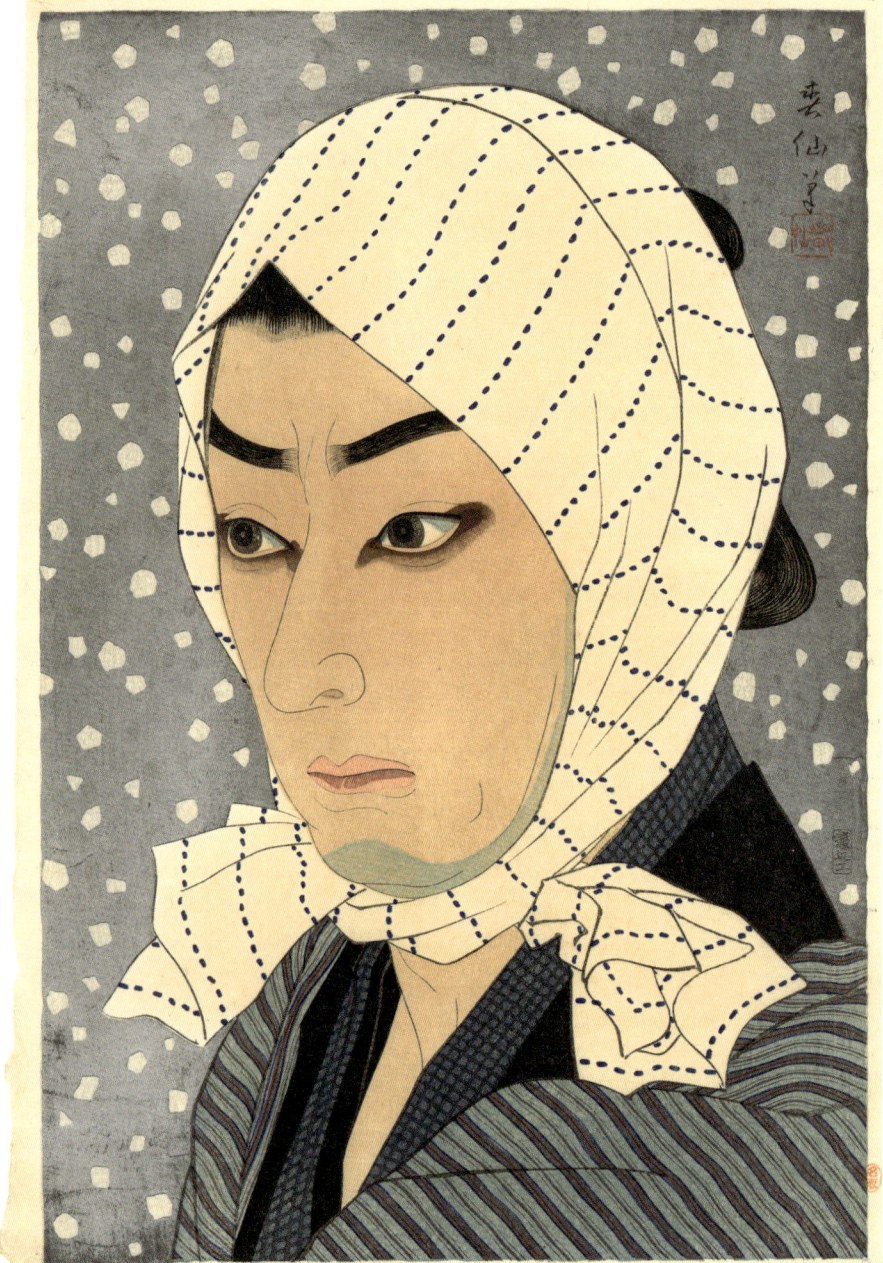

The most representative set of woodblock prints in Shunsen's oeuvre was his series of 36 actor portraits, *A Collection of Shunsen's Creative Print Likeness Portraits*, published together with Watanabe Shōzaburō. The usage of the words 'sōsaku hanga' in the series title was undoubtedly in response to the *sōsaku hanga* movement and its claim to 'creativity'. The actor Ichimura Uzaemon XV (1874–1945) was known for his strong and vibrant presence on stage and generally played the role of 'young lover', even at an advanced age. Here he is shown in the role of Kataoka Naojirō, a *rōnin* and notorious scoundrel, who is ironically known as Naozamurai (Honest Samurai). *Yuki no yūbe Iriya no azemichi* (A Narrow Road in Iriya on a Snowy Evening), commonly known as *Naozamurai*, was originally part of a seven-act play, but in 1910 it premiered as a standalone with Ichimura Uzaemon XV in the lead role. While fleeing from the police, Naozamurai decides to say to goodbye to his mistress, Michitose, who has fallen ill owing to the absence of her lover. He visits her on a snowy spring evening in the quiet town of Iriya, but his plans to spend a last night with Michitose are foiled when a fellow gang member betrays Naozamurai to save his own skin. (JD)

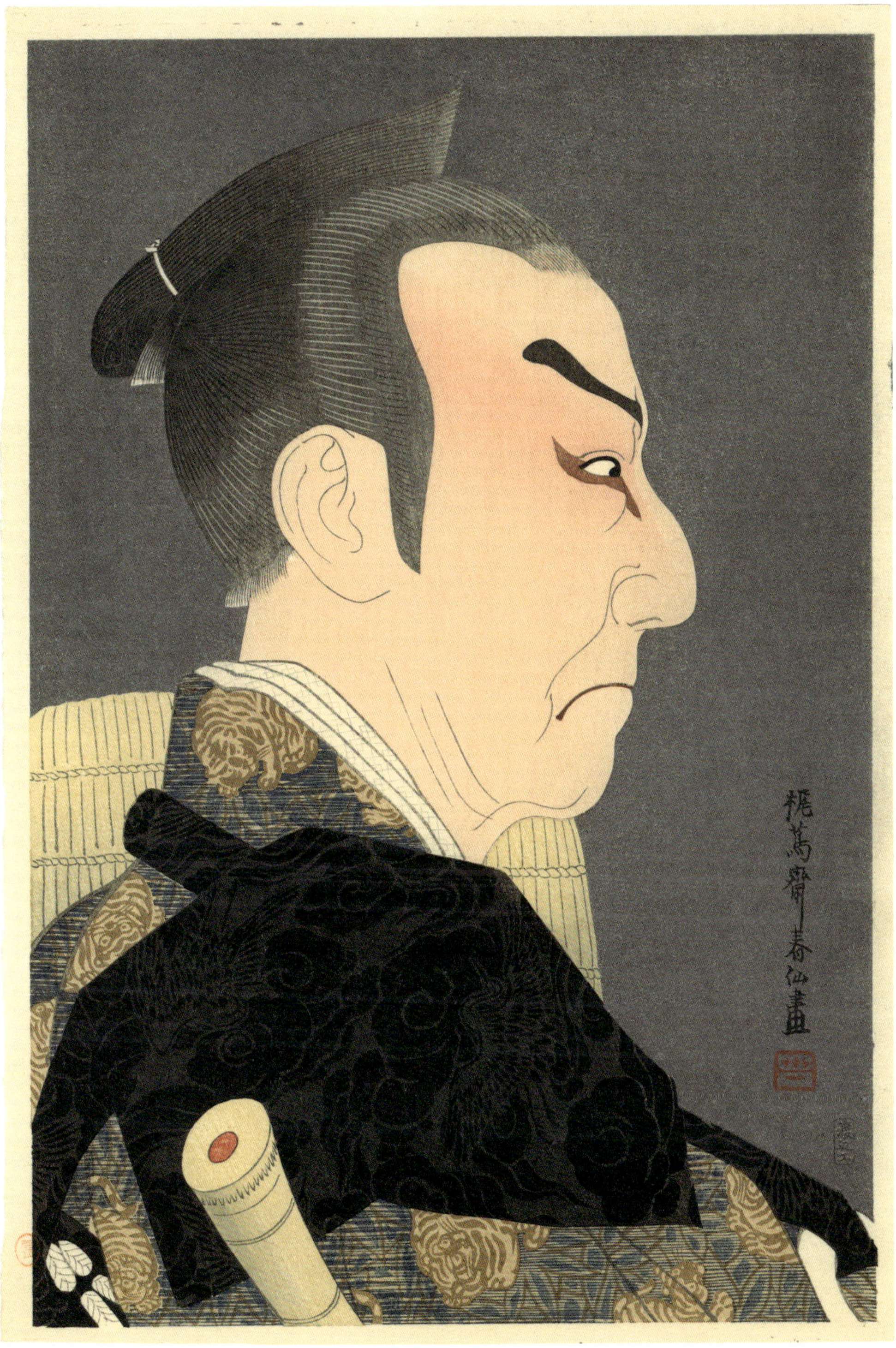

Cat. 119
Natori Shunsen 名取春仙
(1886–1960)

Kataoka Nizaemon XI as Honzō in Act IX [of the play *Kanadehon chūshingura*]

(*Jūissei Kataoka Nizaemon Kyūdanme no Honzō* 十一世片岡仁左衛門 九段目の本蔵)

Series: *A Collection of Shunsen's Creative Print Likeness Portraits* (*Sōsaku hanga Shunsen nigao-e shū* 創作版画春仙似顔絵集)
Date: 1926
Signature: *Bichōsai Shunsen ga*
Artist's seal: *Shun* (square seal below signature), *Natori* (oval approval seal in lower left margin)
Publisher: Watanabe Shōzaburō, distributed through Shunsen Hanga Kankōkai
Size: 39.2 × 27.1 cm
Collection Scholten

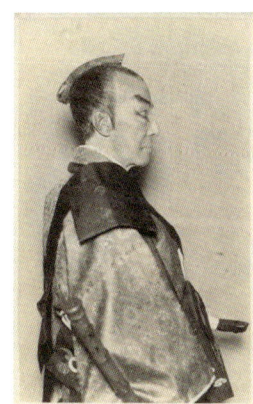

Fig. 5
A photograph of the actor Kataoka Nizaemon XI, c. 1923

The stern-looking profile shown in this print is that of the kabuki actor Kataoka Nizaemon XI (1857–1934) in the role of Kakogawa Honzō, who serves as the chief counsellor to the *daimyō* Wakasanosuke in *The Treasury of the Loyal Retainers*. The play is about 47 *rōnin* (masterless samurai) who have sworn to avenge their lord and is loosely based on historical events in the 18th century. In Act IX of the play, Honzō disguises himself as a travelling monk, right before his self-sacrifice, and here he is recognizable from the straw basket-like *tengai* hat behind him and the *shakuhachi* flute at the bottom margin. Like Yamamura Kōka, Shunsen based his portraits on *buromaido* actor photographs, and in this design the similarity is uncanny (Fig. 5), although the *tengai* hat is an addition by Shunsen.
(JD)

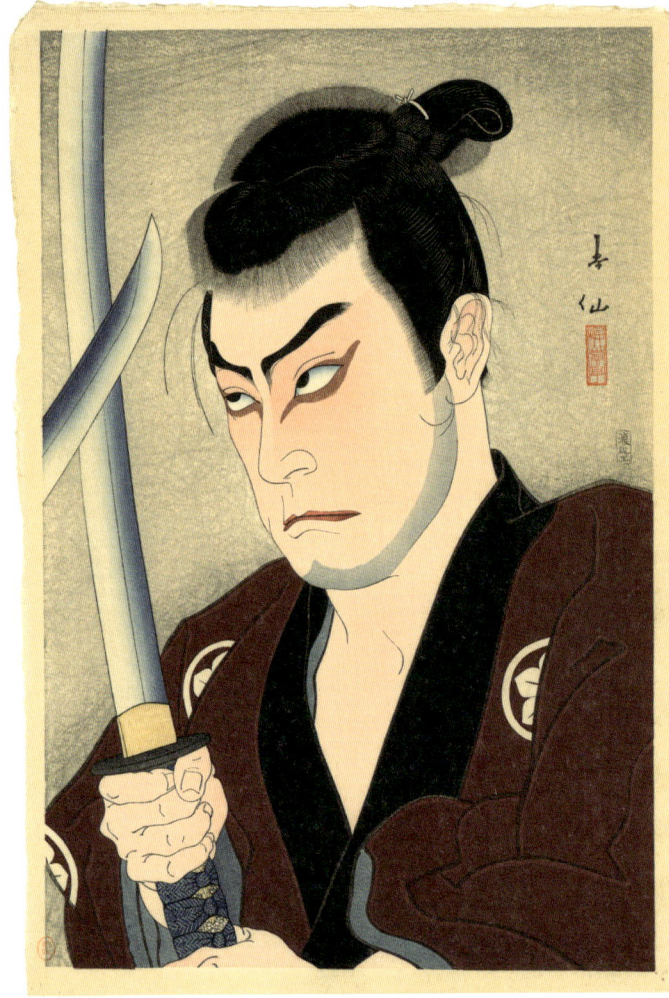

Cat. 120

Natori Shunsen 名取春仙
(1886–1960)

**Ichikawa Sadanji II as the Priest
in [the play]** *Narukami*

(*Nisei Ichikawa Sadanji Narukami
Shōnin* 二世市川左團次 鳴神上人)

Series: *A Collection of Shunsen's
Creative Print Likeness Portraits*
(*Sōsaku hanga Shunsen nigao-e
shū* 創作版画春仙似顔絵集)
Date: 1926
Artist's seals: rectangular *Shunsen* seal
(lower right)/oval, *Natori* seal (lower left
margin)
Publisher: Watanabe Shōzaburō,
distributed through Shunsen
Hanga Kankōkai
Size: 40 × 27 cm
Collection Scholten

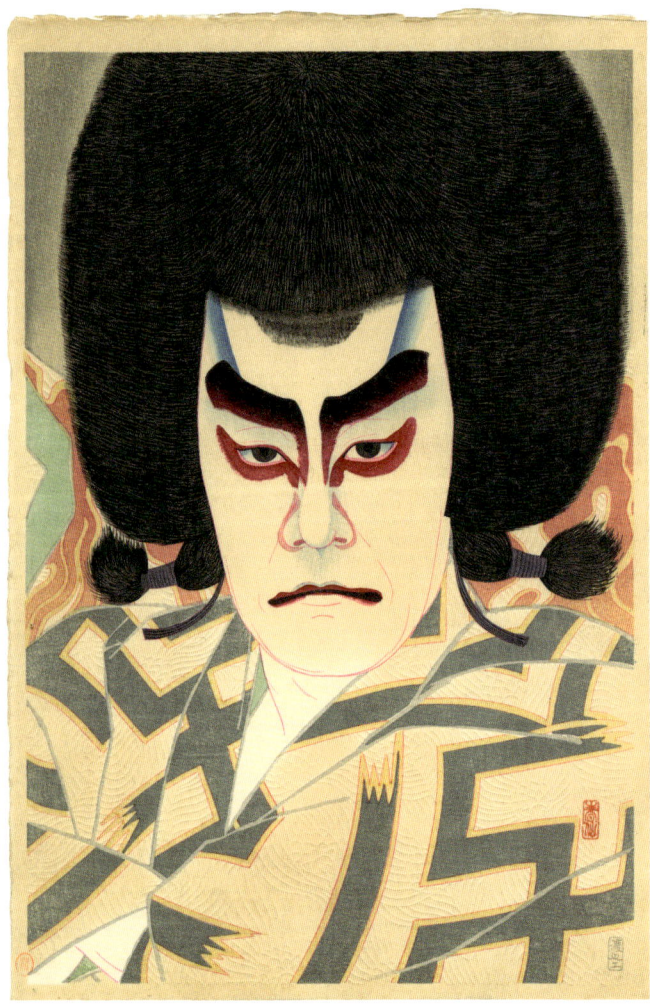

Cat. 121

Natori Shunsen 名取春仙
(1886–1960)

**Sawada Shōjirō as the
Swordsman Hayashi Buhei**

(*Sawada Shōjirō 'Ken' no Hayashi
Buhei* 沢田正二郎「剣」の林武平)

Date: 1927
Series: *A Collection of Shunsen's
Creative Print Likeness Portraits*
(*Sōsaku hanga Shunsen nigao-e
shū* 創作版画春仙似顔絵集)
Signature: *Shunsen*
Artist's seals: rectangular *Bichōsai*
seal (upper right)/oval, *Natori*
seal (lower left margin)
Publisher: Watanabe Shōzaburō,
distributed through Shunsen
Hanga Kankōkai
Size: 39.5 × 27 cm
Collection Scholten

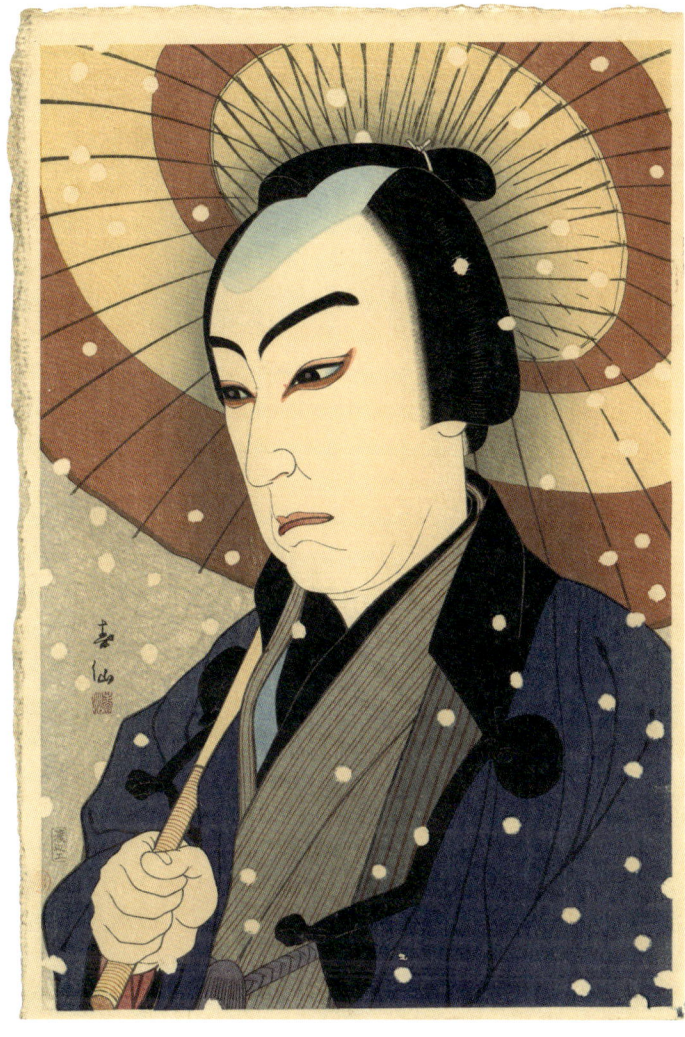

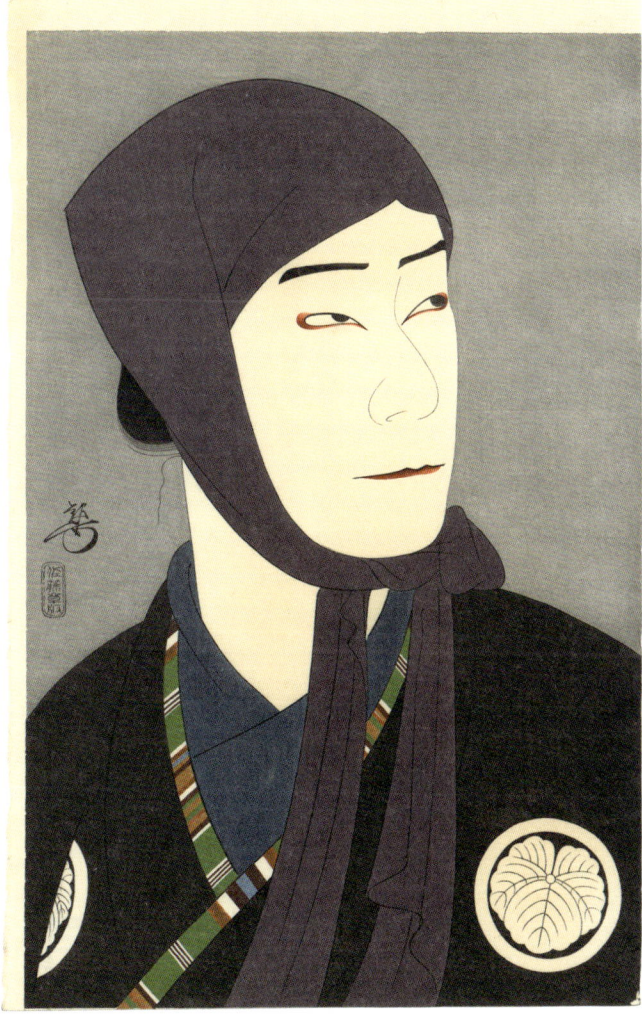

Yoshikawa Kanpō 吉川観方
(1894–1979)

Nakamura Ganjirō I as Kamiya Jihei [in the play *Shinjū ten no Amijima*]

(*Shodai Nakamura Ganjirō no Kamiya Jihei* 初代中村鴈治郎の紙屋治兵衛)

Date: 1922
Signature: *Kanpō*
Edition: 73/200
Publisher: Satō Shōtarō
Block cutter: *Maeda Kentarō*
Printer: *Ōiwa Tokuzō*
Size: 42 × 27.5 cm
Collection Scholten

Natori Shunsen 名取春仙
(1886–1960)

Sawamura Sōjūrō VII as Narihira Reiza in Koisogahara [Act III of the play *Fubuki no hana, Oshizu Reiza*]

(*Nanasei Sawamura Sōjūrō Koisogahara no Narihira Reiza* 七世澤村宗十郎 小磯ヶ原の業平礼三)

Series: *A Collection of Shunsen's Creative Print Likeness Portraits*
(*Sōsaku hanga Shunsen nigao-e shū* 創作版画春仙似顔絵集)
Date: 1927
Signature: *Shunsen*
Artist's seal: *Shunsen*, *Natori* (left margin)
Publisher: Watanabe Shōzaburō, distributed through Shunsen Hanga Kankōkai
Size: 40 × 27 cm
Collection Scholten

Cat. 124

Yoshikawa Kanpō 吉川観方
(1894–1979)

[Ichikawa Sadanji II in the play
Imayō Satsuma uta **as] Gengobei**
of the Takashimaya Guild

(*Takashimaya no Gengobei* 高嶋屋
の源五兵衛)

Series: *Creative Prints by Kanpō, first series*
(*Kanpō sōsaku hanga, dai*
isshū 観方創作版画第壱集)
Date: Autumn 1923
Signature: *Kanpō*
Edition: 25/200 (verso)
Publisher: Satō Shōtarō
Block cutter: *Maeda Kentarō*
Printer: *Ōiwa Tokuzō*
Size: 42.4 × 27.5 cm
Collection Scholten

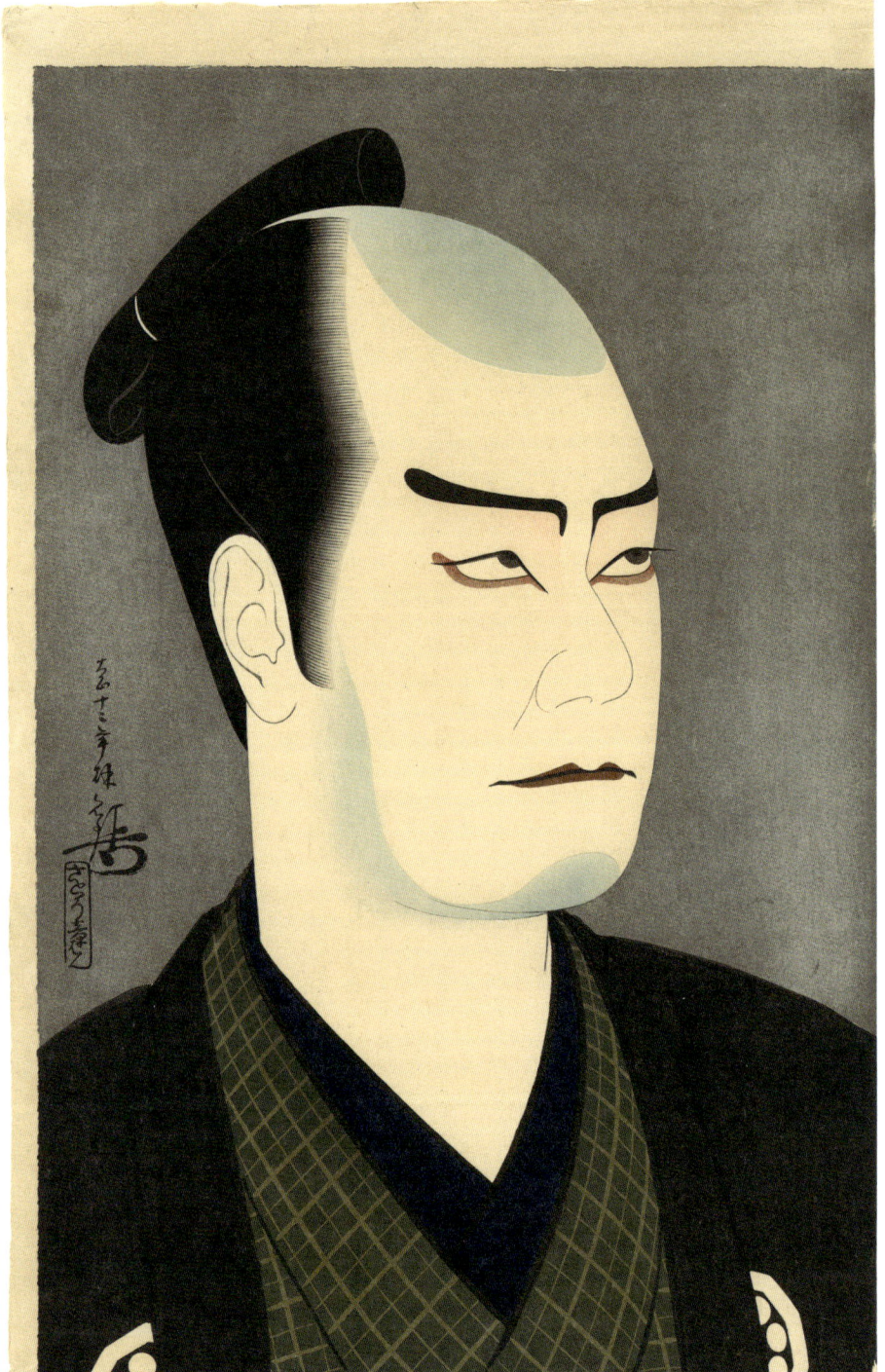

In 1922 Yoshikawa Kanpō was commissioned by the Kyoto publisher Satō Shōtarō to design a series of actor portraits (and at least one *maiko* portrait) in *shin hanga* style called *Creative Prints by Kanpō*. As in Shunsen's set of actor portraits published by Watanabe a couple of years later, the 'creative prints' in the series title was a commentary on the *sōsaku hanga* movement of self-carving and self-printing artists. The unusual titles come from the accompanying folders that do not mention the actors themselves, but rather their actors' guild, followed by their role. This is a portrait of Ichikawa Sadanji II as Hishikawa Gengobei in *Imayō Satsuma uta* (A Modern Satsuma Song), a *shin kabuki* play. *Shin kabuki*, or 'new kabuki', was a new genre that mainly distinguished itself by its playwrights often being modern novelists rather than members of the kabuki establishment. Sadanji II was a reformist and one of the pioneers who actively promoted such new plays. (JD)

Yoshikawa Kanpō 吉川観方
(1894–1979)

[Jitsukawa Enjaku II in the play
Yoshitsune senbon zakura **as]**
Gonta of the Kawachiya Guild

(*Kawachiya no Gonta*
河内屋の権太)

Series: *Creative Prints by Kanpō, first series*
(*Kanpō sōsaku hanga, dai
isshū* 観方創作版画第壱集)
Date: 1923
Signature: *Kanpō*
Edition: 32/200 (verso)
Publisher: Satō Shōtarō
Block cutter: *Maeda Kentarō*
Printer: *Ōiwa Tokuzō*
Size: 41.8 × 27.5 cm
Collection Scholten

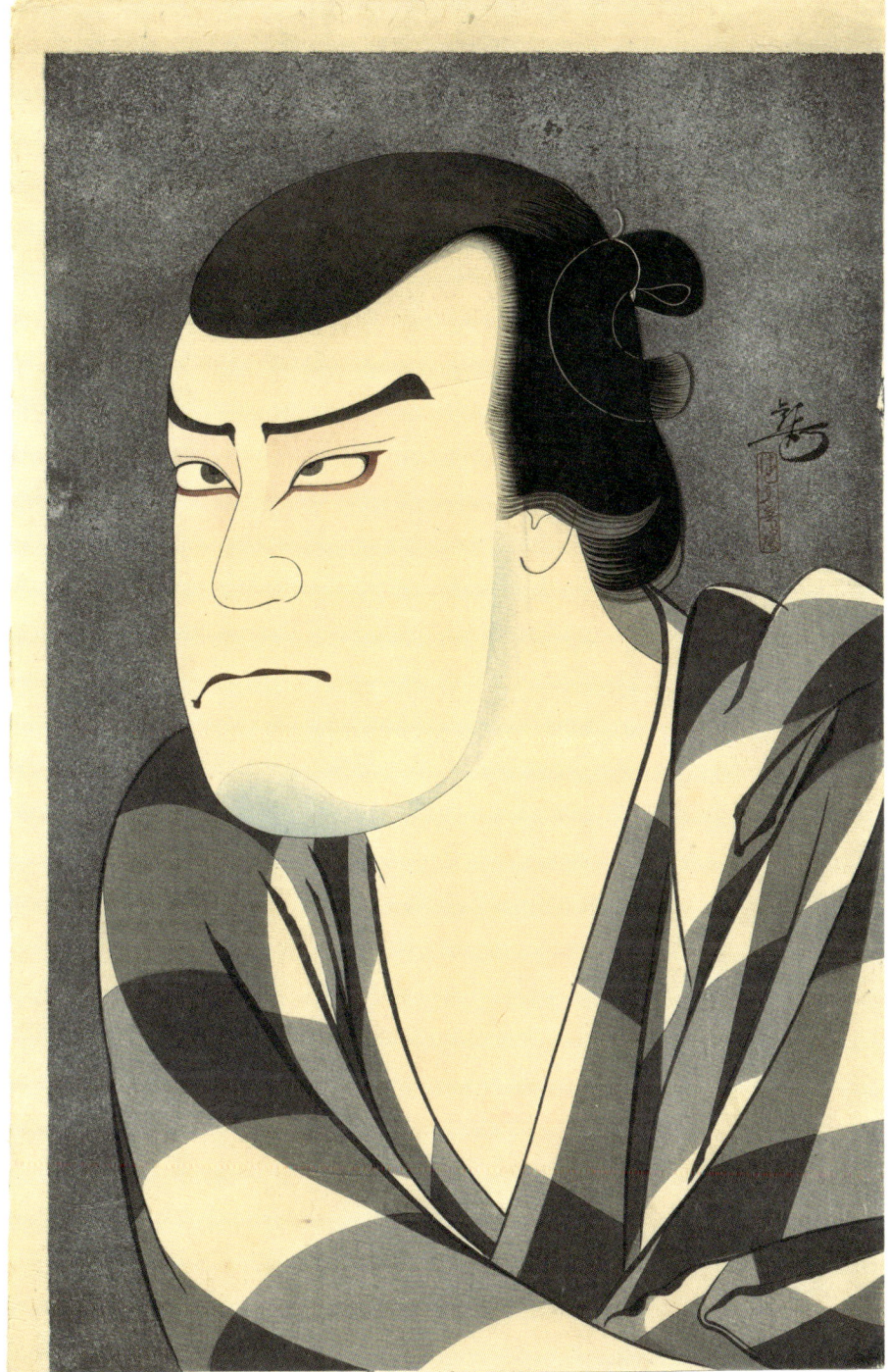

Cat. 126

Shin'ei 新栄 (dates unknown)

Ichikawa Sadanji II as Satsuma Gengobei [in the play *Imayō Satsuma Uta*]

(*Nisei Ichikawa Sadanji no Satsuma Gengobei* 二世市川 左団次の薩摩 源五兵衛)

Series: *Facial Likenesses by Shin'ei*
(*Shin'ei hitsu nigao-e* 新栄筆似顔絵)
Date: 1926
Signature: *Shin'ei hitsu*
Artist's seal: *Ryogoku Ohira ban*
Publisher: Matsuki Heikichi V
Size: 38.7 × 25.6 cm
Collection Darrel Karl

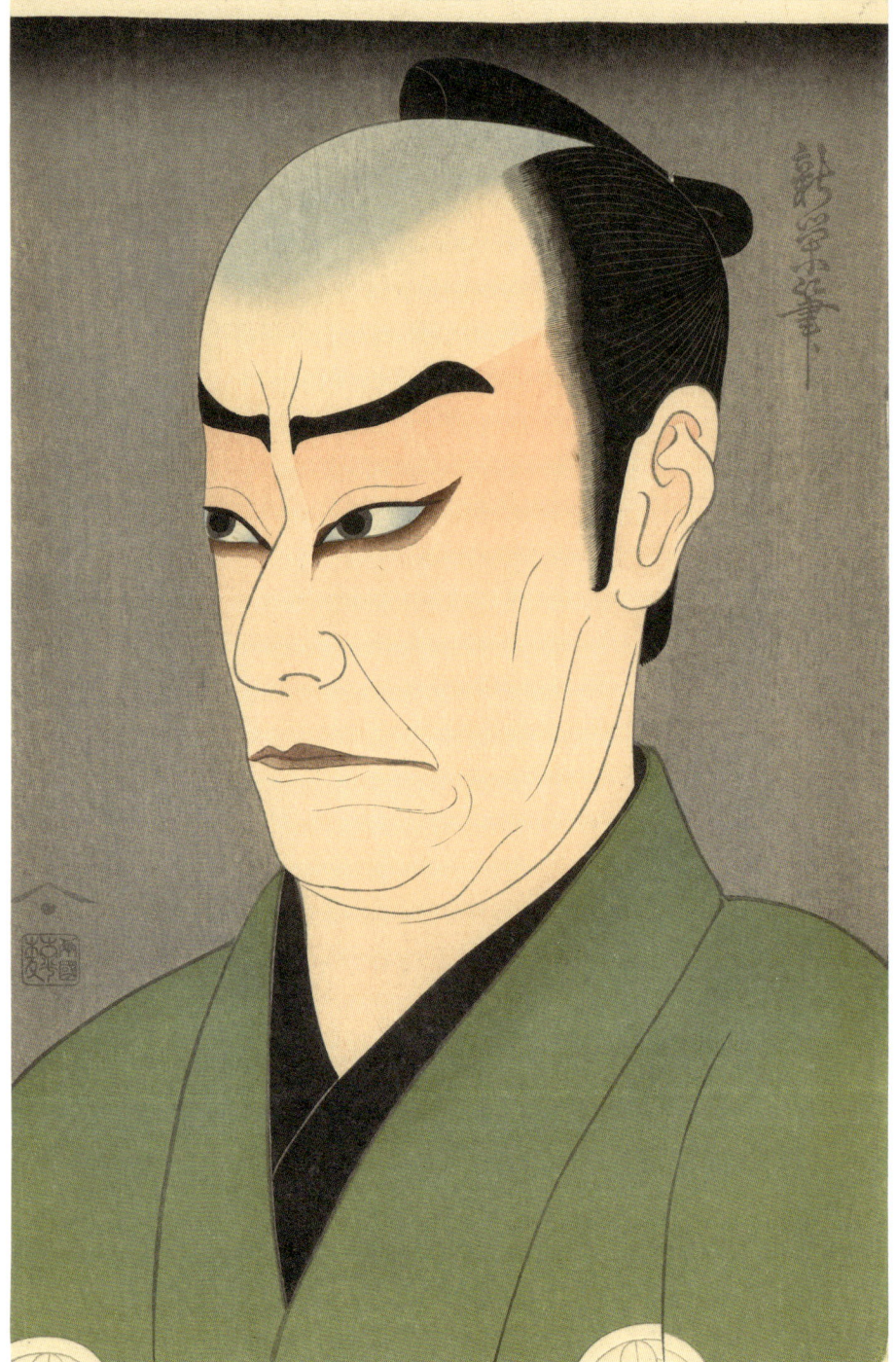

The few existing works by Shin'ei are not dated and do not name the actors nor their roles. The accompanying folders for these prints that do contain this information are now scarce, with only two existing copies in the Waseda University Theatre Museum (WAS 201-0338 & 201-0643). Instead this information can be distilled by looking at similar kabuki portraits. Visually this portrait bears a resemblance to Yoshikawa Kanpō's rendition of Ichikawa Sadanji II as Gengobei of the Takashimaya Guild (Cat. 124). It is likely that the role here is also played by the actor Ichikawa Sadanji II, as at the time he was the sole actor to play this role in Tokyo.

(CU)

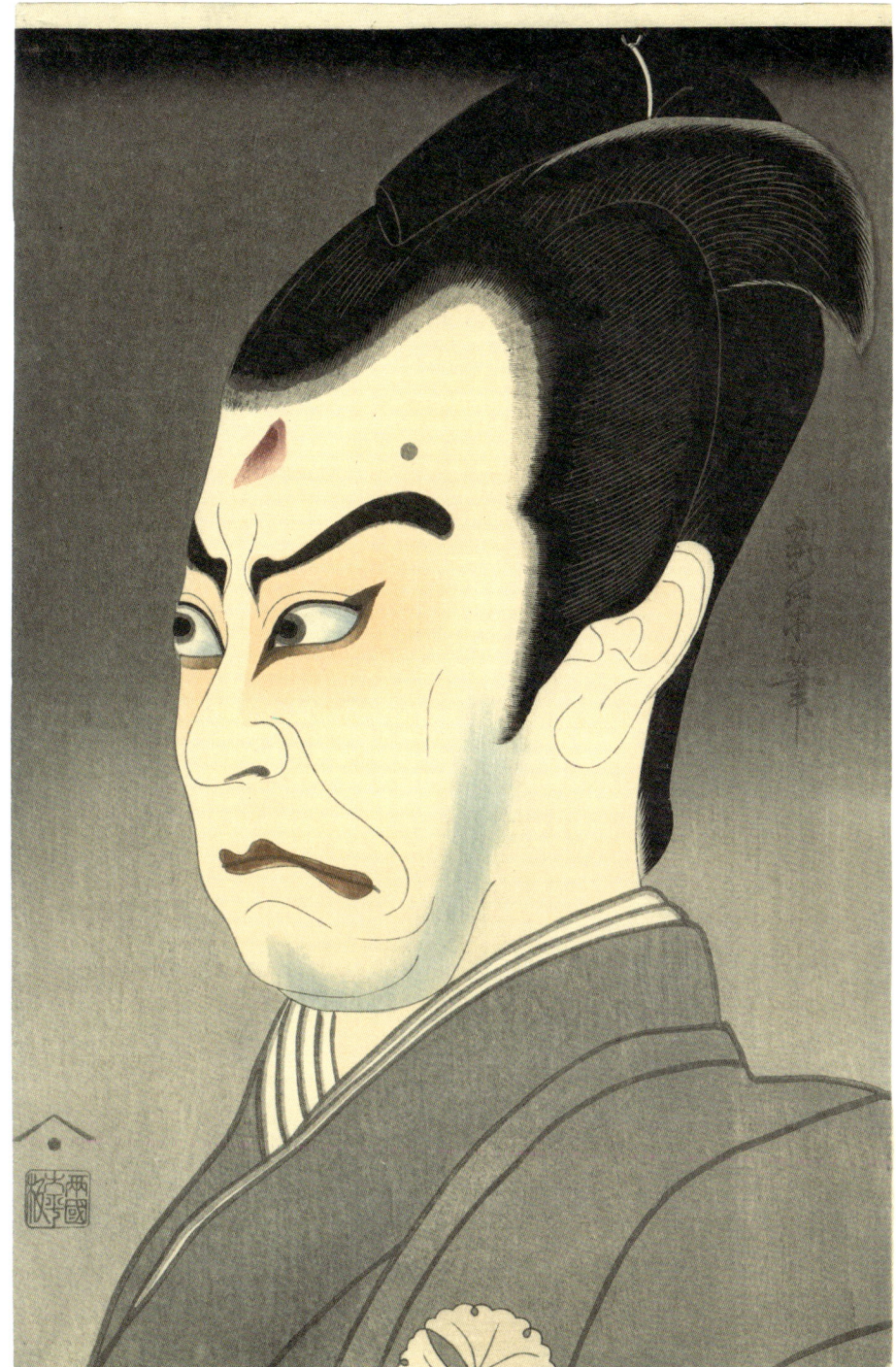

Cat. 127

Matsumoto Kōshirō VII as Nikki Danjō [in the play *Meiboku Sendai Hagi*]

(*Nanasei Matsumoto Kōshirō no Nikki Danjō* 七世松本 幸四郎の仁木弾正)

Series: *Facial Likenesses by Shin'ei*
(*Shin'ei hitsu nigao-e* 新栄筆似顔絵)
Date: 1926
Signature: *Shin'ei hitsu*
Artist's seal: *Ryogoku Ohira ban*
Publisher: Matsuki Heikichi V
Size: 38.7 × 25.7 cm
Collection Darrel Karl

The character Nikki Danjō was an evil magician who could transform himself into a rat. His costume consists of a plain gray kimono, making him instantly recognizable on stage. The transformation into a rat was one of the highlights of the performance: it was achieved through the use of an ingenious trapdoor. This was one of the most famous and spectacular roles in the kabuki repertoire.

The shape and style of the publisher's mark on Shin'ei's prints is a nod to the glory days of the late 18th century when Toyokuni, Sharaku and Kunimasa produced their famous 'large head portraits'. Generally 20th-century publishers positioned their seals discretely in the margins of the prints or unobtrusively in a corner of the design.

(CU)

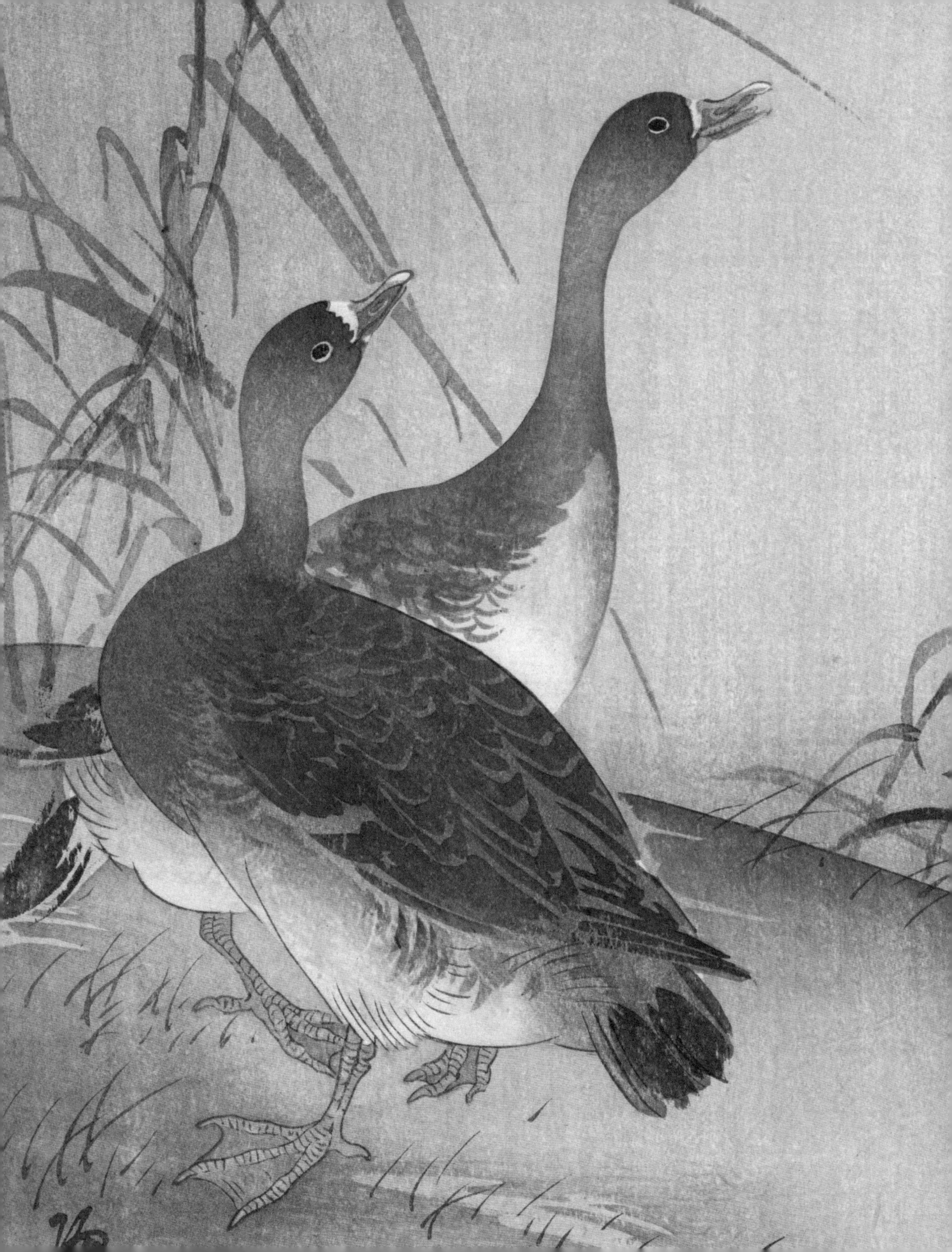

Nature

The *shin hanga* movement reintroduced the genre of the bird-and-flower prints that had been virtually absent from Japanese printmaking since the days of Hiroshige. However, the genre was largely the domain of just one artist – Ohara Koson.

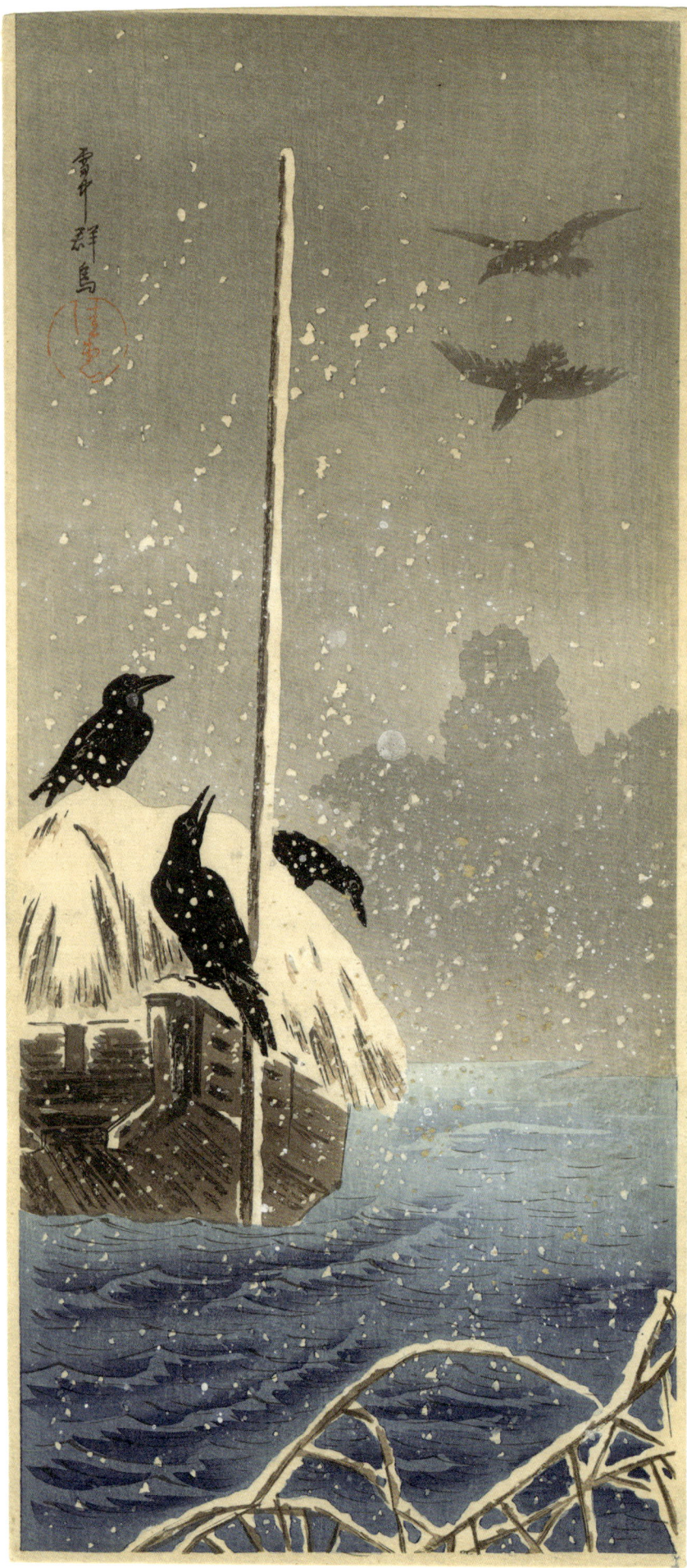

Cat. 128

Takahashi Hiroaki (Shōtei)
高橋弘明 (松亭) (1871–1945)

A Muster of Crows in Snow

(*Setchū muragarasu* 雪中群烏)

Date: before 1923
Artist's seal: *Kakei*
Publisher: Watanabe Shōzaburō
Size: 37.7 × 17 cm
Collection Scholten

A group of crows in the snow, one of the early prints by Hiroaki created for Watanabe, which he sealed under the name Kakei. Previously considered a separate, individual artist, Kakei has only recently been established as one of the (early) names used by Hiroaki.

(CU)

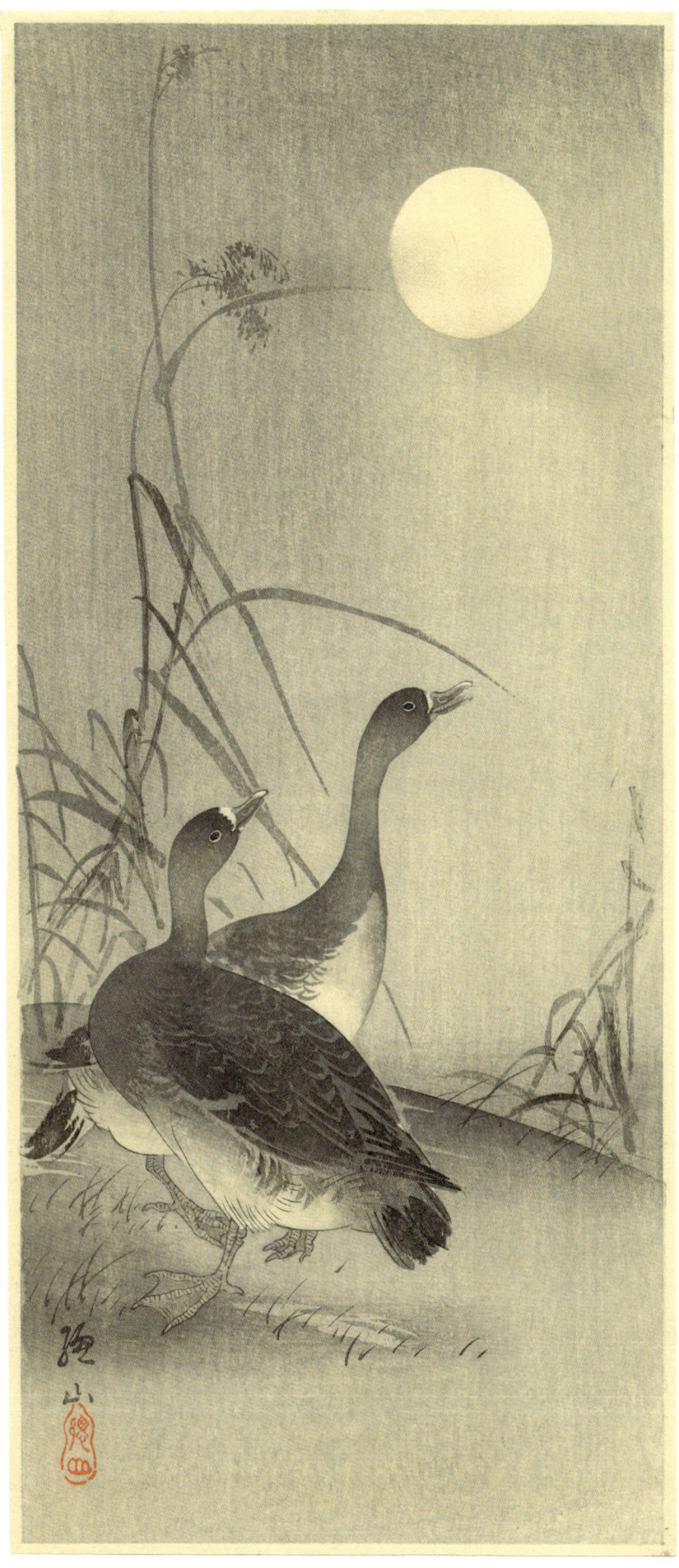

Cat. 129
Itō Sōzan 伊藤総山
(1884–?)

Wild Geese and Autumn Moon

Date: after 1923
Signature: *Sōzan*
Artist's seal: *Sōzan*
Publisher: Watanabe Shōzaburō
Size: 38.2 × 17.1 cm
Private collection, the Netherlands

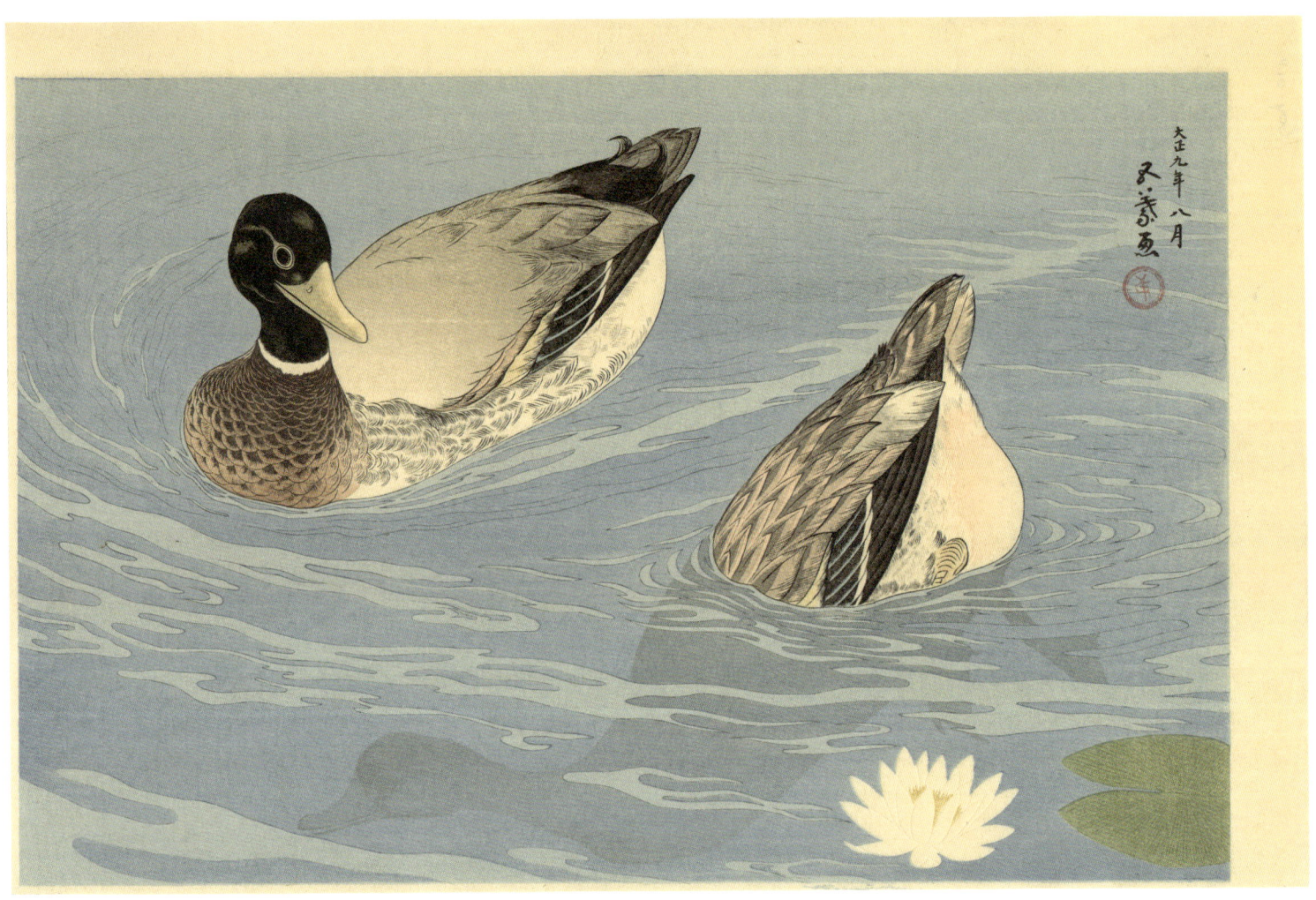

Cat. 130

Hashiguchi Goyō 橋口五葉
(1881–1921)

Pair of Ducks

Date: August 1920
Signature: *Goyō ga*
Artist's seal: *GY*
Publisher: self-published
Block cutter: *Takano Shichinosuke*
Printer: *Akimoto Shōzaburō*
Size: 26.7 × 41 cm
Private collection, the Netherlands

Cat. 131

Ohara Koson (Shōson)
小原古邨 (祥邨) (1877–1945)
White Hawk

Date: c. 1912
Signature: *Koson*
Artist's seal: *Koson*
Publisher: Daikokuya
Size: 34.5 × 18.6 cm
Private collection, the Netherlands

This is an example from Koson's early career working for the publisher Daikokuya, for which he designed several hundred prints in the *tanzaku* (as here) and the *shikishiban* formats.

Here the woodgrain of the woodblock is clearly visible in the background of the print, made possible by a technique known as *itamezuri* ('printing of the plank' [cross-grain]). This rubbing technique lets the *baren* exert more pressure on the print and was frequently used in early prints by Koson to give texture but also create a sense of depth. The subject is often placed at the front of the picture plane, taking up a large part of the composition, against a rather plain background. To make the woodgrain even more distinct, *itamezuri* is often executed on a pale colour paper.

(PO)

Cat. 132

Ohara Koson (Shōson)
小原古邨 (祥邨) (1877–1945)

Scops Owl, Cherry Blossoms and Full Moon

Date: c. 1926
Signature: *Shōson*
Artist's seal: *Shōson*
Publisher: Watanabe Shōzaburō
Size: 39 × 26 cm
S. Watanabe Color Print Co.

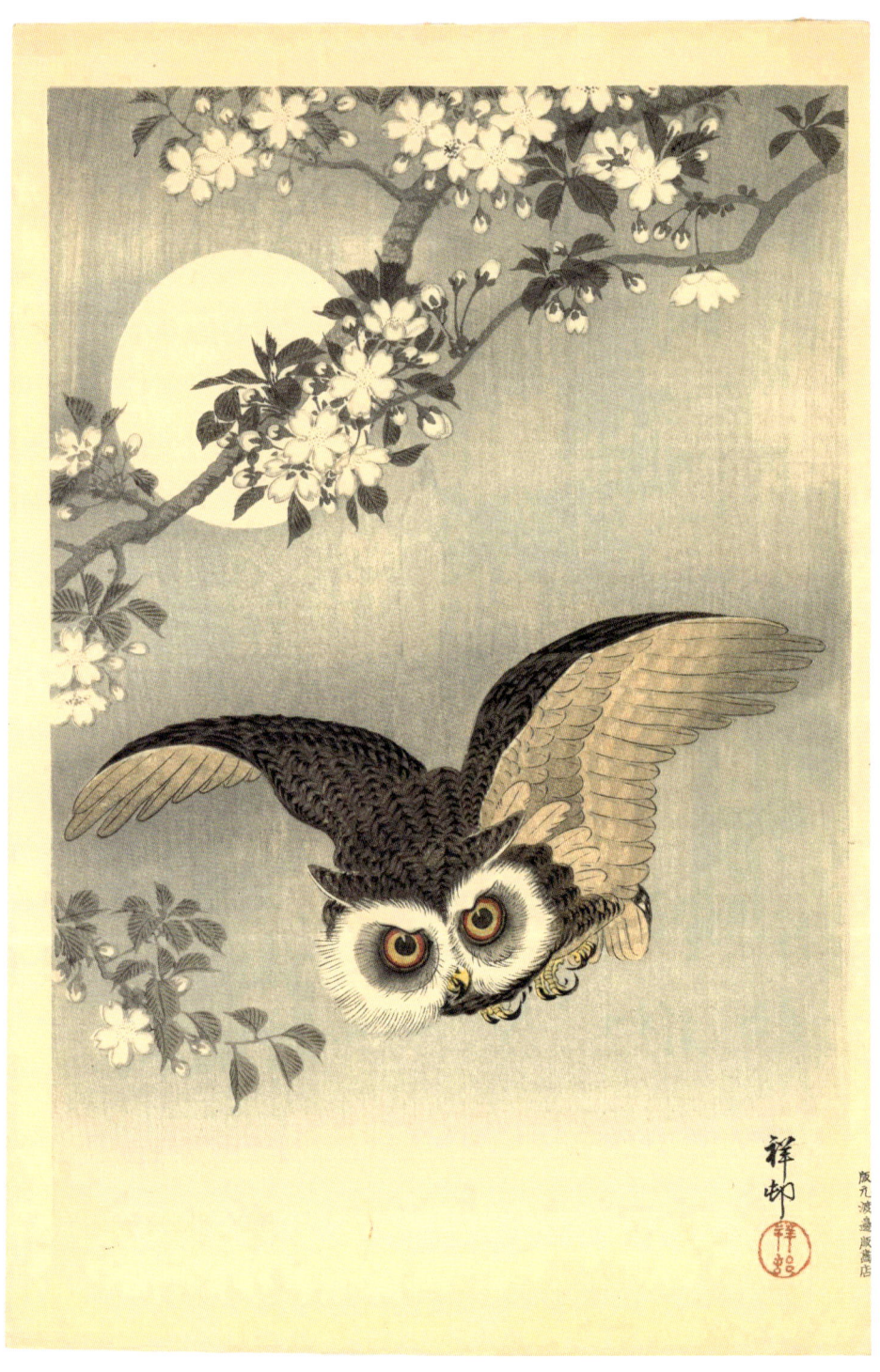

In 1926 Watanabe Shōzaburō recruited Koson to fill the void that the publisher felt existed in his portfolio of nature prints. For the first time Koson worked in the *ōban* format, his colours became brighter and the designs were executed in a less painterly fashion but with more contrast and sharper lines. At this point Koson's signature changed to Shōson.
(CU)

146

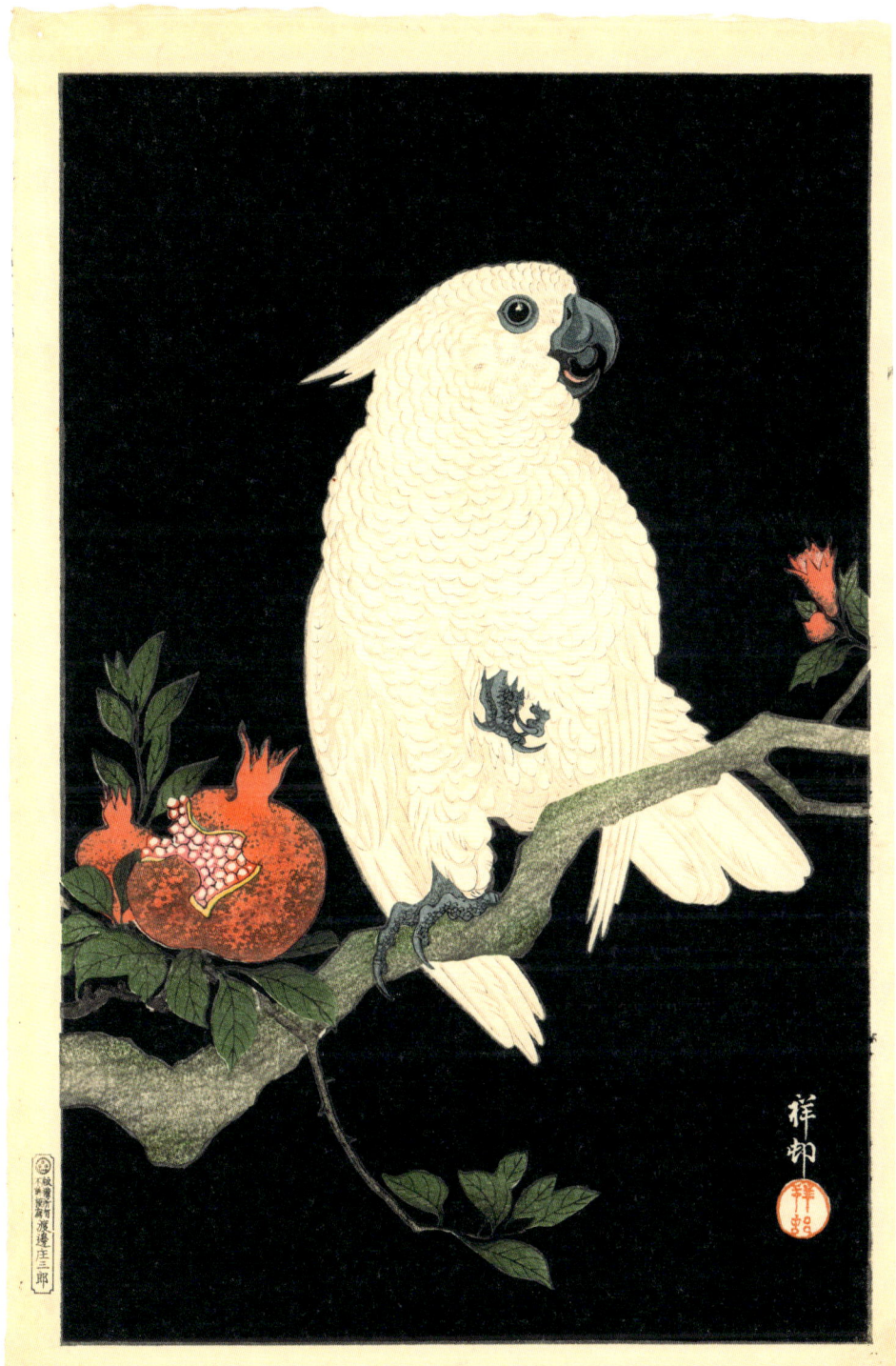

Cat. 133

Ohara Koson (Shōson)
小原古邨 (祥邨) (1877–1945)

Cockatoo and Pomegranate

Date: c. 1926
Signature: *Shōson*
Artist's seal: *Shōson*
Publisher: Watanabe Shōzaburō
Size: 39 × 27 cm
S. Watanabe Color Print Co.

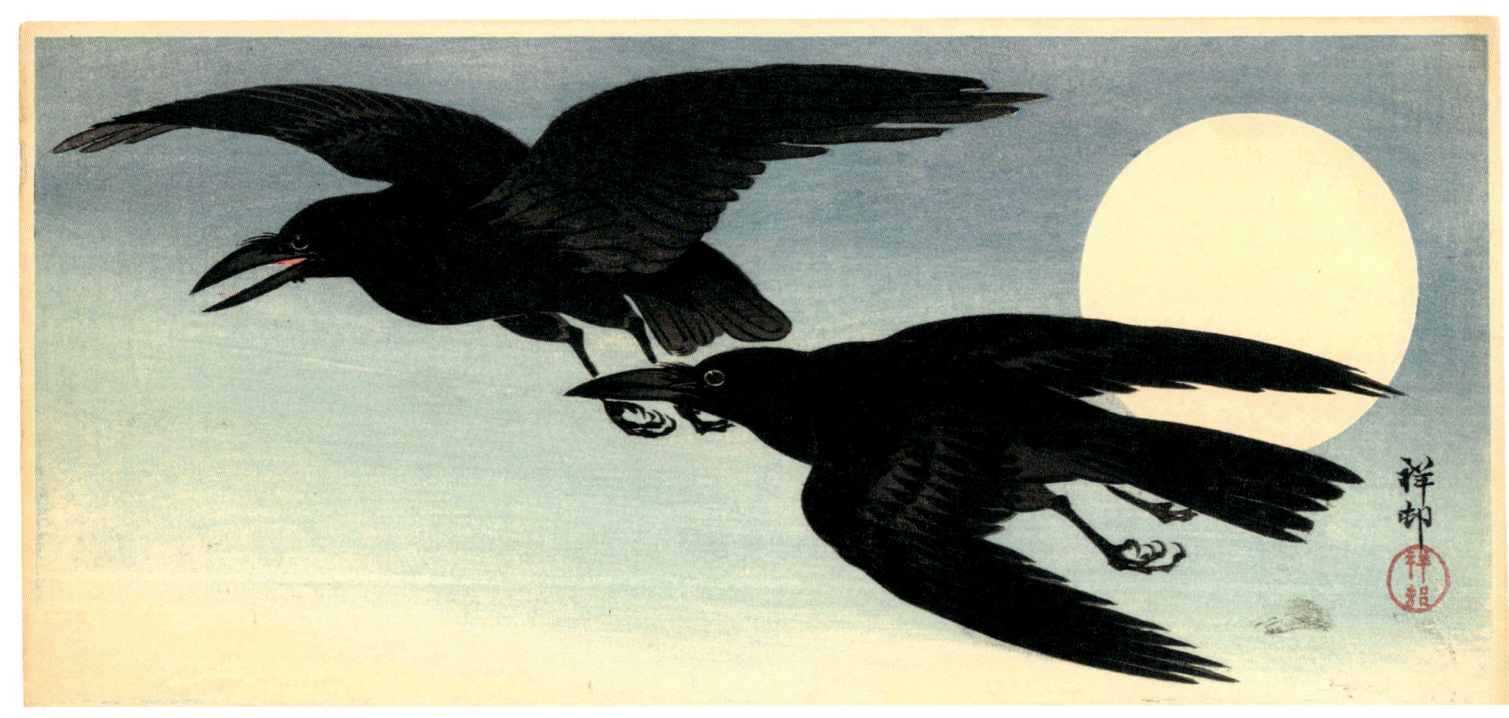

Cat. 134

Ohara Koson (Shōson)
小原古邨 (祥邨) (1877–1945)

Two Crows in Flight against a Full Moon

Date: c. 1926
Signature: *Shōson*
Artist's seal: *Shōson*
Publisher: Watanabe Shōzaburō
Size: 17 × 38 cm
S. Watanabe Color Print Co.

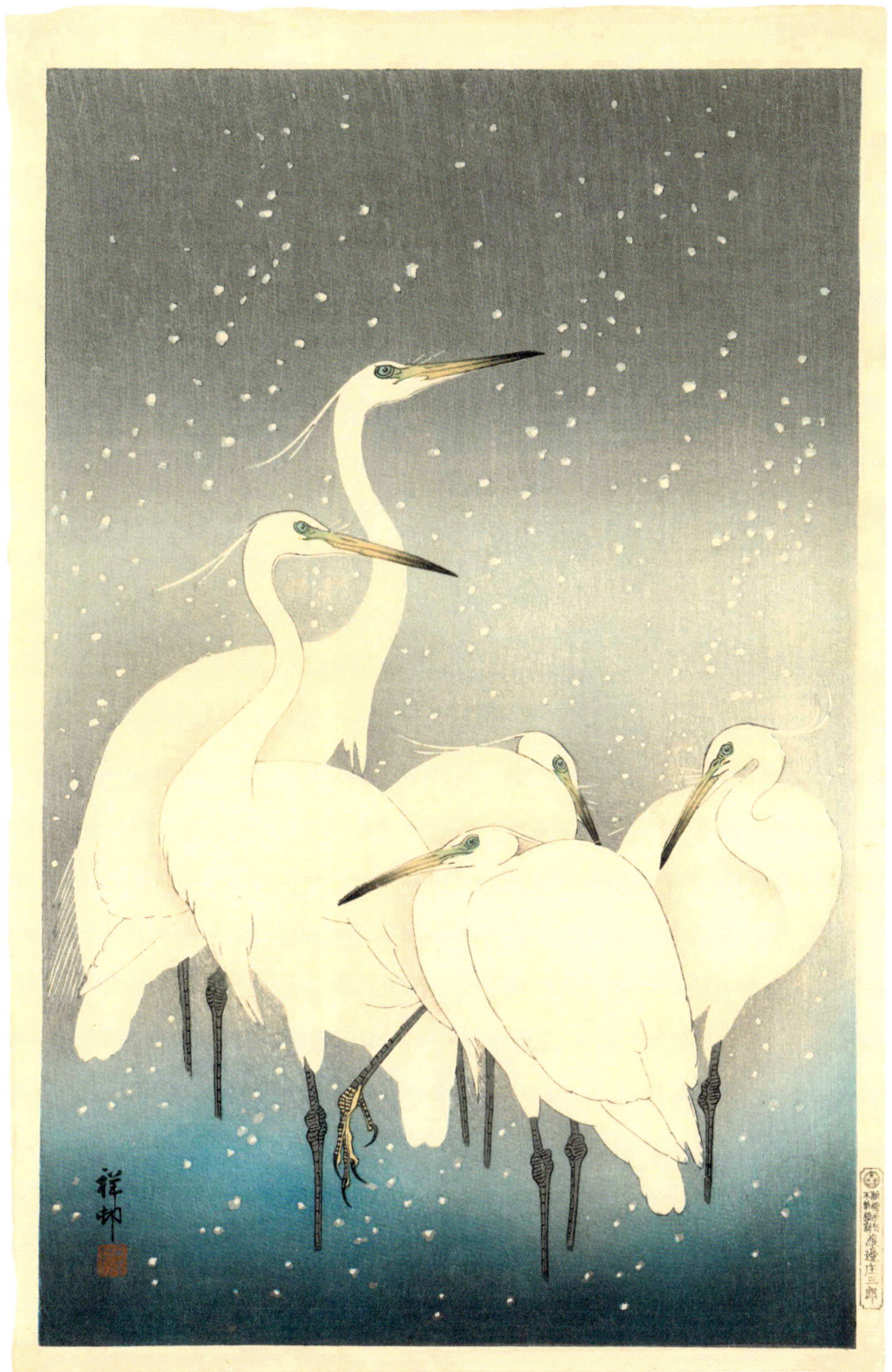

Cat. 135
Ohara Koson (Shōson)
小原古邨 (祥邨) (1877–1945)
A Group of Egrets

Date: c. 1926
Signature: *Shōson*
Artist's seal: *Shōson*
Publisher: Watanabe Shōzaburō
Size: 36 × 24 cm
S. Watanabe Color Print Co.

This is one of Koson's most striking designs. It is worth pointing out the subtleties of the printing: part of the feathers are in gauffrage (embossed), but are made more visible through the application of an additional pink block. The beak has an overprinting of a greenish pigment.

(CU)

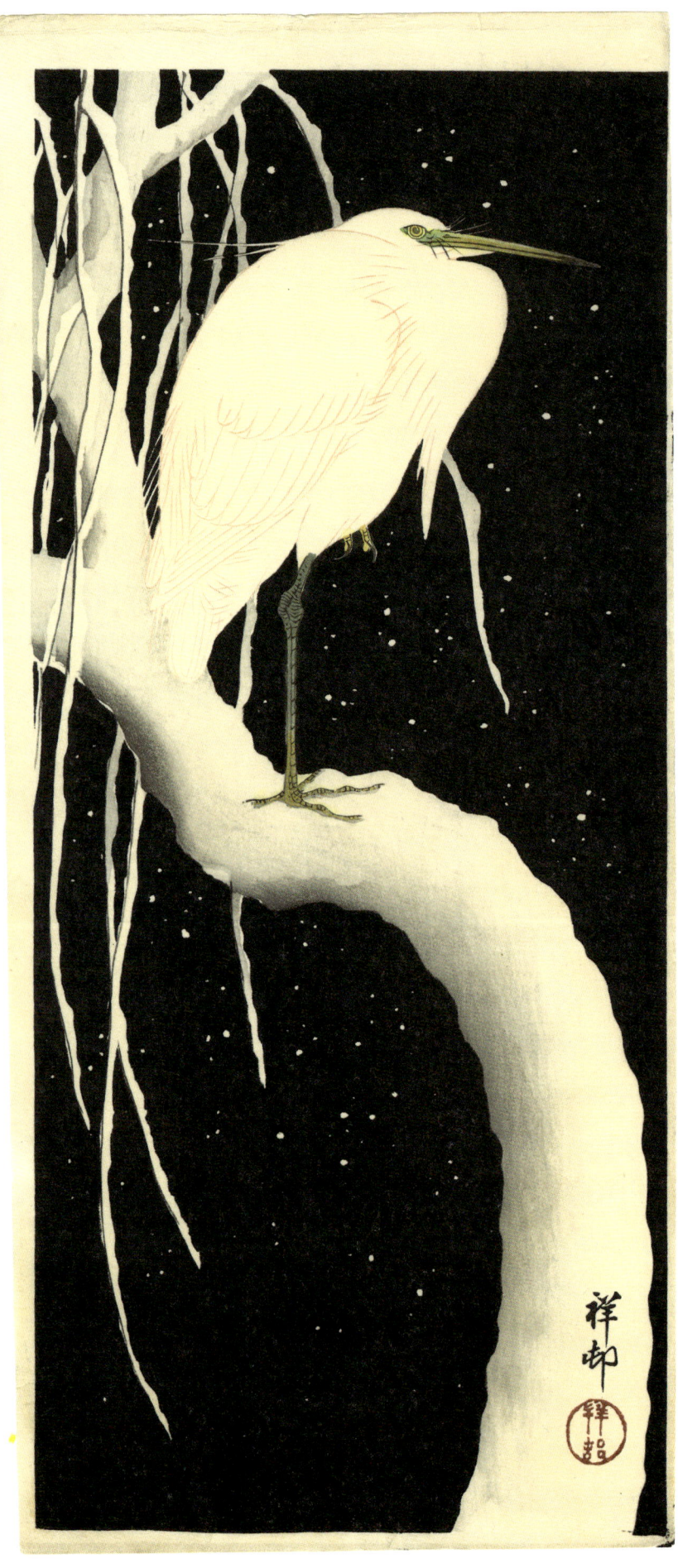

Cat. 136

Ohara Koson (Shōson)
小原古邨 (祥邨) (1877–1945)
Egret on a Snow-Covered Branch

Date: c. 1926
Signature: *Shōson*
Artist's seal: *Shōson*
Publisher: Watanabe Shōzaburō
Size: 37.5 × 17 cm
Private collection, the Netherlands

Although not often found in Edo Period paintings and prints, crows became a popular subject from the Meiji Period onwards. Crows are most often associated with autumn, as in this famous haiku by Matsuo Bashō (1644–94):

on a withered branch
a crow is perched
autumn evening

They are known to be smart animals, and the cawing of a crow on the first day of the new year is seen as a good omen. However, their cawing can also signal the coming of a calamity. They are believed to be messengers of the gods, and to this day rice cakes are offered to crows at Shinto shrines. They are also associated with filial piety: young crows tenderly care for their mother, and the character for piety (*kō*) is homophonic to the sound they make.

It seems that Koson and his publishers were aware of this popularity as he created over thirty designs featuring the large-billed crow (*Corvus macrorhynchos*). These carrion crows are native to Japan, and their far-ranging cries are a characteristic sound of daily life, making their way even into Japanese film and animation.

(PO)

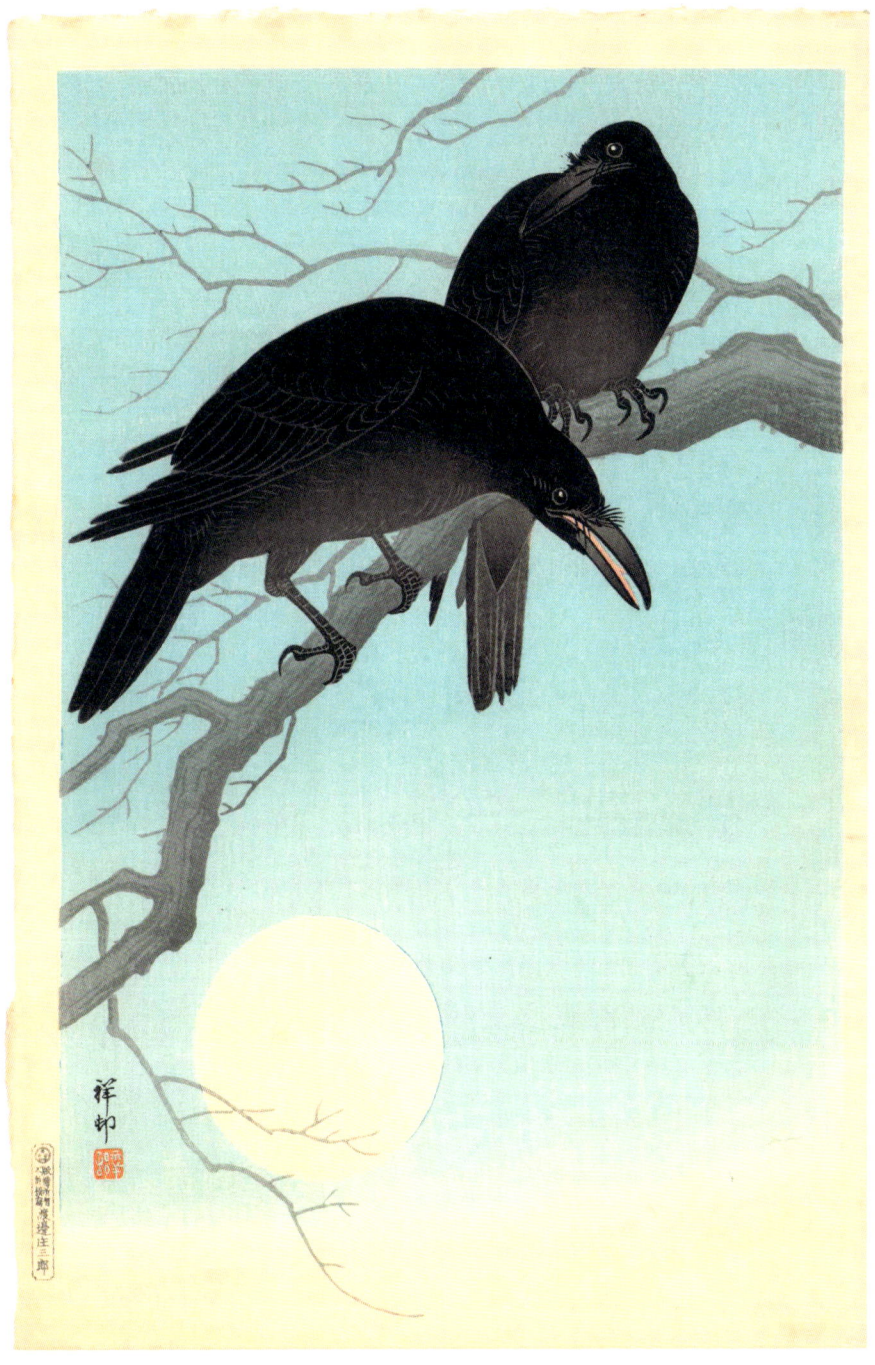

Cat. 137
Ohara Koson (Shōson)
小原古邨 (祥邨) (1877–1945)
Crows in Moonlight

Date: 1927
Signature: *Shōson*
Artist's seal: *Shōson*
Publisher: Watanabe Shōzaburō
Size: 39 × 26 cm
S. Watanabe Color Print Co.

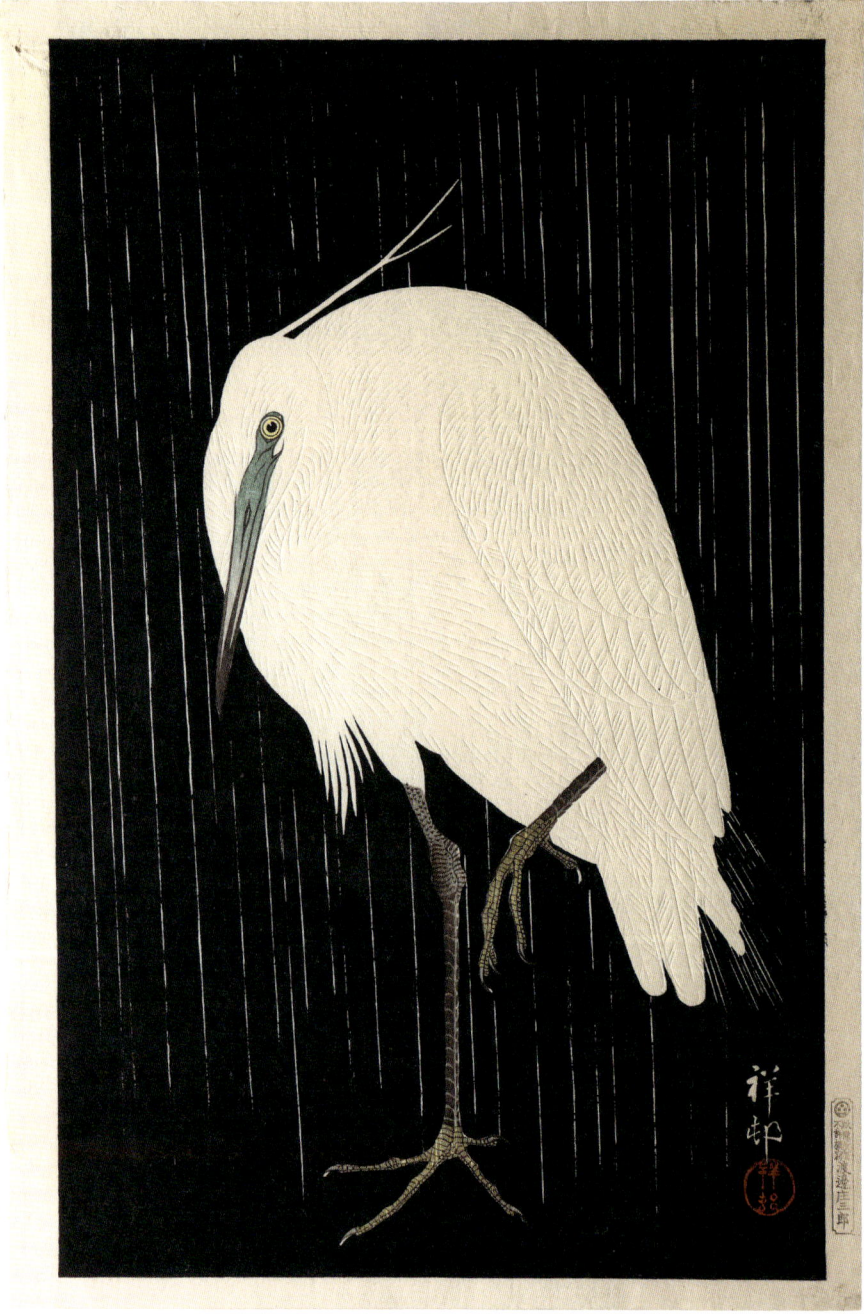

This is one of Koson's most sought-after prints, depicting a little egret (*Egretta garzetta*) standing still, hunched over, while rain comes pelting down, pictured against a pitch-black background. The egret's feathers and body are rendered in blind-printing. In general, Koson's work has quite a naturalistic feel, but this design is one of his more stylized pieces. (PO)

Cat. 138

Ohara Koson (Shōson)
小原古邨 (祥邨) (1877–1945)

Egret in Rain

Date: 1928
Signature: *Shōson*
Artist's seal: *Shōson*
Publisher: Watanabe Shōzaburō
Size: 38.3 × 26.2 cm
Collection RMAH – JP.07298

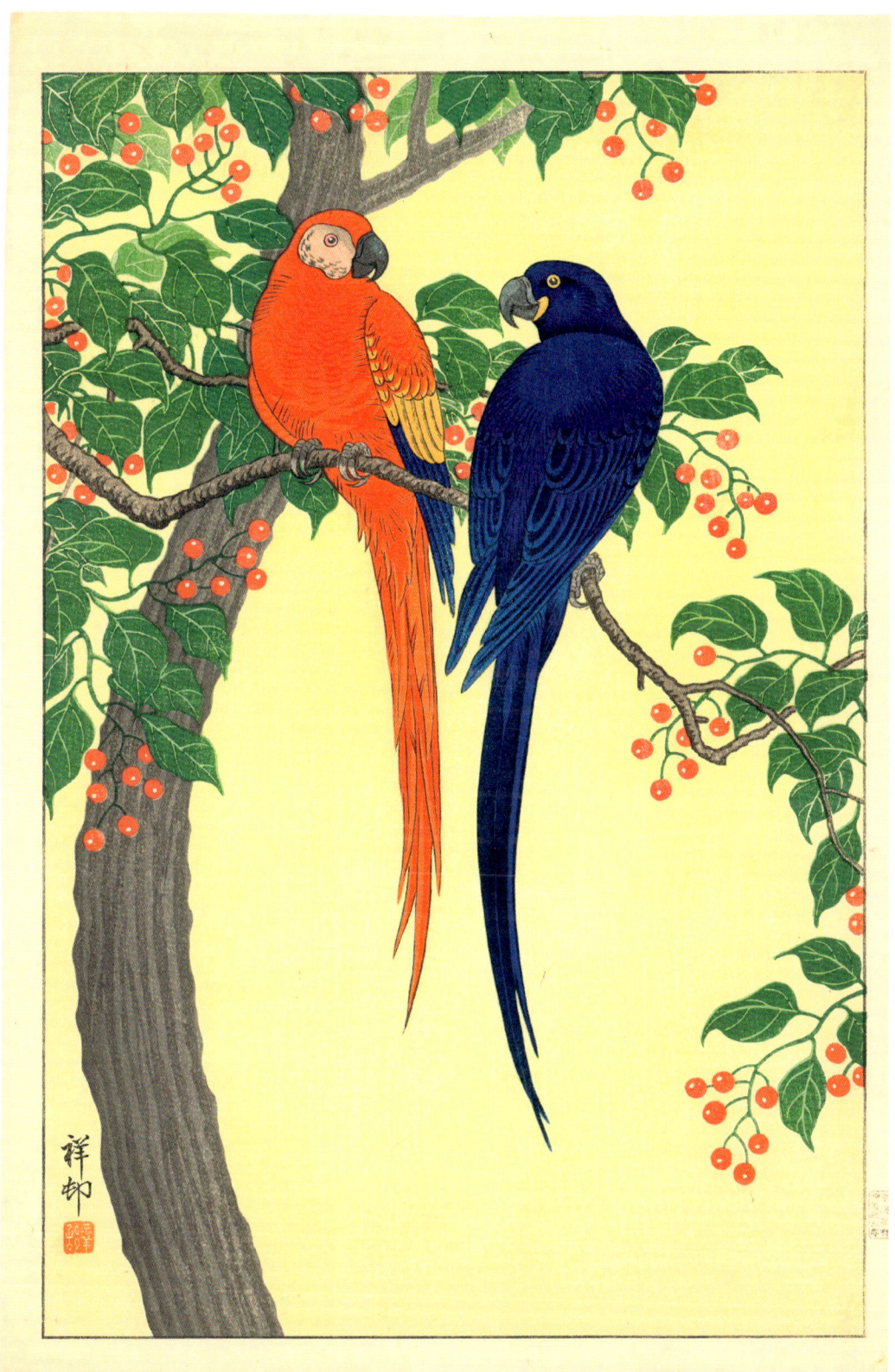

Cat. 139

Ohara Koson (Shōson)
小原古邨 (祥邨) (1877–1945)

Two Macaws

Date: c. 1932
Signature: *Shōson*
Artist's seal: *Shōson*
Publisher: Watanabe Shōzaburō
Size: 39 × 27 cm
S. Watanabe Color Print Co.

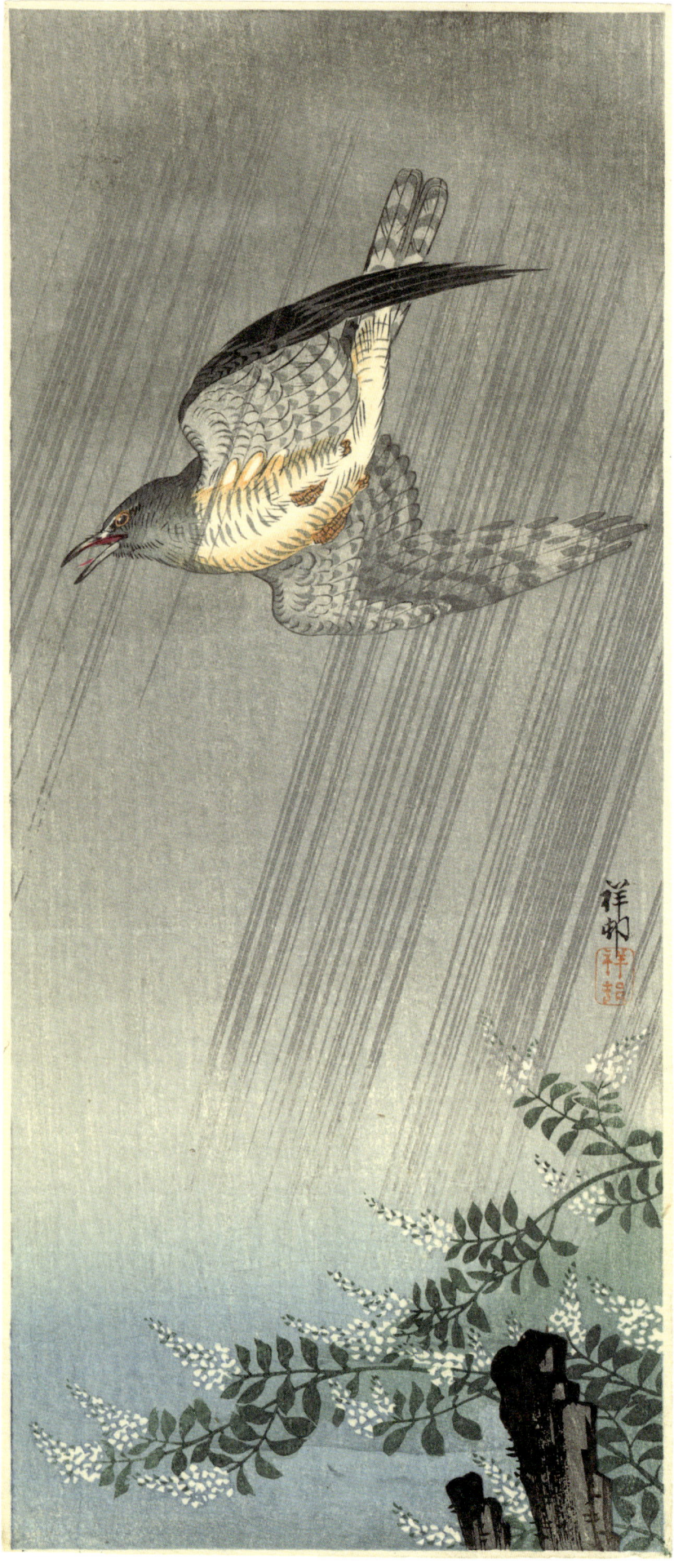

Cat. 140

Ohara Koson (Shōson)
小原古邨 (祥邨) (1877–1945)

Cuckoo in Storm

Date: After 1926
Signature: *Shōson*
Artist's seal: *Shōson*
Publisher: Watanabe Shōzaburō
Size: 37.9 × 17.1 cm
Private collection

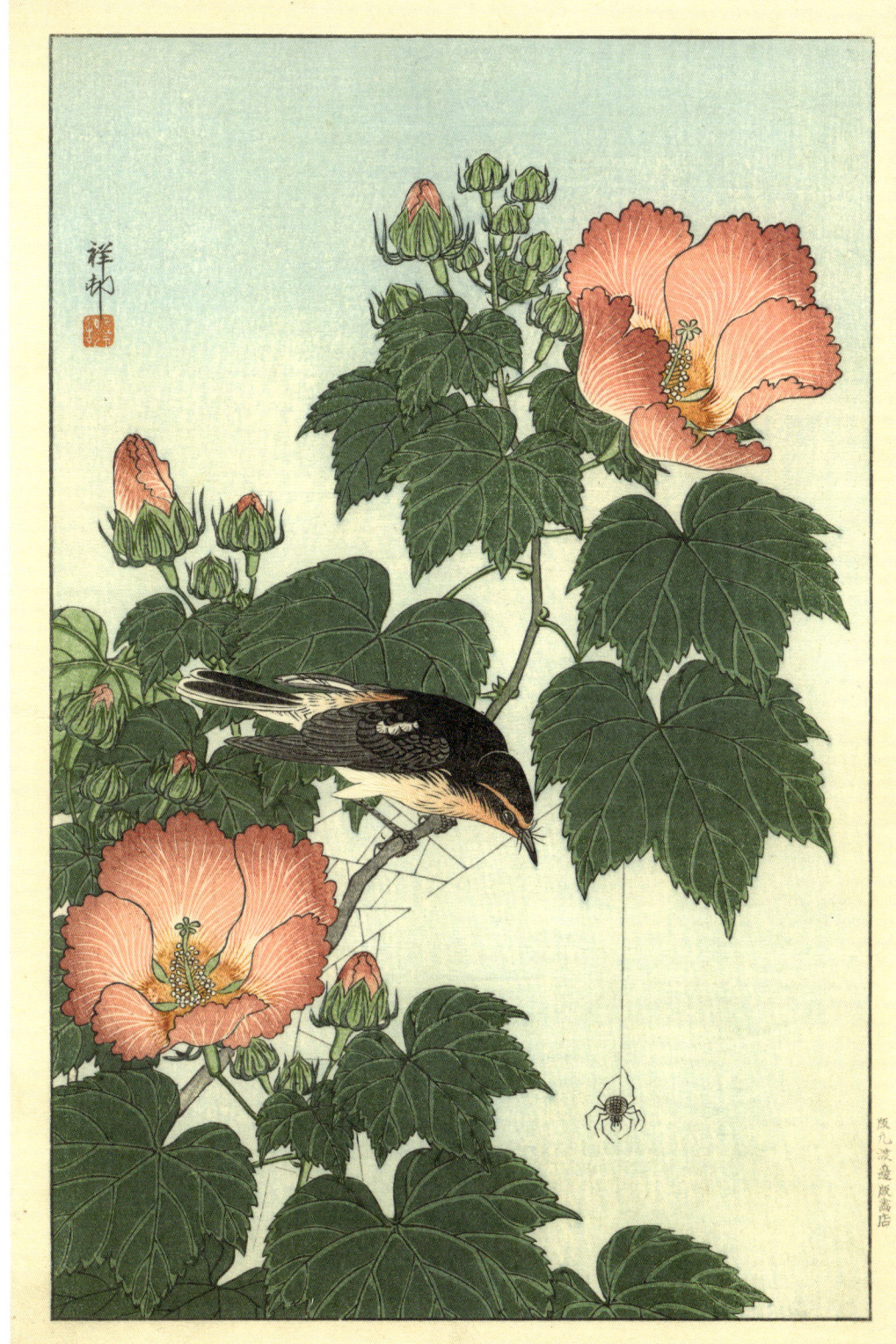

Cat. 141

Ohara Koson (Shōson)
小原古邨 (祥邨) (1877–1945)

**Flycatcher on Rose Mallow
Watching Spider**

Date: n.d. (c. 1942)
Signature: *Shōson*
Artist's seal: *Shōson*
Publisher: Watanabe Shōzaburō
Size: 39.1 × 26.3 cm
Private collection

This is an example of a design by Koson from his years working with the publisher Watanabe Shōzaburō where the depiction of the flowers dominates the design. The gorgeous printing with its beautiful, subtle colour transitions make this a prime example of what Watanabe's printers could achieve. The threatening pose of the bird, about to snatch the spider from its web, adds the necessary tension to the design. (CU)

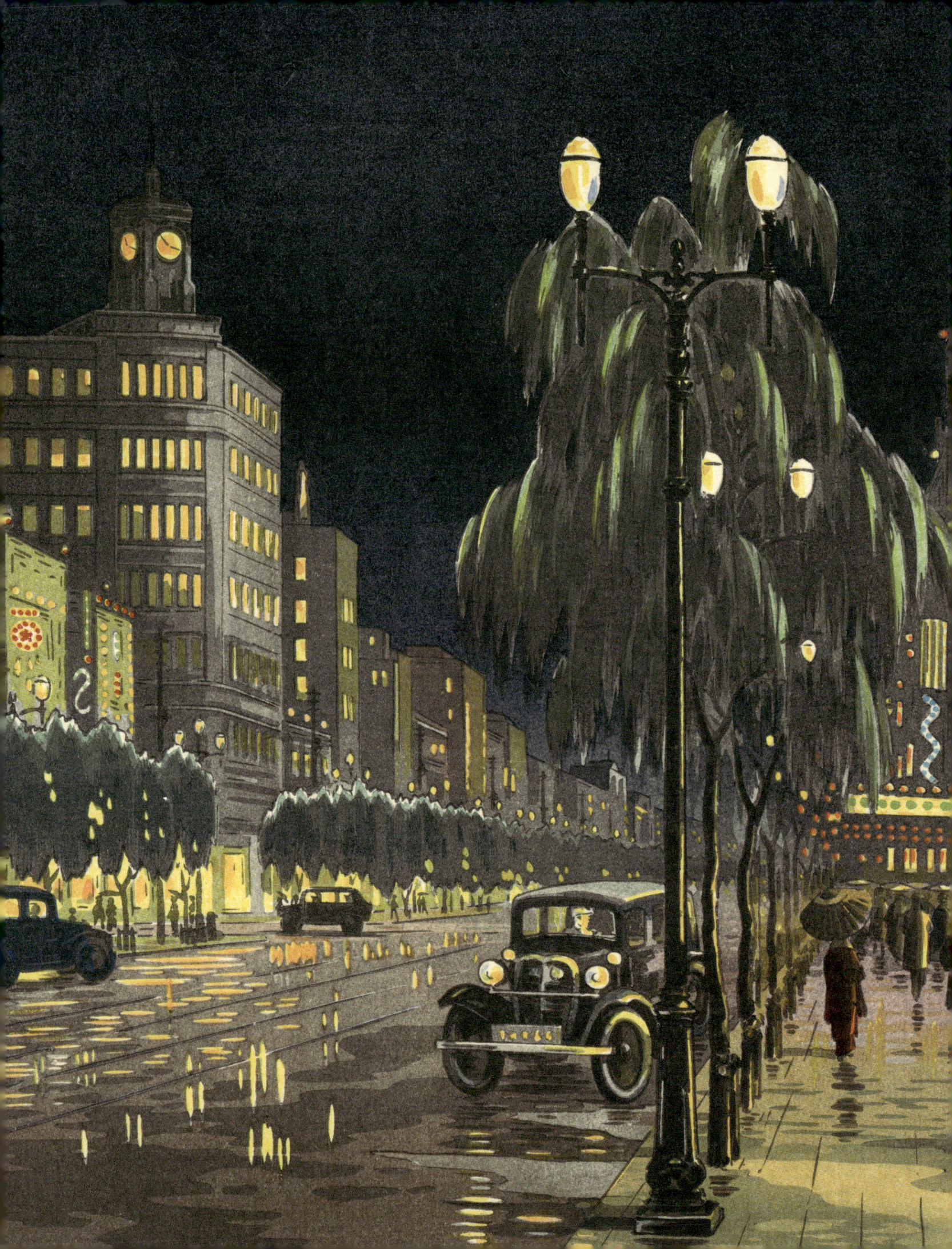

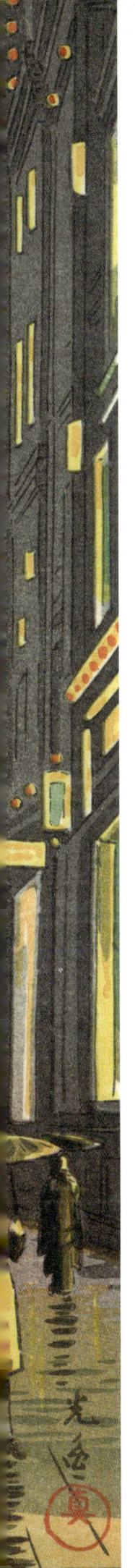

Modernity

Although *shin hanga* artists cannot be considered to belong to the intellectual and artistic avant-garde, they did pay attention to aspects of modernity during the 1920s and 1930s. Modern urban scenes and women dressed after the latest international fashions became a provocative genre.

Yamamura Kōka (Toyonari)
山村耕花 (豊成) (1885–1942)

**Dancing at the New Carlton
Hotel, Shanghai**

(*Odori Shanhai Nyū Karuton shoken*
躍り上海ニューカルトン所見)

Date: 1924
Artist's seal: *Ka* (upper left,
semi-circular seal)
Publisher: Watanabe Shōzaburō for
Yamamura Kōka Hanga Kankōkai
Size: 41.2 × 28.4 cm
Collection Scholten

Kōka is best known for his impressive actor prints but he worked in other genres as well: from bird-and-flower prints, still lifes and landscapes, to modern urban scenes such as *Dancing at the New Carlton Hotel, Shanghai*. He based this design on his painting titled *The New Carlton* (*Nyū Karuton*). It was exhibited in March of the same year, just prior to the release of this print, at the distinguished Mitsukoshi department store, as part of the *Nihon Bijutsuin Shisaku Tenrankai* (Japan Art Institute Trial Piece Exhibitio).

The print radiates modernity, depicting a ballroom with four dancing couples and two fashionable women enjoying a cocktail. Everyone in the ballroom is wearing Western dress, and the women are all sporting short bobbed hair. The print has a fine dusting of mother-of-pearl, adding to its luxurious appearance. This print is considered to be the first woodblock print to depict 'modern women' (so-called *moga*, see also Cat. 144).

Shanghai in the 1920s was a metropolis with a thriving night life, promising fun, modernity and excitement:

The centre of night life is a vast crucible of electric flame. The throb of the jungle tom-tom; the symphony of lust; the music of a hundred orchestras; the swaying of bodies; the rhythm of abandon; the hot smoke of desire – desire under the floodlights; it's all fun; it's life. Joy, gin, and jazz. (*All about Shanghai and Environs* [Shanghai: Shanghai University Press, 1934], p. 76)

(PO)

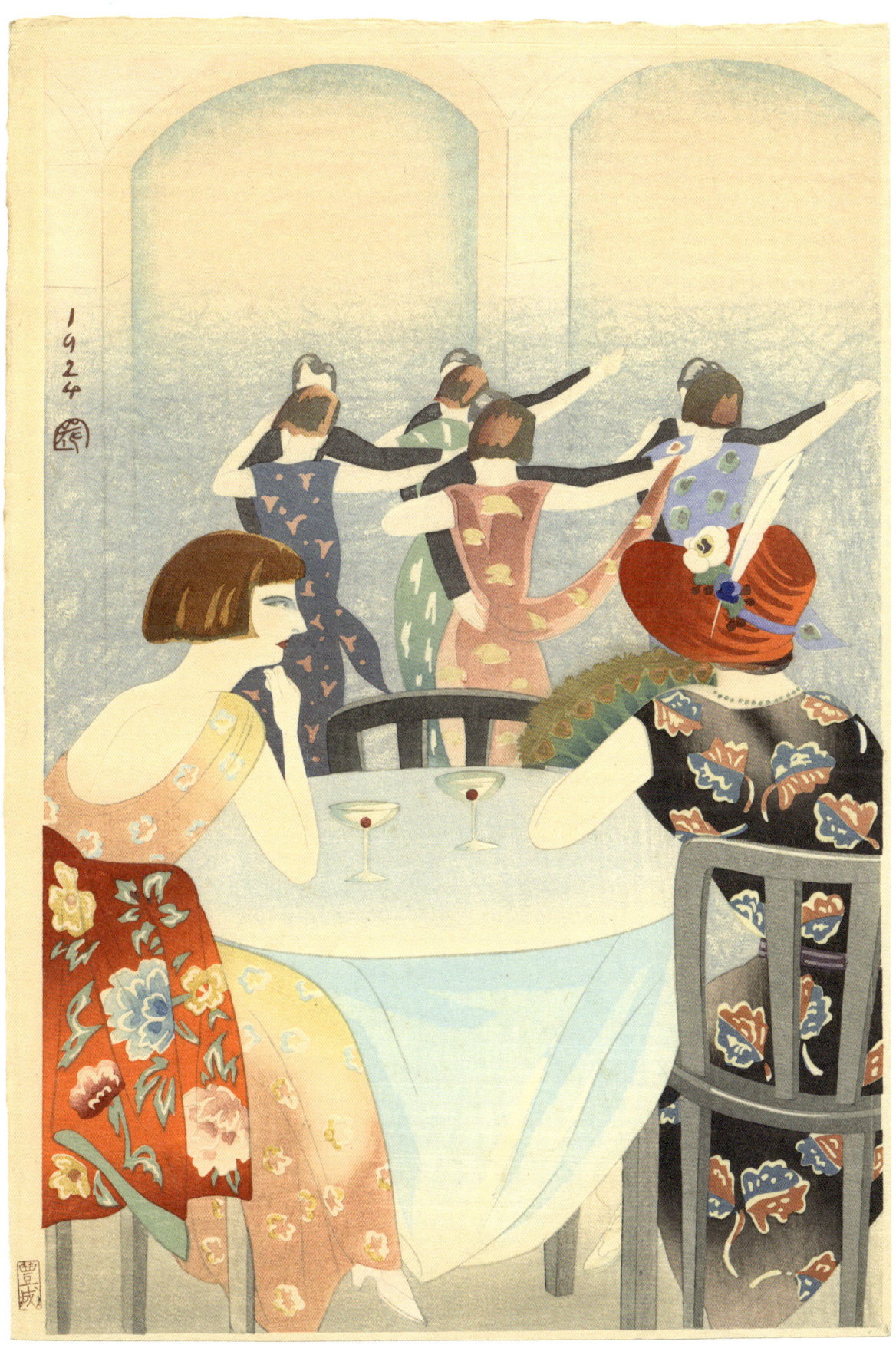

Cat. 143

Takahashi Hiroaki (Shōtei)
高橋弘明 (松亭) (1871–1945)

Nude Playing with a Cat

(*Rafu neko jarashi* 裸婦 猫じゃらし)

Date: c. 1927–30
Signature: *Hiroaki*
Artist's seal: *Hiroaki saku*
Publisher: Fusui gabō (Fusui workshop)
Size: 43.2 × 27.2 cm
Collection Scholten

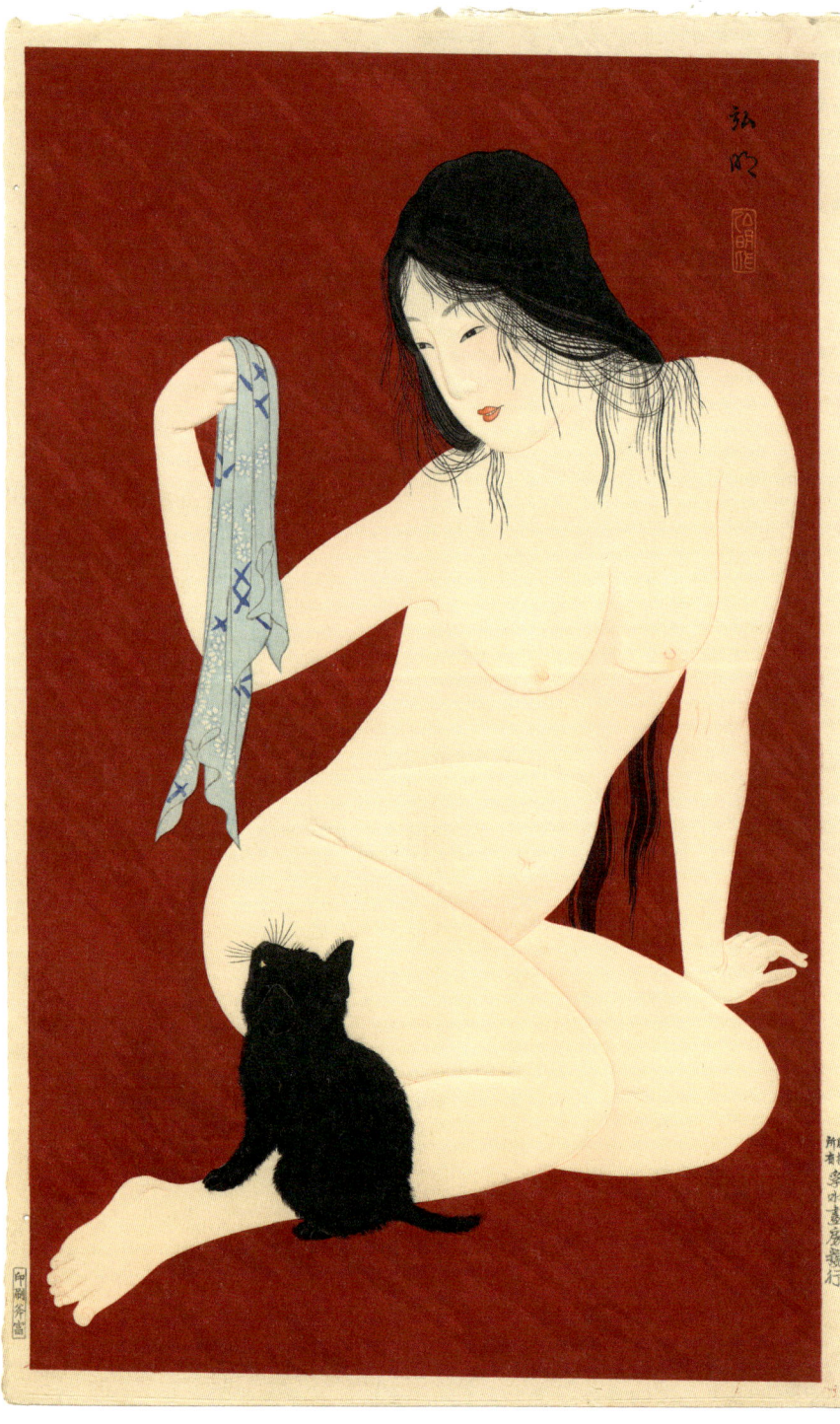

Deviating from his standard subject of the Japanese landscape, Hiroaki produced three nudes between 1927 and 1931 with the publisher Fusui. They are beautifully printed and provocative and now rare; the Fusui headquarters were destroyed during the Second World War, causing the total destruction of print stocks and blocks. Blind-printing (*karazuri*) accentuates the outer lines of the nude's body. The deep-red background and the black in the cat's fur and the woman's hair form a beautiful contrast. (PO)

Completely in tune with the times, Kiyoshi has created an iconic image that embodies the modern woman of the 1920s in Japan. These 'modern women' (*modan gāru*, or *moga* for short) can be seen as the Japanese equivalent of the United States' flappers, Germany's *neue Frauen*, France's *garçonnes* or China's *modeng xiaojie*.

The term *moga* was first introduced in Jun'ichirō Tanizaki's (1886–1965) novel *Naomi* (1924). The modern girl was a symbol of Westernization and modernity: independent both financially and emotionally, and sexually liberated. It was a striking contrast to the 19th-century ideal of the 'good wife, wise mother' (*ryōsai kenbo*), which confined the Japanese woman to the household.

This woman completely looks the part: wearing a polka-dot dress and Western jewellery, she is enjoying a night out in an urban café. She is leisurely resting her elbows on the table, her bobbed hair is loosely pinned back, and she seductively and confidently looks straight towards the viewer, while she smokes a cigarette and drinks a Manhattan cocktail, which, as we can judge from her slightly flushed face, might not be her first. The scarlet background adds to the sensuality and intimate setting and composition, but also to the bold, colourful and graphic quality of this design. It is now seen as one of Kiyoshi's finest works and is one of his most illustrated.

In 1935 Kiyoshi commented on the topic:

There are people who do pictures of the olden days. I don't understand why they do that. I want to depict the society that is changing now – living people, the manners and customs of the environment in front of me [...]. ('Shiranui', *Ukiyo-e geijutsu*, vol. 4, no. 3 [March 1935], pp. 60–61)

(PO)

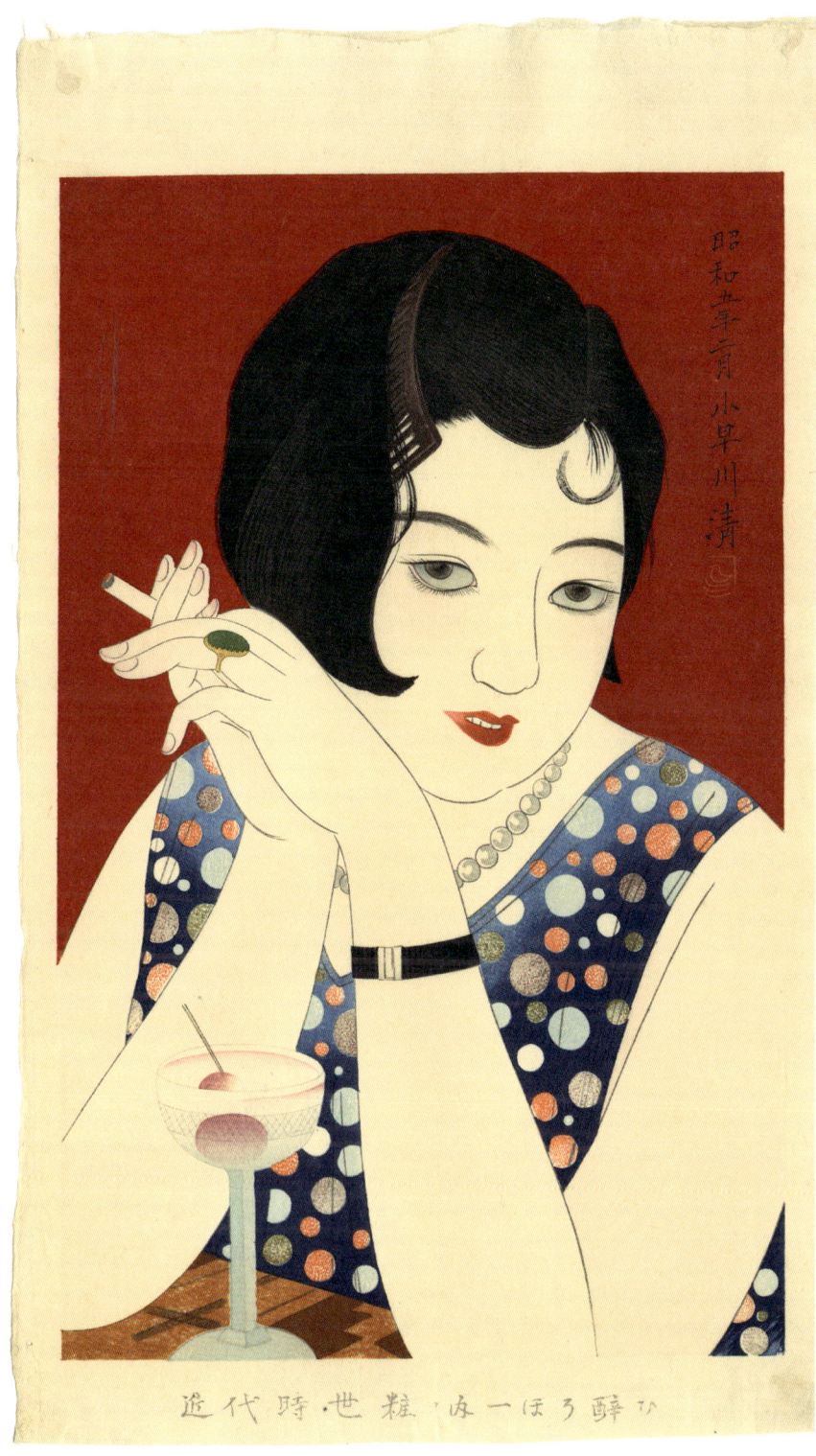

Cat. 144

Kobayakawa Kiyoshi 小早川清
(1899?–1948)

Tipsy (no. 1)

(*[ichi] Horoyoi* [一] ほろ酔い)

Series: *Figures in Contemporary Fashions*
(*Kindai jiseishō no uchi* 近代時世粧ノ内)
Date: February 1930
Signature: *Kobayakawa Kiyoshi*
Artist's seal: bird-shaped seal
Publisher: self-published
Block cutter: *Takano Shichinosuke*
Printer: *Ono Tomisaburō*
Size: 52 × 30 cm
Collection Scholten

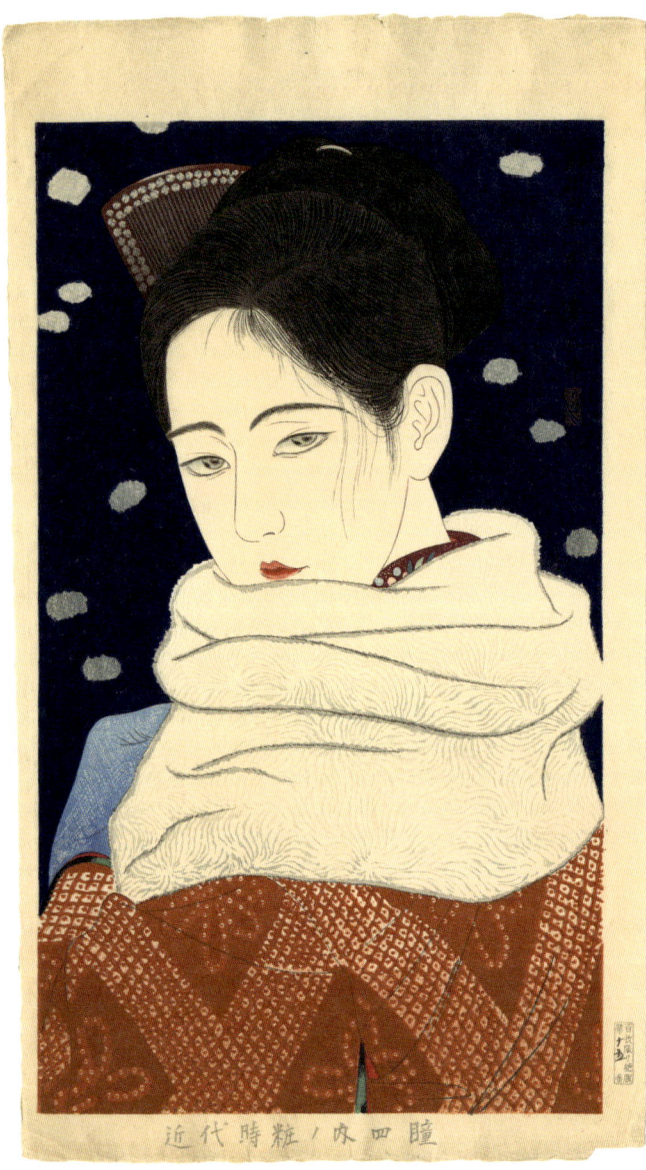

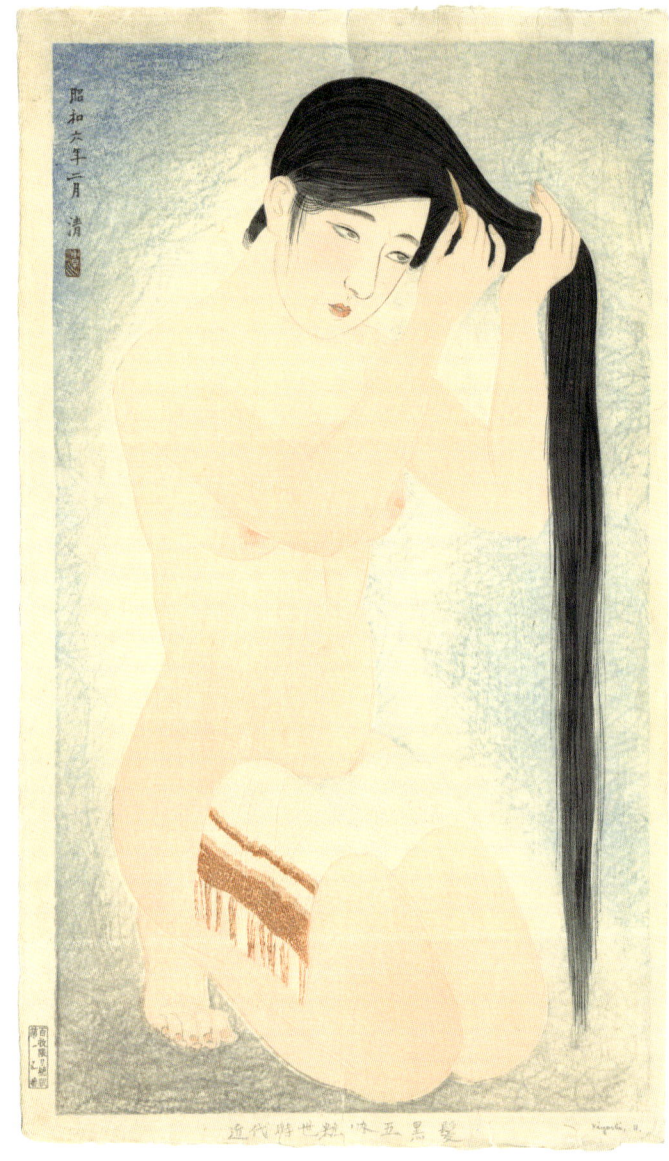

Cat. 145

Kobayakawa Kiyoshi 小早川清
(1899?–1948)

Pupils of the Eyes (no. 4)

(*[yon] Hitomi* [四] 瞳)

Series: *Figures in Contemporary Fashions*
(*Kindai jiseishō no uchi* 近代時世粧ノ内)
Date: January 1931
Signature: *Kiyoshi no saku*
Artist's seal: *Kobayakawa*
Edition: 15/100
Publisher: self-published
Block cutter: *Takano Shichinosuke*
Printer: *Ono Tomisaburō*
Size: 53 × 30 cm
Private collection, the Netherlands

Cat. 146

Kobayakawa Kiyoshi 小早川清
(1899?–1948)

Black Hair (no. 5)

(*[go] Kurokami* [五] 黒髪)

Series: *Figures in Contemporary Fashions*
(*Kindai jiseishō no uchi* 近代時世粧ノ内)
Date: February 1931
Signature: *Kiyoshi*
Artist's seal: *Kobayakawa*
Edition: 15/100
Publisher: self-published
Block cutter: *Takano Shichinosuke*
Printer: *Ono Tomisaburō*
Size: 52.5 × 30.5 cm
Collection Scholten

Kobayakawa Kiyoshi 小早川清
(1899?–1948)
Rouge (no. 6)

(*[roku] Kuchibeni* [六] 口紅)

Series: *Figures in Contemporary Fashions*
(*Kindai jiseishō no uchi* 近代時世粧ノ内)
Date: March 1931
Signature: *Kiyoshi*
Artist's seal: *Kobayakawa*
Edition: 2/100
Publisher: self-published
Block cutter: *Takano Shichinosuke*
Printer: *Ono Tomisaburō*
Size: 54.2 × 30.2 cm
Collection Scholten

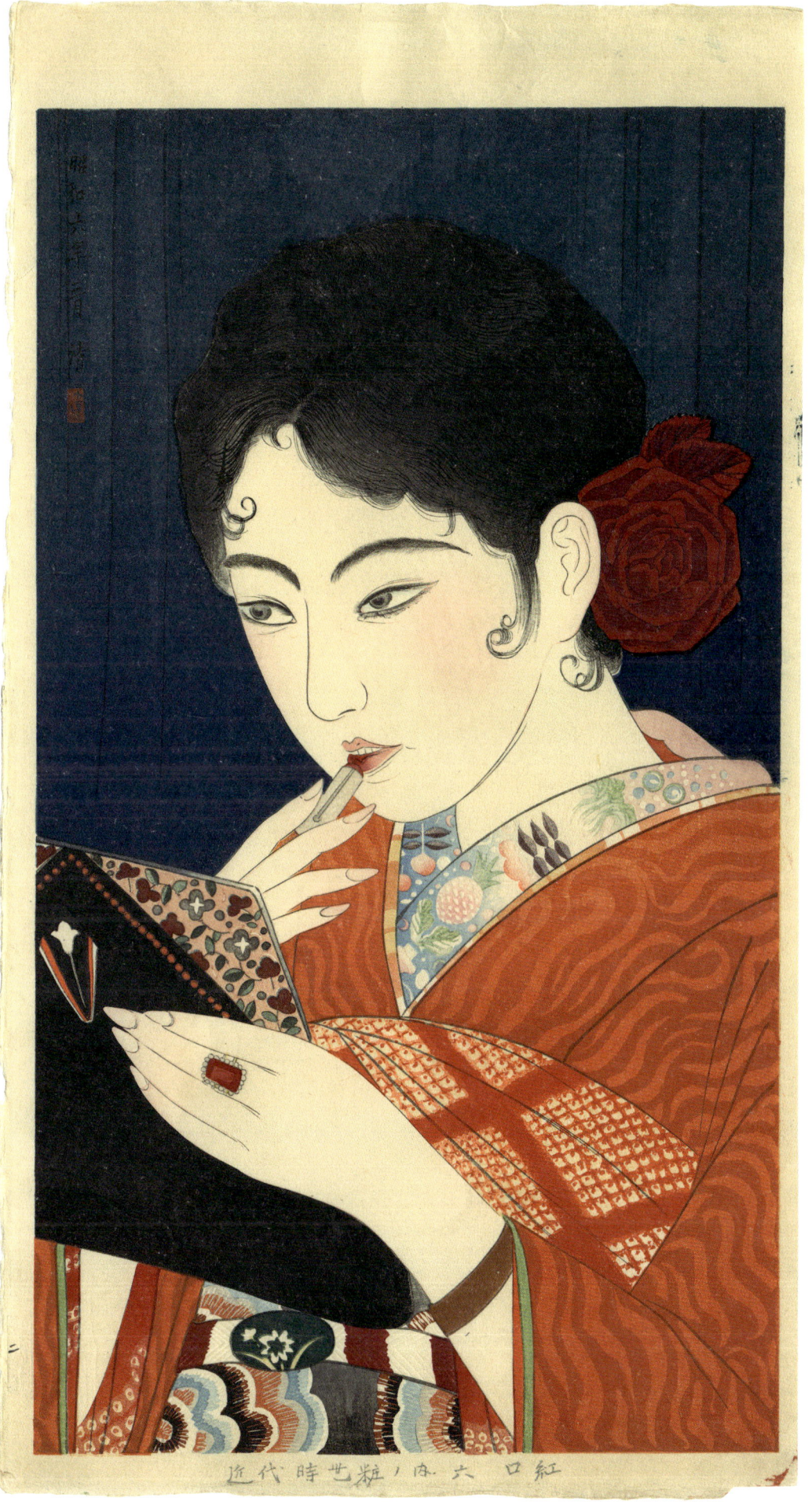

Cat. 148

Kobayakawa Kiyoshi 小早川清
(1899?–1948)

Dance

(*Odori* 踊り)

Date: Spring 1932
Signature: *Kiyoshi*
Artist's seal: *Kobayakawa*
Edition: 54/100
Publisher: Hasegawa
Block cutter: *Takano* (Takano Shichinosuke)
Printer: *Ono Tomi* (Ono Tomisaburō)
Size: 45.5 × 32.5 cm
Collection Scholten

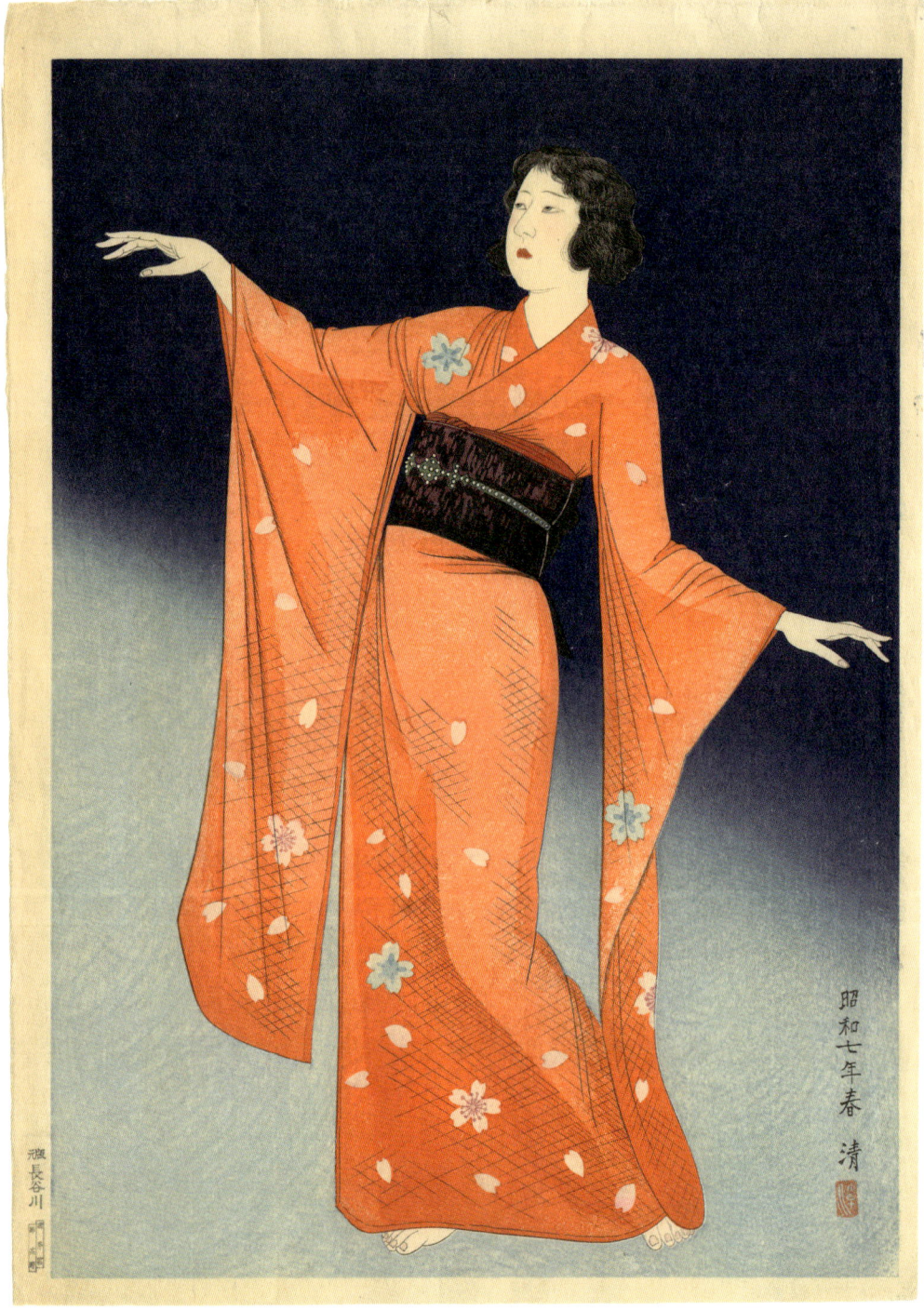

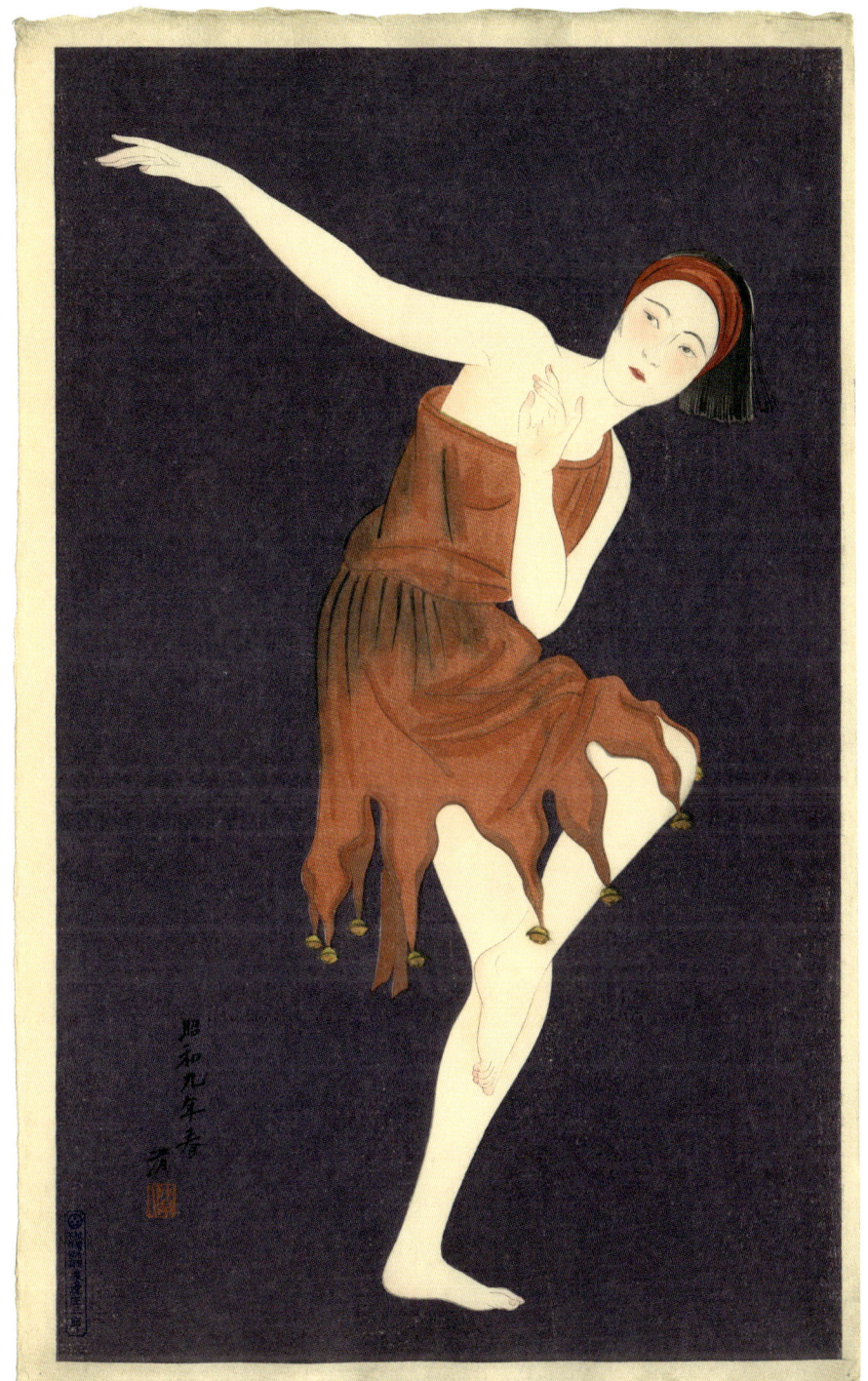

Cat. 149

Kobayakawa Kiyoshi 小早川清
(1899?–1948)

Modern Dance (Western-Style Dancing)

(*Butō* 舞踏)

Date: Summer 1934
Signature: *Kiyoshi*
Artist's seal: *Kobayakawa*
Publisher: Watanabe Shōzaburō
Size: 43.4 × 27.5 cm
Collection Scholten

From the early 1920s onwards, dancing was a popular pastime and more and more dance halls popped up in Tokyo. Two years earlier, Kiyoshi published two other prints of a woman dancing against a minimalistic backdrop: *Dance* (Cat. 148) and *Dancer* (both published by Hasegawa).

In March and April of 1934, various famous European dance companies performed in Japan. Perhaps Kiyoshi was partly inspired by such visits from abroad.

(PO)

Cat. 150

Takahashi Hiroaki (Shōtei)
高橋弘明 (松亭) (1871–1945)
**A Nude Woman in Front
of a Mirror**

(*Kagami no mae no rafu* 鏡の前の裸婦)

Date: c. 1927
Signature: *Hiroaki*
Artist's seal: *Hiroaki*
Publisher: Fusui gabō (Fusui Workshop)
Size: 39.1 × 26.8 cm
Collection Scholten

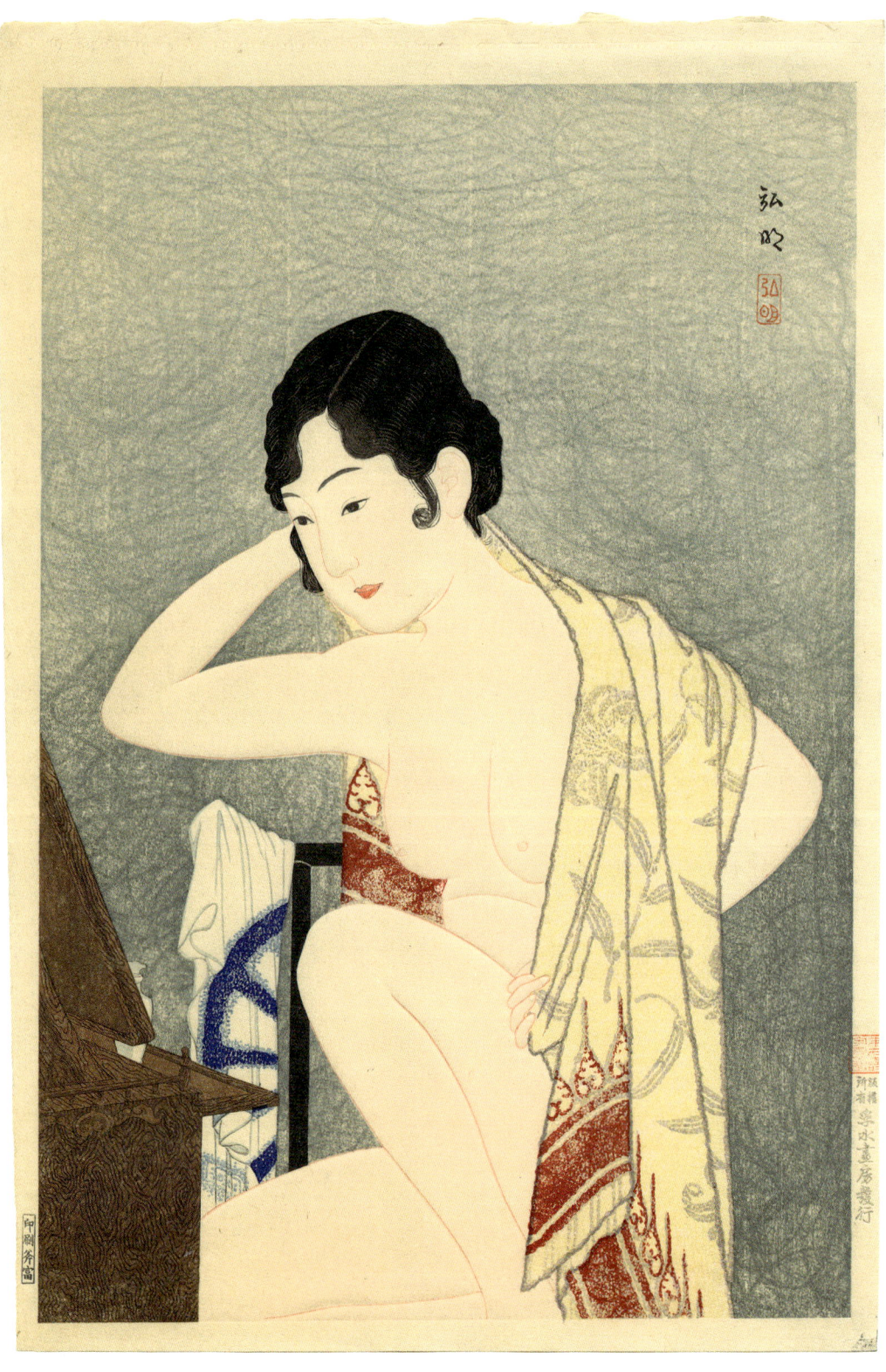

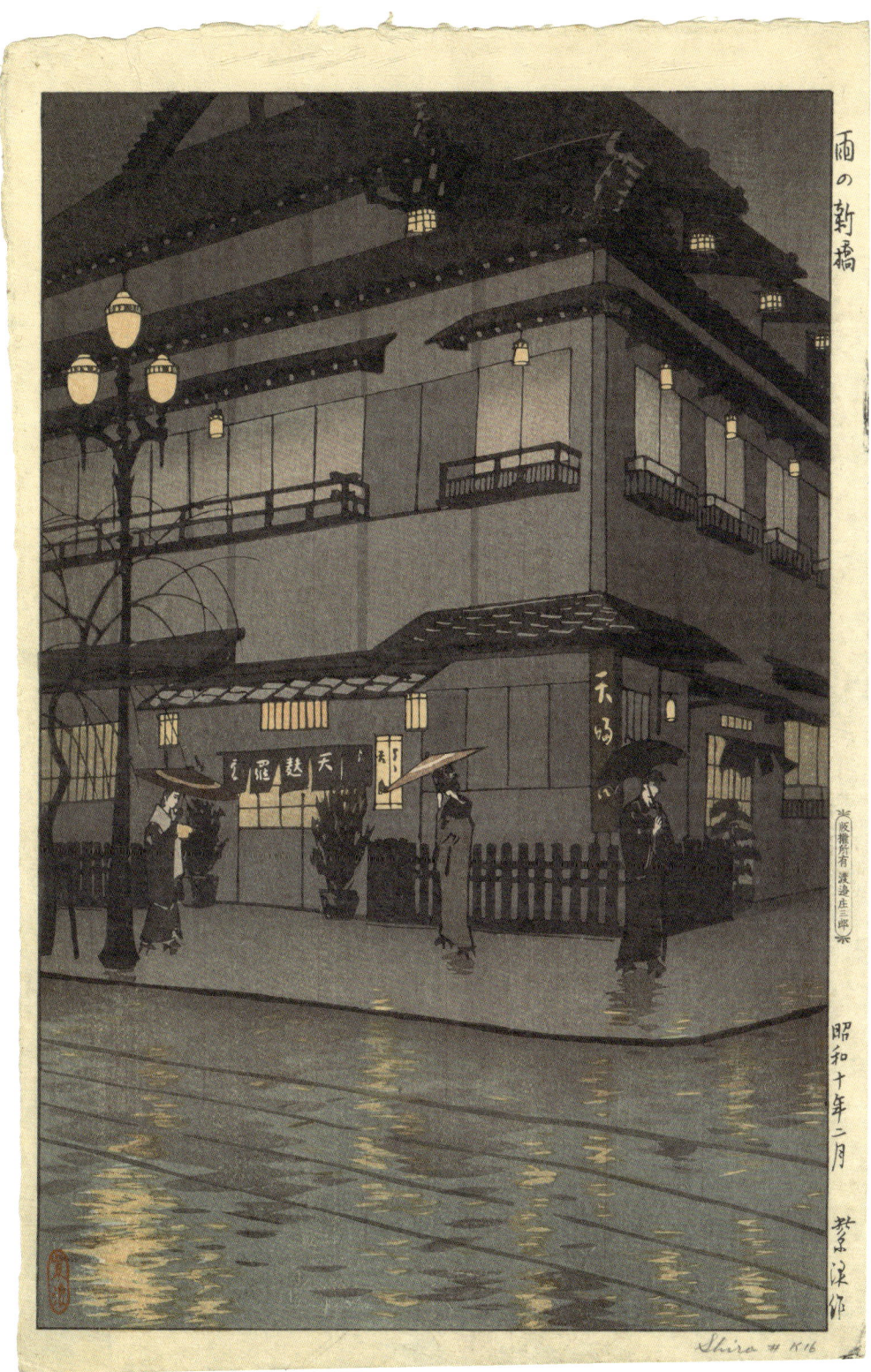

Cat. 151

Kasamatsu Shirō 笠松紫浪
(1898–1991)

Shinbashi in Rain

(*Ame no Shinbashi* 雨の新橋)

Date: February 1935
Signature: Right margin: *Kasamatsu saku*,
lower right margin *Shiro* (romanized)
Artist's seal: *Shirō*
Publisher: Watanabe Shōzaburō
Size: 39 × 26.4 cm
Collection Hein Vijverberg

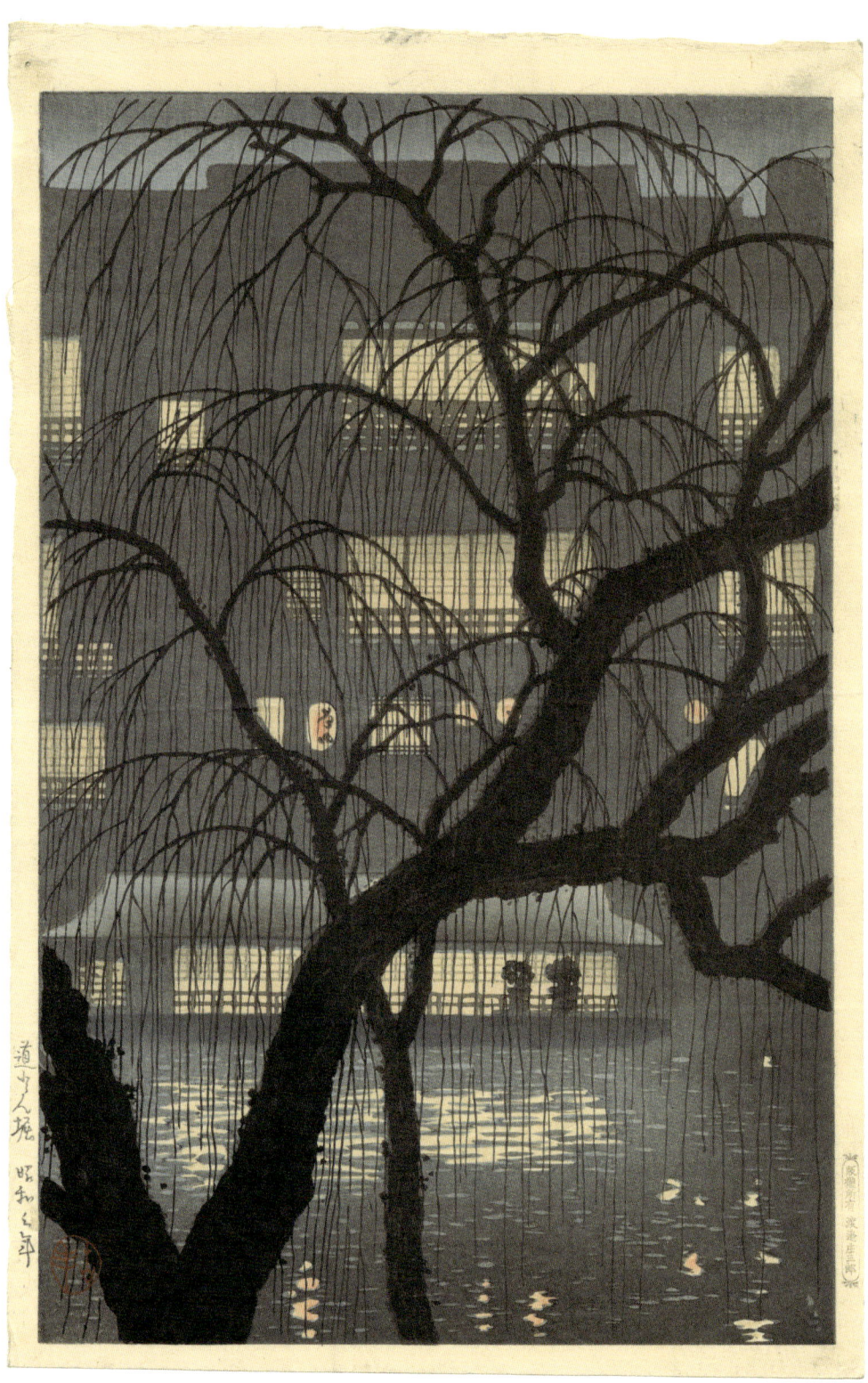

Cat. 152

Uehara Konen 上原古年
(1878–1940)

Dōtonbori

(*Dōtonbori* 道とん堀)

Date: 1928
Artist's seal: *Konen*
Publisher: Watanabe Shōzaburō
Size: 38.8 × 25.7 cm
Collection Scholten

Dōtonbori had been the main entertainment district of Osaka since it was designated as such by the Tokugawa shogunate in 1621, and its broad canal was a much-loved attraction. The allure of its theatres had also ensured a rich variety of restaurants and teahouses that could accommodate the crowds, offering specialties from Osaka, a city also known as 'the Kitchen of the Country'. A common saying associated with Dōtonbori is *kuidaore*, or 'eat until you drop'. Here Konen chose a romantic but modernized rendition of the canal, with bright lights shining through the branches of the willow in the foreground.

(JD)

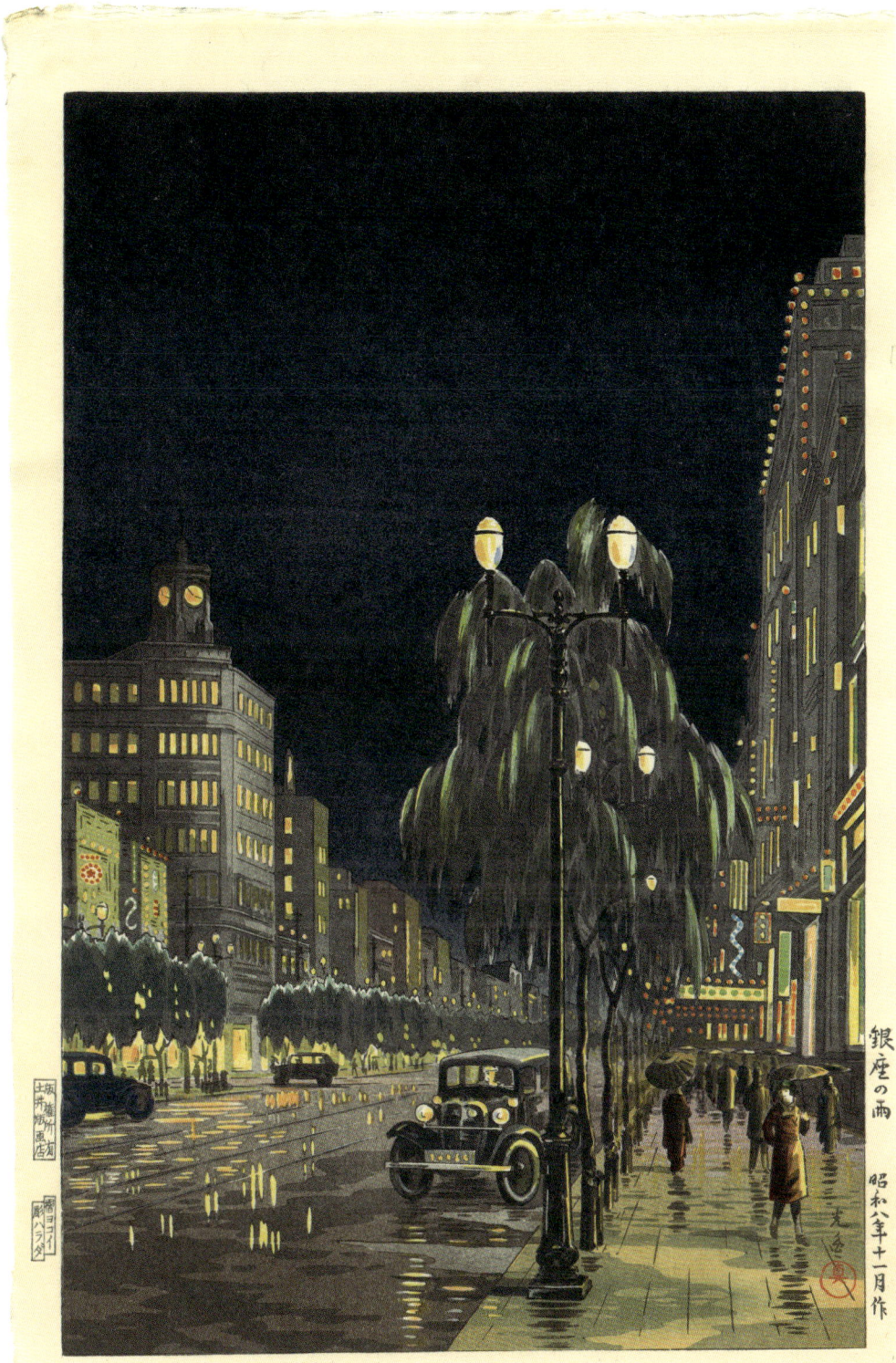

Cat. 153

Tsuchiya Kōitsu 土屋光逸
(1870–1949)

Ginza in the Rain
(*Ginza no ame* 銀座の雨)

Series: *Views of Tokyo*
(*Tōkyō fūkei* 東京風景)
Date: November 1933 (second printing
after 1938, possibly post-war)
Signature: *Kōitsu*
Artist's seal: *Shin*
Publisher: Doi hangaten
(Doi publishing firm)
Block cutter: *Harada* (Harada Kametarō)
Printer: *Yokoi* (Yokoi Giichi)
Size: 39.5 × 26.5 cm
Collection Scholten

Ginza was originally a colloquial name taken after the silver mint office that was established in the area by the Tokugawa government in the 17th century. When the district was completely destroyed by fire in 1872, the Meiji government rebuilt it as a model modern city, with gaslight lanterns and fireproof brick houses. The area was destroyed and reconstructed twice more, in the 1923 earthquake and by the bombings of the Second World War. Despite this history of destruction, Ginza has maintained its status as one of the most luxurious commercial districts in the world. In this design Kōitsu plays with the brightness of the countless neon lights of the modern city, reflected in the wet pavement of the street.
(JD)

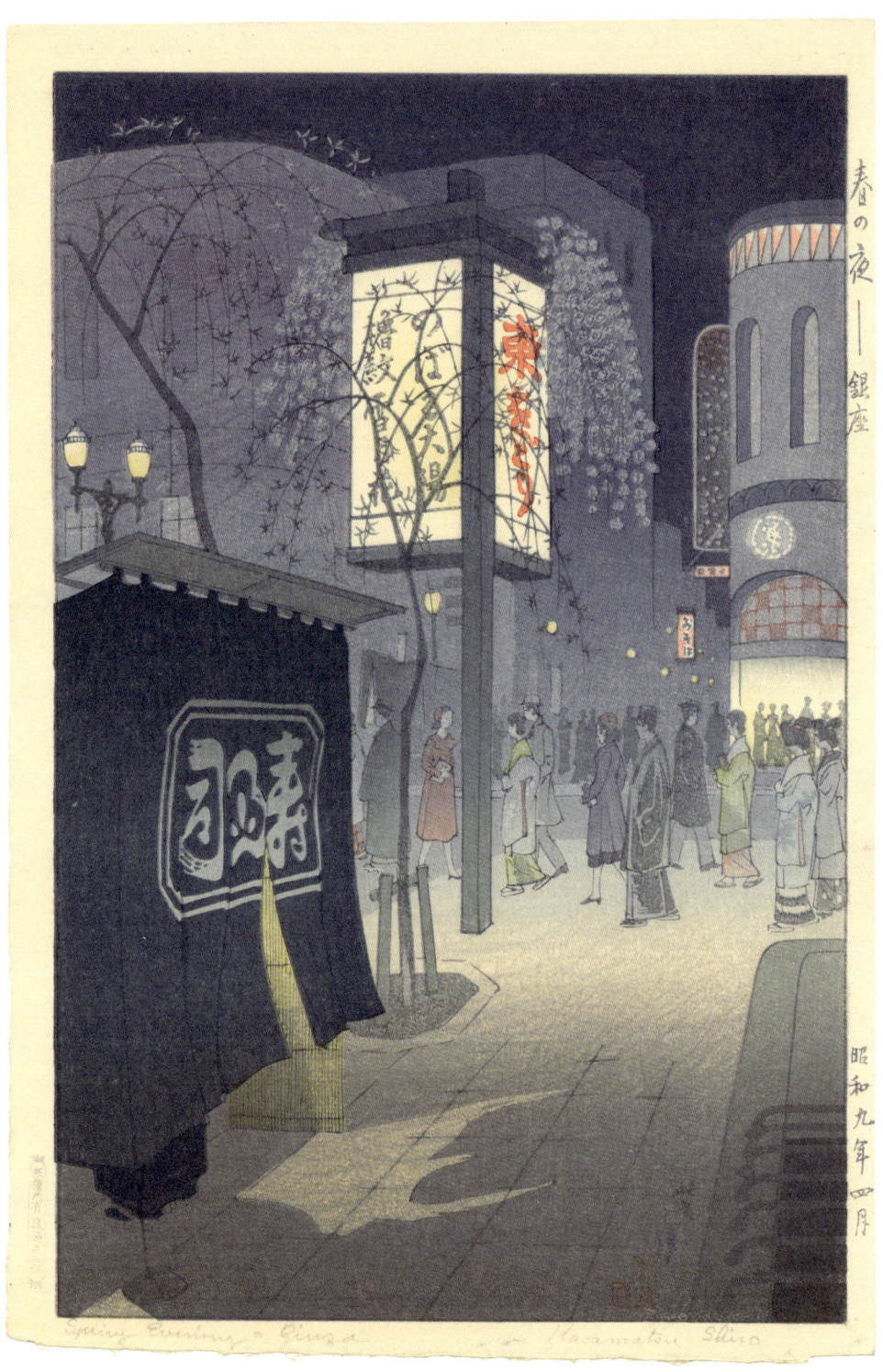

Cat. 154

Kasamatsu Shirō 笠松紫浪
(1898–1991)

Spring Night, Ginza

(*Haru no yoru Ginza* 春の夜 銀座)

Date: April 1934
Signature: *Shirō*
Artist's seal: *Shirō saku*
Publisher: Watanabe Shōzaburō
Size: 38.5 × 25.5 cm
Collection RMAH – JP.07295

Although the street is filled with people, the viewer is placed in a quiet spot and watches the crowd from afar, which, together with the restricted colour scheme, creates a sense of serenity. The tiny traditional sushi stall in the foreground contrasts with the huge neon-lit building blocks in the background. The feet of a sole customer appear from under the stall's *noren*, the cloth divider that is hung at the entrances of shops and restaurants. The red letters in the illuminated sign read *Azuma odori*, a type of dance typically performed in spring. Judging from the thick layers of clothes worn by the people in the background, this scene takes place on a cold early-spring evening.

(JD)

Cat. 155

Kasamatsu Shirō 笠松紫浪
(1898–1991)

**The Great Lantern of the
Kannondō, Asakusa**

(*Asakusa Kannondō daichōchin*
浅草観音堂大提灯)

Date: Spring 1934
Signature: *Shirō*
Artist's seal: *Shirō saku*
Publisher: Watanabe Shōzaburō
Size: 39.5 × 25.7 cm
Collection RMAH – JP.07294

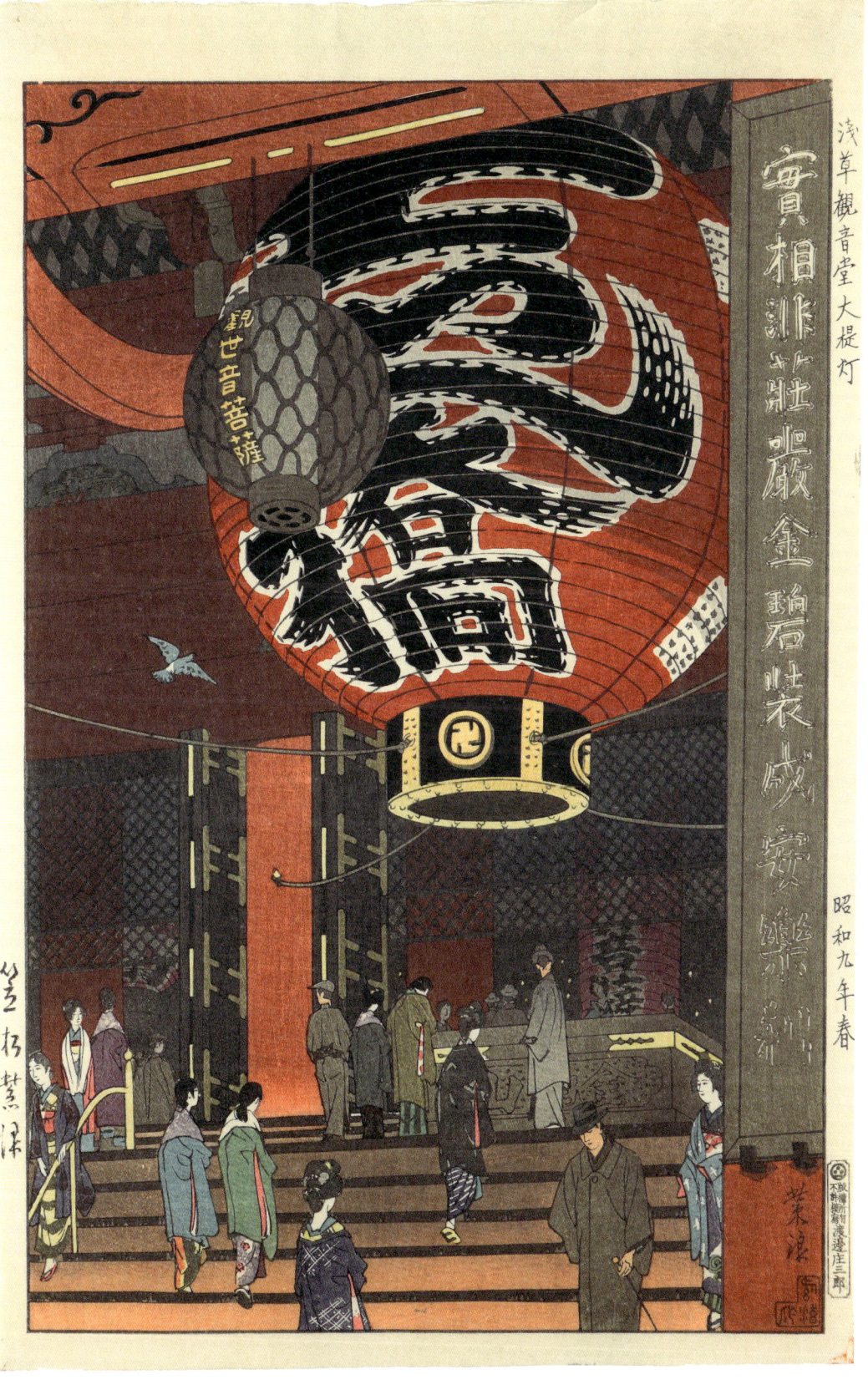

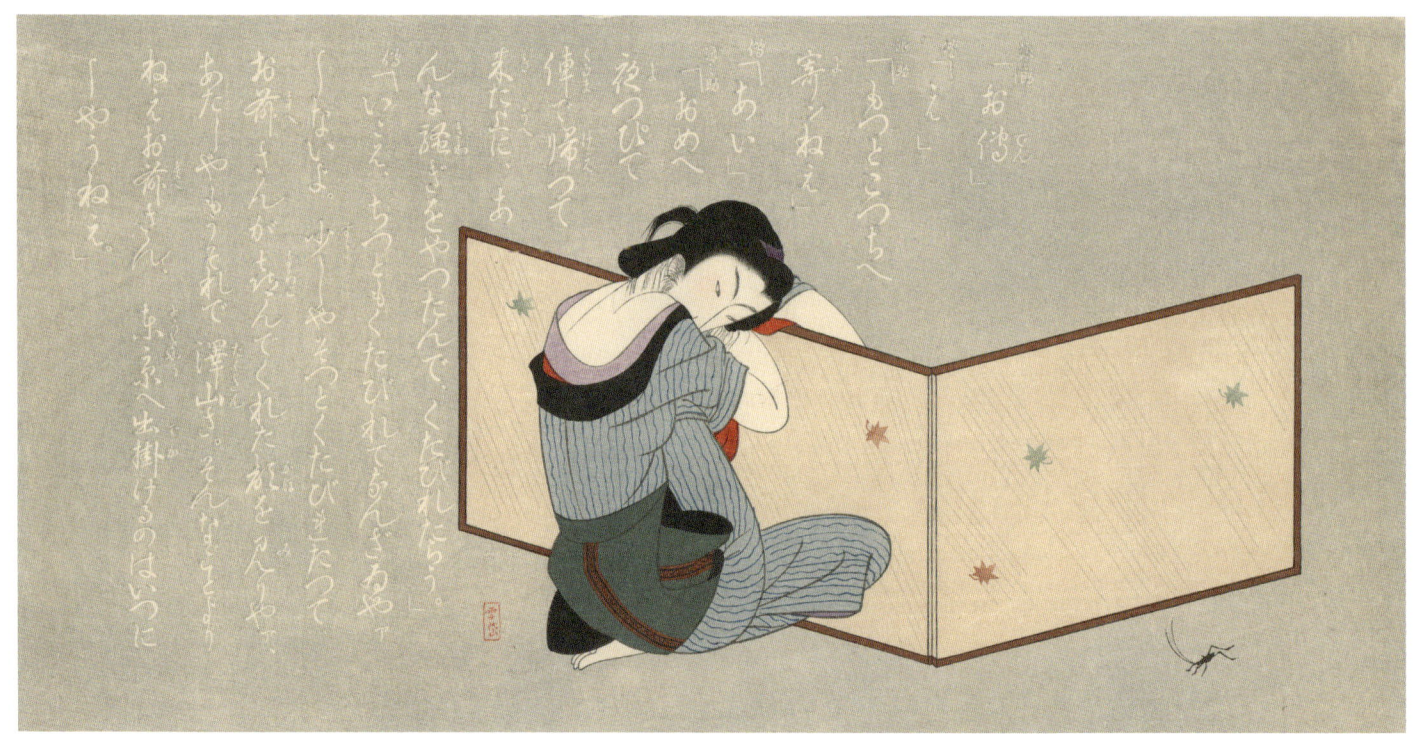

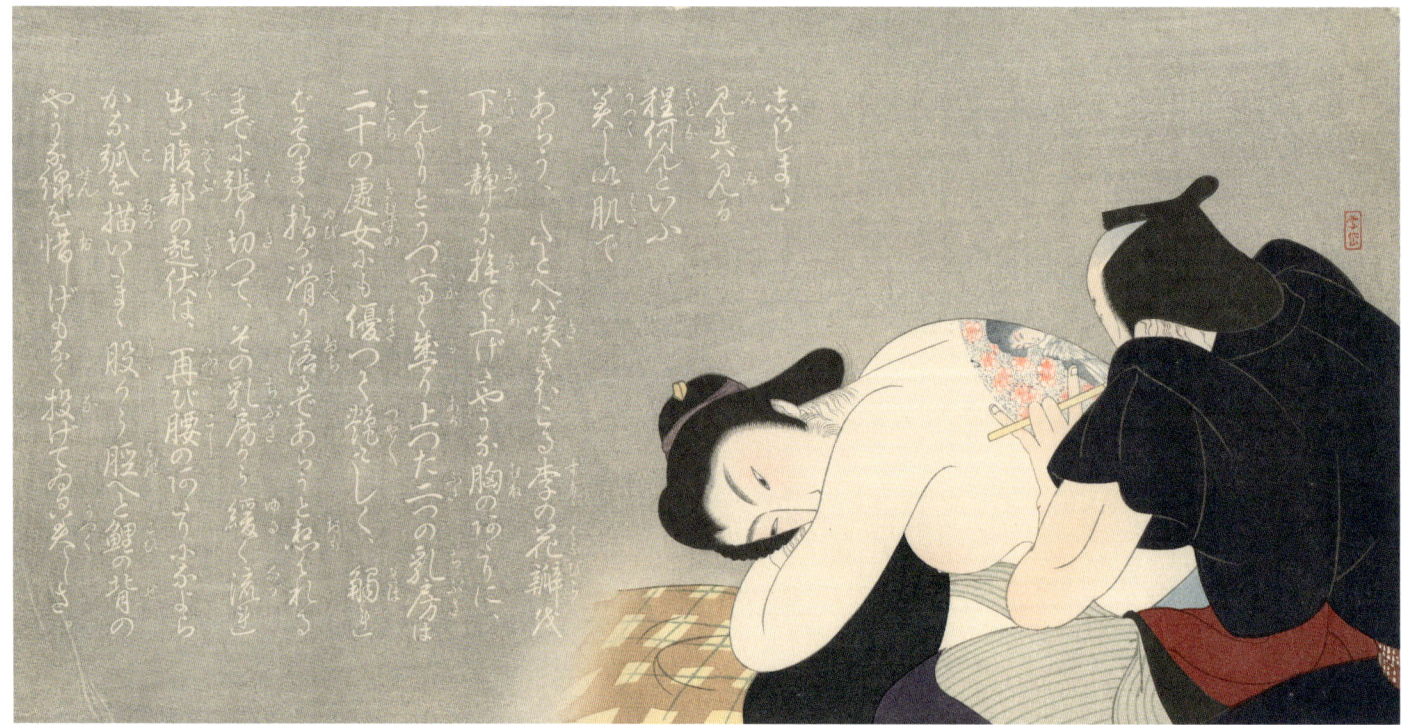

156a

156b

Cat. 156a–d

Komura Settai 小村雪岱
(1887–1940)

Series: *A Legend from Hell*
(*Oden jigoku* お傳地獄)
Date: 1938
Artist's seal: *Settai*
Publisher: privately published
(commissioned by Kunieda Kanji)
Size: 27.5 × 52 cm
Collection Scholten

These four designs by Settai, printed in an exceptional format, clearly deviate in style from other *shin hanga* works. Settai was inspired by the fine delineated style of the 18th-century ukiyo-e master Suzuki Harunobu (1724?–70). *Oden jigoku* (A Legend from Hell) was originally a serialized story written by Kunieda Kanji (1892–1956), with illustrations by Settai, which ran in the newspaper *Yomiuri shinbun* from 1934 to 1935. It was later published as a two-volume book by Chiyoda Shoin in 1935. Kunieda was so impressed with Settai's illustrations that he asked him to create large luxurious prints of a few selected images. Each design is accompanied by a passage from the story.

(JD)

172

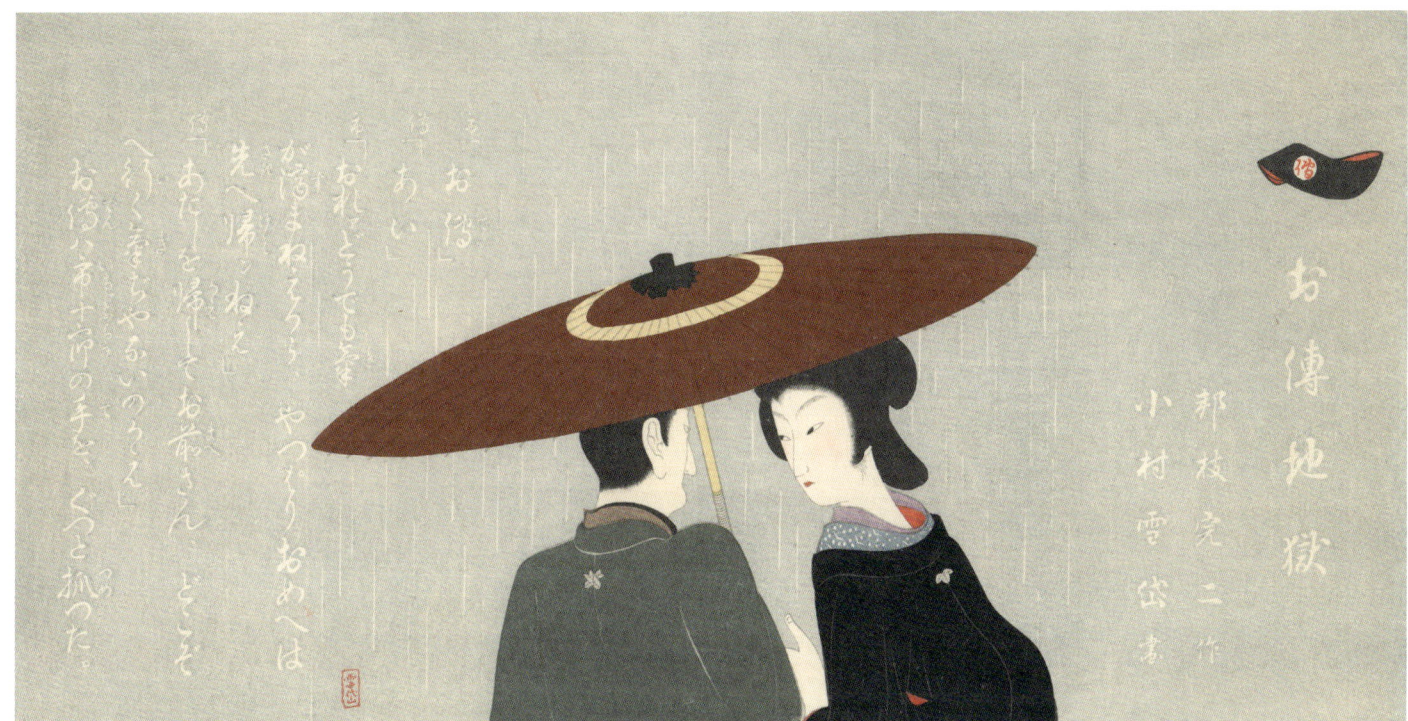

156c

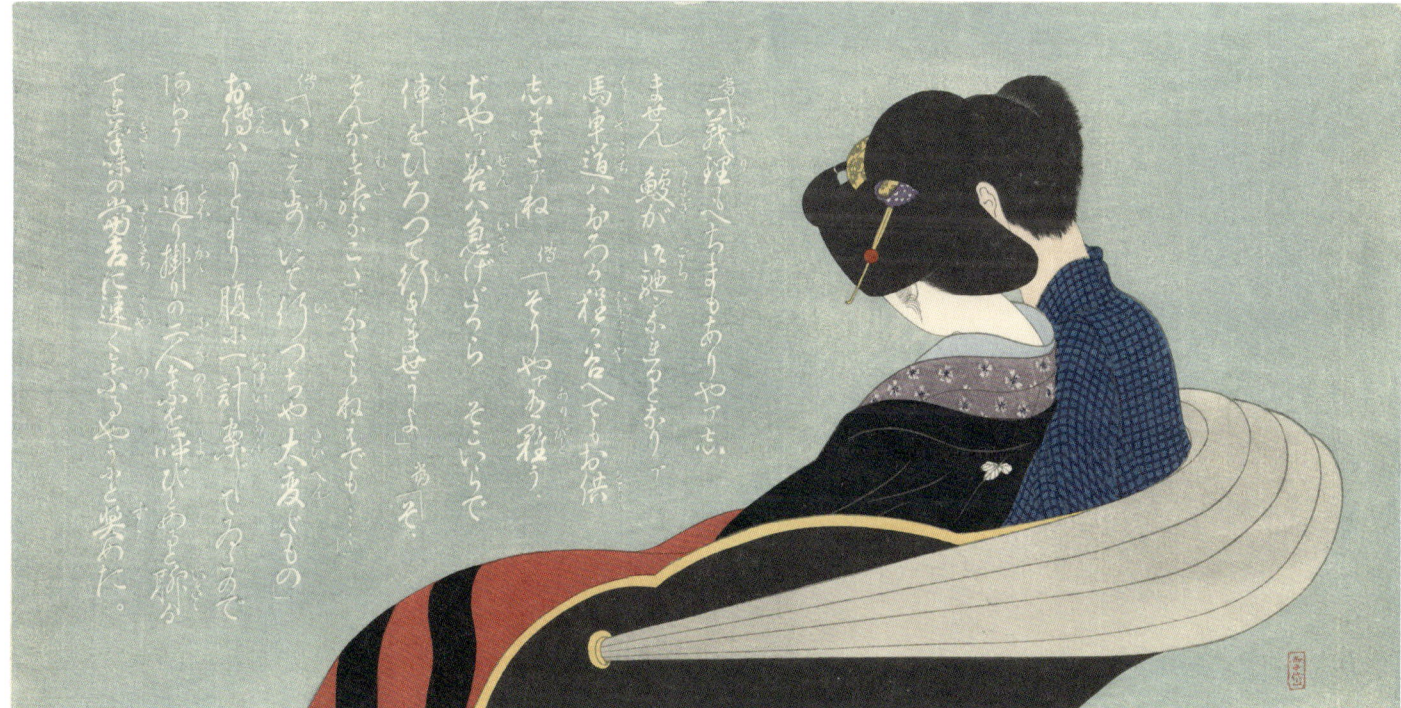

156d

Cat. 156a   Cat. 156c

Folding Screen   **Umbrella**

(*Byōbu* 屏風)   (*Kasa* 傘)

Cat. 156b   Cat. 156d

Tattoo   **Rickshaw**

(*Irezumi* 入墨)   (*Jinrikisha* 力車)

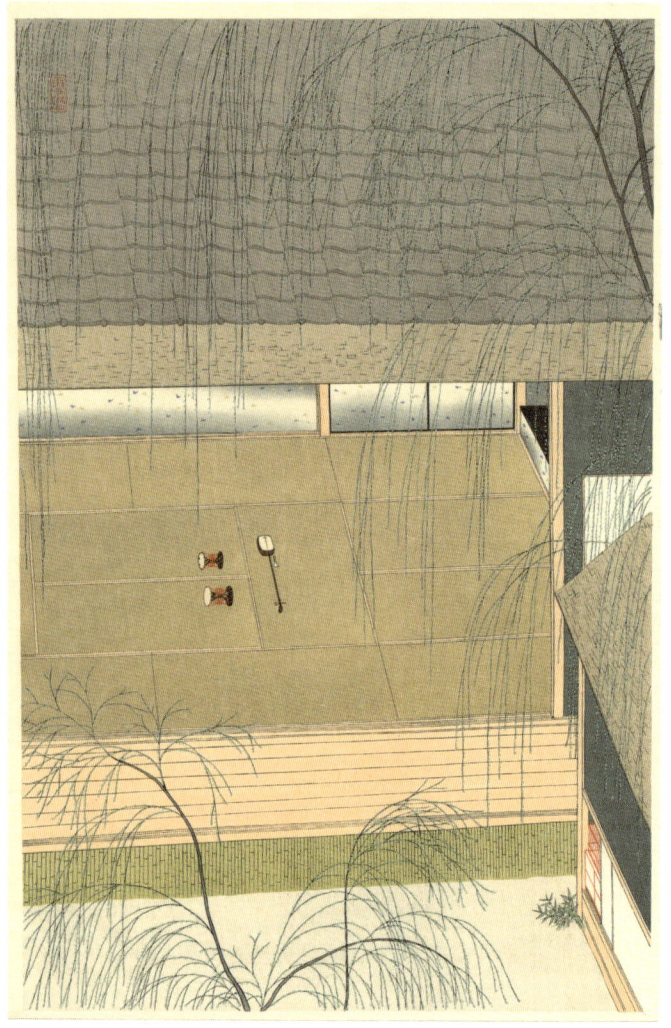

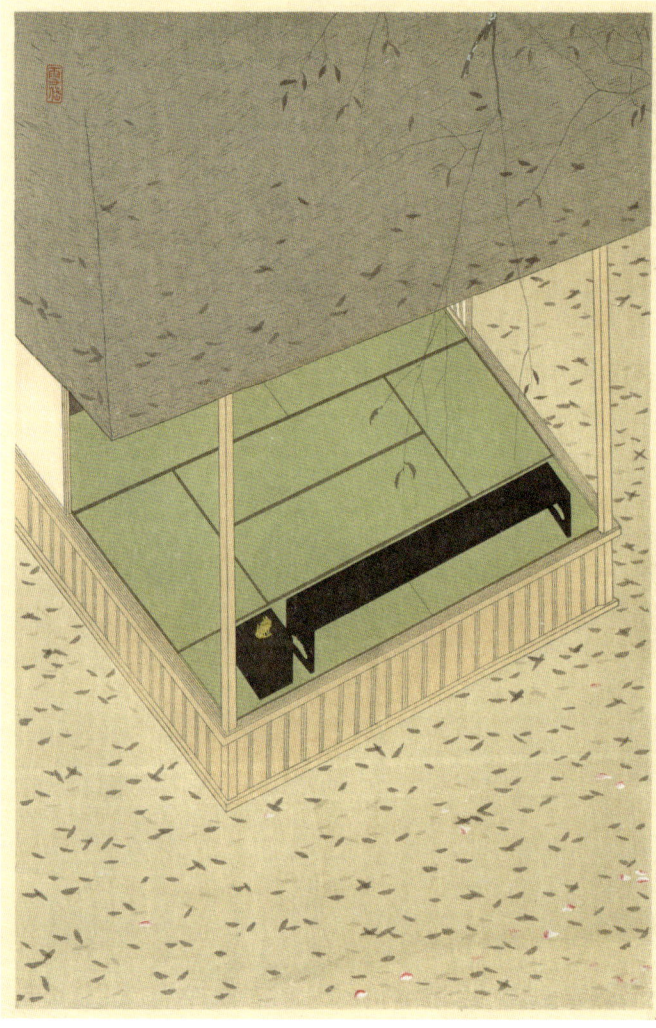

Cat. 157

Komura Settai 小村雪岱
(1887–1940)

Willow

(*Yanagi* 柳)

Series: *A Collection of Prints*
by Komura Settai
(*Komura Settai hangashū* 小村雪岱版画集)
Date: 1942 (posthumously published)
Artist's seal: *Settai*
Publisher: Adachi hanga kenkyūjo
(Adachi Institute of Woodblock Prints)
Block cutter: *Ōgura Hanbei*
Size: 44.5 × 29.3 cm
Collection Scholten

Cat. 158

Komura Settai 小村雪岱
(1887–1940)

Fallen Leaves

(*Ochiba* 落葉)

Series: *A Collection of Prints*
by Komura Settai
(*Komura Settai hangashū* 小村雪岱版画集)
Date: 1942 (posthumously published)
Artist's seal: *Settai*
Publisher: Adachi hanga kenkyūjo
(Adachi Institute of Woodblock Prints)
Block cutter: *Ōgura Hanbei*
Size: 44.5 × 29.3 cm
Collection Scholten

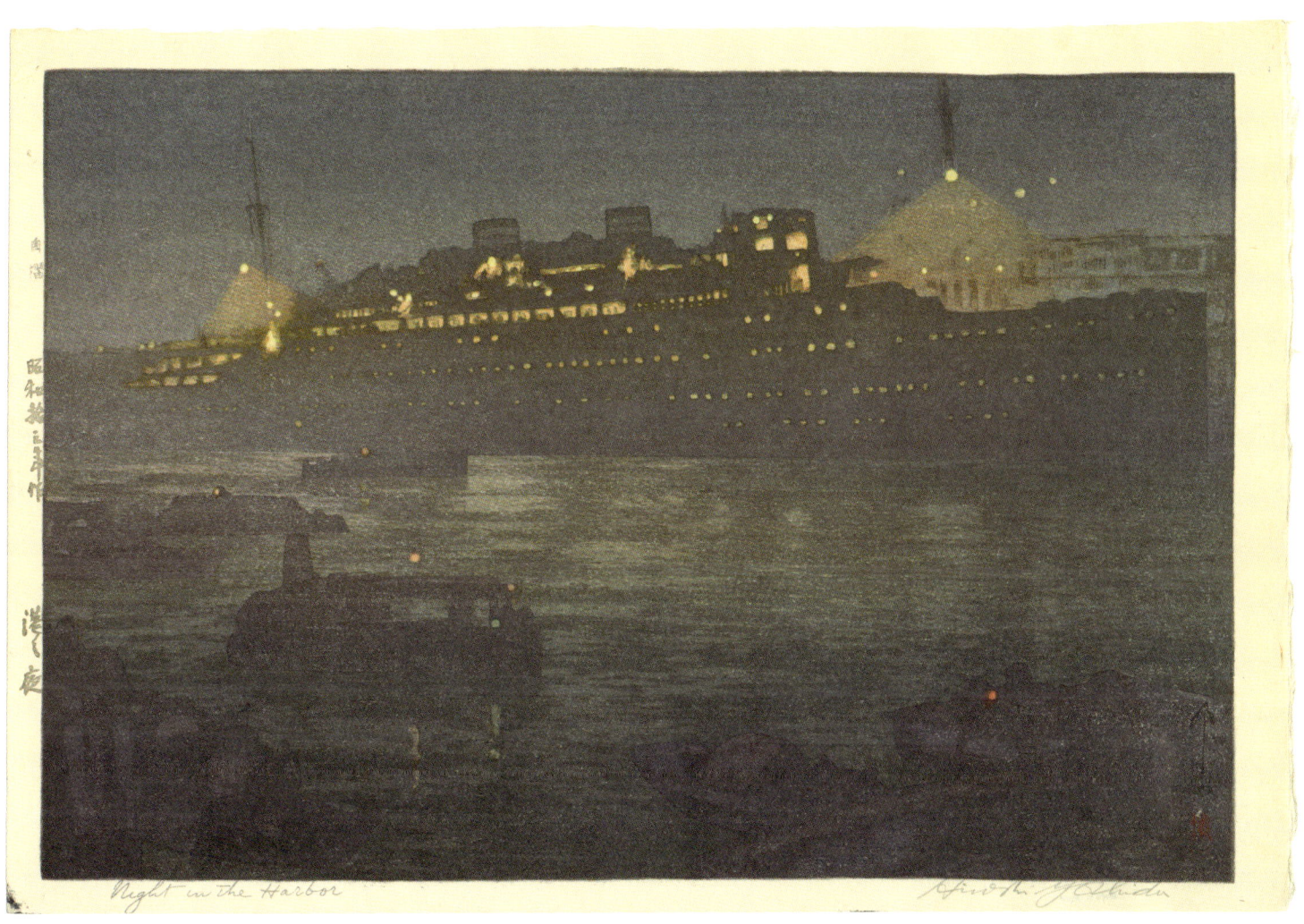

Night in the Harbor

An ocean liner lies in the port of Shanghai at night. Shanghai was the largest harbour in Asia and a booming metropolis, nicknamed the 'Paris of the East, New York of the West'. It is no surprise that in 1937 the first large-scale battle of the Second Sino-Japanese War (1937–45) was fought for control of Shanghai. By the time Yoshida produced this print, Japan had taken most of the city. The Shanghai International Settlement, however, was not annexed until three years later, directly after Japan's surprise attack on Pearl Harbor in December 1941. The settlement had been an enclave within the city where, ever since the days of the infamous 'gunboat diplomacy' carried out by 19th-century Euro-American colonial powers, citizens of various American and European countries enjoyed various privileges such as exemption from Chinese jurisdiction. When the war broke out, ocean liners were used by the Western governments to evacuate their citizens. (JD)

Cat. 159

Yoshida Hiroshi 吉田博 (1876–1950)
Night in the Harbour
(*Minato no yoru* 港之夜)

Date: 1938
Signatures: *Yoshida, Hiroshi Yoshida* (in bottom margin in pencil)
Artist's seal: *Hiroshi*
Publisher: self-published
Printer: self-printed (*jizuri* stamp in left margin)
Size: 27.2 × 40.4 cm
Collection Scholten

Cat. 160

Itō Shinsui 伊東深水 (1898–1972)

Hand Mirror

(*Tekagami* 手鏡)

Date: 1954
Signature: *Shinsui ga*
Artist's seal: *Shinsui*
Publisher: Watanabe Shōzaburō
Size: 50 × 35.3 cm
Collection Scholten

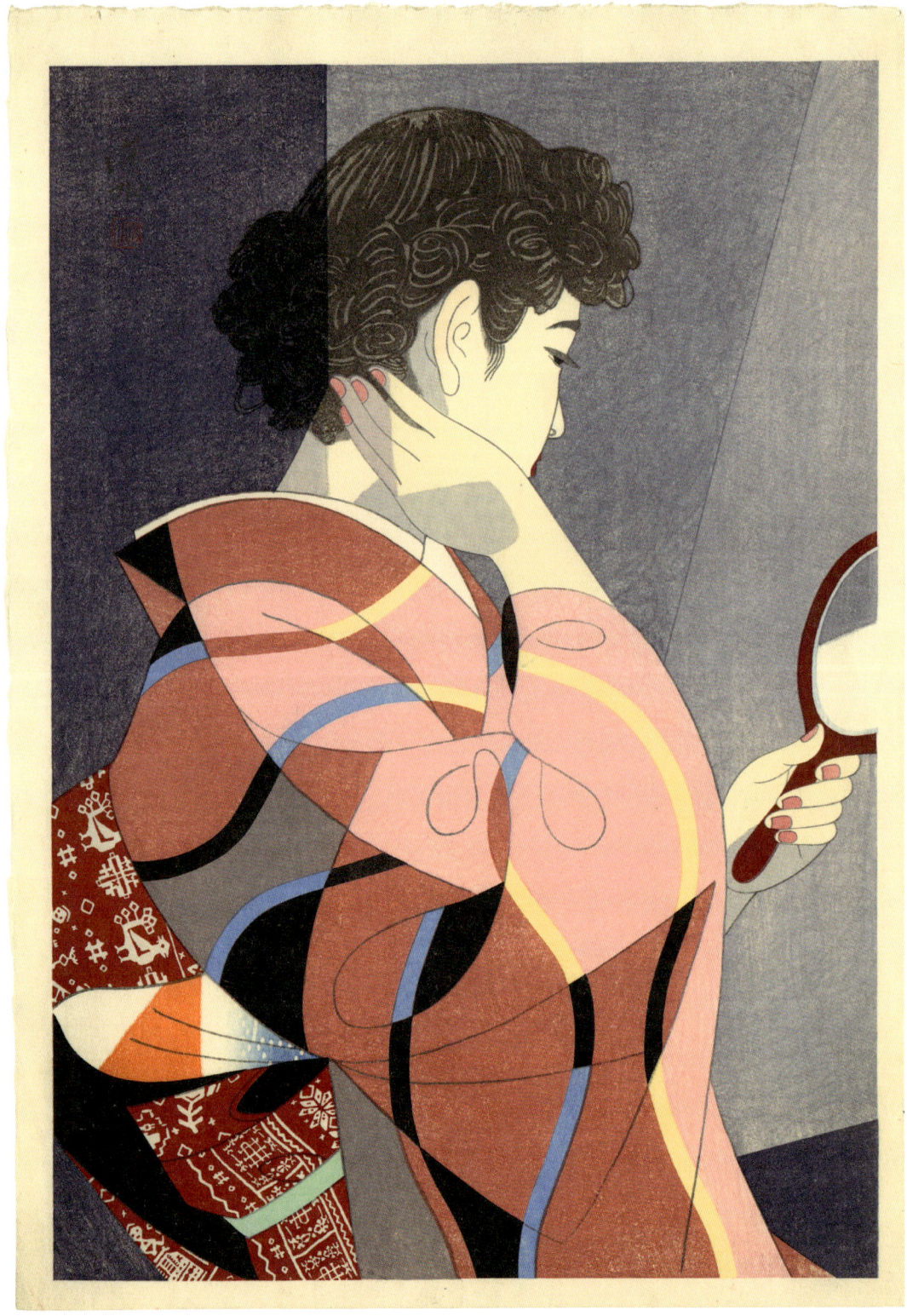

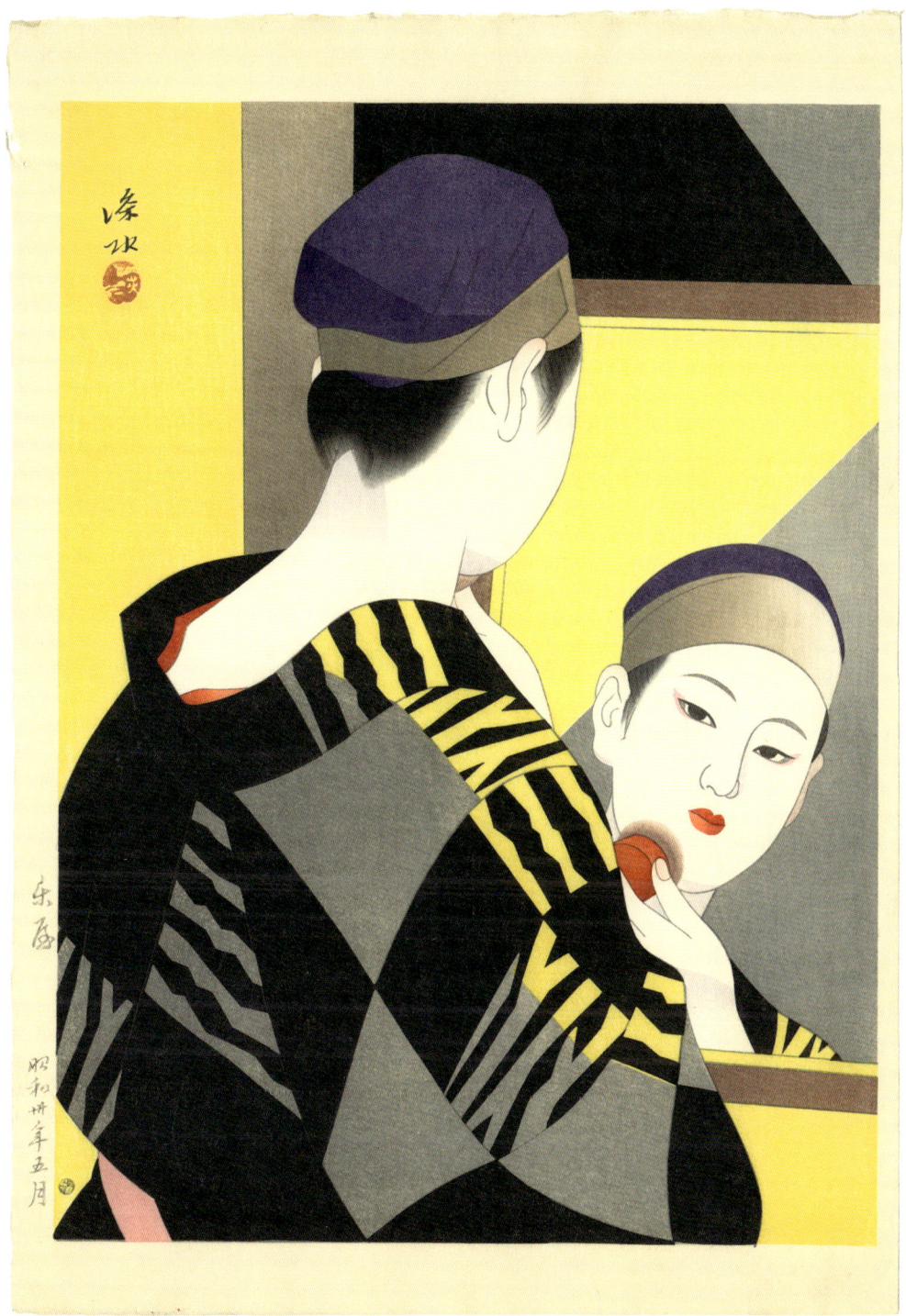

An actress preparing for her show, applying her make-up backstage, was a recurring theme in Shinsui's work (see also Cat. 89). This example features a modern, heavily stylized design in large format. The artist published ten similar prints with mostly modern themes around the same time. Similar to *Hand Mirror* (Cat. 160), the design is characterized by brightly coloured and contrasting areas. This composition is particularly striking due to the bright yellow, which is nicely complemented by grey and black, resulting in a dynamic colour scheme.

(PO)

Cat. 161

Itō Shinsui 伊東深水 (1898–1972)

Backstage

(*Gakuya* 楽屋)

Date: May 1955
Signature: *Shinsui*
Artist's seal: *Shinsui*
Publisher: Watanabe Shōzaburō
Size: 51 × 36 cm
Private collection, the Netherlands

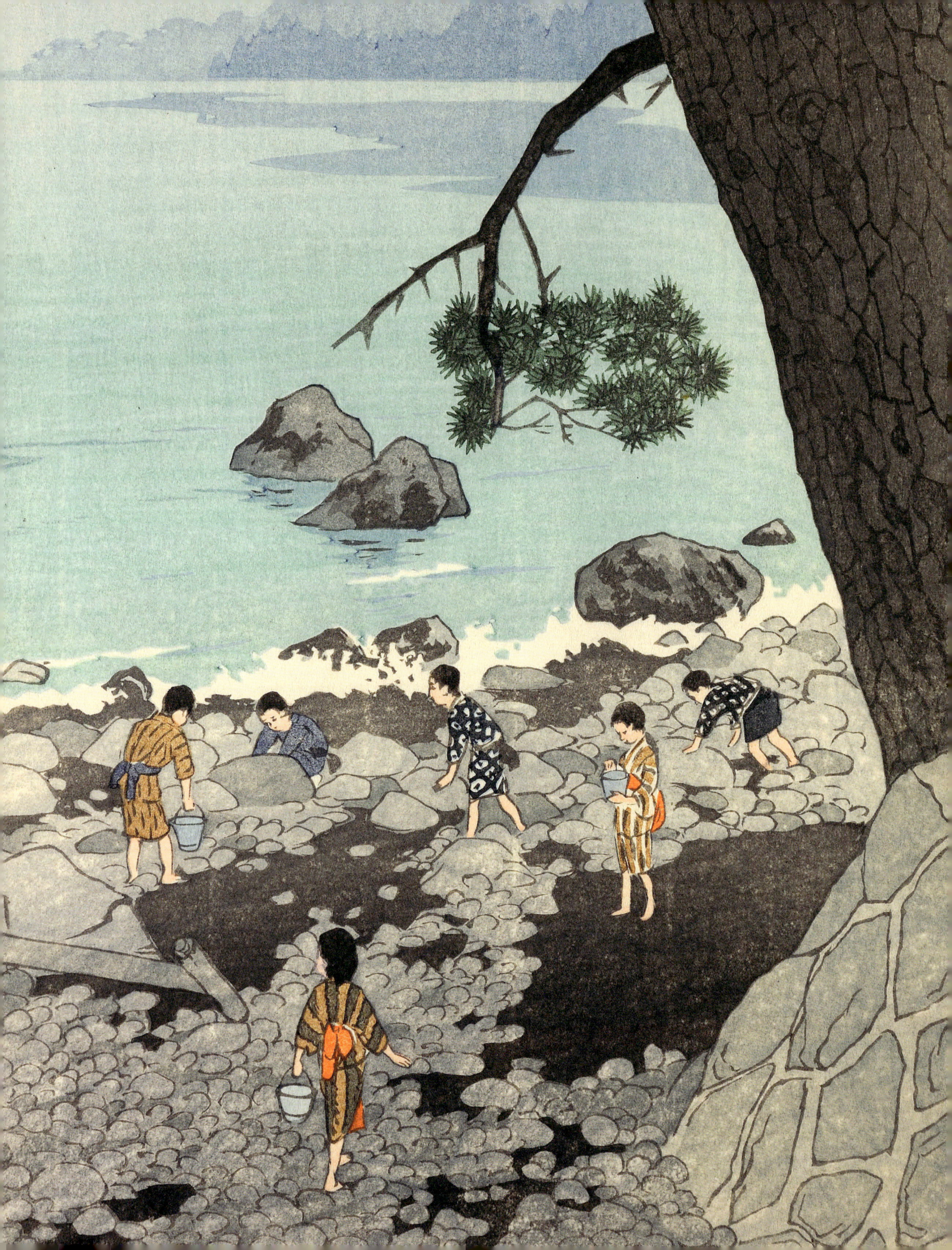

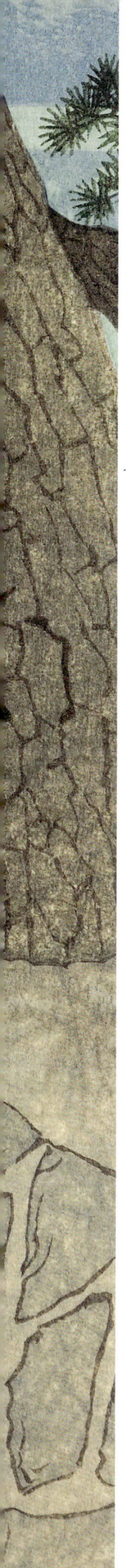

Post-Earthquake Landscapes

Landscape prints remained the bread-and-butter of publishers, as foreign buyers longed for the symbols of a traditional Japan. These stunning prints depicted snow-covered pagodas, moonlit temples and the play of lights on shimmering seas, but commercial success threatened to diminish quality. The war dealt a devastating blow: after 1945 the *shin hanga* movement failed to reinvent itself.

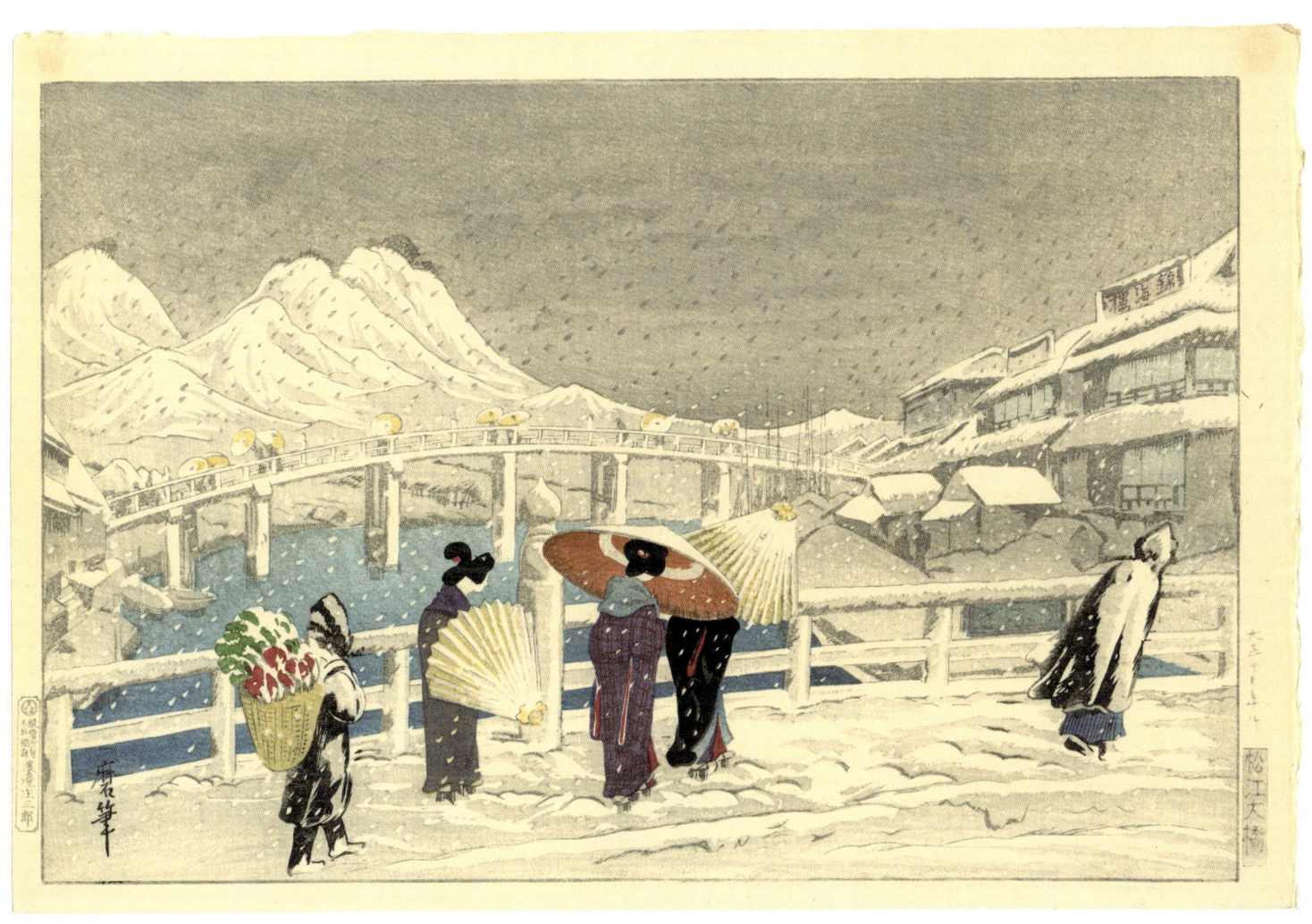

Oda had spent three years in Matsue, Shimane Prefecture, and the city was a recurring theme in his works. San'in, mentioned in the series title, is an old regional name that encompasses the northern coast of the three prefectures at Honshū's western tip: Yamaguchi, Shimane and Tottori. Oda was generally known as a lithographer and *sōsaku hanga* artist who cut and printed his own blocks. This print, however, was issued by Watanabe Shōzaburō in the year after the 1923 earthquake.

(JD)

Cat. 162

Oda Kazuma 織田一磨 (1882–1956)
Matsue Ōhashi Bridge
(*Matsue Ōhashi* 松江大橋)

Series: *Scenes of San'in*
(*San'in fūkei* 山陰風景)
Date: 1924
Signature: *Kazuma hitsu*
Publisher: Watanabe Shōzaburō
Size: 25.8 × 39 cm
Collection Scholten

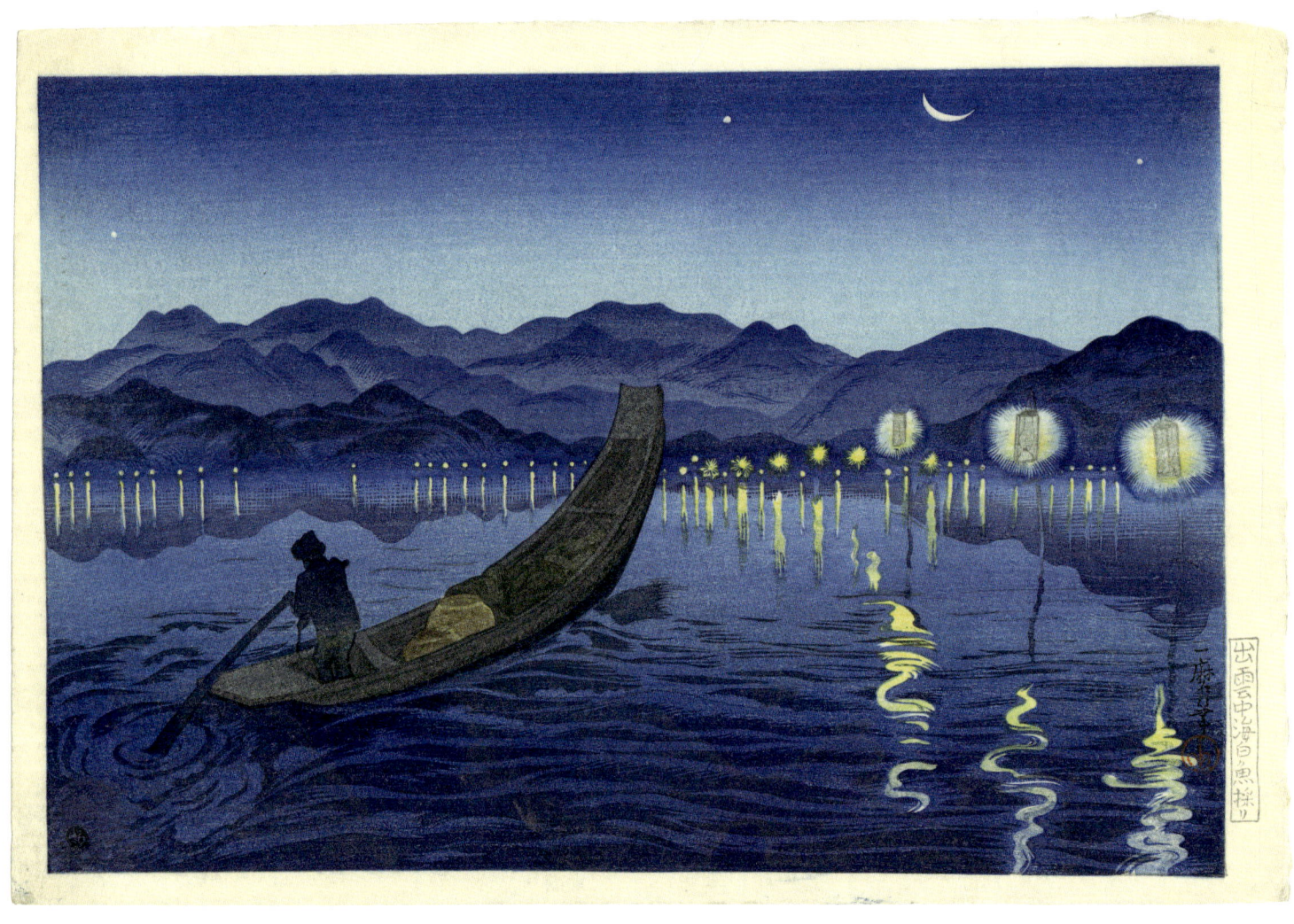

Cat. 163

Oda Kazuma 織田一磨 (1882–1956)

Catching Icefish at Nakaumi, Izumo

(*Izumo Nakaumi shirauo tori* 出雲中海白魚採り)

Series: *Scenes of San'in*
(*San'in fūkei* 山陰風景)
Date: 1924
Signature: *Kazuma hitsu*
Artist's seal: *Oda*
Publisher: Watanabe Shōzaburō
Size: 26.3 × 39.5 cm
Collection Scholten

182

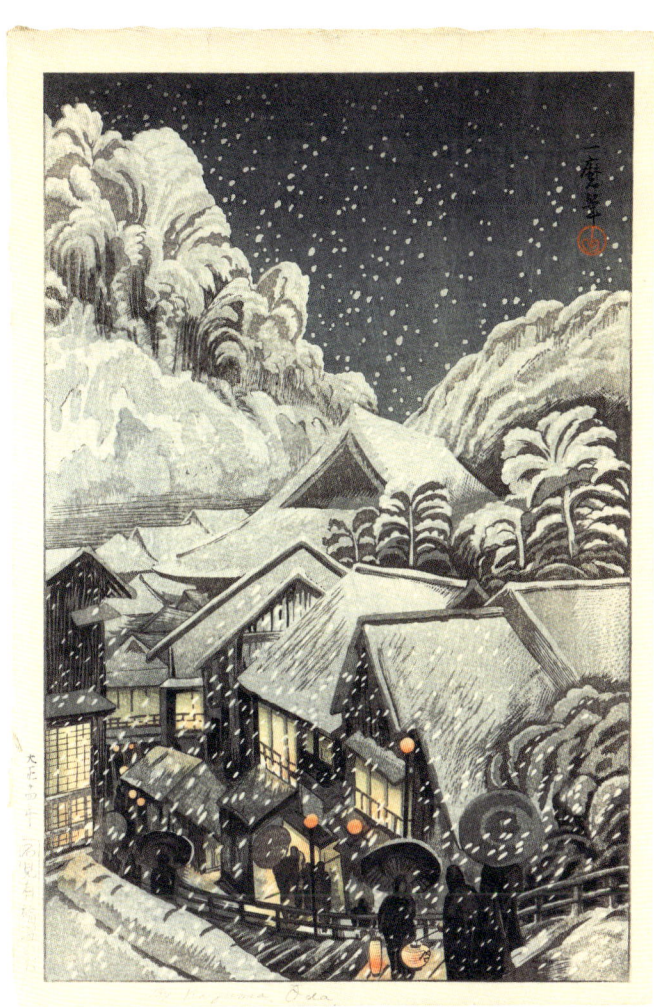

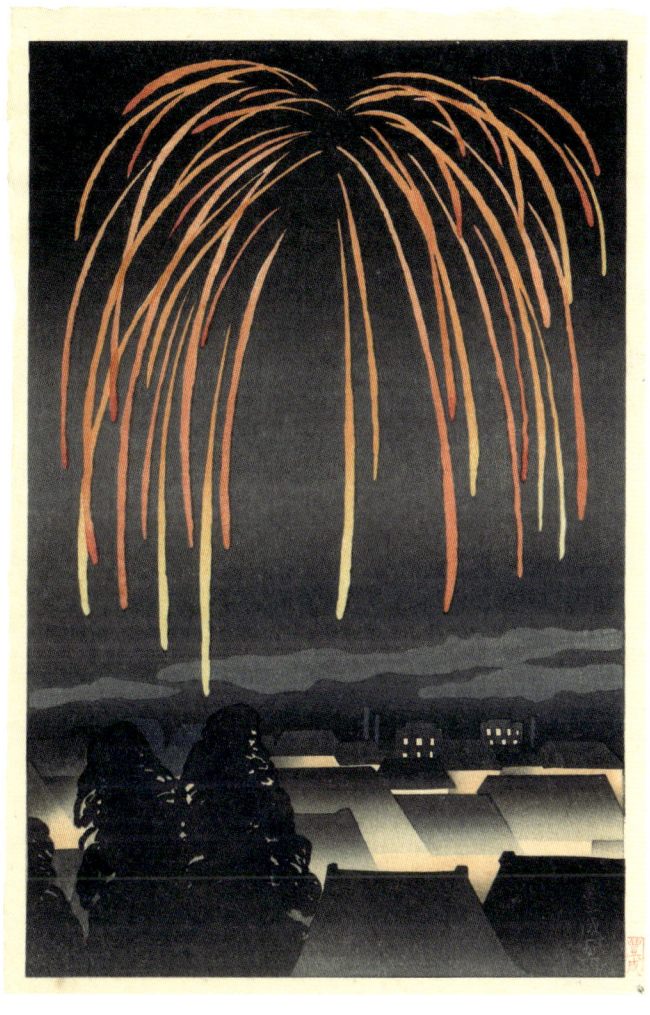

Cat. 164

Oda Kazuma 織田一磨 (1882–1956)
Arifuku Hot Springs, Iwami
(*Iwami Arifuku onsen* 石見有福温泉)

Series: *Scenes of San'in*
(*San'in fūkei* 山陰風景)
Date: 1925
Signature: *Kazuma hitsu* (top right),
By Kazuma Oda (bottom margin in pencil)
Artist's seal: *Oda*
Publisher: Watanabe Shōzaburō
Size: 38.5 × 26.2 cm
Collection RMAH – JP.07274

Cat. 165

Yamamura Kōka (Toyonari)
山村豊成 (豊成) (1885–1942)
Festival Night Fireworks
(*Hōshuku no yoru* 奉祝の夜)

Date: 1924
Signature: *Toyonari ga*
Artist's seal: *Toyonari*
Publisher: self-published
Size: 39.3 × 26.6 cm
Collection Scholten

Cat. 166

Ohara Koson (Shōson)
小原古邨 (祥邨) (1877–1945)

Snow at Yanagibashi

(*Yanagibashi no yuki* 柳橋の雪)

Date: 1927
Signature: *Shōson*
Artist's seal: *Shōson*
Publisher: Watanabe Shōzaburo
Size: 38.4 × 26 cm
Collection Scholten

Two women cross the Yanagibashi (Willow Bridge) over the Kanda River. To protect themselves against the heavy snowfall, they are walking hunched over and hold their umbrellas tight over their heads. Extra snowflakes have been added to the print with the use of *gofun*, a white pigment made of pulverized shells.

(PO)

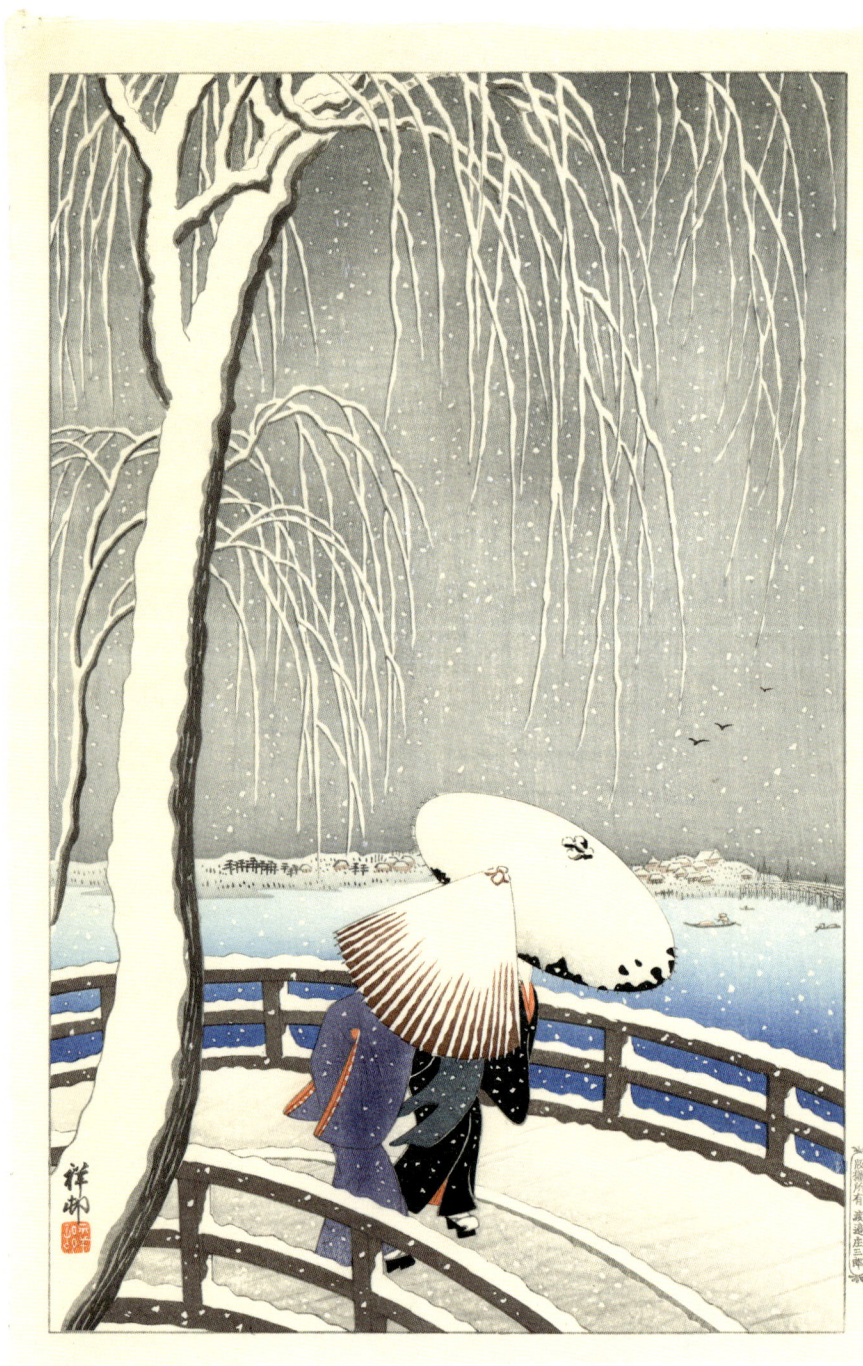

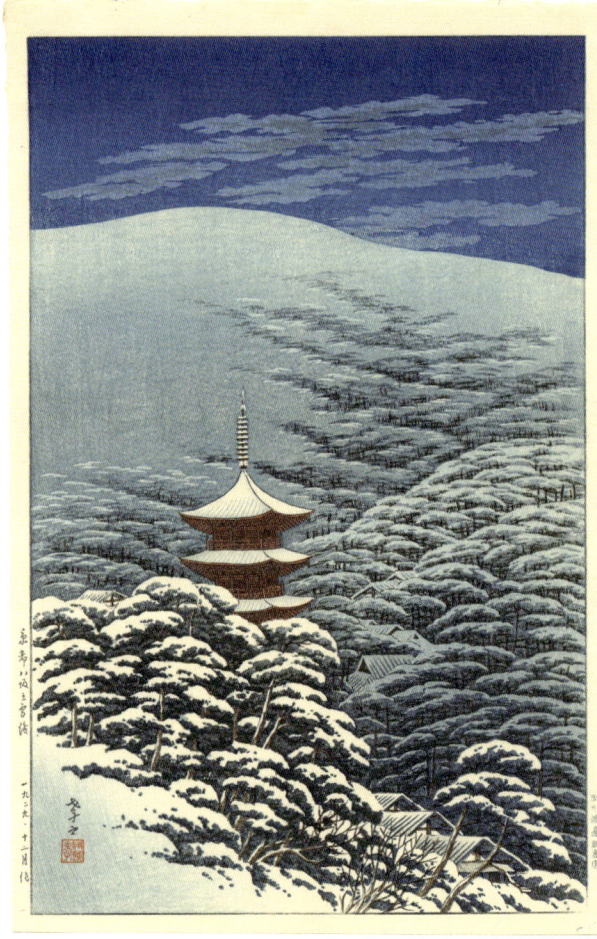

Cat. 167

Itō Takashi 伊藤孝之 (1894–1982)

After a Snowfall, Yasaka Shrine, Kyoto

(*Kyōto, Yasaka no yuki no ato* 京都
八坂之雪後)

Date: December 1929
Signature: *Takashi*
Artist's seal: *Itō Takashi*
Publisher: Watanabe Shōzaburō
Size: 38.6 × 25.5 cm
Private collection, the Netherlands

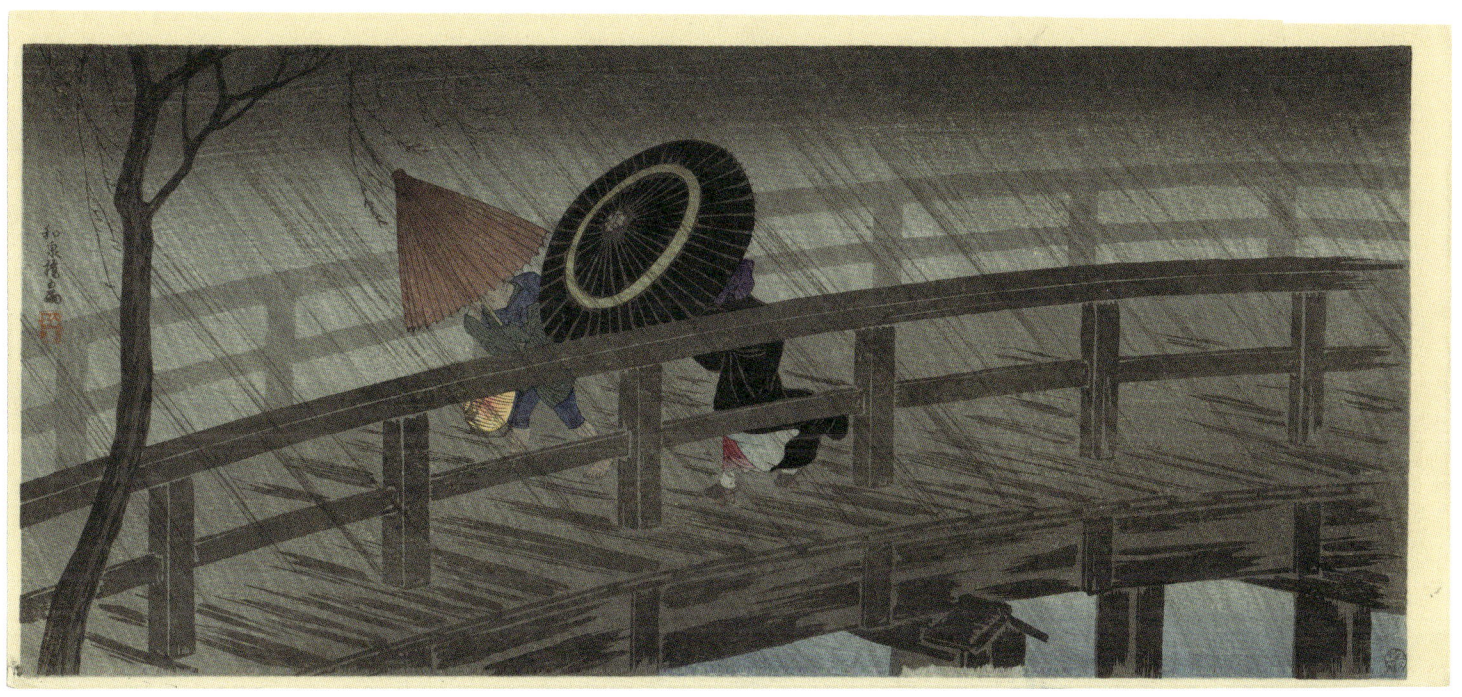

Cat. 168

Takahashi Hiroaki (Shōtei)
高橋弘明 (松亭) (1871–1945)
Night Shower at Izumi Bridge
(*Izumibashi no ame* 和泉橋の雨)

Date: after 1923
Artist's seal: *Shōtei*
Publisher: Watanabe Shōzaburō
Size: 17.5 × 39.2 cm
Collection Scholten

High above the Katsura River, in present-day Yamanashi Prefecture, is the Saruhashi, or 'Monkey Bridge', one of the most famous bridges in Japan. Its original purpose was to allow the crossing of the gorge by travellers along the Kōshūkaidō, one of the five main roads of the Edo Period, connecting Edo (present-day Tokyo) with the Kai and Shinano Provinces. The bridge serves as an excellent example of the Edo Period architectural style of so-called *hanebashi* bridges, in which the walkway rests on stacked cantilevers on both sides of the cliff. This wintry rendition of the Monkey Bridge can be considered one of Hiroaki's masterworks, made possible due to the relative artistic freedom he enjoyed when he made prints for Fusui. In the bottom margin is written 'designed and carved by Hiroaki', although this most probably means that Hiroaki directly supervised the production process rather than actually carving the blocks himself. The print shows superlative craftsmanship, evident in particular in the snow on the trees and roofs and the weather effects in the background. The mottled layers of white and light blue add texture to this snowy scene.

(JD)

Cat. 169

Takahashi Hiroaki (Shōtei)
高橋弘明 (松亭) (1871–1945)
Saruhashi Bridge in Kōshū
(*Kōshū Saruhashi* 甲州さるはし)

Date: December 1931
Signature: *Hiroaki*
Artist's seal: *Shōtei*
Publisher: Fusui gabō (Fusui workshop)
Size: 52.5 × 23 cm
Collection Scholten

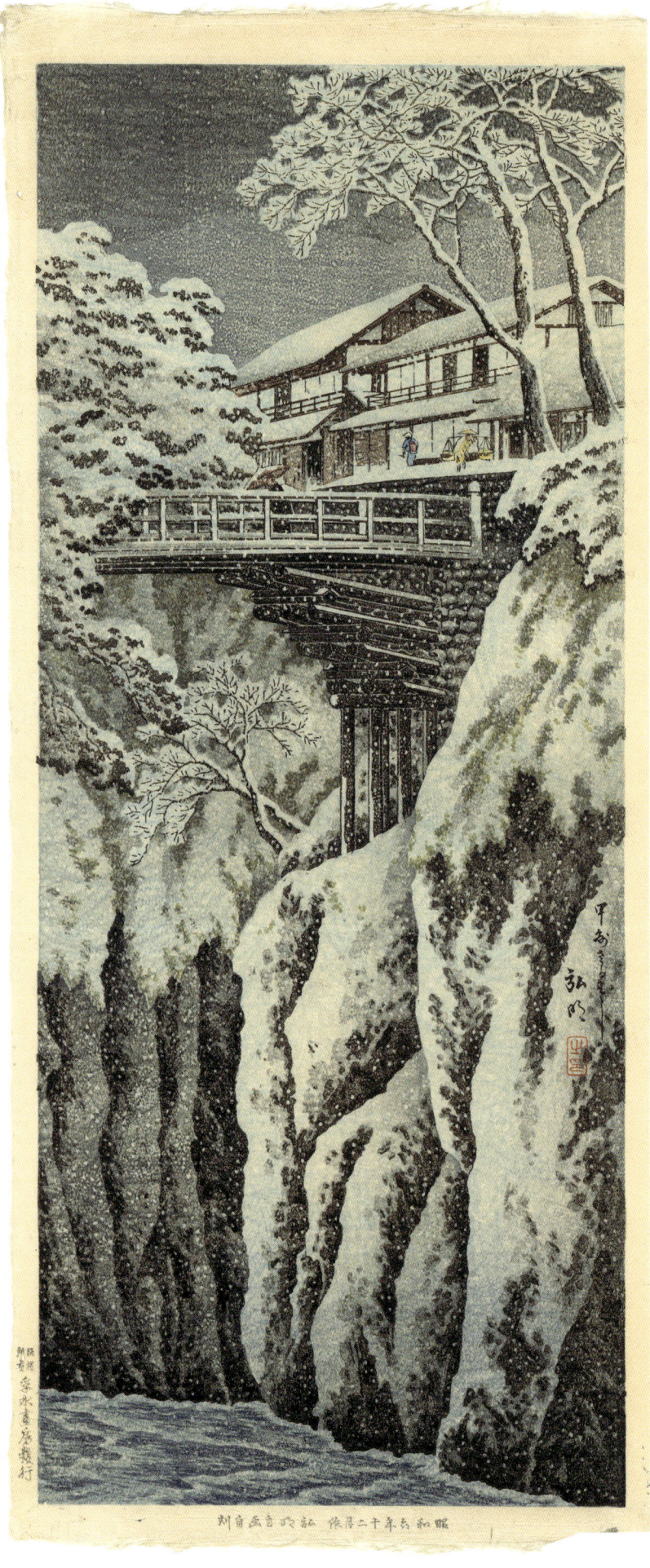

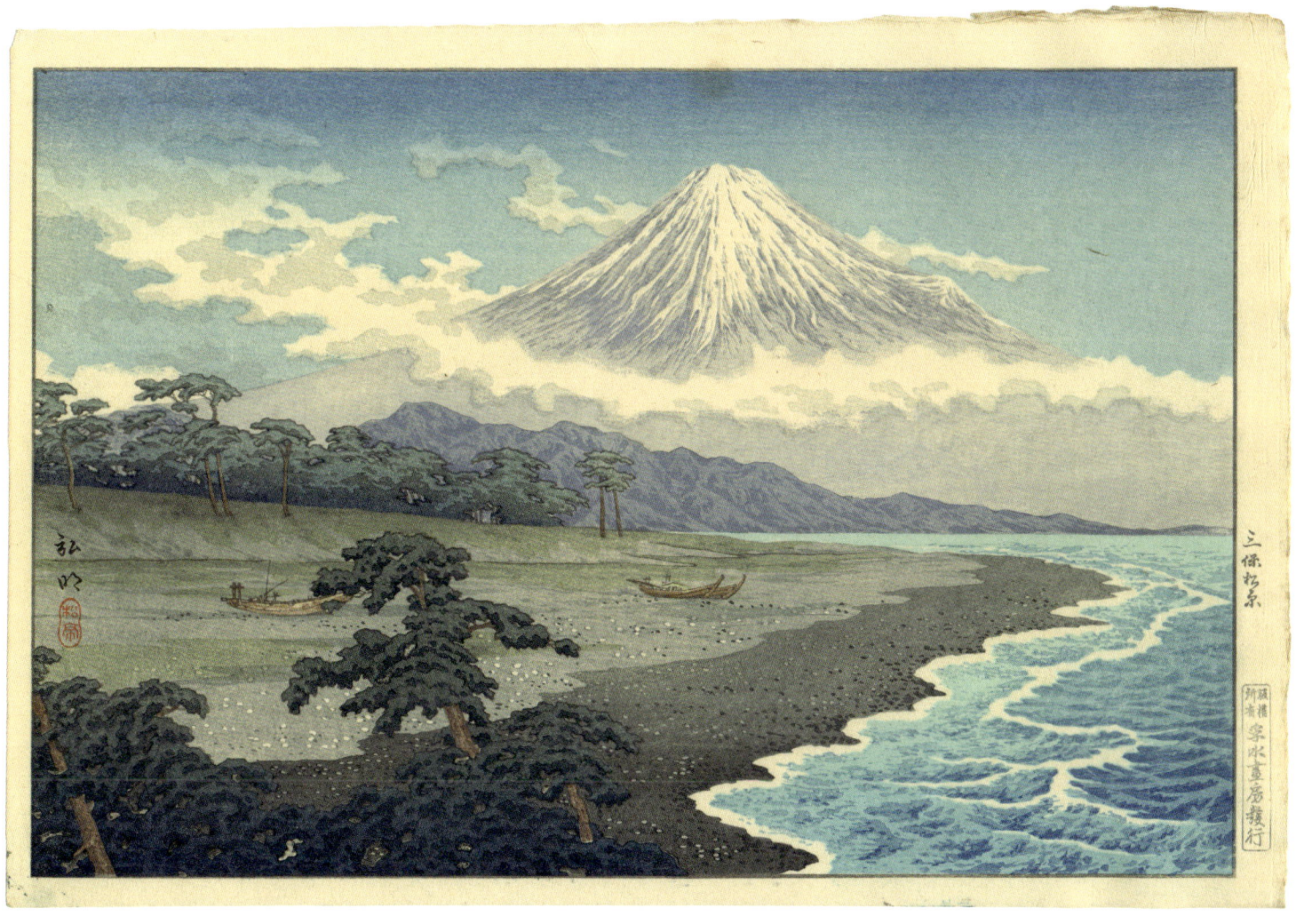

Cat. 170

Takahashi Hiroaki (Shōtei)
高橋弘明 (松亭) (1871–1945)

Senbonhama beach
(*Senbonhama* 千本濱)

Series: *Fuji in the four seasons*
(*Shiki no Fuji* 四季乃富士)
Date: 25 December 1929
Signature: *Hiroaki*
Artist seal: *Shōtei*
Publisher: Fusui gabō (Fusui workshop)
Size: 25.7 × 39.2 cm
Collection Scholten

In December 1929, on Christmas Day, Fusui gabō produced a series of four designs in a portfolio titled 'Fuji in the Four Seasons'. Hiroaki, known for his depiction of famous scenes of Japan since c. 1909, chose Mount Fuji at least 87 times as the subject for his prints.

Although the largest part of Hiroaki's impressive oeuvre was published by Watanabe, during the post-earthquake years he also started collaborating with other publishers, including Fusui gabō, where he also worked as an editor of ukiyo-e reproductions.

(JD)

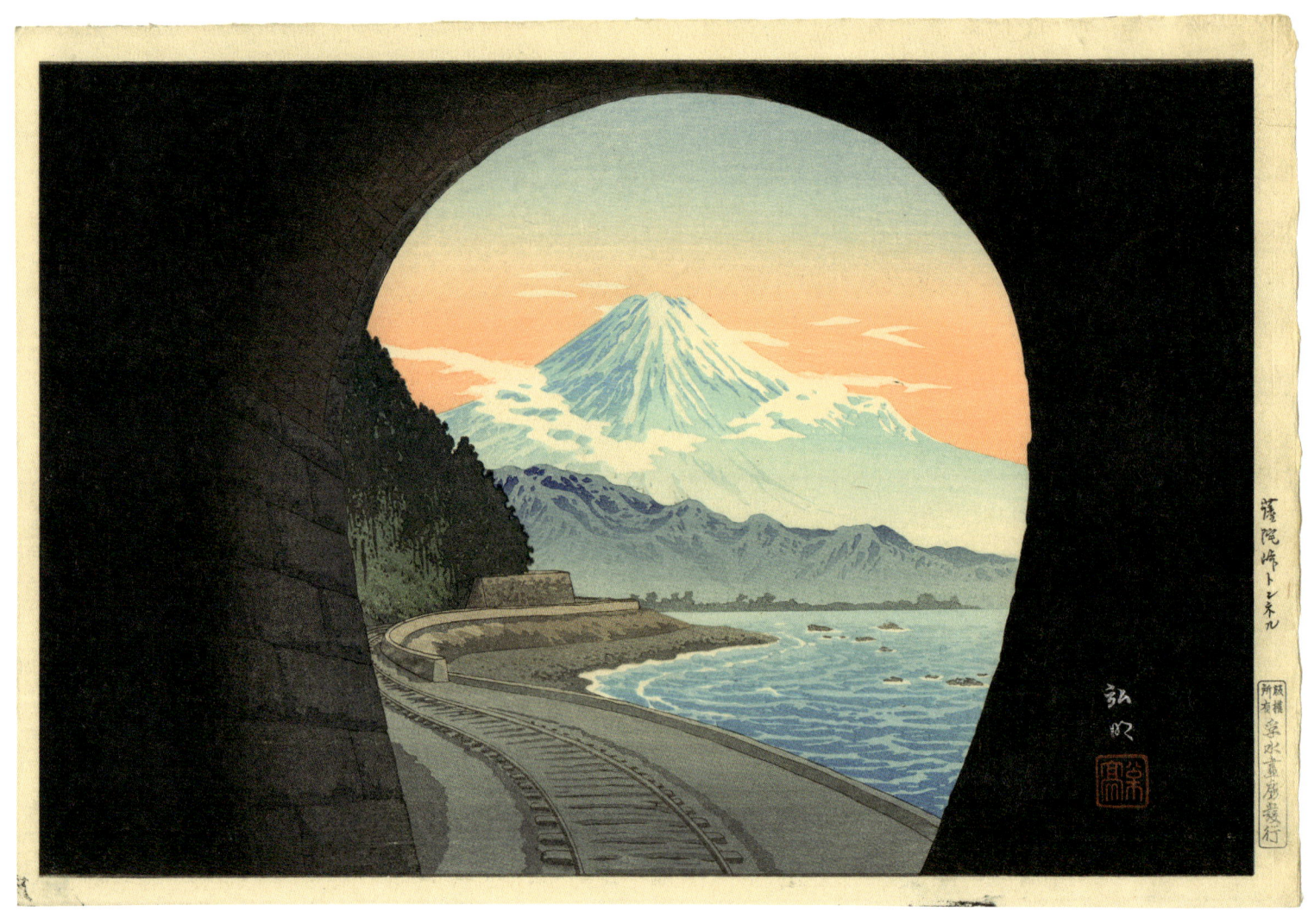

Cat. 171

Takahashi Hiroaki (Shōtei)
高橋弘明 (松亭) (1871–1945)

Satta Pass Tunnel
(*Satta tōge tonneru* 薩陀峠トンネル)

Date: c. 1929–32
Signature: *Hiroaki*
Artist's seal: *Shōtei*
Publisher: Fusui gabō (Fusui Workshop)
Size: 26 × 39.1 cm
Collection Scholten

This view of Mount Fuji was famously depicted in various Tōkaidō series by Utagawa Hiroshige. The most important travel route of Edo Japan was the Tōkaidō road, connecting Kyoto to Edo (modern-day Tokyo). The 'eastern sea route' travelled along the coast of eastern Honshu and was made up of 53 post stations for travellers to refresh and rest. In 1889, the view changed dramatically because the Tōkaidō main line was directed through this small pass along the water's edge between the stations Yui and Okitsu.

(CU)

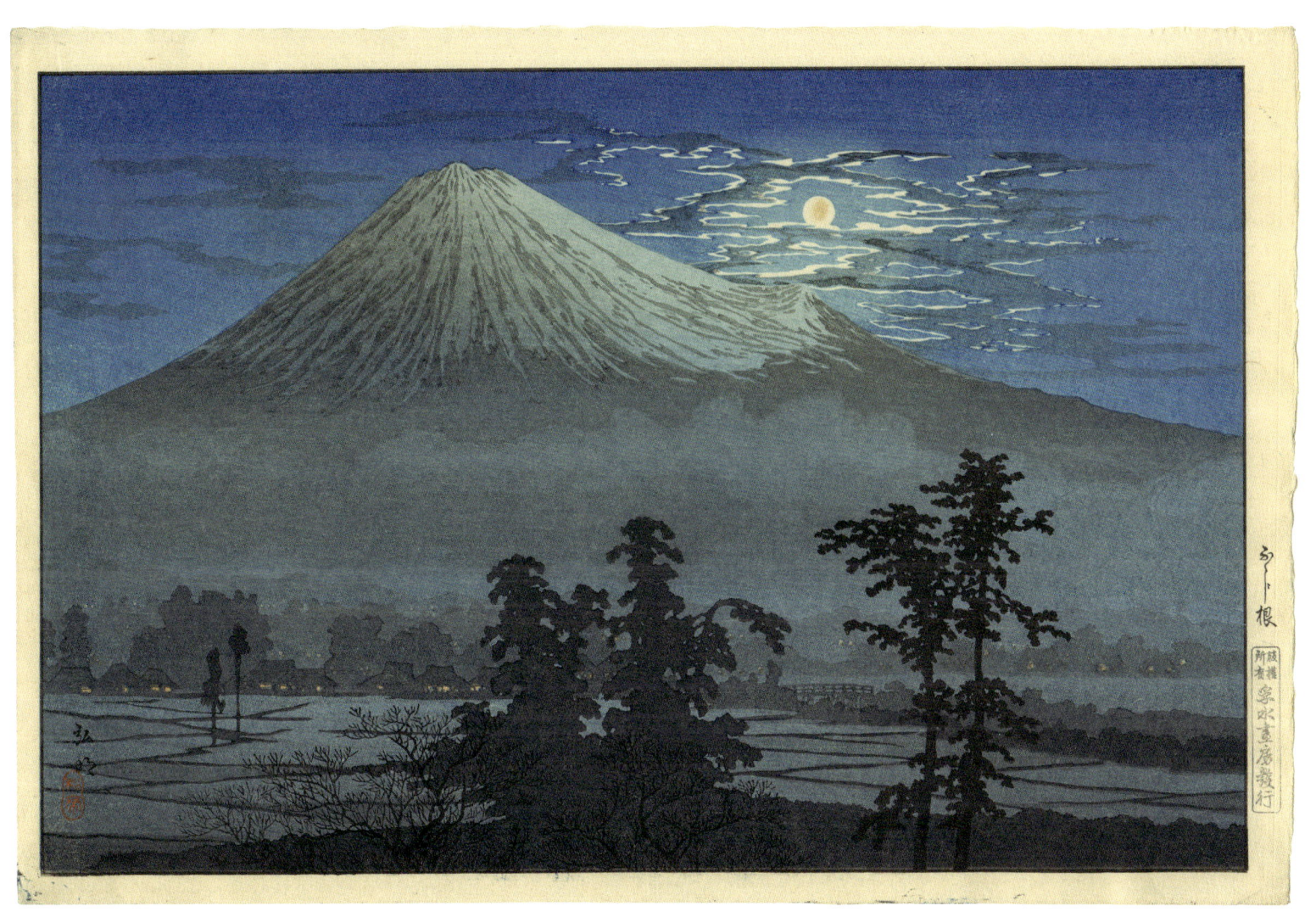

Cat. 172

Takahashi Hiroaki (Shōtei)
高橋弘明 (松亭) (1871–1945)

Fujine

(*Fujine* ふじ根)

Date: After 1923, likely 1929–32
Signature: *Hiroaki*
Artist's seal: *Shōtei*
Publisher: Fusui gabō (Fusui Workshop)
Size: 26 × 39.1 cm
Collection Scholten

Hiroaki mostly designed prints of women and landscapes for Fusui, including these two rare versions in extra-large format of Mount Fuji, towering in the sky, seen from the nearby Ashitaka mountain range. The complete destruction of the Fusui studio during the Second World War increased the rarity of these prints. The vivid details and use of many colour gradients in the rocky cliffs covered by grasses on the left and the current of the river below attest to the great craftsmanship involved in its production. The print exists in two states, one with summery green colours in the grasses and the other showing the yellow and orange tints of autumn. In the summer version, the rocks in the background are always omitted. In the edition illustrated here, a layer of rain is added, the clouds above and the lines of rain created by the motion of the printer's *baren*.

(JD)

Cats. 173a (Summer) – 173b (Autumn)

Takahashi Hiroaki (Shōtei)
高橋弘明 (松亭) (1871–1945)

Foothills of the Mountains at Ashitaka – Summer and Autumn

(*Ashitakayama fumoto* 愛鷹山麓)

Date: January 1932
Signature: *Hiroaki saku*
Artist's seal: *Hiroaki* (alternative characters)
Publisher: Fusui gabō (Fusui workshop)
Block cutter: *Takano Shichinosuke*
Printer: *Ono Tomisaburō*
Size: 52.5 × 36.5 cm
Private collection, the Netherlands

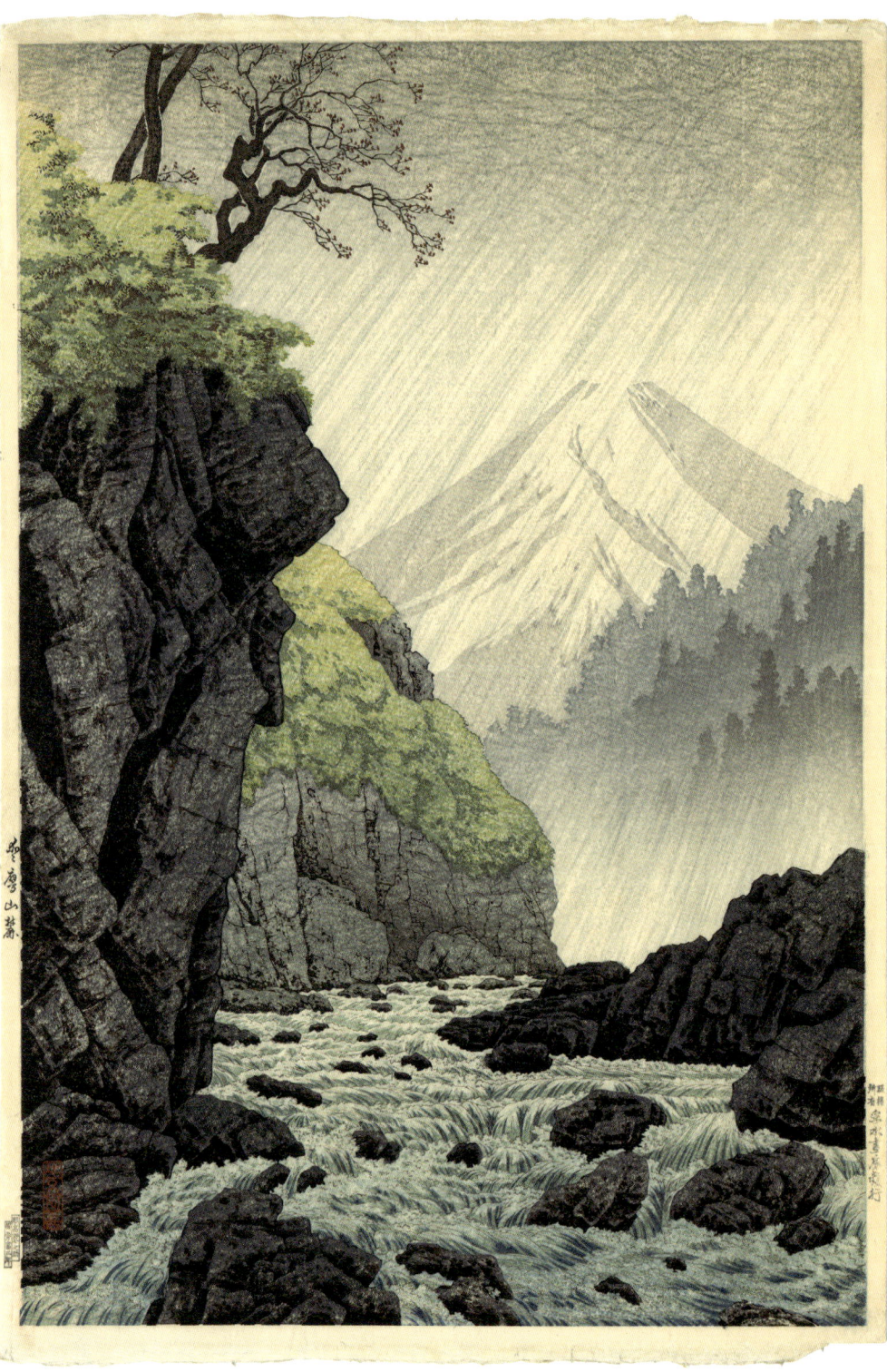

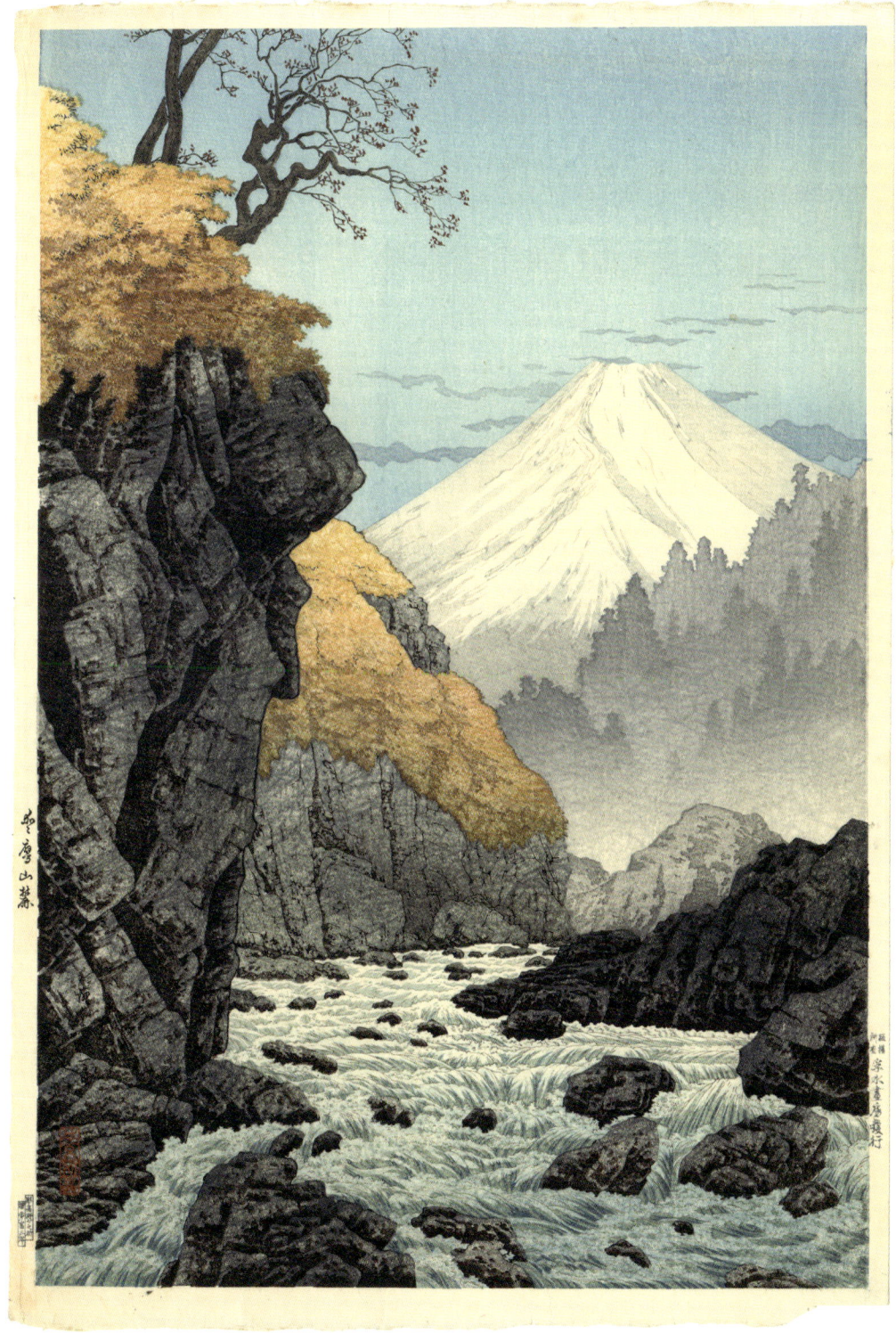

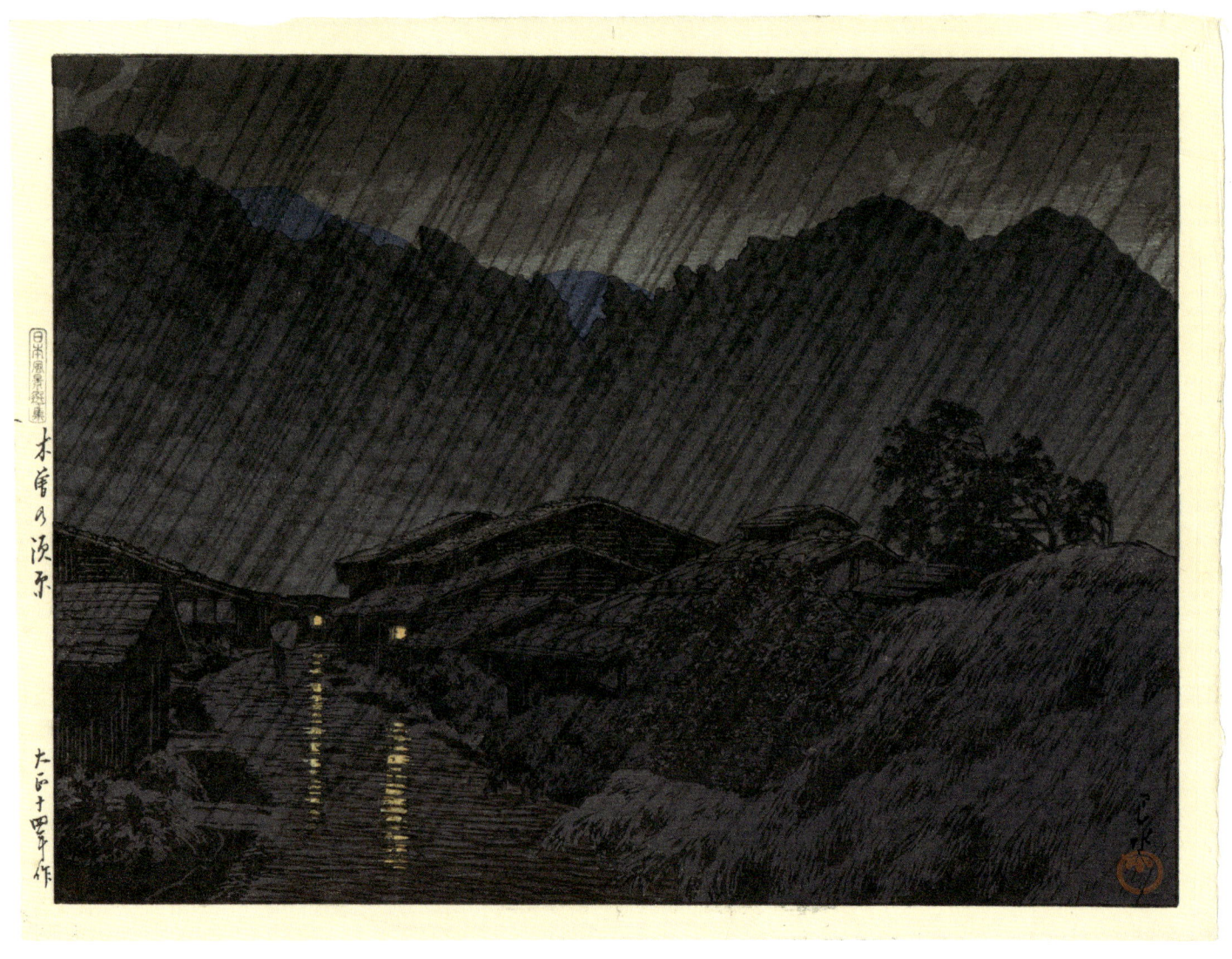

Cat. 174

Kawase Hasui 川瀬巴水 (1883–1957)

Suhara, Kiso

(*Kiso no Suhara* 木曾の須原)

Series: *Selection of Scenes of Japan*
(*Nihon fūkei senshū* 日本風景選集)
Date: 1925
Signature: *Hasui*
Artist's seal: *Kawase*
Publisher: Watanabe Shōzaburō
Size: 22.7 × 30.6 cm
Collection Scholten

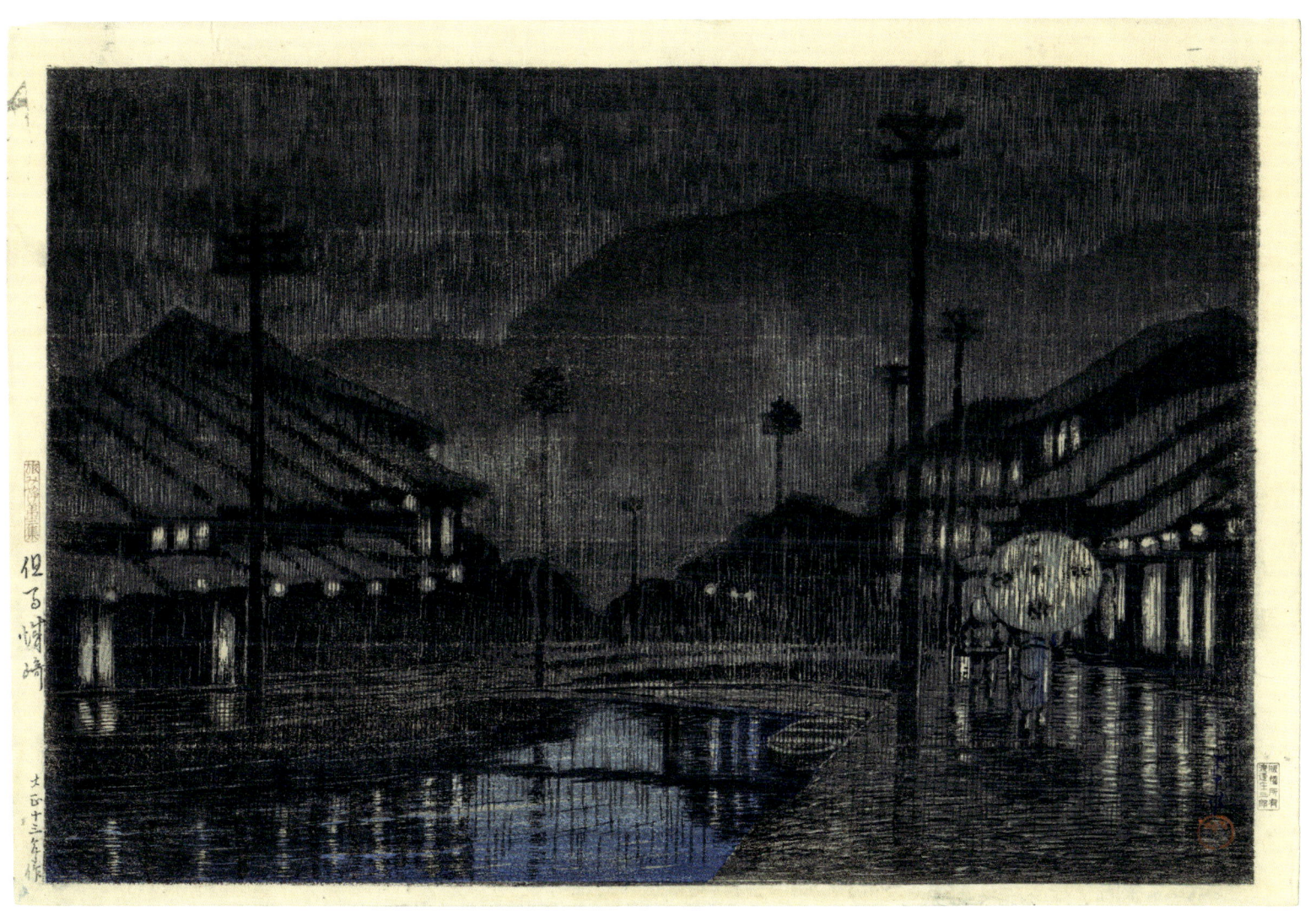

Souvenirs of Travel, third series was a set of 29 prints based on sketches that Hasui made on his first trip shortly after the 1923 earthquake. When all his previous sketchbooks and many of his blocks were destroyed, Watanabe encouraged him to set out again, and Hasui undertook a trip of 102 days visiting many places in central and western Honshū.

(JD)

Cat. 175

Kawase Hasui 川瀬巴水 (1883–1957)

Kinosaki, Tajima

(*Tajima Kinosaki* 但馬城崎)

Series: *Souvenirs of Travel, third series*
(*Tabi miyage dai sanshū* 旅みやげ第三集)
Date: 1924
Signature: *Hasui*
Artist's seal: *Kawase*
Publisher: Watanabe Shōzaburō
Size: 25.7 × 38.5 cm
Collection Scholten

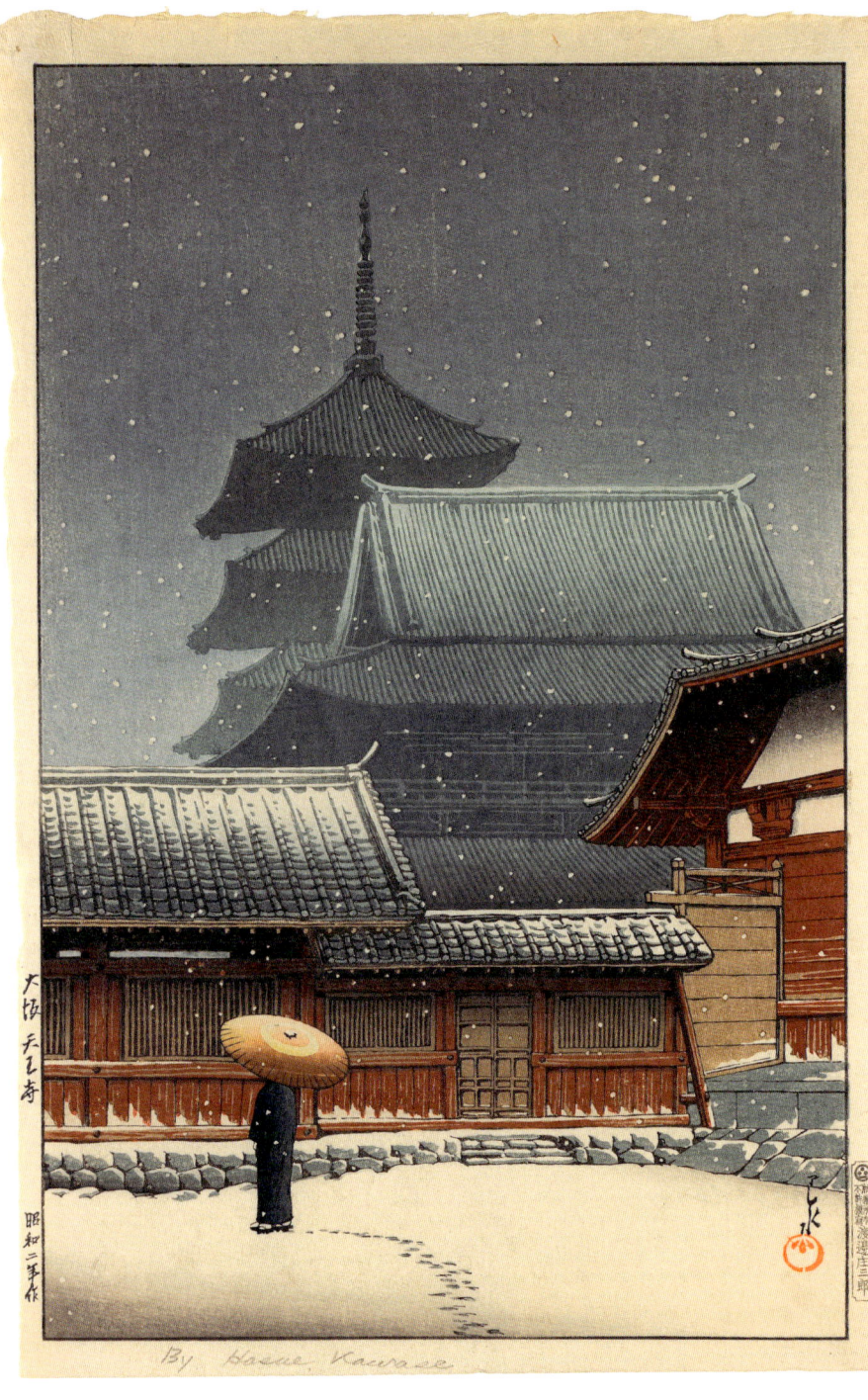

One of Japan's oldest temple sites, the founding of (Shi)Tennō-ji, or Temple of the Four Heavenly Kings, dates back to the institutionalization of Buddhism in Japan under Prince Shōtoku at the end of the 6th century. Since then the temple has been destroyed and reconstructed many times, with its current downsized form built in the post-war Shōwa Period (1960s–70s). The light snowfall, dark colours and the figure with his single trail of footprints make for a serene composition, and a comparison with the blizzard in *Ochanomizu* (Cat. 180), published around the same time, shows how Hasui had truly mastered the variety of the snowscape genre.

(JD)

Cat. 176

Kawase Hasui 川瀬巴水 (1883–1957)

Tennō Temple in Osaka

(*Ōsaka Tennō-ji* 大阪天王寺)

Series: *Souvenirs of Travel, third series*
(*Tabi miyage dai sanshū* 旅みやげ第三集)
Date: 1927
Signature: *Hasui*
Artist's seal: *Kawase*
Publisher: Watanabe Shōzaburō
Size: 38.5 × 25.3 cm
Collection RMAH – JP.07286

Kawase Hasui 川瀬巴水 (1883–1957)

Ioridani Pass, Etchū

(*Etchū Ioridani tōge* 越中庵谷峠)

Date: designed in 1923, published in 1928
Signature: *Hasui*
Artist's seal: *Kawase*
Publisher: Watanabe Shōzaburō
Size: 48.3 × 23.2 cm
Private collection, the Netherlands

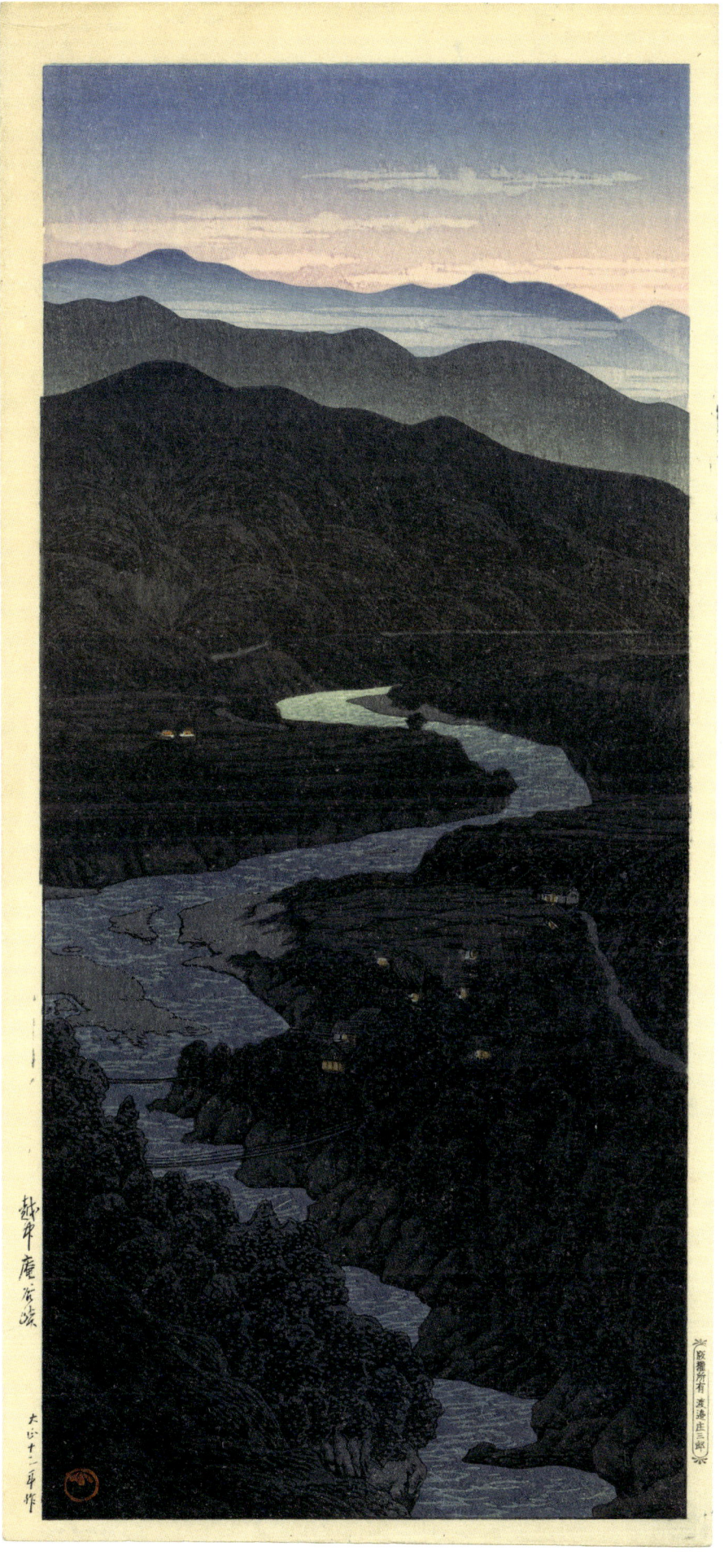

Cat. 178

Kawase Hasui 川瀬巴水 (1883–1957)

Zōjō Temple, Shiba

(*Shiba Zōjōji* 芝増上寺)

Series: *Twenty Views of Tokyo*
(*Tōkyō nijūkei* 東京二十景)
Date: 1925
Signature: *Hasui*
Artist's seal: *Kawase*
Publisher: Watanabe Shōzaburō
Size: 39.3 × 26.6 cm
Collection Scholten

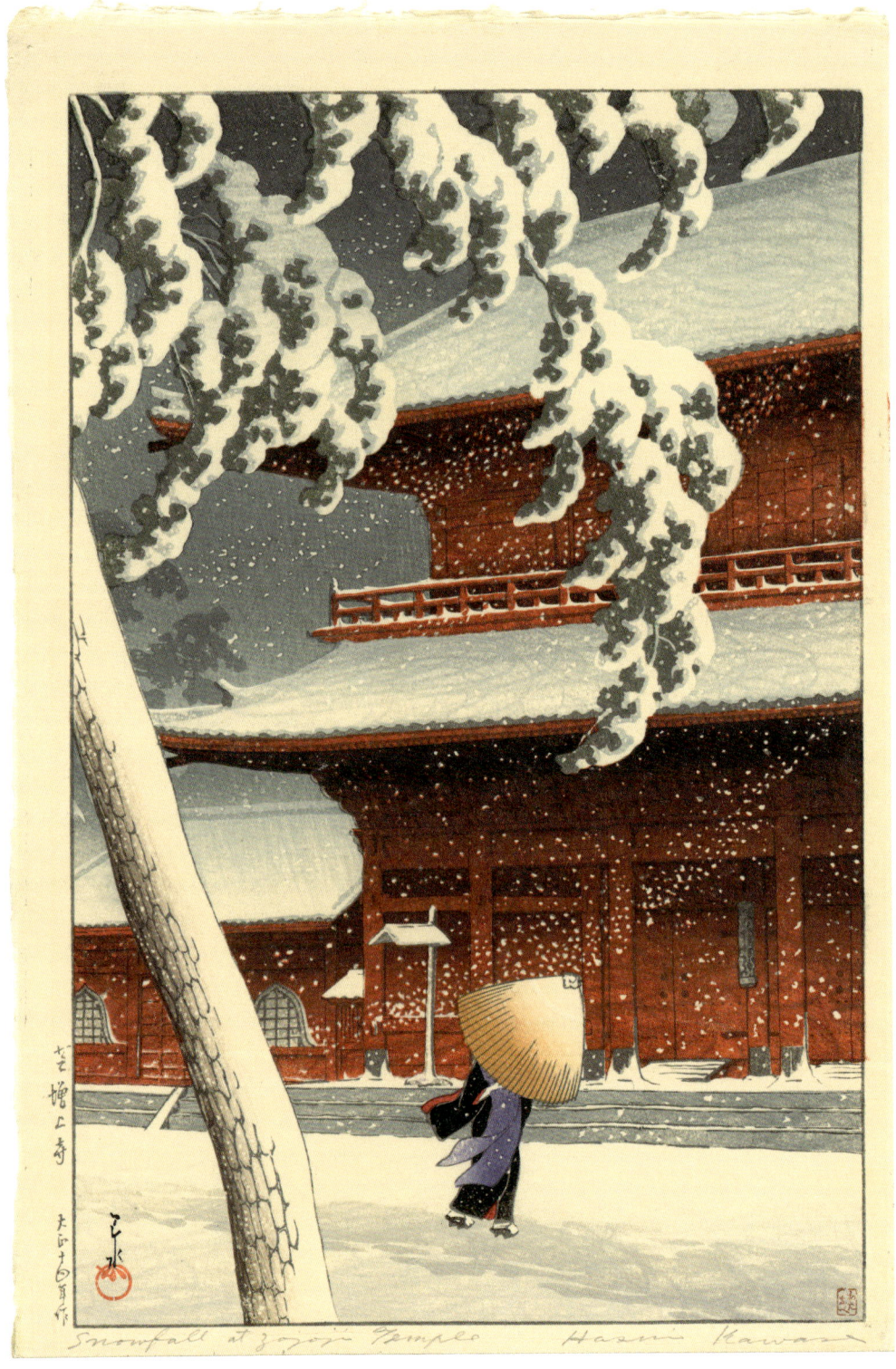

This scene of a woman in a kimono scurrying through a blizzard and shielding herself from the cold with a traditional umbrella is one of Hasui's most popular designs and was printed many times over. In 1933 the Osaka Mainichi publishing company included a reduced-format version in *Japan Today & Tomorrow*, a news magazine targeted at a Western audience. The red building in the background is the main gate of Zōjō temple, one of the city's former two family temples of the ruling Tokugawa shoguns of the Edo Period, the other being Ueno's Kan'ei temple. Built in 1622, the brightly coloured gate has survived Tokyo's history of destruction and demolition. Today it is the temple's only original structure and one of the city's oldest wooden buildings.

(JD)

Cat. 179

Kawase Hasui 川瀬巴水 (1883–1957)

Shin-Ōhashi

(*Shin-Ōhashi* 新大橋)

Series: *Twenty Views of Tokyo*
(*Tōkyō nijūkei* 東京二十景)
Date: 1926
Signature: *Hasui*
Artist's seal: *Kawase*
Publisher: Watanabe Shōzaburō
Size: 38.6 × 26.1 cm
Collection Scholten

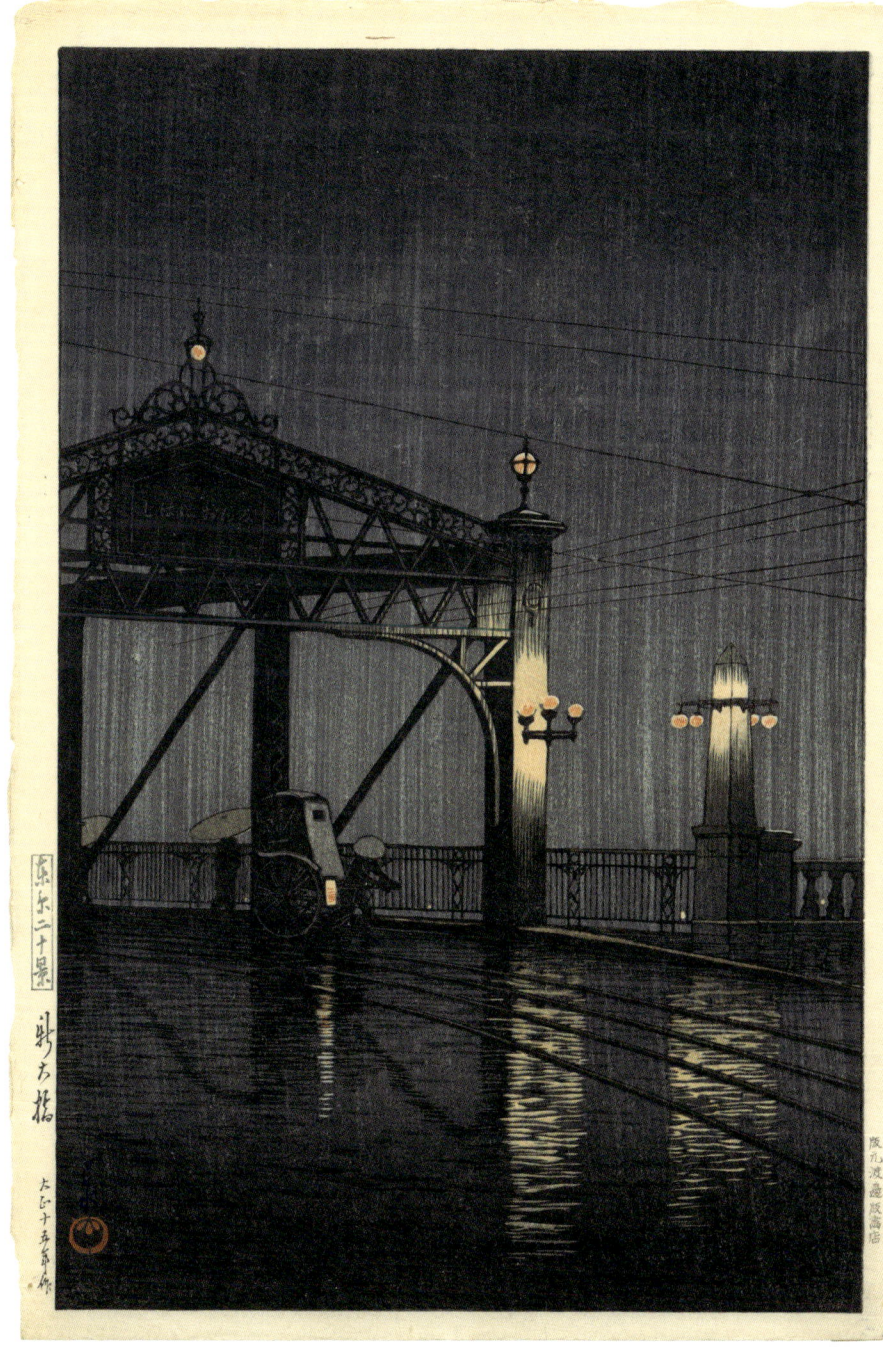

It was not common for Hasui to depict Tokyo's modernizing cityscape. Here a couple of pedestrians and a rickshaw driver cross a Western-style steel bridge during a downpour. The background behind the bridge is no longer visible due to the weather, but a few lights manage to shine through the bridge's railings. The effect of thick rain comes from the *baren*, the tool used by the printer to press the paper on the printing blocks. Since the lines of rain are the result of the printer's hand motions rather than the printing blocks, each print has a unique pattern of rainfall. The steel bridge was built in 1912, a monument to the rapid changes of the Meiji and Taishō Periods. It replaced the old Shin-Ōhashi bridge, made famous by Utagawa Hiroshige's print and later by Vincent van Gogh's copy in oil. The steel bridge survived the war but fell into disrepair in the years after. In order to preserve it, the whole structure was disassembled and brought to the *Meiji-mura* architectural open-air museum near Nagoya, where it was restored to its former glory and can still be crossed by visitors today.

(JD)

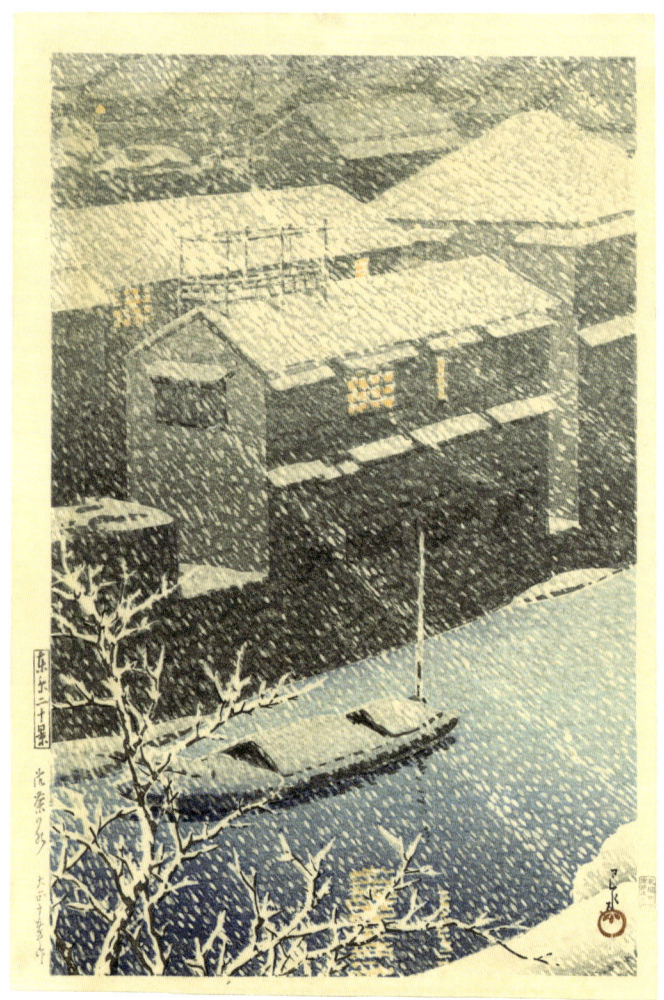

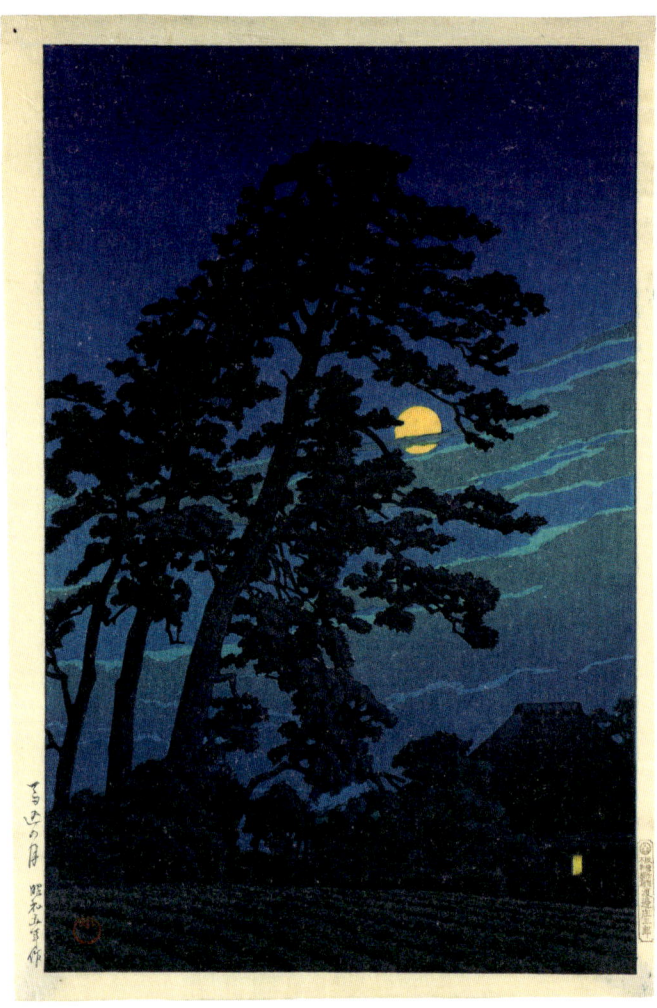

Cat. 180

Kawase Hasui 川瀬巴水 (1883–1957)

Ochanomizu

(*Ochanomizu* 御茶の水)

Series: *Twenty Views of Tokyo*
(*Tōkyō nijūkei* 東京二十景)
Date: 1926
Signature: *Hasui*
Artist's seal: *Kawase*
Publisher: Watanabe Shōzaburō
Size: 39 × 26.5 cm
Private collection, the Netherlands

Cat. 181

Kawase Hasui 川瀬巴水 (1883–1957)

Moon at Magome

(*Magome no tsuki* 馬込の月)

Series: *Twenty Views of Tokyo*
(*Tōkyō nijūkei* 東京二十景)
Date: 1930
Signature: *Hasui*
Artist's seal: *Kawase*
Publisher: Watanabe Shōzaburō
Size: 38.5 × 26 cm
Collection RMAH – JP.07290

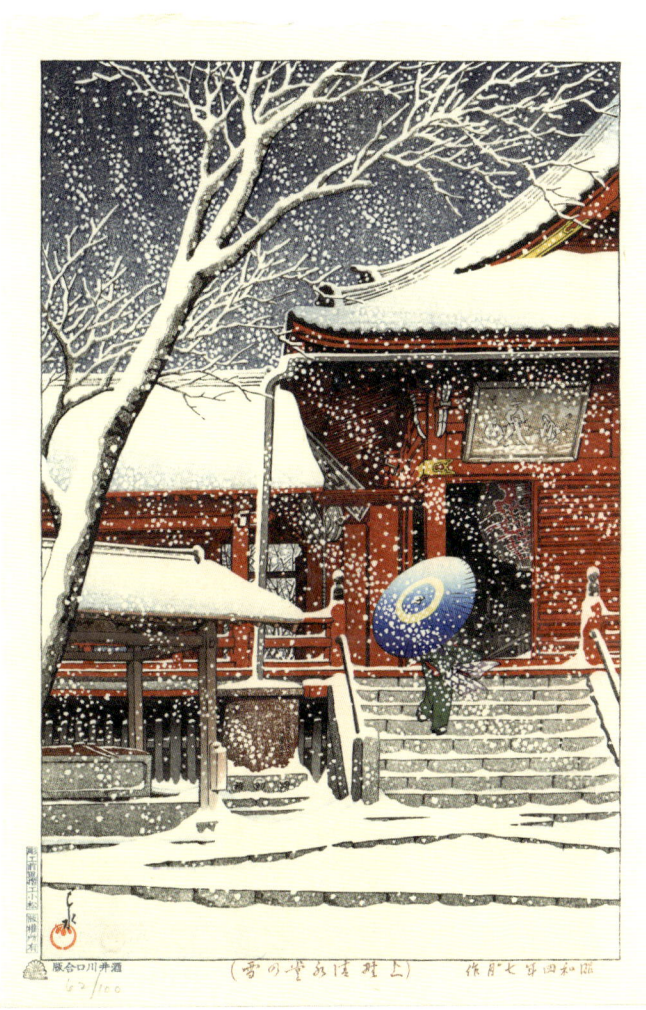

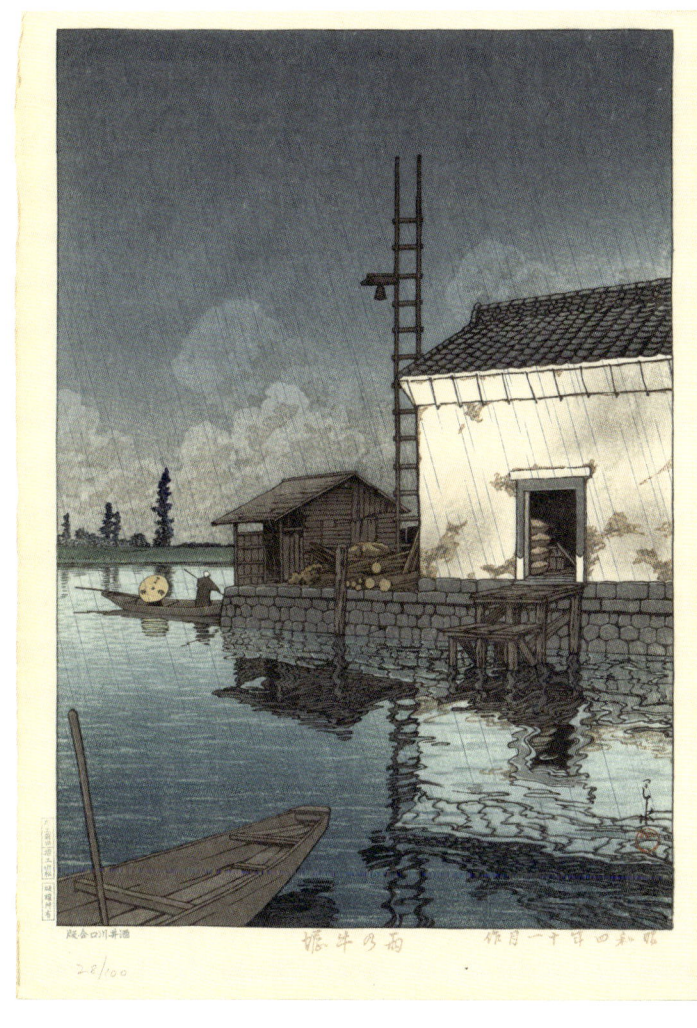

Cat. 182

Kawase Hasui 川瀬巴水 (1883–1957)

Snow at Kiyomizu Hall, Ueno

(*Ueno Kiyomizudō no yuki* 上野清水堂の雪)

Date: July 1929
Signature: *Hasui*
Artist's seal: *Kawase*
Edition: 62/100
Publisher: Sakai-Kawaguchi
Block cutter: *Maeda* (Maeda Kentarō)
Printer: *Komatsu* (Komatsu Wasakichi)
Size: 39.7 × 27.1 cm
Collection Scholten

Cat. 183

Kawase Hasui 川瀬巴水 (1883–1957)

Rain at Ushibori

(*Ame no Ushibori* 雨の牛堀)

Date: November 1929
Signature: *Hasui*
Artist's seal: *Kawase*
Edition: 28/100
Publisher: Sakai-Kawaguchi
Block cutter: *Maeda* (Maeda Kentarō)
Printer: *Komatsu* (Komatsu Wasakichi)
Size: 42.1 × 30 cm
Collection Scholten

One of fifteen designs issued by Sakai-Kawaguchi, with whom Hasui collaborated between 1929 and 1931, and their only one in a narrow format. The first prints were published in issues of 100, with a second edition of 300 prints, and later, after Sakai and Kawaguchi ceased their partnership in 1931, prints appeared without indication of edition size. Ueno's Tōshō-gū was dedicated to Tokugawa Ieyasu (1543–1616), the founder of the Tokugawa dynasty that ruled Japan during the Edo Period (1603–1868). The shrine and the Kan'ei pagoda in the background miraculously survived the fires of the 1923 earthquake and the wartime bombings.

(JD)

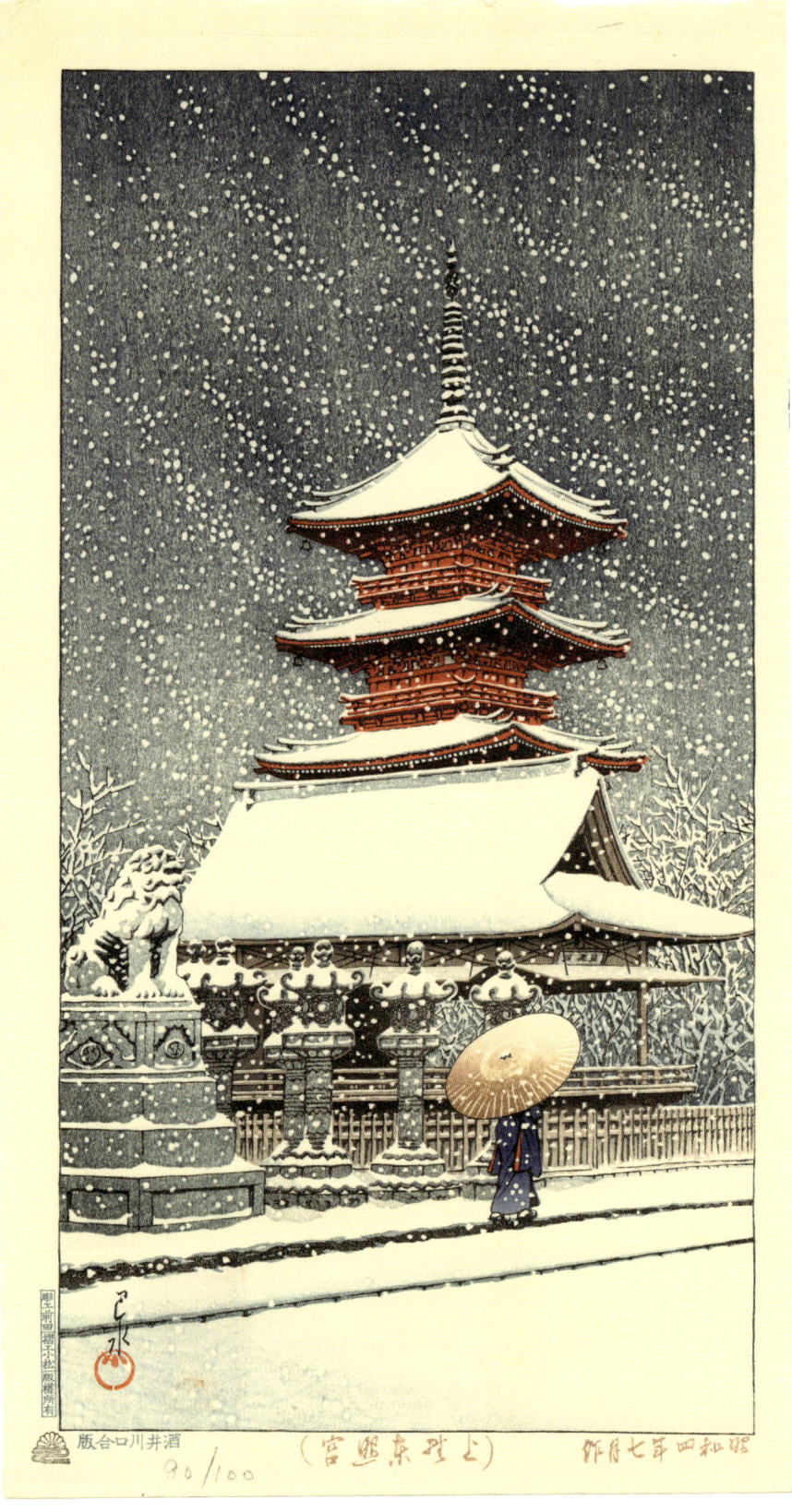

Cat. 184

Kawase Hasui 川瀬巴水 (1883–1957)

Snow at Tōshō Shrine, Ueno

(*Ueno Tōshōgū no yuki* 上野東照宮 の雪)

Date: 1929
Signature: *Hasui*
Artist's seal: *Kawase*
Edition: 90/100
Publisher: Sakai-Kawaguchi
Block cutter: *Maeda* (Maeda Kentarō)
Printer: *Komatsu* (Komatsu Wasakichi)
Size: 38.7 × 21.4 cm
Collection Scholten

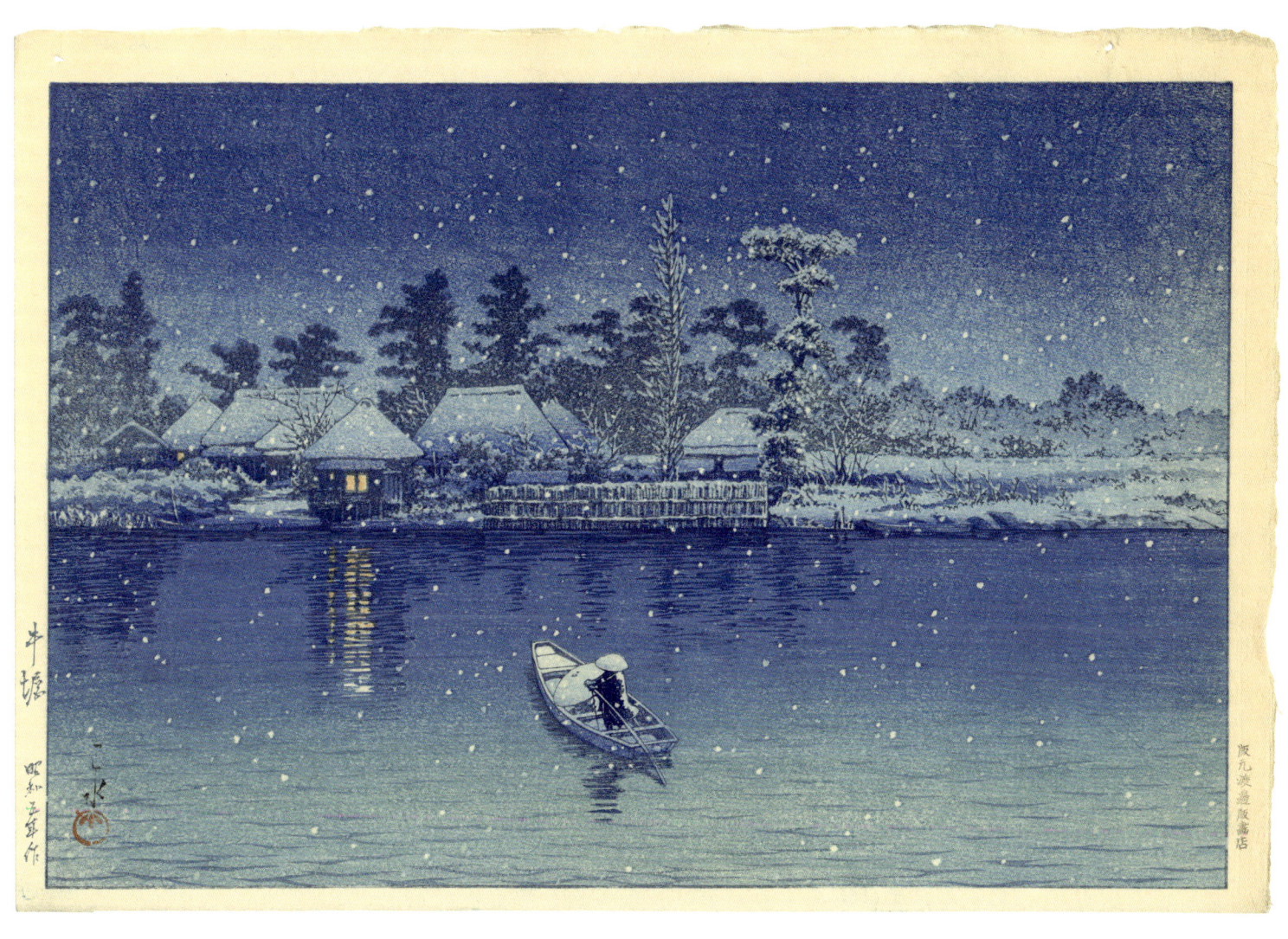

Cat. 185

Kawase Hasui 川瀬巴水 (1883–1957)

Ushibori

(*Ushibori* 牛掘)

Date: 1930
Signature: *Hasui*
Artist's seal: *Kawase*
Publisher: Watanabe Shōzaburō
Size: 26.2 × 38.6 cm
Private collection, the Netherlands

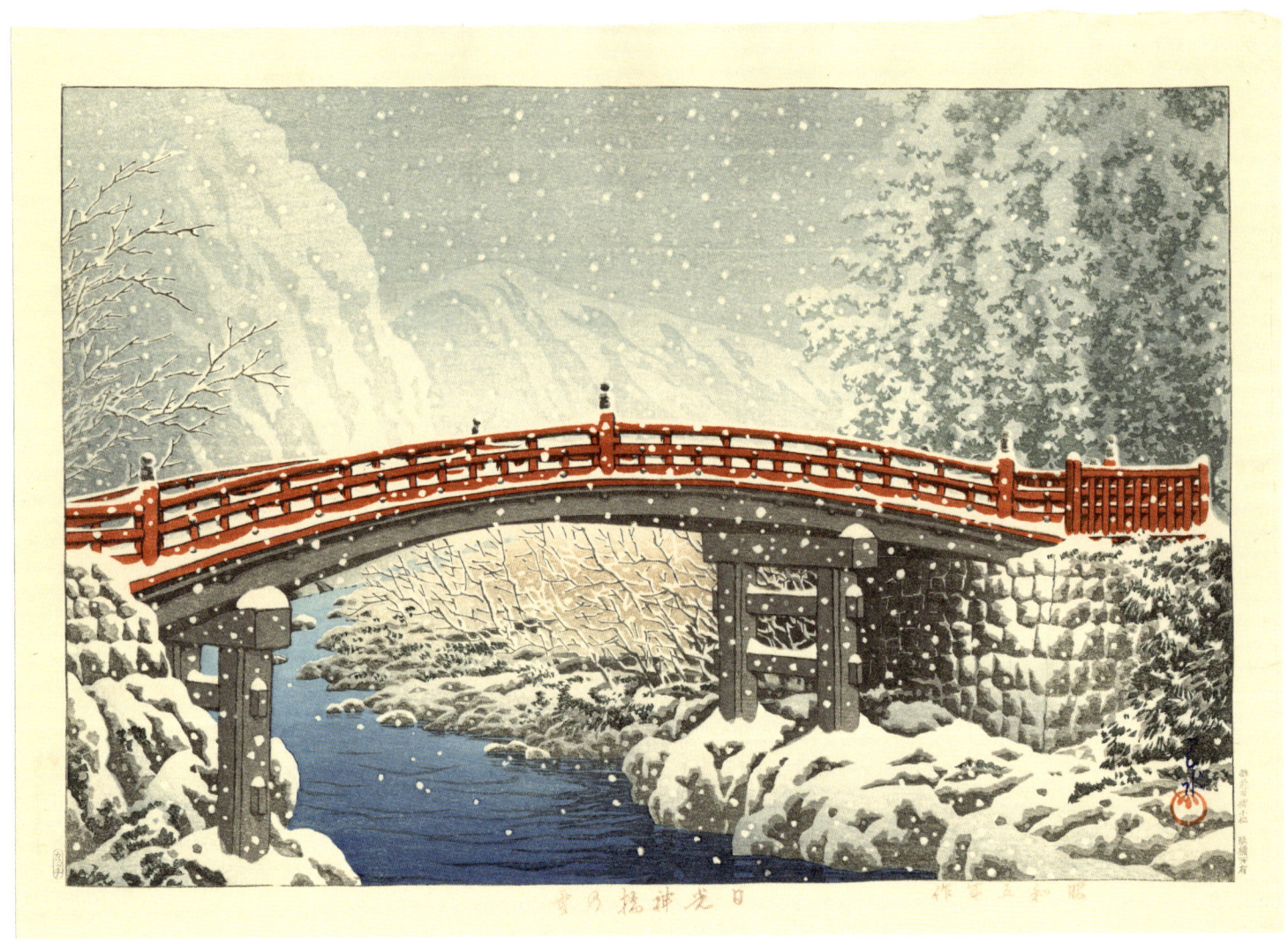

Cat. 186

Kawase Hasui 川瀬巴水 (1883–1957)

**Snow on the Sacred Bridge
at Nikkō**

(*Nikkō shinkyō no yuki*
日光神橋の雪)

Date: 1930
Signature: *Hasui*
Artist's seal: *Kawase*
Edition: 41/350
Publisher: Kawaguchi
Block cutter: *Maeda* (Maeda Kentarō)
Printer: *Komatsu* (Komatsu Wasakichi)
Size: 27.5 × 39.5 cm
Collection Scholten

The Shinkyō, or 'sacred bridge', in Nikkō, crosses the Daiya River and leads to the grounds of Tōshō-gū, a large complex of temples and shrines dedicated to Tokugawa Ieyasu. The bridge dates back to 1636, but it has been destroyed and reconstructed many times since then. During the Edo Period it was accessible only to members of the imperial court and high-ranking officials who came to pay their respects to Tokugawa Ieyasu.

(JD)

Contrary to, for example, Hiroshige, Hasui did not select the traditional famous places (*meisho*), or 'beauty spots', of Japan. He had a preference for remote and serene spots, in which people played a marginal role. This print is a good example.

Set in Mukōjima – today part of Tokyo's Sumida ward – two figures make their way over the water through heavy snowfall. The boatman has already been blanketed by snow, while his passenger has taken shelter under a large umbrella. In the distance another lonely boat is seen on the water. Lit windows hint at more human presence, and the lights reflecting on the water add a sense of warmth and comfort to this otherwise wintry evening scene. Multiple boats lay moored at the quay, already covered by a thick blanket of snow.

(PO)

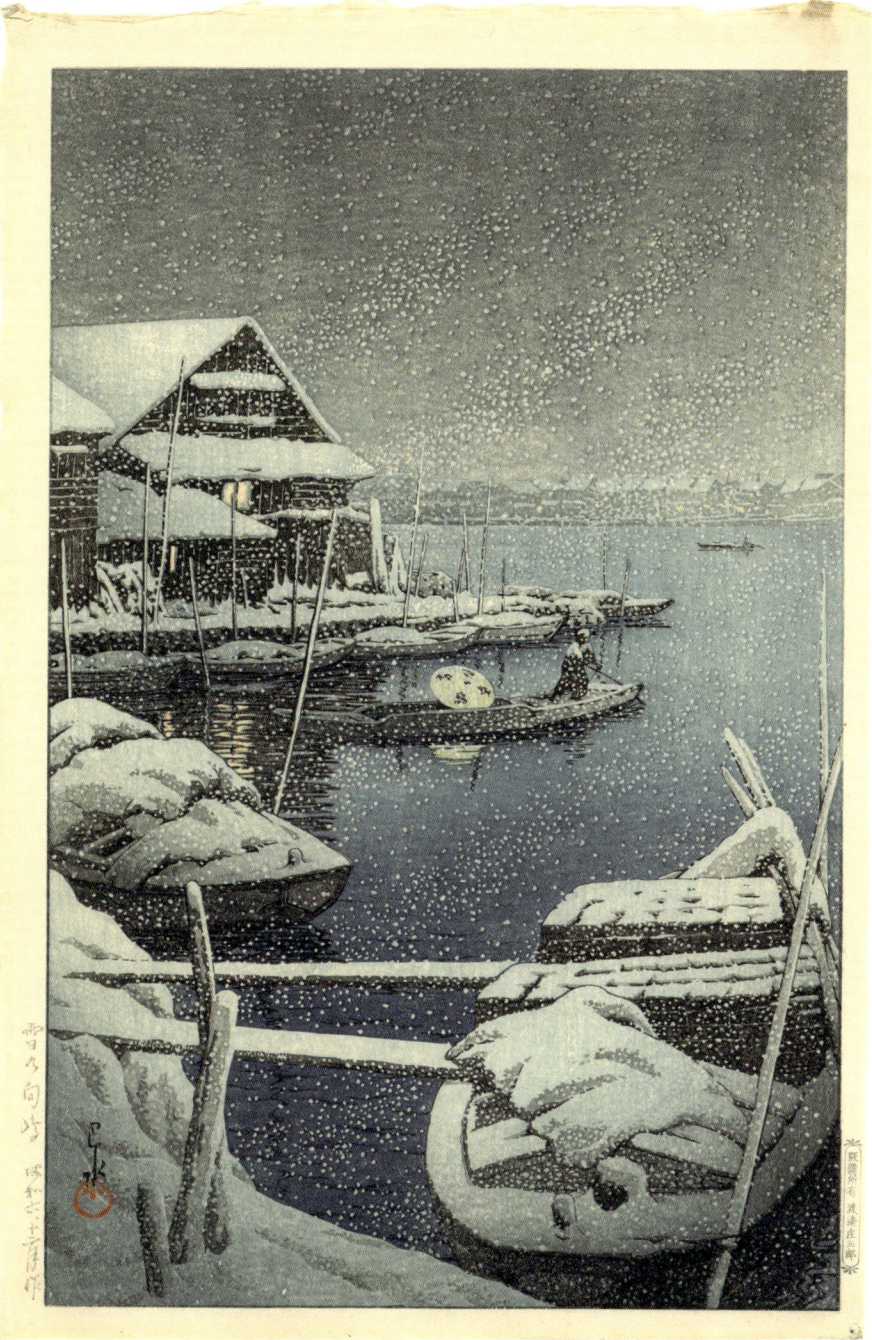

Cat. 187

Kawase Hasui 川瀬巴水 (1883–1957)

Snow at Mukōjima

(*Yuki no Mukōjima* 雪の向島)

Date: December 1931
Signature: *Hasui*
Artist's seal: *Kawase*
Publisher: Watanabe Shōzaburō
Size: 38.8 × 26.4 cm
Collection Scholten

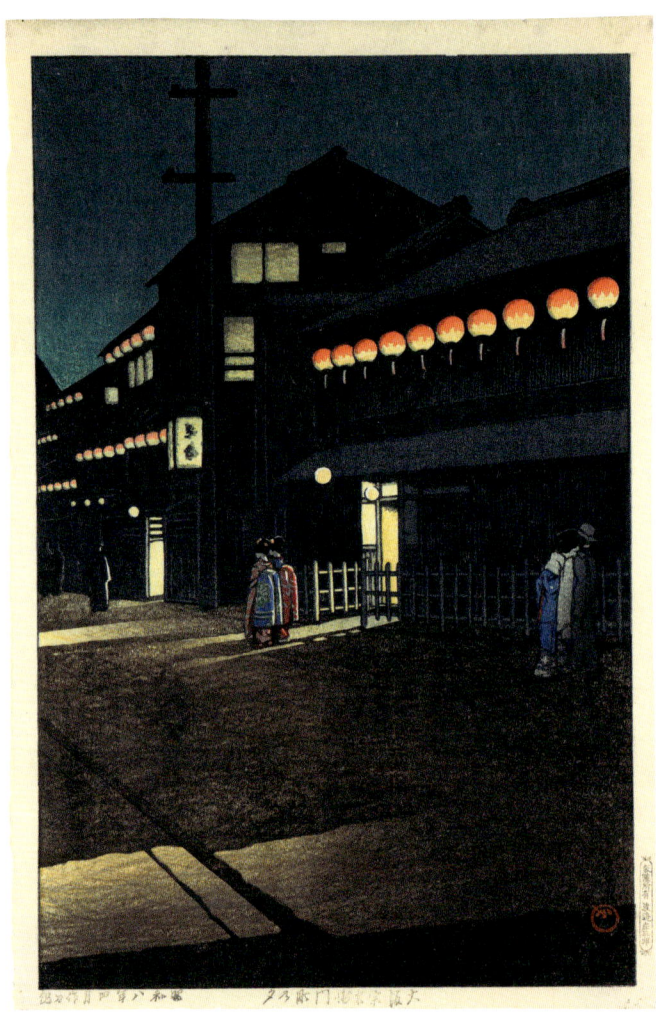

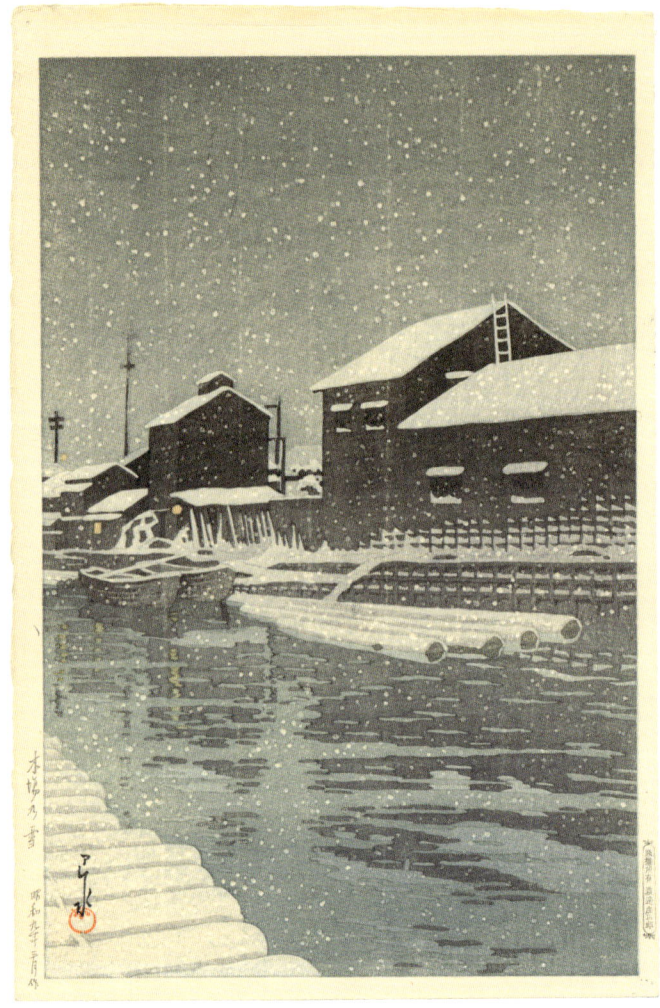

Cat. 188

Kawase Hasui 川瀬巴水 (1883–1957)

Evening at Sōemon-chō in Osaka

(*Ōsaka Sōemon-chō no yū* 大坂宗右
衛門町の夕)

Series: *Collected Views of
Japan II, Kansai edition*
(*Nihon fūkei shū II Kansai hen*
日本風景集 I I 関西篇)
Date: April 1933
Signature: *Hasui*
Artist's seal: *Kawase*
Publisher: Watanabe Shōzaburō
Size: 38.5 × 25 cm
Collection RMAH – JP.07287

Cat. 189

Kawase Hasui 川瀬巴水 (1883–1957)

Snow at Kiba

(*Kiba no yuki* 木場の雪)

Date: March 1934
Signature: *Hasui*
Artist's seal: *Kawase*
Publisher: Watanabe Shōzaburō
Size: 39.9 × 26.8 cm
Collection Scholten

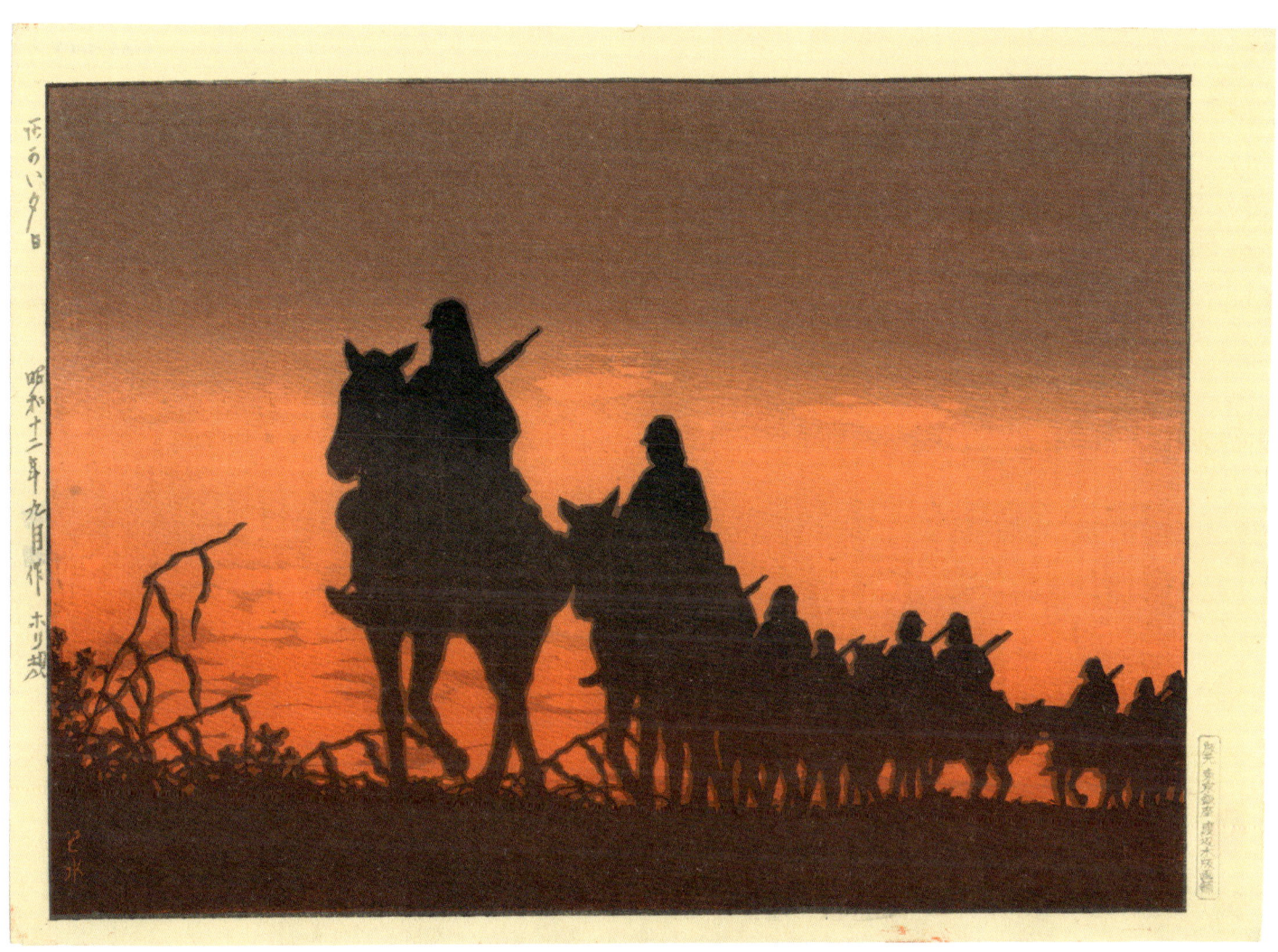

War prints were an uncommon theme in Hasui's oeuvre, but nationalism in the country rose when Japan went to war with China in July 1937. In the same year, Hasui made four designs in the *aiban* format of soldiers at the front in China. According to Watanabe's grandson Shōichirō, during the war years Hasui would take these four prints with him on his sketching journeys to prove to local authorities that he was not a spy but a patriotic countryman. It is said that Hasui based these four designs on photographs from magazines. In this print soldiers on horseback advance into Chinese territory, set against an evening sky. The block cutter was Watanabe Shōzaburō's son, Tadasu.

(JD)

Cat. 190

Kawase Hasui 川瀬巴水 (1883–1957)
The Red Setting Sun
(*Akai yūhi* あかい夕日)

Date: September 1937
Signature: *Hasui*
Publisher: Watanabe Shōzaburō
Block cutter: *Hori Tadasu*
(Watanabe Tadasu)
Size: 25 × 35.2 cm
Private collection, the Netherlands

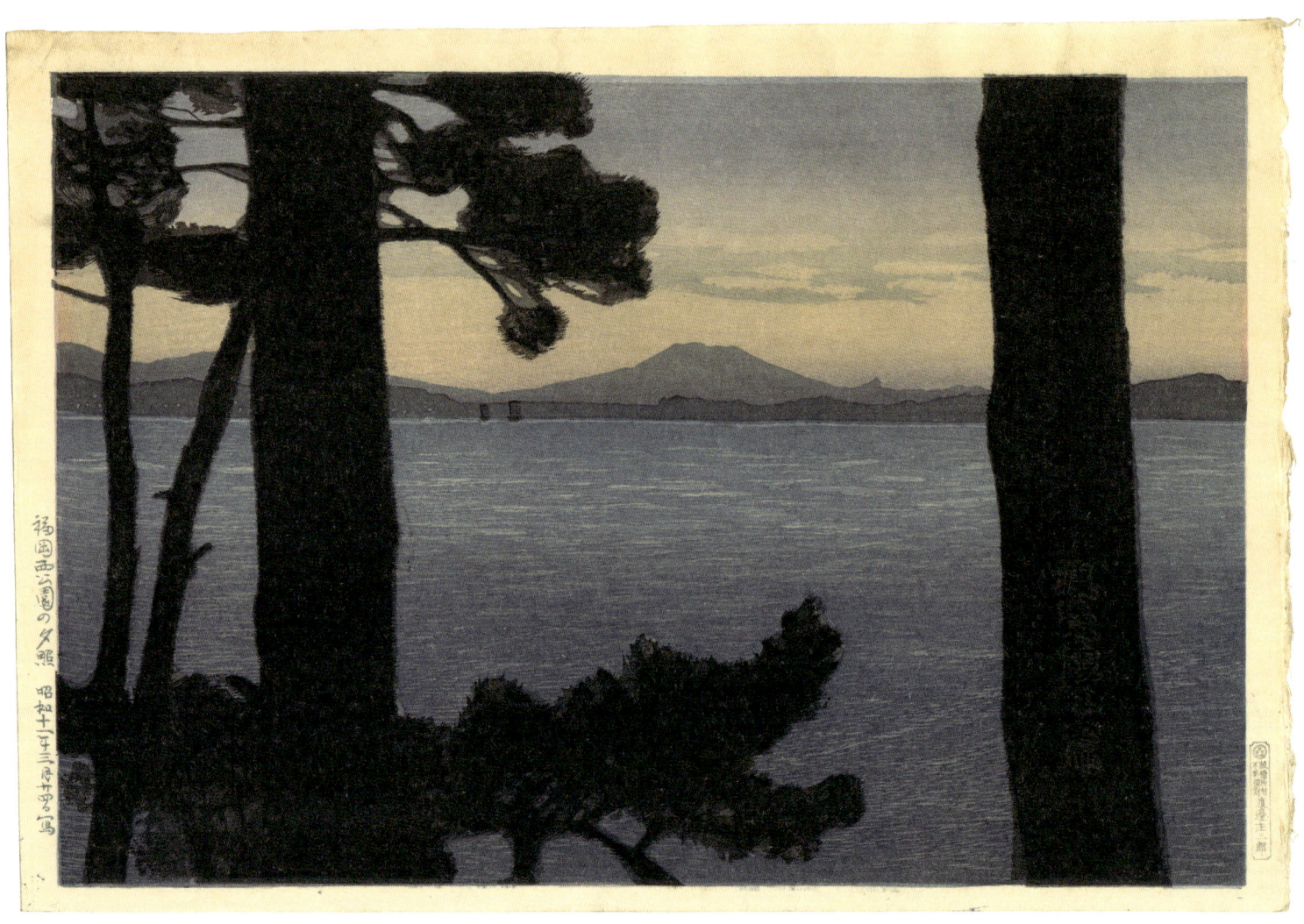

Cat. 191

Watanabe Shōzaburō (Kakō)
渡辺庄三郎 (霞江) (1885–1962)
Sunset at Nishi Park, Fukuoka
(*Fukuoka Nishi Kōen no sekishō*
福岡西公園の夕照)

Date: 24 March 1936
Signature: *Watanabe Kakō kōsaku*
Publisher: Watanabe Shōzaburō
(self-published)
Size: 30 × 44 cm
Private collection, the Netherlands

In the course of the 1930s, the publisher Watanabe Shōzaburō felt that his *shin hanga* prints were becoming too stylized and clichéd, especially those by his main landscape designer, Kawase Hasui. He tried to push his artists to give their designs a slightly rougher touch, somewhat closer to the style of the works produced by the *sōsaku hanga* movement. In the search for a new style, Watanabe personally led the production of two prints based on photographs, and signed them under the artist name Kakō, with the characters derived from the area where he was born, the neighbourhood of Egawa, in Goka, north of Tokyo.

(JD)

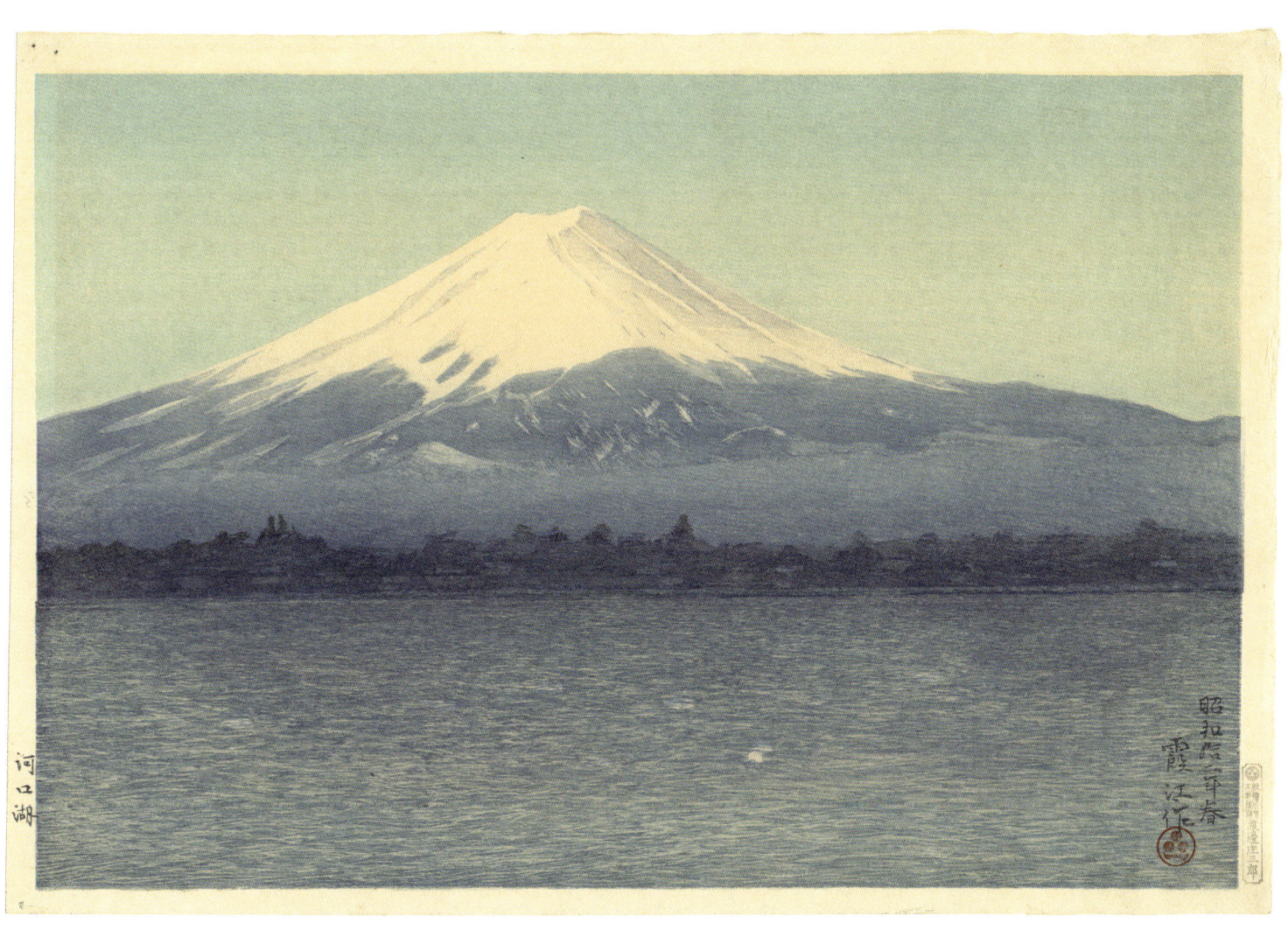

Cat. 192

Watanabe Shōzaburō (Kakō)
渡辺庄三郎 (霞江) (1885–1962)
Lake Kawaguchi
(*Kawaguchi-ko* 河口湖)

Date: Spring 1937
Signature: *Kakō saku*
Artist's seal: Watanabe family crest seal
Publisher: Watanabe Shōzaburō
(self-published)
Size: 29.2 × 43 cm
Private collection, the Netherlands

This and the next print are part of a series of eight designs that Hasui produced depicting scenes of Korea following a trip to that country with four other artists. Japanese colonial rule had been established since 1910, and many Japanese artists visited Korea for longer or shorter periods, either to work or to teach Japanese arts as part of an attempt to assimilate the Korean people. The scholar Narazaki Muneshige has argued that Hasui needed the trip to find new inspiration.

(CU)

Cat. 193

Kawase Hasui 川瀬巴水 (1883–1957)

Hwahong Gate [Buksumun], Suwon

(*Suwon/Suigen Kakōmon* 水原華虹門)

Series: *Eight Views of Korea*
(*Chōsen hakkei* 朝鮮八景)
Date: August 1939
Signature: *Hasui*
Artist's seal: *Hasui*
Publisher: Watanabe Shōzaburō,
distributed through Kansai Bijutsu-sha
Size: 39 × 27 cm
S. Watanabe Color Print Co.

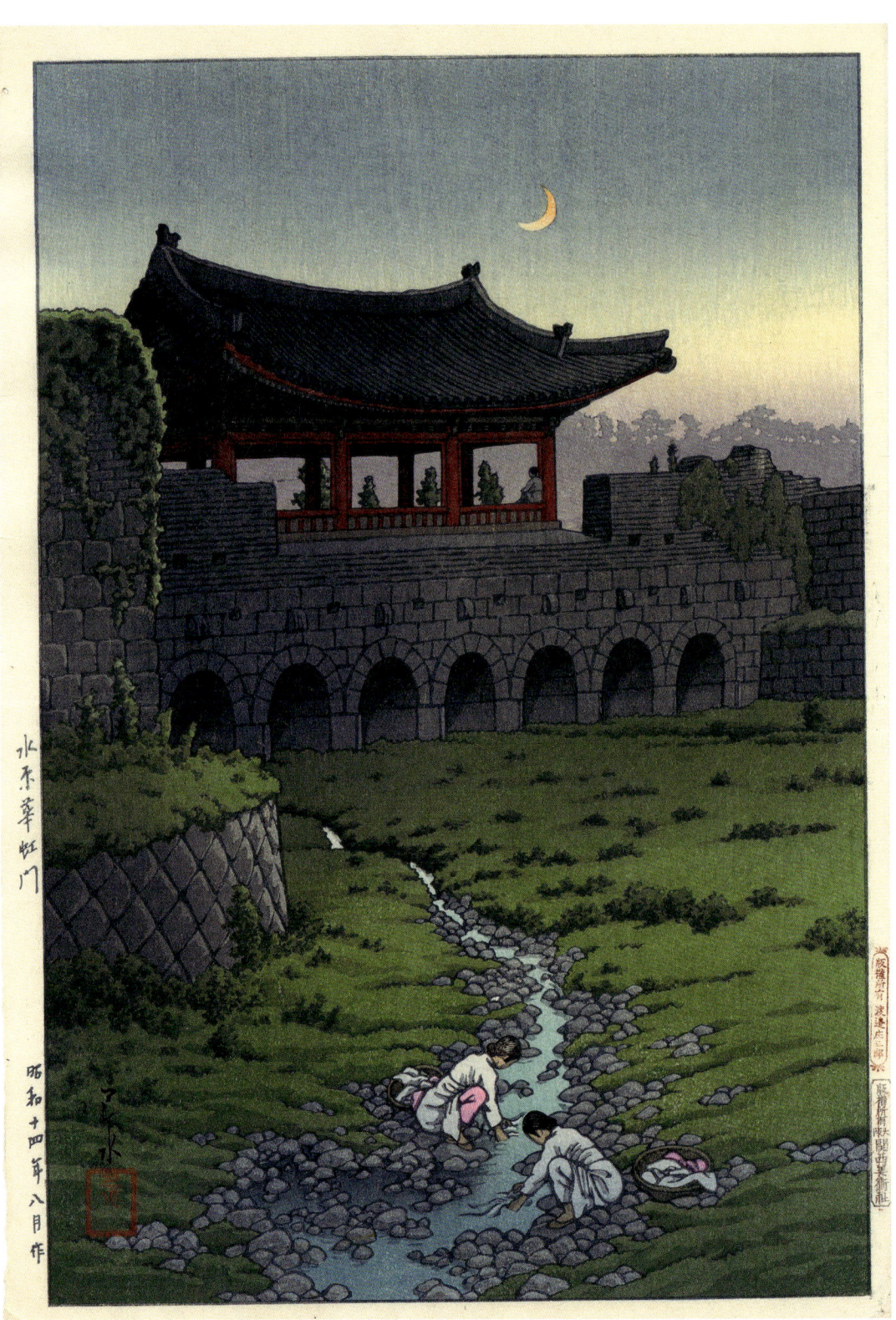

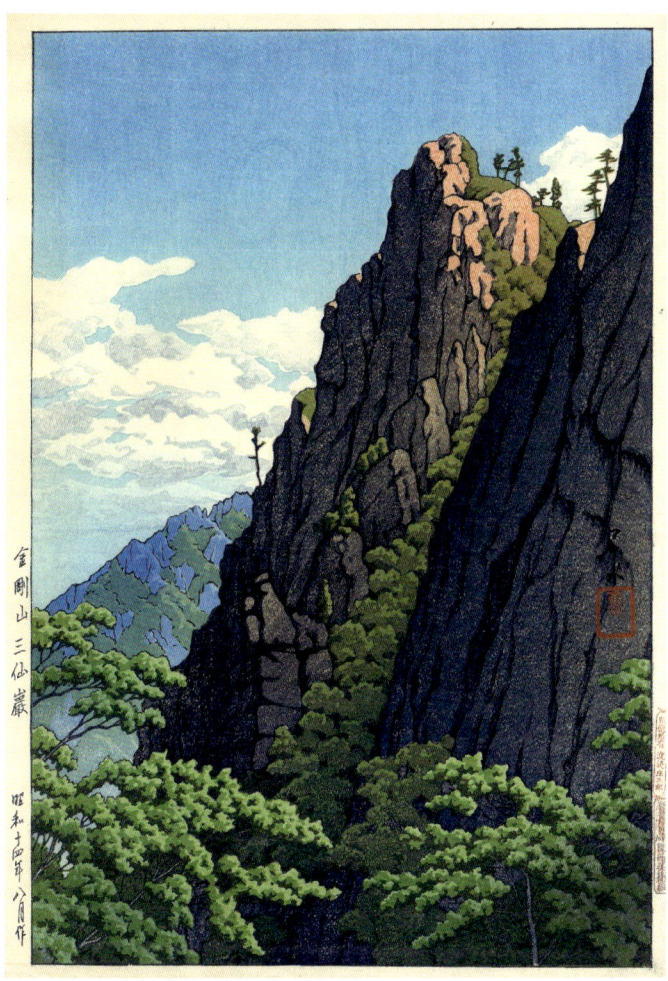

Kawase Hasui 川瀬巴水 (1883–1957)

Shikishima Riverbed, Maebashi

(*Maebashi Shikishima gawara* 前橋敷島河原)

Date: 1942
Signature: *Hasui*
Artist's seal: *Kawase*
Publisher: Watanabe Shōzaburō
Size: 26.2 × 39.2 cm
Collection Scholten

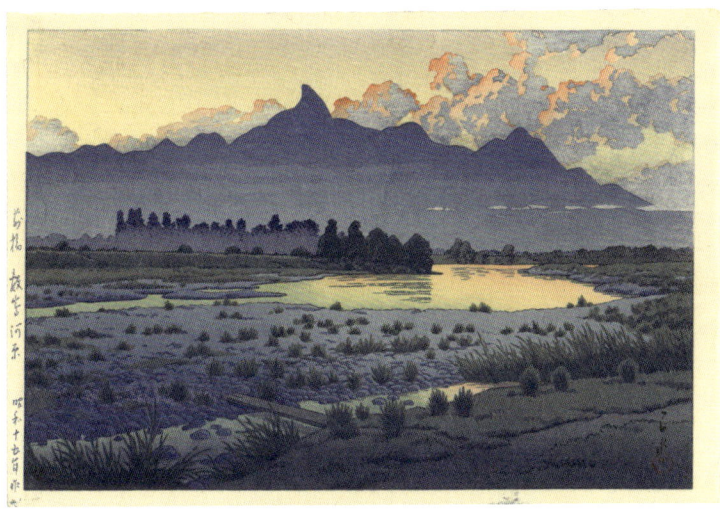

Cat. 194

Kawase Hasui 川瀬巴水 (1883–1957)

Mount Kŭmgang, Samson Rock

(*Kongōsan, Sansengan*
金剛山 三仙巖)

Series: *Eight Views of Korea*
(*Chōsen hakkei* 朝鮮八景)
Date: August 1939
Signature: *Hasui*
Artist's seal: *Hasui*
Publisher: Watanabe Shōzaburō,
distributed through Kansai Bijutsu-sha
Size: 39.3 × 27 cm
S. Watanabe Color Print Co.

Cat. 196

Kawase Hasui 川瀬巴水 (1883–1957)

Hataori, Shiobara

(*Shiobara Hataori* 塩原畑下り)

Date: 1946
Signature: *Hasui*
Artist's seal: *Kawase*
Publisher: Watanabe Shōzaburō
Size: 39.1 × 26.1 cm
Private collection, the Netherlands

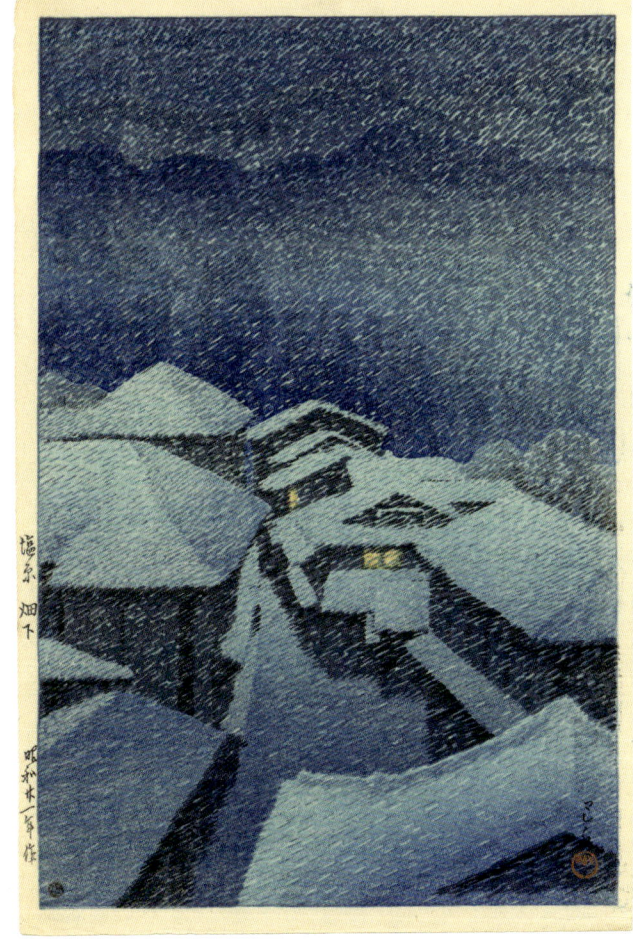

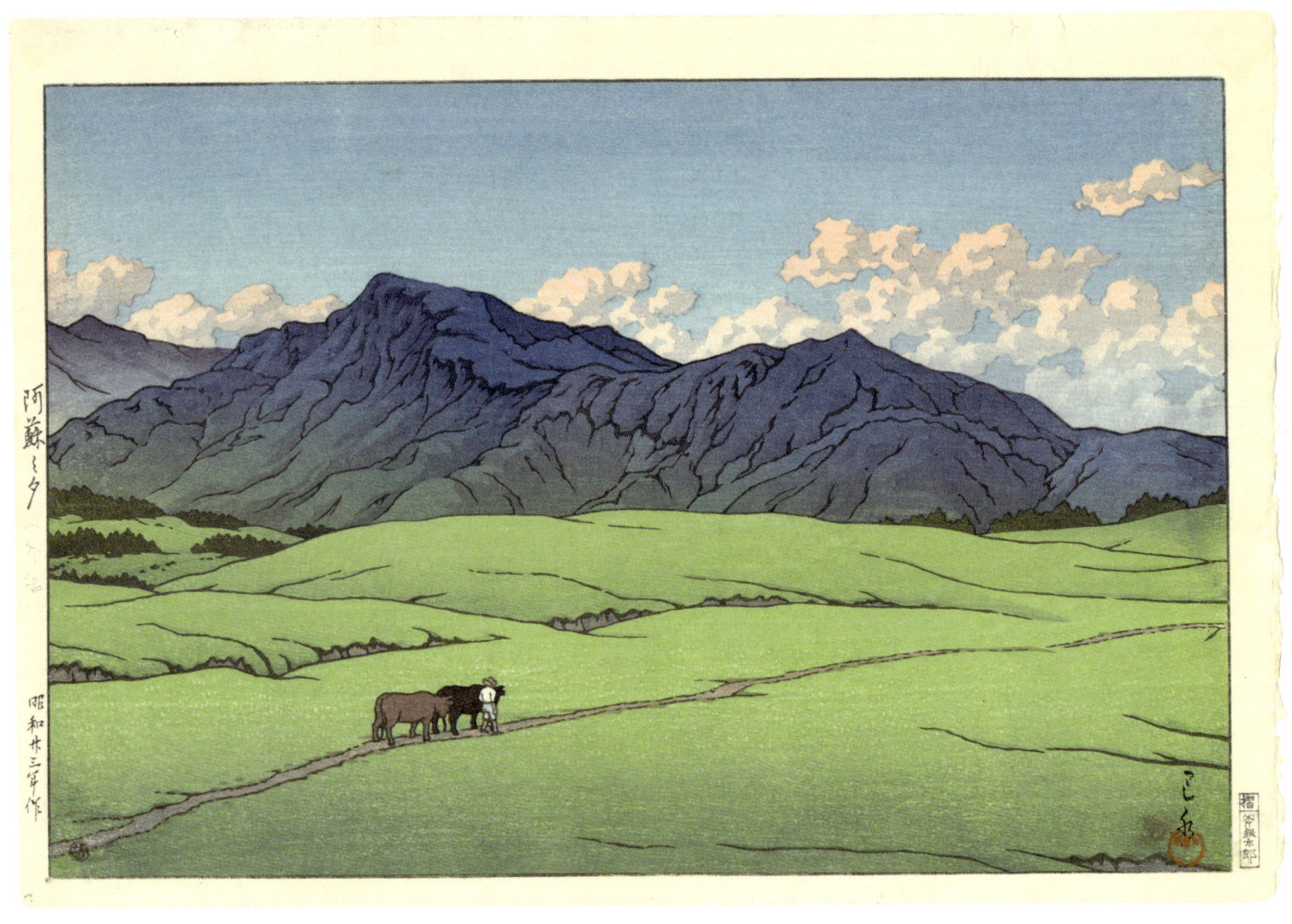

Cat. 197

Kawase Hasui 川瀬巴水 (1883–1957)

Dusk at Aso (outer crater)

(*Aso no yū (gairin)* 阿蘇の勇（外輪）)

Date: 1948
Signature: *Hasui*
Artist's seal: *Kawase*
Publisher: Watanabe Shōzaburō
Size: 26.8 × 39.2 cm
Collection Scholten

Cat. 198

Kawase Hasui 川瀬巴水 (1883–1957)

Ōno, Mito

(*Mito Ōno* 水戸大野)

Date: 1949
Signature: *Hasui*
Artist's seal: *Kawase*
Publisher: Watanabe Shōzaburō
Size: 38.7 × 26.7 cm
Collection Scholten

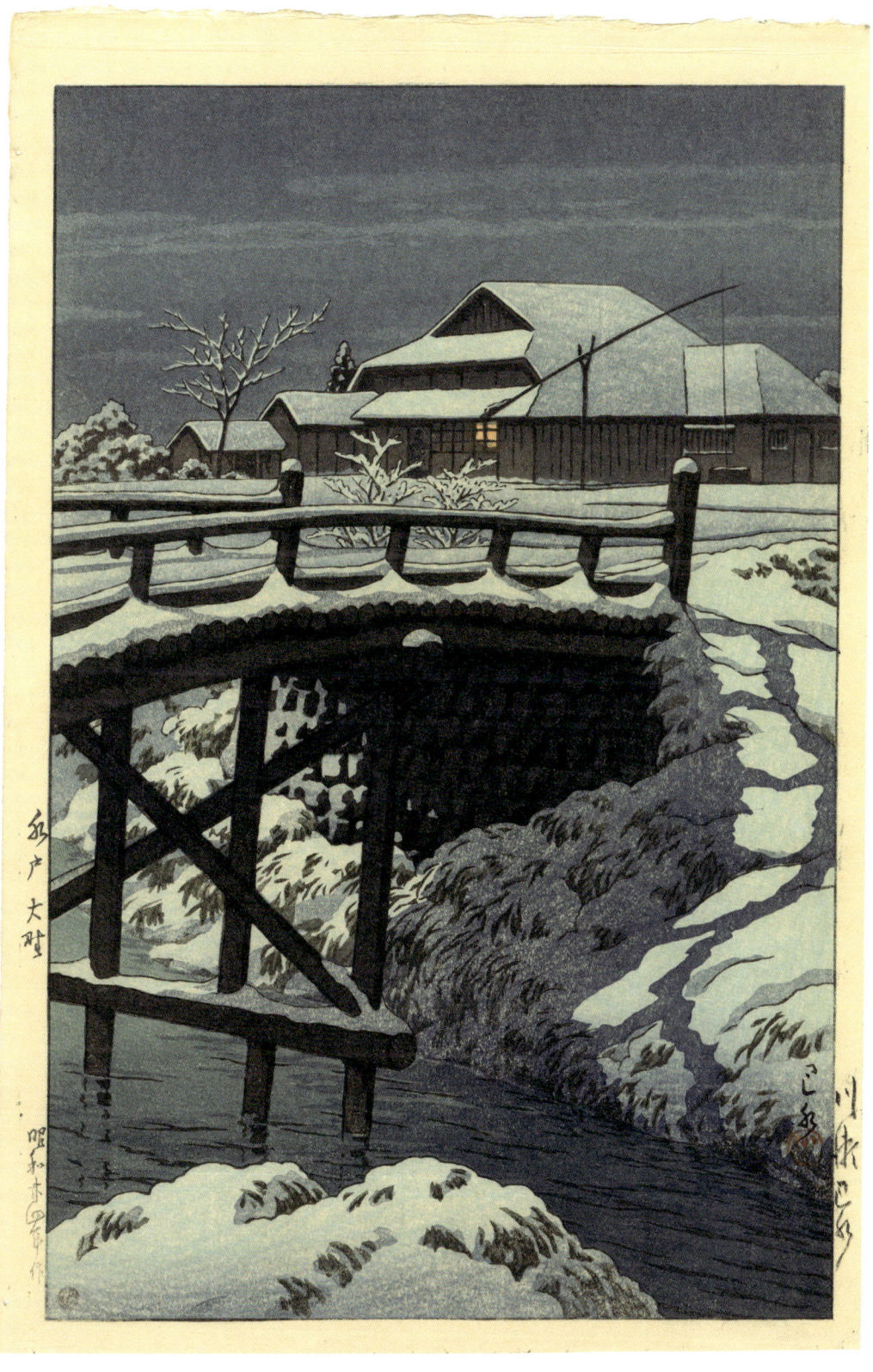

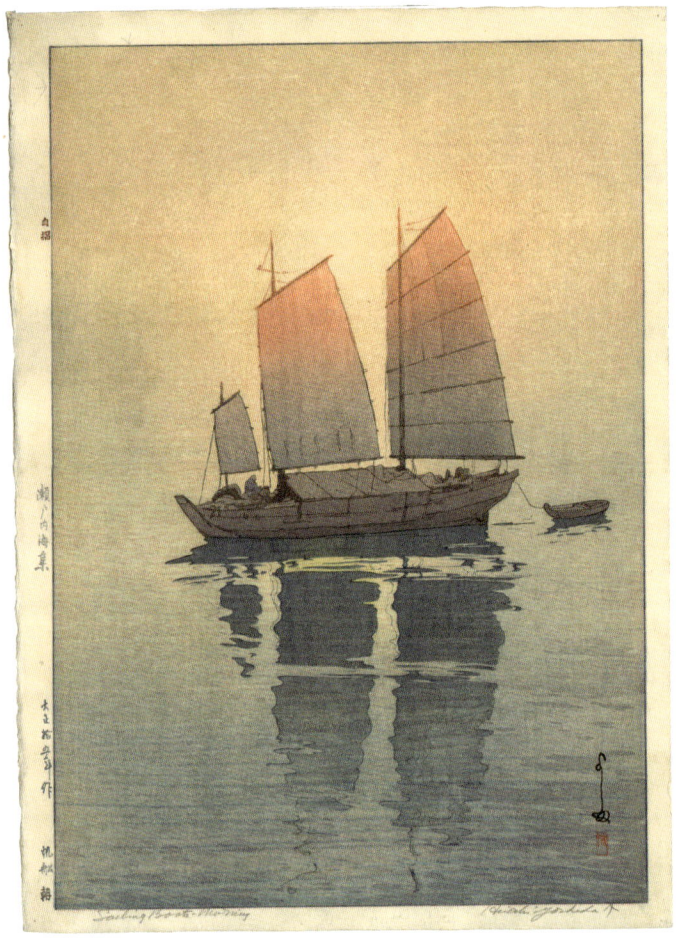

199a

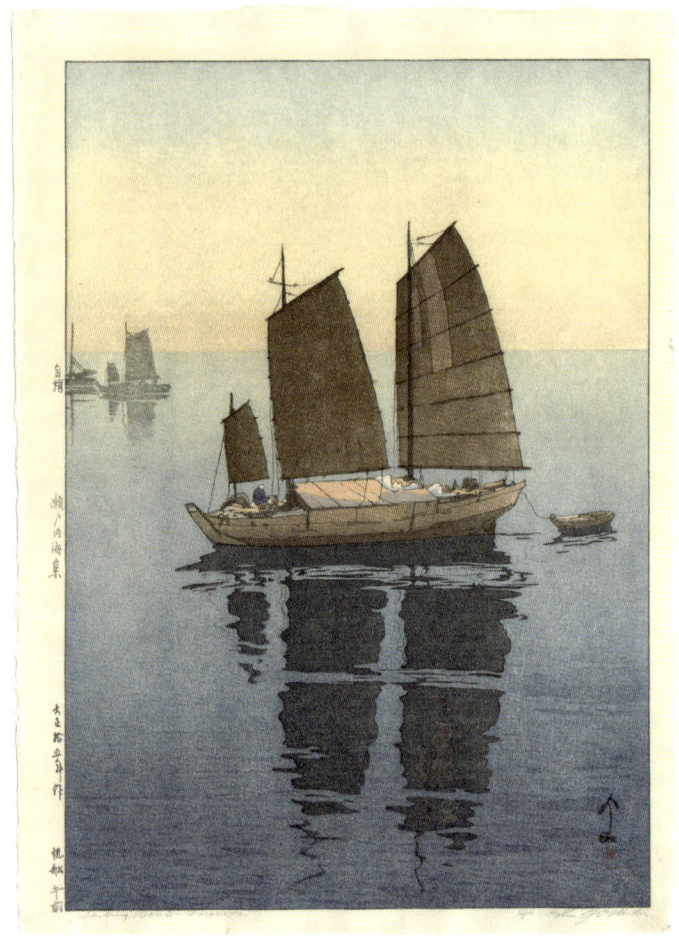

199b

Cat. 199a–f

Yoshida Hiroshi 吉田博 (1876–1950)

Series: *The Inland Sea Series*
(*Seto naikai shū* 瀬戸内海集)
Date: 1926
Signature: *Yoshida*, *Hiroshi Yoshida*
(bottom margin in pencil)
Artist's seal: *Hiroshi*
Publisher: self-published
Block cutter: *Maeda Yūjirō*
Printer: self-printed (*jizuri*
stamp in left margin)
Size: 54.5 × 39.5 cm
Collection Scholten

Cat. 199a

Sailing Boats – Morning

(*Hansen asa* 帆船 朝)

Cat. 199b

Sailing Boats – Forenoon

(*Hansen gozen* 帆船 午前)

Yoshida Hiroshi is known for his stunning *shin hanga* landscape prints, but his turn to the medium of woodblock printing was preceded by oils and watercolours in the field of *yōga*. He discovered that his prints exceeded the commercial success of his watercolours, and decided to focus on woodblock prints. He created his own studio and workshop, and from 1925 onwards he published his prints himself, employing block cutters and printers of the highest level, while remaining closely involved with every step of the production process. While many of his prints were posthumously reprinted, those made during his lifetime should carry the characters *jizuri* (self-printed) in the margin.

Sailing Boats, a masterful set of six prints, is a good example of his experimentation with the woodblock print medium and his skilful use of colour. In 1921 he had made a similar design in three variations published by Watanabe Shōzaburō, but these blocks were destroyed in the Great Kantō Earthquake of 1923. They were extremely successful, and Yoshida decided to make a second edition, enlarging the print size and this time creating six variations.

Using the same woodblocks for all six variants, Yoshida changed the colours to suggest changes of time and weather. Yoshida himself had become aware of the artistic potential of this set, and entered four impressions (*Morning*, *Forenoon*, *Mist* and *Night*) in the government-sponsored Teiten of 1927. They were met with great critical acclaim for their aesthetic beauty and technical brilliance.
(PO)

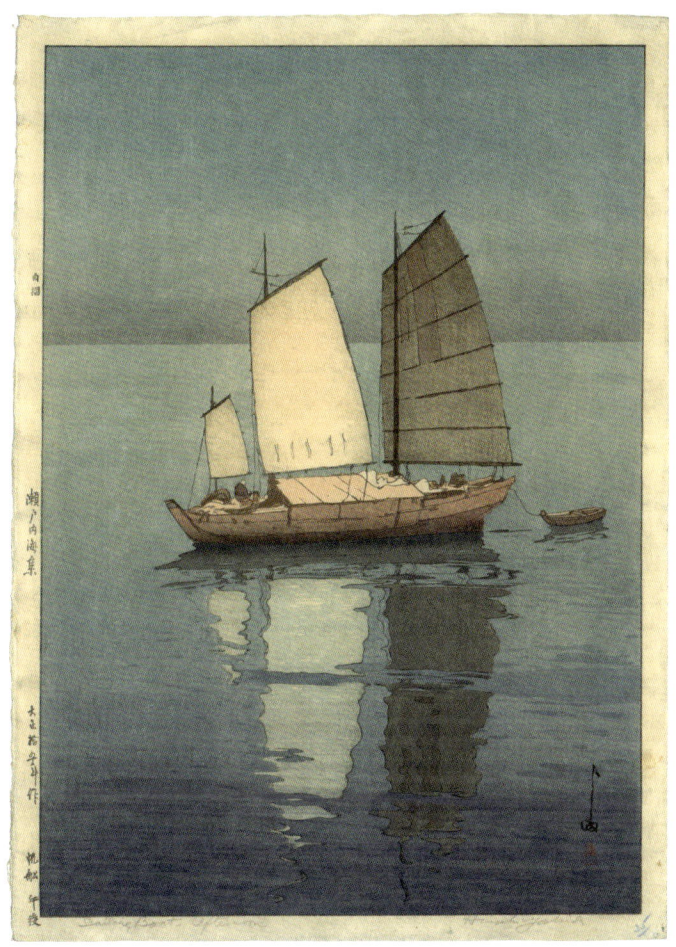

199c

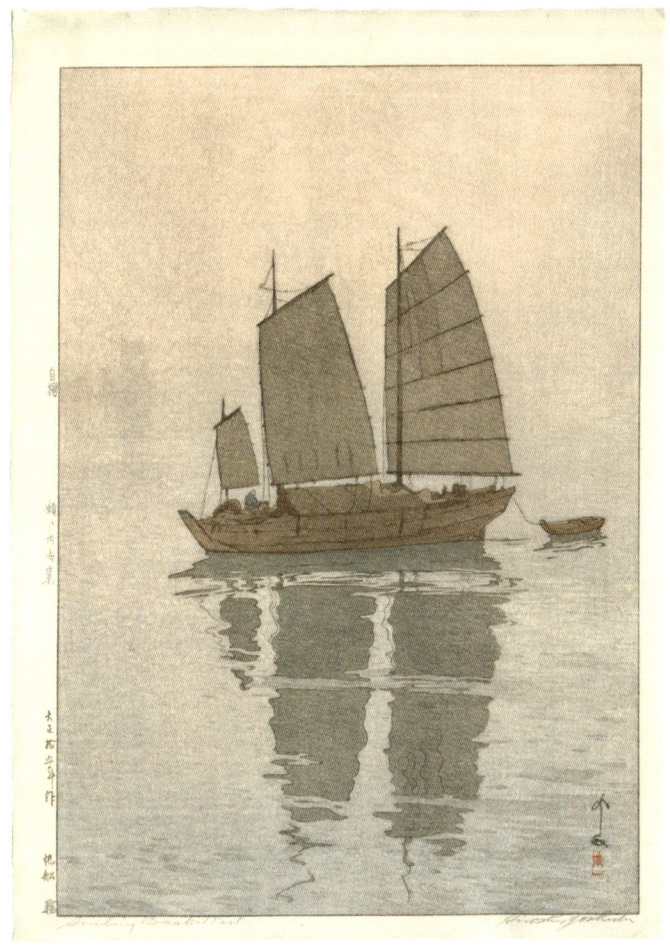

199d

Cat. 199c

Sailing Boats – Afternoon

(*Hansen gogo* 帆船 午後)

Cat. 199d

Sailing Boats – Mist

(*Hansen kiri* 帆船 霧)

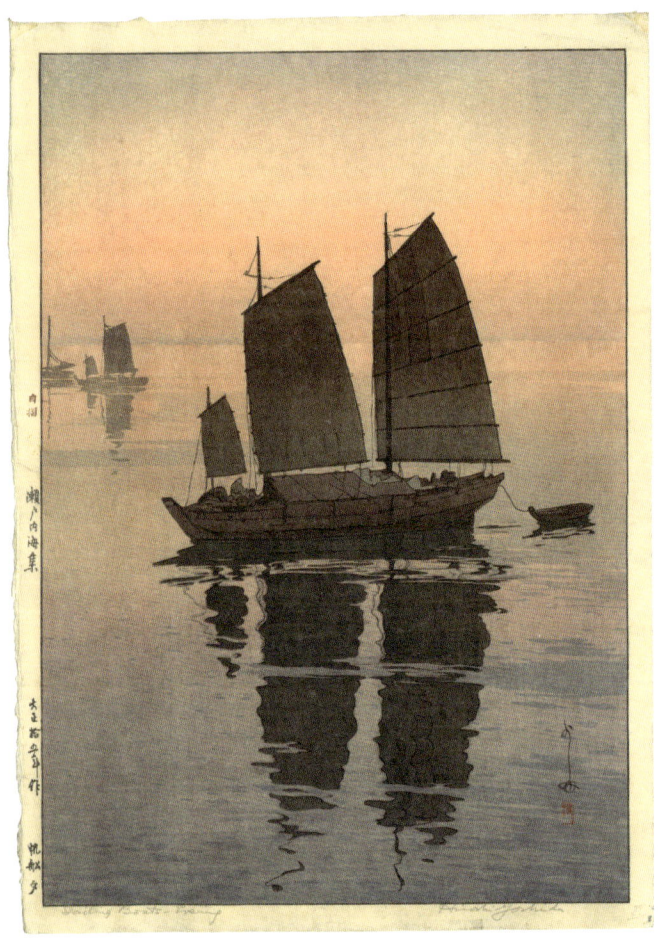

199e

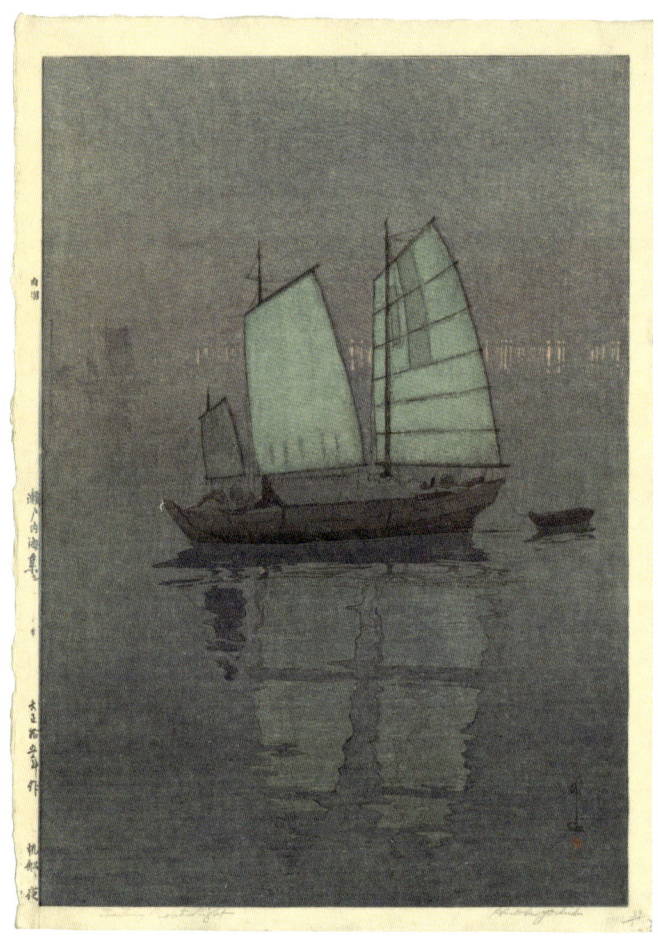

199f

Cat. 199e

Sailing boats – Evening

(*Hansen yū* 帆船 夕)

Cat. 199f

Sailing Boats – Night

(*Hansen yoru* 帆船 夜)

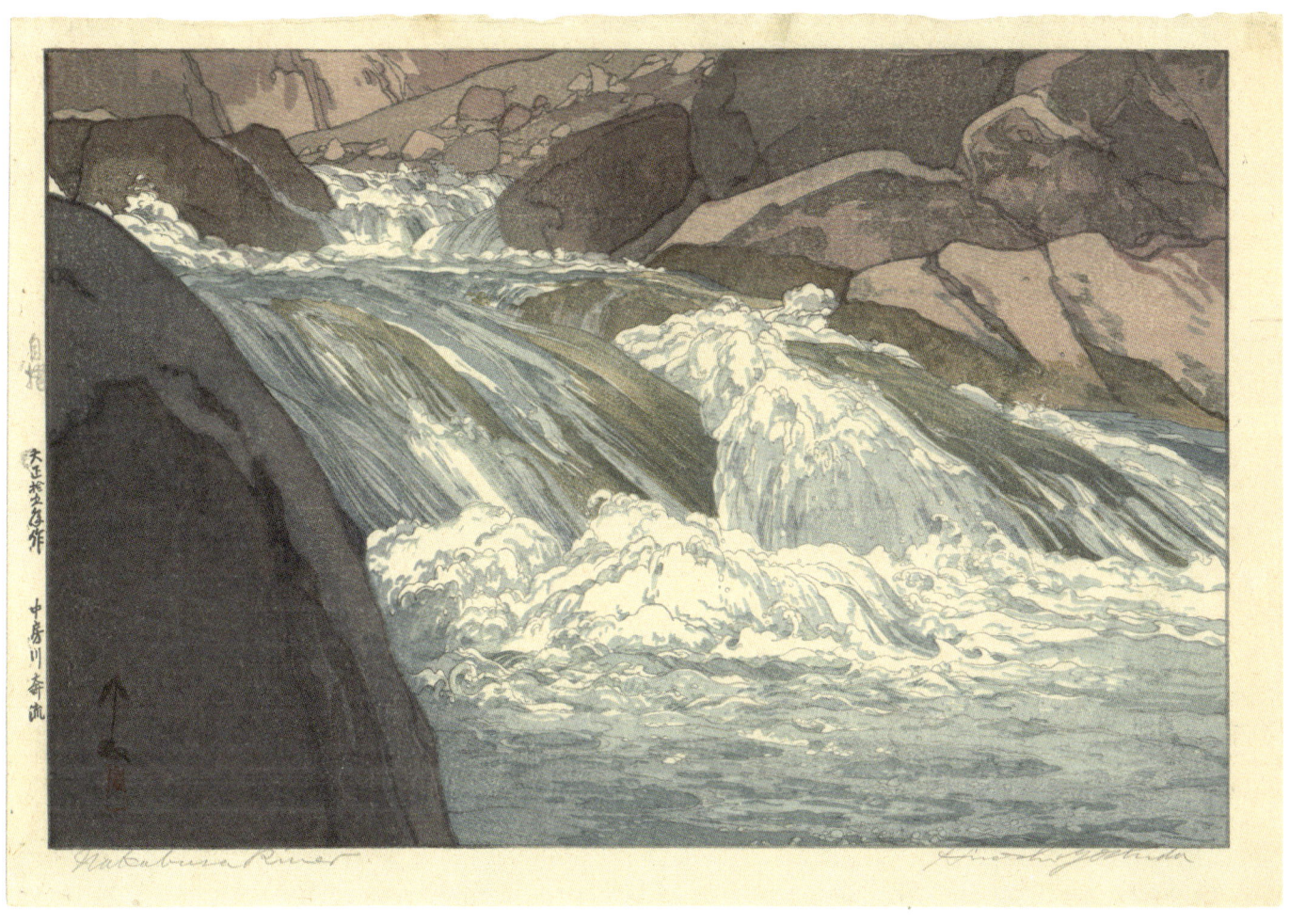

In this print of excellent printing quality, the motion of the water is pictured so vividly that we can almost hear its sound. This was achieved by cutting two key blocks: one for the stream and a separate one for the background. Blind-printing was used to visualize the rushing water. The Nakabusa River originates near the elevation of Mount Otensho, west of Azumino, Nagano Prefecture.
(PO)

Cat. 200

Yoshida Hiroshi 吉田博 (1876–1950)

Nakabusa River Rapids

(*Nakabusagawa honryū*
中房川奔流)

Date: 1926
Signature: *Yoshida, Hiroshi Yoshida*
(bottom margin in pencil)
Artist's seal: *Hiroshi*
Publisher: self-published
Block cutter: *Maeda Yūjirō*
Printer: self-printed (*jizuri*
stamp in left margin)
Size: 27.5 × 40.5 cm
Private collection, the Netherlands

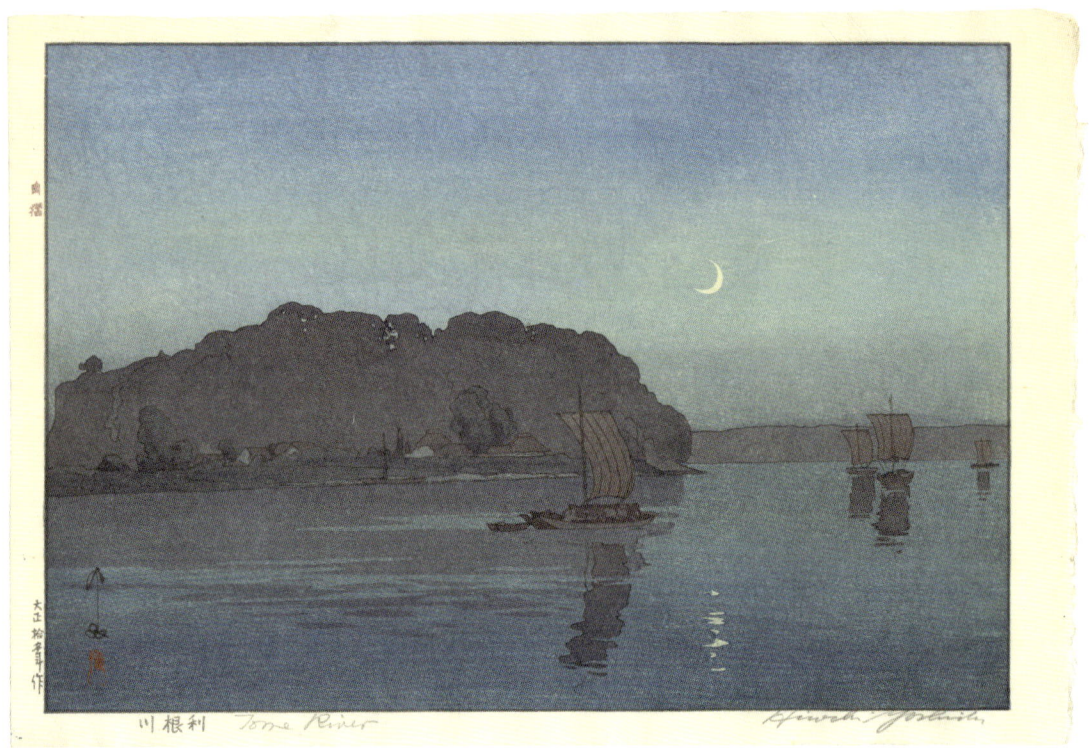

Cat. 201

Yoshida Hiroshi 吉田博 (1876–1950)

Tone River

(*Tonegawa* 利根川)

Date: 1926
Signature: *Yoshida*, *Hiroshi Yoshida*
(bottom margin in pencil)
Artist's seal: *Hiroshi*
Publisher: self-published
Block cutter: *Maeda Yūjirō*
Printer: self-printed (*jizuri*
stamp in left margin)
Size: 27.2 × 40.5 cm
Collection Scholten

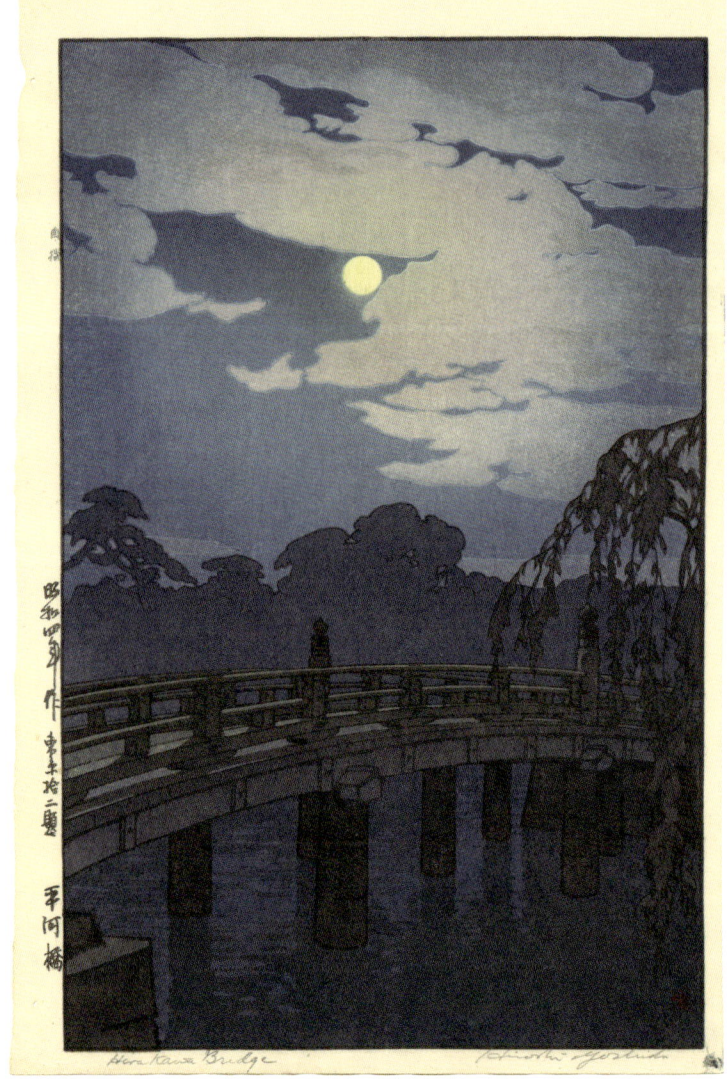

Cat. 202

Yoshida Hiroshi 吉田博 (1876–1950)

Hirakawa Bridge

(*Hirakawabashi* 平河橋)

Series: *Twelve Scenes of Tokyo*
(*Tōkyō jūnidai* 東京拾二題)
Date: 1929
Signature: *Yoshida*, *Hiroshi Yoshida*
(bottom margin in pencil)
Artist's seal: *Hiroshi*
Publisher: self-published
Printer: self-printed (*jizuri*
stamp in top left margin)
Size: 40.2 × 27.3 cm
Collection Scholten

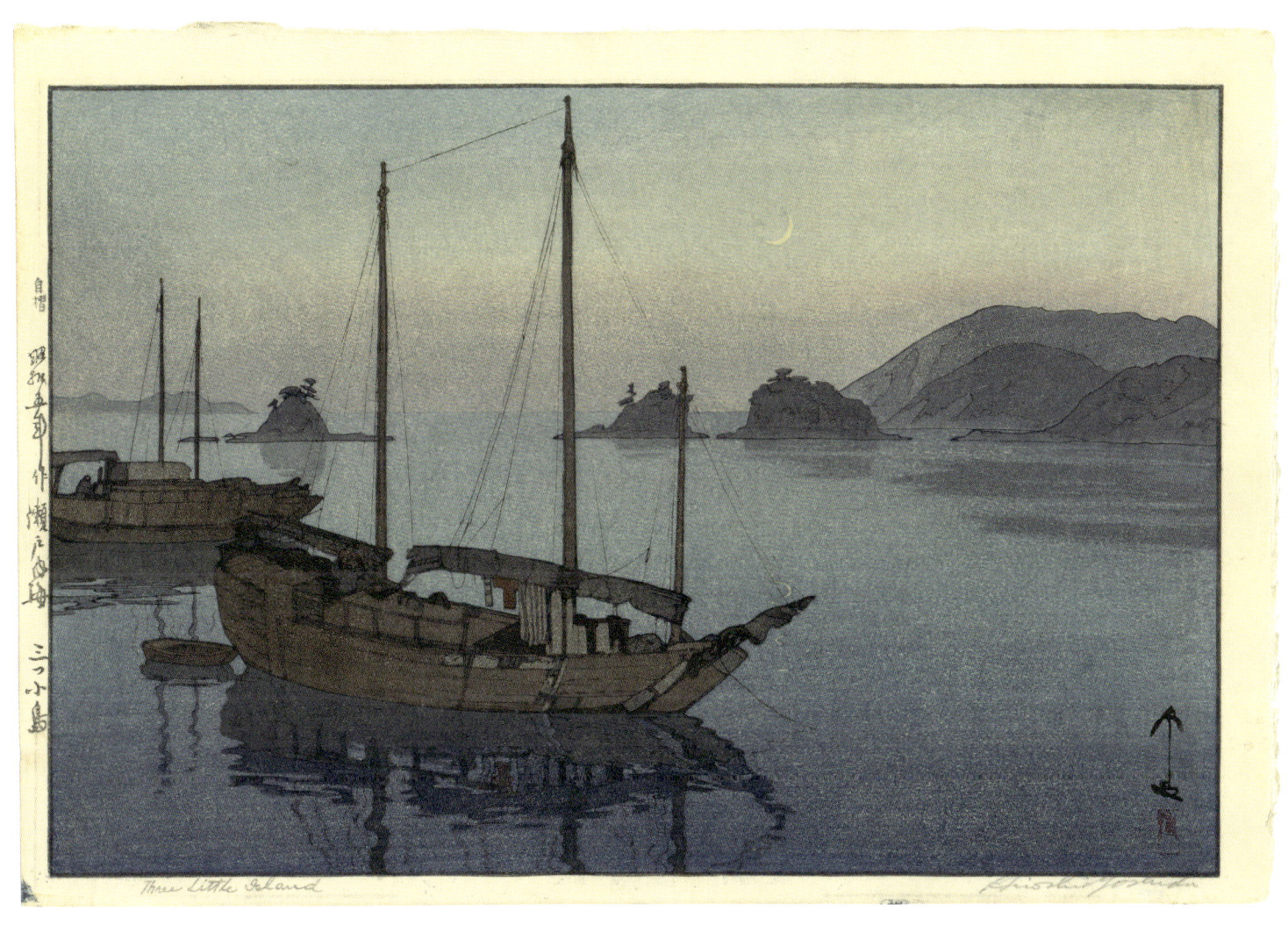

Three Little Island

Hiroshi Yoshida

Cat. 203

Yoshida Hiroshi 吉田博 (1876–1950)

Three Little Islands

(*Mitsu kojima* 三つ小島)

Series: *The Inland Sea Series*
(*Seto naikai* 瀬戸内海)
Date: 1930
Signature: *Yoshida*, *Hiroshi Yoshida*
(bottom margin in pencil)
Artist's seal: *Hiroshi*
Publisher: self-published
Printer: self-printed (*jizuri*
stamp in left margin)
Size: 27 × 40 cm
Collection Scholten

Cat. 204

Yoshida Hiroshi 吉田博 (1876–1950)

Waiting for the Tide

(*Shio machi* 潮待ち)

Series: *The Inland Sea Series*
(*Seto naikai* 瀬戸内海)
Date: 1930
Signature: *Yoshida*, *Hiroshi Yoshida*
(bottom margin in pencil)
Artist's seal: *Hiroshi*
Publisher: self-published
Printer: self-printed (*jizuri*
stamp in left margin)
Size: 27.3 × 40 cm
Collection Scholten

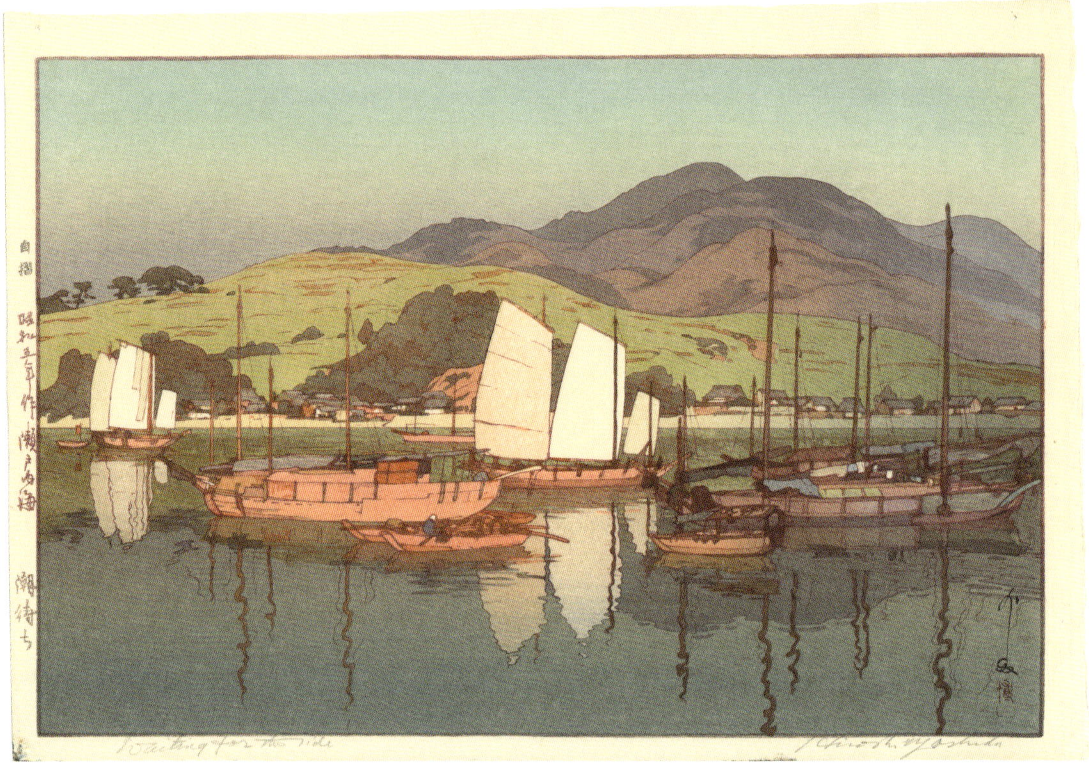

Cat. 205

Yoshida Hiroshi 吉田博 (1876–1950)

Shakujii

(*Shakujii* 石神井)

Date: 1937
Signature: *Yoshida*, *Hiroshi Yoshida*
(bottom margin in pencil)
Artist's seal: *Hiroshi*
Publisher: self-published
Printer: self-printed (*jizuri*
stamp in left margin)
Size: 27 × 40.1 cm
Collection Scholten

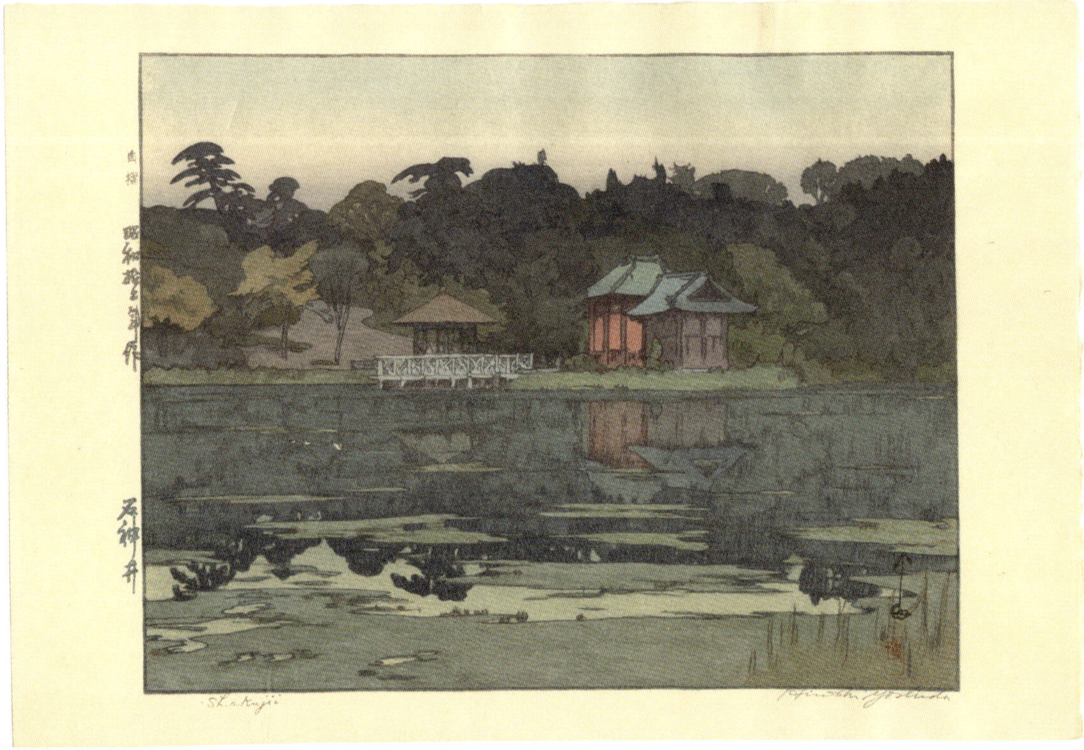

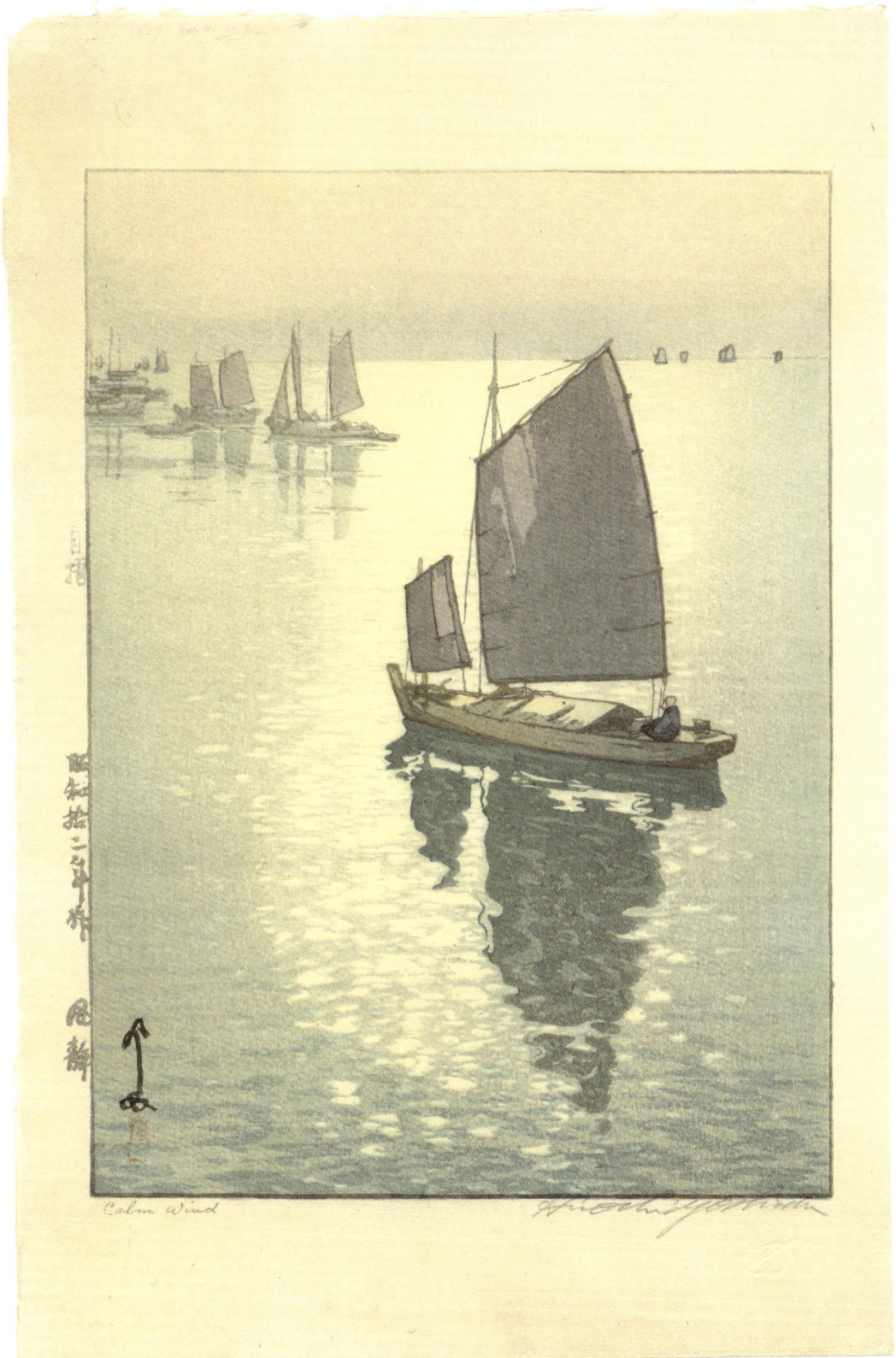

Calm Wind

Cat. 206

Yoshida Hiroshi 吉田博 (1876–1950)

Calm Wind

(*Fūsei* 風静)

Date: 1937
Signature: *Yoshida*, *Hiroshi Yoshida*
(bottom margin in pencil)
Artist's seal: *Hiroshi*
Publisher: self-published
Printer: self-printed (*jizuri*
stamp in left margin)
Size: 40 × 26.8 cm
Collection Scholten

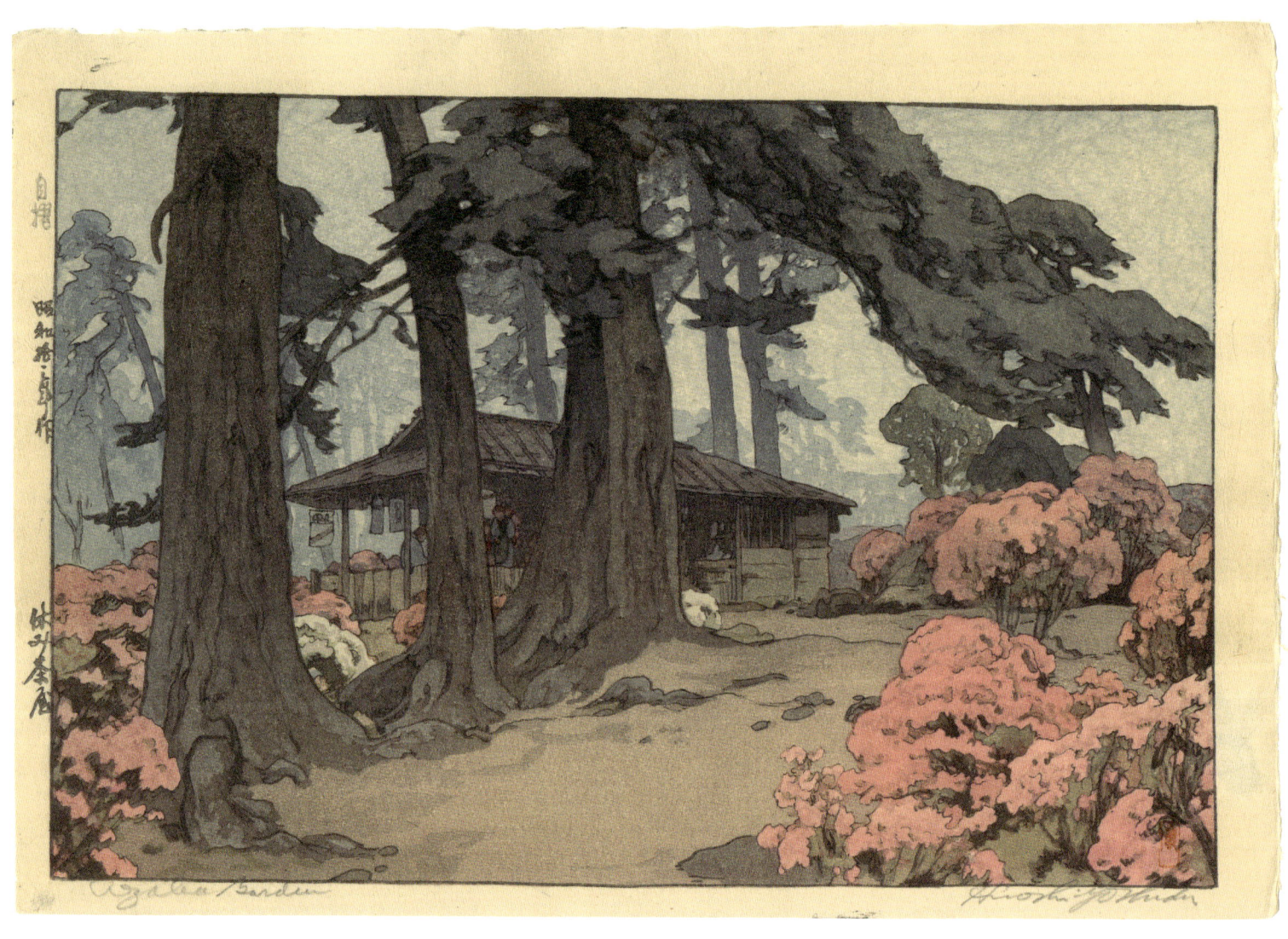

Cat. 207

Yoshida Hiroshi 吉田博 (1876–1950)

Tea (Rest) House

(*Yasumi chaya* 休み茶屋)

Date: 1938
Signature: *Yoshida*, *Hiroshi Yoshida*
(bottom margin in pencil)
Artist's seal: *Hiroshi*
Publisher: self-printed (*jizuri*
stamp left margin)
Size: 28.1 × 40.8 cm
Collection Scholten

The teahouse pictured here is located in Mishima in Shizuoka Prefecture. Catering to a foreign clientele, Yoshida Hiroshi's prints often have two titles: one in Japanese and one in English. Interestingly, at times these titles do not match, as is the case here. Hiroshi has titled the print in the bottom margin in pencil 'Azalea Garden'. Indeed pink azaleas are pictured in bloom next to the teahouse, partly obscured from view by the large trees in the foreground. A dense forest is suggested by the contours of lighter printed trees in the back. It took 51 impressions to create the depth of shades and colours in this composition.

(PO)

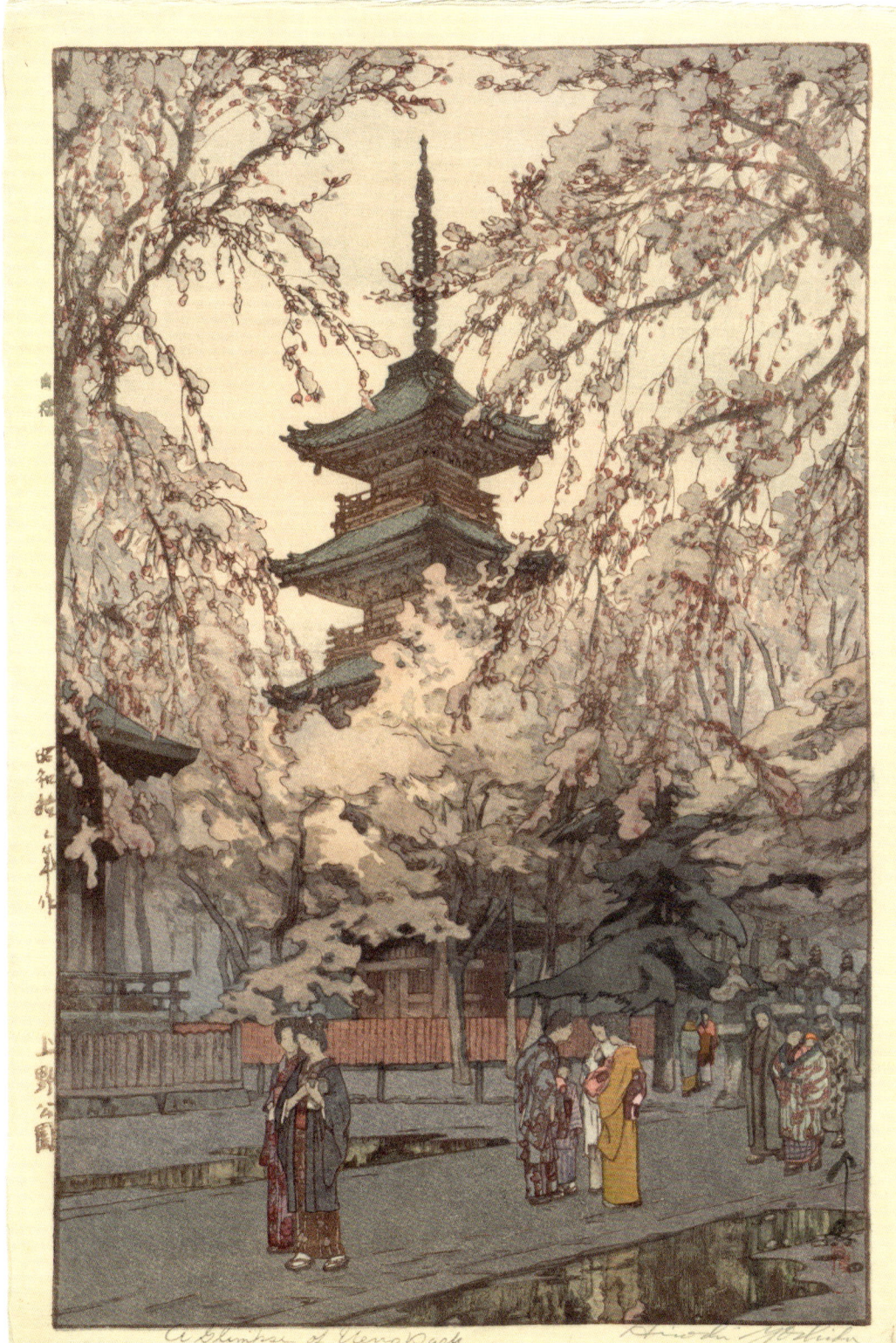

Cat. 208
Yoshida Hiroshi 吉田博 (1876–1950)
A Glimpse of Ueno Park
(*Ueno kōen* 上野公園)

Date: 1937
Signature: *Yoshida*, *Hiroshi Yoshida*
(bottom margin in pencil)
Artist's seal: *Hiroshi*
Publisher: self-printed (*jizuri*
stamp left margin)
Size: 40.2 × 23.7 cm
Collection Scholten

Ueno Park in Tokyo is still a popular spot for viewing cherry blossom. This print seems to be a tribute and celebration of the cherry blossom season: printed in soft pastel tones with a predominantly pink palette, the overall composition has a soft glowing quality. The flowers, together with the pagoda of the Kaneiji Temple and the kimono-clad women make for a very traditional composition that would appeal to both a Japanese as well as a foreign clientele. Note the reflections in the two puddles highlighting the printing mastery of Yoshida Hiroshi.

(PO)

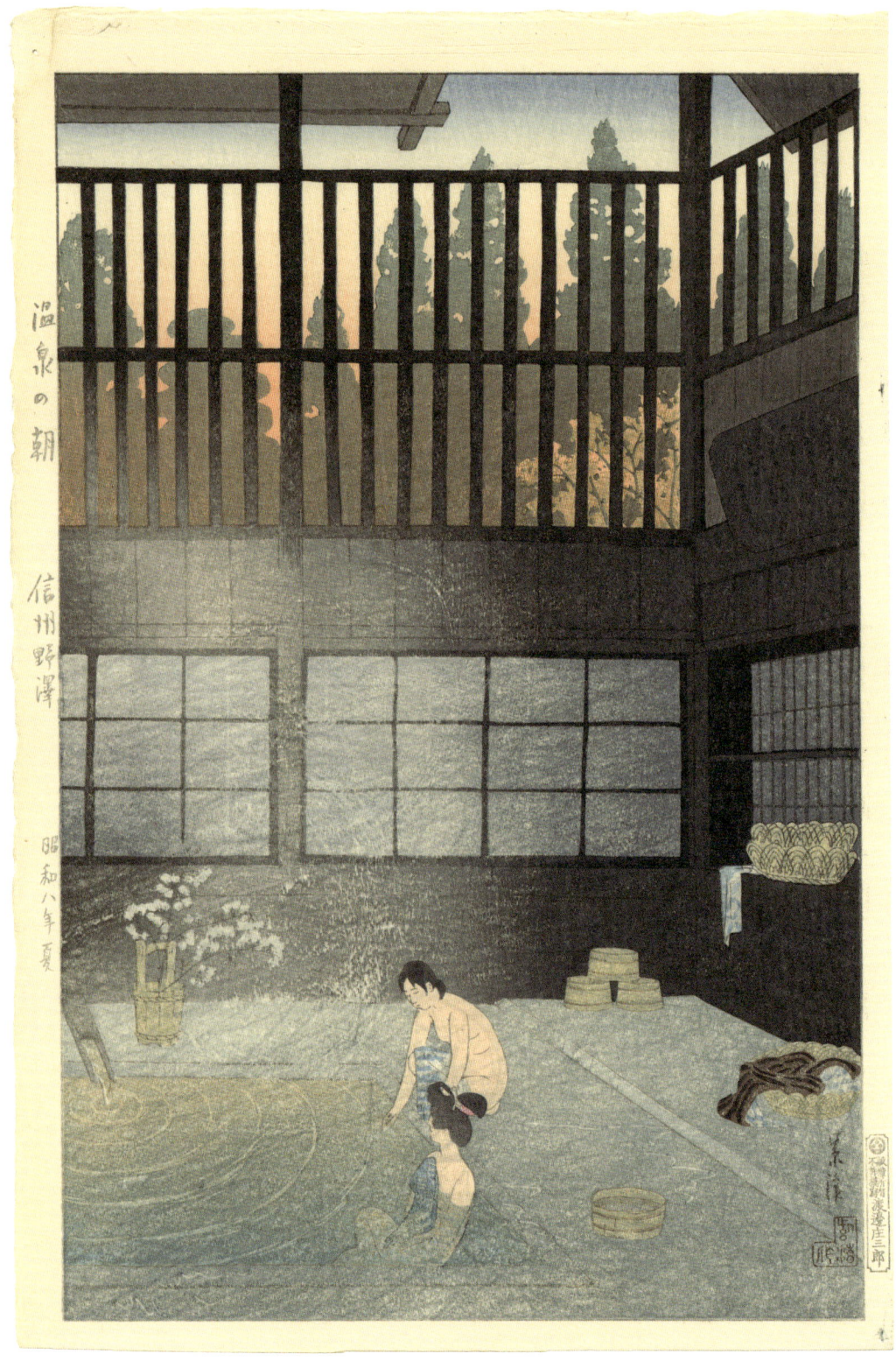

Cat. 209

Kasamatsu Shirō 笠松紫浪
(1898–1991)

**Morning at the Hot Spring,
Nozawa, Shinshū Province**

(*Onsen no asa Shinshū Nozawa*
温泉の朝 信州野澤)

Date: Summer 1933
Signature: *Shirō*
Artist's seal: *Shirō saku*
Publisher: Watanabe Shōzaburō
Size: 38.9 × 26.6 cm
Collection Scholten

Cat. 210

Kasamatsu Shirō 笠松紫浪
(1898–1991)

Morning Calm – Ajiro Promontory, Izu

(*Asanagi Izu Ajiro saki* 朝なぎ
伊豆網代岬)

Date: Spring 1933
Signature: *Shirō*
Artist's seal: *Shirō*
Publisher: Watanabe Shōzaburō
Size: 38.5 × 26 cm
Collection RMAH – JP.07455

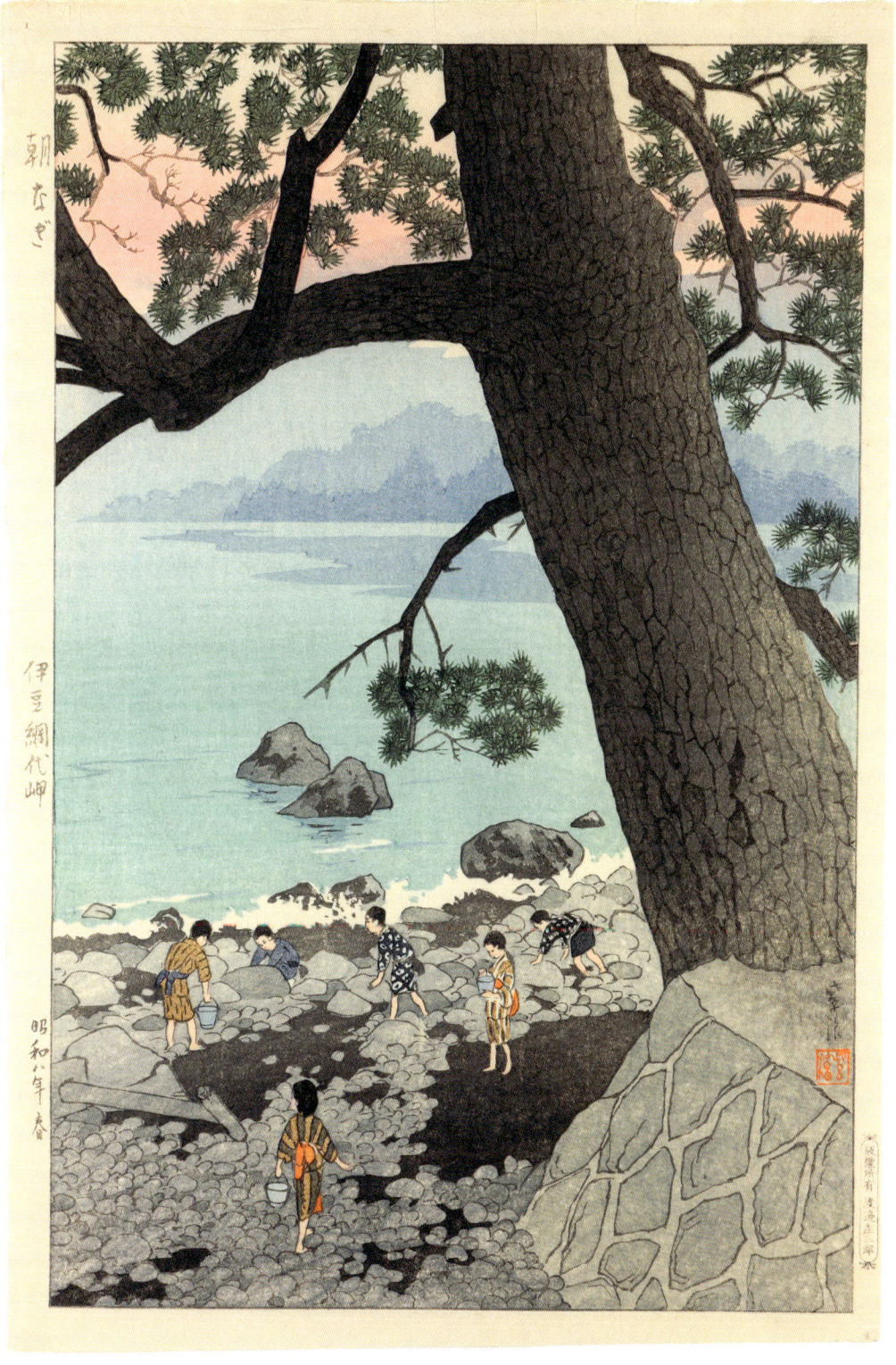

Cat. 211

Kasamatsu Shirō 笠松紫浪
(1898–1991)

Shimoda Town

(*Shimoda no machi* 下田の街)

Date: Summer 1937
Signature: *Shirō ga*
Artist's seal: *Shirō*
Publisher: Watanabe Shōzaburō
Size: 39.5 × 26.5 cm
Collection RMAH – JP.07296

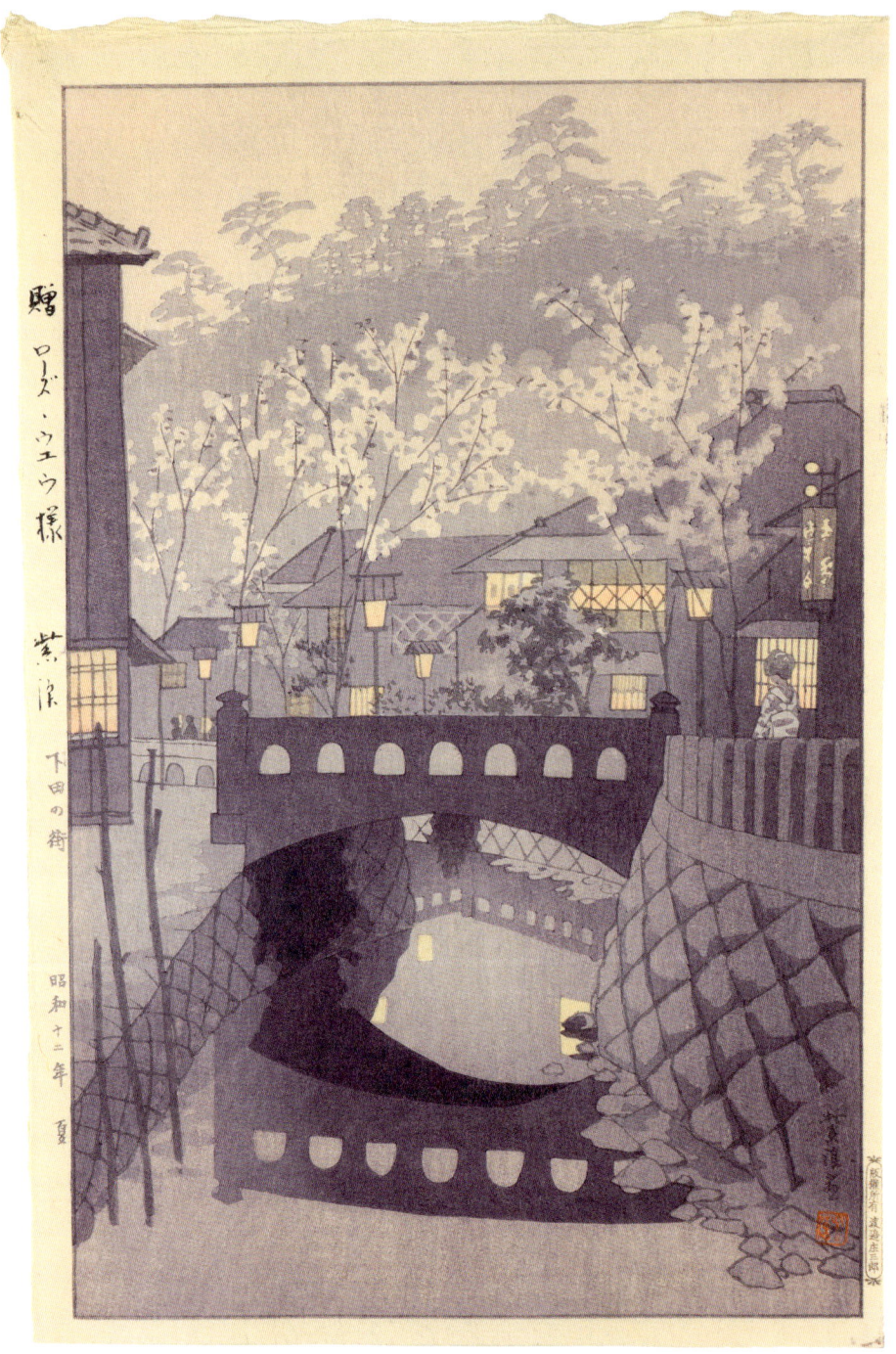

Kasamatsu Shirō designed many scenes in or around cities. Instead of romanticizing the past, his prints tend to highlight the modernization and urbanization of 20th-century Japan.

Shimoda played a central role in the opening up of Japan and the end of Japan's 220-year-old policy of national seclusion (*sakoku*). The 1854 Kanagawa Treaty opened up the ports of Shimoda and Hakodate to US vessels and trade.

(PO)

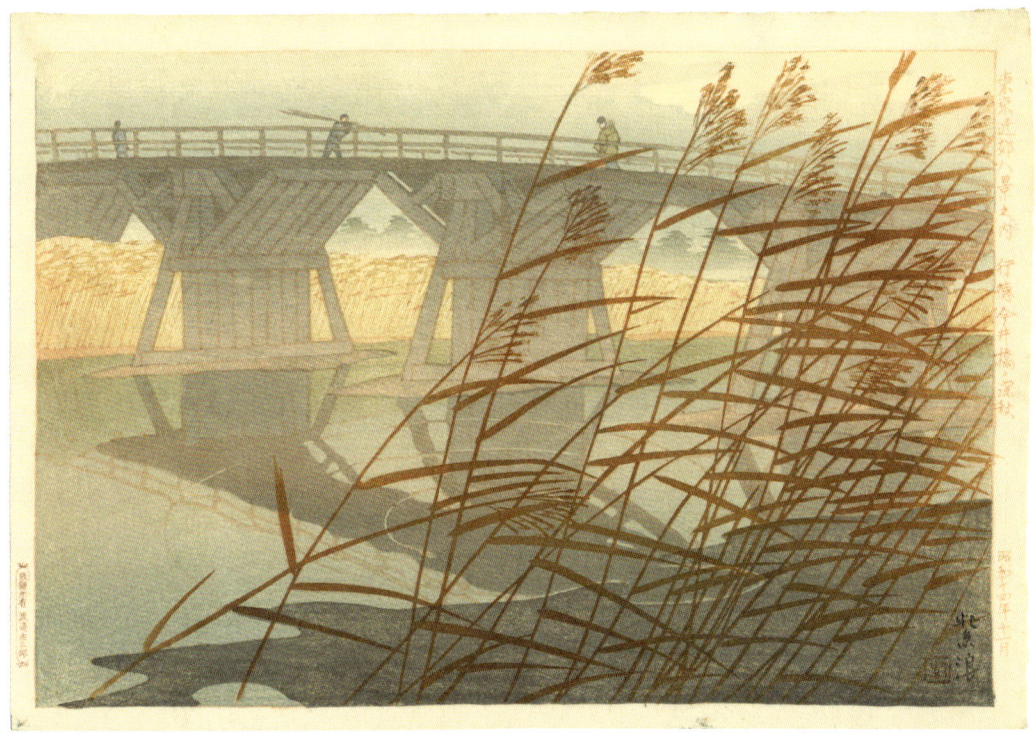

Cat. 212

Kasamatsu Shirō 笠松紫浪
(1898–1991)

The Bridge, Imaibashi, Gyōtoku, in Late Autumn

(*Gyōtoku Imaibashi shinshū* 行徳今井橋ノ深秋)

Series: *Eight Views of the Environs of Tokyo* (*Tōkyō kinkō hakkei no uchi* 東京近郊八景之内
Date: November 1939
Signature: *Shirō*
Artist's seal: *Shi*
Publisher: Watanabe Shōzaburō
Size: 26.4 × 38.5 cm
Collection Scholten

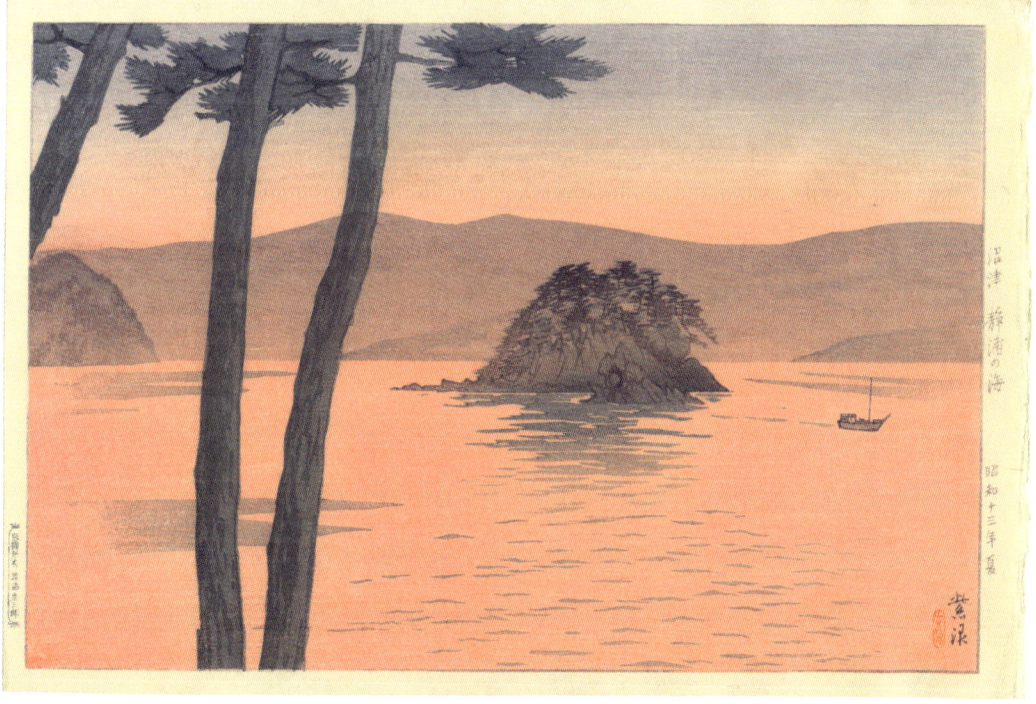

Cat. 213

Kasamatsu Shirō 笠松紫浪
(1898–1991)

The Sea at Shizuura, Numazu

(*Numazu Shizuura no umi* 沼津静浦の海)

Date: Summer 1938
Signature: *Shirō*
Artist's seal: *Shirō*
Publisher: Watanabe Shōzaburō
Size: 25.8 × 38.8 cm
Collection Scholten

Kasamatsu Shirō 笠松紫浪
(1898–1991)

**Kinokunizaka in the Rainy
Season**

(*Kinokunizaka tsuyu* 紀の国坂梅雨)

Date: Summer 1938
Signature: *Shirō*
Artist's seal: *Shi*
Publisher: Watanabe Shōzaburō
Size: 38.1 × 26.3 cm
Collection Scholten

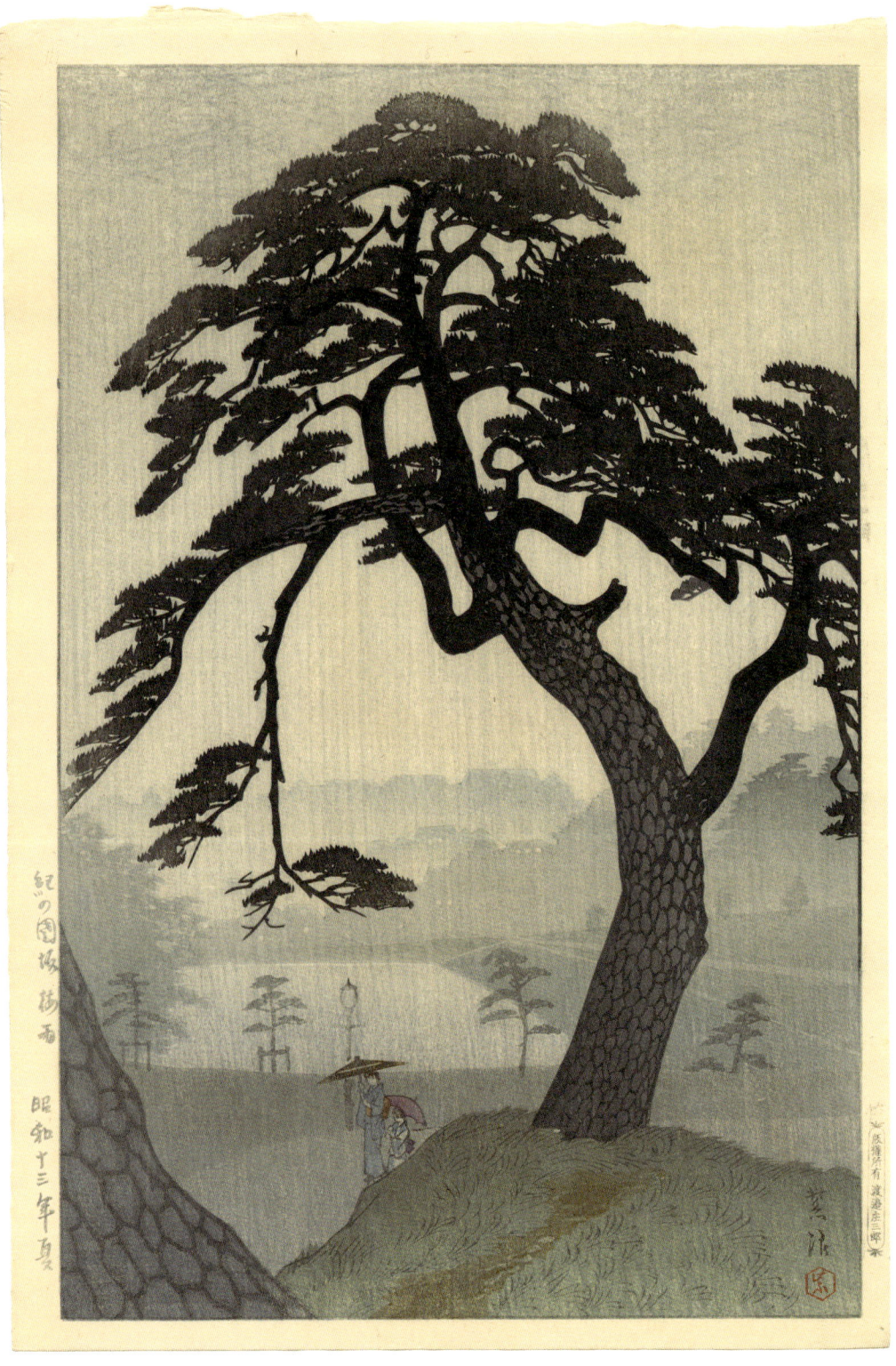

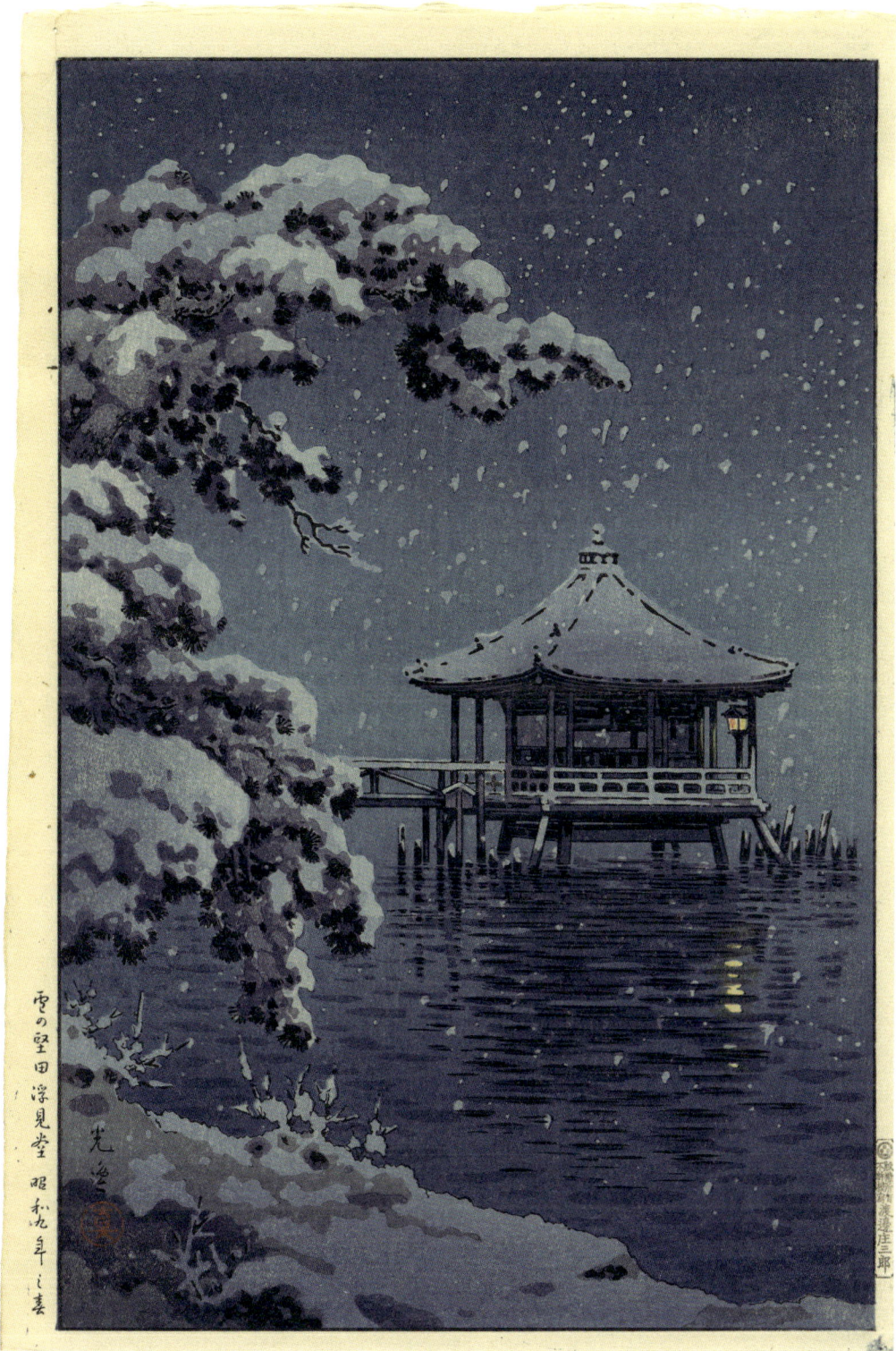

Cat. 215

Tsuchiya Kōitsu 土屋光逸
(1870–1949)

Snow at Ukimidō, Katada

(*Yuki no Katada Ukimidō* 雪の堅田
浮見堂)

Date: Spring 1934
Signature: *Kōitsu*
Artist's seal: *Shin*
Publisher: Watanabe Shōzaburō
Size: 38.5 × 26.5 cm
Collection Scholten

Cat. 216

Tsuchiya Kōitsu 土屋光逸
(1870–1949)

The Futaraasan Shrine at Nikkō

(*Nikkō Futaraasan jinja* 日光二荒
山神社)

Date: c. 1930s
Artist's seal: *Kōitsu*
Publisher: Kawaguchi
Block cutter: *Maeda* (Maeda Kentarō)
Printer: *Komatsu* (Komatsu Wasakichi)
Size: 30 × 41.5 cm
Collection Scholten

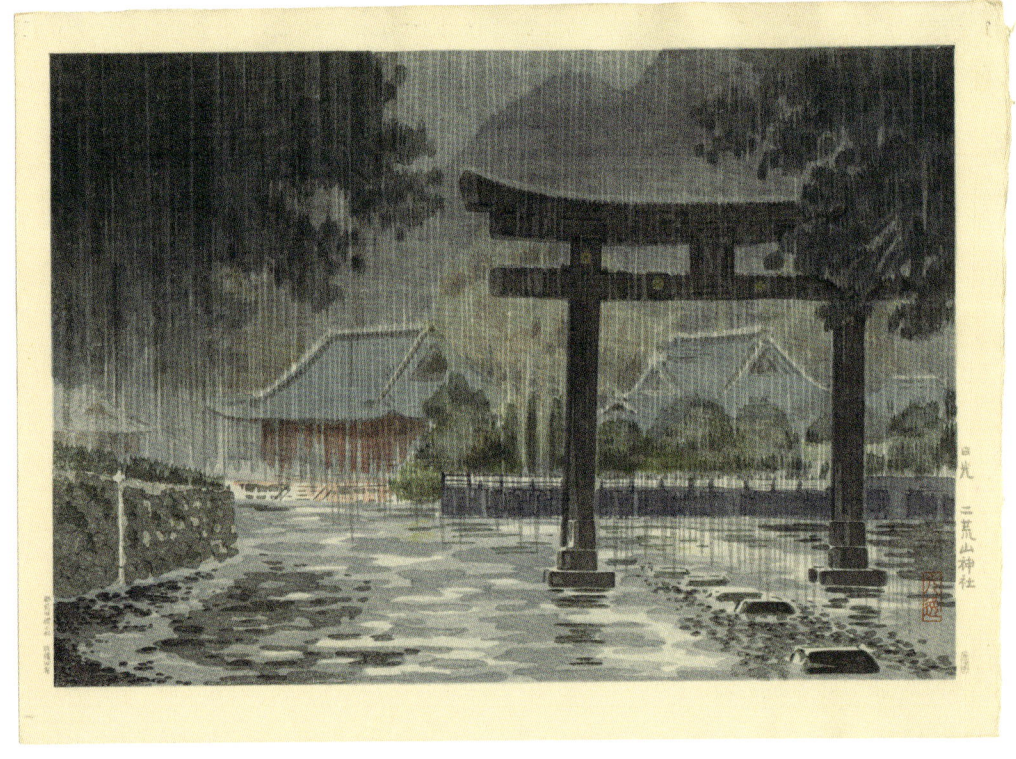

Cat. 217

Itō Shinsui 伊東深水 (1898–1972)

Night Rain at Tago

(*Tago no yau* 田子の夜雨)

Series: *Eight Views of Izu*
(*Izu hakkei no uchi* 伊豆八景之内)
Date: 1939
Signature: *Shinsui*
Artist's seal: *Shinsui*
Publisher: Watanabe Shōzaburō
Size: 27.2 × 39 cm
Collection Scholten

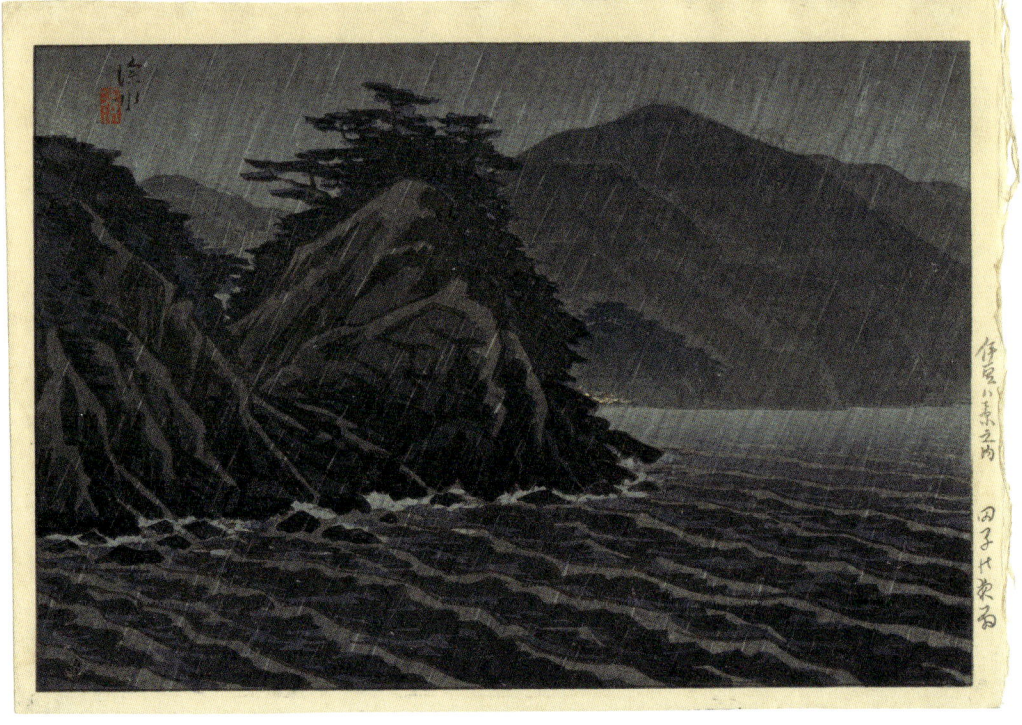

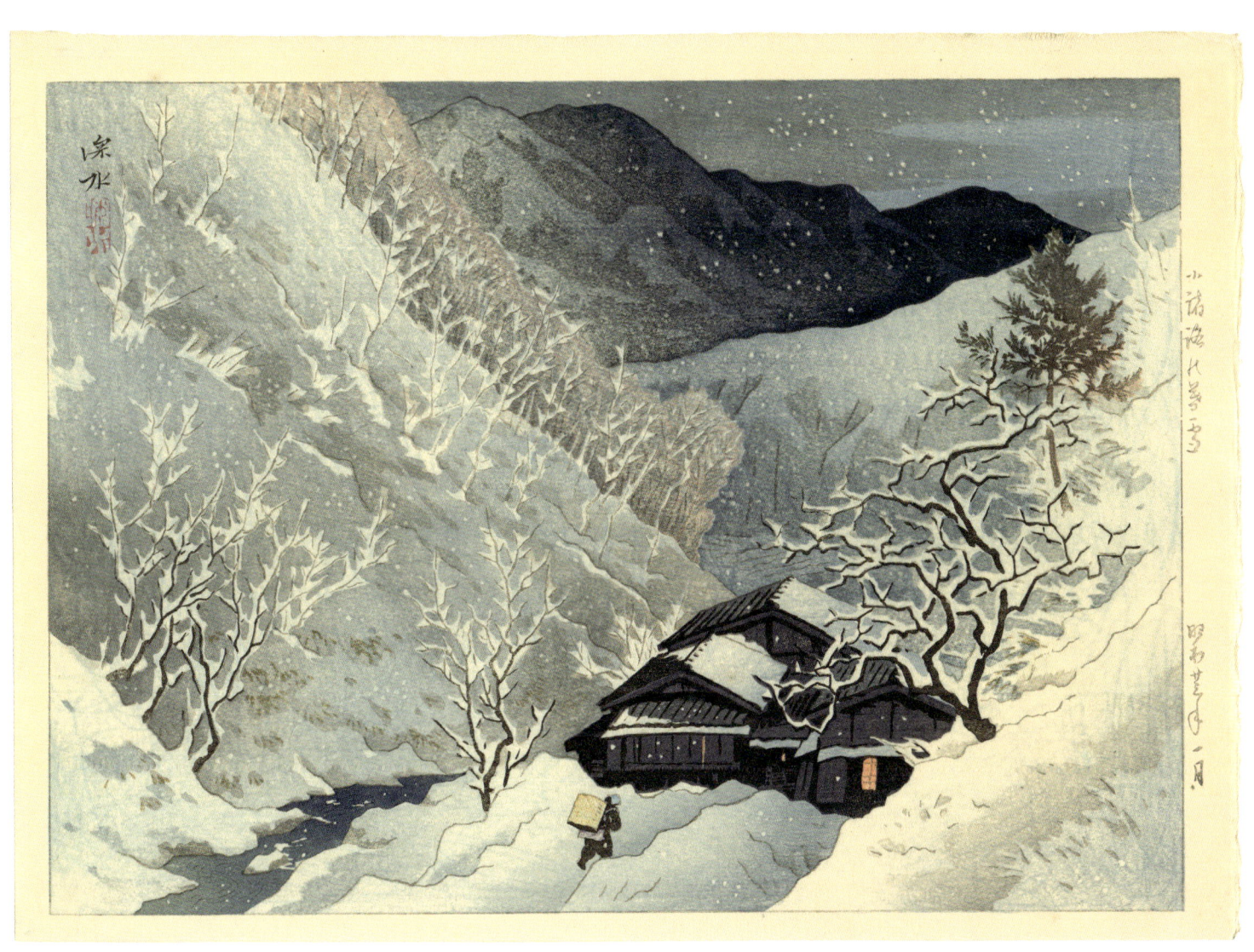

Cat. 218

Itō Shinsui 伊東深水 (1898–1972)

Evening Snowfall, Komoro

(*Komoro doro no bosetsu* 小諸路
の暮雪)

Series: *Ten Views of Shinano*
(*Shinano jikkei* 信濃十景)
Date: January 1948
Signature: *Shinsui*
Artist's seal: *Shinsui*
Publisher: Watanabe Shōzaburō
Size: 28.2 × 39.3 cm
Collection Scholten

Biographies

Charles William Bartlett (1860–1940), born in Bridport, England, enrolled at the Royal Academy of Arts, London, at the age of 23, after a short career in metallurgy. After London, he travelled to Paris to continue his studies at the Académie Julian. He returned to London in 1889 to marry, but soon afterwards his wife and son died in childbirth, and he started travelling and painting round Europe. He became especially known for his watercolours and was one of the founders of the Société de la peinture à l'eau. It wasn't until 1915, after travelling around South and East Asia with his second wife for some two years, that Bartlett came to Japan, where he came into contact with Watanabe Shōzaburō and showed him his sketches. He designed various prints for Watanabe in 1916, among them Indian scenes that are said to have inspired Yoshida Hiroshi. Bartlett left Japan again in 1917 and settled permanently in Hawaii, but he did return for a visit in 1919 when he created 19 more prints for Watanabe, including some Hawaiian scenes. It was actually Bartlett who commissioned Watanabe to publish his sketches in the woodcut medium, and he held ownership of the blocks, which remain in Hawaii to this day.

Friedrich ('Fritz') Capelari (1884–1950) was an Austrian artist who studied at the Akademie der Bildenden Künste in Vienna from 1906. He met several Japanese students who kindled his interest in the region, leading him to travel to various parts of East and South-east Asia before settling in Japan during the 1910s. He had an atelier in Asakusa ward, Tokyo. He met Watanabe Shōzaburō in the latter's shop, Watanabe Hangaten, during a search for ukiyo-e works to use for reference. Soon after, in 1915, in collaboration with Watanabe, he produced his very first prints. Capelari left Japan in 1920. He visited Japan again in the 1930s, but did not produce any new woodblock prints. Besides paintings and prints, he is known to have made wooden sculptures.

Yanagihara Fūkyo (dates unknown) is one of the artists recorded to have worked for Watanabe Shōzaburō's workshop before the Great Kantō Earthquake destroyed it in 1923. No information about the artist is available, and he is known to have produced only two prints for Watanabe.

Hashiguchi Goyō (1881–1921), born Hashiguchi Kiyoshi, came from a family of doctors in Kagoshima who worked for the shogunate during the Edo Period. In the garden of the family household stood a 300-year-old *goyōmatsu* pine tree, from which he later took his artistic name. He is thought to have studied under the Kano painter Uchiyama

Ikkan (1823–97) and the Shijō painter Hirayama Tōgaku (1834–99) during his childhood in Kagoshima. After he travelled to Tokyo in 1899 with his brothers, he became a pupil of the *nihonga* painter Hashimoto Gahō (1835–1908). Later, in 1901, he attended the Tokyo School of Fine Arts where he studied *yōga* (Western-style) painting, and where, in recognition of his talents, he was selected for a scholarship. As a result, from his childhood in Kagoshima up to his graduation in Tokyo in 1905, Goyō received a broad artistic education that covered various genres.

During the second half of the 1910s, Goyō engaged in producing lithographs and woodblock prints for illustrations in magazines and covers for literary works, including those by the famous novelist Natsume Sōseki (1867–1917). He also had an interest in ukiyo-e, and from 1914 onwards he became involved engrossed in collecting, researching and reproducing the works of Old Masters such as Utagawa Hiroshige (1797–1858), Kitagawa Utamaro (c. 1753–1806), and Suzuki Harunobu (1724–70).

Some three years after a short collaboration with the publisher Watanabe Shōzaburō in 1916 that resulted in only one design (see Fig. 4, p. 12 in the Introduction), he started publishing his own prints. Goyō worked with skilled craftsmen recommended to him by Watanabe and supervised the complete production process personally, creating prints of the highest quality. However, his artistic career was cut short by health issues, and he passed away in 1921.

Hirano Hakuhō (1879–1957) was a self-taught *nihonga* painter from Kyoto. Details about the artist's life are scant, and he is mostly known for the handful of beautiful women prints he designed for Watanabe Shōzaburō between 1932 and 1935.

Kawase Hasui (1883–1957) was born into a Tokyo family of craftsmen who made *itokumimono*, a type of braided silk cord used in traditional clothing. The family already had ties to the world of prints, as Hasui's uncle Kanagaki Robun (1829–84) wrote texts for works by famous artists such as Kawanabe Kyōsai (1831–89) and Tsukioka Yoshitoshi (1839–92). At the age of 14, he was instructed by the Shijō painter Aoyagi Bokusen (dates unknown) for a short time, and at 19 he studied under Araki Kan'yū (1850–1920). However, as the eldest son, he was expected to take care of the family business and was forced to quit his studies. It was not until he reached the age of 25 that he was freed from familial obligations and could pursue a career as an artist.

Hasui failed to gain entry to the prestigious studio of Kaburaki Kiyokata, and instead he joined the Aobashi

Institute of Western Painting, where he was taught by the oil painters Okada Saburōsuke (1869–1939) and Kishida Ryūsei (1891–1929). After a second attempt in 1910, he finally entered Kiyokata's studio and was given the artist name Hasui. During the 1910s and 1920s, he participated in various exhibitions while also doing work as a graphic designer for advertisements, books and magazines. In 1918 he was greatly impressed by his fellow student Itō Shinsui's woodblock print series *Ōmi hakkei*, and he approached Watanabe Shōzaburō, who published designs by many of Kiyokata's students. The same year the artist and publisher collaborated on three landscapes based on old sketches of Shiobara, a mountainous region far to the north of Tokyo where Hasui had spent part of his childhood. Watanabe would be his main collaborator throughout his life, but Hasui also made some designs for other publishers. With an oeuvre of almost 700 prints, the majority of which are landscapes, Hasui is among the most prolific print artists of the 20th century.

Takahashi Hiroaki (1871–1945), also known under his artist name Shōtei, was born as Matsumoto Katsutarō in Asakusa ward, Tokyo. During his childhood he began studying under his uncle, the *nihonga* painter Matsumoto Fūko (1840–1923). From 1889, after a short civil service career in his teens doing sketches in the Foreign Affairs department of the Imperial Household, he started making illustrations (*sashi-e*) for woodblock-printed books, magazines and newspapers.

Hiroaki's first work as an ukiyo-e artist started after he was introduced to the publisher Watanabe Shōzaburō. In 1907, one year after Watanabe founded his publishing firm, he commissioned Hiroaki to design single-sheet landscapes. The prints enjoyed great popularity, and from 1907 until the Great Kantō Earthquake in 1923, Hiroaki would produce hundreds of designs. After most of the blocks were destroyed in the earthquake, Watanabe asked him to reproduce the lost designs.

It was not until 1921 that he actually took the name Hiroaki ('Bearer of Good Light', also read as Kōmei), probably in the hope of recovering from poor health. From the mid-1920s until 1942, Hiroaki continued to produce prints. During these years he kept working for Watanabe but also designed for three other publishing firms, Fusui Gabō, Shōbidō Tanaka and Bijutsusha. Hiroaki died from pneumonia in 1945, three years after his last print was published.

Yoshida Hiroshi (1876–1950) grew up in Kurume, Fukuoka Prefecture, where his high-school art teacher Yoshida

Kasaburō (1861–94), who had studied under the Italian painter Antonio Fontanesi (1818–82), recognized his talent. Because Kasaburō had no son, he adopted Hiroshi as heir to the Yoshida family, which traced its lineage back to artists who had served the Nakatsu clan in northern Kyūshū in the late 18th and first half of the 19th century. Hiroshi studied *yōga* in Kyoto for a while in 1893 and, the following year, in Tokyo at the private painting school of Koyama Shōtarō (1857–1916), known as Fudō-sha. Starting in 1899, Hiroshi made several trips abroad and successfully sold his watercolours in both the United States and Europe. From 1903 Kasaburō's daughter Fujio (1887–1987), who was likewise a talented artist, joined him on these trips, and together they held various joint exhibitions. Later, on returning from one such trip in 1907, the two artists married.

Hiroshi did not really become active in producing woodblock prints until his mid-40s, when he started collaborating with the publisher Watanabe Shōzaburō (1885–1962). During the economic difficulties in the wake of the Great Kantō Earthquake of 1923, he discovered that his woodblock prints enjoyed even more commercial success abroad than his watercolours, and he started his own workshop in Japan in 1925. He hired engravers and printers, but personally supervised the production of his prints, and any prints that his workshop published bore the characters *jizuri* (self-printed). Throughout his life Hiroshi was an avid traveller, and he is mostly known for his landscape prints depicting scenes in and outside Japan.

Yoshikawa Kanpō (1894–1979) was a Kyoto-based artist who studied painting as early as 1901, at the age of 7, under Nishibori Tōsui (dates unknown) and later under the famous painter Takeuchi Seihō (1864–1942). He had already participated in Bunten exhibitions when he graduated with honours from the Kyoto Specialist School of Painting in 1918. Besides his activities as a painter, he worked as stage designer and adviser for the Shōchiku kabuki company in Kyoto, played instruments such as the *biwa* and *kokyū*, and was the author of several books about crafts and the performing arts. He was engaged in *shin hanga* printmaking for only a short time, up until 1925, but the few works that he did make were quite successful, especially the kabuki prints published by the Kyoto publisher Satō Shōtarō.

Oda Kazuma (1882–1956) was born in Tokyo into a family of former high-ranking samurai. His family moved to Osaka in 1894, and there his brother Tōu (1873–1933) became a successful painter and lithographic artist. From 1898 Oda learned lithography from his brother and from drawings by the French artist Armand-Théophile Cassagne (1823–1907), while his interest in woodblock printing is said to have been sparked by the works of the Czech artist Emil Orlík (1870–1932). He also started working in a lithographic printing firm in Hiroshima from 1899 and visited Tokyo in 1900 to be taught by the lithographic artist Kaneko Masajirō (1870–1934). He returned to Tokyo in 1903 and studied *yōga* with Kawamura Kiyo'o (1852–1934).

From the late 1900s Oda began to participate in exhibitions, including the first Bunten in 1907, and he carried out printing and design work for various companies and magazines. He was among the founders (and was the sole lithographer) of the Japan Creative Print Association in 1918, and later, in 1929, of the Western-style Print Association, which he formed together with other lithographic and copperplate print artists. As both artist and scholar, he was also active in the production of and research into woodblock prints. Among his woodblock-printed works are landscapes for Watanabe Shōzaburō as well as self-produced 'creative prints', or *sōsaku hanga*. After becoming a recluse during the Second World War, he returned to Tokyo in 1949 and there founded the private Oda Lithography Institute in 1953.

Kobayakawa Kiyoshi (1899?–1948) was born in Hakata, Fukuoka Prefecture, where he studied under the *nanga* painter Ueda Tekkō (1849–1914). He eventually moved to Tokyo to study *bijin-ga*, the beautiful women genre, in the studio of Kaburaki Kiyokata. He had already taken part in Kyōdokai exhibitions in 1918 and had his first real success at the 1924 Teiten exhibition with his painting *Okiku of Nagasaki*. His earliest confirmed woodblock prints date from around the time he departed from traditional *bijin-ga* and shifted towards showing more contemporary scenes, perhaps the most famous of which is *Tipsy*, with its depiction of the 'Modern Girl'. In total, only thirteen surviving prints have been confirmed to have been made by Kiyoshi, of which six were self-published and the other seven issued by various publishers.

Tsuchiya Kōitsu (1870–1949) was born in Hamamatsu, Shizuoka Prefecture, into a family of farmers as Tsuchiya Sahei. At the age of 15, he was sent to a temple in Tokyo to undergo clerical training, but one of the temple priests recognized his talent as an artist and arranged for him to study under the block cutter Matsuzaki Shūmei, an associate of the well-established artist Kobayashi Kiyochika (1847–1915). Soon after, he became Kiyochika's apprentice,

under whom he cultivated his skills in illustration, print design, and the depiction of light and shadow, for which Kiyochika was well known. As much an adoptive family member as a student, Kōitsu remained in Kiyochika's home for 19 years, until around 1903. His first known woodcuts were triptychs depicting the First Sino-Japanese War (1894–95), published by Takekawa Seikichi around 1895. He initially wanted to focus on a career as a lithographer, but this was cut short when he contracted pleurisy, which made the risk of inhalation of metal dust too dangerous. From 1905 onwards he made a steady income by creating hanging scroll paintings destined for export to China, commissioned by the art dealer and publisher Shōbidō Tanaka.

Kōitsu's true engagement with *shin hanga* landscapes did not occur until he was in his early 60s and he met Watanabe Shōzaburō at Kiyochika's memorial exhibition in 1931, which explains why he is considered a second-generation *shin hanga* artist despite being a contemporary of Hasui and Shinsui. Although he produced only some ten woodcuts for Watanabe, he was a prolific landscape artist in the years up until the Second World War, with about 130 designs published by Doi Sadaichi (1876–1945) and 53 for Shōbidō, among others. After the war he did not design any other *shin hanga* prints, but he did continue painting until his death in 1949.

Yamamura Kōka (1885–1942), also known as Toyonari, was born in Shinagawa, Tokyo. He studied under the well-known and self-taught print artist Ogata Gekkō (1859–1920) from 1896 and was given his artist name, with the character *kō* taken from his teacher's name. He graduated from the Tokyo School of Fine Arts in 1907. He was already entering works in exhibitions at the age of 14, and was well connected to various artistic circles, from the theatrical arts to genre painting. He was also an active collector and scholar of ukiyo-e. He designed small-sized actor prints for the five-issue magazine *Shin nigao-e* (New Actor Portraits) in 1915 in a project to advertise the kabuki theatre that also involved other printmakers such as Torii Kotondo and Natori Shunsen. Kōka created print designs for Watanabe Shōzaburō from 1916 until 1924. Although he is mostly known for his actor prints, he also ventured into prints and paintings of landscapes, *bijin*, flowers and birds, still lifes and 'modernity scenes'. The last genre includes some of his best-known works, such as his print of the Carlton Hotel Café in Shanghai.

Uehara Konen (1878–1940) was an artist from Asakusa ward, Tokyo, who studied painting under Kajita Hanko

(1870–1917), a successful painter and *kuchi-e* illustrator, and later under Takahashi Hiroaki's uncle Matsumoto Fūko. His name first appears in exhibitions in 1898, when he was only 20 years old. He designed prints for Kobayashi Bunshichi (1864–1923), a dealer and publisher who catered to foreign audiences with original prints and reproductions of well-known ukiyo-e.

Ohara Koson (1877–1945) was born in Kanazawa, Ishikawa Prefecture, as Ohara Matao. Despite having had a prolific career as an adept *kachō-ga* (bird-and-flower print) artist, with an oeuvre of more than 500 works, details about his life are limited. He is thought to have begun studying at the Ishikawa Prefecture Technical School in 1889. There he became a student of the painter Suzuki Kason (1860–1919), who could trace his artistic lineage back to Kikuchi Yosai (1788–1878), known for integrating styles from several different schools into his own. Matao took the artistic name Koson, taking the second character of his name (*-son*) from his teacher, and moved to Tokyo in the 1890s, where he was introduced into the city's artistic circles.

Besides his participation in several exhibitions with his paintings in the late 1890s and early 1900s, Koson ventured into designing woodblock prints, primarily *kachō-ga*. He was also among the many artists who created dramatic depictions of the events surrounding the Russo-Japanese War of 1904–5. During his early career he designed an abundance of prints for the noted publishing houses Kokkeidō (Akiyama Buemon) and Daikokuya (Matsuki Heikichi V). These early prints by Koson bear no dates, and in those issued by Daikokuya even the publisher's seal is omitted. From 1926 Koson started creating designs for Watanabe Shōzaburō using the name Shōson: it is thought that he used this name exclusively for works issued by Watanabe. Later in his career he switched publisher, working for Kawaguchi Jirō and taking the name Hoson. After his death in 1945, Koson's work did not receive much attention until public interest was renewed through exhibitions held after the turn of the millennium, and he is now regarded as the most important *kachō-ga* artist of the 20th century.

Torii Kotondo (1900–76), born as Saitō Akira, grew up in the Nihonbashi district of Tokyo. His father was Torii Kiyotada VII (1875–1941), who was the seventh head of the Torii school of ukiyo-e artists, known mostly for its actor prints, theatre programmes and billboards for kabuki theatres. Kotondo succeeded his father as the head of the school in 1929. As a teenager he studied *yamato-e* under Kobori Tomone (1864–1931). On his father's advice, he also

entered the studio of Kaburaki Kiyokata (1878–1972), where many representatives of the *shin hanga* school had been mentored.

Kotondo enjoyed a prolific artistic career, engaging in painting, prints and kabuki stage design, and later working as a university lecturer and art consultant for television and cinema. Under the influence of Kiyokata's studio, *bijin* became one of the main themes in Kotondo's works. In contrast to his fellow students, he did not design prints for the publisher Watanabe Shōzaburō, but rather collaborated with the publishing firm Sakai-Kawaguchi and later with Ikeda shoten. His daughter Setsuko succeeded him as the head of the Torii school under the name Kiyomitsu after his death in 1976.

Komura Settai (1887–1940) was born in Kawagoe, Saitama Prefecture, and moved to Tokyo in 1903 to study under the *nihonga* painter Araki Kanpo (1831–1915). He entered the Tokyo School of Fine Arts the next year and was taught by Shimomura Kanzan (1873–1930). After his graduation in 1908, he began to make preparatory drawings (*hanshita-e*) for reproductions published in *Kokka*, Japan's first art journal. He became known for a style that fused modernism and minimalism with ukiyo-e techniques, with particular influence from the Edo Period printmaker Suzuki Harunobu (1724–70). In 1933 Settai made illustrations for *Osen*, a serialized story written by Kunieda Kanji (1892–1956) and published in the Tokyo daily newspaper *Tōkyō asahi shinbun*, enjoying immense popularity. Most of Settai's woodblock prints were published posthumously by the Takamizawa Woodblock Print Company and the Adachi Institute of Woodcut Prints. Because many of the blocks were reused and recut, many different states of Settai's prints exist.

Shin'ei (dates unknown) published seven prints of actors with the fifth generation of the Matsuki Heikichi firm in the 1920s, capturing kabuki actors in dramatic roles. Stylistically his work is close to that of the Kyoto artist, Yoshikawa Kanpō (Cats. 123–25), presenting a strong expressive ōkubi-e ('large head portrait') on a plain background. Very little is known about the artist.

Itō Shinsui (1898–1972) grew up in Fukagawa ward, central Tokyo. At a young age, after his family suffered financial difficulties, he left primary school and found work as a factory worker at the Tokyo Printing Company. His talent as an artist was soon recognized, and he became an apprentice in the company's design department, where he was later introduced to the *nihonga* painter Kaburaki Kiyokata (1878–1972). The young artist was given the name Shinsui when he became a pupil of Kiyokata, who would teach many of the most important figures in the *shin hanga* movement and would be highly influential in its development. Under Kiyokata's wing Shinsui studied feverishly.

In 1916, after enjoying some years of success as a young painter, his works caught the interest of the publisher Watanabe Shōzaburō when they were exhibited by the Kyōdokai, a group consisting of Kiyokata's students. *Before the Mirror* (1916; Cat. 25), their first collaboration, was published soon after and would be followed by many others.

Initially, Shinsui's designs encompassed several themes, including *bijin-ga*, landscapes and genre subjects. But, from 1922 onwards, the vast majority of his oeuvre consists of beautiful women, known for their characteristic downcast gaze. In 1932 some of his landscape designs were used as touristic posters in both Japan and abroad, and in 1943, during the Japanese occupation of the Dutch East Indies, he was sent to the Indonesian archipelago as a war artist and produced several designs depicting local scenes. He continued to have a successful and influential career in the Japanese art world up until his death in 1972.

Kasamatsu Shirō (1898–1991) was born in Asakusa ward, Tokyo, and was one of the pupils in the studio of Kaburaki Kiyokata, which he started attending in 1912. He made his debut as a *shin hanga* artist with four prints published in 1919 by Watanabe Shōzaburō, and another in 1920. After that he focused mostly on *nihonga* painting and did not make any new prints until the 1930s, when he started working with Watanabe again – a collaboration that lasted until the late 1940s. He made many landscapes of scenes in Japanese cities and their immediate outskirts, and more than those by Hasui and other *shin hanga* artists, his designs tended to highlight the process of modernization and urbanization under way in early 20th-century Japan. In the period between 1948 and 1950, he made eight prints, mostly depicting scenes from his stay in Nagano, published by Watanabe Kinjirō (dates unknown), who was a relative of Watanabe Shōzaburō. During the 1950s Shirō started working with the Kyoto-based publisher Unsōdō, for whom he produced more than a hundred prints. The Unsōdō prints are mostly characterized by thick contours, in contrast with Watanabe's fine lines. At around the same time, Shirō ventured into *sōsaku hanga* and produced many self-carved and self-printed works until late into his career. The majority of his oeuvre consists of landscape

prints, but especially from the 1950s onwards he made various *kachō-ga* and prints incorporating Buddhist imagery.

Yamakawa Shūhō (1898–1944) was born in Kyoto but grew up in Tokyo after his family moved there when he was 3 years old. He began to study under the *nihonga* painter Ikegami Shūho (1874–1944) when he was 15. His artistic name, Shūhō, is a combination of the characters *shū*, borrowed from his teacher's name, and *hō*, after his father, Seihō, who was a fabric designer. Later Shūhō entered the studio of Kaburaki Kiyokata, where he studied with other representatives of *shin hanga* and where he befriended Itō Shinsui. He was an accomplished painter, whose works were often displayed in the prestigious imperial Teiten exhibitions. He had a great interest in the performing arts, and dance was a key theme in many of his painted works of beautiful women.

Only a small part of his oeuvre consists of woodcuts. He designed his first four prints in 1927 (of which two were published in 1928) for an obscure firm called Bijutsusha, which, before these *bijin* prints by Shūhō, had published only a few landscapes by Kawase Hasui. He did not produce his next prints until eight years later, when he made several *bijin* prints from the late 1930s up to his last woodcut published in 1942. His *bijin-ga* range from traditional to more modern themes, while a few of his prints also depict Korean women.

Natori Shunsen (1886–1960) was born in Yamanashi Prefecture into a family of textile merchants who moved to Tokyo shortly after Shunsen's birth. His talent was recognized early in his youth and he began studying under the Shijō artist Ayaoka Yūshin (1846–1910). He was given the name Shunsen by his next teacher, the painter, printmaker and illustrator Kubota Beisen (1852–1906). Shunsen started studying under Beisen at the age of 11. He entered the Tokyo School of Fine Arts in 1904, but left within two years. His employment as an illustrator for serialized stories in 1907 for the Tokyo newspaper *Tōkyō asahi shinbun* would pave the way for a successful career in illustrating book covers for famous authors such as Natsume Sōseki.

Shunsen's first woodcuts were for *Shin nigao-e* (New Actor Portraits) magazine, a five-piece project, published in 1915, to raise the profile of the theatrical arts, with further contributions by Yamamura Kōka and Torii Kotondo, among others. Shunsen started designing actor prints for the publisher Watanabe Shōzaburō from 1916. After their first few prints, they would not work together again for some eight years, their collaboration resuming after the Great Kantō Earthquake and thereafter continuing until 1954. The most important work born out of their collaboration was an exclusive set of 36 actor portraits sold through subscription between 1925 and 1929, with an additional ten prints appearing to meet the high demand. Despite a successful career, the last years of Shunsen's life were marked by tragedy when he and his wife lost their daughter to pneumonia in 1958. The couple committed suicide at the family grave two years later.

Itō Sōzan (1884–?) is a fairly unknown artist who specialized in *kachō-ga* (pictures of birds and flowers). From the 1910s until 1926, he designed several prints for Watanabe Shōzaburō. He is also known to have cooperated with Takahashı Shotei around 1915–16 on a small number of now rare landscape prints with *kachō-ga* elements, among others *Irises at Horikiri*.

It is unclear why Sōzan and Watanabe stopped collaborating, but Sōzan's last design for the publisher appeared in the same year as Ohara Koson started working with Watanabe. Some scholars suggest that Sōzan was replaced by Koson as the main *kachō-ga* artist. The 1936 sale catalogue published by Watanabe did include 28 of Sōzan's prints, but without any information on the artist.

Furuya Taiken (1897–1941), born in Asakusa ward, Tokyo, studied painting under the *nihonga* painter Kawai Gyokudō (1873–1957) and was also one of the pupils in Kaburaki Kiyokata's studio. After he was introduced to Watanabe Shōzaburō by his fellow students, he made four prints for the publisher in 1921–22.

Itō Takashi (1894–1982) was born in the suburbs of Hamamatsu, Shizuoka Prefecture. He attended the Tokyo School of Fine Arts and studied painting under Yūki Sōmei (1875–1975). Like many other *shin hanga* artists, he also entered the studio of Kaburaki Kiyokata and designed prints for Watanabe Shōzaburō. Takashi was primarily a painter, but he also designed 85 woodblock prints from the 1920s until the mid-1960s. His oeuvre consists mainly of romantic landscapes. His compositions are characterized by a style that imitates fine brush strokes, and required highly skilled carvers and printers.

Kitano Tsunetomi (1880–1947) was born in Kanazawa and came from a family of former samurai. He began his career in the woodblock print business as a block carver, working for the newspaper *Hokkoku shinpō*. In 1898 he began studying in Osaka under the *nihonga* artist Inano Toshitsune (1858–1907), a former student of the masters Tsukioka Yoshitoshi (1839–92) and Kōno Bairei (1844–95). He received the artistic name Tsunetomi from Inano and became particularly adept in book illustration and poster design. He enjoyed great success as an artist for advertisements in the 1910s, producing lithographic posters for Sakura Beer and the Takashimaya department store. He also designed frontispieces for magazines and worked as an illustrator for the newspaper *Ōsaka shinbun* from 1901. Besides his activities with printed works, he was prominent in painting circles in Kyoto and Osaka. In 1924 he founded the art school and publishing firm Hakuyōsha, where he taught two important female artists, Shima Seien (1892–1970) and Kitani Chigusa (1895–1947). Although his oeuvre does not include many woodblock prints – he was primarily a painter – he is considered an influential figure in the development of 20th-century print design.

Further Reading

Dwinger, Jim, Philo Ouweleen and Chris Uhlenbeck, *Kawase Hasui: Capturing the Soul of Japan* (Brussels: Ludion, 2025).

Brown, Kendall H., *Kawase Hasui: The Complete Woodblock Prints*, 2 vols, ed. *Amy Reigle Newland* (Amsterdam: Hotei Publishing, 2003).

— *Water and Shadow: Kawase Hasui and Japanese Landscape Prints* (Richmond, VA: Virginia Museum of Fine Arts and Leiden: Hotei Publishing, 2014).

Chiba City Museum of Art [Chiba-shi Bijutsukan], ed. *Nihon no hanga II 1911–1920: kizamareta 'ko' no kyōen* [A Feast of Carved 'Individuality'] (Chiba: Chiba City Museum of Art, 1999).

— *Nihon no hanga III 1921–1930: toshi to onna to hikari to kage to* [City and Women, Light and Shadow] (Chiba: Chiba City Museum of Art, 2001).

— *Nihon no hanga IV 1931–1940: Munakata Shikō tōjō* [The Advent of Munakata Shikō] (Chiba: Chiba City Museum of Art, 2004).

Chigasaki City Museum of Art / Tsukimoto Toshiko, *Ohara Koson ten: Hana to tori no Eden – kaikan 20 shūnen kinen Hara Yasusaburō korekushon / Ohara Koson: An Eden of Flowers and Birds – 20th Anniversary Exhibition Hara Yasusaburō Collection* (Chigasaki City Museum of Art, 2018) [includes a supplementary essay by Amy Newland in English and Japanese].

Edo-Tokyo Museum [Edo-Tōkyō Hakubutsukan], ed., *Yomigaeru uki-yo-e: uruwashiki Taishō shin hanga ten / Beautiful Shin Hanga: Revitalization of ukiyo-e* (Tokyo: Edo-Tokyo Museum and Asahi Shinbunsha, 2009).

Folk Museum of Ōta City [Ōta Kuritsu Kyōdo Hakubutsukan] ed., *Takahashi Shōtei (Hiroaki) / Syotei (Hiroaki) Takahashi* (Tokyo: Folk Museum of Ōta City, 2005).

Hamanaka, Shinji, and Amy Reigle Newland, *The Female Image: 20th-Century Prints of Japanese Beauties* (Tokyo: Abe Publishing Ltd and Leiden: Hotei Publishing, 2000).

Herwig, Henk, Arendie Herwig, *Heroes of the Kabuki Stage* (Leiden: Hotei Publishing, 2004).

Iino, Masahito, Kōno Minoru and Hirasawa Kanzō, *Itō Shinsui zenmokuhanga / All the Woodblock Prints of Shinsui Itō* (Tokyo: Executive Committee for the exhibition Itō Shinsui zenmoku-hanga, 1992).

Iwakiri, Shin'ichirō, *Hashiguchi Goyō ten: seitan 130 nen* [Exhibition of Hashiguchi Goyō on the Occasion of his 130th Anniversary] (Tokyo: Tōkyō Shinbun, 2011).

Kasamatsu, Shirō, *Kasamatsu Shirō: zenmokuhanga shū / Kasamatsu Shirō: The Complete Woodblock Prints* (Tokyo: Abe Publishing, 2021).

MacLean, J. Arthur, and Dorothy Blair, *Modern Japanese Prints: The Toledo Museum of Art* (Toledo: The Toledo Museum of Art, 1997) [reprint of the 1930 and 1936 Toledo Museum of Art catalogues].

Marks, Andreas, Chiaki Ajioka, Ishida Yasuhiro, Yuiko Kimura-Tilford, Amy Reigle Newland, Charles Walbridge, Matthew Welch and Yano Haruyo, *Seven Masters: 20th-Century Japanese Woodblock Prints from the Wells Collection* (Minneapolis: Minneapolis Institute of Arts, 2015).

Merritt, Helen, *Modern Japanese Woodblock Prints: The Early Years* (Honolulu: University of Hawai'i Press, 1990).

Merritt, Helen, and Nanako Yamada, *Guide to Modern Japanese Woodblock Prints: 1900–1975* (Honolulu: University of Hawai'i Press, 1992).

Newland, Amy Reigle, Jan Perrée and Robert Schaap, *Crows, Cranes & Camellias: The Natural World of Ohara Koson* (Leiden: Hotei Publishing, 2001).

— *Printed to Perfection: Twentieth-Century Japanese Prints from the Robert O. Muller Collection* (Washington, DC: Arthur M. Sackler Gallery, Smithsonian Institution, in association with Hotei Publishing, Amsterdam, 2004).

Nishiyama, Junko, and Aihata Keiji. *Yoshida Hiroshi: seitan 140 nen* [Yoshida Hiroshi: On the Occasion of His 140th Anniversary] (Tokyo: Mainichi Shinbunsha, 2016).

Ogura, Tadao, H. E. Robison, Yasunaga Kōichi, Yoshida Tōshi and Yoshida Hodak, *Yoshida Hiroshi zenmokuhanga shū / The Complete Woodblock Prints of Yoshida Hiroshi* (Tokyo: Abe Shuppan, 1987).

Putney, Carolyn M., Kendall H. Brown, Koyama Shūko and Paul Binnie, *Fresh Impressions: Early Modern Japanese Prints* (Toledo: Toledo Museum of Art, 2013).

Stephens, Amy Reigle, ed., *The New Wave: Twentieth-Century Japanese Prints from the Robert O. Muller Collection* (London: Bamboo Publishing Ltd and Leiden: Hotei Japanese Prints, 1993).

Takizawa, Kyōji, Murase Kana, Ono Michitaka, Iwakiri Shin'ichirō et al., *Ukiyo-e modān: Shinsui no bijin! Hasui no fūkei! Soshite … / Ukiyo-e Modern* (Tokyo: Tōkyō Shinbun, 2018).

Uhlenbeck, Chris, Amy Reigle Newland and Maureen de Vries, *Waves of Renewal: Modern Japanese Prints, 1900 to 1960 – Selections from the Nihon no hanga Collection, Amsterdam* (Leiden: Hotei Publishing, 2016).

— *Vagues de renouveau: estampes japonaises modernes 1900–1960* (Paris: Fondation Custodia, 2018) [French translation of *Waves of Renewal*].

Watanabe, S. [Shōzaburō], *Catalogue of Wood-Cut Colour Prints of S. Watanabe* (Tokyo: S. Watanabe, 1936).

Useful websites:

www.itosozan.com
www.kabuki21.com
www.koitsu.com
www.mjpap.com
www.myjapanesehanga.com
www.shinhanga.net
www.shotei.com
www.ukiyo-e.org
www.viewingjapaneseprints.net

Glossary

aiban
Print size – approximately 32 × 22 cm.

baren
Round disc used by the printer to press the paper sheets onto the printing blocks.

bijin/bijin-ga
'Beautiful woman' / 'pictures of beautiful women' – genre within Japanese printmaking.

blind-printing
See: *karazuri*.

bokashi
A technique employed by the printer to provide shading or gradual colour transition.

Bunten
Annual art exhibitions held from 1907 by the Fine Arts Reviewing Committee (later the Imperial Fine Arts Academy); later renamed Teiten.

Edo (Tokyo)
The seat of power of the Tokugawa rulers during the Edo Period (1603–1868). One of the largest metropolises in the world during the 19th century, possessing a rich urban culture. Renamed Tokyo in 1868 when the Meiji government established itself there.

-ga
A suffix meaning 'picture by'. Often used as the last character of a signature.

gauffrage
Embossing; see also *karazuri*.

gofun
An opaque white pigment made from pulverized shells; often splashed on a print to imitate effects such as lifelike snowflakes.

jizuri
'Self-printed'.

kabuki
Popular form of theatre that developed in the urban culture of Edo and which was an important subject in Japanese woodblock prints.

kachō-ga
'Pictures of flowers and birds' – a genre within Japanese printmaking.

karazuri
'Empty printing' – a technique whereby an uncoloured pattern is pressed into the paper using a printing block, creating a decoration in relief. Often used in textiles.

key block
Block used to print the outlines of a print. Cut from the finished drawing of the copyist, it is the first block to be printed.

Meiji Period
Era coinciding with the reign of Emperor Meiji (1868–1912), marked by the fall of the Tokugawa shogunate, abolition of the feudal system, and Japan's embrace of 'Westernization', as it modelled itself after Western imperialist powers.

mica
An inorganic pigment created by powdering a silicate mineral. When mixed with glue and printed onto a sheet, mica creates a shimmering surface. Often applied to prints to provide a striking and luxurious background to portraits of women or actors.

nagaban
Print size – long and narrow format of approximately 20 × 53 cm.

nihonga
Japanese-style painting of the late 19th and 20th centuries.

ōban
Print size – approximately 38 × 26 cm. The predominant print size throughout the history of Japanese woodblock prints.

ōkubi-e
'Picture of a large head' – a close-up portrait.

onnagata
'Female form(s)' – male actors in the kabuki theatre who played female roles.

shikishiban
Print size – square format, approximately 23 × 21 cm, often used between 1890 and 1920 for bird-and-flower prints.

shin hanga
'New prints' – a term used to denote the prints resulting from the movement that sought to revitalize traditional printmaking techniques and practices in the early 20th century.

Teiten
See: *Bunten*.

shin kabuki
'New kabuki' – kabuki theatre based on European dramatic models but with kabuki staging.

Shōwa Period
Era coinciding with the reign of Emperor Shōwa (Hirohito) (1926–1989).

sōsaku hanga
'Creative prints' – prints produced by artists who empha-

sized their individual creativity and carried out the entire production process themselves.

Taishō Period
Era coinciding with the reign of Emperor Taishō (1912–1926).

tate-e
Vertical composition, e.g. *ōban tate-e*.

ukiyo-e
'Pictures of the floating world' – an artistic tradition, most commonly expressed through prints, that centres on the depiction of urban life in Edo, often combined with allusions to classical tales. The most notable themes were the pleasure districts and theatres.

yakusha-e
Actor portraits – genre within Japanese printmaking.

yamoto-e
'Japanese painting' – painting developed during the Tang and Heian Periods that is considered the classical Japanese style.

yōga
'Western-style painting'.

yoko c
Horizontal composition – e.g. *ōban yoko-e*.

Colophon

Compilation and editing
Chris Uhlenbeck

With contributions by
Chris Uhlenbeck, Jim Dwinger and Philo Ouweleen

Copy editing
Nausikaä de Blaauw and Robert Anderson
(in association with First Edition Translations Ltd,
Cambridge)

Graphic design
Dylan Van Elewyck

Coordination
Ruth Ruyffelaere

Printing
DZS Grafik

ISBN 978-94-6478-121-2
D/2025/6328/7

Ludion
info@ludion.be
www.ludion.be

Front cover: Torii Kotondo, *Morning Hair*, detail, November 1931
Back cover: Kasamatsu Shirō, *Morning Calm – Ajiro Promontory, Izu*, detail, spring 1933

Note to the reader: dimensions are in centimetres, with height followed by width.

About the authors

Chris Uhlenbeck has been a dealer in Japanese prints for 40 years. He has acted as curator of many exhibitions in the field of Japanese art, starting with the major retrospective exhibition on 20th-century Japanese prints from the Robert O. Muller collection in 1992 for the National Museum of Ethnology in Leiden, the Fondation de l'Hermitage in Lausanne and the Musée Marmottan in Paris. From 2007 to 2017 he was Curator at the Nihon no hanga Museum in Amsterdam. Between 2011 and 2021 he created various exhibitions in the Japan Museum SieboldHuis in Leiden: on Hiroshige (2011), Yoshitoshi (2012), Kuniyoshi (2013), Kunisada (2015) and, most recently, on Gekkō (2021). In 2016 he was involved in the major ukiyo-e exhibition held at the Royal Museums of Art and History in Brussels and in 2018 in the exhibition *Van Gogh and Japan*, staged at the Van Gogh Museum, Amsterdam.

Jim Dwinger is a scholar of Japanese art history, with a specialization in woodblock prints. He works as a researcher and editor in that field. He is currently employed by Hotei Japanese Prints in Leiden and is a member of the editorial board of *Andon, Journal of the Society for Japanese Art*. An excerpt from his master's thesis appeared in *Andon* 109 (June 2020), titled 'Positive Perceptions of Tokugawa Rule in Meiji Prints'.

Philo Ouweleen obtained her master's degree in Japanese Studies at Leiden University. Specializing in Japanese arts and media, she first worked as a Japanologist at Japan Museum SieboldHuis, and is currently employed at Hotei Japanese Prints in Leiden. An article based on her master's thesis was published in *Andon* 106 (December 2018), titled 'Through the Photographic Lens: Japanese Photographers Visualizing the Triple Disaster'. Ouweleen also gives lectures about Japanese visual culture, from modern animation to woodblock prints. Her fascination with Japanese art history is also reflected in her own work as a visual artist.